Introduction to Counseling and Guidance

Fourth Edition

Robert L. Gibson

Marianne H. Mitchell

Indiana University

Merrill,
an imprint of Prentice Hall
Englewood Cliffs, New Jersey   Columbus, Ohio

Library of Congress Cataloging-in-Publication Data
Gibson, Robert L. (Robert Lewis).
  Introduction to counseling and guidance / Robert L. Gibson, Marianne H. Mitchell.—4th ed.
    p.   cm.
  Includes bibliographical references and index.
  ISBN 0-02-341741-2
  1. Counseling.   II. Mitchell, Marianne. II. Title.
BF637.C6G48   1995
158'.3—dc20   94-34593
                                                  CIP

Cover art: Nicholas Hill
Editor: Kevin M. Davis
Production Editor: Julie Anderson Tober
Photo Editor: Anne Vega
Text Designer: Bill Harrington
Cover Design: Gryphon III
Production Buyer: Patricia A. Tonneman
Electronic Text Management: Marilyn Wilson Phelps, Matthew Williams, Jane Lopez, Karen L. Bretz

This book was set in Goudy Old Style by Prentice Hall and was printed and bound by Book Press, Inc., a Quebecor America Book Group Company. The cover was printed by Phoenix Color Corp.

 © 1995 by Prentice-Hall, Inc.
A Simon & Schuster Company
Englewood Cliffs, New Jersey 07632

Earlier editions © 1986, 1990 by Macmillan Publishing Company; entitled *Introduction to Guidance* copyright © 1981 by Macmillan Publishing Company

All photos by Cunningham/Feinknopf except photo on p. 2, courtesy of Bettman Archives.

Printed in the United States of America

10 9 8 7 6 5 4 3 2 1

ISBN: 0-02-341741-2

Prentice-Hall International (UK) Limited, *London*
Prentice-Hall of Australia Pty. Limited, *Sydney*
Prentice-Hall of Canada, Inc., *Toronto*
Prentice-Hall Hispanoamericana, S. A., *Mexico*
Prentice-Hall of India Private Limited, *New Delhi*
Prentice-Hall of Japan, Inc., *Tokyo*
Simon & Schuster Asia Pte. Ltd., *Singapore*
Editora Prentice-Hall do Brasil, Ltda., *Rio de Janeiro*

About the Authors

Dr. Robert L. Gibson is Professor of Education, Department of Counseling and Educational Psychology at Indiana University, Bloomington, Indiana. In addition to his experiences as a counselor educator, he has been a high school teacher, counselor and director of guidance, as well as a college counselor. His service activities include Chairperson of the Guidance and Counseling Committee of the North Central Association of Schools and Colleges; member of the state guidance advisory committee in two states; president of two state counseling associations; treasurer of the Association for Counselor Education and Supervision (ACES); plus various state and national committee memberships.

His research activities include directing funded international research projects in the areas of pupil academic achievement, common educational problems of youth, and school dropouts. Recent studies include an assessment of prevention programs in elementary schools and opinions of school programs of counseling and guidance.

Dr. Gibson is Co-Director of Indiana University's programs in Bermuda and Scotland.

Dr. Marianne H. Mitchell is Professor of Education, Department of Counseling and Educational Psychology, Indiana University, Bloomington, Indiana. She has served as President of the American Counseling Association and as President of the Association of Counselor Education and Supervision.

Dr. Mitchell's research activities include international investigations of pupil personnel services, pupil achievement and common educational problems in the United States, the United Kingdom, and Europe. She has been the principal investigator in studies of career information delivery systems, career placement programs, and adolescent girls' attitudes towards vocational education. She serves as a consultant to the Ministries of Education and Health and Social Services in Bermuda and to Moray House Institute, Edinburgh, Scotland.

Dr. Mitchell is Co-Director of Indiana University's programs in Bermuda and Scotland.

Preface

This book is primarily designed for use in introductory counseling and guidance courses and in related fields for those who seek a comprehensive overview of counseling services. In this text, readers will find a broad general discussion rather than the in-depth treatment that students majoring in counseling can anticipate later in their specialized preparatory courses.

The objectives of this book are to provide the reader with an overview and general understanding of (1) historical perspectives and current activities of counselors, (2) the role and function of counselors in a variety of settings, (3) techniques utilized by counselors, (4) the organization of counseling programs, and (5) legal and ethical guidelines.

Although counselors in both school and nonschool settings adhere to basically the same principles and practices, it is recognized, through special attention in Chapter 3 (schools) and Chapter 4 (community and agency), that counselors are functioning in a variety of settings. We therefore believe that those interested in counseling in both school and nonschool settings will find this book to be an appropriate introduction.

The initial chapters lead the reader from the historical background of the counseling movement through traditional and current activities. These activities are then translated into the counselor's role and function in both school and nonschool settings (Chapters 3 and 4). Chapter 5 focuses on the primary and distinguishing activity of counselors—individual counseling. Chapters 6 through 10 discuss other basic activities of counselors (group counseling, assessment through standardized and nonstandardized techniques, career counseling, and consultation). Chapter 11 discusses the current trend of increased counselor attention to prevention and wellness. Chapters 12 and 13 address development and management of counseling and guidance programs and their improvement through accountability, evaluation, and research. The final chapter presents legal and ethical considerations. Throughout this text we have sought to raise the reader's multicultural awareness. Special issues and current concerns of the profession have also been addressed.

As an introductory text, we have written and revised this book in a relatively informal style in the hope that it is readable and enjoyable as well as informative. Your comments, suggestions, and reactions will be most welcome.

ACKNOWLEDGMENTS

We would like to acknowledge all those who have contributed directly and indirectly to the undertaking and completion of this book. These include, of course, the helpful staff of Prentice Hall and Merrill Publishing Company, particularly our past and present editors, Lloyd C. Chilton, Robert Miller, Linda Sullivan, and Kevin Davis. Special thanks go to Julie Tober, Production Editor, and Laura Larson, copyeditor, whose helpful comments, diligent attention to detail, and timely packages kept us to the production schedule! We would also like to acknowledge the valuable comments of our reviewers, Clayton J. Arceneaux, University of Southwestern Louisiana; Ronald D. Bingham, Brigham Young University; Brenda Freeman, University of Wyoming; Robert C. Nielsen, North Dakota State University; and Lee J. Richmond, Loyola College in Maryland.

We are extremely grateful to the many considerate authors and publishers who granted us permission to quote from their publications. It is also appropriate to acknowledge the many useful suggestions from our departmental colleagues at Indiana University and our fellow counselor–educators who volunteered their time and comments for our guidance. In addition, we have been appreciative of the critical comments of our graduate students (who undoubtedly had in mind the well-being of their counterparts of the future). We are particularly thankful for the patient and persistent assistance of our graduate assistants, past and present, Dr. L. Lynn Krebs, Ms. Patricia J. Parrett-Mader, Ms. Gilda Broadwell. A very special note of appreciation must be given to our graduate assistant of the past several years, Ms. Camille Sexton-Villalta, whose conscientious contributions to preparing this current edition were especially helpful. In conclusion, we would like to acknowledge our close friends and families who have endured "the worst of times" and are now looking forward to "the best of times."

R.L.G.
M.H.M.

Brief Table of Contents

Contents

Chapter 3

The School Counselor's Role and Function   44

Chapter 4

Counselors in Community and Agency Settings   96

Chapter 10

The Counselor as Developmental and Educational Consultant   354

Chapter 14

Ethical and Legal Guidelines   448

Appendix A
Role Statement: The School Counselor   464

Appendix B
Ethical Standards   467

Introduction to Counseling and Guidance

Chapter 1

Historic Perspectives

COUNSELING: A RESPONSE TO HUMAN NEEDS

Many of you have recently decided to prepare for careers as counselors; some of you may be considering such a decision; still others may be interested in counseling because you are in or are preparing to enter various careers in which some introductory knowledge of this field may be helpful. In this process you probably asked yourself, Why have I selected this field? On occasion, you also may have even thought, Why do I have to work? Both are age-old questions that are vital to society and that have been discussed and researched extensively over the years.

Perhaps an equally important question but one not raised quite as frequently or researched as extensively is, Why do certain careers exist? What were the factors that led to their demand and creation? The answers to these questions are fairly obvious concerning such fields as medicine and law, for the need for physicians and lawyers in society has been clearly and universally recognized since the earliest recordings of civilizations. Less clear to many, however, is the role of less well-known occupations, such as ornithologists, demographers, and cytotechnologists. Although a popular understanding and acceptance of the need for all careers are not necessary or expected, those studying the general areas encompassed by counseling will benefit from understanding the nature of the societal needs to which counseling and counselors are responding and, in turn, understanding the nature of those responsibilities and responses.

This first chapter, therefore, briefly reviews the historic antecedents leading to the development of counseling programs and the professional careers they represent. You may determine whether counseling and counselors are a response to human needs or just another fancy that will pass when the need is examined more closely and critically.

OUR HERITAGE FROM THE PAST

It is quite possible that the earliest (although unconfirmed) occasion in which humans sought a counselor was when Adam reaped the consequences of his eating the apple in the Garden of Eden. There is no proof of this early beginning to counseling, but an abundance of evidence suggests that persons throughout the ages have sought the advice and counsel of others believed to possess superior knowledge, insights, or experiences.

Perhaps the first counterparts of the present-day counselor were the chieftains and elders of the ancient tribal societies to whom youths turned or were often sent for advice and guidance. In these primitive societies the tribal members shared fundamental economic enterprises such as hunting, fishing, and farming. No elaborate career guidance programs were developed—or needed—because occupational limitations were usually determined by two criteria: age and sex. Later, as skills became more recognizable and important to societies, the occupational determinant of inheritance became common. Thus, potters passed on the secrets and skills of their trade to their sons, as did the smiths and carpenters. Women passed on their skills to their daughters; however, their occupational opportunities were limited.

A study of early primitive life can lead one to conclude that most of the conflicts existing in present-day society regarding career decision making were absent. This absence of a career decision-making dilemma, however, should not be interpreted to mean that workers did not enjoy or take pride in a "job well done." Even the earliest evidence of humankind's existence indicates that pride and pleasure resulted from developing and demonstrating one's skills—in developing one's "human potential."

In the early civilizations, the philosophers, priests, or other representatives of the gods and religions assumed the function of advising and offering counsel. The historic origins of "developing one's potential" may be identified in the early Grecian societies, with their emphasis on developing and strengthening individuals through education so that each could fulfill a role reflecting their greatest potential for themselves and their society. It was believed that within the individual were forces that could be stimulated and guided toward goals beneficial to both the individual and the community. Of these early Greek "counselors," Plato more than any other person is generally recognized as one of the first to organize psychological insights into a systematic theory. Belkin (1975) notes that Plato's interests

> were varied, and he examined the psychology of the individual in all of its ramifications: in moral issues, in terms of education, in relation to society, in theological perspective, and so on. He dealt with such questions as "What makes a man virtuous—his inheritance, his upbringing, or his formal education" (Meno), "How can children be most effectively taught" (Republic), and "Which techniques have been successfully used in persuading and influencing people in their decisions and beliefs" (Gorgias). But it is not the specific questions themselves that prove important to counselors, but, rather, the method that Plato used to deal with these questions, a method which, more than any other in the history of human thought, sets the way for the counseling relationship. It is a dramatic method, in which profound questions are dealt with through the dynamics of very real human interactions, a method in which the characters are as important as the things they say. (p. 5)

The second great counselor of the early civilizations was Plato's student, Aristotle, who made many significant contributions to what was to become the field of psychology. One of these was his study of people interacting with their environment and others. Also, Hippocrates and other Greek physicians offered the opinion that mental disorders were diseases originating from natural causes. Physicians' treatments (bleeding, purging, etc.) were hardly humane except by comparison.

Later, in ancient Hebrew society, individuality and the right of self-determination were assumed. The early Christian societies emphasized, at least in theory if not always in practice, many of the humanistic ideals that later became basic to democratic societies and, in this century, the counseling movement.

Philosophers who were also educators, such as Luis Vives (1492–1540), recognized the need to guide persons according to their attitudes and aptitudes. Foreshadowing the more recent women's equity movement and the earlier women's liberation movement, "Vives in his *De subventione pauperum* (Bruges, 1526) even demanded that girls should be prepared for useful occupations" (Mallart, 1955, p. 75).

In the Middle Ages attempts at counseling increasingly came under the control of the church. By the early Middle Ages the duty of advising and directing youth had become centered in the parish priest. At that time education was largely under church jurisdiction. Sporadic efforts at placing youth in appropriate vocations occurred during the rise of European kingdoms and the subsequent expansion of the colonial empires. Books aimed at helping youths choose an occupation began to appear in the 17th century (Zytowski, 1972). One notable effort by the Italian Tomasco Garzoni was nearly 1,000 pages and treated various professions and occupations in great detail. His publication *La Piazza Universale ai Tutti le Professioni del Mundo* (*The Universal Plaza of All the Professions of the World*) had 24 Italian editions and was translated into Latin, German, and Spanish. Zytowski labeled it the *Occupational Outlook Handbook* of the 16th and 17th centuries (Zytowski, 1972).

In the 17th century a number of picture books also appeared depicting different occupations. One of the more popular publications was Powell's *Tom of All Trades; Or the Plain Path Way to Preferment*, published in 1631 in London. "Powell gives much information on the professions and how to gain access to them, even suggesting sources of financial aid and the preferred schools in which to prepare" (Zytowski, 1972, p. 447).

Also during this time, René Descartes (1596–1650) and others began to study the human body as an organism that reacted or behaved to various stimuli. These studies were to be forerunners for later, more accurate and scientific psychological studies.

In the 18th century Jean-Jacques Rousseau (1712–1778) suggested that the growing individual can best learn when free to develop according to his or her natural impulses; he advocated permissiveness in learning and learning through doing. At approximately the same time, the famous Swiss educator Johann Pestalozzi (1746–1827) expressed the belief that society could be reformed only to the extent that the individual in that society was helped to help him- or herself develop.

For centuries, however, many with mental illnesses, as well as those with physical illnesses, went underground and retreated. While the wealthy could afford the attention of physicians, most mentally ill patients were almost always treated in the home. Those poor who received any treatment at all were treated in hospitals run by religious orders. For the first 75 years of this new nation, the United States of America, few public facilities existed for the treatment of the mentally ill.

The newly independent United States did have leading citizens with a "counseling viewpoint." "One of its most versatile citizens, Thomas Jefferson, called for a plan to recognize and educate its male youth as a source of national leadership" (Gibson & Higgins, 1966, p. 4). The second president, John Adams, called for laws for the liberal education of youths, especially of the lower classes. He felt that no expense for this purpose could be thought extravagant.

The most famous U.S. educator of the 19th century, Horace Mann, included in his *Twelfth Annual Report* a notation of the advantages of the American common school system, advantages that were to be conducive to the development of counseling and guidance programs in U.S. education in the next century. Mann reported that "in teaching the blind and the deaf and dumb, in kindling the latent spark of intelligence that lurks in an idiot's mind, and in the more holy work of reforming abandoned and outcast children, education has proved what it can do by glorious experiments" (Johansen, Collins, & Johnson, 1975, p. 280). Mann also believed that education should have as one of its objectives the reform of society, and he continually stressed this view in his reports to the Massachusetts Board of Education.

In the wake of the political scandals of the Grant administration and other evidence of the decay of Christian morals, methods of moral instruction and moral education became significant in the later 1800s. In 1872, the noted educator A. D. Mayo stated that morality and good citizenship were indistinguishably intermingled and that moral education in the public schools should be based on concepts, principles, and models drawn from the Christian tradition of U.S. society.

During this period, the biologist Herbert Spencer (1820–1903) set forth his concept of adjustment (Hinshaw, 1942). This biological concept held that forms of life that do not adapt to their environment eventually become extinct. From this, Spencer concluded that perfect life consisted of perfect adjustment. In other words, biological adjustment is a criterion of life. Adaptive behavior is that which maintains life.

Also important to the scientific study of behavior and of special significance to the eventual development of counseling as a psychologically based profession was the emergence of the field of psychology itself during the latter part of the 19th century. Preceded by physicists and physiologists who were conducting experimental investigations that led to reliable information on physical and physiological aspects of behavior, similar investigations launched psychology as a separate science in the late 1800s. Psychology's formal beginnings as a separate science occurred in 1879 when Wilhelm Wundt opened his Psychological Institute at the University of Leipzig. This was the beginning of the movement toward a systematic inquiry into human behavior rather than aimless and often biased observation. With William James (1892–1920) as its early American leader, psychology emerged over the next 100 years as a recognized discipline with its own distinct areas of specialization, inquiry, and training.

The rise of psychiatry as a specialty of medicine was another important and relevant development of this period. This field led to a decline in the support of moral treatment for mental disorders, since psychiatry advocated organic treatment for organic causes. During this same time, the state mental hospital movement, led by Dorothea Dix, resulted in the development of these institutions and the removal of much of the care for at least the seriously mentally ill from local communities (Goshen, 1967).

As the United States entered the 20th century, its society was growing more complex, and finding one's appropriate place within it and adjusting to it were becoming increasingly complicated. Many adults were turning to such traditional sources of guidance as their family physician, minister, or employer. However, it would appear that the 20th century was ripe for a considered and genuinely scientific approach to meeting many human needs. The time was "now" for the development of counseling and other psychologically oriented programs to meet these needs. Let us now examine how these emerged in schools and institutional and agency settings in this century.

THE DEVELOPMENT OF COUNSELING AND GUIDANCE IN U.S. EDUCATION

History is often made when a person with an idea coincides with a need and an opportunity. In 1908, Frank Parsons organized the Boston Vocational Bureau to provide vocational assistance to young people and train teachers to serve as vocational counselors. These teachers were to aid in the selection of students for vocational schools and assist students in choosing a vocation wisely and making the transition from school to suitable work. Soon thereafter, Parsons (1909) published *Choosing a Vocation,* a predecessor to this and other basic books in the field. In this publication he discusses the role of the counselor and techniques that might be employed in vocational counseling. This publication is divided into three areas: personal investigation, industrial investigation, and the organization and the work.

Parsons's book is interesting reading even today, and few would find fault with what he considered to be three factors necessary for the wise choice of a vocation:

> (1) a clear understanding of yourself, your aptitudes, abilities, interests, ambitions, resources, limitations, and other causes; (2) a knowledge of the requirements and conditions of success, advantages and disadvantages, compensation, opportunities, and prospects in different lines of work; and (3) true reasoning on the relations of these two groups of facts. (p. 5)

Parsons goes on to suggest that in initiating the personal investigation, the client should first make an extensive self-study by answering questions on a "schedule of personal data." The counselor then fills in the details by reading between the lines. Parsons states that this approach will give clues to possible flaws such as defective verbal memory and slow auditory reactions. Such a client would make a poor stenographer, or as he puts it, "would have difficulty in becoming an expert stenographer" (p. 7). The inventory suggested by Parsons includes such items as "How far can you walk? Habits as to smoking? Drinking? Use of drugs? Other forms of dissipation? How often do you bathe?"

An unusual feature of the intake interview was the observations Parsons suggests regarding the client's physical appearance:

> While I am questioning the applicant about his probable health, education, reading, experience, et cetera, I carefully observe the shape of his head, the relative development above, before, and behind the ears, his features and expression, color, vivacity, voice, manner, pose, general air of vitality, enthusiasm, et cetera.
>
> If the applicant's head is largely developed behind the ears, with big neck, low forehead, and small upper head, he is probably of an animal type, and if the other symptoms coincide, he should be dealt with on that basis. (p. 7)

Parsons advocates getting the client to see him- or herself exactly as others do and giving the client recommendations about methods that can be used for self-improvement—for example, reading suitable books to develop analytical power. Parsons also recommends using biographies of famous people and finding commonalities with the client in biographic details as a form of inspiration.

Parsons insists that counselors be thoroughly familiar with all relevant details concerning job opportunities, the distribution of demand in industries, and courses of study. A detailed analysis should be made of industrial opportunities for men and women, including location and demand, work conditions, and pay. A similar detailed approach was to be given to opportunities in vocational schools.

Parsons also explains the need to train vocational counselors. This training was to be accomplished in one to three terms, and the applicants were to have some relevant occupational background and maturity. In addition to sound judgment, character, and maturity, Parsons (1909) believes the vocational counselor should have the following traits:

1. A practical working knowledge of the fundamental principles and methods of modern psychology.
2. An experience involving sufficient human contact to give him an intimate acquaintance with human nature in a considerable number of its different phases; he must understand the dominant motives, interests, and ambitions that control the lives of men, and be able to recognize the symptoms that indicate the presence or absence of important elements of character.
3. An ability to deal with young people in a sympathetic, earnest, searching, candid, helpful, and attractive way.
4. A knowledge of requirements and conditions of success, compensation, prospects, advantages, and disadvantages etc., in the different lines of industry.
5. Information relating to courses of study and means of preparing for various callings and developing efficiency therein.
6. Scientific method analysis and principles of investigation by which laws and causes are ascertained, facts are classified, and correct conclusions drawn. The counselor must be able to recognize the essential facts and principles involved in each case, group them according to their true relations, and draw the conclusions they justify. (pp. 94–95)

Parsons's pioneer efforts and publications were popular and succeeded in identifying and launching a new helping profession: the guidance counselor. Today, Parsons is generally referred to as the "father of the guidance movement in American education," but he probably did not envision the growth of the movement from the several dozen counselors he trained to the more than 50,000 counselors functioning in schools alone 70 years later.

By 1913, the fledgling "guidance" movement (as it was initially called) had grown sufficiently in numbers and specialization to warrant the organization of the National Vocational Guidance Association and initiate, 2 years later, the publication of the first guidance journal, appropriately titled *Vocational Guidance*. The term *guidance* was the popular designation for the counseling movement in schools for well over 50 years. However, in recent generations *guidance* has been sometimes viewed as an outdated label. Additionally, the early years of the movement had a vocational orientation that was primarily concerned with those aspects of youth guidance dealing with vocational choice, preparation, and placement. (Sixty years later, many of the same characteristics would once again be reasserted in the career education and guidance movements.) Hence, in these early years the movement was often referred to as one of "vocational guidance."

According to Rockwell and Rothney (1961), other early leaders in the guidance movement in the United States were Jessie B. Davis, Anna Y. Reed, Eli W. Weaver, and David S. Hill. Their contributions should also be noted.

Davis's approach was based on self-study and the study of occupations. His descriptions of counseling (Rockwell & Rothney, 1961) seem to suggest that students should be "preached to" about the moral value of hard work, ambition, honesty, and the development of good character as assets to any person who planned to enter the business world. In their discussion of early pioneers of the guidance movement, Rockwell and Rothney (1961) suggest:

Davis's position within the social gospel philosophy was enhanced by his use of the "call" concept of the ministry in relation to the way one should choose a vocation. When an individual was "called," he would approach it with the noblest and highest ideals which would serve society best by uplifting humanity. (p. 351)

In the same era, Anna Reed was an admirer of the then prevailing concepts and ethics of the business world and the free enterprise system. She believed that guidance services could be important to the Seattle school system as a means of developing the best possible educational "product." Contrary to today's philosophy, she placed the system's (business world) needs above those of the individual. As a result, the guidance programs she developed were designed to judge a person's worth by the employability of that individual.

Another early leader, Eli Weaver, succeeded in establishing teacher guidance committees in every high school in New York City. These committees worked actively to help youths discover their capabilities and learn how to use those capabilities to secure the most appropriate employment (Rockwell & Rothney, 1961).

The fourth of these early pioneers, David S. Hill, was a researcher in the New Orleans school system who used scientific methods to study people. Because his research studies pointed out the wide diversity in student populations, he advocated and worked for a diversified curriculum complemented by vocational guidance. He viewed this model as most appropriate if the individual student were to develop fully.

In the first quarter of the 20th century, two other significant developments in psychology profoundly influenced the school guidance movement: (a) the introduction and development of standardized, group-administered psychological tests and (b) the mental health movements.

The French psychologist Alfred Binet and his associate Theodore Simon introduced the first general intelligence test in 1905. In 1916, a translated and revised version was introduced in the United States by Lewis M. Terman and his colleagues at Stanford University, and it enjoyed widespread popularity in the schools. However, when the United States entered World War I and the armed services sought a measure that would enable them to screen and classify inductees, the first so-called group intelligence measure, the Army Alpha Test, was subsequently administered to thousands of draftees. The possibilities of applying these and other psychometric techniques to pupil assessment resulted in the rapid development and expansion of standardized testing in education in the decade immediately following World War I.

The 1920s was a lively decade in many ways. That noble experiment, Prohibition, was launched; in turn, such names as Al Capone and "Baby Face" Nelson appeared in the nation's newspaper headlines. Socially, the jazz age, flappers, and bathtub gin were in vogue. For the professional educator, the progressive movement ensured a lively educational era as well. This movement, the thought of which would influence the further development of a people-oriented philosophy, stressed the uniqueness and dignity of the individual pupil, emphasized the importance of a facilitating classroom environment, and suggested that learning occurred in many ways. Many of today's counselors would have embraced the progressive education suggestions that pupils and teachers should plan together, that the child's social environment should be improved, that the developmental needs and purposes of the student should be considered, and that the psychological environment of the classroom should be a positive, encouraging one.

Organized guidance programs began to emerge with increasing frequency in secondary schools in the 1920s and more often than not modeled themselves after college student personnel programs, with titles of deans (separately for boys and girls, of course) and similar accompanying functions of discipline, school attendance, and related administrative responsibilities. As a result, many programs of this decade began to have a remedial emphasis, as pupils who experienced academic or personal difficulties were sent to their deans for help modifying their behavior or correcting their deficiencies. Nevertheless, a counselor of the mid-1920s, if projected by a time capsule into a school counselor's meeting 70 years later, could converse easily with his present-day counterparts—at least to the point of their concerns and involvement in vocational or career counseling, the use of the standardized testing instruments, assistance to students with their educational planning, the need for a more caring school environment, and their role as disciplinarians and quasi-administrators.

It is also probable that the elementary school counseling movement had its beginnings in the mid-1920s and early 1930s, stimulated by the writings and efforts of William Burnham. Faust (1968b) indicates that Burnham emphasized the important role of the teacher in the mental health of children in the elementary school. Efforts to develop guidance in elementary schools during this period were scarcely noticeable, but a few notable programs were undertaken. One of these, in Winnetka, Illinois, established a department of elementary counseling with resource personnel for guidance. These personnel included (although not all on a full-time basis) psychiatrists, psychometrists, psychologists, an educational counselor, a psychiatric social worker, and supporting clerical services. Their basic responsibilities were counseling, child study, psychotherapy, pupil analysis, parental assistance, and referrals.

College campuses also began to reflect the influences affecting the guidance movement in the 1920s as student personnel workers began utilizing standardized tests for admission and placement purposes. A few institutions even began to offer vocational guidance.

By the end of the 1920s, it was evident that the early guidance pioneers believed that there was a need for guidance services and the school was the proper institution for the delivery of these services. Some even thought that pupil guidance should encompass all grades.

It is also important to note that the word *counseling* was rarely used during these early years as the label *guidance* was broadly applied to those activities utilized to "guide" students and other clients into appropriate educational choices and career decisions. The reversal in popularity of these labels is noted by Hoyt (1993) in his article "Guidance Is Not a Dirty Word." Perhaps the first delineation of counseling as a psychological process was expressed with the publication of *Workbook in Vocations* by Proctor, Benefield, and Wrenn in 1931 (cited in Lewis, Hayes, & Lewis, 1986).

While in the 1930s the American public debated the policies of FDR and the threat of Hitler to world peace, the "guidance" movement continued to develop to the point at which it was becoming increasingly popular as a topic for discussions and debate in educational circles. Questions and criticisms concerning guidance activities were increasingly noted in the professional literature of the era. Educational associations appointed committees to study the movement, and many issued reports with descriptions and definitions of guidance and guidance services. The New York State Teachers Association published a report in 1935 in which guidance was defined as "the process of assisting individuals in making life adjustment. It is needed in the home, school, community, and in all other phases of the individual's environment" (p. 10).

As in the 1960s, when concern was often expressed about the interchangeability of the words *guidance* and *counseling,* in the 1930s a similar concern was expressed over the interchangeability of the terms *student personnel* and *guidance.* Adding to the confusion, leading spokespeople for the movement during that period, such as John Brewer (1932), used the terms *education* and *guidance* synonymously.

Sarah M. Sturtevant (1937) sought to deal with some of these growing concerns by addressing some of the questions regarding the developing secondary school guidance movement: What do we mean by the guidance movement? What are the essentials of a functioning guidance program? What personnel and what qualifications should guidance workers have for a good guidance program? and the inevitable question, What are the costs of individualizing education? These questions would not be outdated more than 50 years later.

During the late 1930s and early 1940s, the trait-factor approach to counseling became increasingly popular. This often-labeled "directive" theory received stimulus from the writings of E. G. Williamson (*How to Counsel Students: A Manual of Techniques for Clinical Counselors,* 1939) and others. Whereas critics of this measurement-oriented approach claimed it was rigid and dehumanizing, Williamson stresses its worth: "You are trying to improve your understanding by using data with a smaller probable error of estimate, such as test data—instead of judgments, which have a much larger probable error of estimate: variability" (Ewing, 1975, p. 84).

Also during the 1930s, possible directions for guidance in the elementary school were put forth by the child study movement, which took the position that it was the teacher's role to provide guidance for each pupil in the self-contained classroom. Publications by Zirbes and others described the ways in which the learning experiences of children could be guided. The intensive study of each child was recommended, with the objective of understanding how children achieved or failed to achieve certain developmental tasks. This approach was a popular one that found some following at the secondary school level and ultimately led to the suggestion of "every teacher a guidance worker."

As the United States emerged from World War II, the counseling and guidance movement appeared to be taking on new vitality and direction. A significant contributor to this new direction, with an impact on counseling in both school and nonschool settings, was Carl R. Rogers (1902–1987). Rogers set forth a new counseling theory in two significant books, *Counseling and Psychotherapy* (1942) and a refinement of his early position, *Client-Centered Therapy* (1951). In *Counseling and Psychotherapy,* Rogers offers nondirective counseling as an alternative to the older, more traditional methods. He also stresses the client's responsibility in perceiving his or her problem and enhancing the "self." This self theory soon was labeled nondirective because it appeared to be the opposite of the traditional counselor-centered approach for dealing with client problems.

Rogers's suggestion that the client assume the major responsibility for solving his or her own problem rather than the therapist solving the client's problem provoked the first serious theoretical controversies in the school guidance and counseling movement. Rogers's follow-up publication, *Client-Centered Therapy,* was the result of this continued research and application effort. The book promotes the semantic change from nondirective to client-centered counseling but, more importantly, places increased emphasis on the growth-producing possibilities of the client.

Perhaps more than any other person, Rogers influenced the way in which American counselors interact with clients. Furthermore, his view of the client as an equal and his positive view of a person's potential seem more consistent with the American way of life and democratic traditions than the European-based theories.

> The extent of [Rogers's] influence was most marked by the overnight replacement of testing by counseling as the key guidance function. In turn, counseling would rise to such eminence in the next few years that it would compete and contend with guidance in regard to the use of the counselor's time and the overall purpose of counseling and guidance. What began as an adjunct tool of guidance would now raise a challenge for ascendancy in its own right. (Aubrey, 1977, p. 292)

Over the years Rogers continued to research, test, revise, and challenge others to test his theory. In summary, it might be analogous to compare Carl Rogers's impact and contributions to the counseling movement in this century with Henry Ford's contribution to the development of the automotive industry.

Another dimension to the techniques of counselors of the late 1940s and one to which Rogers, again, was a significant contributor was group counseling. Others, utilizing research data gathered by the armed services and their investigations into small-group dynamics, developed a theoretical framework within which school counselors could integrate the skills and processes of individual counseling with the dynamic roles and interactions of the individual in a group setting.

Other opportunities also appeared on the horizon for the counseling and guidance movement. Feingold (1947), writing in *School Review,* called for a new approach to guidance. He indicated that guidance counselors cannot stop with mere educational direction—they must go beyond that goal, must provide guidance, "not only for the anointed, but for those pupils who really need it—the pupils who run afoul of rules and regulations" (p. 550). Feingold and others also called for "guidance of the whole child," an outgrowth of the child study movement of the 1930s. Three years later, Traxler (1950), writing in the same publication, identified emerging trends in guidance:

1. More adequate training of guidance personnel.

2. Guidance as an all-faculty function.

3. Closer cooperation with home and community agencies.

4. Orderly accumulation and recording of individual information.

5. Use of objective measures.

6. Differential prediction of success on the basis of test batteries that yield comparable scores in broad areas.

7. Increased interest in improved techniques in the appraisal of personal qualities of pupils and the treatment of maladjustment.

8. Trend toward "eclectic" guidance (rather than directive/nondirective).

9. Recognition of the relationship between remedial work and guidance.

10. Improved case study techniques.

11. Availability and better use of occupational–educational information. (pp. 14–23)

In 1957, the Soviet Union made headlines around the world by successfully launching the first earth satellite, *Sputnik I*. An indirect but nevertheless significant result of this accomplishment was the "lift-off" of the counseling and guidance movement in the United States. This boost came about through legislation resulting from the public's criticism of education and its failure to supply trained personnel for careers deemed vital for the national well-being. This legislation, labeled the National Defense Education Act and passed in September 1958, became a most important landmark in American education, as well as the guidance movement, for its acknowledgment of the vital link among our national well-being, personnel needs, and education.

This act provided special benefits for youth guidance in 5 of its 10 titles or sections. Of these, perhaps Title V was the key to the upsurge in counseling and guidance program development. Gibson and Higgins (1966) indicate that this provided for "(1) grants to states for stimulating the establishment and maintenance of local guidance programs, and (2) grants to institutions of higher education for the training of guidance personnel to staff local programs" (p. 7).

Gibson and Higgins go on to point out that 6 years later (September 1964), the impact of the act could be detected in announcements from the U.S. Department of Health, Education and Welfare, which pointed out that the act had, in that short period of time, achieved the following:

1. Made grants to states of approximately $30 million, thereby helping bring the number of full-time high school counselors from 12,000 (one for every 960 students) in 1958 to 30,000 (one for every 510 students) in 1964.

2. Through the end of the 1964–1965 academic year, supported 480 institutes designed to improve counseling capabilities, which were attended by more than 15,700 secondary school counselors and teachers preparing to become counselors.

3. From 1959 to 1964, made it possible for 109 million scholastic aptitude and achievement tests to be given to public secondary school students and over 3 million to private secondary school students.

4. Helped 600,000 students obtain or continue their college education with federal loans.

5. Trained 42,000 skilled technicians to meet critical manpower needs.

6. Granted 8,500 graduate fellowships, a first step toward meeting the need for many more college teachers. (p. 7)

Stimulated by this rapid growth in counseling and guidance, standards for the certification and performance of school counselors were developed and upgraded; the criteria used by accrediting associations for school guidance program evaluation were strengthened; and noticeable progress was made in counselor training. Many writers in the field noted that guidance had come of age, that there was a "new era."

For example, Donovan (1959) wrote about a new era for guidance in which he pointed out that "the testing expert and professional counselor enter the picture to give scientific aid in getting each child in touch with those teachers and courses best calculated to free his abilities" (p. 241). He and others further discussed the movement from an era of mass education to one in which each child was treated as an individual with "counseling personnel becoming indispensable auxiliaries to administrators and teachers" (p. 241).

The following year, Klopf (1960) called for an expanding role for the high school counselor. He pointed out that "as populations increase, schools will become larger and taxes become greater in most communities. Instructional services will increase in communities, but guidance programs may not increase accordingly" (p. 418). He suggested that new uses and approaches to homeroom group guidance, small discussion groups, and group counseling needed to be explored. He also suggested that guidance workers should view themselves not only as counselors but as individuals concerned with total learning, including the personal and social relations of the student:

> If he has a knowledge of individual behavior, the social structure of the school and the community and awareness of the world of today and the future, this in all the ongoing activities of the school he should share. (p. 418)

In the 1960s one of the most important developments for the school counseling and guidance movement was the *Statement of Policy for Secondary School Counselors* (1964), which was developed and approved as an official policy statement by the American School Counselor Association (ASCA). This effort to specify the role and function of the school counselor involved more than 6,000 school counselors plus teachers, school administrators, and other educators.

C. Gilbert Wrenn's classic contribution of the 1960s, *The Counselor in a Changing World*, also examined the counselor's role in a society with changing ideas about human behavior and changing schools. Wrenn (1962) noted the growing complexity of the counselor's task:

> It is not enough for the counselor to understand youth in isolation, as it were. More than ever before, the counselor must understand not only the student, but himself and his adult contemporaries as they attempt to adjust to a rapidly changing technology and world order. (p. 8)

C. Harold McCully (1965) implied that if school counselors were to move toward bona fide professionalization, "they cannot afford to define their function on the basis of a retrospective analysis of what counselors have done in the past as technicians" (p. 405). He forecast needed new directions in which the counselor functioned as a consultant and agent for change, directions that would require substantive study of the dynamics of cultural and social change.

By the 1970s the school guidance counselor had inherited a series of stereotypes, the value and validity of which had to be determined. What historians recorded about guidance in the 1970s attested to their concern for these stereotypes and their behavior in dealing with them. These stereotypes were as follows:

> *The Stereotype of Responsibility*. The belief by parents and others that counselors have certain responsibilities such as ensuring that the student takes the "right" courses, selects the appropriate college, takes necessary standardized examinations, meets application deadlines, and so forth.

The Stereotype of Failure. The belief that the counselor is responsible for keeping individuals from failing—that the counselor is a buffer between success and failure. As a predictor of outcomes that determine decisions, the counselor can assess risks and chances for success or failure.

The Stereotype of Occupational Choice. Perhaps more consistent and widespread than any other is the view of the counselor as the person who can tell a student what occupation to enter—who can make this "once-in-a-lifetime" decision for individuals. After all, the counselor is the one with the various interest and aptitude tests and occupational fields—and one is constantly referred to as the person to see about industrial, armed services and educational recruitment materials. (Munson, 1971, pp. 16–17)

In 1973, the Report of the National Commission on the Reform of Secondary Education published its report, with 32 recommendations for the improvement of secondary education. Although the majority of these held implications for the functioning of the secondary school counselor, the following were of particular importance:

❖ Recommendation 6, dealing with bias in counseling

❖ Recommendation 9, focusing on career education

❖ Recommendation 10, emphasizing suitable job placement as a part of career education

❖ Recommendation 12, recommending alternative routes to high school completion

During the mid-1970s and early 1980s, a number of developments influenced counselors in schools and frequently in other settings as well. As noted in more detail in Chapter 13, the accountability movement of this period resulted in many school counseling programs developing more relevant databased programs usually based on objective needs assessments. A major publication of this period, *Guidance and Counseling in the Schools* (Herr, 1979), was the outgrowth of a national survey directed by Dr. Edwin L. Herr and jointly sponsored by the American Personnel and Guidance Association* and the Counseling and Guidance Office of the U.S. Department of Education.

While state certification laws have in recent generations governed the credentialing of counselors in schools in all states, school counselors also became increasingly interested in the movement to license counselors for practice outside school settings. To date, 41 states plus the District of Columbia have passed legislation to license counselors (Alabama, Arizona, Arkansas, California, Colorado, Delaware, Florida, Georgia, Idaho, Illinois, Iowa, Kansas, Louisiana, Maine, Maryland, Massachusetts, Michigan, Mississippi, Missouri, Montana, Nebraska, New Hampshire, New Jersey, New Mexico, North Carolina, North Dakota, Ohio, Oklahoma, Oregon, Rhode Island, South Carolina, South Dakota, Tennessee, Texas, Utah, Vermont, Virginia, Washington, West Virginia, Wisconsin, and Wyoming), and others are preparing to follow suit.

In 1983, the presidentially appointed National Commission on Excellence in Education issued its report, entitled *A Nation at Risk.* This report cites as its primary evidence the decline in standardized achievement test results and has resulted in recommendations

---

*The American Personnel and Guidance Association officially changed its name to the American Association for Counseling and Development (AACD) in 1983. Then, in 1992, the AACD changed its name to the American Counseling Association.

for longer school days, more effective school discipline, a return to basics, and more. Although there are no specific references to school counseling programs, many inferences for such programs could be drawn.

However, another significant report, *Keeping Options Open*, published in 1986, focuses entirely on school counseling and guidance programs. Noting that the school reform movement ignored guidance and counseling, the report states:

> The country's future economic health provides a powerful imperative for improvement of guidance and counseling functions in the schools. We would add what we believe is another equally important argument—the entitlement of children to a public education that meets their abilities and needs. Flagrant violations of justice too often have been inflicted on minority groups in this country. The promise of equal educational opportunity has been made, but not kept. Better counseling and guidance services in schools constitute an important element in making that promise a reality for all students. (College Entrance Examination Board, 1986, p. 2)

The 2-year study of the College Boards Commission will be discussed in Chapter 3.

THE DEVELOPMENT OF INSTITUTIONAL AND AGENCY COUNSELING PROGRAMS

The mental health movement, like the vocational guidance movement, owed much of its impetus in the early 1900s to the efforts of one man. This was Clifford Beers, who was neither a physician nor a psychologist but for several years a patient in a mental institution suffering from schizophrenia. During his confinement Beers (1908) wrote:

> I soon observed that the only patients who were not likely to be subjected to abuse were the ones least in need of care and treatment. The violent, noisy, and troublesome patient was abused because he was violent, noisy, and troublesome. The patient too weak, physically or mentally, to attend to his own wants was frequently abused because of that very helplessness which made it necessary for the attendants to wait upon him. Usually a restless or troublesome patient placed in the violent ward was assaulted the very first day. This procedure seemed to be a part of the established code of dishonor. The attendants imagined that the best way to gain control of a patient was to cow him from the first. In fact, these fellows—nearly all of them ignorant and untrained—seemed to believe that violent cases could not be handled in any other way. (pp. 164–165)

In another statement, Beers (1908) wrote:

> Most sane people think that no insane person can reason logically. But that is not so. Upon unreasonable premises I made most reasonable deductions, and at that time when my mind was in its most disturbed condition. Had the newspapers which I read on that day which I supposed to be February 1st borne a January date, I might not then, for so long a time, have believed in special editions. Probably I should have inferred that the regular editions had been held back. But the newspapers I had were dated about two weeks ahead. Now if a sane person on February 1st receives a newspaper dated February 14, he will be fully justified in thinking something wrong, either with the publication or with himself. But the shifted calendar which had planted itself in my mind meant as much to me as the true calendar does to any sane busi-

nessman. During the seven hundred and ninety-eight days of depression I drew countless incorrect deductions, and essentially the mental process was not other than that which takes place in a well-ordered mind. (pp. 57–58)

These and similar descriptions aroused the public to initiate humanitarian reforms and scientific inquiry into the problems of mental illnesses and their treatment. With the help of a few psychologists of the time, such as William James and Adolph Meyer, the mental hygiene movement was launched to educate the general public on a better appreciation of the plight and treatment of disturbed persons.

At the same time the viewpoint that persons are products of both their environment and their heredity was reemerging. As a result, a new type of institution for dealing locally with mental illness was gaining support. This institution was to become the forerunner of our present-day community mental health center. It was called a psychopathic hospital. According to Bloom (1984):

> It was to be located in the community, and it was to provide treatment rather than custodial care. The rationale for the psychopathic hospital was based on a set of what were then quite radical ideas. First, it was believed that patients should be identified and treated soon after the onset of their disorder. Second, it was believed that patients should not be isolated from their families, friends, and other sources of support. Third, it was believed that patients' families could provide very useful information to those persons responsible for the patients' treatment and that such information would be far easier to obtain if the treatment facility were in the community. Finally, the psychopathic hospital was designed to stimulate in local physicians an increased interest in the problem of mental illness. (p. 15)

During the same time, community aftercare services for former psychiatric patients emerged, and local hospitals began to develop psychiatric diagnostic and outpatient clinics. Community efforts also increased to raise the standards of treatment and prevention of mental disorders and to establish local clinics for disturbed children. As the public became increasingly aware of the extent and impact of mental illness, the possibility of preventive or early treatment began to be discussed.

World War I not only stimulated the development and postwar usage of standardized group psychological tests, it also resulted in two acts significant to the development of one of the early specializations in counseling, rehabilitation counseling. The first of these, the Civilian Vocational Rehabilitation Act (Public Law 236, 1920), was followed in 1921 by Public Law 47. The latter created the Veteran's Bureau and provided, among other benefits, a continuation of vocational rehabilitation services for veterans, including counseling and guidance:

> The counseling provided for veterans was one of the most important features of the Veterans Administration's vocational rehabilitation and education program. It had been observed early in the vocational rehabilitation program for the disabled veterans of World War I that good vocational counseling and guidance was of crucial importance. The lesson was not overlooked in the legislation for World War II veterans and in the implementation of that legislation. All Public Law 16 trainees were required to select their vocational objectives only after formal vocational evaluation and counseling. Those training under Public Law 346 could receive counseling services if they requested them. (Obermann, 1965, p. 190)

The term *rehabilitation counselor*, however, did not appear in professional literature until the late 1930s. Since then, rehabilitation counseling has generally come to be recognized as basically psychological counseling that specializes in the rehabilitation of persons with physical as well as social and emotional problems. In the history of its development, the practice of rehabilitation counseling seems to have gone through several models, described by Jacques (1969) as

1. Vocational agent, trainer, or worker model.
2. Vocational counselor or coordinator of services model.
3. Psychotherapeutic model.
4. Community-centered team counselor model. (p. 17)

The quarter century from 1904 to 1929 was a period of rapid growth in solid scientific research in many different areas. As Mueller (1979) reports:

While there may have been an overly optimistic view of the fruits of mathematization and postulational procedures, it was a period in which the foundations for such techniques as factor analysis, test theory, scaling, etc., were broadly expanded. In areas such as physiological and sensory psychology, human and animal learning, and social and abnormal psychology, the empirical bases of psychology as science were made as firm in that period as they have ever been. This period established psychology as a provable science, not just an "in-principle" science. (p. 20)

During the first half of this century, the community mental health movement reflected a good deal of diversity and encompassed both ideological and practical features. Jeger and Slotnick (1982) note:

As a philosophy, it has its roots in the fields of social psychiatry and public health, which recognized the iatrogenic effects of institutionalization, redefined "mental illness" as a social problem, advocated alternatives to hospitalization and called for community change for purposes of preventing mental health problems. As a methodology, community mental health refers to specific programs that sought to translate this ideology into practice. (p. 15)

After World War II a series of federal legislative acts defined the mandates of agencies and in so doing provided operational definitions of community mental health practices. The federal government's first major entrance into the public mental health arena began with the passage of the National Mental Heath Act of 1946, which established the National Institute of Mental Health, thus announcing the federal government's interest and involvement in public mental health.

The National Mental Health Act also encouraged each state to designate a single agency as the state mental health authority and initiated a state grant-in-aid program to assist these authorities in the improvement of community mental health services.

In 1944 the Veterans Administration (VA) established centers to provide counseling for those receiving benefits under the GI Bill, which provided training and education for veterans. Many counselors were trained in VA-supported counseling services on college campuses. The VA did much to broaden and professionalize the role of the vocational counselor. In 1951, the VA established the position of counseling psychologist, in line with newer concepts from psychology and related disciplines (Borow, 1964, cited in Humes, 1987, p. 16).

During and immediately after World War II, counselors also found increasing opportunities in the VA vocational rehabilitation and educational services as these were rapidly expanded to accommodate the needs of U.S. Armed Services personnel and ex-service personnel.

In 1955, a significant statistic was noted when the initial decline in the number of patients in state mental institutions was recorded. This decline was to continue steadily over the next 20 years despite increases in the number of admissions. This trend had obvious implications for the growth of local mental health services.

Also in the 1950s, another counseling specialty began to emerge in the form of marriage and family counseling. Although historically this movement appeared to have been initiated in the early 1930s, the dramatic post–World War II increase in the separation and divorce rate of young couples led to rapid developments in marital therapy. In the 1960s, dramatic increases in new styles of coupling, marriage, and living together further stimulated interest in providing professional counseling assistance to couples and families. During this period marital therapy moved increasingly from individual analysis to conjoint marital therapy (Brown & Christensen, 1986).

The trauma of the Vietnam War and the postwar era for many veterans and their families created another population needing mental health counseling. Also during the 1960s and 1970s, increased substance abuse and public awareness of the extent and seriousness of the problem at all age levels led to research, the development of training programs, and the growth of another area of specialization for counselors. Special attention to preparing specialists for correctional counseling and counseling the elderly reflected a concern for the needs of these populations as well.

This period after World War II also saw a rapid expansion of community mental health services. In 1955 Congress passed a Mental Health Study Act, which established a joint commission on mental illness and health. This study resulted in a report entitled *Action for Mental Health* (1961), which led in 1963 to the Community Mental Health Centers Act (Public Law 88-164) (Jeger & Slotnick, 1982).

The initial 2,000 centers were expected to provide five essential services:

1. Inpatient (for short-term stays);

2. Outpatient;

3. Partial hospitalization (i.e., day and/or night hospitals);

4. Emergency care (i.e., 24-hour crisis services); and

5. Consultation (i.e., indirect service) and community education (i.e., prevention).

For a center to be considered "comprehensive," five additional services were required: (a) diagnostic, (b) rehabilitation, (c) precare and aftercare, (d) training, and (e) research and evaluation (Jeger & Slotnick, 1982).

The Community Mental Health Centers Amendments of 1975 (Public Law 94-63) redefined the notion of a comprehensive community mental health center from the five minimum and five optional services to a mandated set of 12 services. They include the five originally established services plus seven additional services as follows:

1. Special services for children;

2. Special services for the elderly;

3. Preinstitutional screening and alternative treatment (as pertains to the courts and other public agencies);

4. Follow-up for persons discharged from state mental hospitals;

5. Transitional living for persons discharged from state mental hospitals;

6. Alcoholism services (prevention, treatment, and rehabilitation); and

7. Drug abuse services.

In addition, the 1975 amendments also obligated centers to allocate 2% of their operating budgets for program evaluation.

The mandated delivery of these 12 services was further modified in the Community Mental Health Extension Act of 1978 (Public Law 95-622). Specifically, new centers were required to provide six services (inpatient, outpatient, emergency, screening, follow-up of discharged inpatients, and consultation/education) and were allowed to phase in gradually the remaining 6 of the 12 services over their initial 3 years of operation (i.e., partial hospitalization, children's services, elderly services, transitional halfway houses, alcohol abuse, and drug abuse services).

In considering all the various provisions for services mandated by legislation during the past 17 years, we can convey the spirit of the community mental health movement. The 10 characteristics delineated by Bloom (1984) as differentiating community mental health from "traditional" clinical practice can serve to identify both the ideological and operational aspects of the movement:

❖ First, as opposed to institutional (i.e., mental hospital) practice, the *community* provides the practice setting.

❖ Second, rather than an individual patient, a *total population* or community is the target; hence the term *catchment area* to define a given center's area of responsibility.

❖ A third feature concerns the type of service delivered, that is, offering *preventive services* rather than just treatment.

❖ *Continuity of care* among the components of a comprehensive system of services constitutes the fourth dimension.

❖ The emphasis on *indirect services*, that is, consultation, is the fifth characteristic.

❖ A sixth characteristic lies in the area of *clinical innovations*—brief psychotherapy and crisis intervention.

❖ The emphasis on *systematic planning* for services by considering the demographics of a population, specifying unmet needs, and identifying "high-risk" groups represents a seventh characteristic.

❖ Utilizing new *person-power resources,* especially nonprofessional mental health workers, constitutes the eighth dimension.

❖ The ninth dimension is defined in terms of the *community control* concept, which holds that consumers should play central roles in establishing service priorities and evaluating programs.

❖ Finally, the tenth characteristic identifies community mental health as seeking *environmental causes* of human distress, in contrast to the traditional intrapsychic emphasis. (Jeger & Slotnick, 1982, p. 17)

Although a majority of community mental health workers might agree that these characteristics reflect the orientation of community mental health, there is much less agreement on the emphasis of these concepts in practice. (Bloom, 1984, p. 38)*

In the 1970s, significant federal legislation in the form of the Mental Health Systems Act passed Congress and was signed into law by President Carter. In addition to continuing many of the provisions of the original act, other provisions broadened the scope of care for disturbed children and adolescents. The election of President Reagan in 1980, however, led to new economic policies at the federal level, which included repealing the budgetary authorizations of this act. As a result, in the 1980s, states and local communities were increasingly called on to assume the financing of mental health care facilities and programs.

The United States entered the 1990s with great fanfare—fanfare that trumpeted the many accomplishments of the first 90 years of the 1900s and triumphs anticipated in the remaining 10 years. Not to be overlooked or forgotten, however, was the fact that the nation faced significant societal problems that affected millions of its citizens.

These problems included the ever-increasing AIDS epidemic; the continuing addiction of millions to drugs and alcohol; the alarming numbers of abused children and spouses; increases in teen pregnancies, teen suicides, and teens engaged in criminal activities; the persistent school dropout problem; the disgraceful numbers of homeless; the resurfacing of various forms of prejudice; a "bankruptcy" of values ranging from the political to the private sector; and a myriad of career needs affecting all age groups and socioeconomic levels. We could be labeled a nation on the verge of being psychologically and sociologically "at risk."

Further, in examining these problems we would note that many of these issues require not only remedial treatment but, even more importantly, preventive efforts of our profession if they are to be ameliorated to any degree. Treatment or punitive actions cannot alone "stem the tide." Only prevention has the prospect for diminishing the numbers of potential victims of nearly all these social ills. In this context, then, we can conclude that most of these problems are in our "ballpark." Of all the helping professions, counselors, more than any other, have access to and work with populations and emphasize prevention as well as early intervention and treatment.

Thus, as we close out the 1990s, we see the opportunity for counseling to become *the* helping profession and respond to society's needs in the coming years. The chapters that follow will acquaint you with the skills and knowledge counselors must acquire to serve society's mental health needs and the settings in which counselors will function to provide their services in meeting these great challenges in the years ahead.

SUMMARY

We have examined the need of humankind, from the time of Adam down through the ages, for advice and counsel, to understand themselves and their relationships to their fellow human beings, and to recognize and develop their own potential. In responding to these needs, the chieftains and elders of the ancient tribal societies were perhaps the first forerunners, the ancient counterparts, of the present-day counselor. Later, in the early civilizations, the philosophers, priests, or other representatives of the gods were seen in roles offering advice and counseling. Often "treatment" for the mentally ill was cruel, even when administered by physicians. The role of religion in the counsel and advice of the young in particular, but not exclusively, continued through the Middle Ages, supplemented by sporadic efforts of talent identification and development and even planned career placement. From the Middle Ages onward, teachers also were increasingly expected to provide "guidance" for their pupils, often of the most directive kind. To supplement these efforts, books began to appear with increasing frequency from the 18th century onward that focused on providing advice and counsel to youth in meeting many of the problems of the times, especially those concerning occupational choice. Meanwhile, many leading statesmen, philosophers, scientists, and educators were laying a philosophical groundwork that would eventually support and nurture an embryonic movement to establish psychology as a science and academic discipline in its own right, with an impact on school and community settings.

The school counseling and guidance movement, which for many years was unique to U.S. education, in its beginnings had a vocational guidance emphasis but was shortly to be influenced by a multitude of other movements, especially psychological testing, mental health, and progressive education. Later in the 20th century, the interdisciplinary character of the movement was further emphasized through influences from such movements as group dynamics, counseling psychology, education of the gifted, career education, and placement.

The public or community aspects of the mental health movement initially focused on home confinement and treatment, if at all. An early significant development was the establishment of mental hospitals, in the United States in the 19th century, by state support for the establishment of state mental hospitals. However, at the turn of the century (1908), the mental health movement was stirred by the writings of Clifford Beers, and local mental health treatment centers began to emerge. These community aftercare services were the forerunners of the present-day community mental health centers.

Three significant legislative acts that further stimulated the counseling movement were the Civilian Vocational Rehabilitation Act (1920), the Mental Health Study Act (1955), and the Community Mental Health Centers Act (1963). Later in this century, public need led to the development of specializations in marriage and family, substance abuse, corrections, and elderly counseling.

Over the years the movement has not been without its pioneers and heroes. Of course, the great humanistic teachers of history—Christ, Mohammed, Buddha—and farsighted leaders such as Plato, Aristotle, Pestalozzi, Rousseau, and Charlemagne would have been charter members and undoubtedly elected officers of any counseling association of their time in history. In the United States, one can easily envision Franklin, Jefferson, Lincoln, and the Roosevelts receiving honorary life memberships in the American Counseling Association for their contributions to the eventual growth of the movement. But the real heroes have been persons such as Parsons, Beers, Davis, Reed, Weaver, and Hill—those early, persistent, and farsighted pioneers of the movement whose efforts were later recognized and advanced and then further enriched by the giants of the last half of the 20th century: Carl R. Rogers, E. G. Williamson, and C. Gilbert Wrenn.

It is said that a movement must have a cause and leadership to survive. This brief review of some historic highlights of the development of counseling and guidance in the United States should indicate that neither has been lacking. As the past illuminates the future, it is possible to predict that regardless of the wonderful scientific and technological advances that await humankind, many persons will search out the counsel and advice of the trained, while others will still seek self- and other understandings for the development of their potential or the solution of their problems. Also, as we look at the current major social concerns in society, we see unprecedented opportunities for the counseling profession to serve society. Let us therefore proceed to the next chapter to examine some of the activities of the trained professional counselor.

DISCUSSION QUESTIONS

1.   Discuss factors and events that influenced your decision to enter or consider entering the counseling profession.

2.   Have you had your fortune told? If so, who and when, how accurate, and what results? Which do you believe is most likely to be accurate in predicting futures: palmists, astrologists, graphologists, or others? Defend your selection.

3.   In what ways has standardized testing changed as you perceive it since the Frank Parsons–Clifford Beers era? Why is it so popular even though controversial today?

4.   What led to the creation of the National Defense Act of 1958?

5.   National and state legislative acts have had significant impact on the counseling profession. What current legislation might you suggest that would affect the field of counseling?

6.   Discuss differences and similarities in the historic development of counseling in schools versus counseling in agency and institutional settings.

CLASS ACTIVITIES

1.   Go to the library and find the earliest article you can on the subject of counseling and guidance. Report your article, its date, author, publication, and content to the class.

2.   Break the class into small groups and have them discuss the following: Identify significant characteristics of today's society and examine these to see whether they have implications for the development of any new careers or occupations. What are the implications of these developments for the counseling profession?

3.   Have the class members each select and write down any historic leader's name; then allow 15 minutes for a one-page description of how the leader would have benefited from counseling at some particular point of his or her career. Permit a few students to read their description in class.

4.   Review current newspapers and popular publications for reports or articles that would imply a useful role that the counseling profession can play in responding to human needs in today's society.

5.   Go to the library and examine the major journals in the field of guidance and counseling today. Select three journals and examine issues that are focused on today and compare them with the issues discussed 20 and 30 years ago. What changes do you see in the contents?

SELECTED READINGS

Adler, A. (1959). *Understanding human nature.* New York: Premier Books.

Anastasi, A. (1954). The measurements of abilities. *Journal of Counseling Psychology, 1,* 164–168.

Conant, J. (1959). *The American high school today.* New York: McGraw-Hill.

Cross, H. I. (1964). The outcome of psychotherapy: A selected analysis of research findings. *Journal of Consulting Psychology, 28*, 413–417.

Dugan, W. (1962). An inward look: Assumptions and expectations. *Counselor Education and Supervision, 1*, 174–180.

Dymond, R. F. (1953). Can clinicians predict individual behavior? *Journal of Personality, 22*, 151–161.

Ellis, A. (1957). Outcome of employing three techniques of psychotherapy. *Journal of Clinical Psychology, 13*, 334–350.

Gummere, R. (1988). The counselor as prophet: Frank Parsons. *Journal of Counseling and Development, 66*, 402–405.

Howard, G. S. (1992). Behold our creation! What counseling psychology has become and might yet become. *Journal of Counseling Psychology, 39*, 419–442.

Kinzer, L. (1961). The educated counselor. *Journal of Counseling Psychology, 8*, 14–16.

Meyerson, L., & Jack, M. (1962). A behavioral approach to counseling and guidance. *Harvard Educational Review, 4*, 382–402.

Murphy, G. (1955). The cultural context of guidance. *Personnel and Guidance Journal, 34*, 4–9.

Odegaard, C. (1987). A historical perspective on the dilemmas confronting psychologists. *American Psychologist, 42*, 1048–1051.

Tiedeman, D. V., & Field, F. L. (1962). Guidance: The science of purposeful action applied through education. *Harvard Educational Review, 32*, 483–501.

Whiteley, J. (Ed.). (1984). Counseling psychology: A historical perspective. *The Counseling Psychologist, 12*, 1–126.

Williamson, E. G. (1964). An historical perspective of the vocational guidance movement. *Personnel and Guidance Journal, 42*, 854–859.

RESEARCH OF INTEREST

Campbell, D. P. (1965). Achievements of counseled and non-counseled students twenty-five years after counseling. *Journal of Counseling Psychology, 12*, 287–293.

Abstract

During the mid-1930s, 400 students who had obtained counseling at a university counseling center were matched individually with noncounseled students of similar academic and socioeconomic background. One year later comparisons revealed that counseled students had significantly better grades and had made a better adjustment to college. Few comparisons can be made between the pairs 25 years later because of historic factors and experimental mortality. Remaining comparisons revealed a mild difference in achievement in favor of counseled over noncounseled students 25 years later.

Truax, C. B. (1966). Reinforcement and nonreinforcement in Rogerian psychotherapy. *Journal of Abnormal Psychology, 71*, 1–9.

Abstract

Explores the possibility of important reinforcement effects from therapy encounters with a client-centered therapist. Four eclectic and one analytic clinical psychologist rate three therapist behaviors identified as potential reinforcers and nine patient behaviors identified as theoretically significant, from an unbiased sample of 40 typewritten (TPT, Therapist, Patient, Therapist) interaction units. Findings support the Skinnerian view that reinforcement occurs and influences behaviors in Rogerian therapeutic encounters.

Chapter 2

Traditional and Current Activities of Counselors

In studying any profession, one may ask, What is the profession of . . . [i.e., counseling]? What do they [i.e., counselors] do? The objective of this chapter is to respond to those questions. We begin by examining counseling as a helping profession and then identify activities through which the professional counselor carries out his or her responsibilities.

COUNSELING AS A HELPING PROFESSION

In examining counseling as a profession, we begin by identifying counseling as a helping profession, a concept that forms the basis for the role and function of the counselor in today's society. A helping profession may be described as one in which the members are specially trained and licensed or certified to perform a unique and needed service for fellow human beings. Helping professionals serve; they are recognized by the society as the sole professional providers of unique and needed services.

The helping professions include medicine, law, dentistry, education, psychology, and social work. The roots of each lie in the nature of humankind and society, past and present. It is on these bases that services are determined and programs for providing these services are developed. We will briefly review some of the basic concepts of humankind and society as a basis for the helping profession in general and the profession of counseling in particular.

In the instance of the helping professions, including counseling, it is appropriate to begin with the very foundation of their existence—namely, the client. This client has certain distinguishing characteristics that provide a basis for the profession of counseling and the institutions and agencies through which this profession contributes its special knowledge and skills. Although any attempt to characterize such a versatile and ever-changing species as human beings is perilous, we have certain stable yet unique traits that set us apart from other living species. In the main these are what we might term the "privileges" of the human race. They provide not only the basis or focus of our "being" but the basis for our "doing" as well. They also suggest roles that human beings can play in helping their fellow human beings. These distinguishing characteristics include the following:

❖ *Humans are among the weakest species at birth.*
We are born without the genetically imprinted behaviors possessed by many forms of life. Young animal life in the forests and jungles of the world can survive without adult help; young human life cannot. Our early survival, for years, is dependent solely on the attention, care, and affection of others. The human need for love and care and the degree to which it is provided becomes a critical basis for the lifelong adjustment or lack of it for the individual.

❖ *Humankind has the greatest potential for growth and development of all the species.*
The brain itself triples in physical size and multiplies even more in capacity. This brainpower, coupled with a surplus of energy (over all other species), gives us almost limitless possibilities. The realization of human potential does not, however, rest with the individual alone but depends also on many environmental variables and assistance in recognizing and developing one's potential.

❖ *Humankind has the highest level of communication skills, skills that enable us to express our thoughts in detail to many others; to teach our language to others (even other animal species at certain levels); to record, send, and receive.*

These dual capacities, sending and receiving, in both word and gesture, yield the bases for human relationship skills and for love and affection, which in turn form the primary stimulus for the human race. This ability to relate to others thus becomes the core of a happy, well-adjusted life.

❖ *The human species exhibits a wider range of differences than any other.*

These differences not only clearly distinguish each human from every other human but also multiply the potential of the society and stimulate the advancement of civilizations. The concept of individual differences provides the rationale for client analysis in the helping professions.

❖ *Human beings manipulate and are manipulated by their environment.*

Thus, the behavior of a human being cannot be adequately understood apart from the environmental context within which it occurs. Thus, environmental analysis is becoming increasingly important to the professional counselor.

❖ *Humankind is the only living organism that captures the time stream.*

We can recall the past, act in the present, and plan for the future. This gives us the capability for building on our past experiences, avoiding past mistakes, anticipating the future, and planning for the development of our potential.

❖ *Humankind has the ability to reason and to gain insight.*

These twin factors enable us to make reasoned choices among alternatives and to change. This aptitude for planned individual change is significant in the important arenas of individual development and social adjustment (relationships with one's peers). Our ability to understand ourselves and act rationally also contributes to the maturing process.

From images of the human species, McCully (1969) draws inferences for counseling and other helping relationships as follows:

1. All [people] at birth possess the potential for the distinguishing characteristics of the human species; and

2. The environmental conditions the individual experiences from birth on may either nourish or suppress their realization. (pp. 134, 135)

In light of these premises, we can suggest at even this early point in our discussion that a fundamental basis for counseling program development must be rooted in our understanding of the characteristics and needs of all our clientele, plus an understanding of the environment that shapes them. For counselors, this implies learning in human growth and development and our sociocultural foundations.

Societal needs and expectancies also play an important role in a profession's development and functioning. The brief historic review in Chapter 1 indicated some of the social influences on the counseling profession.

COUNSELING AS A DISCIPLINE

While examining our "roots" and the emergence of counseling as a helping profession, it is also appropriate to note the foundations for counseling as a discipline. Much of this foundation has been derived from the field of psychology. The contributions from psychology have included counseling theory and process, standardized assessment, individual and group counseling techniques, and career development and decision-making theories.

Specialty areas within the field of psychology have further contributed to a knowledge base for counselors to draw on. These include *educational psychology* and its studies of learning theories and human growth and development and their implications for educational settings. *Social psychology* helps us understand the impact of social situations on individuals, including the environment's influence on behavior. *Ecological psychology* is also concerned with the study of environments and how individuals perceive and are shaped by, as well as influence in turn, their environments. *Developmental psychology* helps us understand why and how individuals grow and change over their life span.

While acknowledging that our strongest disciplinary ties are to the field of psychology, we must also recognize the important contributions of other sciences to the counseling profession. For example, sociology has contributed to our understanding of human groups and their influence on human behavior. Anthropology has provided counselors with insights into the cultures of peoples, cultures that in turn provide guidelines for the behaviors and viewpoints of their members. (Chapter 8 will discuss the contributions of sociology and anthropology to human assessment.) Biology has helped us understand the human organism and its uniqueness. The health professions have made us aware of the importance of wellness and prevention.

TRADITIONAL ACTIVITIES

The historic review of the counseling movement in Chapter 1 noted the contributions of the many disciplines and influences that have consistently been expanding their areas of emphasis. Noted were eras of vocational or career guidance, mental health, standardized testing for client analysis, education as guidance, group activities, and the identification and college placement of the gifted. Other "movements of the times" included the community mental health agency movement, the counseling psychology movement, the development of specialized counseling programs for rehabilitation, substance abuse, correctional, marriage and family, and elderly counseling, the reemphasis of the impact of environment on the individual's growth and development, and a currently renewed stress on preventive intervention. However, despite the relatively short period of time that counseling has existed as a profession, certain traditional activities, basic principles, and identifiable patterns of program organization have emerged. An understanding of these can provide some insights into the not infrequently asked question, "How come counselors do what they do the way they do it?"

Since many of the early training programs emphasized school counselor preparation, many influential texts had this orientation as well. These authors tended to discuss counselor functions in terms of "services." For example, over 25 years ago, Froehlich (1958), in discussing counseling and guidance services to pupils in schools, identified basic services to pupils in groups and individually, services to the instructional staff, services to the administration, and research services. Due to the National Defense Education Act (NDEA) of 1958, the 1960s were a period of rapid growth of counseling programs, especially in schools. Publications of that period, such as that by Hatch and Costar (1961), also noted that

> it seems more desirable to think of the guidance program as a program of services—services which can be defined, recognized, administered, and evaluated. It is then possible to define a guidance program as a program of services specially designed to improve the adjustment of the individual for whom it was organized. (p. 14)

These authors go on to make the following suggestions:

❖ Guidance services are for all concerned.

❖ Guidance services are for all school levels.

❖ Guidance services are primarily preventive in nature.

❖ The teacher plays a major role in the guidance program.

❖ The program of guidance services needs trained personnel.

❖ The program of guidance services requires coordination.

❖ The guidance program uses and improves on present practices.

❖ Guidance services are not an added activity.

❖ Guidance services are a group of facilitating services.

❖ The training background of guidance workers presupposes certain elements.

Hatch and Costar conclude their first chapter by identifying the following services as desirable for a school counseling program:

❖ Pupil inventory service

❖ Information service

❖ Counseling service

❖ Placement service

❖ Follow-up and evaluation service

Other references of this period include Zeran and Riccio (1962), who identify basic services as analysis of the individual, counseling, placement, and follow-up and informational services. Gibson and Higgins (1966) note that although semantics and labels varied, the basic services were usually identified as pupil analysis, individual counseling, informational activities, group guidance, placement and follow-up, and evaluation and research.

Later, in the 1980s, Shertzer and Stone (1981) enumerated components of guidance programs in schools as follows: (1) an appraisal component; (2) an information component; (3) a counseling component; (4) a consulting component; (5) a planning, placement, and follow-up component; and (6) an evaluation component. Blocher and Biggs (1983) note, in their discussion of counseling in community settings, that counseling psychologists engage in individual and small-group counseling centered around concerns involving educational and vocational planning, personal problem solving and decision making, family problems, and other activities related to personal growth, prevention, consultation, and, at times, as a psychological educator. They state that assessment strategies must be developed and mastered that permit an understanding of individuals as they interact in natural environments. Finally, counselors must understand processes of human development as they apply to both individuals and social organizations.

In summary, these and numerous other authors over the years have pointed toward certain traditional or basic activities for counselors across all settings, although emphasis may vary, of course. Those prominently identified include individual assessment, environmental assessment, individual counseling, group counseling and guidance, career development, placement, and follow-up. Currently, these "traditional" activities have expanded to include consultation, research, accountability, and prevention. Preventive intervention has also received renewed attention. These areas are discussed briefly in the sections that follow and will be considered in greater detail in later chapters.

Individual Assessment

Individual assessment is that activity that seeks, systematically, to identify the characteristics and potential of every client. This activity is often considered a primary skill of the professional counselor because it provides a database for more readily understanding the person in the counseling setting, the effective planning of group counseling activities that reflect client interests and needs, the development of responsive career and human potential development programs, and the organization of systematic placement and follow-up programs. Often referred to as *individual inventory, assessment,* or *appraisal*, this activity promotes the client's self-understanding as well as better understandings by counselors and other helping professionals.

This activity received initial stimulus as a result of the standardized testing movement. Even today, standardized test results are the most frequently used objective data in individual analysis. Other popular and traditional techniques are observation and observation reports, self-reporting techniques such as the autobiography, and, in recent years, an increasing use of values clarification techniques. It should be noted that other helping professional specialists also have diagnostic skills and responsibilities. For example, a school counselor will often consult with school psychologists and psychometrists as specialists in psychological assessment, including individual testing, and with school social workers as specialists in environmental and case study analysis. Chapters 7 and 8 will discuss these and other techniques for human resource assessment in greater detail.

Counseling

Individual counseling, since the early days of the counseling movement, has been identified as the core activity through which all the other activities become meaningful. *Counseling* is a one-to-one helping relationship that focuses on a person's growth and adjustment and problem-solving and decision-making needs. It is a client-centered process that demands confidentiality. This process is initiated by establishing a state of psychological contact or relationship between the counselor and the counselee and progresses as certain conditions essential to the success of the counseling process prevail. Many practitioners believe that these include counselor genuineness or congruence, respect for the client, and an empathic understanding of the client's internal frame of reference.

Although each counselor will, in time, develop his or her own personal theory to guide personal practice, established theories provide a basis for examination and learning. Effective counseling not only requires counselors with the highest levels of training and professional skills but a certain type of person as well. Counseling programs will suffer in effectiveness and credibility unless counselors exhibit understanding, warmth, humaneness, and positive attitudes toward humankind. Chapter 5 will discuss individual counseling in more detail.

Group Counseling and Guidance

Groups have become increasingly popular as a means of providing organized and planned assistance to individuals for a wide range of needs. Counselors provide such assistance through *group counseling* or *group guidance*. In schools, students have been organized into groups for what might be called guidance purposes since long before any counseling or guidance label was bestowed on the activity. The organization of courses and group meetings to dispense primarily occupational information can be traced back to before the evolution of the counseling movement. Homeroom grouping served a guidance as well as an administrative function long before being labeled as such. However, in 1934, a textbook by H. C. McKown bore the title *Home Room Guidance*. With the increasing importance and attention given to extracurricular activities in schools in the 1920s and 1930s, some suggested these activities also were a type of group guidance experience.

Although various activities from time to time have been given the label group guidance, the most consistent definition of this service is one that views it as an activity designed to provide individuals with information or experiences that promote their career or educational understandings and personal social growth and adjustment. Some traditional group guidance activities that have become familiar to most high school students are career days, college days, and orientation days.

In recent generations, group counseling has also been viewed as a basic but different activity from group guidance. Whereas group guidance focuses on providing information and developmental experiences, group counseling tends to focus more on the problem-solving and adjustment needs of persons through a process very similar to individual counseling. Gazda (1984) makes distinctions between group guidance and group counseling in the school setting as follows:

Group Guidance

Group guidance was organized to prevent the development of problems. The content included educational–vocational–personal–social information not otherwise systematically taught in academic courses. The typical setting was the classroom. Typical class size ranged from approximately 20 to 35. Providing accurate information for use in improved understanding of self and others was the direct emphasis in group guidance; attitude change frequently was an indirect outcome or goal. The leadership was provided by a classroom teacher or counselor who utilized a variety of instructional media and group dynamics concepts in motivating students and in obtaining group interaction. Instructional media included unfinished stories, puppet plays, movies, films, filmstrips, guest speakers, audio and videotaped interviews, student reports, and the like. Group dynamics concepts referred to the process employed in group guidance, such as sociodramas, buzz groups, panels, and other related techniques. (p. 6)

Group Counseling

Whereas the goal of group guidance is to provide students with accurate information that will help them make more appropriate plans and life decisions and in this sense is prevention oriented, group counseling is growth engendering and prevention and remediation oriented. Group counseling is prevention oriented in the sense that the counselees or clients are capable of functioning in society but may be experiencing some "rough spots" in their lives. If counseling is successful, the rough spots may be successfully smoothed with no serious personality defects incurred.

Group counseling is growth engendering insofar as it provides the participants incentive and motivation to make changes that are in their best interest (that is, the participants are motivated to take actions that maximize their potential through self-actualizing behaviors).

Group counseling is remedial for those individuals who have entered into a spiral of self-defeating behavior but who are nevertheless capable of reversing the spiral without counseling intervention. However, with counseling intervention, the counselee is likely to recover, and recover more quickly and with fewer emotional scars.

Although the content of group counseling is very similar to group guidance—including educational, vocational, personal, and social concerns—a number of other factors are quite different. First *group guidance* is recommended for all students on a regularly scheduled basis; *group counseling* is generally recommended only for those who are experiencing continuing or temporary problems that information alone will not resolve.

Group guidance makes an *indirect* attempt to change attitudes and behaviors through accurate information or an emphasis on cognitive or intellective functioning; group counseling makes a *direct* attempt to modify attitudes and behaviors by emphasizing total involvement. Group guidance is applicable to classroom-size groups, whereas group counseling is dependent upon the development of strong group cohesiveness and the sharing of personal concerns, which are most applicable to small, intimate groups. (pp. 7–8)

We might conclude that group guidance activities are most likely to be found in schools. Group counseling will be popular in agency and institutional settings and utilized somewhat, though not as frequently as group guidance, in school settings, while group psychotherapy will most frequently occur in clinics and agency or institutional settings. Group counseling and other group responsibilities of the counselor will be discussed in greater detail in Chapter 6.

Career Assistance

Counselors in both school and nonschool settings are asked to provide career planning and adjustment assistance to clients. In some agencies, such as community career centers and career centers for special populations, the focus is almost exclusively on the career needs of individuals. Counselors in government employment offices and rehabilitation services have an obvious responsibility to provide career counseling and guidance. Even those counselors in more broadly based programs such as community agencies, secondary schools, and institutions of higher education are expected to provide for the career-oriented needs of the populations they are designed to serve.

Since their earliest inception, both the school guidance movement and the counseling psychology movement have had a strong vocational influence. Traditionally, this activity has been viewed as one in which standardized tests were used for career assessment and planning. Descriptive materials and media were accumulated, organized, and then disseminated through planned group activities, as well as used in individual advising and counseling.

For many years in school settings this activity was referred to as the *information service* (providing occupational and educational information). In the 1970s the concept of this basic service was broadened and a new (now more appropriate) label assigned: *career guidance*. This term seemed more compatible with the rapidly developing career education movement and also represented in the minds of many (but not all) a broadening of the school counseling program's responsibility in the career development of school-aged youths. This approach is a developmental one that suggests certain experiences and understandings at each stage of one's growth that will provide for the building of appropriate foundations for later career planning and decision making.

Currently, the availability of various computer-based programs and other technological advances is significantly changing the career assistance resources available to counselors and how they use them in interactions with those they serve.

Placement and Follow-Up

Placement and follow-up have more traditionally been a service of school counseling programs, with an emphasis on educational placement in courses and programs. In actual practice this has meant that many school counselors have had responsibility for student scheduling, a very time-consuming task that has been viewed with considerable controversy as an administrative rather than a counseling function. Another aspect of educational placement is those activities associated with college admissions.

The other obvious component of the placement service—employment placement—has had much less emphasis and planning in schools, as we discovered in a national survey of school placement activities (Gibson, Mitchell, Stockton, Gerster, & Shafe, 1977). This type of placement seeks to match students seeking part-time or regular employment with available jobs. It also frequently involves a form of referral as well, in which the individual is referred to a particular job setting.

Follow-up activities are a means of assessing the effectiveness of a program's placement activities. Placement and follow-up activities have taken on increasing significance in schools in which career education and planning are emphasized. Of course, employment counselors and rehabilitation counselors are very active in the referral, placement, and follow-up of their clients. Also, as counselors are increasingly employed in business and industrial settings, these procedures will be an important aspect of their services. Counselors in all settings should use follow-up procedures for assessing counseling outcomes. Placement and follow-up activities are discussed further in Chapter 9.

Referral

Referral is the practice of aiding clients in finding needed expert assistance that the referring counselor cannot provide. This assistance provides the client with a higher level of training or special expertise related to the client's needs. Counselors in all settings will find it an advantage to their clients to establish a network of qualified helping professionals for referral purposes. Of course, counselors themselves will be the recipients of referrals from their various work settings and the populations they are expected to serve.

Consultation

Consultation is a process for helping a client through a third party or helping a system improve its services to its clientele. The former, usually labeled *triadic consultation*, is popular in working with parents of troubled children or teachers of problem pupils. The latter, appropriately labeled *process consultation*, focuses primarily on the processes that an agency or institution may be using to carry out its mission. Thus, consultation is a form of outreach in which counselors function as team members to assist individual clients or systems that serve clients.

In community and other agency settings, consultation is receiving increased attention as a way of preventing severe mental illnesses. In fact, the Community Mental Health Centers Act requires centers to provide consultation as one of five essential services. In school settings, especially elementary schools, the counselor is being increasingly used as a consultant to teachers and parents. Consultation is discussed in greater detail in Chapter 10.

Research

Research is necessary to the advancement of the profession of counseling. It provides a major source of empirically based hypotheses relevant to the ultimate goal of implementing effective counseling. It is a means for producing additional knowledge in our field, providing factual data to reinforce or guide the counselors' professional judgments, and seeking answers to questions of professional concern. Research results and the research process are important to program managers and other counselors who find it advantageous to have factual data to reinforce or guide their professional judgment.

Whether one is an active researcher or not, a counseling professional cannot afford to ignore or gloss over the important research in the field. It is important to recognize that different client populations, more diverse and usually more intense client problems, plus greater variation in staff backgrounds and, hence, treatment approaches, offer counselor–researchers the opportunity for unique and significant investigations. The Community Mental Health Center Amendment of 1975 emphasizes research with local application.

Interest has grown recently in *outcome research*—research that measures the outcomes of various counseling practices and activities. The Counseling and Human Development Foundation has sponsored recent studies of counseling outcome research. The professional publications of the American Counseling Association and the American Psychological Association regularly report the findings of counseling research studies. A brief sampling of counseling research studies is provided at the end of each chapter in this text, and research is discussed in general in Chapter 12.

Evaluation and Accountability

Although *evaluation* and *accountability* are not synonymous terms, they are interrelated and counselors and counseling programs are expected to engage in both. *Evaluation* is a means or process for assessing the effectiveness of the counselor's activities. It is fundamental to the verification and improvement of professional and program performance.

The use of the term *accountability* is an outgrowth of demands that schools and other tax-supported institutions and agencies be held accountable for their actions. In other words, some evidence of accomplishments must be provided in return for tax investments. Accountability also implies that these accomplishments must be provided in return for tax investments and that these accomplishments be relevant to the purpose for which the agencies or organizations were established.

Accountability establishes a basis for relevance, effectiveness, and efficiency. In this context, evaluation can be viewed as a component of the accountability model. More attention is given to accountability and evaluation in Chapter 13.

Prevention

The past 20 years have seen a substantial number of reports of important studies that examined the promotion of mental health through primary prevention using a social-psychological perspective. These include the Hahnemann Group (Spivack & Shure, 1974), the Connecticut Group (Allen, Chinsky, Larcen, Lochman, & Selinger, 1976), Project Aware (Thomson-Rountree & Woodruff, 1982), and the Rochester Pilot Program (1976–1977) (Weissberg & Gesten, 1982). The protective factors that operate in children's responses to stress and disadvantage have also been used to profile "invulnerable," that is, stress-resistant children (Garmezy, 1978; Rutter, 1980).

These and other studies suggest that a most attractive alternative to traditional remedial mental health practices is primary prevention, which seeks to prevent the occurrence of the disorder in the first place. Such an alternative suggests a shift in focus to the settings and life conditions that shape early adaptation. In this regard, the school and family are those social institutions that most profoundly affect early human development. Increasingly, this focus is on the school as a vital ongoing shaping force with organizational advantages for the initiation and development of mental health programs for primary prevention.

Thus, potential benefits for society may be derived from devising programs in schools that facilitate positive mental health interacting with a mastery of cognitive development. Since basic human needs, both sociological and psychological, are to a large measure met either successfully or unsuccessfully in major social institutions, for youth the schools become not only a resource for intellectual achievement but institutions that, in a larger and more important sense, shape the entire social group, subject to its experiences. As such, the schools have a major role in the promotion of positive mental health. In this effort, a significant contribution can be made through effective primary intervention strategies.

Community and other mental health-oriented agencies are becoming active in working with families to "head off" anticipated stresses, as well as in working with other stress-prone groups, such as divorced individuals, widows and widowers, and so forth. We can anticipate that counselors in a wide range of settings will be increasingly called on to develop and implement prevention strategies for serving their clientele. Chapter 11 gives further attention to prevention and wellness.

Closely allied with prevention is the concept of *wellness*, which recognizes both the mental and physical well-being of the individual. While the professional counselor may assist clients more directly in becoming mentally healthy, the possible interrelationships between mental and physical health cannot be overlooked. Counselors will, therefore, work to establish linkages with health care professionals. Too, as we are concerned with the total well-being of the individual, we may consider the *holistic approach* to counseling, which embodies the dimensions of body, mind, spirit, and emotions.

BASIC PRINCIPLES

Principles tend to form a philosophical framework within which programs are organized and activities developed. They are guidelines that are derived from the experiences and values of the profession, and they represent the views of the majority of the profession's membership. As such, they become fundamental assumptions or a system of beliefs regarding a profession and its role, function, and activities.

For Schools

Indicated here are some principles suggesting how school counseling programs can make their contributions more effectively:

1. School counseling and guidance programs should be designed to serve the developmental and adjustment needs of all youth.

2. The school counseling program should be concerned with the total development of the students it serves. This program also recognizes that individual development is a continuous, ongoing process; therefore, school counseling programs must themselves be developmental.

3. Pupil guidance must be viewed as a process that is continuous throughout the child's formal education.

4. Trained professional counseling personnel are essential for ensuring professional competencies, leadership, and direction (which does not imply that paraprofessionals cannot make worthwhile contributions).

5. Certain basic activities are essential to program effectiveness, and these must be specifically planned and developed if they are to be effective.

6. The school counseling program must reflect the uniqueness of the population it serves and the environment in which it seeks to render this service; thus, like individuals, each school guidance program will be different from other programs.

7. Relevant to the preceding point, the school counseling program should base its uniqueness on a regular, systematic assessment of the student clientele's needs and the characteristics of the program's environmental setting.

8. An effective instructional program in the school requires an effective program of pupil counseling and guidance. Good education and good guidance are interrelated. They support and complement each other to the student's advantage.

9. Relevant to statement 7, teacher understanding and support of the school counseling program is significant to the success of such programs.

10. The school counseling program is accountable. It recognizes the need to provide objective evidence of accomplishments and the value of those accomplishments.

11. The school counselor is a team member. The counselor shares a concern and programs for youths with psychologists, social workers, teachers, administrators, and other educational professionals and staff.

12. The school counseling program must recognize the right and capability of the individual to make decisions and plans.

13. The school counseling program must respect the worth and dignity of the individual—every individual.

14. The school counseling program must recognize the uniqueness of the individual and the individual's right to that uniqueness.

15. The school counselor should be a role model of positive human relations—of unbiased, equal treatment.

Although counseling is a relatively young profession, counselors are developing traditions, establishing their role and worth, and will cope resourcefully and imaginatively with the demands of the future. The following discussion considers some traditions, activities, and effective counseling program organization and functioning.

For Community Agencies

Counseling programs in community and other institutional or agency settings represent a wide range of approaches for delivering services. The development and implementation of these services is based on certain underlying assumptions and basic principles.

The basic assumption that community involvement is essential for relevant and accountable community mental health agencies has implications for the basic principles of those agencies that are community based. Bloom (1984) has suggested seven such principles for the guidance of professional personnel employed in community mental health agencies as follows (these might be paraphrased slightly for noncommunity-based mental health agencies):

Principle 1: Regardless of where your paycheck comes from, think of yourself as working for the community.

Principle 2: If you want to know about a community's mental health needs, ask the community.

Principle 3: As you learn about community-mental-health-related needs, you have the responsibility to tell the community what you are learning.

Principle 4: Help the community establish its own priorities.

Principle 5: You can help the community decide among various courses of action in its efforts to solve its own problems.

Principle 6: In the event that the community being served is so disorganized that representatives of various facets of the community cannot be found, you have the responsibility to find such representatives.

Principle 7: You should work toward the equitable distribution of power in the community.* (pp. 429–431)

SUMMARY

Most of the basic principles and traditional activities enumerated here have, as Chapter 1 suggested, a historic relationship with the development of the counseling movement. Although the organization of these activities into program formats differs across the various settings, the mention of the importance of individual assessment, one-to-one counseling, group activities, career information and placement, and follow-up would evoke a ringing round of applause from our professional forebears. Additionally, in recent generations we have come to view consultation as an expected professional service, and the current emphasis on prevention indicates it will be a major role for counselors in the future.

Traditions are the hallmarks of a profession. They are often seen as indexes of the professional maturity of a discipline and synonymous with the guiding principles for a profession. They represent guidelines for newcomers (and reminiscences for the "old timers") to the profession. They become powerful determinants of the profession's goals and actions and, in time, extremely resistant to elimination or alteration. Thus, although sometimes a call for drastic change (even elimination of counseling programs in some settings) will arise, it is not the fundamental beliefs or traditional activities of the counselor that must change but rather how the activity is interpreted or viewed and carried out that will determine the merits of a counseling program in any setting.

Relevancy is a key to the success or failure of a program's activities and services. For example, it is doubtful that the counseling skills and understandings that we possessed when we first entered the profession would be relevant to the demands of today's youths, and it is certain that both the concept of careers and the career information at our disposal then would not be in any way relevant today. As C. Gilbert Wrenn stressed in his classic book *The World of the Contemporary Counselor* (1973), "the need of the counselor is to attempt to understand contemporary youth and the world in which they live" (p. 3). That is relevancy—seeing and understanding the current environment that surrounds our clients as well as our clients themselves.

We move from this broad overview of counselor activities to more specifically examining how counselors may function in school settings (Chapter 3) and community and agency settings (Chapter 4).

DISCUSSION QUESTIONS

1. When you hear the term *professional*, what does this imply to you? What does the label *profession* mean to you?

2. Discuss characteristics attributable to those in the helping professions (medicine, law, dentistry, education, psychology, and social work) and how these characteristics help and/or hinder professional performance.

*From *Community Mental Health: A General Introduction,* 2nd edition, by B. L. Bloom. Copyright © 1984 (1977) by Brooks/Cole Publishing Company, a division of International Thomson Publishing, Inc., Pacific Grove, CA 93950. Reprinted by permission of the publisher.

3. Do some current societal needs have implications for new directions in educational or societal services? Identify and discuss.

4. List five environmental variables that positively influenced the development of your human potential as well as five environmental variables that detracted from your human potential growth. Next, examine present environmental variables.

5. Are there traditions you associate with other professions such as medicine and law? Discuss these and how you believe they may have evolved.

6. Are there any special responsibilities that a "profession" has to the public? Identify and discuss.

7. In view of current societal needs, what changes in the traditional counselor role and function might be envisioned, if any?

CLASS ACTIVITIES

1. Organize the class into small groups to interview professionals in the professions of medicine, dentistry, law, nursing, and teaching. Interviews should seek information regarding (a) training, (b) regulation of the profession by the profession, and (c) traditions of the profession. Report findings orally to the class.

2. Have class members interview counselors in various settings to ascertain the major activities they typically engage in as professional counselors. Report these findings to the class.

3. Organize the class into small groups and have each group member discuss his or her contact with counseling programs and the perceptions of those programs for each of the educational levels: elementary, secondary, and higher education. Have each group come up with a list of recommendations based on its experiences for improving counseling programs in educational settings.

SELECTED READINGS

Aubrey, R. F. (1982). A house divided: Guidance and counseling in 20th century America. *Personnel and Guidance Journal, 61,* 198–204.

———. (1985). A counseling perspective on the recent educational reform reports. *The School Counselor, 33,* 91–99.

Herr, E. L. (1982). *Why counseling?* [Monograph]. Washington, DC: American Personnel and Guidance Association.

Herr, E. L., & Pinson, N. M. (1982). *Foundations for policy in guidance and counseling.* Alexandria, VA: American Association for Counseling and Development.

Hutson, P. W. (1962). On professionalism. *Personnel and Guidance Journal, 41,* 63–64.

McCully, C. H. (1962). The school counselor: Strategy for professionalization. *Personnel and Guidance Journal, 40,* 681–689.

Miller, G. M. (1988). Counselor functions in excellent schools: Elementary through secondary. *The School Counselor, 36,* 88–93.

Tiedeman, D. V. (1980). Status and prospect in counseling psychology: 1962. In J. M. Whiteley (Ed.), *The history of counseling psychology* (pp. 125–132). Monterey, CA: Brooks/Cole.

Whiteley, J. M. (1980). Counseling psychology in the year 2000 A.D. *Counseling Psychologist, 8,* 2–62.

RESEARCH OF INTEREST

Decker, W. H. (1986). Occupation and impressions: Stereotypes of males and females in three professions. *Social Behavior and Personality, 14,* 69–75.

Abstract

Stereotypes of persons in three predominantly sex-typed professions and of "average persons" were studied. Males were perceived as more autonomous and effective but less acceptable than females only when target occupation was unspecified and data of both subject-sexes were combined. Females were generally rated equal or superior to males.

Dees, M. S., III, Buck, P., Walker, C. E., & Nicewander, A. (1985, August). *Survey of the public perception of psychology, psychologists, and psychiatrists*. Paper presented at the Annual Convention of the American Psychological Association, Los Angeles.

Abstract

The public perception of psychology, psychologists, and psychiatrists has not been examined for 20 years. Participants for this study were randomly selected from an urban area (Oklahoma City) and a rural area (Okarche, Oklahoma). Questionnaires about the usefulness and competency of these professionals were administered by telephone; half of the questionnaires used the term *psychologist* ($N = 225$) and the other half substituted the word *psychiatrist* ($N = 225$). Additionally, urban psychologists ($N = 47$) and psychiatrists ($N = 25$) responded to the questionnaire as if they were members of the public. Psychiatrists are favored for intelligence testing, career counseling, sexual dysfunction, and alcohol and drug abuse, while psychologists were favored for stress management. The findings indicate that the perception of psychologists' competence had improved since a 1965 study, but confusion about professional domain continues. Rural residents also recognize the need for psychiatrists and psychologists, but they desire less information than urban residents about a potential therapist. The psychologists and psychiatrists who responded to the questionnaire report that the public have greater confidence in their abilities to solve problems than the public report.

Lemkau, J. P. (1983). Women in male-dominated professions: Distinguishing personality background characteristics. *Psychology of Women Quarterly, 8,* 144–165.

Abstract

Compares 64 women in atypical professions with 71 women in sex-typical professions. Results suggest those in atypical professions are more likely to be firstborn and to mention positive influences of men on their careers. Factors related to atypical choice may relate to academic achievement.

Livneh, C. (1988). Characteristics of lifelong learners in the human service professions. *Adult Education Quarterly, 8,* 149–159.

Abstract

The Characteristics of Lifelong Learners in the Professions instrument was administered to 195 human service professionals, and responses were subjected to principal components analysis, Varimax rotation, and multiple-regression analysis. Two factors emerge as potential predictors of lifelong learning: educability and future orientation.

Prochaska, J. O., & Norcross, J. C. (1982). The future of psychotherapy: A Delphi poll. *Professional Psychology, 13,* 620–627.

Abstract

Predicts psychotherapy trends in the next decade by using Delphi poll. Thirty-six therapists and researchers completed a 100-item questionnaire assessing possible changes in therapeutic interventions, psychotherapists, therapy modalities, theoretical orientations, research findings, and professional issues. Results indicate that therapy will become more cognitive-behavioral, present centered, problem specific, and briefer; cathartic, aversive, and dynamic approaches are expected to decrease. Family and marital therapy are predicted to markedly increase; long-term individual modalities are expected to markedly decrease. Optimistic forecasts include an increase in women and minority therapists, accelerated services to under-served populations, coverage under national health insurance, and standard implementation of peer review. One emerging pattern suggests that psychotherapists' efforts at change will become more similar to self-change processes that are used by people in their natural environment.

Chapter 3

The School Counselor's Role and Function

Counselors in any work setting need to be aware of what services school counselors and school counseling provide. Therefore, a purpose of this chapter is to orient potential counselors, including those interested in school settings, to the

- ❖ training of counselors,
- ❖ credentialing of counselors, and
- ❖ role and function of counselors and their supporting professionals in different educational settings.

TRAINING PROGRAMS FOR COUNSELORS

As previously noted, counseling and guidance programs in schools are an educational development of this century, and they have, until recently, been unique to the U.S. and Canadian educational systems. The same is true of training programs for counselors. Similarly, since the initial years of the National Defense Education Act (1958–1960), both the number and size of counselor training programs have grown rapidly. The supporting facts indicate that in 1964 there were 327 institutions of higher education supporting counselor preparation programs with 706 faculty. Hollis and Wantz (1994) report that by 1992 this number of accredited programs was 798. Also, if you had entered a counselor training program in 1964, you could have anticipated a training staff of slightly more than two full-time faculty members; however, if you delayed your entry until 1990, you could have expected, on the average, a staff of eight full-time faculty members.

Because many of you may already be enrolled in programs of counselor education, the initial discussion of this chapter may serve only to remind you to see your adviser about the course work that lies ahead or how your own program may differ or be similar to others. We are certain, however, that you recognize the significant relationship between what you are trained to do and your role and function once you are on the job. Also, as Thomas (1973) notes in *The Schools Next Time:*

> Control of the lower schools (elementary and secondary) by the colleges is again obvious when one remembers that all certified school personnel are college trained—they cannot be licensed without such training. Teachers, counselors, and administrators are all enculturated with the biases of academia. (p. 216)

As a means of putting into perspective who functions at what level and with what training or expertise, Table 3–1 indicates that persons with appropriate experience or training and the skills to communicate can function at the advice-giving level. In the school setting, for example, all teachers and most staff would qualify as advisers for many occasions and should serve in this important role in the school's program of pupil guidance. At the second level, special training to at least the master's degree is required, which provides the school counselor with special expertise as a counselor. Such expertise sets the counselor apart from other professionals in the school setting and establishes the unique qualifications to interact with or on behalf of students in meeting their routine development, adjustment, planning, and decision-making needs. The third level repre-

TABLE 3–1 Levels of Training and Responsibility

Level	Training	Responsibility
First	Appropriate educational and/or experience background	Advising; information giving
Second	Master's degree in counseling and guidance	Developmental and normal adjustment counseling
Third	Doctorate in counseling and guidance or counseling psychology	Serious personality disorders

sents the highest degree of professional training available, usually an earned doctorate. As practicing counselors, these professionals are most frequently used as resource personnel for referrals and consultation. Their clients usually have serious personality disorders requiring intensive and long-term counseling. In addition to counseling, these higher-trained counselors may also seek careers in research or university teaching or in supervisory positions.

Additional insights into the relationship between levels of training and the counselor's role and function as represented by initial employment may be noted in Tables 3–2 and 3–3, which depict the initial placement of graduates of master's degree programs of counseling in community, mental health, marriage and family, rehabilitation, and school counseling.

TABLE 3–2 Counselor Placement First Year After Graduation Listed in Rank Order for 1993: Community, Mental Health, Marriage and Family, and Rehabilitation Counselors.

Employment Category	Community and/or Mental Health Majors		Marriage and Family Majors	Rehabilitation Majors
	Community Counselors	Mental Health Counselors		
Public Agency	49%	48%	37%	50%
Private practice/ agency	24%	25%	37%	28%
Advanced Graduate placement	10%	14%	12%	5%
Managed Care	8%	7%	9%	7%
Other	8%	6%	4%	8%

Source: From J. W. Hollis and R. A. Wantz (1994), *Counselor Preparation 1993–95. Vol. II: Status, Trends, and Implications* (8th ed.), p. 85, 102, 113. © Accelerated Development, Inc. Used by permission.

TABLE 3–3 School Counselor: Placement First-Year After Graduation, Listed in Rank Order for 1993

Employment Category	Average percent of graduates of school counseling majors
Elementary	29%
Middle	23%
Secondary	34%
Advanced graduate placement	7%
Other	7%

Source: From J. W. Hollis and R. A. Wantz (1994), *Counselor Preparation 1993–95. Vol. II: Status Trends, and Implications* (8th ed.), p. 122. © Accelerated Development, Inc. Used by permission.

In examining the content of training programs available, one cannot help but note course content consistent among master's programs across the United States and Canada. In the United States much of this conformity is undoubtedly the result of state certification patterns for school counselors, which reflect, with little deviation, an expectancy of training to perform the traditional basic services noted in Chapter 2.

A number of counselor training institutions also offer a specialist or 6th-year degree. In many states this degree qualifies one with appropriate experience for director or supervisor of guidance or director of pupil personnel services certificates. The current trend toward a 2-year master's degree will probably result in the elimination of the specialist degree in many institutions. Brown and Pate (1983) suggest that this trend will go far to establish a distinction between those who want some level of human relations training and those who have a commitment to a career.

Approximately 175 counselor training institutions in the United States and Canada offer programs leading to an earned doctorate. These programs tend, according to the nature of the program, to prepare their candidates for positions in mental health clinics, hospitals, crisis and therapy agencies, for positions on university counselor education faculties, in college and university counseling centers, and for rehabilitation counseling, student personnel work in higher education, and other agency or institutional settings. Some may also elect to enter private practice. Variations in program emphasis and preparation patterns are more commonplace than at the master's level. Also, in many institutions, several counselor education or related programs may exist because of specialized training (i.e., departments of counselor education, rehabilitation counseling, counseling psychology, marriage and family, etc.).

THE CREDENTIALING OF SCHOOL COUNSELORS

Today, counselors seem to be used with ever-increasing frequency in a variety of settings. There are home buyer counselors, financial counselors, landscape counselors, used car counselors, and diet counselors. There are also counselors who may be distinguished from the first group on the basis of certification or legal licensure. These include legal counselors, investment counselors, psychological counselors, and school guidance counselors. Differences between licensure and certification will be discussed later in this chapter. The licensure or certification indicates that the holder has successfully completed and has been examined on learning and experience criteria recommended by the representative professional organizations and the appropriate licensing boards or agencies. The late C. Harold McCully, in his classic discussion "The School Counselor: Strategy for Professionalization" (1962), suggested 11 characteristics of a profession, stating:

> A profession is an occupation in which the members of a corporate group assure minimum competence for entry into the occupation by setting and enforcing standards for selection, training, and licensure or certification. (p. 682)

Advantages

The following advantages accrue from some sort of a credentialing process:

1. *Credentialing protects the public against those who would masquerade as possessing certain skills and training.* A number of years ago, an article in the old *Look* magazine entitled "Beware of the Psycho-Quacks" gave examples of the various guises for preying on the public under counseling and psychological titles. Many have read the book or seen the movie *The Great Imposter,* in which one individual successfully assumed a variety of professional careers. Although such reports sometimes amuse and often attract admirers for those who have "beat the system," very few people would knowingly like to be seen by a physician who is not a physician, a lawyer who is not a lawyer, or a counselor who is not a counselor. These examples remind us of the need for some sort of a procedure that protects the public against professional misrepresentation and fraud.

2. *It provides, at the very least, minimally accepted training and experience requirements.* Credentialing and training requirements (and experiences) are closely interrelated. This interrelationship provides for a common core of learning experiences and achievement expectancies. These are related to the profession's concept of preparatory standards for entry into the profession. These standards are not only helpful to candidates considering entry into training programs and protect them from misleading training schemes, but they also reassure employers as well as the general public who use the services.

3. *Credentialing can provide a legal base for the protection of the membership of the profession.* Because credentialing suggests standards that benefit the public, law-making bodies are prone to provide the profession and its membership with certain legal forms of protection. For example, individuals cannot legally practice medicine without a license, and lawyers legally have the right of privileged communication with their clients. In many states, the right to enter private practice in such fields as psychology and professional counseling is limited by law.

4. *It may provide a basis for special benefits.* In addition to legal benefits, credentialed professionals may also qualify for certain financial benefits. Physicians' and lawyers' fees may qualify for insurance payments. Physicians, including psychiatrists, also qualify for national health insurance payments such as Medicaid. Psychologists may also qualify as mental health providers for insurance payments in some states. Credentialed school counselors have, on occasion, been qualified to receive special training grants to increase their

qualifications. Because credentialing qualifies individuals for membership in professional organizations, they become eligible for the benefits such memberships provide (e.g., special training, publications, group insurance).

Types of Credentialing

Two common methods are used to credential practitioners of a profession such as counseling: *certification* and *licensure*. Differences between certification and licensure have been described by Forster (1977):

> *Certification:* This is a process of recognizing the competence of practitioners of a profession by officially authorizing them to use the title adopted by the profession. Certification can be awarded by voluntary associations, agencies, or by governmental bodies, some of which are recognized by state laws. In school counseling, certification is usually handled by an office within the state government's department of education or its branch for executing public instruction matters. Certification officials commonly check transcripts for evidence that the applicant has completed required courses from preparation programs that are known to be acceptable.
>
> *Licensure:* This is a process authorized by state legislation that regulates the practice and the title of the profession. Because of its legislative base, licensure subjects violators to greater legal sanctions than does certification. Licensure is generally considered to be more desirable when a substantial proportion of a profession's practitioners are in private practice, because of the broader coverage and greater potential for using sanctions against violators. Licensure boards are usually established with quasi-legislative power to make rules and examine applicants who seek licenses. (p. 573)

Another activity that has significance for the credentialing process, whether it be certification or licensure, is *accreditation*. Accreditation, according to Forster (1977), is a process

> whereby an association or agency grants public recognition to a school, institute, college, university, or specialized program of study that has met certain established qualifications or standards as determined through initial and periodic evaluations. "Program approval" is another name for accreditation. In some professions, graduates of accredited preparation programs are considered credentialed. Sometimes a registry is used by a profession to list graduates of accredited programs. (p. 573)

Most programs preparing school counselors are accredited by their regional accrediting associations. Counselor training programs in schools or colleges of education may also have accreditation by the National Council for Accreditation of Teacher Education (NCATE), and programs both within and outside education may qualify for approval by the Council for Accreditation of Counseling and Related Educational Programs (CACREP), which is affiliated with the American Counseling Association. Doctoral programs preparing counseling psychologists may seek accreditation by the American Psychological Association (APA). In addition, many state departments of public instruction accredit higher education training programs within their jurisdictions.

The Issue of Licensure

During the 1970s, credentialing became one of the major issues facing the counseling profession. Although school counselor certification existed in all states before 1970, the issue of licensure became of greater concern as the APA moved to secure legal recognition of the more or less exclusive rights of psychologists and those trained in psychological counseling programs to engage in and identify themselves in practice as counselors. Many counselors trained in counselor education programs viewed this as limiting their options to primarily school or certain agency settings. A major focus of the legislative efforts of the APA has been to establish psychology as a profession to provide health services (and as previously noted, qualifying them for insurance reimbursements).

In the 1980s the American Personnel and Guidance Association, now the American Counseling Association, became increasingly active in providing certification options for counselors through their certification arm, the National Board for Certified Counselors, Inc. (NBCC). A national examination has been developed and a national registry of mental health care providers published listing those who have met the specified qualifications for training, experience, and examination. The content areas of the NBCC examination reflect the knowledge and skills necessary to carry out the traditional activities supporting the role and function of the professional counselor:

- ❖ Appraisal of persons
- ❖ Group dynamics, processing, and counseling
- ❖ Human growth and development
- ❖ Lifestyle and career development
- ❖ Professional orientation
- ❖ Research and evaluation
- ❖ Social and cultural foundations
- ❖ The helping relationship

Concurrently, the American Counseling Association has been politically active in securing legal recognition for counselors licensed through the NBCC. A number of states currently have licensure (41 in 1994), with success anticipated in more states in the remaining 1990s. As part of the growing trend toward licensure, other counseling groups such as marriage and family, drug, alcohol, and rehabilitation counselors are now licensed or certified in many states. Since a variety of training programs, despite different orientations, can claim to train counselors—such as counseling psychologists, school counselors, marriage counselors, rehabilitation counselors, and others—the movement toward licensure has been viewed in many instances as an effort to limit and restrict the practice of counseling to those who come from a particular training background.

In general, most of those in the counseling profession believe that the movement toward licensure is one that will protect both the public and the profession in the long run. The issues primarily center on what training is necessary for what role and function and under whose jurisdiction or approval.

Certification and the School Counselor

As previously mentioned, all states require certification for those who will be school counselors. Generally very similar across states, these requirements account for the considerable degree of reciprocity by which candidates certified in one state may be eligible for certification in another state. For example, the vast majority of certification programs require a counselor's minimal completion of a master's degree. Also, most certification patterns require course work appropriate to the basic guidance services. That includes courses in appraisal or, sometimes, standardized testing, career and educational information, career guidance or career development, individual counseling, group guidance and counseling, and principles of counseling and guidance. Courses in consultation and organization of school counseling programs are also frequent requirements. In addition, some sort of supervised practicum experience is typically required. In 3-year preparation programs, internships are required. Many states also demand 1–3 years of prior teaching experience for certification to counsel in schools. An increasing number of states have, however, recently amended their certification requirements to provide for an alternative experience to teaching, such as an internship.

It is probably a "chicken or egg" situation to attempt to determine whether training influences practice or vice versa, and we do not intend to bias that argument. We have, by choice, discussed training and resulting certification first. In the paragraphs that follow, counseling practices in various educational settings will be described. One may note the relationship between these practices and training patterns previously presented. Remember, though, that this discussion is a brief overview only; greater detail will be provided later.

THE ROLE AND FUNCTION OF COUNSELORS IN SCHOOL SETTINGS

An Overview

The counselor's role and function, as described in an official American School Counselor Association statement, is presented in Appendix A.

One view of the role and function of school counselors may be based on how they spend their time. A study by Partin (1993) identified school counselors' perceived distribution of time by elementary, middle/junior high, and senior high school (Table 3–4).

Individual counseling, guidance activities, consultation, and group counseling are major activities as measured by time commitments. Administrative and clerical responsibilities increase from elementary to senior high school. In fact, Partin (1993) notes in his study that "for senior high counselors, paper work, scheduling, and administrative tasks are seen as significant time robbers that deter counselors from allotting more time for individual and group counseling" (p. 279).

The variety in school settings, of course, will account for some differences in the ways counselors may carry out their roles. However, some common influences determine the role and function of counselors, regardless of the setting. The first of these is what might be called *professional constants* or determinants that indicate what is appropriate and not appropriate to the counselor's role. These include guidelines and policy statements of professional organizations, licensing or certification limitations, accreditation guidelines and requirements, and the expectancies of professional training programs. In addition to these professional constants, personal factors inevitably influence role and function. These include the interest of the counselor, such as what he or she likes to do; what he or she

TABLE 3–4   Counselors' Perceived Distribution of Time

Activity	Elementary		Middle/Junior High		Senior High	
	M%	*SD*	*M%*	*SD*	*M%*	*SD*
Testing, appraisal	6.29	6.70	7.27	5.39	6.68	4.02
Guidance activities	24.19*	21.16	13.18[a]	11.75	11.47[a]	8.23
Individual counseling	27.31	18.99	28.60	13.91	30.96	16.56
Group counseling	11.21	8.19	12.44	11.94	8.77	6.26
Professional development	3.64	2.92	3.78	2.70	4.55	2.98
Consultation	12.10	6.45	13.50	8.11	11.32	6.24
Resource coordination	5.43	4.58	6.38	5.38	6.11	3.30
Administrative & clerical	7.02[a]	7.42	11.83[a]	10.16	17.27*	13.06
Other, nonguidance activities	4.43	12.99	5.08	5.31	3.98	7.18

[a]Means are significantly lower than means marked with an asterisk (*).
$p < .05$.

Source: From R. L. Partin, "School Counselors' Time: Where Does It Go?" *School Counselor, 40*(4), 1993, p. 278.
© American Counseling Association. Reprinted with permission. No further reproduction authorized without written permission of the American Counseling Association.

gets encouraged to do and is rewarded for doing by the school, community, or his or her peers; what the counselor has resources to do; what the counselor perceives as the appropriate role and function for a given setting; and finally, how life in general is going for the counselor. The counselor's attitudes, values, and experiences both on and off the job can influence how he or she views the job.

Counselors and other professional helpers are recognizing more and more that traditional roles and delivery systems in human services may have imposed real limitations on their ability to deal directly and effectively with clients' critical needs. We would also note the current call for counselors and counseling programs to become increasingly active in preventive interventions and developmental guidance. Thus, as we further view the role and function of counselors, we are seeking to integrate for you, our reader, not only those concepts that have proven themselves over the years but also current and promising directions that seem necessary for the counselor to remain a viable entity in the school setting.

The Elementary School Counselor

Elementary schools are a powerful socializing force in human development. For better or worse, virtually all members of modern society carry important imprints of their elementary school experiences throughout their lives. In this setting the young pupil is expected to acquire basic mastery of increasingly difficult bodies of knowledge as well as learn to meet the school's behavior and social expectancies. Failure to learn generates behavioral problems just as inappropriate behaviors and social skills handicap learning.

TABLE 3–5 Rank Ordering of Elementary School Counselor Activities as Indicated by 996 School Counselors

Rank	Activity	Percentage Engaging in Activity
1	Individual counseling	98
2	Group guidance and counseling	81
3	Consultation with parents	79
4	Consultation with teachers	78
5	Classroom guidance instruction	65
6.5	Pupil assessment	39
6.5	Coordination, referral, and consultation with community agencies	39

Source: Reprinted from R. L. Gibson, "Prevention and the Elementary School Counselor," *Elementary School Guidance and Counseling, 24,* p. 34. © 1989 American Counseling Association. Reprinted with permission. No further reproduction authorized without written permission of the American Counseling Association.

In the 1970s it became increasingly evident that the developmental requirements of elementary-age youth were often neglected and even unrecognized (Stevens & Phil, 1982; White, 1985). As a result, a number of states (12 in 1993) have mandated elementary school counseling. Humes and Hohenshil (1987) suggest that this trend will continue inasmuch as there now appears to be a reawakened interest in elementary school counselors as primary mental health providers.

The characteristics of the elementary pupil and the elementary school dictate certain elements in program organization that distinguish elementary school counseling programs from those at other educational levels. Thus the elementary school counselor's role and function will also reflect these differences. The differences, however, are not so much in what the elementary school counselors do but in *how* they do it.

For example, counselors and other elementary school specialists must work closely and effectively with classroom teachers, and guidance activities, usually classroom oriented, are a major time consumer (see Table 3–5). This context naturally leads to an emphasis on consultation and coordination. In addition to counseling, coordination, and consulting functions, the elementary school counselor has responsibilities for pupils' orientation, assessment, and career development needs.

Counselor

Although one-to-one counseling in the elementary school may take correspondingly less of the counselor's time than counseling at other levels, the counselor should be available to meet individually or in groups with children referred by teachers or parents or identified by the counselor or other helping professionals as being in need of counseling.

In recent years, however, the elementary school counselor has also been asked to participate in the resolution of contemporary mental health problems, such as latchkey children, child abuse, substance abuse, and suicide. Thus, the developmental needs of all children may be seen as secondary to crisis intervention for some pupils by school administrators and parents. This new priority has had an impact on preservice and in-service training needs because there is a current public demand in counselor education programs for courses related to social problems. (Sheeley & Jenkins, 1985, as cited in Humes & Hohenshil, 1987, p. 40)

Consultant

As a consultant, the counselor may confer directly with teachers, parents, administrators, and other helping professionals to help an identified third party, such as a student, in the school setting. In this role, the counselor helps others assist the student–client in dealing more effectively with developmental or adjustment needs.

Coordinator

Elementary school counselors have a responsibility for the coordination of the various guidance activities in the schools. Coordinating these with ongoing classroom and school activities is also desirable. As the only building-based helping professional, the elementary school counselor may be called on to coordinate the contributions of school psychologists, social workers, and others. Other coordination activities could include intraschool referrals and interagency referrals.

Agent for Orientation

As a human development facilitator, the elementary school counselor recognizes the importance of the child's orientation to the goals and environment of the elementary school. It is important that the child's initial education experiences be positive ones. In this regard the counselor may plan group activities and consult with teachers to help children learn and practice the relationship skills necessary in the school setting.

Assessment

The counselor in the elementary school can anticipate being called on to interpret and often gather both test and nontest data. To the counselor will also fall the task of putting these data into focus not only to see but to be able to interpret the child as a total being. Beyond the traditional data used for pupil understanding, the counselor should also understand the impact of culture, the sociology of the school, and other environmental influences on pupil behavior.

Career Developer

The importance of the elementary school years as a foundation for the child's later significant decisions underscores the desirability of planned attention to the elementary pupil's career development. Although the responsibility for career education planning rests with the classroom teachers, the elementary school counselor can make a major contribution as a coordinator and consultant in developing a continuous, sequential, and integrated program.

TABLE 3–6   Major Program Emphasis in 96 Elementary School Counseling Programs

Rank	Program Emphasis	Percentage of Programs
1	Prevention	81
2	Developmental	78
3	Remediation and crisis intervention	64
4	Enhancement	22

Source: From Gibson, R. L., "Prevention and the Elementary School Counselor," *Elementary School Guidance and Counseling, 24*(1), p. 34. © 1989 American Counseling Association. Reprinted with permission. No further reproduction authorized without written permission of the American Counseling Association.

Agent of Prevention

In the elementary school are early warning signs of future problems for young children: learning difficulties, general moodiness (unhappiness, depression), and acting-out behaviors (fights, quarrels, disruptions, restlessness, impulsiveness, and obstinacy) (Finkel, 1976). Conyne (1983), Dodge (1983), and others have cited accumulating evidence to demonstrate that children who cannot adjust during their elementary school years are at high risk for a variety of later problems. Further, substance abuse, violence among peers, vandalism, problems associated with latchkey children, and so forth have increased among elementary school pupils.

A study (Gibson, 1989) of 96 elementary school programs recommended as "outstanding" by their state departments of public instruction indicated that prevention was a major program emphasis in 81% of these programs. Elementary school counselors will be increasingly called on and challenged to develop programs that seek to anticipate, intervene in, and prevent the development of these problems. (See Table 3–5 for a rank ordering of elementary school counselor activities as indicated by counselors.)

An Overview of the Elementary School Counselor's Role

Some additional insight into the role and function of the elementary school counselor may also be provided by examining the results of the previously noted study (Gibson, 1989), which notes major program emphasis (see Table 3–6). The benefits of counseling programs in elementary schools are outlined in Table 3–7.

The following description of a day in the life of an elementary school counselor was written by Dr. Sherry K. Basile, at that time an elementary school counselor at Berkeley Elementary School, Monck's Corner, South Carolina (currently an assistant professor of education at Indiana University).

> Children are scattered on the sidewalks, laughing, playing, crying, some hugging poles. It's early morning and as I walk through the safety of the gate, I am welcomed with a deluge of hugs from what seems like a thousand arms. In the distance there are faces with eyes eagerly waiting their turn for mine to acknowledge theirs.

TABLE 3–7 Benefits of Counseling Programs in Elementary Schools

The Elementary School exists to provide:	The Counseling Program in the Elementary School can contribute by:	This implies the following:
1. Foundations for learning and living	1. Providing classroom guidance to enhance learning and relate learning to preparation	1.1 Classroom guidance 1.2 Consultation with teachers and administrators
2. Transmission of our culture and historical heritage	2. Developing multicultural awareness: pride in our cultural diversity and respect for the uniqueness of all cultural/ethnic groups	2.1 Classroom guidance activities 2.2 Consultation with teachers and administrators 2.3 Group guidance and counseling
3. Development as a social-psychological being	3. Providing for the socialization (social development) of all children, including respect for self and others	3.1 Group guidance and group counseling focusing on prevention, development, and remediation 3.2 Individual counseling 3.3 Consultation with parent
4. Preparation for citizenship	4. Providing for the development of each individual's human potential	4.1 Career development 4.2 Individual assessment 4.3 Talent and skill enhancement

Source: From Gibson, R. L., Mitchell, M. H., and Basile, S. K. *Counseling in the Elementary School: A Comprehensive Approach*, p. 20. Copyright © 1993 by Allyn and Bacon. Reprinted by permission.

The elementary school is a gloriously fulfilling environment for a school counselor. In my opinion the elementary school counselor is the ultimate human resource for hundreds of children. We are perceived by them as an adult who never judges or belittles them. We are their friend. Children depend on us to be loving, understanding, happy, always willing to help, incredibly flexible and genuine. In essence we are our positions.

Truly, our jobs are energizing and rewarding. In the lives of many children, we are possibly the only positive force. Our presence in schools allows all children to experience feeling warm and fuzzy and accepted.

The multifarious position of an elementary school counselor begins as I enter the gate of the school yard. Following my regal entrance into the building, most often I am greeted by teachers who need consultation on discipline problems or to refer a child. They follow me inside. Once in my office, I can find paper and pencil to take necessary notes.

With all their needs met, I get ready for the parent conference that is scheduled next. Many parents work and are unable to come in after school, so they prefer early morning appointments. Teachers may or may not be included depending on the issue.

This type of conference is intervention. When a problem or concern exists, the counselor intervenes, for example, by suggesting ways of modifying behavior or some other form of problem solving.

In addition to intervention, another major thrust is toward prevention. The purpose and underlying hope is to help children, early in their lives, to become problem solvers, to develop self-confidence, to become more responsible and thoroughly practice being the best they can be.

We incorporate prevention strategies primarily through classroom guidance activities. In my school, teachers are allowed to choose either the first period of the day or their period before lunch for classroom guidance.

It is now time to gather audiovisual equipment and scurry off to a classroom. Sometimes I pack a cassette player, puppets, posters, handout sheets, books, stickers, but always high energy and a smile. Also, the rule at my school is that, as the counselor walks by, it is not acceptable to get out of line to give hugs. They all raise their hand for a high-five as I walk by their line. This saves the teacher frustration from lining up again, and I am not late for my scheduled activity.

As I open the door and enter the classroom, there's clapping and happy glowing faces. The children are thrilled that I have come to be with them. The teachers sit in the back of the room or at their desks. I invite the children to enter the world of affective education—feelings, thoughts, decision making, understanding who they are and how to be the best they can be. Through clever and outwardly unacademic techniques of teaching, whether it is musical or magical, the children gain understanding of themselves and life skills that will forever be useful to them. In addition, they are uplifted, excited, and eager to learn.

On my way back to the office, I am inevitably stopped by a teacher or two for a quick suggestion or a follow-up comment on a child they referred. Since I am often stopped on my way to or from a classroom, it is necessary to invite them to come to my office at their activity period or after school.

With a few minutes before my next scheduled activity, I stop in the attendance office to welcome any new students who have registered.

Next is a small-group counseling session consisting of children who have been referred for similar reasons. My group size is limited to six children. Guidelines for conducting group counseling are followed.

After group, there are phone calls to return to parents, district office personnel, the school psychologist, doctors, or other counselors.

Now it's time to administer a series of screening tests and counsel with individuals before leaving for the next classroom guidance presentation. If time permits I will join a class for lunch. It's always a treat for children when the counselor shares extra time.

After lunch, again there are phone calls to return and messages that need attention. It may be necessary to visit a classroom to do an observation or go to the rescue in an emergency situation. This time is also used for paperwork. On days when I make an abuse or neglect report to the Department of Social Services, three copies of the report must be made and sent to appropriate agencies. Afternoons are scheduled for individual and small-group counseling also.

After children leave for the day, typically there is a constant flow of teachers in the guidance office. This time is also used for parent–teacher conferences and staffings of children into programs for students with disabilities.

On days when the school psychologist is working in my school, I work closely with her as a liaison for teachers who have referred children for psychological testing. Teachers depend on the counselor to make accurate reports to the school psychologist related to the special needs of their children. It is often advisable to set up times for her to observe in these classrooms.

After testing and proper discussion of test results, we set up staffing dates and parent conferences to explain test scores and recommendations. I send letters of invitation to parents and teachers a week in advance of the meetings. Administrators are also included in these staffings.

By now, the school day has come to an end. I pack my school bag, exchange hugs, and say my good-byes. It could be an evening when I'm conducting a parenting class at school. If so, things at home are put into fast-forward so I can leave again for school. There are parents who are a little nervous yet eager to learn how to better care for their children and relieved that other parents share their woes. Parenting groups are very supportive and encouraging ways to reach the children. Our jobs are made easier because of them.

Elementary school counselors are special, caring people who are dedicated to educating children in the affective domain. We help them become more self-confident, productive, and successful adults. Our day is ended with a feeling of accomplishment because of the constant feedback we get from children, parents, and teachers about the difference we make in the lives of people they care about. Elementary school counselors: every child deserves one!

The Middle/Junior High School Counselor

In the 1970s there was a trend from the elementary, junior, senior high school organizational concept to the elementary, middle, senior high school concept. These changes have not been without their attending controversies, but the middle school in concept and function may not really be all that different from the more traditional junior high school. For example, many contend that the junior high school was originally conceived as an institution to meet the developmental and transitional needs of youth from puberty to adolescence, from elementary to secondary school. Early in the middle school movement, a rationale for the middle school concept was based on data indicating that modern youth reach physical, social, and intellectual maturity at a younger age than did previous generations and that the junior high school may no longer meet the developmental needs of these students.

Regardless of whether a school system adopts a middle school type of intermediate school or stays with the more traditional junior high school, either institution will reflect such characteristics as providing for (a) the orientation and transitional needs and (b) the educational and social-developmental needs of their populations. In such a setting, middle or junior high school counselors will be actively involved in the following roles.

Student Orientation

This would include the initial orientation of entering students and their parents to the programs, policies, facilities, and counseling activities of their new school and, later, their pre-entry orientation to the high school they will attend.

Appraisal or Assessment Activities

In addition to typical school record and standardized test data, counselors may increasingly encourage the use of observation and other techniques to identify emerging traits of individual students during this critical development period. Values clarification activities may also be increasingly used for assessment and developmental purposes during this time.

Counseling

Both individual and group counseling should be used by school counselors at this level. In practice, it appears that middle and junior high school counselors tend to use group counseling more frequently than individual counseling.

Consultation

Counselors will provide consultation to faculty, parents, and, on occasion, school administrators regarding the developmental and adjustment needs of individual students. Counselors will also consult with other members of the school system's pupil personnel services team.

Placement

Counselors are usually involved in course and curricular placement of pupils, not only within their own schools but also cooperatively with their counterparts in the feeder secondary schools.

Thornburgh (1986), drawing on the developmental tasks of middle grade students, suggests that middle school counselors should include in their competencies the following:

- ❖ Counselors must have a general information base with respect to the developmental characteristics of middle graders.
- ❖ Counselors must understand the specific developmental tasks middle graders feel the need for or are expected to achieve.
- ❖ Counselors must be knowledgeable about the specific individual with whom they are interacting.
- ❖ Counselors must understand the perspective of the student.
- ❖ Counselors should teach skills that encourage decision-making. (pp. 175–176)

An Overview of the Middle School Counselor's Role

William Crowe, a counselor at Tri-North Middle School in Bloomington, Indiana, indicated his activities for a day in the life of a middle school counselor.

Typical Day's Activities of a Middle School Counselor

- ❖ Arrived at school at 7:15 A.M.
- ❖ Sent notes to teachers about parent conferences requested by a parent—delivered in mailboxes
- ❖ Sent two phone progress reports out to teachers at parent's request
- ❖ Gave copy of schedule to student from my computer
- ❖ Spoke to wrestling coach about upcoming match in which I would be doing announcing tomorrow
- ❖ Opened jammed locker for student
- ❖ Checked list and reminded principal to announce today's Career Seminar for period 3
- ❖ 8:00: period 1—group activity with at-risk group
- ❖ Spoke with teacher about her mother passing away
- ❖ Talked with practicum student about where to meet a student; gave him my office
- ❖ Visited with social worker about student not attending school
- ❖ Returned parent phone call about scheduling

- ✤ Held three-way conference with teacher, student, and myself about problems in class at student's request
- ✤ Introduced and helped coordinate Career Seminar in auditorium
- ✤ Gym supervision 1—10:45–11:00
- ✤ Lunch with coworker while discussing achievement test plans for upcoming ISTEP and CTBS (Indiana Statewide Testing for Educational Progress and Comprehensive Test of Basic Skills, respectively)
- ✤ Gym supervision 2—11:35–11:50
- ✤ Teacher visit about problem student
- ✤ Returned three calls about tomorrow's field trip to organize lunch and award ceremony and transportation
- ✤ Did conflict resolution with two boys at assistant principal's request
- ✤ Saw two students about schedule concerns
- ✤ Saw student about conflicts with others at student's request
- ✤ Received three packets of in-school mail containing schedule requests from current sixth graders for next year; processed and gave to students to file
- ✤ Parent call about schedule for next year
- ✤ Student requesting tutorial help
- ✤ Saw student about poor attitude and problems at home at teacher's request
- ✤ Received two phone calls about tomorrow's field trip
- ✤ School over for students at 2:30 P.M.
- ✤ Curriculum Council meeting after school canceled due to ice storm; left school at 3:35

The Secondary School Counselor

Of all the educational levels in which counselors serve, the secondary school is the one in which counselors and the general educational public (teachers, pupils, parents) are most likely to have some consistent understanding of "what the school counselor does." Although the role and function of the secondary school counselor has expanded over the years, it is clearly the most traditional and readily identified, even though it has been more frequently and seriously challenged than that of elementary or collegiate counselors. However, despite these challenges, any drastic or "overnight" changes are unlikely. Secondary school counseling programs in the future will still be built around the traditional basic services. Although the emphasis and techniques will undoubtedly change, the role and function of the secondary school counselor will continue to be built around the traditional expectancies discussed in Chapter 2. These expectations are, for the most part, confirmed in a study of the goals of secondary school guidance programs reported by Moles (1991) (see Table 3–8).

In a study of teacher opinions of secondary school counseling programs, Gibson (1989) reports that teachers view the most important functions of counselors as (a) providing individual counseling, (b) offering career planning assistance and information, (c) administering and interpreting standardized test results, and (d) assisting in college guidance and placement.

TABLE 3–8   Goals for Guidance Programs: Means of Rankings

Goal	Currently Emphasized	Desired by Guidance Staff	Desired by School Administrators	Desired by Teachers	Desired by Parents
Help students with their academic achievement in high school[a]	2.7	2.6	3.2	3.6	2.9
Help students plan and prepare for post-secondary schooling	2.7	2.3	2.4	2.1	2.2
Help students with personal growth and development	2.5	3.1	2.4	2.6	2.6
Help students plan and prepare for their work roles after high school	2.0	2.0	2.0[a]	1.7	2.3

Note. 1 is lowest, and 4 is highest emphasis.
[a]Phrased as "Help students improve their achievement in high school courses" in the question for columns 2–5.

Source: From Moles, O. C. (1991). "Guidance Programs in American High Schools: A Descriptive Portrait." *School Counselor, 38*(3), p. 167. © American Counseling Association. Reprinted with permission. No further reproduction authorized without written permission of the American Counseling Association.

The roles and functions of the secondary school counselor are not dissimilar to those of counselors in the elementary and middle/junior high schools. The differences occur in how counselors in the secondary school discharge their role and function and in the various emphases appropriate to the secondary school setting. For example, the emphasis at the secondary school level shifts drastically from the preventive to the remedial in dealing with many common counseling concerns. Many of these concerns are potentially serious life problems, such as addiction to drugs and alcohol, sexual concerns, and interpersonal relationship adjustments. Furthermore, there is less client emphasis on preparing for decisions and more emphasis on making decisions. These include decisions about an immediate or impending career or further education, relationships with the opposite sex and perhaps marriage, and developing personal values systems.

In addition to these different emphases in contrast to counseling needs at other educational levels, counselors anticipate more emphasis on consultation and a broader understanding of the impact of environment on students' behavior; a shifting emphasis toward a closer relationship with the classroom teacher in the school environment, as opposed to the traditional "medical" model (in which the client in need comes to the office for a "prescription"); and, finally, a change in emphasis from a reactive to proactive change agent in both the school and the community.

Delores "De" Klocke, a counselor at North Side High School in Fort Wayne, Indiana, lists her activities in a typical day as a high school counselor.

Typical Day's Activities of a High School Counselor

❖ Typically arrive at 7:00 A.M. and leave at 5:00 P.M.

❖ Host parent calls to explain her foreign student's broken elbow and premature return to Brazil

❖ Coordinator of Career Academy calls to see whether student who was recommended for the special program and put on a waiting list last semester is still interested in participating

❖ Student from Czech Republic discusses schedule change

❖ Student from Germany adds two classes to his schedule for second semester; checked with teachers for approval

❖ Senior brings in college application and wants school recommendation completed by "tomorrow"

❖ Local employer calls for recommendation for a 1993 graduate who is seeking employment

❖ Interpretation of PSAT/NMSQT test results to 200+ juniors and sophomores

❖ Conference with former parent (her daughter graduated in 1979; currently her granddaughter is a freshman at NSHS) who is concerned with her granddaughter's well-being

❖ Conference with a sophomore who is interested in participating in an international exchange program for his junior year

❖ Conference with senior who needs help with college application

❖ Phone call from senior parent re FAFSA form and Financial Aids Workshop

❖ Conference with senior (returning from a semester of study in Japan at our sister city school) who will be returning for his eighth semester at North Side; also needed help with college applications

❖ Conference with senior and Student Assistance Counselor re possible abuse by parent

❖ Conference with parent (whose daughter graduated in 1993) and daughter's fiancé who wants to get GED certificate

❖ Phone conversation with soccer coach who had borrowed a videotape of soccer game from one of our Spanish exchange students and had not returned it

❖ Conference with female junior who is interested in hosting a Japanese girl

❖ Phone conversation with former student (who was a peer facilitator and now a teacher at South Side High School) who is interested in starting such a program at his school and wanted some help in writing his proposal

❖ Conference with Japanese businessman who brought me a present from parents of one of our exchange students

❖ Conference with a journalism student who was writing an article on the FAFSA and financial aid

❖ Chat with senior football player whom I had moved, at his request, from an Essentials of English class to an Academic English class, checking on his grades; currently earning a B+

❖ Conference with sophomore soccer player to see whether his family would consider taking the Rotary Exchange student from Turkey for the second semester

❖ Phone conversation with counselor from Educational Opportunity Center re one of our students

❖ Phone conversation with probation officer re a senior at Wood Youth Center who has registered for the SAT and wants to take it; dilemma is that this would be an exception if they let him: "he could escape"

❖ Phone conversation with chief probation officer downtown to discuss the student's being transported to North Side to take the SAT test

❖ Appointment downtown with Media Services person in Fort Wayne Community School Channel 20 re production of a videotape about PURSUITS career development program (which I coordinate)

❖ Phone conversation with Educational Testing Service re providing test center for the PLUS Academic Abilities Assessment Program (for sixth graders)

❖ Conference with parent of junior dropout re plans to reenter school next semester

❖ Area coordinator for Center for Cultural Interchange needs signature for student from Argentina who will enter North Side High School second semester

❖ Phone conversation with Indiana University Admissions Office re appeal process for senior who was not admitted; followed up with letter confirming the telephone conversation

❖ Phone conversation with mother of senior transfer student who is experiencing adjustment problems

❖ Parent request for progress reports for student; advised secretary to prepare reports

❖ Conference with teacher re need to find "shadowing" sites for Advanced Biology students

❖ Phone conversation with tutor at Benet Learning Center re a student he is tutoring

❖ Conversation with North Side graduate who is currently a professor at Earlham College

❖ Conference with parent of sophomore re college opportunities for minority students

❖ Discussion with athletic director re NCAA Clearinghouse for student–athletes

❖ Prepared memo for science and math teachers re National Engineers Week and the need to recommend seniors who are serious about pursuing a career in engineering

❖ Senior Interview (all counselors assist in interviewing each senior individually)

❖ Phone conversation with Purdue nutritionist who will teach the "Have a Healthy Baby" class

❖ Case conference with student–athlete, his mother, and a teacher to discuss inappropriate behavior and attitude

❖ Conference with student re possibility of sexually transmitted diseases; referral to Board of Health; appointment scheduled

❖ Letter to mayor re nomination of student for Mayor's Youth Achievement Award

❖ Letter and applications completed for Hoosier Girls state delegates and alternates

❖ Meeting with two community consultants and Student Assistance Counselor re plans for conflict management training sessions

❖ Conference with *Journal-Gazette* reporter re teens and "Sexuality in the 1990s"

❖ Phone conversation with two counselors in our feeder middle schools arranging for home stays for eleven Japanese middle school students and one teacher

❖ Financial Aid Workshop, 7–9 P.M. with 96 parents participating

This is a typical day!

Additional Responsibilities on a Regular Basis

Monthly Meetings:

Faculty Advisory Committee (first Tuesday 2:45–4:00)

Faculty meetings (first Thursday, during teachers' plan periods)

Family and Children's Service board meeting (third Thursday, 11:30–1:00); PR Committee meets second Tuesday for lunch

Sister Cities Committee (first Wednesday, 5:00–6:15)

Integrated Guidance Program staff (first Thursday, 8–10 A.M.)

Curriculum and Instruction Division (second Tuesday, 8–10 A.M.)

Other Meetings:

North Side High School administrative staff and guidance staff meet weekly for about 2 hours each

Performance Based Accreditation Steering Committee meets weekly at 7 A.M.; School Climate Committee (which I chair) meets weekly at either 7 A.M. or 2:45 P.M.

Peer facilitator training, 7 A.M. on Tuesday, Thursday, Friday

PURSUITS (career development program) board meets quarterly; I serve as coordinator of this program, which is funded by a private foundation, currently serves all high schools in Allen County and 11 Fort Wayne Community Schools middle schools, and pilots a career development program for elementary schools

Dave Hefner International Exchange Fund Board meets twice a year; I serve as president

Indiana Counseling Association Foundation meets yearly; I serve as treasurer

North Side Area Guidance Leadership Project (3-year project funded by the Lilly Endowment) core team meets quarterly; North Side High School CAIT (Child Advocacy/ Inquiry Team) meets regularly

❖ Regularly attend professional conferences and workshops as well as serve on various ad hoc committees (e.g., the State of Indiana GED Study Group)

❖ Supervise test center for the American College Testing, Scholastic Aptitude Testing, ASE Technician Test, PLUS, and U.S. Postal Service exams

❖ Prepare college applications/scholarship recommendations on an ongoing basis (usually after school and on weekends)

❖ Attend/supervise various fine arts programs, athletic events, dances, and other programs

Counselors in Vocational Schools

The image and significance of vocational education changed markedly in the 1970s. Once regarded as a "dumping ground" for the unwilling or unable student (with facilities usually appropriate to this image), vocational education programs have made a dramatic turnaround. Today they are some of the finest educational facilities in the country, attracting students at all ability levels and preparing them for jobs in demand. School counselors need to become aware of both the nature of vocational education programs and the opportunities available to those who complete them. Additionally, counselors in preparation need to recognize some differences in the role and function of the counselor in the vocational school.

Counselors in Higher Education

A wide variety of counseling services are available to students in programs of higher education across the United States and Canada. Some of these counselors function in specialized facilities such as career centers and college admissions and placement offices. The majority of counselors, however, are employed in university counseling, mental health, or psychological service centers. These centers typically offer personal, academic, and vocational counseling, although group counseling has increased in popularity in recent years. Many of these centers are interdisciplinary in terms of staffing.

A noticeable trend in the activities of college counseling center programs is their move to assist larger numbers of students on their campuses through such activities as outreach programs, special workshops, residence hall groups, and peer counseling. On some campuses, counselors are also becoming more active in consultation with their faculty peers, campus administrators, and leaders of student organizations.

Counseling Services in Community and Junior Colleges

Counselors in community colleges play a significant role in the educational, social, and emotional development of the student. They provide a variety of services for students with distinct socioeconomic and cultural backgrounds and varying levels of academic abilities and motivation toward education (Paradise & Long, 1981).

Community and junior colleges are often challenged with the task of educating students who have not developed the necessary skill to engage in adequate college work (Higbee, Dwinell, McAdams, GoldbergBelle, & Tardola, 1991). Higbee et al. explain that these students generally had not planned to attend college and therefore failed to choose an academic curriculum in high school, may have dropped out of high school and later decided further education was necessary, have been absent from the academic setting for an extended period of time, experienced poor instruction or a weak curriculum in high school, or have little motivation. They insist that counseling services for these students must address intellectual as well as emotional development by focusing on the following issues:

- ❖ Academic policies and procedures
- ❖ Study skills
- ❖ Time management strategies
- ❖ Communication skill development
- ❖ Cultural pluralism
- ❖ Relationship enhancement
- ❖ Stress reduction
- ❖ Health and wellness
- ❖ Career exploration
- ❖ Decision-making skills
- ❖ Goal-setting strategies
- ❖ Motivational strategies
- ❖ Personal empowerment strategies

Counseling services are noted by Burnham and Satcher (1990) as among the services provided for enhancing the educational opportunities of individuals with learning disabilities in over 40 community colleges in Mississippi, Alabama, Georgia, Tennessee, and Alabama. Activities offered include advising, remedial skills courses, training programs, support groups, orientation programs, career development, and study skills courses. Through involvement in such activities, students have a stronger chance of gaining the most from their education and becoming involved in a career that contributes not only to societal needs but also to their own image of themselves as an important, contributing factor in our society. Delco (1988) claims that enhancement of this self-image is just as important as enhancement of educational skills and that counselors play a vital role in promoting this positive self-image.

As the U.S. economy has become more and more dependent on technology, community colleges are playing a significant role in the training and retraining of the work force for businesses and industries (Hirshberg, 1991). Hirshberg identifies the activities of management and technical assistance for new and small businesses, tech prep programs with high schools, cooperative education programs, partnerships with state agencies, and customized and contract job training for industries as roles of community colleges in promoting the economic development of our society. She emphasizes further the important role that counseling services play in promoting the appropriate education and training of students in these programs.

Quimbita (1991) maintains that community colleges are in a position to take a significant role in increasing the number of individuals in scientific careers as well as promoting diversification in terms of ethnic and gender composition. Vocational counseling and career guidance services are among the strategies she identifies as being utilized by community colleges in successfully recruiting and educating more women and minorities into 2-year college science, math, and engineering programs.

TEACHER AND ADMINISTRATOR ROLES IN THE SCHOOL COUNSELING PROGRAM

The Role of the Classroom Teacher

Although it seems heresy to the counseling profession, schools have existed and could continue to exist without the benefit of counselors. Many students possibly would not achieve their potential, solve their problems, or make appropriate decisions and plans, but nonetheless most of them would learn, progress, and be viewed as educated. It is also possible for schools to exist without the presence of an even more prominent member—the school principal. Although teachers would be even more overburdened with administrative responsibilities and their teaching effectiveness would undoubtedly suffer, students would still be taught, learn (perhaps at a slower rate), graduate (even without the principal's handshake), and be viewed as educated.

Schools without teachers, however, cease to be schools. They become, instead, detention centers, social clubs, or temporary shelters, but they are not schools, and any learning that takes place would be both incidental and accidental. It therefore becomes obvious, and has been since the beginning of schooling, that the teacher is the most important professional in the school setting. Teacher support and participation are crucial to any program that involves students. The school counseling program is no exception. Further, today's teachers, as indicated in a study (Gibson, 1990), feel that they should have responsibilities in the school counseling program beyond those performed in the classroom. Gibson (1990) also notes:

> Notwithstanding changing roles and calls for new directions, it can be concluded that secondary school teachers continue to believe that counseling and guidance programs make a positive contribution to the total program of their schools. Interviews further confirmed that teachers have high respect for the skills and dedication of the counselors in their schools. This was especially noted in those schools in which counselors interacted with every teacher on a one-to-one basis at least once per semester. (p. 254)

It is therefore important to examine the role and function of the classroom teacher in the counseling program, recognizing, of course, that differences may be anticipated at differing educational levels and in different educational settings.

Role as a Listener–Adviser

Most classroom teachers see their pupils every day, 5 days a week, for at least 45 minutes per day on the average of 180 school days per year, often for several years, all of which represents a staggering amount of contact time exceeded by no other adults except parents, and that exception does not always hold true. The inevitable result is that the teacher, more than any other professional in the school setting, is in the position to know the students best, to communicate with them on an almost daily basis, and to establish a relationship based on mutual trust and respect. The teacher thus becomes the first line of contact between the student and the school counseling program—a contact in which the teacher will frequently be called upon to serve in a listening/advising capacity.

Role as a Referral and Receiving Agent

The classroom teacher is, inevitably, the major source of student referrals to the school counselor. Because the counselor's daily personal contacts with students are necessarily limited, the counselor's personal awareness of students needing counseling is similarly limited. The counseling program must therefore depend on an alert faculty to ensure that students with counseling needs will not go unnoticed and uncounseled. School counselors need to encourage their teacher colleagues to actively "search" for these students, since much evidence exists to suggest that only "the tip of the iceberg" has been touched in efforts to identify all students with serious counseling needs.

Of course, simply identifying these students to a counselor may not be enough. In many instances, the teacher must orient and encourage the student to seek counselor assistance. Nor does the teacher's responsibility necessarily end when the student has entered a counseling relationship. The teacher may still be involved, if only in the role of supporting the student's continuation with the counseling process. Teachers may also anticipate a role as a receiving agent, not only for those students they have referred but for others in their classes as well. In such situations, the teacher in a sense "receives" the counseled student back into the classroom environment and, it is hoped, supports and reinforces the outcome of the counseling. The importance of this reinforcer role cannot be overemphasized.

Teachers can also play a valuable role as members of study teams for pupils they refer.

Role as a "Human Potential Discoverer"

Each year teachers witness a talent parade through their respective classes. Although teachers may lack sufficient training, experience, or versatility to identify the special talents of the vast majority of students, most teachers have the expertise to identify those who may have some special talents for their own particular career specialty. That expertise multiplied across the many career specialties represented in most school programs represents a near army of talent scouts that should ensure that each student will have his or her talents and potentials identified and his or her development encouraged and assisted. This teacher role as a discoverer of human potential is significant in fulfilling not only a mission of the school counseling program but also in meeting the responsibility of education to the individual and society.

Role as a Career Educator

Closely related to the foregoing is the teacher's central role in the school's career education program. Because career education is recognized as a part of students' total education, it is important also to recognize the classroom teacher's responsibility to integrate career education into teaching subject matter. Career education cannot succeed without career guidance and vice versa. The success of the career guidance program therefore is tied to the success of the career education program, a success that rests largely with the classroom teacher.

The career education responsibilities of the teacher include developing positive attitudes and respect for all honest work, a challenging responsibility in view of the many adult-imposed biases with which the student is constantly confronted. Additionally, the teacher must promote the parallel development of positive student attitudes toward education and its relationship to career preparation and decision making. Students must also have the opportunity to examine and test concepts, skills, and roles and to develop values appropriate to their future careers. The security of the classroom group provides an ideal setting for these experiences.

Role as a Human Relations Facilitator

The potential for success of any school counseling program depends to a considerable degree on the climate of the school, an environment that is conducive to the development and practice of positive human relations. The influence of the classroom teacher on that environment is dominant, as ably expressed by Haim Ginott:

> I have come to the frightening conclusion
> I am the decisive element in the classroom
> It is my personal approach that creates the climate
> It is my daily mood that makes the weather

As a teacher I possess tremendous power to make a child's life miserable or joyous
I can humiliate or humor, hurt or heal
In all situations it is my response that decides whether a crisis will be escalated or de-escalated,
and a child humanized or dehumanized. (cited in Gross & Gross, 1974, p. 39)

Among the research emphasizing the importance of a favorable classroom and school environment for learning is that reported in Benjamin Bloom's book *Human Characteristics and School Learning* (1976). Bloom suggests that it is possible for 95% of the students to learn all that the school has to teach at or near the same achievement level. His research indicates that most students will be very similar in both learning and their motivation to learn when they are provided the favorable conditions or environment for learning. On the other hand, his research also demonstrates that when the environment in the classroom is unfavorable, differences occur that widen the gap between high and low achievers. In this role as a human relations facilitator, the classroom teacher has the opportunity to be a model to demonstrate positive human relations. The teaching and practicing of these skills should occur as a regular procedure in the classroom as the teacher plans and directs group interactions that promise positive human relationship experiences for each participant.

Role as a Counseling Program Supporter

Someone once said, "Counselors are the most human of all humans." Be that as it may, counselors, like all humans, need and respond to the encouragement and support of their fellow beings. Therefore, a significant contribution that the classroom teacher can make to the school counseling program is one of counselor encouragement and support and the creation of a motivating environment. Support can be especially influential in determining how pupils view and use the services of the school's counseling program. Teachers' reactions also do not go unnoticed by school administrators and supervisors. Of course, evidence of teacher support for counseling ideally should extend to parents and others in the community as well.

Despite the importance of the classroom teacher in any school counseling program at any educational level, evidence indicates that in far too many settings, the classroom teacher is still only incidentally involved in the program. Many classroom teachers may feel uncertain about the goals of their school programs and lack communication and involvement in the counseling programs. In such situations, the student is the real loser, and both the counselor and the teacher must share the blame.

Because the school counseling program is the responsibility of counselors, they must initiate communications and interaction with their teaching faculties; they must actively pursue teachers' involvement and assistance; and they must exemplify their claim to human relations expertise. Blum (1986) suggests the importance of the counselor having visibility—being seen—and sociability—being known by the teachers in their school. They must also recognize that although most teachers are willing to accept their role in the school counseling program, as many studies have indicated, they may lack some understanding of what that role and function are.

Of course, not all teachers will or can be "all things," as suggested in this section. Hopefully, most can and will accept many of the roles, however. These role opportunities also can be enhanced by preparing teachers to recognize, accept, and enjoy their roles in the school counseling program. Unfortunately, most teachers do not seek and are not required to take course work in counseling and guidance and, therefore, are limited in realizing their full potential as team members.

The Role of the Chief School Administrator

Whether a building principal or a university president, the chief on-site administrator is potentially (and usually) the most singularly important person in the development of any educational program in his or her respective setting. Most staff members of schools (including principals and college presidents) think of chief administrators in terms of power—what the chief administrators permit them to do and not to do. Studies (Gibson, Mitchell, & Higgins, 1983) have noted that administrative support was ranked in the highest-priority category in the establishment and development of school counseling programs. The studies emphasize the significant role the school principal and other educational leadership can and should play in any program of counseling within their jurisdiction. This role may be appropriately expressed through leadership, consultation, advice, and resource support. Some of the characteristics of these activities are described next.

Role as a Program Leader and Supporter

The leadership behavior of the school principal on behalf of the school counseling program is a major determinant of the program's prospects for success. Because school administrators represent the educational leadership in both the school and the community, they have the responsibility of giving clear, open, and recognized support for the school program. This will include responsibilities for communicating program characteristics, achievements, and needs to school boards and others within the educational system and to the tax-supporting public.

Role as a Program Consultant and Adviser

The chief school administrator has the best overview of all activities and planning within the institution. This position enables the chief administrator to make a valuable contribution to the school counseling program as adviser and consultant on school needs that can be served by the school program, school policies that affect counseling program functioning, resolution of problems encountered by the program, and procedures or directions for program development and improvement.

Role as a Resource Provider

Chief school administrators are usually responsible for the institution's budget—its makeup and utilization. In this role, they provide advice and direction to all school programs regarding budget expectations, staffing possibilities, facilities, and equipment. They may also be aware of possible external resources such as state or federal funding, which the school counseling program may wish to explore.

THE COUNSELOR AND RELATIONSHIPS WITH OTHER HELPING PROFESSIONS

As already noted, one of the school counselor's important roles is as a team member. Unlike the gifted athlete who may have to limit membership to one team, the counselor may play on several teams. One of the most important and logical of these is the *pupil personnel services* or *helping professions* team. This team typically includes the school psychologist, social worker, speech and hearing specialists, and health personnel. To work effectively with each other, members of these teams must understand the expertise and responsibilities of their team members and how they support each other. This is not always easy because their roles often seem to overlap, especially at the elementary school level. The All Handicapped Children's Act of 1975 has had the most consistent influence over the past 15 years in role determination for elementary school personnel. Unfortunately, most training programs do little in the way of interdisciplinary planning or training. Therefore, it becomes the responsibility of the school counselor and other helping professionals to initiate and develop positive, cooperative working relationships consistent with the team concept.

The School Psychologist

Current estimates indicate that over 22,000 school psychologists are practicing in the United States today (Fagan & Wise, 1994). These psychologists received their professional preparation in one of the approximately 230 training programs that emphasize the application of knowledge in psychological and educational foundations to the academic, behavioral, and social problems that students experience in a school setting.

During the 1970s and 1980s the number of school psychologists increased dramatically in public schools as a result of state and federal laws mandating free and appropriate educational services for students with disabilities. As a result of the expansive growth in special education, the role and services provided by most school psychologists have been heavily tied to federal and state requirements for comprehensive evaluation of students to determine eligibility for special education services. Federal laws such as the Individuals with Disabilities Education Act (IDEA) indicate that the services of school psychologists include assessment, consultation, and the provision of psychological services to students with disabilities and their families (Humes & Hohenshil, 1987). Consistent with these mandates, recent studies have reported that school psychologists spend approximately 50% of their time involved in assessment-related activities, with the remaining 50% evenly distributed across consultation and intervention activities (Smith, 1984; Reschly & Wilson, 1993).

As the focus in special education and other remedial education programs switched during the 1980s from eligibility and identification to intervention and prevention for students with mild disabilities and others at risk for school failure, school psychologists became increasingly involved in intervention and remediation programs for all students. The school psychologists' skill with individual assessment tools—including measures of cognitive ability; academic achievement; and behavioral, personality, or adaptive behavior—are often used to meet specific student needs and deliver possible intervention alternatives. Increasingly, these assessment skills are expanding beyond individual test administration to include interviewing, observation, and alternative techniques such as curriculum-based assessment.

School counselors will often work directly with school psychologists in providing psychological and support services to students with disabilities, families, and classroom teachers working with these students. Thus, school counselors and school psychologists will frequently work collaboratively on building-level and student support teams that consult with teachers and parents and provide direct services to students with academic and/or behavioral problems in school.*

The School Social Worker

Crouch (1979) defines social work as "the attempt to assist those who do not command the means to human subsistence in acquiring them and in attaining the highest possible degree of independence" (p. 46). The school social worker provides helping services for those children who are unable to make proper use of their educational opportunities and who find it difficult to function effectively in the school environment. In this role, the social worker is a referral source for those children who appear to have emotional or social problems that are handicapping their learning and social adjustment to school. The school social worker has special interviewing and casework skills that are used within a school-child-parent context. The school social worker works closely with community agencies and nonschool professional helpers, such as physicians, lawyers, and ministers.

Meares (1977) reports a study that ranked the importance of the tasks performed by school social workers. Four major interrelated priority activities were identified: (a) clarifying the nature of the child's problem and the parameters of social work services; (b) assessing the child's specific problem; (c) facilitating better relationships among school, community, and pupils; and (d) educational counseling with the child and his or her parents. Most activities emphasize the importance of the liaison role. Thus, there has been a transition from the primarily clinical casework approach to serving children in schools to that of home–school–community liaison and educational counseling with the child and parents.

The school social worker is an important member of the school services team. Counselors and other helping professionals may depend on the social worker to provide better understanding of the child, especially in regard to the home environment and the nature of the pupil's behavioral problems.

Special Educator

In 1975 the Education for All Handicapped Children Act (Public Law 94-142) was signed into law. The intent of this law was to provide normal and integrated educational opportunities for children with disabilities. A major impact of the act was the intent to educate the

---

*All information on school psychology was provided by Nancy Waldron, Ph.D., assistant professor, Indiana University.

student in the least restrictive environment, which resulted in the "mainstreaming" of most students with disabilities into regular classrooms. The regular classroom teacher was also made responsible for the progress of such students in his or her classroom, and the law forbade any categorical labels (i.e., *emotionally disturbed, retarded,* etc.). Other aspects of the law provided for due process or the equal protection of the rights of people with disabilities and individualized programs designed to maximize the potential of each student.

One outcome of these provisions has been the addition of the special educator to the school's helping services team. Obviously, the school counselor has special skills in terms of assessment and placement, individual counseling, group guidance, and career assistance that can help this population. Consulting with parents can also be useful. In all of these aspects the school counselor will work closely with the special educator and others concerned with maximizing the educational opportunities for these students.

School Health Personnel

Most school systems employ professional health services personnel, at least on a part-time basis. Most common are the school nurse and the dental hygienist; a number of school systems also employ school physicians. Your personal recall of these helping professionals may consist of memories of immunization shots, opening your mouth to say "Ahh," the taste of the tongue depressor, and the admonition of the dental hygienist when she discovered you weren't brushing regularly. Such memories are fairly characteristic of the role of these providers of basic, preventive health services for all schoolchildren. These professionals also identify children who need special medical treatment or referrals for the correction or alleviation of defects. Counselors will find these medical specialists a resource for making referrals and determining whether or to what extent physical ailments or defects are an obstacle to a student's anticipated development or adjustment.

Psychiatrists

Psychiatrists are physicians with specialized training in the treatment of behavioral abnormalities. As physicians, psychiatrists are permitted by law to use drugs and other physical means of treatment for mental problems. Counselors often suggest to parents that they refer their son or daughter to a psychiatrist if it is suspected that the child may have an emotional disturbance requiring the use of medication. Many psychiatrists perform an important consultative role to pupil personnel workers as well.

> It is clear that there are many overlapping functions—especially among school counselors, school psychologists, and school social workers, particularly in the elementary school. There remains a uniqueness to each specialty, however. The question to be answered, then, is: Who does what? It can be argued that there is enough work to spread around if the dollars and jobs exist. Student non-adjustment and incidence of social ills suggest that there are not enough mental health professionals. Then what is the issue? The problem seems to be territoriality. The three specialties (elementary school counselors, school psychologists, school social workers) remain eager to protect professional boundaries even though similarities are acknowledged when actual situations require broad services to pupils. Perhaps the main solution to the teamwork dilemma is a multidisciplinary examination of organizational patterns and line-staff relationships. (Kameen, Robinson, & Rotter, 1985, cited in Humes & Hohenshil, 1987, p. 43)

Working together as a "team" is clearly desirable, enabling each helping professional to enhance the contributions of the other.

COMPUTERS AND COUNSELING IN THE SCHOOLS

Cooperation among the various helping professions has been enhanced significantly by the advent of computer technology in recent generations. This development has promoted abundant use of computers in schools today, and counselors are currently offering a variety of computer-assisted services to students.

Crosbie-Burnett and Pulvino (1990) state that during the early 1980s, counselors utilized computers exclusively for vocational counseling but presently are also using computers in attempts to increase student self-awareness, improve study skills, enhance decision-making and problem-solving skills, and assist students in preventing and coping with difficult stress.

Walz (1987) points out that the major impact of computer-assisted career guidance programs is that they complement and supplement the activities of the counselor who is involved in individual as well as group work. He refers to technology as a "two-edged sword" that allows the counselor to perform tasks with more ease and precision (provide occupational information) or to perform tasks that counselors are not capable of doing (provide immediate feedback from an assessment device).

As Casey (1992) indicates, computers are used by counselors in school for a variety of testing, administration, career, and personal counseling activities. He points out that initially counseling-specific software was utilized for these purposes. He describes more recent adaptations of software not originally intended for counseling purposes that have been successfully used by school counselors working with "at-risk" students, including involving them in writing poetry on word processors and creating art products in the development of cooperative learning materials with peers and being trained as computer resource tutors for teachers and fellow students. In addition, several counselors are consulting with teachers in order to develop intergenerational communication between at-risk youth and senior citizens through live computer activities and electronic mail (Henderson, 1989).

Many counselors, realizing the influence of home entertainment software such as Nintendo, have utilized video games in attempts to enhance the relationship-building process with students. For example, the Print Shop game is used to encourage the expression of feelings among resistant clients; Wheel of Fortune and MacConcentration are used with students with learning disabilities to encourage their engagement with the counselor and to provide the opportunity for success in the counselor's presence. Nonverbal games such as the Hot Air Balloon are used by counselors who do not speak the same language as the student in order for the two to find a commonality between themselves without having to speak.

Clearly, video games have become a dominant aspect in many students' lives. Gifford (1991) identifies six attributes of such games that contribute to their success as counseling and learning tools: They (a) encourage free play by allowing children to exercise fantasies without the limitations of the real world; (b) encourage easy movement between electronic "microworlds" from one graphic environment to another; (c) provide instant replays of performances that allow students to study, edit, or make another attempt at a task in a safe environment that supports risk taking; (d) let children be in control even to the point where they can turn the game off when frustrated; (e) serve as partners with the students in the learning process; and (f) provide an opportunity to work toward a clear goal that enhances motivation.

Another application of computer-assisted counseling involves a "MacMentoring Project." In attempting to reconnect disenfranchised youth back to school through this program, counselors have successfully facilitated the students' development of greater self-esteem while also teaching them transferable computer skills (Casey & Ramsammy, 1992). Students involved have shown improvement on task behaviors, gained knowledge and skills in word processing and computer graphic procedures, and benefited from a nondirective relationship with the counselor as the computer facilitates the counseling relationship.

The computer is a vital resource in the educational system, and all students must become knowledgeable and comfortable with the use of this tool. Campbell and Dobson (1987) explain that often students may experience computer anxiety, avoid interacting with computers, and consequently eliminate present educational opportunities as well as future employment choices. They insist that counselors must take the initiative in identifying these students and implementing appropriate interventions that would assist students in dealing with these problems. Crosbie-Burnett and Pulvino (1990) support Campbell and Dobson's contention that children who are not computer competent will be at a significant disadvantage in school as well as the job market. They recommend a multimodal group counseling approach through which counselors are able to help those who are uncomfortable with computers to become more confident and familiar with computers. The program is called "PRO-TECH" (Crosbie-Burnett & Pulvino, 1990) and is based on

P—practice on the computer
R—risk-taking imagery and behaviors through the computer
O—organization and planning of computer projects
T—tactile exploration with the computer
E—emotions associated with trying new things
C—cognitions or developing positive self-talk
H—helping others learn

Through involvement in such group activities, students have the opportunity to realize that others have similar fears and doubts as they do about using computers, have access to supportive individuals during their process of learning about computers, and, as a result, experience increased feelings of self-efficacy in regard to computer use. Counselors play a significant part in providing an environment through which students can become less threatened and more motivated in terms of working with computers.

School counselors also have a major role in serving as the communications link in schools, as they are responsible for communicating such information as school policies, graduation requirements, and special programs and activities being offered (Lucking & Mitchum, 1990). Lucking and Mitchum identify the computer as a necessary resource that facilitates this communication to students, parents, administrators, and other interested parties. They refer to *desktop publishing,* a term "given to the production of documents with a recent generation of software and newly developed printer technology" (p. 270), as a computer tool providing high-quality printed material. Desktop publishing allows the counselor to produce high-quality documents, avoid the expense of commercial documents, and have more time for providing counseling services to students.

Although computers are a valuable resource for students, counselors, and other school personnel, caution must be taken in ensuring that computer utilization also integrates the human aspect of learning and development. Pyle (1985) discusses the necessity for the counselor to use computer technology both effectively and humanely, while Walz and Bleur's (1985) imperatives for counselors involved in computer-assisted activities with students are also important to keep in mind:

> Do not expect miracles out of computer use.
> Examine software carefully for its intended purpose.
> Be creative in applying software to the counseling situation.
> Integrate computer interventions with other counseling interventions.

Computers will be most beneficial when the counselor is able to utilize carefully chosen computer-assisted interventions that will facilitate attending to the students' special needs. When these needs are ignored, computer technology may actually be detrimental for students.

Assessment of students is a common task for school counselors. Computerized programs are available to assist in analyzing all available assessment data, generating hypotheses, making interpretations, and suggesting recommendations about the examinee. Sattler (1992, p. 790) warns that anyone utilizing such computerized assessment strategies must be aware of their limitations. Among these limitations are that "computerized reports are usually based on one, two, or three tests; they usually do not take into account either the examinee's unique clinical history or the complete assessment results (Matarazzo, 1986)." Counselors are still the ones responsible for communicating results in a nontechnical and understandable manner. If a computer report is used by a counselor who is untrained regarding the limitations and use of such reports, results might be misinterpreted and interventions would be based on inaccurate conclusions. This situation would clearly pose the potential for more harm than good for the student.

Of further concern in regard to using computer-assisted counseling strategies is the aspect of confidentiality. Abuse of confidentiality is more likely when student information is maintained on electronic data storage systems, although counselors can avoid problems in this area by using identification codes and passwords and placing restrictions on individuals who may have access to student information (Zunker, 1990). School counselors must take serious precautions in order to ensure the maintenance of confidentiality regarding student information.

The American Counseling Association (1988) addresses this concern of confidentiality and other issues regarding computer use in their ethical guidelines. (See Appendix B for the *American Counseling Association Ethical Standards*.) Wilcoxon (1992) emphasizes that "there is perhaps no greater area of featured specificity throughout the 1988 (ACA) Ethical Standards than those standards addressing the use of computers and related technological advances as adjuncts to counseling" (p. 5). She identifies sections B.6, B.9, B.16, B.19, B.20, C.4, C.5, and C.13 as applying specifically to counselor use of computer technology. Important points regarding each of these follow.

Under Section B: Counseling Relationship, B.6 states that in using the extensive data storage and processing capacities of computers, counselors must ensure that information is both appropriate and vital for services being offered, information is destroyed once it is no longer useful in providing services, and the best computer security methods available are used in restricting access to appropriate staff involved in client or student care. Section B.9 states that as part of the counseling relationship, counselors must provide clients with information that appropriately explains the limitations of computer technology use.

Regarding client use of computer applications, B.16 explains that counselors must ensure that clients are intellectually, emotionally, and physically able to use the computer applications appropriately; the application procedures being utilized are appropriate for the client's needs; the client is aware of the purpose and operation of the computer activity with which she or he is involved; and follow-up of client computer application use is provided in order to correct possible concerns, such as client misconceptions or inappropriate use. Follow-up also must be provided as a means for assessing subsequent client needs. Section B.20 addresses requirements for counselors who have developed programs for use by clients as self-help or stand-alone software. The ethical guidelines state that the counselor must ensure that these software programs must have been originally developed with the purpose of functioning in a stand-alone manner and have not been modified from software that was originally developed with the requirement that a counselor be available for support while in use. The applications must include, within the program, statements in regard to intended user outcomes, suggestions for software usage, descriptions of conditions in which self-help software might not be appropriate, as well as a description of how and when counseling services might be beneficial. The counselor is also ethically responsible for including information regarding her or his qualifications as the developer, the development process, the validity of the software, and operating instructions.

Section C of the *American Counseling Association Ethical Standards* (1988) deals with measurement and evaluation. Section C.4 maintains that counselors using computer-based test interpretations must have been trained regarding the construct being measured and the specific instrument being used prior to utilizing the computer application. Section C.5 specifies that when a computer is used for test administration and scoring, the counselor must ensure that both the administration and scoring programs are functioning properly in order that clients will be provided with accurate assessment results. In terms of the development of computer-based assessment interpretations geared at supporting the assessment process, Section C.13 applies. It explains that when the counselor has developed these interpretations her- or himself, she or he must ensure that the validity of the interpretations is established before commercial distribution of such computer-based applications.

Computers are clearly a valuable tool in the schools for both the students and staff. It is essential that both students and staff become involved in computer-assisted learning activities. However, computer technology has its limitations and will not work effectively for students if used inappropriately. Mudore (1988) emphasizes that ethical use of computers requires that the counselor use the computer with discrimination and actively advocate computer use that will promote the rights and privacy of students. A thorough understanding of the ethical guidelines regarding the counseling process and computers is a must for the school counselor in order to ensure that this takes place. *Ethical Principles of Psychologists and Code of Conduct* of the American Psychological Association (1992) can also be referred to in becoming more knowledgeable of these issues (see Appendix C).

PATTERNS OF COUNSELING PROGRAM ORGANIZATION IN EDUCATIONAL SETTINGS

Because we noted earlier in this chapter that school counseling programs must reflect the differences in their populations and settings, it is appropriate to assume that these differences will also result in differing organizational structures for programs. Consequently, it must be recognized that there are many successful yet differing patterns of program organization for all educational levels. Furthermore, these structures differ according to the educational levels (elementary, middle, secondary, or higher education) they serve. This chapter attempts to briefly illustrate only a few of the most traditional and popular program formats.

Organizational Patterns in Elementary Schools

As has been already noted in the discussions of the historic development of guidance in U.S. education, counseling programs are just beginning to emerge in the elementary schools of this country, despite the fact that there have been supporters of this concept for more than 50 years. Because there are no established, traditional organizational formats with which the subject of elementary counseling programs might be comfortably introduced, let us examine some possible considerations.

In determining appropriate approaches to program organization and development in the elementary school, elementary educators have considered those characteristics and goals of the elementary school, especially those that highlight the special role of the elementary school as an educational institution. These include the missions of orienting the elementary school child to the educational environment and providing the elementary school pupil with the basic educational–developmental experiences that are essential for future development. Other special characteristics of the elementary school are also important as considerations in the organization and development of their counseling programs, including the following:

1. Most elementary schools are centered on the homeroom teacher. The elementary pupil is in a self-contained classroom with one teacher for most of the day, and the pupil is with this teacher for at least one academic year. As a result, pupil and teacher get to know each other better in the elementary school than in schools at higher levels.

2. Learning through activity is emphasized. Physical activity and exercises related to learning are characteristic of the elementary school.

3. The elementary school pupil is a member of a reasonably stable group. Although some school populations are relatively transient, it is common for a child to be with the same group of fellow pupils for most of each school year and, in many elementary school situations, many of the same children throughout the elementary school years.

4. Elementary schools are usually smaller and less complex than secondary schools.

5. Parental interest and involvement are generally greater at the elementary level.

Further reflected in the educational approach and structure of the elementary school are the characteristics of elementary school children. Anyone who has ever set foot in an elementary school must have noted that there is no such thing as the "typical" elementary school pupil. Parents and teachers who interact with these children on a daily basis can further testify to the difficulties of characterizing this age group. Indeed, the common characteristic all elementary school youth share is that no two are alike. Despite this, it is not inappropriate to briefly note some broadly recognized needs and characteristics of this youthful population, even though there have been and will continue to be innumerable studies made and volumes written about the needs of children.

As a basis for guidance in the elementary school, we will view these needs from two standpoints: (a) basic needs that continuously demand satisfaction and (b) developmental needs that must be met during different life stages.

People's basic needs have been presented by Maslow (1970) in a hierarchy or priority ordering of needs in which the higher-order needs will emerge only when the lower-order needs have been fairly well satisfied. Maslow points out that the best way to repress the higher motivation of humankind is to keep individuals chronically hungry, insecure, or unloved. According to Maslow's theory, as the teacher and counselor view the elementary pupil and the ability to become self-actualized and develop potential, the teacher or counselor must be concerned with, and aware of, the degree to which the pupil's lower-order needs are being met.

The developmental needs of humankind, according to his life stage, have been well presented by Havighurst (1953) in his popular "developmental tasks." Counselors and teachers in the elementary school should take note of the following developmental tasks for middle childhood:

1. Learning physical skills necessary for ordinary games

2. Building wholesome attitudes toward oneself as a growing organism

3. Learning to get along with age mates

4. Learning an appropriate masculine or feminine social role

5. Developing fundamental skills in reading, writing, and calculating

6. Developing concepts necessary for everyday living

7. Developing conscience, morality, and a scale of values

8. Achieving personal independence

9. Developing attitudes toward social groups and institutions

The presentations of Maslow and Havighurst stress both the personal and the cultural nature of the needs of children as they grow and develop. There is also an implied "developmental task" for educational programs: the task of providing learning experiences appropriate to the needs, both basic and developmental, of the elementary school child.

In addition to the needs of children, plans for counseling in the elementary school should take into consideration the following characteristics of the student:

1. The elementary school student is experiencing continuous growth, development, and change.
2. The elementary school student is constantly integrating experiences.
3. The elementary school student is relatively limited in the ability to verbalize.
4. The reasoning powers of the elementary school pupil are not fully developed.
5. The ability of the elementary school pupil to concentrate over long periods of time is limited.
6. The enthusiasm and interest of the elementary school pupil can be easily aroused.
7. The decisions and goals of the elementary school pupil serve immediate purposes—he or she does not yet make long-range plans.
8. The elementary school pupil displays feelings more or less openly.

The implications of these characteristics and needs for programs of counseling in the elementary school must be reflected in both counseling program structure and counselor role and function.

On the basis of these identifiable features of the elementary school and the characteristics and needs of elementary school students, any program in the elementary school that focuses on the student, to be successful, must have not only the approval of but also significant involvement of the faculty: It must be teacher centered. Furthermore, close and frequent contact with parents must be anticipated, especially in the primary years. Any program that relies too heavily on "talking at" the elementary school student, even when supplemented with films and other media or material aids, is doomed to failure. The elementary school is activity oriented, and the counseling program in this setting must "do as the Romans do." Finally, the elementary school years are noted as developmental years. The elementary school guidance program must therefore respond accordingly with a developmental rather than a remedial emphasis—an emphasis that suggests, for example, less individual adjustment counseling and more developmental group guidance activities.

Organizational Patterns in Secondary Schools

Since their early, sometimes timorous, sometimes tenuous beginnings in the 20 years after Parsons, through their experimental growth years of the 1930s and 1940s, into the boom years of the 1950s and 1960s, school programs of counseling and guidance have been almost the exclusive property of high schools in the United States. Although different influences and emphases in both the secondary school and the counseling and guidance movement have often altered concepts of program structure and function, the movement maintained a steady growth in both numbers and professionalization through the last half of this century and developed recognizable images of program structure, role, and function. These, however, may also be more readily understood if one renews acquaintance with the characteristics of the secondary school and the high school student as well.

Although adolescence is identified as that period between puberty and adulthood, nothing defies standard definition or description more than the adolescent. They are as varied, unpredictable, and uncontrollable as their peer group permits. They give meaning to the expression "generation gap," of which many adolescents are proud and, before it is over, for which many adults are thankful. Most persons view their adolescent years as different from those of today. They probably were, for adolescents today not only exhibit a wide variation in individual characteristics, but the group characteristics also seem to change rapidly from generation to generation. As an extreme example, many may recall that some of their grandparents seemed to go directly from childhood to work and adulthood. They completed their 8–10 years of schooling and went to work. Today, some youth stretch their adolescence into their 20s, resisting growing up or accepting responsibility, and rejecting independence. For all who are concerned with youth during these magical years, for those who may hope to "ease their passage," it is important to recognize some of the characteristics of adolescents:

1. It is a period of continuous physical growth, not the least of which is the awakening of sexual impulses. Girls discover boys, and boys discover girls who discover boys. "Puppy" love becomes a serious crush that becomes "undying love" (at least for the moment).

2. It is a period of movement toward maturity with all its implications for independence, responsibility, and self-discipline—a period often very trying to parents who want to keep little Sasha tied to her mother's apron strings or Johnnie still passing the football to old "butter fingers" Dad.

3. Reveling in their newly acquired independence and the discovery of their rapidly developing abilities to reason and hypothesize, many adolescents exaggerate their ability to solve "the problems of the world" and those that are personal for them. At the same time, many become critical of adult solutions to social problems, lifestyles, and values but deny that adults are in a position to evaluate life among the adolescents.

4. Furthermore, with the acquisition of the privileges of adulthood—independence, responsibility, and self-direction—there is a movement from childish to adult forms of expression, reaction, and behavior. For better or worse, adult behavior is mimicked and often exaggerated.

5. Self-selected (not adult-imposed) peer group memberships are important to the adolescent. The peer group becomes the center of most of their significant social–recreational activities and, in the eyes of many parents (and many authorities as well), their initial sex education "program." Also, while demanding their independence from parents and other adult controls, adolescents in turn may surrender much of their independence and individuality to peer group conformity.

6. It is a period when they seek direction, a set of values, and their own personal identity. The latter demands treatment as an individual—a demand that the home and school often appear to overlook. In the quest for this new identity, the adolescent encounters, with peers, many of the common problems of this journey. Although a multitude of studies have investigated the priority concerns of youth, most of these tend to be outdated immediately after their publication. Recognizing this limitation, we would use three categories to classify a consensus of common adolescent problems from current studies:

a. *Developing as a social being.* This includes problems of one-to-one personal relationships, particularly dating, love, sex, and marriage. It also involves group living and acceptance and, in general, the development of human relationship skills.

b. *Developing as a unique being.* The adolescent is concerned with the development and recognition of the uniqueness of individuals. It is a time when they are seeking to develop their own value system and often find they face value conflicts. Anxieties are frequently created as a result of constant demands to "measure up" made by evaluative testing and other appraisal techniques that appear to standardize them. They are also concerned when they fail to gain parental or other support for their "new self."

c. *Developing as a productive being.* In this regard, youth are concerned with their educational adjustments and achievements, their career decisions, future educational directions, impending financial needs, and employment prospects. Many become concerned because school is not providing them with a marketable skill. Others feel that staying in school is delaying earning a living.

Let us now briefly note some of the significant characteristics of the secondary school. Although there are, of course, many exceptions to any attempt to characterize schools at any level, the following are generally appropriate for many secondary schools in the United States and Canada.

1. Secondary schools are generally large, complex institutions populated by a heterogeneous student body. The size and complexity of the secondary school have implications for both counseling program development and program activities. Since the larger student bodies tend to be more heterogeneous, often representing many cultural minority groups, the identification of these groups and the response to their needs can represent a major challenge to the program.

2. Secondary school faculties represent a variety of academic specialties. The secondary school faculty member tends to concentrate on a particular subject area. As a result, the secondary school faculty represents a variety of specializations, which provides a reservoir of resources that the school counseling program may use in the career, educational, and personal–social development of students.

3. Secondary school years are important decision-making years for the individual student. During a student's secondary schooling, one is usually confronted with at least two lifetime-influencing decisions. The first of these decisions that many youth make during this period of time is whether to complete their secondary schooling. Various dropout studies indicate that approximately one fourth of high school youth make the decision to leave school before finishing their secondary school program. In addition, many students make important decisions regarding careers or choice of college. The wide variety of course offerings and activities available in most secondary schools prompts a nearly continuous series of minor decisions for the students as well. They may also be confronted with significant personal decisions regarding sex and marriage, use of tobacco, alcohol, and drugs, and friends and friendship.

4. Secondary schools are subject-matter oriented. Schedules and classes tend to be formal and rigidly organized in many secondary schools, with considerable emphasis on acad-

emic standards, homework, and grades (rather than personal growth). Emphasis on standardized test achievements and school discipline can be expected. The homeroom that many students have experienced in the elementary school years ceases to exist in most high schools, except as an administrative checkpoint. As a result, at a time when students are accelerating their development as social beings, the secondary school structure often tends to inhibit this growth and development by placing them in a series of formal, academically oriented subject-matter class experiences. At the same time, many schools fail to provide students with an organized scheduled group (such as homeroom) where they might develop social skills and attitudes. This suggests a challenge to the subject-matter teacher and the counselor to work cooperatively to incorporate social development experiences into the academic program.

5. School spirit, or esprit de corps, is usually more evident in secondary schools than in any other educational institution. This school spirit is usually reflected in the quest for winning athletic teams, championship bands, and other public indications of excellence. Often the competition among students for participation in significant school events is keen. Social divisions may often arise between those who have "made it" and those who have not in terms of these activities. On the positive side, however, school spirit in competitive activities can often be a potential factor in motivating students to remain in school, making them seek higher academic achievements, and promoting pride in the school. Recently, frequent suggestions and efforts have been made to increase the visibility of academic competition as well.

6. The school principal is the single most influential person in the secondary school setting. Decisions, policy development, and practices all emanate or are subject to the approval of the school principal. Unlike the elementary school principal, the secondary principal is frequently assisted by several assistant principals, supervisors, department heads, and specialty chairs. In addition, probably no other person is so significant in establishing the tone or atmosphere of the school and its inhabitants.

Although the adolescent and the adolescent's school have many characteristics in common, wide variations also prevail between them. Counseling programs in secondary schools seem to reflect these ambivalences as counselors engage in many of the same basic activities but within a variety of organizational structures. Figures 3–1 through 3–3 present three of the more traditional organizational models of school counseling programs. Bigger schools in larger school systems may have resource specialists and specialized services (computer and data processing, test scoring) available in the administrative offices of the school system. These resources are available to supplement the efforts of the local building counselors. On the other hand, small schools may often have to share counseling and other specialized personnel. These personnel may operate out of the central administrative offices of the school system and be available on certain days to each school that shares their assignment.

Organizational Patterns in Institutions of Higher Education

Although the popular view from the "Ivory Tower" seems to most frequently focus on the football stadium, the pretty coeds, and, sometimes (but rarely), the distinguished profes-

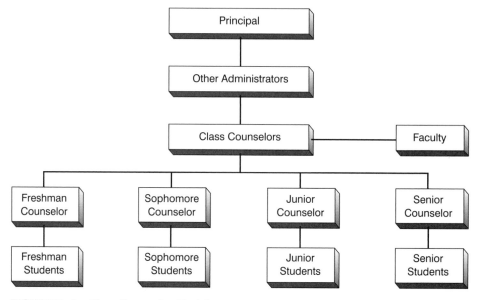

FIGURE 3–1   Class Counselor Model

sor, a serious look at most college and university campuses confirms the existence of counselors and attending programs of counseling and other student services or student development, as it is now called. As might be anticipated, these programs are as unusual or as traditional as the institutions they represent. The burgeoning junior and community college movement appears to be developing programs that often suggest "open marriage" between elements of secondary school counseling programs and traditional university student personnel services programs. Four-year colleges and universities maintain, although often with interesting innovations, programs based on traditional student personnel services models—programs in which counseling services are frequently provided through

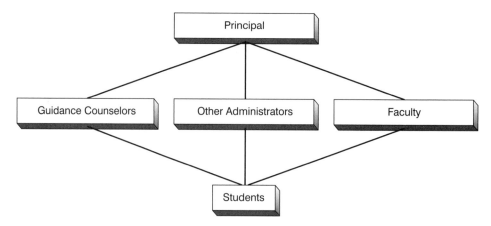

FIGURE 3–2   Guidance Counselor (Generalist) Model

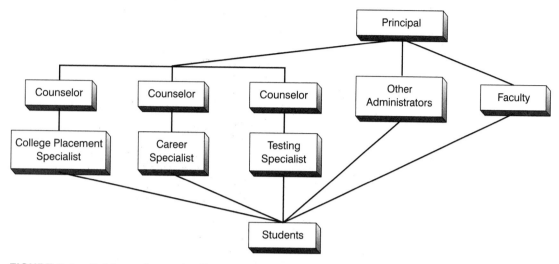

FIGURE 3–3   Guidance Counselor (Specialist) Model

campus counseling centers or clinics, residential counselors, and career counseling offices. Today, the field has grown to over 100 graduate preparation programs producing over 1,200 graduates per academic year at the master's and doctoral level (Johnson, 1993).

Figure 3-4 illustrates an organizational chart for a 4-year college with counseling services provided as a part of the student services of the college or university. Figure 3-5 displays counseling services as a unit of a large university program.

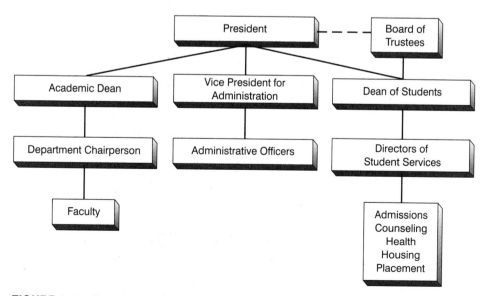

FIGURE 3–4   Organization Chart for a 4-Year College

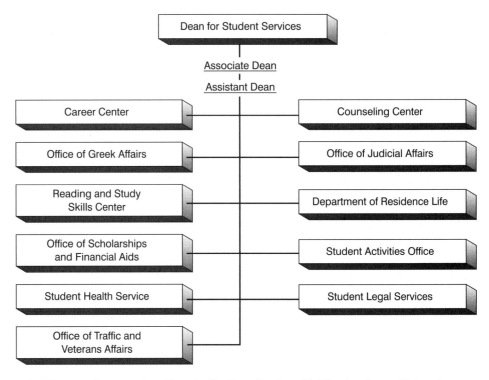

FIGURE 3–5 Organization Chart for Student Services Division in a Large University (Indiana University)

FUTURE DIRECTIONS FOR SCHOOL PROGRAMS OF COUNSELING

All of us engage in predicting the future. Much of our speculation on what lies ahead is, of course, short-range—we predict that the weather will be better tomorrow, the price of coffee will go up again next month, or the football team will be a winner next fall.

Predicting the future is fun, but it is also risky, especially if one is bold enough to put these speculations in print. However, despite the many uncertainties attending even the most scientific efforts (and highly reputable scientific institutes are engaged in such studies today), we still read our horoscopes, have our palms read or handwriting analyzed, read the annual New Year's predictions, and note that books such as Naisbitt and Aburdenes's *Megatrends 2000* (1990) have become international best-sellers.

Although the high level of interest in knowing what the future holds in store for us and our societies does not appear to have diminished over the centuries, both the nature and need for future insights have undergone significant change. We have noted the emergence since World War II of a futuristic science, with an emphasis on scientific, database, and computer-assisted forecasting, and the development of organizations such as the Institute for the Future (Middletown, CT), the World Future Society (formed in

Washington, DC), and the Hudson Institute (Indianapolis). The need for some form of reasonably accurate future forecasting has become increasingly evident.

One indicator that change will probably take place in a product, activity, or organization is strong and significant criticism of their present state. For example, even those who "see no evil, hear no evil, speak no evil" are well aware of the volume and intensity of critical changes leveled at education over the years, criticisms that have and will continue to promote change in the future.

For example, increased emphasis on basics was called for by President Reagan's 1984 Task Force on Education. The publication of this task force, *A Nation at Risk* (Bell, 1983), led to a nationwide educational reform movement characterized by a return to no-nonsense basics, greater attention to student discipline and management, and measurement of student growth through standardized achievement testing. Of special interest to school counselors was the report of the College Entrance Examination Board's Commission on Precollege Guidance and Counseling, *Keeping the Options Open* (1986), which found:

❖ Adequate counseling and guidance services are essential for all students, particularly for those who suffer disadvantages from poverty, discrimination, and family stress or disruption.

❖ Counseling is a profession in trouble. (Too often counselors are assigned tasks—administrative routines, maintaining records, and supervising students—that make inadequate use of their special skills and talents. In many states the student/counselor ratios are rising beyond the level at which counselors can perform effectively.)

❖ Provision for guidance and counseling follows an all too well-established pattern in the distribution of public services: Those with the least at home often get the least help from public institutions and programs. (College Entrance Examination Board, 1986, pp. 2–3)

The College Board Commission (1986) made four priority recommendations for future action in our schools:

1. Establish a broad-based process in each local school district for determining the particular guidance and counseling needs of the students within each school and for planning how best to meet these needs.

2. Develop a program under the leadership of each school principal that emphasizes the importance of the guidance counselor as a monitor and promoter of student potential, as well as coordinator of the school's guidance plans.

3. Mount programs to inform and involve parents and other members of the family influential in the choices, plans, decisions, and learning activities of the student.

4. Provide a program of guidance and counseling during the early and middle years of schooling, especially for students who traditionally have not been well-served by the schools. (pp. 5–6)

The board also made four other major recommendations that involve a variety of actors and institutions outside the schools and provide essential support for school-based change:

❖ Strengthen collaboration among schools, community agencies, colleges, businesses, and other community resources to enhance services available to students.

❖ Establish a process in each state to determine the guidance and counseling needs of specific student populations and give support to local initiatives that address these needs.

❖ Increase support of federal programs that help disadvantaged students to enter and remain in college.

❖ Revise the training of school counselors to include the specific skills and knowledge necessary to enable them to take a more central role in schools. (College Entrance Examination Board, 1986, p. 6)

We must also recognize that a "new wave" of counselors will be entering our schools in the last years of this century as many of the National Defense Education Act (NDEA)-trained counselors of the 1960s move into retirement. This, coupled with the increased demand, nationwide, for elementary school counselors, could result in an acceleration in employment opportunities for counselors in schools. Revised training and certification requirements are also occurring in many states.

This new generation of counselors must be computer competent and alert to the technological advancements of the "information age" that have implications for their practice. Electronic learning and multimedia approaches, among others, will dramatically influence new approaches to learning. New curricular emphases will include increased attention to technological and vocational curricula, plus renewed attention to the arts. The schools may also stress the importance of environmental conservation. Increased international orientation may also be anticipated. A longer school day and school year may be part of future school systems in the United States. Finally, the schools are being envisioned as centers for life-long learning.

As in the past, counselors will continue to counsel and consult and give attention to the career development needs of student populations. These needs, however, will be dramatically different from the past "one person, one career" approach as we view a century when individuals entering the work force (with the exception of the professions) can anticipate *at least* three distinctly different careers over their working lifetime. Many of these will require a return to educational settings, adapting to new technologies, and movement to new geographic locations. School career programs must prepare youthful workers for both adaptability and flexibility. Counselors must ensure that youth are prepared for tomorrow's career world rather than yesterday's.

There will be a greatly increased program emphasis on prevention and early intervention, with special attention to such societal concerns as child abuse, substance abuse, teen pregnancies, AIDS and other human sexuality concerns, and the seemingly perennial problems of school dropouts and youth unemployment. The increasing recognition that prevention programs are needed—and more promising—than the after-the-incident treatment of these social issues will present school counselors with unprecedented opportunities to establish their uniqueness and, at the same time, their unprecedented value to society. Too, counselors will be expected, as the school's human relations experts, to take a much more active role in preventing prejudice by promoting multicultural understandings and relationships. As noted previously, we are a profession dedicated to caring and respecting the worth of every individual. Further, as a discipline, we are experts in communications and human relations. Thus, our values and skills would suggest an increasingly important role for the profession of counseling in promoting positive and productive relationships among all racial/cultural/ethnic and religious populations.

The urgent need for counselor involvement is further suggested by the recognition that while considerable progress has been made in legislative enactments and judicial decisions, much more remains to be accomplished at the levels of personal awareness, understanding, respect, and acceptance. The urgency for this progress is further highlighted when we note that over 25% of our population is currently estimated to represent minorities. This is projected to increase to 32% by 2010 and 47% by the year 2050 (U.S. Department of Commerce, Bureau of Census, 1993). Here again, we note that the elimination of prejudice and the substitution of respect and understanding in human relations must begin in the school setting. To achieve this goal, counselors must themselves be models of awareness, understanding, and acceptance.

Counselors of the 2000s will also be expected to be more professionally competent in assessing differing environments (i.e., community, school, etc.) and their impact on their clients. Accountability mandates will demand increased counselor knowledge in the areas of measurement and standardized testing. The rapidly developing field of family therapy will influence school counseling in the immediate decades ahead. In this regard, Peeks (1993) writes:

> The changes occurring in the fields of counseling and education are traversed within the walls of U.S. public schools. As counseling has made a shift toward the systems paradigm, the student is viewed as a part of a larger unit, his family. As education makes a shift toward expanded effectiveness, parents are viewed as an important and integral part of the educational process. Both of the changes acknowledge the importance of a student's extended social unit to the success of his or her education. Students are first members of a family. (p. 248)

Counselors in schools will be called upon in the near future to direct more attention to family lifestyles and their impact on school youth. Peeks (1993, p. 249) predicts:

> The increasing changes in education and the expanded counseling function will bring counseling and education closer together within the context of the schools. It is predicted that the schools of the future will become family centers (Cetron, 1985), where family health and employment services are offered for stress-laden families. A typical school district may provide training for students ages 3 to 21 years and for adults 21 to 80-plus years. These expanded services will be offered either through satellites or widely expanded professional staffs. Schools will need programs to protect children against the ravages of social disorganization and family collapse (London, 1987). The establishment of such programs will necessitate family involvement in the context of the school by school counselors who understand the powerful systemic connection between the student and family. Parent involvement in the school in almost any form seems to produce measurable gains in student achievement (Henderson, 1988).

Additionally, it is clearly evident that by 1998 the vast majority of homes in the United States with children will be either dual-career or single-parent homes. The implications of these new models of family life are many, not the least of which will be "what happens to the children?" So far, there has been little planning to provide for these "latchkey" youth. Obviously, the failure to make adequate provisions guarantees disastrous consequences to both the individual and society. School counseling programs must take the lead in developing comprehensive and effective programs for all school youth, including latchkey children.

According to Peeks (1993), it is also important in the decades ahead for counselors to work for parental involvement in their child's academic efforts.

> Decades of research document that families are critically important to the academic success of students. Studies have shown that, for most students, the schools they attend make less difference to academic success than the families from which they come (Gandara, 1989). Further research has shown that parent–school conferences not only enhance family–school relationships, but that they also have an impact on student performance. (Turnbull & Turnbull, 1990, p. 248)

We believe that school counselors of the future increasingly will be called on to engage in research in their settings to hasten the solutions to many constant youth problems such as those previously noted. Only through an all-out professional effort involving those "on the scene" can we hope to make real headway in dealing with these problems.

THE ECOLOGY OF THE SCHOOL

In discussing the ecology of the school, we are, in fact, examining the climate of the school, its environment. Ecological psychology, has, since the early pronouncements of Kurt Lewin (1936), stressed the importance of the environment on individual behavior. The growing field of specialists in ecological psychology are concerned with how individuals perceive, are shaped by, value, influence, and are influenced by their environments.

Certainly, the school is a significant environment and one that will influence the behavior, values, and plans of its student inhabitants. However, Conyne (1987) notes that only recently has increased interest in the application of this viewpoint to the practice of counseling been noted. Within this context, school counselors can improve their understanding of their student–client population by recognizing the following concepts:

1. Environment is a significant influence on behavior. Therefore, school counselors must understand this influence if they are to predict, modify, or prevent undesirable behaviors in their student clientele.

2. Since stable, long-term settings such as the school pass on expectations and norms for behaviors, values, and attitudes, school counselors, with their teaching colleagues, must plan accordingly.

3. Environmental understandings provide a basis for the development of meaningful prevention programs.

4. Students, like all others, strive for optimal environments in which to develop adequate self-concepts, fulfill their needs, and maximize their potential. Such settings provide supportive relationships and a "climate" that is motivational and enjoyable.

Schools and students cannot be understood on the basis of records and data (i.e., test scores, grades, attendance, etc.) alone. They are performers on the stage of life. To understand the roles they are playing, we must understand the setting. Ecological psychology thus helps us better understand students by understanding their psychological interplay with their environment.

SUMMARY

An article in *Better Homes and Gardens* noted that "if you graduated from high school before 1960, chances are the only school counselors you have known are your child's" (Daly, 1979, p. 15). This chapter assumes that most of those who graduated from high school before 1960 also knew little about how their counselors were trained or licensed and had little familiarity with their role and function. Perhaps this very lack of understanding has led the counseling professionals in the past decade to move more energetically into the public communications arena to "tell what they're about," upgrade their training, and seek protection of their profession from unqualified intruders through certification and licensure. Much has been accomplished in a short period of time if one considers that at the turn of this century there were no counselors in schools. More than 90 years and approximately 150,000–200,000 school counselors later, we can identify tremendous progress in training, certification, and practice.

Counselor training today is available at the master's, specialist, and doctoral levels, with the possibility of undergraduate and postdoctoral courses as well. All states specify some type of counselor preparation or certification for employment in school settings, with the exception of postsecondary institutions. These requirements in general reflect role and function expectancies. Differing characteristics of various school levels, settings, and clientele, by necessity, result in variations in that role and function. However, school counselors cannot "go it alone." They must view themselves as "member players" on the school "team" and work for the cooperation and contributions of teachers, administrators, and other helping professionals who are vital to the success of any school counseling program.

Finally, we noted that school counselors and school counseling programs must be able to adapt to the demands of the future if they are to become or remain relevant and valuable to the populations they are intended to serve. This is, of course, no less true for counselors functioning in various community and agency settings. Chapter 4 will describe counselors in these various settings.

DISCUSSION QUESTIONS

1. Discuss contacts that you can recall during your schooling with differing helping professionals (i.e., school psychologist, school social worker, school counselor, school nurse, and other health personnel). Compare the role of each of these in the school program.

2. As a potential counselor, are there some special preparations or subject matters that you would like to see as a part of your training program? Identify and present a rationale.

3. Should school counselors be required to have teaching experience? Why?

4. Discuss your own elementary, junior/middle, and/or high school counseling programs as you experienced them.

5. What do you envision the professional activities of a school counselor will be in the year 2025?

6. How should school counseling and guidance programs respond to major societal programs such as substance abuse, child abuse, AIDS, school dropouts, underemployment, juvenile groups, latchkey children, and the homeless? Are there other major societal problems that school counseling programs should address? If so, what are these problems, and how should school counseling programs respond to them?

CLASS ACTIVITIES

1. "Shadow" a school counselor for a day or two and report your observations to the class.

2. Interview a teacher, school principal, or other helping professional regarding their relationship and contribution to the school counseling program. Report your findings.

3. Assume you (the class) are a group of "experts" called together to formulate a "model" school counselor preparation program for the first years of the twenty-first century.

SELECTED READINGS

Bell, T. (1983). *A nation at risk: The imperative for educational reform.* Washington, DC: The National Commission on Excellence in Education.

Castronovo, N. R. (1990). Acquired immune deficiency syndrome education on the college campus: The mandate and the challenge. *Journal for Counseling and Development, 68,* 578–580.

Cetron, M. J. (1985). *Schools of the future: How American business and education can cooperate to save our schools.* Sponsored by the American Association of School Administrators. New York: McGraw-Hill.

College Entrance Examination Board. (1986). *Keeping the options open.* New York: Author, Commission on Precollege Guidance and Counseling.

Cummings, N. A. (1990). The credentialing of professional psychologists and its implication for the other mental health disciplines. *Journal of Counseling and Development, 68,* 485–490.

Dennis, D. L., Buckner, J. C., Lipton, F. R., & Levine, I. S. (1991). A decade of research and services for homeless mentally ill persons. *American Psychologist, 46,* 1129–1138.

Gibson, R. (1990). Teacher opinions of high school guidance programs: Then and now. *The School Counselor, 37,* 248–255.

Helms, B., & Ibrahim, F. (1985). A comparison of counselor and parent perceptions of the role and function of the secondary school counselor. *The School Counselor, 32,* 266–274.

Hutchinson, R. L., Barrick, A., & Groves, M. (1986). Functions of secondary school counselors in the public schools: Ideal and actual. *The School Counselor, 34,* 87–91.

Ibrahim, K., Helms, B., & Thompson, D. (1983). Counselor role and function: An appraisal by consumers and counselors. *The Personnel and Guidance Journal, 61,* 597–601.

Kelly, J. A., Murphy, D. A., Sikkema, K. J., & Kalichman, S. C. (1993). Psychological interventions to prevent HIV infection are urgently needed: New priorities for behavioral research in the second decade of AIDS. *American Psychologist, 48,* 1023–1034.

McAuliffe, G. J. (1992). A case presentation approach to group supervision for community college counselors. *Counselor Education and Supervision, 31,* 163–174.

Milburn, N., & D'Ercole, A. (1991). Homeless women. *American Psychologist, 46,* 1161–1169.

Neukrug, E. S. (1991). Computer-assisted live supervision in counselor skills training. *Counselor Education and Supervision, 31,* 132–138.

Rafferty, Y., & Shinn, M. (1991). The impact of homelessness on children. *American Psychologist, 46,* 1170–1179.

Robbins, S. B., Lese, K. P., & Herrick, S. M. (1993). Interactions between goal instability and social support on college freshman adjustment. *Journal of Counseling and Development, 71,* 343–348.

Schmidt, J. J., & Osborne, W. (1982). The way we were (and are): A profile of elementary counselors in North Carolina. *Elementary School Guidance and Counseling, 16,* 163–171.

RESEARCH OF INTEREST

Corders, L. D., & Drury, S. M. (1992). Comprehensive school counseling programs: A review for policymakers and practitioners. *Journal of Counseling and Development, 70,* 487–498.

Abstract

Provides an overview of the components of effective school counseling programs which have surfaced over the period from 1960–1990. Results and discussion are categorized in seven sections, including core principles of school counseling programs, program resources, interventions utilized by programs, evaluation procedures, written policies, program climate, and renewal process.

Brooks, D. K., & Gerstein, L. H. (1990). Counselor credentialing and interprofessional collaboration. *Journal of Counseling and Development, 68,* 477–484.

Abstract

Presents the history and development of the counselor credentialing process. Includes aspects of standards, accreditation, certification, and licensure as well as future trends in the licensure movement pertaining to preparation and training, examinations, accountability, and consumer protection. Collaboration and reimbursement are also discussed.

Campbell, N. J., & Dobson, J. E. (1987). An inventory of student computer anxiety. *Elementary School Guidance and Counseling, 22,* 149–156.

Abstract

Presents the development of an instrument designed to identify computer-anxious students in grades 4 through 8. Also provides counselors with information regarding proper use of the instrument. Discusses computer use in schools as well as grounds for counselors to utilize computers in their work in schools.

Casey, J., & Ramsammy, R. (1992, February). *Macmentoring: Using technology and counseling with at-risk youth.* Paper presented at the Annual Conference of the California Association for Counseling and Development, San Francisco.

Abstract

Describes the "MacMentoring Project," which was designed to reconnect disenfranchised youth back into school through activities focused on enhancing self-esteem while also teaching them transferable computer skills. Among the subjects ($N = 45$), improvements of on-task behaviors, expression of creativity, benefits from a nondirective counseling strategy, and success at meeting expectations were demonstrated.

Chapman, D. W., O'Brien, C. J., & De Masi, M. E. (1987). The effectiveness of the public school counselor in college advising. *Journal of College Admissions, 115,* 11–18.

Abstract

First-time applicants to the New York State Tuition Assistance Program completed the Student Survey on High School Guidance Counseling. Student–counselor contact was low, and mostly initiated by the counselor. Most students who used counselors used them as sources of information about college and financial aid but felt that they played an indifferent role in the college decision process.

Fagan, T. K., & Jenkins, W. M. (1989). People with disabilities: An update. *Journal of Counseling and Development, 68,* 140–143.

Abstract

Provides information regarding disabling conditions in school-age and adult populations. Presents changes in federal legislation and interpretations of this legislation. Focuses extensively on adult disabling conditions and rehabilitation services.

Fisher, P. J., & Breakey, W. R. (1991). The epidemiology of alcohol, drug, and mental disorders among homeless persons. *American Psychologist, 46,* 1115–1128.

Abstract

Discusses recent research regarding the prevalence of alcohol, drugs, and mental (ADM) disorders and the personal characteristics of homeless substance abusers and individuals with mental disorders. Emphasizes that these individuals are impacted by extreme poverty; underutilization of public entitlements; isolation from family, friends, and other networks of support; frequent contacts with correctional agencies; and poor overall health. Concludes that awareness of those issues must take place in advocating more suitable services for persons experiencing homelessness.

Gray, L. A., & Saracino, M. (1989). AIDS on campus: A preliminary study of college students' knowledge and behaviors. *Journal of Counseling and Development, 68,* 199–202.

Abstract

Examines the probable relationship between knowledge about AIDS, subjective perceptions regarding the risk of contracting AIDS, and sexual behavior of undergraduate college students ($N = 459$). Data analysis indicates no relationship between accurate knowledge about AIDS and sexual activity. Recommendations are made regarding AIDS educational and counseling approaches among college students.

Kameen, M. C., Robinson, E. H., & Rotter, J. C. (1985). Coordination activities: A study of perceptions of elementary and middle school counselors. *Elementary School Guidance and Counseling, 20,* 97–104.

Abstract

Examines 193 counselors' perceptions of their coordination activities. Results indicate counselors spend the majority of time in information dissemination and maintenance and testing and placement coordination. The authors feel more time should be spent in guidance, in-service, and community activities.

Leigh, B. C., & Stall, R. (1993). Substance use and risky sexual behavior for exposure to HIV. *American Psychologist, 48,* 1035–1045.

Abstract

Reviews research literature on the relationship between substance use and high-risk sexual behavior through global association studies, situational association studies, and event analysis procedures. Concludes that both sex and substance abuse are complicated behaviors and wonders whether related comprehension of the dynamics of the relationship is necessary.

Lombana, J. H. (1989). Counseling persons with disabilities: Summary and projections. *Journal of Counseling and Development, 68,* 177–179.

Abstract

Presents the findings of various articles pertaining to counseling individuals with disabilities and the progress recently made regarding provision of services to these individuals. Also discusses issues of concern in counseling persons with disabilities and provides guidelines for counselors in their future work with persons with disabilities.

Mooney, S. P., Sherman, M. F., & Lo Presto, C. T. (1991). Academic locus of control, self-esteem, and perceived distance from home as predictors of college adjustment. *Journal of Counseling and Development, 69,* 445–448.

Abstract

Examines the academic locus of control, self-esteem, and geographic distance from home (actual and perceived) as predictors of college adjustment for female college freshmen ($N = 88$). Results indicate that internal academic locus of control, high levels of self-esteem, and a belief that the distance from home was "just right" for the individual related to personal, academic, social, and attachment adjustment.

Olson, M. J., & Dilley, J. S. (1988). A new look at stress and the school counselor. *School Counselor, 35,* 194–198.

Abstract

Reviews research on school counselors' stress. Concludes stress is not so much a function of conflict between roles that are differentially endorsed by different publics as it is of the sheer number of roles that are strongly endorsed. Claims mental health and quality of work of counselors is adversely affected by the stress of inability to meet demands.

Stone, W. H., Jr., Thompson, S. D., & Lacount, D. M. (1989). Attitudes of high school counselors toward computers. *School Counselor, 36,* 281–285.

Abstract

Examines the attitudes of high school counselors (*N* = 86) toward computers. Uses the Computer Attitude Scale developed by Loyd and Gressard (1985). Results demonstrate that at least 62% of counselors have positive attitudes regarding computers, found them useful, and felt confident using them.

Vacc, N. A., & Loesch, L. C. (1993). A content analysis of opinions about the National Counselor Exam. *Journal of Counseling and Development, 71,* 418–421.

Abstract

Explores the degree of professional satisfaction among candidates (*N* = 363) taking the National Counselor Examination (NCE) between 1986 and 1990. Responses refer to specific test items, overall content of the examination, professional value of the examination, and the examination process. Both negative and positive comments are reported.

Wiggins, J. D., & Moody, A. H. (1987). Student evaluations of counseling programs: An added dimension. *School Counselor, 34,* 535–561.

Abstract

Evaluates school counseling programs in seven junior high and four senior high schools by focusing on student perceptions of various parts of the counseling program and then relating these evaluations to reported time–task emphasis of counselors. Counselors who spend the most time in direct delivery of services through individual and group counseling are rated as most effective.

Wilson, N. S. (1986). Counselor interventions with low-achieving and underachieving elementary, middle, and high school students: A review of the literature. *Journal of Counseling and Development, 64,* 628–634.

Abstract

Reviews experimental studies and evaluates the effects of counselor interventions on the grade point average of underachieving or low-achieving students in elementary, middle, and high schools. Includes characteristics of programs associated with improved achievement.

Chapter 4

Counselors in Community
and Agency Settings

Many of you may eventually consider employment as counselors in community, agency, or other "nonschool" professional situations. The objective of this chapter is to acquaint you with the counselor's role and function in a variety of these settings. These include community mental health agencies, employment and rehabilitation agencies, correctional settings, and marriage and family practice. Pastoral counseling, counseling for veterans, sports counseling, gerontology counseling, and private practice are also discussed.

TRAINING PROGRAMS FOR COUNSELORS IN COMMUNITY AND AGENCY SETTINGS

The training of counselors for the various community and agency settings is very similar to the training of school counselors, and in the past there was little distinction in many master's degree programs with the possible exceptions of practicum and internship settings and a few specialized courses. However, new standards for the preparation of counselors in specialty areas as officially indicated by appropriate professional organizations have resulted in an increase in specialized courses. In some training programs counselors may be trained in separate departments or in programs with distinctly different emphases. Even greater distinctions will be noted at the doctoral degree level, where preparation tends to focus on the anticipated professional work setting.

The Council for Accreditation of Counseling and Related Educational Programs (CACREP; 1994) specifies that community agency counselor preparation programs will require a minimum of 48 semester or 72 quarter hours of graduate course work. This course work will include studies in each of eight common core areas: human growth and development, social-cultural foundations, helping relations, group work, career and lifestyle developments, appraisal, research, and program evaluation and professional orientation. Programs in mental health counseling and/or marriage and family counseling/therapy are comprised of graduate-level study, with a minimum of 60 semester-hour or 90 quarter-hour credits. Additional course work is required in three specialty areas: foundations of community counseling, contextual dimensions for community counseling, and knowledge and skills for the practice of community counseling. A 600-hour internship in a community setting is also required.

Further insights into both training and on-the-job functioning may also be noted by examining the provisions of the Community Mental Health Centers Act of 1963, which provided for the establishment of a network of mental health centers throughout the nation. Each center was to provide at least the five basic services of (a) in-patient care; (b) out-patient care; (c) partial hospitalization; (d) emergency care; and (e) consultation, education, and information.

Blocher and Biggs (1983), in discussing counseling psychology in community settings, define counseling psychology as a subdiscipline of the science of psychology and a specialty in the practice of professional psychology. As a discipline, counseling psychology draws upon and contributes to psychological knowledge, particularly in the following domains:

1. Vocational behavior, including the development of vocational interests, attitudes, values, and aptitudes and their relationship to vocational satisfaction and effectiveness.

2. Human cognition and cognitive development and their relationships to problem-solving, decision-making, and judgment.

3. Human learning and behavior change particularly in their relationships to the acquisition, transfer, and maintenance of coping and mastery behaviors through the life span.

4. Human communication and interpersonal behavior, especially within family and other primary group settings that influence developmental processes.

5. The nature of optimal person/environment fit, especially in family, educational, work, and other community settings as these impinge on the health, happiness, and continuing growth of members.

As a professional practitioner, the counseling psychologist draws upon the science of human behavior to help people in a variety of settings and situations. The counseling psychologist engages in individual and small-group counseling around a variety of concerns involving educational and vocational planning, personal problem-solving and decision-making, family problems, and other activities related to the enhancement of personal growth and effectiveness. Such counseling also focuses on the prevention, removal, or remediation of obstacles to personal growth as these exist in the interaction between the individual and the environment.

The counseling psychologist also consults with individuals, organizations, and institutions in the society to help enhance the quality of physical, social, and psychological environments as these affect the growth of those who work, study, or live within them.

The counseling psychologist often engages in training a variety of people in basic interpersonal and life skills that can improve their functioning in significant social roles. The counseling psychologist also functions at times as a psychological educator, who shares with a variety of others, important psychological skills and knowledge needed to help them function more effectively in helping situations and to move to higher levels of personal and social development.* (pp. 15–16)

Thus, as we proceed to examine the role of the counselor in a variety of community, agency, and institutional settings, we emphasize that these counselors deal with the developmental and growth needs of clients as well as the more traditional remedial and adjustment concerns.

THE IMPORTANCE OF LICENSURE

As previously noted in Chapter 3, the movement toward licensure is one that, in the long run, will protect both the public and the profession. Licensure is particularly important to many professional counselors practicing in community agencies or private practices, in which client reimbursement is significant to the agency's or individual's fiscal wellness. This reimbursement, usually referred to as "third-party payment," is based on insurance companies' and Medicare provisions to pay for services rendered to clients by eligible (licensed) providers. This process of licensure in each state is established by legislative action. State licensure boards administer the legislated licensing program.

*Reprinted from Blocher, D. H., & Biggs, D. A., *Counseling Psychology in Commnity Settings.* © 1983 Springer Publishing Company, Inc., New York 10012. Used by permission.

Currently, counseling psychologists may be credentialed in any of the 50 states. To be eligible for such licensure, candidates must hold an earned doctorate in psychology, have completed a predoctoral internship, and have passed the national licensure examination and whatever special examination an individual state may require.

Professional counselors trained in programs of counselor education may currently secure licensure in 41 states, plus the District of Columbia. While this process differs from state to state, it typically requires candidates to have an earned master's degree and often to have passed the National Board for Certified Counselors examination. Graduates of programs accredited by CACREP may, in some instances, be eligible to take this examination while completing their graduate training program, rather than having to wait to gain experience before being eligible to take the examination.

COMMUNITY AND MENTAL HEALTH AGENCIES

Community mental health agencies provide counseling services for the general population within a specified geographic locale. Many community mental health agencies have been initiated under the provisions of the previously mentioned Community Mental Health Act of 1963, which provides initial funding for such centers that must be developed following the guidelines of the National Institute of Mental Health. These agencies were designed to provide preventive community mental health services. Typically, such centers offer inpatient and outpatient services, emergency services, and educational and consultation services. Many centers also provide partial hospitalization services, diagnostic services, and precare and aftercare in the community through programs of home visitations, foster home placement, and halfway houses.

Senator Edward M. Kennedy notes (1990):

Experience has demonstrated that a number of key features must be included in any effective community-based program of care for the seriously mentally ill. They include the following:

1. Quantitative analysis of the population to be served, so that the number of people to be helped and their specific needs can be determined.

2. Case management, so that someone is responsible for coordinating and monitoring necessary services.

3. A program of support and rehabilitation to provide services appropriate for each client's age, functional level, and individual needs. Psychotherapy, regular social contact to assist reintegration into the community, vocational training, supervised work, and assistance in obtaining and keeping competitive employment should be available to adults, and an appropriate range of services should also be available to children. The goal is to enable individuals to function at the maximum feasible level.

4. Medical treatment and mental health care, available on a continuum from day hospitalization to periodic appointments, to regulate medication and monitor mental status.

5. Assistance to families who often provide the frontline care for the mentally ill in the community and who are often left to cope with the severe strains of mental illness without assistance from the society at large.

6. Housing services, ranging from half-way houses with staff in residence who provide continuous supervision to largely independent living. Outreach to the homeless mentally ill should be seen as an essential part of these services. (pp. 1238–1239)

Belkin (1988) notes that counseling in the community differs from general private practice and counseling in an academic or agency setting in four respects:

1. It is located in a setting that is easy for community members to reach, and that is viewed by the community as being associated with them. This differs from having to take a car, train, or bus to some distant, possibly downtown location, which may be viewed as threatening, alien, or hostile.

2. The community facility is generally geared to specific problems of the community. For example, in a community where there is a high rate of substance abuse, addiction prevention and drug rehabilitation programs may be instituted to deal with the problems of drug abuse. Certain kinds of problems that are common to all communities would, of course, be included in all such facilities.

3. The professional and paraprofessional staff at such centers is trained to relate to the community members. This can take place on many different levels. For instance, in a Spanish-speaking community, you would have staff who not only can speak and understand the Spanish language, but who also understand the cultural uniqueness of the constituency (Blatt, 1976).

4. There is a willingness to experiment with counseling modalities that are less traditional than those the counselor may otherwise employ. Because of special population needs, it is often necessary to design innovative and creative programs to reach large numbers of the population.

There are several other key differences that should be pointed out as well. Because of its location in the community and dependence on community members as clientele, such a center tends to view the client as a *consumer* of services. This attitude encourages a flexibility and responsiveness, especially when it is observed that members' needs are not being adequately met.

Also, whereas many counseling activities are focused on the individual client's needs, community counseling places emphasis on setting up programs that can benefit *the community as a whole,* as well as individual community members.* (pp. 460–461)

The Agency Team

In most community mental health agencies, counselors are employed as team members with other helping professionals. These typically include psychiatrists, clinical and counseling psychologists, and psychiatric social workers. Psychiatrists are usually considered to be the leaders of the team, inasmuch as they have a medical background and may perform physical examinations, prescribe drugs, and admit people to hospitals in the treatment of behavior abnormalities. In addition to basic medical training, certification as a psychiatrist typically requires 3 years of residency in a psychiatric institution plus 2 years of further practice.

Counseling or clinical psychologists are prepared in programs that require a minimum of 3 academic years of full-time resident graduate study, plus a full year's internship in an appropriate setting. Although emphases in programs will vary somewhat from institution to institution and depend on whether one is trained in a clinical or counseling psychology program, the psychologist receives general training in basic psychology, counseling and psychotherapy, psychological assessment, and psychological research.

Some contend that the difference between clinical and counseling psychology has never been entirely clear, but distinctions do exist. One distinction might be that clinical psychologists appear to work more frequently with behavioral abnormalities and personality reorganization, whereas counseling psychologists emphasize a better understanding of the adjustment problems of normal persons.

Psychiatric social workers are trained minimally to the master's degree level in 2-year programs. One year of this program is devoted to supervised internship in a clinical or hospital setting. Social workers are trained to help people experiencing economic or other problems. This assistance is facilitated through welfare and other programs. The psychiatric social worker, however, is more frequently found in hospital or community mental health settings. In such settings, they may gather data regarding patients and their families and often will work with the patient's family in assisting the client's adjustment. In many community mental health centers, psychiatric social workers may also conduct treatment of a nonmedical nature.

Counseling in the Agency Setting

What is it like to counsel in an agency setting? The following represents a "day" in the professional life of a counseling psychologist, Louise Dunn, Ph.D., at the South Central Community Mental Health Agency, Bloomington, Indiana.

Typical Day of a Counselor at a Community Mental Health Center

8:00 A.M.   Pick up any messages with secretary regarding schedule changes, important meetings scheduled

8:05 A.M.   Drop by Medical Records and get three charts for clients scheduled to be seen today

8:10 A.M.   Review case notes for client 1 scheduled at 8:30

8:30 A.M.   Meet with client 1 for 50 minutes—27-year-old married woman with two children dealing with the recent death of her father; grief issues

9:20 A.M.   Summary report on client 1

9:45 A.M.   Make phone calls: (1) social worker assigned to case seen yesterday regarding special services needed for client's child; (2) psychiatrist regarding referral of client needing psychiatric evaluation for current functioning

10:00 A.M. Meet with new client for scheduled intake

11:15 A.M. Rewrite intake notes for new client just seen for presentation of client in team meeting later today

11:45 A.M. Call client seen 2 days ago to give information about a new support group formed for AMAC (adults molested as children) victims

12:00 P.M.   Lunch and pick up new messages

12:30 P.M.   Go over notes in preparation for presentation of morning's intake to team—and previous case notes for client to be seen at 2:00 P.M.

1:00 P.M.   Team meeting: meet with adult outpatient team; listen to the presentation of five new cases; pick up two of the new cases to fill two slots left by client terminations; present new case to team (client seen at intake earlier)

2:00 P.M.   Meet with client 2—36-year-old recently divorced male with two small children, having problems coping with new situation

3:00 P.M.   Write case summary notes for client 2

3:20 P.M.   Make phone calls: (1) confirm appointment regarding phone message from client; (2) call new clients picked up in team to schedule appointment—able to reach one and set up appointment; other unavailable: dictate letter to other client to be typed by secretary

3:45 P.M.   Go to Center Library to seek a reference for assertiveness training as refresher to use with client scheduled the next day

4:00 P.M.   Meet with client 3—72-year-old woman complaining of morning dizziness and anxiety attacks

4:50 P.M.   Write case summary notes for client 3

5:10 P.M.   Return charts to Medical Records

5:15 P.M.   Leave for the day

Counselors in community settings deal with widely diverse populations and a wide variety in both the type and nature of human concerns. These range from continuous developmental needs of people to crises requiring immediate emergency attention. Pietrofesa, Hoffman, Splete, and Pinto (1978) identify the general types of counseling situations with which community counselors deal as the following:

1. *Crisis*—Is likely to involve issues related to concerns about suicide, drugs, or rejection by a loved one. The counselor is involved in individual counseling with the client, providing personal support as well as gathering additional support and/or referral of the client to appropriate resources.

2. *Facilitative*—Is likely to involve issues related to job placement, career/academic concerns, and marital adjustment. The counselor, through individual counseling with the client, uses techniques such as reflecting, informing, interpreting, confronting, and providing direction.

3. *Prevention*—Involves issues such as sex education, self-awareness, career awareness, and drug awareness. The counselor provides information, refers the client to relevant programs, and counsels the client regarding content issues and process issues related to the preventative program.

4. *Developmental*—Involves issues related to life span development such as self-concept development for children, midlife career adjustment, and death and dying. The counselor uses values clarification techniques, processing of decision-making procedures, and exploration of personal development and relationship issues.

In addition to community mental health agencies, what might be labeled alternative and nontraditional yet related community counseling services have developed over the past several generations. These nontraditional service centers have had a variety of titles, but most of them can be categorized under the labels of hot lines or crisis centers, "drop in" or open-door centers, and specialized counseling centers such as those catering to drug and alcohol abusers or careers dealing with special populations such as women, minorities, or the aged.

❝ Hot lines or crisis phones have been one of the most popular and older alternative services offered. They are frequently staffed by nonprofessionals or paraprofessionals with, in some settings, professional volunteers available or a professional supervisor on call. Usually hot lines or crisis phones are designed to provide sympathetic and helpful listeners and reliable information for dealing with common concerns such as drug overdoses, suicide, spouse abuse, alcoholism, and mental breakdown.

It is obviously desirable that crisis situations be handled by trained, professional counselors. Table 4-1 lists some suggestions made by Belkin (1981) for counselor behavior in a crisis situation.

Open-door or drop-in centers provide havens for persons who need a place to come to and, in larger cities, to get off the streets—a place where they can feel secure and receive sympathetic attention and counseling assistance. Some of these centers actually provide minimal accommodations where a person can "sleep it off." For the most part, however, they simply offer an opportunity for the person to have emergency counseling assistance. In many of these centers, record keeping is at a minimum, and clients may not even be required to give their name or other personal data unless they wish.

In a number of more populous communities, various specialized counseling service centers are on the increase. These centers tend to serve special populations, defined either by the nature of the problem, such as alcohol or drug addiction, spouse abuse, marital relations, or sexual problems; or by age classifications or racial or religious groups. These specialty centers tend to be staffed by a mixture of professionals, paraprofessionals, and volunteers. Facilities are equally diverse. For example, the Norfolk, Virginia Redevelopment and Housing Authority has established a system of community-based counselors who function with aides to assist individuals and families living in 11 public housing parks in that city. These counselors and their aides give support to residents in crisis situations and provide the information they need to cope with their problems, including the rules and regulations of the housing authority. Counseling activities tend to focus particularly on strengthening families.

EMPLOYMENT COUNSELING

In 1933, the Department of Labor established the Employment Security offices, which were to provide job placement and attending advising or counseling functions for the unemployed. Counseling was more specifically provided for in the G.I. Bill of 1944, which provided job counseling for veterans returning from World War II. By the 1960s, the Department of Labor was encouraging the states to upgrade their counselors to the professional or master's degree level of training:

TABLE 4–1   Do's and Don'ts in Crisis Intervention Counseling

Do's	Don'ts
1. Remain calm and stable. Prepare yourself psychologically for the turbulence of emotion that is soon to flow from the client.	1. Don't try to "cheer up" the client, to tell him that his problems are not as bad as they seem, to reassure him unless he specifically requests these types of interventions (which is, by the way, the exception rather than the rule).
2. Allow the client full opportunity to speak. Attempt to determine the type of crisis, its precipitating forces, and its severity. Interrupt only when it is for the client's benefit, never to relieve yourself of distressing feelings being induced by the client.	2. Don't ask the suicidal client to abandon his plans. Always make such a request a temporary delay.
3. When indicated, ask object-oriented questions. These should, if asked properly, have a calming effect upon the client. If they fail to have such an effect, the counselor should consider the possibility that he is asking ego-oriented questions.	3. Don't attempt to solve the total personality adjustment difficulty. Some counselors make the error of minimizing the crisis itself and attempting to get the client to speak about more "fundamental" things.
4. Deal with the immediate situation rather than its underlying, unconscious causes that may be left for later. "In the crisis period," Brockopp (1973) points out, "the person is open to change; the sooner we can work with him, the more likely we are able to minimize the possible deterioration of the personality and to develop an effective solution which will improve the personality functioning of the individual."	
5. Have readily available local resources to assist the counselor: community, medical, legal, etc.	

Source: From Gary S. Belkin, *Practical Counseling in the Schools,* 2nd ed., p. 439. Copyright © 1981, Wm. C. Brown Communications, Inc., Dubuque, Iowa. All rights reserved. Reprinted by permission.

In the fall of 1970, the Manpower Administration initiated a massive inservice training program for selected employment service personnel. Originally, 88 colleges and universities in 33 states participated in the training program. Approximately 2,500 employment service personnel were initially involved in the training. The training was intended to increase the overall skill level of the trainees in dispensing employability assistance to those persons comprising the client population of the U.S. Public Employment Service. It was assumed by Manpower officials and participating university faculty that training in basic counseling skills and the behavioral sciences would improve the general quality of service rendered the public by employment service workers. (Phelps, Peer, & Canada, 1973, pp. 173–174)

Within the Department of Labor, an employment counselor is defined as one who performs counseling duties and who meets the minimum standards for employment counselor classification.

Brown and Feit (1978) describe the services that an employment counselor should offer:

The employment counselor needs to be aware of and familiar with a number of placement service skills. These would include (1) securing job leads, (2) recording job specifications, (3) referring clients to employers, (4) assessing client level of motivation, (5) assessing client readiness for employment (Goeke & Salomone, 1979) as well as (6) surveying of job opportunities. (pp. 176–183)

Although the focus of employment counselors, as with other employees of the employment security offices, is appropriate job placement of its clientele, the counselors are expected in the process to counsel clients on personal problems and assist them in developing attitudes, skills, and abilities that will facilitate their employment. Counselors are also involved in data gathering from their clients and administering and interpreting standardized tests. Employment counselors tend to consider the National Employment Counselors Association (an affiliate of the American Counseling Association, formerly the American Counseling and Development Association and the American Personnel and Guidance Association) their professional organization.

The National Employment Counselors Association (1975) presents the following basic competencies that the employment counselor must develop in order to carry out employment counseling responsibilities effectively:

Employment Counselor Competencies

Relationship skills. The ability to establish a trusting, open, and useful relationship with each counselee, accurately interpreting feelings as well as verbal and nonverbal expressions, and conveying to the applicant this understanding and whatever pertinent information and assistance is needed.

Individual and group assessment skills. The ability to provide ongoing assessment in individual and group settings involving the appraisal and measurement of the counselee's needs, characteristics, potentialities, individual differences, and self-appraisal.

Group counseling. The ability to apply basic principles of group dynamics and leadership roles in a continuous and meaningful manner to assist group members to understand their problems and take positive steps toward resolving them.

Development and use of career-related information. The ability to develop and use educational, occupational, and labor market information to assist counselees in making decisions and formulating occupational plans.

Occupational plan development and implementation. The ability to assist the counselee in developing and implementing a suitable employability plan that helps move the jobseeker from current status through any needed employability-improvement services, including training and related supportive services, into a suitable job.

Placement skills. The ability to ascertain and to communicate understanding of employers' personnel needs, to make effective job development contacts, and to assist the counselee in presentation of qualifications in relation to the employer's needs.

Community relations skills. The ability, based on extensive knowledge of the important service delivery systems in the community, to assist counselees in obtaining the services needed.

Work load management and intra-office relationships skills. The ability to coordinate the various aspects of the total counseling program in the employing agency, resulting in a continuous and meaningful sequence of services to counselees, agency staff, and the community.

Professional development skills. The ability, based on interest in furthering professional development, to engage in activities that promote such development individually and within the profession, and to demonstrate by example the standards and performance expected of a professional employment counselor. (pp. 152–153)

Employee Assistance Counselors

More and more counselors practice in business and industrial work settings. The impact of substance abuse on the work force, plus a heightened recognition of the importance of employees' general mental health to productivity, stimulated the initial development of many programs. Economic opportunity and labor legislation also created opportunities. However, as counselors proved their worth in the industrial sectors, many programs expanded their activities to include career assistance, retirement planning, educational guidance, and family counseling. Additionally, the rapidly changing nature of the employment picture for the rest of this century will continue to create challenges for employers and employees alike and their employee assistance programs.

CORRECTIONAL COUNSELING

Practitioners of correctional counseling are employed in various law enforcement settings, ranging from those involved with first-time juvenile probationary offenders to persons incarcerated in penal institutions. Counselors in these settings usually have training backgrounds in counseling, psychology, sociology, criminal justice, or forensic studies. Their duties include counseling and interviewing; the use of various analytical techniques, including the use of standardized testing; referrals; parole recommendations; and placement. In some juvenile institutional settings, counselors may be employed as "live-in advisers." Counselors working with young offenders work closely with police officers and other authorities.

Examples of counselors functioning in juvenile correctional institutions may be found in the differential treatment approach of the Kennedy Youth Center of Morgantown, West Virginia, and the Indiana Boys' School, Plainfield, Indiana. These and other similar institutions utilize the differential treatment approach, which seeks to take into account individual differences in matching inmates with counseling staff on the basis of personality or behavioral categories. In other correctional settings, counselors function as key agents in converting closed, traditional punitive systems into those that are more positive, helping, and rehabilitative. In these settings, the emphasis is on the formation of positive interpersonal climates and open lines of communication among the various members of the prison community, including inmates and correctional officers, or guards. An example of such an activity is described in an article by Wittmer, Lanier, and Parker (1976) in which prison officers (guards) in Florida participated in a race-relations training program with an emphasis on communications.

Counselors in the field of correctional counseling may join the International Association of Addictions and Offender Counselors, a division of the American Counseling Association.

REHABILITATION COUNSELING

History reflects the admiration that society has always held for those who have overcome physical disabilities to achieve notable success: the man (Franklin D. Roosevelt) who was paralyzed by polio in both legs at age 39 but later became president of the United States and a wartime world leader, the woman (Helen Keller) who was deaf and blind from the age of 2 but became a successful author and lecturer, the deaf musician (Ludwig van Beethoven), and the amputee actress (Sarah Bernhardt), to name but a few. Clifford Beers, who was mentioned in Chapter 1, is an example of individual triumph over mental illness.

The achievements of these and others, despite their disabilities, were notable, but history has failed to record the tragic losses in human potential that were allowed to occur because of lack of attention, other than medical, for people with disabilities. Since World War II, however, rehabilitation counseling has expanded into public agencies so that these individuals may receive special counseling assistance in overcoming their disabilities.

The functions of a rehabilitation counselor enumerated by Muthard and Salomone (1969) in terms of eight major classes of role behavior have often been considered to be a definitive description of rehabilitation-counselor role behavior (Berven, 1979). These eight classes of role behavior include (a) placement, (b) affective counseling, (c) group procedures, (d) vocational counseling, (e) medical referral, (f) eligibility—case finding, (g) test administration, and (h) test interpretation. As of 1980, the Council of Rehabilitation Education has suggested that professional rehabilitation counselors be skilled in (a) counseling, (b) assessment, (c) vocational placement, (d) communication, (e) the understanding of disabilities, and (f) occupational and vocational analysis.

According to Hosie, Patterson, and Hollingsworth (1989), rehabilitation counselors have increasingly begun providing services to individuals with learning disabilities, head injuries, chronic mental illness, sensory impairments, and life-threatening conditions such as AIDS. Fagan and Jenkins (1989) point out that the Rehabilitation Services Administration includes mental illness, alcoholism, and drug abuse among the disabling conditions addressed with clients.

Rehabilitation counselors help clients overcome deficits in their skills. They may work with a special type of client, such as the deaf, the blind, the mentally ill, or the physically disabled or, in some settings, all of these plus people with other kinds of disabilities as well.

For example, vocational rehabilitation counseling seeks to help clients with disabilities prepare for gainful employment, frequently assisting in appropriate job placements. In recent decades, much effort has been expended on the rehabilitation of substance abusers, with counselors prominent in both inpatient and outpatient facilities. We have also noted increased efforts to rehabilitate those with mental disabilities. Rehabilitation counselors also work with ex-offenders in preparing for adjustment to life in society's mainstream.

The role of rehabilitation counselors is a complex one; they provide a broad range of psychological and career-oriented services and work with and often coordinate the efforts of community agencies on their clients' behalf. They also function as resource persons who seek to encourage the optimum adjustment and development of their clients.

Capuzzi and Gross (1991) note:

> Academic training of counselors whose interest lies in working with clients with disabilities is accomplished almost invariably through Rehabilitation Counselor Education (RCE) programs. These training programs are typically graduate (master's level) programs and are offered by Counselor Education or Counseling Psychology departments. The programs normally require two years of academic and clinical training when completed on a full-time basis.
>
> The curriculum content pursued in most of these training programs has been developed and verified by the Council on Rehabilitation Education (CORE). CORE was established in 1971 as an accreditation body to oversee the academic and clinical training of rehabilitation counselors and to promote effective delivery of rehabilitation services to people with disabilities. Of the approximately 100 RCE programs in the United States, 75 are currently CORE-accredited. These programs must show evidence of a graduate-level curriculum that provides its trainee with a course of study that includes, but is not limited to, the following knowledge and/or skill areas: (1) history and philosophy of rehabilitation; (2) rehabilitation legislation; (3) organizational structure of the rehabilitation system (public and private, nonprofit and for-profit service delivery); (4) counseling theories, approaches, and techniques; (5) case management; (6) career development and career counseling theories and practices; (7) vocational evaluation, occupational analysis, and work adjustment techniques; (8) medical aspects of disability; (9) psychosocial aspects of disability; (10) knowledge of community resources and services; (11) rehabilitation research; and (12) legal and ethical issues in rehabilitation counseling.
>
> In addition, rehabilitation counseling trainees are required to participate in supervised practicum and internship experiences totaling a minimum of 600 clock hours in approved rehabilitation sites.* (pp. 436–437)

MARRIAGE AND FAMILY COUNSELING

Although the marriage vows read "until death do us part," the high divorce rate in the United States indicates that thousands of couples have decided they cannot wait that long to split up. In addition, thousands of other couples suffer through phases of their marriages or seek adjustment to marriage difficulties by means other than separation or divorce. Although not based on empirical studies, the report by the popular advice colum-

---

*From Capuzzi, David, and Gross, Douglas R., *Introduction to Counseling*. Copyright © 1991 by Allyn and Bacon. Reprinted by permission.

nist Ann Landers indicates that the top four items on her readers' list of the 10 most common problems concern marriage and family.

Certainly, an abundance of statistical empirical evidence indicates that family discord and divorce is continuing to increase. The stresses of the actual divorce process for spouses and children and the later adjustment requirements for all involved are well documented and include such problems as the feelings of failure that often accompany divorce and other emotions such as anger, regret, and depression. Adjustment problems may also arise in terms of separation, child rearing, and single-parent roles. In addition to these emotional and psychological stresses, there are also those practical concerns that center on the legal issues and financial responsibilities for persons in divorce or separation. Also, the adjustment problems of children in the divorcing of parents cannot be overlooked. Concerns about loyalty, parental dating, and custody can have severe psychological consequences, especially when coupled with the feelings of guilt and devalued self-concept commonplace in children of divorce.

We can conclude that the traditional image of the "home" and "family" as a cozy nest of love, security, togetherness, and never-ending happiness has been severely battered (as have many of the nest's inhabitants) in recent generations. The need for counselors who can effectively counsel outside the one-to-one relationship, who can work in this new dimension—the family or family system—has evolved. Yet, providing effective counseling assistance to families and couples in today's complex and stressful society is a challenging and often difficult task, frequently complicated by advice from nonprofessionals, cultural traditions, and environmental pressures.

Only within the past several decades has marriage and family therapy emerged as a counseling specialty. While individual counseling focuses on the individual person and his or her concerns, family therapy tends to focus on "the family system." Even if only one member of the family is being counseled, if the counseling is concerned primarily with the family system, it can be viewed as family counseling.

> Family and couples counseling/therapy is a treatment approach which views and treats the family as a system. The system has properties all its own: a set of rules, assigned and ascribed roles for its members, an organized power structure, intricate overt and covert forms of communication, and elaborate ways of negotiating and problem solving that permit various tasks to be performed effectively (Goldenberg & Goldenberg, 1991). Family counselors/therapists engage in the clinical practice of treating individuals, couples, or families. Regardless of the number of clients being treated, the family counselor conceptualizes problems in terms of the systems perspective. The family counselor therefore focuses on the context in which individuals exist and intervene on the relational level. (Carlson, 1993, p. 63)

Family therapy focuses on the communication process, power balances and imbalances, influence processes, structures for conflict resolution, and the current functioning of the family system as a system. The goal of family therapy is to effect change not simply in an individual within the family but rather in the structure of the family and the sequencing of behavior among its members (Okun & Rappaport, 1980).

Three major approaches to marriage and family counseling are identified by Blocher and Biggs (1983):

1. The first of these major foci for family counseling could be termed the Communications Approach. This approach is centered on the task of teaching family members to communicate more effectively and so increasing the sensitivity and awareness of family members to each other's needs and concerns. Treatment models based upon this approach have been described by therapists such as Satir (1964) and Gordon (1970).

   Family counseling interventions within this approach emphasize structured communications exercises, direct analyses of family communications processes, and teaching of models of communication based upon open and honest two-way communication. The communication approach to family counseling is based upon a number of fundamental concepts and assumptions about social interaction processes. (p. 250)

2. The structural approach to counseling of families is a logical extension of the application of general systems theory to the study of family life. In a sense, the structural approach looks at family functioning in terms of basic organizational principles. Family structure refers to the pattern of roles, relationships, rules and responsibilities established for accomplishing family tasks.

   Counseling interventions drawn from this (general systems) research tend to emphasize the family as a hierarchical system with parents or parent surrogates being responsible for the managerial or executive functions. In families experiencing difficulties, the exercise of these functions is often observed to be confused and inappropriate. In particular, many such families are found to involve children in parental conflict to the detriment of both the child's emotional well-being and the overall effectiveness of the family.

   Treatment generally includes a careful analysis of family decision-making processes and prevailing ways of handling conflict. Parents are often taught child management techniques and attitudes that clearly differentiate between the roles and responsibilities of children and parents. Children are encouraged to play age-appropriate roles and to stay out of parental conflict situations as much as possible.

   Family counselors in this model serve, in a sense, as organizational consultants who analyze family interaction processes and present new and more effective organizational arrangements. (pp. 256, 257)

3. A third basic approach to family counseling concerns what can be called family community transactions (Bronfenbrenner, 1979). This approach is especially relevant to the counseling psychologist in community practice in that it focuses on the degree to which families are able to utilize and contribute to needed resources that exist in the community.

   Research [has supported] an approach to providing family services which has been developed that is sometimes called "family networking." This approach emphasizes helping to break down barriers between families and community resources. It often involves building positive, cooperative relationships between parents and teachers. It may concentrate on helping families relate positively to neighbors or to restore extended family relationships. It may involve helping to organize support or action groups around the specific needs of single parents, tenants, insecure neighborhoods, or others. The approach may help families utilize the services of already organized community groups such as Parents Without Partners, Big Brothers, Big Sisters, or other community resources.* (pp. 258–259)

We must continue to recognize the rising numbers of dual-career couples, single-parent families, and latchkey children as issues in family living that are more characteristic of

*Reprinted from Blocher, D. H., & Biggs, D. A., *Counseling Psychology in Commnity Settings,* 1983. © 1983 Springer Publishing Company, Inc., New York 10012. Used by permission.

recent generations. These stresses, plus those accompanying the necessitated major career changes predicted for most adult workers in the immediate decades ahead, would indicate complex factors challenging marriage and family counselors.

An outgrowth of the increased recognition of the extent and popularity of marital problems has been the development of a specialty area within the field of marriage counseling. This group, represented by the American Association of Marriage and Family Therapy, includes memberships from diverse professional preparation backgrounds, including psychiatrists, psychologists, law, and the ministry. Another representative organization of this group is the National Council on Family Relations.

Many counselor education programs offer courses in the marriage and family area. Two studies, Peltier and Vale (1986) and Gladding, Burgraf, and Fennell (1987), surveying marriage and family course offerings in counselor education, both reported the most frequently offered course was family counseling. Other popular courses were marriage counseling, human sexuality, and marriage/family counseling. For those who wish to specialize in the field of family therapy, credentials can be earned in one of two ways. An individual can complete an advanced degree in one of the traditional disciplines, such as clinical psychology, counseling, pastoral counseling, expressive therapies, social work, or psychiatry. Either within the course of study for that degree or after completing the degree, the student must complete specific course work that meets the educational requirements for a degree in marriage and family counseling.

PASTORAL COUNSELING

From the standpoint of sheer numbers and geographic coverage, pastoral counseling provides a significant mental health resource. Not only are clergy members generally available to listen to the concerns and personal problems of their parishioners, but they also are frequently the first source to which people in trouble turn. In fact, many churches

> offer extensive counseling on marriage, divorce, widowhood, drug abuse, and family problems in line with their traditional community helping services. The American Association of Pastoral Counseling has procedures for certifying individuals on the basis of their clinical and behavioral science education plus supervised clinical training leading to fellow and diplomate status. In addition, the association has an accrediting process for preparation programs.* (Brammer, Shostrom, & Abrego, 1989, p. 366)

Churches are also increasingly utilizing professional counselors in their youth programs. In recognition of the mental health function of the clergy, many theological training programs include courses in pastoral counseling, related psychology, and general counseling subjects. Special programs have also been developed in clinical pastoral education for theology students and clergy wanting further training. Although many of these specialized programs are comparatively short-term, others provide intensive training in clinical settings.

*From L. M. Brammer, E. L. Shostrom, and P. J. Abrego, *Therapeutic Psychology: Fundamentals of Counseling and Psychotherapy* (5th ed.). Copyright © 1989 by Prentice-Hall. All rights reserved. Reprinted by permission.

GERONTOLOGY COUNSELING

The "graying of America" is the phrase frequently used to note the dramatic increase in the older population. The *U.S. Bureau of the Census Current Population Reports* noted that the group 65 years of age and older constitutes approximately 11% of our total population, contrasted to 4.1% in 1900, with predictions of continued increases well beyond the turn of the century. "People now live from two thirds to three fourths of their lives as older persons. In the next 20 years, one in five persons in the United States will be over the age of 60 (American Association of Retired Persons, 1988)" (Myers, 1992, p. 35).

With increased representation has also come an increased sensitivity to the needs, including counseling, of this special population. Also, as this group becomes more politically potent and active, the aged themselves are demanding the same range of social services and attention to their needs that are provided for other age groups.

> Development in later life can be viewed from at least two perspectives: developmental sequences and life transitions. The developmental perspective assumes a unidirectional, stepwise progression of events. Certain tasks must be mastered for successful development. The positive theme here is that development occurs and can be fostered throughout the life span. Older persons are not viewed as static, rigid, or poor prospects for therapeutic change. . . .
>
> Gerontologists, those who study older persons, have devoted much attention to the study of successful aging. Those who age successfully tend to have a strong sense of life satisfaction, high self-esteem, and positive morale. Persons who do not age successfully experience depression and low self-esteem. (Myers, 1990, p. 248)

As more people live longer, they are often required to move into untested roles. The greater the difference in role and the less knowledge beforehand about this role, the more marginal that person will feel (Schlossberg, 1984). Without clear-cut expectations in many areas of their lives, older people may frequently feel confused by the role shifts brought on by aging or retirement. Counseling can assist such persons in coping with these and other adjustment and development needs.

These trends are further reflected in the growth of course offerings in counselor preparation programs and substantive increases in professional publications addressing the counseling of older individuals. It is also now possible for gerontological counselors to be certified.

> Any National Certified Counselor (NCC) may apply for specialty certification as a National Certified Gerontological Counselor (NCGC). The certification does not require an examination, but a review of training, experience, and supervisory evaluations. A 2-year "alternate entry period" was established at the time the credential became available to encourage practicing counselors to seek certification.
>
> As of January 1, 1993, all applicants will meet these criteria (NBCC, 1990): (a) 2 years of professional gerontological counseling experience; (b) three graduate courses in gerontology (or the equivalent in 120 hours of related gerontological counseling continuing education), and a 600-hour internship or supervised experience (25% of which is with or on behalf of persons age 55 or older) or a 600-hour internship or supervised experience in a gerontological setting; (c) completion of a self-assessment of competence; and (d) two professional assessments of competence. The NCGC certification is awarded after a successful review of credentials and competencies. (Myers, 1992, pp. 37–38)

PRIVATE PRACTICE

The possibility of establishing a full-time private practice has appealed to an increasing number of counselors, while many, employed by other institutions or agencies, have done so on a part-time basis. Those interested in private practice may consider whether they wish to practice alone or in a partnership or group practice. They must also determine whether to enter general practice or specialize (i.e., addictions, career, children, etc.).

A basic consideration in entering private practice is whether one's professional interest and expertise are relevant to a sufficient client population in the geographic area of practice to adequately support the private practitioner. Legal and ethical guidelines are also critical. The importance of licensure and eligibility for third-party payment must also be examined. A 1992 study of professional developmental needs of 288 mental health counselors (Wilcoxon & Puleo, 1992) reported that two top professional concerns were (a) third-party reimbursement (54.5%) and (b) licensure (46.5%). Other concerns that the individual private practitioner must address are fiscal (fees, billing policies, insurance, office overhead), logistical (office location, hours, furnishings, record keeping, secretarial help), and public relations or communications, including advertising of services.

FUTURE DIRECTIONS

In 1980, *The Counseling Psychologist* had a special theme issue (vol. 8, no. 4) entitled "Counseling Psychology in the Year 2000." In this issue, Whiteley (1980) concludes:

> In order to have an increased impact in the changed world of 2000 A.D., counseling psychology will have to enlarge its substantive bases to include environmental psychology and environmental planning; life-span developmental psychology including aging, developmental tasks, and transitions between phases of life; the psychology of men and women, the growth of men and women within relationships, sex roles, parenting, sexuality, and child rearing; more refined approaches to building a psychological sense of community; assertion training and social organization; self-renewal; psychobiology; information and computer science; and, finally, systematic study of the expected future and its alternatives. (p. 7)

In 1987, Division 17, the Counseling Psychology division of the American Psychological Association, held its third national conference focusing on the theme "Planning the Future." Rude, Weissberg, and Gazda (1988) note:

> Across the five work groups that comprised the Third National Conference for Counseling Psychology a number of common themes emerged. Discussions of identity affirmed the value of the scientist-practitioner model and of traditional strengths such as prevention, life-span development, and skill-building as well as innovative and nontraditional functions. Among the ideas that were endorsed by multiple work groups were strategies to enhance counseling psychology's visibility and political strength and to build mechanisms for proactive planning into governance. Ways to improve the training of counseling psychologists by enhancing rigor, scientific thinking, professional identity, and ability to work in diverse and emerging settings also received substantial attention. Overall, deliberations of the groups resulted in substantial convergence and a set of specific goals and plans for the future. (p. 423)

Details of the conference were reported when another special issue of *The Counseling Psychologist* (Fretz, 1988) featured the theme and reports from this conference on "Planning the Future":

> Leona Tyler (1980) discussed the implications for the year 2000: "It means that counseling psychology (and counseling psychologists) will be dealing with the significant reality problems of that day, just as they have been oriented toward the reality problems of the 40's, 50's, 60's, and 70's.
>
> What are these reality problems of 2000 likely to be? (Fortunately, I can treat this as an academic exercise.) No one really knows, of course, but it is useful to speculate. Here are my speculations concerning those trends that are likely to involve counseling psychologists:
>
> 1. The single-cycle sequence of family life, education, work and labor-force retirement will break down. Education will be a life-long process, interspersed and interacting with work and family.
> 2. There will be more explicit attention to a broader scope of life skills. Just as we now have organized training in educational skills and job skills, so there will be organized training in family skills, community skills, recreational skills, and so on.
>
> Mental health will be a recognized aspect of our total health system. Just as we go to the dentist twice a year and have an annual medical exam, so we will periodically go to the psychologist for a 'psychological check-up.'
>
> In all of the above, counseling psychologists, with their history of dealing with the normal, everyday reality problems of the entire spectrum of age and level of adjustment will have an increasingly important role to play. They will be located in a variety of settings—educational institutions, government, community and social agencies, and private business and industry. And if psychology ever develops a 'general practitioner' (as I think it will) professional training in counseling psychology will be the best preparation for this role." (p. 22)

Many of these predicted futures of a decade ago are already emerging as reality. We would note also that advancements in "futuristic science," as in other fields, are making it possible to be increasingly accurate in seeing the future.

For community, agency, and other counselor settings, it is appropriate to note that the increased attention to prevention, multicultural, family, and career issues will apply to nonschool counselor settings as well. For example, the growing European and Asian economic competition plus U.S. companies threatening to take their production to where work forces are more efficient and/or cheaper will mandate the United States' development of a world-class work force. This will necessitate training and retraining, plus worker transitions to new careers and locations. For orderly and meaningful career planning and development, career counseling should be increasingly in demand in the public sector.

Because of the potential for at least temporary unemployment or underemployment and the accompanying frustrations, people abuse, substance abuse, and crime will continue to be national social concerns unless the major nonschool institutions of society (government, business, and industry) demonstrate more caring through counselor-directed human assistance programs.

Counselors in nonschool settings must be prepared for the "fall-out" from an older work force; a drastic scaling down of traditional promotional opportunities in many fields; more women in management positions; the downsizing of government, military, and related industries leaving the former workers of these organizations seeking new options; and the creation of a large pool of workers in temporary or transitional jobs.

Thus, while the future will present many opportunities for counselors, whether we as a profession serve the population will depend to a large degree on how vigorous and successful we are in communicating to the political and general publics our capabilities and readiness for rendering our much-needed services in the decades ahead.

SUMMARY

You have a problem, and you need to see a counselor, but you are no longer in school, and, besides, your old school counselor is too busy with the current student body. So what are your options? This chapter has suggested a number of these opportunities both for employment as counselors and assistance for clients in nonschool settings.

Community mental health agencies are perhaps the most versatile in terms of their readiness to deal with a wide range of developmental as well as remedial needs. Also, the staffing of these agencies is usually more diverse, often including professionals trained in medicine and social work as well as psychology. If one is seeking less conventional settings, many communities have crisis centers, hot-line counseling, open-door agencies, centers for human growth, and other nontraditional approaches to providing mental health services.

If your problem is one of career decision making or job placement, you might want to seek the assistance of a government employment office counselor (unlike private employment agencies, government employment offices charge no fees and are more likely to employ trained counselors). Additionally, career counseling centers, both government and nongovernment sponsored, are available in a number of communities. These specialized centers are also popular on college campuses.

Of course, if you are confined to a correctional institution, your only option may be your institutional counselor. Unfortunately, in many such institutions counseling personnel may not be employed.

For assistance in overcoming a physical or mental disability, rehabilitation counselors can be a valuable resource because they are specially trained to work with the developmental needs of people with disabilities. Veterans can seek such assistance through the Veterans Administration, of course, and other "rehab" counselors may be found in community and other governmental agencies and hospitals. A small number are in private practice.

If your problem is marriage or family related, there can be help for you, too, since marriage and family counseling is a growing area of specialization. Like many people, you may turn to your family clergy. The likelihood is increasing that your minister, priest, or rabbi will have received some counseling preparation in his or her ministerial studies or will have some assistant specially trained to provide counseling services. Another source of counseling assistance, if you are a member of the armed services, would be your service counselor. If you are among our older readers, specialized counseling assistance may also be available to help you plan for your retirement or other needs.

A final option—one that would probably cost you more dollars—is to seek out a counselor in private practice. Large population centers, university-oriented communities, and upper-socioeconomic suburbs are the most likely habitats of the private practitioners. Obviously, evidence of appropriate training, such as licensure, is important for private practitioners.

Having examined the historic development of our profession, the activities of counselors, and their role and function in various school and nonschool settings, we now move to a more detailed examination of specific counselor services and activities. We shall begin in the next chapter with our most important skill and service: individual counseling.

DISCUSSION QUESTIONS

1. Discuss your familiarity with the role and function of counselors in nonschool settings.

2. Discuss differences in lifestyle one might anticipate among

    a. school counselors,

    b. correctional counselors, and

    c. counselors in private practice.

3. Should all counselors for school and nonschool settings come under one broad general counseling license? Discuss.

4. Should counselors in community agencies be involved in such community problems as substance abuse, crime and delinquency, the homeless, unemployment, and so on? If so, in what way?

5. Discuss the growth of specialty areas in the counseling profession (i.e., marriage and family, sports, gerontology, etc.). Are there other areas of counseling specialization that you see emerging in the next 25 years?

6. Suggest prevention or enrichment program ideas for nonschool counseling agencies.

CLASS ACTIVITIES

1. "Shadow" a marriage and family counselor, an employment counselor, a counselor in private practice, or a counselor in an agency or institutional setting, and report your experiences to the class.

2. Interview a minister, rabbi, or priest regarding the counseling aspects of their assignment.

3. Visit your local community mental health center and prepare a written report covering the following topics:

    a. Scope of jurisdiction

    b. Services offered

    c. Population served

    d. Internal administrative hierarchy

    e. Fees charged

    f. Sources of funding

4. Survey a small sample of your community population to ascertain their perceptions of the profession of counseling and their awareness of local counseling agencies and services. Discuss the implications of your findings.

SELECTED READINGS

Bobby, C. L., & Kandor, J. R. (1992). Assessment of selected CACREP standards by accredited and nonaccredited programs. *Journal of Counseling and Development, 70,* 677–684.

Craig, R., & Messell, M. (1986). The mentally ill offender: Punishment or treatment? *State Legislative Report, 11,* 370–373.

Duncan, B. L., & Frasher, J. (1987). Buckley's scheme of schemes as a foundation for teaching family systems theory. *Journal of Marital and Family Therapy, 13,* 299–305.

Egbert, A. (1985). Employment counseling for the handicapped can be easier through linkages. *Journal of Employment Counseling, 22,* 31–38.

Haight, D. A. (1992). The pursuit of quality: A look into the future of CACREP. *Journal of Counseling and Development, 70,* 688–694.

Humphries, K., & Rappaport, J. (1993). From the community mental health movement to the war on drugs: A study in the definition of social problems. *American Psychologist, 48,* 892–901.

Johnson, T. R., & Helwig, A. A. (1982). Counseling: Practices and practitioners. *Journal of Employment Counseling, 19,* 147–157.

Marlowe, H. A., Jr., Marlowe, J. L., & Willetts, R. (1983). The mental health counselor as case manager: Implications for working with the chronically mentally ill. *American Mental Health Counselors Association Journal, 5,* 184–191.

Parker, W. M., & McDavis, R. J. (1983). Attitudes of Blacks toward mental health agencies and counselors. *Journal of Non-White Concerns in Personnel and Guidance, 11*(3), 89–98.

Quackenbos, S., Privette, G., & Klentz, B. (1985). Psychotherapy: Sacred or secular? *Journal of Counseling and Development, 63,* 290–293.

Rubin, S. E. (Ed.). (1984). Roles and functions of certified rehabilitation counselors [Special issue]. *Rehabilitation Counseling Bulletin, 27,* 199–245.

Schlossberg, N. (1984). *Counseling adults in transition.* New York: Spring.

Seligman, L., & Dougherty, E. (1987). Establishing and maintaining a private practice. *Counseling and Human Development, 19*(5), 1–11.

Vacc, N. A. (1992). An assessment of the perceived relevance of the CACREP Standards. *Journal of Counseling and Development, 70,* 685–687.

Watkins, C. E., Jr., Lopez, F. G., Campbell, V. L., & Himmell, C. D. (1986). Contemporary counseling psychology: Results of a national survey. *Journal of Counseling Psychology, 33,* 301–309.

Worthington, E. L. (1986). Religious counseling: A review of published empirical research. *Journal of Counseling and Development, 84,* 421–431.

RESEARCH OF INTEREST

Benjamin, B. A. (1992). Career counseling with couples. *Journal of Counseling and Development, 70,* 544–549.

Abstract

Examines a career counseling model that takes into account the couple dynamics active in the career choice process of the adult individual. Describes facilitative elements of career counseling with couples, the role of couple assessment, precautions in counseling couples, and future directions.

Bernal, G. (1987). Families with depression, school, marital, family and situational problems: A research note. *American Journal of Family Therapy, 15,* 44–51.

Abstract

Reports improvement rates for families in family therapy for depression, school, family, marital, and situational problems. Marital problems showed the lowest rate of improvement, while depression improved in fewer sessions. Family and situational problems improved most with the help of many sessions.

Brown, S. D. (1983). Coping skills training: Attitude toward mental illness, depression, and quality of life one year later. *Journal of Consulting and Clinical Psychology, 30,* 117–120.

Abstract

The results of this follow-up study reveal that a coping skills curriculum of progressive relaxation, anxiety management, assertiveness, and self-reinforcement are effective with participating clients.

Charlesworth, E. A., & Dempsey, G. (1982). Trait anxiety reductions in a substance abuse population trained in stress management. *Journal of Clinical Psychology, 38,* 764–768.

Abstract

A stress management training program delivered to hospitalized drug-abusing patients results in significant decreases in stress-related symptoms such as insomnia, anger, and anxiety.

Cooper, S. E. (1986). The effects of group and individual vocational counseling on career indecision and personal indecisiveness. *Journal of College Student Personnel, 27,* 39–42.

Abstract

Decreases in career indecision and personal indecision are found in both group and individual vocational counseling for a sample of 34 students.

Crane, D. R., Griffin, W., & Hill, R. D. (1986). Influence of therapist skills on client perceptions of marriage and family therapy outcome: Implications for supervision. *Journal of Marital and Family Therapy, 12,* 91–96.

Abstract

Marriage and family therapy training clinic clients rate their therapist's skill level on several therapist variables including "experience," "confidence," "concern," and how well the treatment seemed to fit their view of the problem. Suggestions for using these results in supervision of beginning therapists are given.

Dion, G. L., & Anthony, W. A. (1987). Research in psychiatric rehabilitation: A review of experimental and quasi-experimental studies. *Rehabilitation Counseling Bulletin, 30,* 177–203.

Abstract

Describes studies on the outcomes of psychiatric rehabilitation in terms of setting predominant focus of the intervention outcome measures and interventions used. Shows the effectiveness of rehabilitation interventions for decreased recidivism, increased time spent in the community, higher rates of employment and productivity, greater skill development, increased satisfaction, and lowered costs.

Giblin, P. (1986). Research and assessment in marriage and family enrichment: A meta-analysis study. *Journal of Psychotherapy and the Family, 2,* 79–96.

Abstract

Attempts to integrate and evaluate existing enrichment research literature, using meta-analysis. Eighty-five studies from 1971 to 1982 of premarital, marital, and family enrichment, representing 3,886 couples or families, were gathered and their results statistically aggregated. Results show that enrichment programs affected the lives of participants, particularly in the areas of communications skills and constructive problem-solving techniques. Participants underwent negative changes initially. Findings are discussed in terms of overall enrichment effectiveness as well as salient program, design, and measurement characteristics.

Giblin, P., Sprenkle, D. H., & Sheehan, R. (1985). Enrichment outcome research: A meta-analysis of premarital, marital and family interventions. *Journal of Marital and Family Therapy, 11,* 257–271.

Abstract

Presents findings from meta-analysis of 85 studies of premarital, marital, and family enrichment, representing 3,886 couples or families. Findings are discussed in terms of overall enrichment effectiveness and salient program, subject, design, measurement, and analysis characteristics. The most powerful factors related to outcome were measurement variables.

Hardin, S. I., & Yanico, B. J. (1983). Counselor gender, type of problem, and expectations about counseling. *Journal of Counseling Psychology, 30,* 294–297.

Abstract

Investigates subject expectations for counseling as a function of counselor gender, problem type, and subject gender. Subjects (N = 200) responded to the Short Form Expectations about Counseling. Women scored higher on motivation and openness. Men scored higher on directiveness and self-disclosure. Results conform to sex-role stereotypes regarding interaction styles.

Hefner, C. W., & Prochaska, J. O. (1984). Concurrent vs. conjoint marital therapy. *Social Work, 29,* 287–291.

Abstract

Evaluates couples (N = 27) randomly assigned to conjoint or concurrent therapy to compare treatment effectiveness with regard to intrapersonal and interpersonal problems. Results show no differences between the two treatments on any of the outcome measures.

Hosie, T. W., West, J. D., & Mackey, J. A. (1993). Employment and roles of counselors in employee assistance programs. *Journal of Counseling and Development, 71,* 355–359.

Abstract

Examines employment and roles of master's-level counselors in employee assistance programs (EAPs) as well as the services offered by the diverse EAP organizations. Found that master's-level counselors were similar to individuals with master's degrees in social work in employment rate and percentages among EAP staff. Differences in the roles of counselors among the EAP types are presented.

Prout, H. T., & Demartino, R. A. (1986). A meta-analysis of school-based studies of psychotherapy. *Journal of School Psychology, 24,* 285-292.

Abstract

Applies the meta-analysis technique to school-based studies of psychotherapy. Thirty-three controlled studies were identified that met the criteria for meta-analysis. Although research efforts in this area offer a relatively small number of appropriate studies, the results of the meta-analysis indicate that psychotherapy in the schools can be viewed as at least moderately effective. Evidence was also found of the greater efficacy of group and behavioral theory interventions and interventions that target observed behaviors and problem-solving abilities.

Silverman, W. H., & Beech, R. P. (1984). Length of intervention and client assessed outcome. *Journal of Clinical Psychology, 40,* 475–480.

Abstract

Explores the relationship between length of intervention and client-assessed outcome in clients (N = 47) seen in an outpatient program of a community mental health center. Results indicate no differences between single-session and multiple-session clients in terms of demographic background, presenting problems, assessments of agency helpfulness, or problem improvement.

Chapter 5

Individual Counseling

Counseling is, of course, the single most important activity in which counselors engage. They are called counselors not because they give tests, offer career planning information, or provide consultation, but because they counsel. Counseling is a skill and process distinguished from advising, directing, perhaps listening sympathetically, and appearing to be interested in many of the same concerns as professional counselors. To introduce this topic, the objectives of this chapter are to (a) orient you to traditional and popular theories of counseling, (b) introduce and briefly discuss the counseling process, and (c) examine some basic counseling skills.

Individual counseling has, since the early days of the movement into both school and nonschool settings, been identified as the heart of any program of counseling services. All other professional activities of the counselor lead to this most important function. Test results, career information, and autobiographies are all relatively meaningless if they do not provide information that enhances the effectiveness of the counseling process.

Many definitions are available to students of counseling. There are semantic differences, of course, but most definitions begin by suggesting that individual counseling is a one-to-one relationship involving a trained counselor and focuses on some aspects of a client's adjustment, developmental, or decision-making needs. This process provides a relationship and communications base from which the client can develop understanding, explore possibilities, and initiate change. In this setting, it is the skill of the counselor that makes positive outcomes possible. The counselor's skills and knowledge provide the appropriate framework and direction that maximize the client's potential for positive results. Untrained and unskilled helpers, regardless of their best intentions, cannot duplicate the functions of the professional counselor.

George and Cristiani (1990) point out several elements that are common to these definitions:

> One is the notion that counseling is aimed at helping people make choices and act on them. A second is the notion of learning, although there are some sharp differences as to what facilitates learning and how learning occurs. Still another element is that of personality development, with relatively little agreement as to how personality development is best facilitated. (p. 2)

THEORIES OF COUNSELING

Since the various definitions of counseling differ little in actual meaning, one might assume that all counselors function similarly in like situations; that, like so many robots, we would all respond similarly, interpret client information in the same manner, and agree on desired outcomes in specific counseling situations. Thus, a chapter on counseling techniques might read like a cookbook in which recipes were specified for the kinds of situations and the kinds of outcomes desired for these situations. Of course, nothing could be further from the truth. As definitions vary in counseling, the approaches that professional counselors use vary even more. Although the variety of these approaches may, at times, confuse the beginning student and the general public as well, it is fair to say that unlike recipes, they have proven useful in the provision of counseling services to various populations. These approaches are usually distinguished and described under their theoretical labels.

Theoretical models for counseling have their origins in the values and beliefs of persons who, in turn, have converted these into a philosophy and a theoretical model for counseling. These values and beliefs form a rationale for what one does, how one does it, and under what circumstance. As Brammer, Shostrom, and Abrego (1989) note:

> Theory helps to explain what happens in a counseling relationship and assists the counselor in predicting, evaluating, and improving results. Theory provides a framework for making systematic observations about counseling. Theorizing encourages the coherence of ideas about counseling and the production of new ideas. Hence, counseling theory can be very practical by helping to make sense out of the counselor's observations. What behaviors exemplify the scientific attitude? A counselor or psychotherapist who proceeds through daily tasks without asking the following questions is not likely to progress in therapeutic effectiveness, nor is he or she likely to contribute new ideas to the profession. The scientific attitude leads to questions such as: What is happening here? What is my model? What are my assumptions? What accounts for this event? What will happen if I try this? Unscientific counselors who do not ask themselves these vital questions are likely to feel smug about their counseling methods, a dangerous attitude to take.* (pp. 6–7)

Of course, for the established theories, research has played an important part in bridging the gap through verifying or "proving" theoretical premises:

> The application of counseling theory is quite different from the application of theory in the physical sciences. Physical theories can be applied with little regard for the element of human interaction, but counseling theory, which is applied in the give and take between and among persons, must be integrated into the counselor's philosophy and personality. To apply theory in counseling as one applies it in the physical sciences would result in a view of oneself and the client as objects, with the consequent loss of the human element so essential to the success of a counseling relationship. (Boy & Pine, 1982, p. 38)

This progress from theory to practice is depicted in Figure 5-1.

In the next section, brief descriptions of some of the popular counseling theories will be presented. Counselors in training, and certainly the proactive professional counselor, should be knowledgeable about the popularly recognized theories of counseling—their premises, characteristics, differences or similarities, and implications for practice. It should be stated, however, that these and other recognized theories in the field of counseling provide only a base that the practicing counselor will modify in order to suit the unique situation in which he or she functions and his or her unique personality.

As McWhirter and McWhirter (1991) note:

> There are three ways in which counseling theories can help counselors in their quest to help others. First, the theory contributes to a greater understanding of an individual's behavior. It provides a way of organizing relevant, available, and observable data about a client into a framework that allows greater unity and greater predictability. Second, the theory suggests guidelines that provide signs of success or failure of counseling activities. Essentially, the theory becomes a "working model" to explain what clients *may* be like and what *may* be helpful to them. Built into the "working model" is an appreciation of what constitutes success or failure.

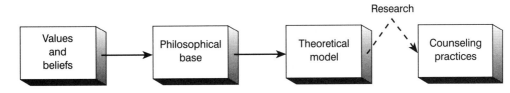

FIGURE 5–1 Bridging the Gap from Theory to Practice

> The end result is twofold: helpers reach a deeper and richer understanding of what their client *is* like, and their theory is enriched in ways that make it more useful in working with future clients. Finally, and perhaps most important for the practitioner, the theory directly influences the strategy of change that counselors select to use with their client as well as the counseling procedures that are most applicable with a given client or with a particular presenting problem. (McWhirter & McWhirter, 1991, as seen in Capuzzi & Gross, 1991, p. 71)

As these traditional theories of counseling are examined, it is important to recognize their roots in European and North American cultures. The pioneering theorists did not consider multicultural perspectives in their origins. Thus, all these theories can be enhanced by multicultural awareness and considerations. In fact, the counselor's failure to recognize the unique cultural background of clients from diverse backgrounds will handicap their interaction with their clients. All this suggests that counselors consider the extended background—family, support networks, coping styles, and so forth—plus the cultural context of the client for integration into their theoretical orientation.

Finally, we believe that eventually every counselor will adopt that theory or combination of theories, plus a multicultural perspective, that is most appropriate for him or her; with which he or she is most comfortable and effective; and that reflects what he or she is as a person *and* a professional.

Psychoanalytic Theory

For beginning counselors, the study of psychoanalytic theory is more important from a historic perspective rather than as a model for adoption. Certainly the name Sigmund Freud has been prominently associated with the practice of psychoanalysis and psychotherapy throughout this century. He was the first to develop and popularize a comprehensive theory of personality development that included both a theory and method of therapy. This in turn offered those who followed Freud a solid ideological theory and methodology of treatment on which to build. This fact alone assured him a place in the history of counseling and psychotherapy (Wallace, 1986).

Corey (1986) notes that

> Freud gave psychology a new look and new horizons. For instance, he called attention to psychodynamic factors that motivate behavior, focused on the role of the unconscious, and developed most of the first therapeutic procedures for understanding and modifying the structure of one's basic character. Freud stimulated a great deal of controversy, exploration, and further development of personality theory and laid the foundation on which later psychodynamic systems rest. His theory is a benchmark against which many other theories are measured. (pp. 11–12)

In Freud's view, the development of personality, including the various defense mechanisms and how an individual uses them, is largely dependent on the course of her or his psychosexual development. Much of this development occurs during the first 5 years of life, after which there is a period of relative calm for 6 years. Then, during adolescence the process becomes very active once again. Another of Freud's major assumptions is that at any point in a person's development a person moves through an orderly sequence in which one body area gives way to another; the order of this sequence is the same for everyone. The third major assumption is that failure to complete this normal sequence will result in serious personality problems.* (Hansen, Stevic, & Warner, 1986, p. 30)

Psychoanalytic theory views the structure of personality as separated into three major systems; the *id,* the *ego,* and the *superego*. Hereditary factors are represented by the id, which functions in the inner world of one's personality and is thus largely unconscious. The id is usually viewed as the original system of personality that is inherent and present at birth. Many believe that the id is ruled by the "pleasure principle," and thus it seeks to avoid tension and pain, seeking instead gratification and pleasure. As Corey (1986) notes, it is "the spoiled brat of personality" (p. 13).

The ego is viewed as the only rational element of the personality. The ego also has contact with the world of reality. Because of this contact with reality, it controls consciousness and provides realistic and logical thinking and planning.

The superego represents the conscience of the mind and operates on a principle of moral realism. It represents the moral code of the person, usually based on one's perceptions of the moralities and values of society. As a result of its role, the superego in a sense is responsible for providing rewards, such as pride and self-love, and punishments, such as feelings of guilt or inferiority to its owner.

In this triangle, the superego, because it resides largely in the subconscious, is most aware of the impulses of the id and seeks to direct the ego to control the id. As a result, psychoanalytic theory views tension, conflict, and anxiety as inevitable in humans and that human behavior is therefore directed toward reduction of this tension. In the psychoanalytical context, then, the reduction of tension becomes a major goal of counseling. Because personality conflict is present in all people, nearly everyone can benefit from professional counseling. Inasmuch as the psychoanalytic approach requires insights that in turn rely on openness and self-disclosure, multiculturally oriented counselors would be aware that these traits are sometimes seen as signs of immaturity by some Asian, African, and Native Americans. We would conclude by noting that the psychoanalytic approach does require extensive training.

Individual Psychology

Individual psychology is often called Adlerian therapy, since its initial developer was Alfred Adler, a colleague of Freud who disputed with Freud on some basic issues; this disagreement led Adler to break away entirely from Freud's circle. The works of Adler have had, in turn, a profound impact on many therapists, acknowledged by persons such as Albert Ellis, Victor Frankl, Rudolf Dreikurs, Rollo May, and William Glasser.

*From J. C. Hansen, R. R. Stevic, and W. R. Warner (1986), *Counseling: Theory and Process* (4th ed.). Copyright © 1986. Used by permission of James C. Hansen.

Individual psychology sees the person as a unity, an indivisible whole, and focuses on the unique individuality of persons (Manaster & Corsini, 1982). Adler's view of humans offered a refreshingly optimistic focus. At the core of his theory was the belief that there exists within the human being an innate drive to overcome perceived inferiorities and develop one's potential, self-actualize, and that given a healthy environment, this growth will take place.

What is it that keeps a person from moving in a fast and easy manner toward this full realization of self? For Adler it was feelings of inferiority. A person permits him- or herself to experience these feelings through three sources: (a) our biological dependency and dependency in general as infants, (b) our image of ourselves in relationship to the grandeur of the universe, and (c) organ inferiority. The drive within ourselves, however, enables us to compensate for these feelings and strive for superiority and perfection.

Adler's theory is sometimes referred to as *socioteleological,* for, as noted, it sees persons as constantly in the process of striving toward goals. This is not done, however, in isolation but with other people. This concept, called *Gemeinschaftsgefuhl* (usually translated as "social interest"), is central to the growth and actualization of the individual as well as of the good of the society. Because social interest is viewed as an innate aptitude, it must be consciously developed over time (Manaster & Corsini, 1982). Social interest or developing one's ability to give and take is accomplished through the "life tasks" in which all human beings participate. These include (a) work, (b) friendship, and (c) love (Sweeney, 1989).

When a person comes for therapy, it is in one or more of these areas that he or she is experiencing incongruence and discomfort. The counseling process then is seen as a means by which the therapist and counselee work together to help the counselee develop awareness as well as healthier attitudes and behaviors so as to function more fully in society on the more useful side of life. Developing social interest is seen as the salient variable of one's mental health.

The Adlerian counseling process involves four stages: (a) establishing relationship, (b) diagnosis, (c) insight/interpretation, and (d) reorientation. In the first session the counselor establishes a relationship with the client through a subjective/objective interview in which the client is helped to feel comfortable, accepted, respected, and cared about. Through an "objective" component of the interview, the client is encouraged to explain what specifically has helped him or her determine the need for counseling. The client is asked to discuss how things are going in each of the life task areas. Also during this first session the counseling process is explained and discussed with the client. The diagnostic stage involves the "lifestyle interview," a formal assessment procedure that looks at things such as family constellation, perceptions of self in relationship of siblings, perceptions of parents, early recollections, and recurrent dreams.

The interpretation phase is the time during which the counselor and the client develop insight from the lifestyle interview into the client's "basic mistakes" by analyzing and discussing the convictions, goals, and movement that the client developed early in life and the ensuing thought, emotional, and behavioral patterns and attitudes.

The reorientation stage is perhaps the most critical, for it is in this stage that the therapist helps the counselee to move from "intellectual" insight to actual development and expression of healthier attitudes and behaviors. Here the client—with the counselor's support, encouragement, and direction—actively pursues changing unhealthy ways of thinking, feeling, and behaving to ways that are more satisfying and healthy for him- or herself and society.

Wallace (1986) believes:

> The application of Adler's theory in one-to-one therapy has declined somewhat over the years, but there has been a marked increase during the last two decades in the application of Adler's theory in the classroom, marriage and family counseling, and child-rearing practices. Some of the leaders responsible for the renewed interest in individual psychology and psychotherapy are Ansbacher, Dinkmeyer, Dreikurs, Mozak, and Sweeney. (pp. 79—80)

Client-Centered Theory

Client-centered (now frequently referred to as person-centered) counseling is another historically significant and influential theory. This theory was originally developed and described by Carl R. Rogers as a reaction against what he considered the basic limitations of psychoanalysis. As a result of his influence, this particular approach is often referred to as "Rogerian counseling":

> This person-centered approach focuses on the client's responsibility and capacity to discover ways to more fully encounter reality. Clients, who know themselves best, are the ones to discover more appropriate behavior for themselves.
>
> The person-centered approach emphasizes the phenomenal world of the client. With accurate empathy and an attempt to apprehend the client's internal frame of reference, therapists concern themselves mainly with the client's perception of self and of the world.
>
> Rogers proposes the hypothesis that certain attitudes on the therapist's part (genuineness, nonpossessive warmth and acceptance, and accurate empathy) constitute the necessary and sufficient conditions for therapeutic effectiveness. Person-centered theory holds that the therapists' function is to be immediately present and accessible to the client and to focus on the here-and-now experience created by their relationship. (Corey, 1982, p. 82)

In understanding the client or person-centered approach to counseling, it is helpful to be aware of the personality basis for this theory, as presented by Rogers (1959a) in the form of 19 propositions. The lead statements for each of these propositions are as follows:

1. Every individual exists in a continually changing world of experience of which he is the center.

2. The organism reacts to the field as it is experienced and perceived. This perceptual field is, for the individual, "reality."

3. The organism reacts as an organized whole to this phenomenal field.

4. The organism has one basic tendency and striving—to actualize, maintain, and enhance the experiencing organism.

5. Behavior is basically the goal-directed attempt of the organism to satisfy its needs as experienced, in the field as perceived.

6. Emotion accompanies and in general facilitates such goal-directed behavior, the kind of emotion being related to the seeking versus the consummatory aspects of the behavior, and the intensity of the emotion being related to the perceived significance of the behavior for the maintenance and enhancement of the organism.

7. The best vantage point for understanding behavior is from the internal frame of reference of the individual himself.

8. A portion of the total perceptual field gradually becomes differentiated as the self.

9. As a result of interaction with the environment, and particularly as a result of evaluational interaction with others, the structure of self is formed—an organized, fluid, but consistent conceptual pattern of perceptions of characteristics and relationships of the "I" or the "me," together with values attached to these concepts.

10. The values attached to experiences and the values which are a part of the self-structure, in some instances, are values experienced directly by the organism, and in some instances are values introjected or taken over from others, but perceived in distorted fashion, *as if* they had been experienced directly.

11. As experiences occur in the life of the individual, they are either (a) symbolized, perceived, and organized into some relationship to the self; (b) ignored because there is no perceived relationship to the self-structure; (c) denied symbolization or given a distorted symbolization because the experience is inconsistent with the structure of the self.

12. Most of the ways of behaving which are adopted by the organism are those which are consistent with the concept of self.

13. Behavior may, in some instances, be brought about by organic experiences and needs which have not been symbolized. Such behavior may be inconsistent with the structure of the self, but in such instances the behavior is not "owned" by the individual.

14. Psychological maladjustment exists when the organism denies to awareness significant sensory and visceral experiences, which consequently are not symbolized and organized into the gestalt of the self-structure. When this situation exists, there is a basic or potential psychological tension.

15. Psychological adjustment exists when the concept of the self is such that all the sensory and visceral experiences of the organism are, or may be assimilated on a symbolic level into a consistent relationship with the concept of self.

16. Any experience which is inconsistent with the organization or structure of self may be perceived as a threat, and the more of these perceptions there are, the more rigidly the self-structure is organized to maintain itself.

17. Under certain conditions, involving primarily complete absence of any threat to the self-structure, experiences which are inconsistent with it may be perceived, and examined, and the structure of self revised to assimilate and include such experiences.

18. When the individual perceives and accepts into one consistent and integrated system all his sensory and visceral experiences, then he is necessarily more understanding of others and is more accepting of others as separate individuals.

19. As the individual perceives and accepts into his self-structure more of his organic experiences, he finds that he is replacing his present value system—based so largely upon introjections which have been distortedly symbolized—with a continuing organismic valuing process.* (pp. 483–524)

In the counseling relationship, six conditions account for personality change in the client. These were presented by Rogers (1959a, 1967):

*From C. R. Rogers (1959), "A Theory of Therapy, Personality and Interpersonal Relationships as Developed in the Client-Centered Framework" in S. Koch, *Psychology: A Study of Science*, Vol. 3. Copyright © 1959. Reprinted with permission of McGraw-Hill, Inc.

1. Two people (a therapist and a client) are in psychological contact. (1967, p. 73)

2. The client is experiencing a state of anxiety, distress, or incongruence.

3. The therapist is genuine (truly himself or herself) in relating to the client.

4. The therapist feels or exhibits unconditional positive regard for the client.

5. The therapist exhibits empathetic understanding of the client's frame of reference and conveys this understanding to the client.

6. The therapist succeeds to a minimum degree in communicating empathetic understanding and unconditional positive regard to the client. (1959a, p. 213)

Some of the changes expected from a successful utilization of this approach are these:

❖ The person comes to see himself differently.

❖ He accepts himself and his feelings more fully.

❖ He becomes more self-confident and self-directing.

❖ He becomes more the person he would like to be.

❖ He becomes more flexible, less rigid, in his perceptions.

❖ He adopts more realistic goals for himself.

❖ He behaves in a more mature fashion.

❖ He changes his maladjustive behaviors, even such a long-established one as chronic alcoholism.

❖ He becomes more acceptant of others.

❖ He becomes more open to the evidence, both to what is going on outside of himself, and to what is going on inside of himself.

❖ He changes in his basic personality characteristics in constructive ways. (Rogers, 1959b, p. 232)

Thus, the client-centered model is optimistic or positive in its view of humankind. Clients are viewed as being basically good and possessing the capabilities for self-understanding, insight, problem solving, decision making, change, and growth.

The counselor's role is that of a facilitator and reflector. The counselor facilitates a counselee's self-understanding and clarifies and reflects back to the client the expressed feelings and attitudes of the client. Giving information for problem solving in a client-centered context is not usually considered a counselor responsibility. The client-centered counselor also would not seek to direct the mediation of the counselee's "inner world" but rather to provide a climate in which the counselee could bring about change in him- or herself. As Ivey, Ivey, and Simek-Downing (1987) note, "a central task of the counselor is to understand and empathize with the unique experiential world of the client" (p. 275).

In recent years, another label, *self-theory*, has been increasingly used instead of the traditional client-centered, nondirective, or Rogerian labels. This has probably resulted from the emphasis on enhancement of the self, the capacity of one's self, self-actualization, and self-perceptions. Regardless of one's choice of label, this theory, originated by Rogers, continues to exert its influence on the field of counseling.

From a multicultural frame of reference, Ivey, Ivey, and Simek-Morgan (1993) indicate the emphasis in Rogerian theory on ideal self and real self tends to obscure relational and broader environmental issues. As such, you may find it helpful to add a broader focus when working with many clients. For example, it would be within the Rogerian tradition to help clients focus on *real relationships* and *ideal relationships*. Such a focus would help individuals think of themselves as persons in relation to significant others. This focus would entail a change in the style of counseling and therapy usually associated with Rogers. But when one considers Rogers's life development, one would suspect that these concepts are not too distant from where he was heading at the end of his life. Clearly, Rogers was focusing on a more *ideal world* as contrasted with the *real world* (*Umwelt*). (p. 304)

Behavioral Theory

Behavioral theory and conditioning can be traced directly from Pavlov's 19th-century discoveries in classical conditioning. Important foundations for the behavioral approach later were discovered from the system of psychology called behaviorism, founded by American psychologist John B. Watson (1913) and expressed initially in his article "Psychology as the Behaviorist Views It."

Significant research and publication on the subject were conducted by Watson, Thorndike, and others, but it was not until B. F. Skinner systematically refined and developed his principles of behaviorism that the behavioral theory moved toward its current popularity. The behaviorist views behavior as a set of learned responses to events, experiences, or stimuli in a person's life history. The behaviorist believes that behavior can be modified by providing appropriate learning conditions and experiences. The experimental origins of the behaviorist's approach explain their indifference to concepts that cannot be empirically observed or measured. Thus, rather than being concerned with the emotional dynamics of behavior characteristics of the insight approaches of either Freudians or Rogerians, the behaviorist focuses on specific behavioral goals, emphasizing precise and repeatable methods.

For the behaviorist, counseling involves the systematic use of a variety of procedures that are intended specifically to change behavior in terms of mutually established goals between a client and a counselor. The procedures employed encompass a wide variety of techniques drawn from knowledge of learning processes. A current leader in behavioral psychology, John D. Krumboltz (1966), places these procedures into four categories:

1. *Operant Learning.* This approach is based on the usefulness of reinforcers and the timing of their presentation in producing change. Reinforcers may be concrete rewards or expressed as approval or attention.

2. *Imitative Learning.* This approach facilitates acquisition of new responses by exposure to models performing the desired behaviors.

3. *Cognitive Learning.* This technique fosters learning of appropriate responses by simply instructing the client how he may better adapt.

4. *Emotional Learning.* Involves substitution of acceptable emotional responses for unpleasant emotional reactions, using techniques derived from classical conditioning. (pp. 13–20)

Behaviorists also believe that stating the goals of counseling in terms of behavior that is observable is more useful than stating goals that are more broadly defined, such as self-understanding or acceptance of self. This means that counseling outcomes should be identifiable in terms of overt behavior changes. Krumboltz (1976) suggests three criteria for counseling goals:

1. The goals of counseling should be capable of being stated differently for each individual client.

2. The goals of counseling for each client should be compatible with, though not necessarily identical to, the values of his counselor.

3. The degree to which the goals of counseling are attained by each client should be observable. (pp. 172–173)

Three examples of behavioral change appropriate to counseling are the altering of behavior that is not satisfactory, the learning of the decision-making process, and problem prevention. Krumboltz (1976) indicates that the consequences of the behavioral statements of counseling goals would include the following:

1. Counselors, clients, and citizens could more clearly anticipate what the counseling process could and could not accomplish.

2. Counseling psychology would become more integrated with the mainstream of psychological theory and research.

3. The search for new and more effective techniques of helping clients would be facilitated.

4. Different criteria would have to be applied to different clients in assessing the success of counseling. (pp. 175–176)

Blackham and Silberman (1980) have developed an operant paradigm consisting of six steps:

1. Define and state operationally the behavior to be changed.

2. Obtain a baseline or operant level of the behavior that is considered desirable to promote or change.

3. Arrange the learning or treatment situation so that the desirable behavior will occur.

4. Identify potential reinforcers.

5. Shape and/or reinforce the desired behavior.

6. Maintain records of the reinforced behavior to determine whether response strength or frequency has increased. (pp. 33–35)

Counselors utilizing behavioral theory assume that the client's behavior is the result of conditioning. The counselor further assumes that each individual reacts in a predictable way to any given situation or stimulus, depending on what has been learned. Ivey et al. (1993) warn:

The behavioral approach can run into problems in multicultural situations over the issue of *control*. Early ventures in behavioral psychology often gave the therapist, counselor, or teacher almost complete power, and decisions sometimes focused on controlling the client rather than helping the client control him- or herself. Behavioral psychology has been forced to overcome some of these early problems and the resultant fears among minority clients and their advocates. (p 219)

Gilliland, James, and Bowman (1989) point out:

> Most modern behavioral counselors approach the helping process from a much broader perspective than was the case a few years ago. Rather than viewing the counselor as the expert who scientifically develops and imposes behavior-modifying processes on the client, the modern approach strives to involve the client in the analysis, planning, process, and evaluation of his or her behavior-management program. Modern behavioral counselors seek to help the client extinguish a wide range of maladaptive behaviors and learn adaptive behaviors needed to establish and maintain targeted goals and consequences. The counselor collaborates with the client. The counselor is expected to have training and experience in human behavior modification and also to serve as consultant, teacher, adviser, reinforcer, and facilitator. (p. 163)

Rational Emotive Therapy

As is often the case, a person, for instance, Carl R. Rogers, is associated with the formulation and development of a theory—in this case client-centered therapy. A comparatively recent example is the rational emotive therapy (RET) movement developed by Albert Ellis. This theory is based on the assumption that people have the capacity to act in either a rational or irrational manner. Rational behavior is viewed as effective and potentially productive, whereas irrational behavior results in unhappiness and nonproductivity. Ellis assumes that many types of emotional problems result from irrational patterns of thinking. This irrational pattern may begin early in life and be reinforced by significant others in the individual's life as well as by the general culture and environment. According to Ellis, people with emotional problems develop belief systems that lead to implicit verbalizations or self-talk resting on faulty logic and assumptions. And what a person tells him- or herself is intimately related to the way that person feels and acts.

The basic foundation of Ellis's theorizing is contained in this ABCDEF paradigm. Ivey et al. (1993) note:

> Perhaps Ellis's most important contribution is his A-B-C theory of personality, which can be summarized as follows:
>
> A—the "objective" facts, events, behavior that an individual encounters.
>
> B—the person's beliefs about A.
>
> C—the emotional consequences, or how a person feels and acts about A. (p. 259)

The D-E-F's of the paradigm are aimed at the promotion and maintaining of change. *D* indicates the counselor's disputing of the client's irrational thoughts, *E* refers to the presumed consequences of the therapist's interventions, and *F* stands for the new feelings the client has regarding the situation.

In summary, the basic assumption of the RET approach to counseling is that most

> people in our society develop many irrational ways of thinking. These irrational thoughts lead to irrational or inappropriate behavior. Therefore, counseling must be designed to help people recognize and change these irrational beliefs into more rational ones. The accomplishment of this goal requires an active, confrontive, and authoritative counselor who has the capacity to utilize a whole variety of techniques. (Hansen et al., 1986, p. 202)

The RET therapist does not believe that a personal relationship between the client and counselor is a prerequisite to successful counseling. In fact, the therapist may frequently challenge, provoke, and probe the irrational beliefs of the client. In the relationship the counselor is viewed more as a teacher and the client as a student. As a result, procedures may include not only teaching and related activities such as reading or other assignments but also questioning and challenging, even confrontation tactics, contracts, suggestions, and persuasion. RET can be applied not only to individual therapy but also to group therapy, marathon encounter groups, marriage counseling, and family therapy.

While RET therapists may challenge clients, such confrontations with minority clients should not bring into question the client's cultural values and background.

Reality Therapy

Another popular theory of counseling is that of reality therapy, largely developed by William Glasser. Glasser's approach is a fairly straightforward one that places confidence in the counselee's ability to deal with his or her needs through a realistic or rational process. From a reality therapy standpoint, counseling is simply a special kind of teaching or training that attempts to teach an individual what he should have learned during normal growth in a rather short period of time.

Glasser (1984) suggests that reality therapy is

applicable to individuals with any sort of psychological problem, from mild emotional upset to complete psychotic withdrawal. It works well with behavior disorders of the aged and the young, and with drug- and alcohol-related problems. It has been applied widely in schools, corrections institutions, mental hospitals, general hospitals, and business management. It focuses on the present and upon getting people to understand that they choose essentially all their actions in an attempt to fulfill basic needs. When they are unable to do this they suffer, or cause others to suffer. The therapist's task is to lead them toward better or more responsible choices that are almost always available. (p. 320)

Glasser (1981) conceptualizes reality therapy in eight steps:

1. Make friends or get involved, or get along; create a relationship or gain rapport.

2. Deemphasize the patient's history and find out what you are doing *now*.

3. Help the patient learn to make an evaluation of his or her behavior. Help the patient find out if what he or she is saying is really *helpful*.

4. Once you have evaluated the behavior, then you can begin to explore alternative behaviors—behaviors that may prove more helpful.

5. Get a commitment to a plan of change.

6. Maintain an attitude of "No excuses if you don't do it." By now the patient is committed to the change and must learn to be responsible in carrying it out.

7. Be tough without punishment. Teach people to do things without being punished if they do not; it creates a more positive motivation.

8. Refuse to give up. Once clients realize the counselor will not give up, they feel more support and work proceeds with more efficiency and promise.

Reality therapy focuses on present behavior and, consequently, does not emphasize the client's past history. When using this approach, the counselor functions as a teacher and a model. Reality therapy emphasizes a major psychological need that is present throughout life: the need for identity. It includes a need for feeling a sense of uniqueness as well as separateness and distinctiveness. This need for identity is considered to be universal among individuals in all cultures (Corey, 1982).

Reality therapy is based on the anticipation that the client will assume personal responsibility for his or her well-being. The acceptance of this responsibility, in a sense, helps a person achieve autonomy or a state of maturity by which he or she relies on his or her own internal support. Whereas many of the counseling theories suggest that the counselor should function in a noncommittal way, reality therapists praise clients when they act responsibly and indicate disapproval when they do not.

Reality therapy has

direct implications for school situations. Glasser first became concerned about children's learning and behavior problems while he was working with delinquent girls at the Ventura Schools for Girls of the California Youth Authority. He noted the almost universal history of school failure among these girls, and this finding led him to the public schools as a consultant. Glasser (1965) developed the concepts for helping children in problem solving that he described in his book *Reality Therapy.*

As he continued his work in the public elementary schools, he became convinced that the stigma of failure permeated the atmosphere in most schools and had a damaging effect on most children in schools. The elimination of failure in the school system and the prevention, rather than merely the treatment, of delinquency became two of his goals.

Glasser (1969) believes that education can be the key to effective human relating, and, in his book *Schools Without Failure,* he proposed a program to eliminate failure, emphasize thinking instead of memory work, introduce relevance into the curriculum, substitute discipline for punishment, create a learning environment where children can maximize successful experiences that will lead to a success identity, create motivation and involvement, help students develop responsible behavior, and establish ways of involving the parents and the community in the school. (Corey, 1977, p. 158)

Belkin (1988) comments:

The reality therapist considers behavior against an objective standard of measurement, which he or she calls "reality." This reality may be a practical reality or a moral reality. In either case, the reality counselor sees the individual as functioning in consonance or dissonance with that reality.* (p. 255)

It is important to make a plan through which the client can improve his or her behavior. This plan should lead to behavior that enables the client to gain satisfaction and, even at times, favorable recognition as well.

Transactional Analysis

Transactional analysis is a cognitive-behavioral approach that assumes a person has the potential for choosing and redirecting or reshaping his or her own destiny. Eric Berne did much to develop and popularize this theory in the 1960s. It is designed to help a client review and evaluate early decisions and to make new, more appropriate choices:

> Transactional analysis stresses understanding the transactions between people as a way to understand the different personalities that comprise each of us. Each of these personalities behaves in a distinct pattern and at various times is in control of the person. When one of the personalities (ego states) is in rigid control and is unwilling to relinquish that control at appropriate times, it is said to be pathological. (Pietrofesa, Hoffman, Splete, & Pinto, 1984, p. 92)

Thus, transactional analysis (TA) places a great deal of emphasis on the ego, which, from this viewpoint, consists of three states: parent, adult, and child.

> Each of these three states can take charge of the individual to the point that his or her observable behavior indicates "who's in charge" (adult, parent, or child). The client is assisted in gaining social control of his or her life by learning to use all ego states where appropriate. The ultimate goal is to help the client change from inappropriate life positions and behaviors (life scripts) to new more productive behaviors while coming from an "I'm o.k." position.* (Gibson et al., 1993, p. 74)

An essential technique in TA counseling is the contract that precedes each counseling step. This contract between counselor and counselee is a way of training or preparing people to make their own important decisions.

Hansen et al. (1986) discuss Dusay and Steiner's (1971) belief about the contract when they emphasize that it must meet the following requirements:

1. Both the counselor and the client, through Adult-Adult transactions, must mutually agree on the objectives.

2. The contract must call for some consideration. The counselor gives professional skill and time as his consideration. In some agency situations the client gives money, in others he signs a contract that commits his time and effort as his consideration.

3. The contract defines the competencies of both parties. On the part of the counselor, it means stating that he does have the skill to help with this problem; on the part of the client, it means that he is of mind and age sound enough to enter the contract.

4. Finally, the objective(s) of the contract must be legal and within the ethical limits adhered to by the counselor.† (pp. 91–92)

In addition to the contract technique, transactional analysis also utilizes questionnaires, life scripts, structural analysis, role-playing, analysis of games and rituals, and "stroking." Although not a counseling technique, TA sessions are tape-recorded in their entirety.

At each stage of counseling the decision to go ahead is squarely up to the counselee. (This is the way the counselor protects him- or herself from implications that the counseling is being forced on the counselee.) The counselor may specify conditions to client participation in contracts, such as requiring the counselee to define, in advance, what advantage might ensue from their joint effort.

---

*From Gibson, Robert L., Mitchell, Marianne H., and Basile, Sherry K., *Counseling in the Elementary Schools*. Copyright © 1993 by Allyn and Bacon. Reprinted by permission.

†From J. C. Hansen, R. R. Stevic, and W. R. Warner (1986), *Counseling: Theory and Process* (4th ed.). Copyright © 1986. Used by permission of James Hansen.

Transactional analysis, of course, focuses on the individual, but it is a procedure for counseling persons within a group setting. Transactional analysis counselors feel that the group setting facilitates the process of providing feedback to persons about the kind of transactions in which they engage. The counseling group, then, represents a microcosm of the real world. In this setting, the individual group members are there to work on their own objectives, and the counselor acts as the group leader.

Gestalt Counseling

"Gestalt therapy, developed by Frederick Perls, is a therapeutic approach in which the therapist assists the client toward self-integration and toward learning to utilize his energy in appropriate ways to grow, develop, and actualize" (George & Cristiani, 1995, p. 66). The primary focus of this approach is the present—"the here and now." This approach implies that the past is gone and the future has yet to arrive; therefore, only the present is important.

Gestalt counseling also has as its major objective the integration of the person. In popular terminology, this might be called "getting it all together." Perls (1948) writes:

> The treatment is finished when the patient has achieved the basic requirements: a change in outlook, a technique of adequate self-expression and assimilation, and the ability to extend awareness to the verbal level. He has then reached that state of integration which facilitates its own development, and he can now be safely left to himself. (p. 58)

In order to achieve this togetherness, the counselor seeks to increase the client's awareness. As a result, the counselor functions in a way that provides the client with an atmosphere conducive to the discovery of client needs, or what the client has lost because of environmental demands, and in which the client can experience the necessary discovery and growth:

> To facilitate this process, counselors utilize the most important tool they have: themselves. A counselor, fully aware of herself in the now, engages the client in a here and now interaction. The counselor does not interpret, probe, preach about reality; rather she interacts with the client in the now. (Hansen et al., 1986, p. 141)

Gestalt counselors believe that people always act to organize stimuli into total pictures or wholes. Several of the principles developed to explain this process have been stated by Hansen et al. (1986):

> *Principle of Closure:* When we perceive a figure that is incomplete, our mind acts to finish the figure and perceives it as complete.
>
> *Principle of Proximity:* The relative distance of stimuli from each other within the perceptual field determines how they are seen.
>
> *Principle of Similarity:* The similarity of stimuli in the perceptual field causes us to group them together.

Each of these three principles illustrates how the human mind seeks to make sense from the vast array of stimuli in the phenomenal field by pulling things together. The important point is that the stimuli have meaning only as they are organized in the mind by the individual. (p. 130)

Cited by Hansen et al. (1986), Passons (1975) lists eight assumptions about the nature of humans that act as the framework for Gestalt counseling:

1. Individuals are composite wholes made up of interrelated parts. None of these parts—body, emotions, thoughts, sensations, and perceptions—can be understood outside the context of the whole person.

2. Individuals are also part of their own environment and cannot be understood apart from it.

3. People choose how they respond to external and internal stimuli; they are actors, not reactors.

4. People have the potential to be fully aware of all their sensations, thoughts, emotions, and perceptions.

5. Individuals are capable of making choices because they are aware.

6. Individuals have the capacity to govern their own lives effectively.

7. People cannot experience the past and the future; they can experience only themselves in the present.

8. People are neither basically good nor bad.* (pp. 132–133)

From these assumptions we can conclude that the Gestalt therapist has a positive view of the individual's capacity for self-direction. Furthermore, the client must be encouraged to utilize this capacity and take responsibility for his or her own life—and do that *now*, in the present; they must experience the here and now. Counseling techniques may include "how" and "what" questions, confrontations, "I" statements, and sharing awareness with clients emphasizing "this moment."

Integrated Theories

In recent years we have seen continued efforts not only to reinforce and expand on the many traditional theories of counseling but, additionally, to develop new multidimensional and integrated models. One of these, Actualizing Counseling and Psychotherapy, presented by Brammer and Shostrom (1982), represents a creative synthesis approach to counseling theory and human growth. Actualizing counseling is based on the following assumptions:

1. Each person is a unique human being seeking actualization even though he or she shares much "human nature" in common with others. A better term is Buber's "particularity" principle, a unique "thou" seeking to be realized.

2. While the actualizing principle has a futuristic quality in the "becoming" sense, it takes place in the moment-to-moment growth process. Hence, the "here and now" becomes the temporal focus of the process.

3. Human behavior is not determined by events (external and internal) as much as by one's own cognitive representations of events.

---

*From J. C. Hansen, R. R. Stevic, and W. R. Warner (1986), *Counseling: Theory and Process* (4th ed.). Copyright © 1986. Used by permission of James Hansen.

4. While much of human behavior is determined by personal history and forces beyond one's control, the actualizing process assumes that one's future is largely undetermined and one has wide ranges of freedom to choose.

5. The assumption of freedom places corresponding responsibility on the person for his or her own actualizing. One cannot depend upon others or blame others for one's growth or lack of it. Even though growth takes place in a social context, each person alone is responsible for his or her own life.

6. While some primitive behaviors are reflexive, hence largely genetically determined, and some are the result of chemical and neurological changes, a fundamental assumption of actualizing counseling is that social behavior is learned and changes in behavior follow an active learning process.

7. Most human learning is not automatic but, rather, is mediated through cognitive processes such as symbolic coding and selective attention.

8. Actualization is achieved primarily in social interaction with a counselor, teacher, minister, group, friend, or family; but it also can be achieved through self-help methods, such as meditation and imagery. Social interaction becomes the main vehicle for conditions of actualization, such as honesty with feelings, awareness of self, freedom of expression, and trust in one's self and others.

9. A reciprocal interaction takes place between thoughts, emotions, and actions such that a change in one tends to bring about a change in the others. Each person decides intentionally which modality begins the change process—thought, feeling, or action. To go from intention to action the person must move beyond awareness and intention to commitment.

10. Each personality contains the paradoxical state of polar opposites which are expressed and forced to awareness and action in the actualizing process. Examples are dependence and independence, affection and aggression, support and criticalness.* (pp. 80–81)

Ivey et al. (1987) note that an integrated knowledge of skills, theory, and practice is essential for culturally intentional counseling and therapy. Further,

Skills form the foundation of effective theory and practice: The culturally intentional therapist knows how to construct a creative decision-making interview and can use microskills to attend to and influence clients in a predicted direction. Important in this process are individual and cultural empathy, client observation skills, assessment of person and environment, and the application of positive techniques of growth and change.

Theory provides organizing principles for counseling and therapy: The culturally intentional counselor has knowledge of alternative theoretical approaches and treatment modalities. Practice is the integration of skills and theory: The culturally intentional counselor or therapist is competent in skills and theory, and is able to apply them to research and practice for client benefit.

Undergirding integrated competence in skills, theory, and practice is an intentional awareness of one's own personal worldview and how that worldview may be similar to and/or different from the worldview and personal constructions of the client and other professionals.† (p. 413)

---

*From Brammer, L. M., & Shostrom, E. L. *Therapeutic Psychology: Fundamentals of Counseling and Psychotherapy.* Copyright © 1982 by Prentice-Hall. Reprinted by permission.

†From Ivey, A. D., Ivey, M. B., and Simek-Downing, L., *Counseling and Psychotherapy: Integrating Skills, Theory, and Practice,* p. 413. Copyright © 1987 by Allyn and Bacon. Reprinted by permission.

TABLE 5–1 A Classification of Pyschotherapy Theorists, Goals, and Processes According to an E-R-A Model

	Emotionality	**Rationality**	**Activity**
Theorists	Rogers Perls Frankl	Berne Ellis Alexander Kelly Sullivan	Dreikurs Wolpe Dollard and Miller
Goals	Awareness and acceptance of self in conflict and of inner resources Awareness of negative feelings	Strengthening of ego functioning Awareness of negative thoughts	Transfer of therapy Symptom removal Learning to respond and to control the environment
Processes	Acceptance Support of client's autonomy	Recognition and interpretation of the unconscious material Manipulation of client anxiety	Active initial questioning Reeducation about emotional conflicts

Source: L'Abate, L. (1981). "Classification of Counseling and Therapy Theorists, Methods, Processes, and Goals: The E-R-A Model, *Personnel and Guidance Journal, 59*(5), p. 264. © American Counseling Association. Reprinted with permission. No further reproduction authorized without further permission of the American Counseling Association.

Eclectic Counseling

The eclectic approach to counseling is one of long-standing tradition and equally long-standing controversy. It is also an approach that appears to have increased in popularity in the 1980s, as reported by Brabeck and Welfel (1985). It originally provided a safe, middle-of-the-road theory for those counselors who neither desired nor felt capable of functioning as purely directive or nondirective counselors.

Defenders of the theory, on the other hand, suggested eclecticism as an approach that allowed each individual to construct his or her own theory by drawing on established theories. It has often been suggested that the eclectic counselor can choose the best of all counseling worlds. Others contend that eclecticism encourages counselors to become theoretical "jacks of all trades." Certainly, the many theoretical models currently available can be confusing in the absence of a model for theory and technique selection. One such classification system is presented in Table 5–1. Another model, using the same categories of emotionality, rationality, and activity (Ulrici, L'Abate, & Wagner, 1981, p. 264), is noted in Table 5–2.

In a conversation with the authors, Camille Sexton-Villalta, a research assistant at Indiana University, noted that through an eclectic approach, the counselor is able to develop a more personally meaningful point of view that integrates his or her own style and is better suited for him or her than other formal approaches. In doing this, however, the counselor must be aware that her or his approach may have deficiencies that need to be addressed.

TABLE 5–2 Classification of Intervention Methods According to the E-R-A Model

Emotionality	Rationality
Methods focus on experimental exercises that differentiate feeling states of solitude and solidarity	Methods focus on the development of conscious understanding that supports reality based controls
1. Developing interpersonal awareness through individual exercises of mediation fantasy trips, imaginary dialogues, here-and-now awareness	1. Teaching new facts, concepts, and theories through lectures, readings, and discussions
2. Developing awareness of interpersonal relationships through interactional task of role play, sculpting, etc.	2. Relating past influences to present functioning through cognitive recreation of past events (e.g., psychoanalytic dialogues, genograms, and rational reevaluations)
3. Developing bodily awareness through physical exercises of creative movement and interpersonal body contacts	3. Developing insight to differentiate feelings from actions through analysis of one's present and past relationships (e.g., working through transference, understanding defense operations, and ego controls)
4. Teaching skills of interpersonal sensitivity and communication through lectures, readings, demonstrations, and practice exercises	4. Teaching skills of rational thinking and ego control through lectures, discussions, and practice at rational problem solving and decision making

Behavioral Activity	Systemic Activity
Methods focus on the application of scientific principles to shape and control behavior	Methods focus on adjusting dimensions of cohesion and adaptability that maintain family functioning
1. Solving behavioral problems through experimental analysis—quantifying behavior, determining controls, and implementing interventions	1. Establishing appropriate boundaries for cohesion and autonomy through
2. Teaching and increasing desired behavior and extinguishing inappropriate behavior through techniques of	a. Directives given in session (e.g., interactions, blocking others, bringing members of the social network)
a. Respondent conditioning (e.g., stimulus pairing, desensitization)	b. Behavior assignments for daily context (e.g., rituals, paradoxical exercises, age-appropriate tasks, activities to support coalitions or limit enmeshment)
b. Operant conditioning (e.g., positive reinforcement, punishment)	2. Restructuring operations in response to situational stress or developmental change through
3. Teaching desired behavior through social learning (e.g., modeling, films)	a. Assigning linear tasks to directly change operations (e.g., rescheduling, assigning family duties)
4. Increasing and maintaining behavior through evaluative feedback	b. Assigning paradoxical tasks that emphasize operations problems (e.g., role reversals, behavioral extremes)
5. Practice application of learned behavior through role play and simulated exercises	
6. Implementing desired behavior or its approximation through behavioral tasks performed in daily context	
7. Teaching behavioral principles through lectures, models, and practice exercises	

Source: From Ulrici, Donna, L'Abate, Luciano, and Wagner, Victor (pp. 308–309), "The E-R-A Model: A Heuristic Framework for Classification of Skill Training Programs for Couples and Families" (1981), *Family Relations, 30*(2), 307–315. Copyright © 1981 by the National Council on Family Relations, 3989 Central Ave. NE, Minneapolis, MN 55421. Reprinted by permission.

Brammer and Shostrom (1982) recommend that each counselor and psychotherapist must ultimately develop a point of view that is uniquely his or her own.

Developing one's own view is a very demanding lifelong task. In addition to knowing current theories of personality structure and behavior change, counselors must know their own assumptions about the nature of man and the process of knowing, their own values and views of the good life, and their models of the mature well-functioning person. This goal is accomplished through self-study of client/counselor relationships and personal therapeutic experiences resulting in increased self-understanding. These understandings and assumptions are then related to one's goals for counseling, which in turn are matched with strategies and methods to reach those goals most effectively. One borrows from other theorists in the sense that one stands on their shoulders to reach higher levels of understanding and effectiveness in practice. Then, one synthesizes these pieces incrementally into a unified system which is comfortable and effective in a particular setting. Finally, one tests the theory in practice and formulates hypotheses which can be tested experimentally. The results then are incorporated into one's system, or one revises the system. (p. 38)

As summarized in Table 5–3, Brammer and Shostrom (1982) also believe:

Counselors and psychotherapists can take one of three positions: identify with one of the theories already published and tested in practice, develop an eclectic position, or strive for a personalized creative synthesis of theory and practice. (pp. 33–34)

We conclude our discussion of eclecticism by noting Wallace's (1986) warning:

Student-counselors cannot shelve their responsibility for constructing a personal theory of counseling by turning it into an intellectual game or academic exercise. Their obligation to their clients is far too real for that. Developing an eclectic approach to therapy requires an enterprising juxtaposition and a genuine confrontation of their work with the values, thoughts, and research of others. And, while independence of observation and thought is essential to an eclectic stance, so are understanding, respect, and tolerance for other theorists. Before students in search of a personal theory of counseling and psychotherapy can choose the best, they must become fully aware of all that are available—no small achievement in a discipline overburdened with diverse and contradictory theories. The eclectic approach, then, is no shortcut to theory formulation. Indeed, when properly traveled, it is a most difficult path to follow. (p. 310)

GOALS OF COUNSELING

Another approach to viewing the various theoretical models is to examine goals in relationship to theories. Table 5–4 presents a framework in the form of counseling goals that are presented through a developmental continuum. It incorporates various counseling models and integrates Maslow's (1970) hierarchy of needs.

In Table 5–4 the continuum moves from the top (primary goals/needs) to the bottom (secondary goals/needs).

It is proposed that client goals/needs that are most basic (at the top of the continuum) need to be addressed in counseling before a client can work effectively on higher level goals/needs (at the bottom of the continuum). The continuum is seen as fluid, however, and a counselor might well be working up and down the continuum at different times with a client. (Bruce, 1984, p. 259)

TABLE 5–3 Comparison of Basic Approaches to Theory Building

Established Single Theory	Eclectic Approaches	Creative Synthesis
Main Characteristic		
Integrated set of assumptions related directly to strategy and method	Strategies and methods from several approaches applied selectively to clients	Application of broad and varied strategies and methods related to a synthesized theory evolved and "owned" by the practitioner
Examples		
Freud's Psychoanalytic Theory Rogers' Client-Centered Theory	Thorne's Integrative Psychology Lazarus's Structural Eclecticism	Assagioli's Psychosynthesis Shostrom's Actualizing Therapy
Advantages		
Ready-made system of assumptions Extensive experience and data base Consistency of theory and method	Collection of various methods Flexibility of choice methods Wide agency application of methods	Continues synthesizing, extending, and amplifying personal system Discourages competition Fosters therapist's identity with own views
Limitations		
Tendency toward restricted view of data Often a closed system Encourages hero worship Fosters competition and divisiveness	Encourages uncritical choosing Deemphasizes integrative theorizing Tends toward faddism Additive collection of what works for now Imitative and limited creativity	A continuous lifelong task Tends to be idealistic Futuristic—ahead of its time Requires continuous creativity Requires trust in self Risky—requires standing on one's own
Illustrative Comments by Practitioners		
"Client-centered theory speaks to me." "Ellis is my hero." "I dig Freud." "I am analytic." "I stick with the tried and true."	"I use what works." "I'm flexible." "I try many methods." "I like TA methods but not the basic assumption." "Everyone says something important."	"I'm constantly reevaluating my ideas." "I develop my own theory to fit me." "I try to keep open and take some risks." "I trust my own observations and judgments."

Source: Brammer, L. M., and Shostrom, E. L., *Therapeutic Psychology: Fundamentals of Counseling and Psychotherapy*, p. 34. Copyright © 1982 by Prentice-Hall. Reprinted by permission.

TABLE 5–4   Continuum of Counseling Goals

Counseling Process Goals	Corresponding Counseling Process Models	Maslow's Hierarchy of Needs, Expanded (Physiological Needs)
Ego development (Inception) Anxiety reduction Personal adjustment	Clinical/analytical model Ego psychotherapy	Security/safety needs Dependency Ego defenses
Socialization Role/self-identity Social adjustment Behavior change	Behavioral counseling Behavior modification Reality therapy	Belongingness needs Affiliation Identification Character development

Developmental competence
  Resolving developmental
    conflicts and challenges
Coping/mastery
Problem solving
Decision making
Self-sufficiency
	Developmental counseling
	Adlerian counseling
	Transactional analysis
	Rational-emotive therapy
	Problem solving
	Decision making
		(Developmental/cognitive needs) to know and under-stand, curiosity

Self-esteem
  Self-awareness
Self-acceptance
Self-confidence
Congruence of self
	Client-centered/relationship
	  counseling
		Esteem needs, values devel-opment

Self-realization
  Actualizing potential:
    Intellectual, emotional,
    social, spiritual
	Gestalt counseling
	Existential counseling
		Actualization needs

Source: Reprinted by Bruce, P., "Continuum of Counseling Goals: A Framework for Differentiating Counseling Strategies," *Personnel and Guidance Journal, 62,* 1984, p. 260. © American Counseling Association. Reprinted with permission. No further reproduction authorized without further permission of the American Counseling Association.

Obviously, counseling goals may also be more simply classified in terms of counselor goals and client goals or the immediate, intermediate, or long-range goals of therapy. Regardless of how one chooses to classify counseling goals, counseling, like all other meaningful activities, must be goal driven, have a purpose, or seek to attain an objective. Broadly speaking, counseling goals may also be separated into the following categories:

Developmental Goals: Developmental goals are those wherein the client is assisted in meeting or advancing her or his anticipated human growth and development (that is, socially, personally, emotionally, cognitively, physical wellness, and so on).

Preventive Goals: Prevention is a goal in which the counselor helps the client avoid some undesired outcome.

Enhancement Goals: If the client possesses special skills and abilities, enhancement means they can be identified and/or further developed through the assistance of a counselor.

Remedial Goals: Remediation involves assisting a client to overcome and/or treat an undesirable development.

Exploratory Goals: Exploration represents goals appropriate to the examining of options, testing of skills, and trying new and different activities, environments, relationships, and so on.

Reinforcement Goals: Reinforcement is used in those instances where clients need help in recognizing that what they are doing, thinking, and/or feeling is okay.

Cognitive Goals: Cognition involves acquiring the basic foundations of learning and cognitive skills.

Physiological Goals: Physiology involves acquiring the basic understandings and habits for good health.

Psychological Goals: Psychology aids in developing good social interaction skills, learning emotional control, developing a positive self-concept, and so on.* (Gibson et al., 1993, pp. 87–89)

Cormier and Hackney (1993) note that:

goals serve three important functions in the counseling process. First, goals can have a motivational function in counseling. Secondly, goals can also have an educational function in counseling in that they can help clients acquire new responses and three, goals can also meet an evaluative function in counseling whereby the client's goals help the counselor to select and evaluate various counseling strategies appropriate to the client's goals.† (pp. 103–104)

The Counseling Process

Having briefly introduced some of the popular counseling theories, let us now move on to examine the translation of these theories into action. This "action" is frequently referred to as the counseling process. This process is usually specified by a sequence of interactions or steps. Although various authors will conceptualize these stages or phases differently because of different theoretical models, there is considerable agreement that initially the process is concerned with relationship establishment, followed by some method of problem identification and patterns of exploration, leading to planning for problem solution and remediation and concluding with action and termination. Cormier and Hackney (1993) identified the stages as follows:

1. Relationship establishment
2. Problem identification and exploration
3. Planning for problem solving
4. Solution application and termination

*From Gibson, Robert L., Mitchell, Marianne H., and Basile, Sherry K., *Counseling in the Elementary School.* Copyright © 1993 by Allyn and Bacon. Reprinted by permission.

†From Cormier, L. Sherilyn, and Hackney, Harold, *The Professional Counselor.* Copyright © 1993 by Allyn and Bacon. Reprinted by permission.

Pietrofesa, Hoffman, Splete, and Pinto (1984) also present stages of the therapeutic process. A brief description of each of these stages will be helpful.

Relationship Establishment

As often stated in definitions, counseling is a relationship. Furthermore, it is defined as a helping relationship. It therefore follows that if it is to be a relationship that is helpful, the counselor must take the initiative in the initial interview to establish a climate conducive to mutual respect, trust, free and open communication, and understanding in general of what the counseling process involves.

Within a formal context Brammer (1988) asserts that this relationship takes the form of an interview—a structured helping relationship to which many variables contribute. Figure 5–2 illustrates these variables.

Although responsibility will later shift increasingly to the client, at this stage the responsibility for the counseling process rests primarily with the counselor. Among the techniques the counselor may use are those designed to relieve tensions and open communication. Both the counselor's attitude and verbal communications are significant to the development of a satisfactory relationship. In the latter instance, all the counselor's communication skills are brought into play. These include attentive listening, understanding, and feeling with the client.

Among the factors that are important in the establishment of this counselor-client relationship are positive regard and respect, accurate empathy, and genuineness. These conditions imply counselor openness, an ability to understand and feel with the client, and valuing the client. As Hackney and Cormier (1988) suggest, much of what is accomplished in counseling is dependent on the quality of the relationship. This counselor-client relationship serves not only to increase the opportunity for clients to attain their goals but also to be a potential model of a good interpersonal relationship, one that clients can use to improve the quality of their other relationships outside the therapy setting.

Counselors must keep in mind that the purpose of a counseling relationship is to meet, insofar as possible, client needs (not counselor needs). The counseling process within this relationship seeks to assist the client in assuming the responsibilities for his or her problem and its solution. As viewed by Okun (1987):

> a helping relationship that benefits the helpee is a mutual learning process between the helpee and one (or more) other persons. The effectiveness of the relationship depends on (1) the

FIGURE 5–2   The Helping Relationship in the Interview
Source: From Brammer, L. M., *The Helping Relationship: Process and Skills.* Copyright © 1988 by Allyn and Bacon. Reprinted by permission.

helper's skill in communicating his or her understanding of the helpee's feelings and behaviors; (2) the helper's ability to determine and clarify the helpee's problem; and (3) the helper's ability to apply appropriate helping strategies in order to facilitate the recipient's self-exploration, self-understanding, problem-solving, and decision-making, all of which lead to constructive action on the part of the helpee. (p. 21)

The establishment of a relationship that is seen as helpful to the client must be achieved early in the counseling process, inasmuch as this will often determine whether the client will continue.

Eisenberg and Delaney (1983) suggest that the essential goals of the initial counseling interview are

For the Counselor:

Stimulate open, honest, and full communication about the concerns needing to be discussed and the factors and background related to those concerns.

Work toward progressively deeper levels of understanding, respect, and trust between self and client.

Provide the client with the view that something useful can be gained from the counseling sessions.

Identify a problem or concern for subsequent attention and work.

Establish the "gestalt" that counseling is a process in which both parties must work hard at exploring and understanding the client and his or her concerns.

Acquire information about the client that relates to his or her concerns and effective problem resolution.

For Most Clients:

Stimulating self-examination.

Generating some specific task for the client to do, or some specific issue to think about before the next counseling session. (p. 75)

Problem Identification and Exploration

Once an adequate relationship has been established, clients will be more receptive to the in-depth discussion and exploration of their concerns. At this stage, clients assume more responsibility, because it is their problem and their willingness to communicate as much of the nature of the problem to the counselor that will determine to a large extent the assistance the counselor can give.

During this phase, the counselor continues to exhibit attending behavior and may place particular emphasis on such communication skills as paraphrasing, clarification, perception checking, or feedback. The counselor may question the client, but the questions are stated in such a way as to facilitate the continued exploration of the client's concern. Questions that would embarrass, challenge, or threaten the client are avoided. Throughout this phase the counselor will recognize cultural differences and their implications in terms of how techniques should be modified to be culturally appropriate.

During this stage, the counselor is seeking to distinguish between what might be called surface problems and those that are more complex. The counselor also strives to determine whether the stated problem is, in fact, the concern that has brought the client to the counselor's attention. This may be a time for information gathering. The more usable information the counselor has, the greater the prospects of accurate assessment of the client's needs. It is therefore helpful for counselors to recognize the various areas of information that must be tapped.

The information index in Figure 5–3 represents the main sources of information for the counselor.

According to Cavanaugh (1982):

> Continuum A-B represents the time dimension. Information about the person's past helps the counselor understand how the person got where he or she is. Information about the present indicates how well the person is functioning currently, and information about the future tells the counselor who the person wishes to become. As these pieces of information are brought together, they can give a reasonably good picture of who the person is and why the person is seeking help.
>
> Continuum C-D reflects the importance of getting both intrapsychic and interpersonal information. Intrapsychic information consists of learning about the person's perceptions of reality; his inner conflicts and how they are handled; the relationship between who the person is, thinks he is, and wants others to think he is; as well as the person's beliefs, values, and hopes. Interpersonal information comprises the dynamics involved in how the person relates with others, whether these relationships are satisfying or dissatisfying to the person or to the people with whom he or she relates.
>
> Continuum E-F denotes what the person thinks and feels about herself, others, and relevant events. It is not only important to know the content of the person's thoughts and feelings but to recognize how they interact and perhaps conflict. For example, when asked how she viewed her father, a woman responds, "I have nothing but the utmost respect for him." When she is asked how she feels about her father, she replies, "I resent him more than words can say."
>
> The information index highlights cautions in information gathering. Typically, people seeking help lure counselors into talking about the past, discussing interpersonal relationships, and focusing on ideas. The counselor who is successfully lured will have a fragmented and inaccurate picture upon which to make a clinical evaluation. (p. 106)

During this stage, some counselors may use appraisal techniques such as standardized tests for problem diagnosis. Subproblems may also be identified. During this stage, the client not only explores experiences and behaviors but also may reveal feelings and the

FIGURE 5–3

An Information Index
Source: M. E. Cavanaugh, *The Counseling Experience: A Theoretical and Practical Approach* (1982), p. 106. Copyright © 1982 Brooks/Cole Publishing Co., Pacific Grove, CA. Used by permission.

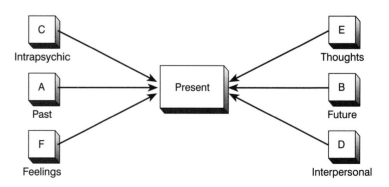

relationship of concern to the way he or she is living life in general. The counselor, on the other hand, is seeking to secure as much relevant data as possible and to integrate it into an overall picture of the client and his or her concern. The counselor also shares these perceptions with the client. A goal of this stage is for both the counselor and the client to perceive the problem and its ramifications similarly. Another goal of the counselor during this stage is to help the client develop a self-understanding that recognizes the need for dealing with a concern—the need for change and action.

Obviously, this is a busy stage of the counseling process. As Blackham (1977) describes it, this second stage is when much of the real work occurs, with intensive exploration and counselor analysis. Blackham explains that facilitative conditions arise that promote client understanding of the basis of problems as well as the formulation of action plans for resolving problems. Although problem-solving activities are likely to be initiated during this stage, the major steps in implementing the activities take place in the third stage.

The following goals and guidelines for this stage are identified by Blackham (1977):

1. Explore and analyze each problem area.

2. Specify client problems behaviorally and state them in a form that makes them possible to resolve. Problems are stated in terms of client behavior that can be learned or changed in the context of the person's present life circumstances.

3. Analyze each problem in terms of variables that influence or maintain it. For example, if the client has a behavior or interpersonal problem, identify the significant people in the client's life and analyze the interactions or contingencies (stimulus/response-consequence relationships) that maintain the inappropriate response.

4. Determine the severity of client problems and make arrangements for referral if they are beyond the counselor's competence.

5. Arrange client problems in terms of priorities; decide which problem will be worked on first.

6. Extend the facilitative conditions that best promote problem exploration, client understanding, and problem-solving activity.

7. Recognize and deal effectively with transference, countertransference, and resistance.

8. Formulate procedures that will resolve client problems effectively or promote the desired behavior change. (p. 203)

Blackham (1977) continues:

Successful counseling and therapeutic outcomes are not only a function of method and counselor's characteristics. Client problems and characteristics may also play an important role. Both clinical experience and research seem to suggest that counseling prognosis tends to be more positive under the following conditions:

1. Client problems are recent rather than long-standing, and the client has some expectation of improvement.

2. The symptoms the client exhibits and the degree of distress or anxiety present are handicapping or incapacitating.

3. The client voluntarily seeks help and is willing to explore problems and invest time and effort to change.

4. The client has normal intelligence or higher, has adapted reasonably well in the past, and his present family or circumstances of living do not negate or jeopardize counseling or change efforts.

5. The client's problem has no hereditary, constitutional, or endocrine basis.

6. The client's problems or symptoms do not produce major secondary gains. That is, the client's nonadaptive behavior should not provide excessive personal gratification or be intentionally encouraged or reinforced by significant others.

7. The client has experienced some satisfying interpersonal relationships in the past with parents or parent figures and is able to form an appropriate relationship to the counselor. (pp. 196–197)

Finally, we would note the five-stage decisional counseling model presented by Ivey et al. (1993):

The central theoretical point of the five-stage model is that *counseling and therapy are not only about decisions, but the interview itself also may be structured using a decision-making framework.* Mastering the five-stage interview, gaining an understanding of key empathic dimensions, and developing competence in interviewing microskills will give you a framework for understanding many different approaches to helping theory.

You can structure a very effective interview using the following five stages as a model or checklist:

1. Establishing rapport and structure ("Hello" and "This is what we'll be doing today.")

2. Gathering data and identifying assets ("What's the problem or concern?" and "What are your strengths?")

3. Determining outcomes ("What do you want to have happen?")

4. Generating alternative solutions ("What are we going to do to generate new ideas?")

5. Generalizing and transferring learning ("Will you do it?") (pp. 76–77)

Planning for Problem Solving

Once the counselor has determined that all relevant information regarding the client's concern is available and understood and once the client has accepted the need for doing something about a specific problem, the time is ripe for developing a plan to solve or remediate the concern of the client.

At this point, effective goal setting becomes the vital part of the counseling activity. Indicated here are seven specific criteria from Dyer and Vriend (1977) for judging effective goal setting in counseling:

1. Mutual agreement on goals is vital.

2. Goal specificity promotes goal achievement.

3. On-target goals are relevant to the self-defeating behavior of the goal setter.

4. Effectively set goals are achievable and success-oriented.

5. Effectively set goals are quantifiable and measurable.

6. Effectively set goals are behavioral and observable.

7. Goals have been effectively structured when a client understands them and can restate them clearly. (pp. 470–471)

Dyer and Vriend (1977) go on to suggest that the counselor can ask the following evaluative questions:

Am I helping this client to set goals that are: (a) High in mutuality? (b) Specific in nature? (c) Relevant to the client's self-defeating behavior? (d) Achievable and success-oriented? (e) Quantifiable and measurable? (f) Behavioral and observable? (g) Understandable and repeatable? (p. 471)

In the further development of this plan, the counselor recognizes that the client will frequently not arrive at basic insights, implications, or probabilities as fast as the counselor will. However, most counselors will agree that it is better to guide the client toward realizing these understandings him- or herself rather than just telling the client outright. To facilitate the client's understanding, the counselor may use techniques of repetition, mild confrontation, interpretation, information, and, obviously, encouragement.

The outcome of this process is aimed at allowing the client to identify as many solutions as possible, project the consequences of each solution, and finally set the priorities of these solutions.

Solution Application and Termination

In this final stage, the responsibilities are clear-cut. The client has the responsibility for applying the determined solution, and the counselor, for determining the point of termination. In the first instance, the counselor has a responsibility to encourage the client's acting on his or her determined problem solution. During the time that the client is actively engaged in applying the problem solution, the counselor will often maintain contact as a source of follow-up, support, and encouragement. The client may also need the counselor's assistance in the event things do not go according to plan. Once it has been determined, however, that the counselor and the client have dealt with the client's concern to the extent possible and practical, the process should be terminated. As noted before, this responsibility is primarily the counselor's, although the client has the right to terminate at any time. The counselor usually gives some indication that "the next interview should just about wrap it up" and may conclude by summarizing the main points of the counseling process. Usually, the counselor will leave the door open for the client's possible return in the event unexpected additional assistance is needed. Because counseling is a learning process, the counselor hopes that the client has not only learned to deal with this particular problem but has also learned problem-solving skills that will decrease the probability of the client's need for further counseling in the future.

In concluding this section on the counseling process, we are aware of our frequent reference to the client's "problem," and we would like to remind our readers that problems are not always based on perceived inadequacies or failures requiring remediation and restorative therapy. Clients can have equally pressing needs resulting from concerns for developing their human potential—for capitalizing on their strengths. In these instances the emphasis is on development, growth, or enhancement rather than remediation.

COUNSELING SKILLS

Thus far in this chapter we have discussed the importance of the counselor having a theoretical framework within which to function and a knowledge of the process or stages through which client counseling moves. Equally important are the skills that the counselor must possess to apply a given theory and implement the process.

The skills of counseling have their roots in both theory and process and have been reinforced through both practice and research. The counselor acquires these skills through learning and practice. We have grouped these under the categories of communications skills, diagnostic skills, motivational skills, and management skills, recognizing that there will be overlap and interrelations among these as well as between skills and process.

Communications Skills

Nonverbal Communications Skills

All of us communicate nonverbally. Through the use of facial expressions, body posture, and physical movements we send messages, usually intentional but sometimes not intentional. We also usually "read messages" that others communicate to us in a similar manner. In our society, nonverbal language is a popular means of communication, and in counseling, it is a social interaction process important to both the counselor and the counselee. For example, from the onset and throughout the counseling process, visual clues will influence the client's perception of the counselor. As noted earlier in this chapter, one of the nonverbal ways in which the counselor deals with this factor is by exhibiting attending behavior, by communicating nonverbally, "I am interested in you and your concerns, I respect you and I'm going to give you my undivided attention," and so forth. Attending behaviors accomplish several purposes:

1. *Communication of Individual Attention.* Attending behaviors communicate nonverbally, "I am listening to you and only you." They can act as a reinforcement for the client to continue to speak.

2. *Communication of Respect.* Counselors, by attending, communicate respect for the client, as if to say, "What you say is so important, I will attend to you."

3. *Modeling of Effective Behavior.* Counselors can act as models for their clients. Through their modeling behavior, counselors are afforded the opportunity to demonstrate effective interpersonal skills for clients. After several sessions, counselors will often report how clients have altered their own attending behaviors. With the modeling concept, counselees learn to utilize attending behaviors outside the counseling framework.

4. *Improvement of Counselor Discrimination.* Good attending behavior can actually help counselors focus on the client. It helps to maintain alertness and to provide for more effective discrimination. (Pietrofesa et al., 1984, pp. 270–271)

Gazda, Asbury, Balzer, Childers, and Walters (1977) categorize nonverbal behaviors into four modalities. It should be emphasized that nonverbal behaviors are highly idiosyncratic; interpretation of these clues must be tentative and based on the context in which they are sent.

1. **Nonverbal Communication Behaviors Using Time**

Recognition

Promptness or delay in recognizing the presence of another or in responding to his or her communication

Priorities

Amount of time another is willing to spend communicating with a person

Relative amounts of time spent on various topics

2. **Nonverbal Communication Behaviors Using the Body**

Eye contact (important in regulating the relationship)

Looking at a specific object

Looking down

Steady to helper

Defiantly at helper ("hard" eyes), glaring

Shifting eyes from object to object

Looking at helper but looking away when looked at

Covering eyes with hand(s)

Frequency of looking at another

Eyes

"Sparkling"

Tears

"Wild-eyed"

Position of eyelids

Skin

Pallor

Perspiration

Blushing

"Goose bumps"

Posture (often indicative of physical alertness or tiredness)

"Eager," as if ready for activity

Slouching, slovenly, tired looking, slumping

Arms crossed in front as if to protect self

Crossing legs

Sits facing the other person rather than sideways or away from

Hanging head, looking at floor, head down

Body positioned to exclude others from joining a group or dyad

Facial expression (primary site for display of affects; thought by researchers to be subject to involuntary responses)

No change

Wrinkled forehead (lines of worry), frown

Wrinkled nose

Smiling, laughing

"Sad" mouth

Biting lip

Hand and arm gestures

Symbolic hand and arm gestures

Literal hand and arm gestures to indicate size or shape

Demonstration of how something happened or how to do something

Self-inflicting behaviors

Nail biting

Scratching

Cracking knuckles

Tugging at hair

Rubbing or stroking

Repetitive behaviors (often interpreted as signs of nervousness or restlessness but may be organic in origin)

Tapping foot, drumming or thumping with fingers

Fidgeting, squirming

Trembling

Playing with button, hair, or clothing

Signals or commands

Snapping fingers

Holding finger to lips for silence

Pointing

Staring directly to indicate disapproval

Shrugging shoulders

Waving

Nodding in recognition

Winking

Nodding in agreement, shaking head in disagreement

Touching

To get attention, such as tapping on shoulder

Affectionate, tender

Sexual

Challenging, such as poking finger into chest

Symbols of camaraderie, such as slapping on back

Belittling, such as a pat on top of head

3. Nonverbal Communication Behaviors Using Vocal Media

Tone of voice

Flat, monotone, absence of feelings

Bright, vivid changes of inflection

Strong, confident, firm

Weak, hesitant, shaky

Broken, faltering

Rate of speech

Fast

Medium

Slow

Loudness of voice

Loud

Medium

Soft

Diction

Precise versus careless

Regional (colloquial) differences

Consistency of diction

4. Nonverbal Communication Behaviors Using the Environment

Distance

Moves away when the other moves toward

Moves toward when the other moves away

Takes initiative in moving toward or away from

Distance widens gradually

Distance narrows gradually

Arrangement of the physical setting

Neat, well-ordered, organized

Untidy, haphazard, careless

Casual versus formal

Warm versus cold colors

Soft versus hard materials

Slick versus varied textures

Cheerful and lively versus dull and drab

"Discriminating" taste versus tawdry

Expensive or luxurious versus shabby or spartan

Clothing (often used to tell others what a person wants them to believe about him/her)

Bold versus unobtrusive

Stylish versus nondescript

Position in the room

Protects or fortifies self in position by having objects such as desk or table between self and other person.

Takes an open or vulnerable position, such as in the center of the room, side by side on a sofa, or in a simple chair. Nothing between self and other person.

Takes an attacking or dominating position. May block exit from area or may maneuver other person into boxed-in position.

Moves about the room.

Moves in and out of other person's territory.

Stands when other person sits, or gets in higher position than other person.* (pp. 89–92)

Verbal Communications Skills

Strange as it may seem, we will initiate our discussion of verbal communications skills by discussing listening. Listening, however, is a prerequisite to effective verbal communicating. Listening also is implied in attending behavior, but because of its importance, we would emphasize the point again. Cavanaugh (1982) makes this point:

> Listening is the basis of a counselor's effectiveness. The one behavior that effective counselors do most is listen. Without listening, counselors cannot know who the person in counseling really is and, without this knowledge, cannot help him or her. Unfortunately, listening is one of the most difficult behaviors in which human beings participate. (p. 194)

Effective listening enables counselors to adroitly manipulate their verbal counseling skills. These skills include using attending responses that indicate to the client you are listening (i.e., "I understand," "I see") and what we might label as "stimulus responses," those that encourage the client to continue to comment (i.e., "Can you tell me more about that?" "Could you clarify that for me?" "Please continue if you wish.").

Effective listening is mandatory for feedback, another important verbal (as well as nonverbal) communication skill. Feedback is the verbalization of the counselor's perceptions and reactions to the client's behaviors, feelings, concerns, actions, expressions, and so forth. It offers the client the opportunity in turn to feedback-react—perhaps validate or expand on the counselor's feedback. It offers the counselor the opportunity to periodically summarize and validate what has transpired and ensure that both counselor and counselee are accurately "receiving" each other's messages, before moving further in the counseling process.

---

*From Gazda, George M., Asbury, Frank R., Balzer, Fred J., Childers, William C., and Walters, Richard P., *Human Relations Development*. Copyright © 1977 by Allyn and Bacon. Reprinted by permission.

Also important in verbal communications is the art of questioning. Skill in questioning involves timing, wording, and type of questions. The skillful counselor does not inject questions that will stop, alter or "slow down" a client's open discussion of a concern. Questions are injected to keep the discussion moving (i.e., "Why do you think they reacted that way to your behavior?"); to clarify (i.e., "What do you mean?" "Am I right in understanding you?"); and to validate (i.e., "How do you know? Give me an example.").

The type of question used should be appropriate to the desired outcome from asking it. Open questions (i.e., "How did you feel about that?") provide opportunities for the client to express feelings, provide greater detail, and gain new insights, while closed questions (i.e., "Will you go back next week?") get an answer rather than an evasive or rambling reply. The counselor may also decide when to use direct questions (i.e., "Tell me, are you an alcoholic?") or nondirect questions (i.e., "What do you think about alcoholism today?"), which do not directly identify the client with a problem or issue.

Effective communication is also facilitated by knowing what not to do. George and Cristiani (1995) list these barriers to communications:

1. Giving advice

2. Offering solutions

3. Moralizing and preaching

4. Analyzing and diagnosing

5. Judging or criticizing

6. Praising and agreeing; giving positive evaluations

7. Reassuring (pp. 126–128)

Diagnostic Skills

Other chapters in this book document the importance and the basic techniques of diagnosis. We would simply indicate in this section on counseling skills that effective counseling requires skill in accurately diagnosing and understanding the client, client concerns, and the relevant environmental influences. Counselors must therefore be skillful in the use of both standardized psychological measures and nonstandardized techniques for diagnosis.

Motivational Skills

The goals of counseling usually represent some form of behavior or attitudinal change. Client movement toward counseling goals will often be dependent on the skill of the counselor in motivating the client. This may require a sensitivity to cues that stimulate motivation for the client, or it may require the use of influence (see Table 5–5). Ivey et al. (1987) believe:

> When you become an active participant in the interview, you can influence and speed the change process. Through your knowledge of theory and skills, personal life experience, and specific understanding of the unique client and his or her culture, you can share more of yourself and your knowledge to the benefit of your client. (p. 78)

TABLE 5–5   Influencing Skills

Skill	Description	Function in Interview
Interpretation	Provides an alternative frame of reference from which the client may view a situation. May be drawn from a theory or from one's own personal observations. *Interpretation may be viewed as the core influencing skill.*	Attempts to provide the client with a new way to view the situation. The interpretation provides the client with a clear-cut alternative perception of "reality." This perception may enable a change of view which in turn may result in changes in thoughts, constructs, or behaviors.
Directive	Tells the client what action to take. May be a simple suggestion stated in command form or may be a sophisticated technique from a specific theory	Clearly indicates to clients what action counselors or therapists wish them to take. The prediction with a directive is that the client will do what is suggested.
Advice/information/ other	Provides suggestions, instructional ideas, homework, advice on how to act, think, or behave	Used sparingly, advice and related skills may provide client with new and useful information. Specific vocational information is an example of necessary use of this skill.
Self-disclosure	The interviewer shares personal experience from the past or may share present reactions to the client	Closely allied to feedback, this skill emphasizes counselor "I statements." Self-disclosure may build trust and openness leading to a more mutual relationship with the client.
Feedback	Provides clients with specific data on how they are seen by the counselor or by others	Provides concrete data that may help clients realize how others perceive behavior and thinking patterns, thus enabling an alternative self-perception.
Logical consequences	Explains to the client the logical outcome of thinking and behavior. "If, then."	Provides an alternative frame of reference for the client. This skill helps clients anticipate the consequences or results of their actions.
Influencing summary	Often used at or near the end of a session to summarize counselor comments, most often used in combination with the attending summarization	Clarifies what has happened in the interview and summarizes what the therapist has said. Designed to help generalization from the interview to daily life.

Management Skills

We conclude our discussion of the counseling skills that counselors should possess by noting the importance of the counselor's "management" of the counseling process. This includes, first of all, attention to the environment and physical arrangements in which the counseling takes place. Once the counseling process begins, the counselor has the responsibility for managing this process: keeping it moving, "on track," and progressing. A sense of both timing and time management are important. An awareness of the client's well-being and managing the process in this context are another kind of management task. Management also means managing your own contributions to the process, recognizing and working within your professional limitations. Finally, determining the point and method of termination plus any follow-up and evaluation are primarily the counselor's responsibilities.

SPECIAL COUNSELING POPULATIONS

Counselors in nearly all settings deal with a variety of individual problems and concerns. Because increasing attention is being given to certain populations, it seems appropriate to note several of these "special" clients.

Substance Abusers

Increases in the use of alcohol and drugs and the ill effects of the abuse of these substances are well publicized. These social ills are spelled out in such dramatic numbers as 9 million estimated alcoholics, 550,000 heroin addicts, and 4 million regular users of marijuana. Nor is the outlook for future generations bright, as data indicate 3 million teen alcoholics, 5 out of 10 adolescent users of marijuana, and 1 out of 10 having tried cocaine (U.S. Department of Education, 1986). Persons are considered abusers of any substance when it is used to the extent that it causes or threatens damage to the individual or society or both.

Individuals who abuse alcohol are labeled *alcoholics*. An alcoholic is an individual who has habitually consumed alcohol to the point where he or she can no longer control his or her intake of alcohol or stop drinking for any appreciable period of time. Although a variety of classification systems may be used, the American Psychiatric Association recognizes the following types of alcoholism:

> *Episodic excessive drinking.* If alcoholism is present and the individual becomes intoxicated as frequently as four times a year, the condition should be classified here. Intoxication is defined as a state in which the individual's coordination or speech is definitely impaired or his behavior is clearly altered.

> *Habitual excessive drinking.* This diagnosis is given to persons who are alcoholic and who either become intoxicated more than 12 times a year or are recognizably under the influence of alcohol more than once a week, even though not intoxicated.

> *Alcoholic addiction.* This condition should be diagnosed when there is direct or strong presumptive evidence that the patient is dependent on alcohol. If available, the best

directive evidence of such dependence is the appearance of withdrawal symptoms. The inability of the patient to go one day without drinking is presumptive evidence. When heavy drinking continues for three months or more it is reasonable to presume addiction to alcohol has been established. (Kinney & Leaton, 1978, p. 42)

Belkin (1988) points out:

Some drugs are inherently dangerous and may always be considered instances of drug abuse unless taken under the supervision of a physician. Heroin, a synthetic derivative of morphine, is a highly addictive substance with no legitimate medical uses. Crack, a derivative of cocaine, gained a deadly prominence during the mid-1980s. The hallucinogenic (psychedelic) drugs produce gross distortions of reality, hallucinations, and erratic behavior and thinking. Barbiturates and other depressant drugs produce a feeling of relaxation and blissfulness that enables the user to forget all the problems that must be faced in life. Such drugs are highly addictive and may result in fatality upon withdrawal. Cases of suicide under the influence of barbiturates are not uncommon. Amphetamines are stimulant drugs that result in great feelings of optimism as well as mania. They are used by adolescents as sleep inhibitors, appetite suppressants, and for relief of depression. Prolonged use of amphetamines may result in hallucinations, psychosis, and violent behavior.* (p. 322)

Beginning in the mid-1970s, alcohol has been the single most abused drug in adolescent culture. It is estimated that more than 3 million teenagers today are alcoholics, most of them enrolled in schools. No one knows exactly why this is, but it may represent an ironic adolescent rebellion against the prevailing adult acceptance of marijuana.

The manifest symptoms of alcohol abuse among teenagers are as evident or more evident than the symptoms of drug abuse, which at times may be obscure. The adolescent problem drinker is likely to have a high absentee rate, appear intoxicated in class, and fall behind in schoolwork. It is not uncommon to find a flask of alcohol concealed on the person of the student, and the student may even imbibe during the class itself, so strong is the drive and so weak the control. The counselor, rather than responding punitively, should recognize the serious medical-psychological nature of this problem and encourage the student to seek help.† (Belkin, 1988, p. 323)

The counselor may be involved in prevention, intervention, and crisis treatment or remediation. However, it is important to stress the importance of specialized training for counselors who are working with substance abusers. Kottler and Brown (1985) suggest that the reason

for studying a specialty such as drug counseling is that traditional therapeutic interventions tend not to work. Insight into the reasons underlying self-destructive behavior in the form of drug and alcohol abuse is not sufficient to alter the behavior. Clients with drug and alcohol problems are so immune and resistant to change that sometimes very dramatic and creative interventions must be found. (p. 241)

In addition to having a thorough, well-grounded understanding of the drug problem, he or she should also be engaged in a continual interaction with teachers, ministers, juvenile

*From Gary S. Belkin, *Introduction to Counseling,* 3rd ed. Copyright © 1988 Wm. C. Brown Communications, Inc., Dubuque, Iowa. All rights reserved. Reprinted by permission.

†From Gary S. Belkin, *Introduction to Counseling,* 3rd ed. Copyright © 1988 Wm. C. Brown Communications, Inc., Dubuque, Iowa. All rights reserved. Reprinted by permission.

authorities, industrial personnel managers, and others who can assist in the implementation of prevention, early intervention, and/or addictive treatment programs.

In many programs, both individual and group counseling are used. In some settings, counseling teams have been found to be effective for group counseling. It is also obviously important that counselors who work with drug and alcohol abuse have more than a superficial knowledge of the causes, symptoms, and potential outcomes of the problem. Furthermore, in many individual situations, medical treatment may be needed, and referral to or "teaming" with a psychiatrist may be necessary.

Counselors in all settings therefore need to be aware of the resources available for the treatment of substance abuse clients. These may include emergency clinics, specialized centers, hospital care (both inpatient and outpatient), halfway houses, crisis centers, and special assistance groups such as Alcoholics Anonymous and Narcotics Anonymous. Counselors working with such populations generally have a specialized knowledge of the pharmacological, physiological, psychological, and sociocultural aspects of the use of alcohol and drugs.

Women

In recent generations, considerable attention has been focused on the effects of sex-role stereotyping and its detrimental effects, particularly on women. Yet, according to Ohlsen (1983):

> there are many obstacles that block women from realizing their full potential as human beings. Today's woman has been socialized to live in a world which no longer has the same demands as the world of yesterday. The obstacles are multidimensional and complex; some are outside of the woman's control, i.e., sex, race, ethnicity, and social stereotypes. Others she can directly influence if she is able to interpret her life experiences in such a way that she becomes empowered to appreciate herself as a whole being. She can learn how to use these resources to influence change in her personal and career relationships. (p. 242)

Although federal and state legislation has sought to promote opportunities for women to achieve their potential by stimulating legal equality of the sexes, abundant evidence indicates a lack of consistency at both the national and state levels in the application and enforcement of such legislation.

Women are still encountering problems and stereotypes in achieving their sex-role identity and career destinies without the impediments of sexual bias. Maccoby and Jacklin (1974) point out some of the most common sex-role stereotypes accepted within U.S. society:

1. Females are more susceptible to persuasion than males.

2. Females have lower self-esteem.

3. Females excel in rote learning and simple repetitive tasks, whereas males perform better in tasks that require higher learning cognitive processing and the inhibition of previously learned responses.

4. Males are more analytic.

5. Females are more affected by heredity and males by the environment.

6. Females lack achievement motivation.

7. Females are more fearful, timid, and anxious.

8. Males are more active; females are passive.

9. Males are more competitive.

10. Males are dominant; females are dependent.

11. Females are more compliant.

12. Females demonstrate more nurturing behavior.

13. Females are more emotional.

14. Males are more aggressive.

15. Females have greater verbal ability; males have greater mathematical ability.

According to the extensive research review reported by Maccoby and Jacklin, only two stereotypes (numbers 14 and 15) have been supported by empirical evidence; however, all have popular support in U.S. society. Thus, the counselor's role in counseling women is often further complicated not only by the woman's perception of what is appropriate for her but also by society's suggestion that her opportunities are limited by her sex.

Another complicating factor in counseling women is the multiple role expectations held for women. Counselors must be particularly alert not to reinforce these biases through sexist behavior or verbalization. With increasingly greater numbers of women seeking counseling, especially in periods of career planning and decision making, there is a need to be alert that sexist counseling does not limit their career opportunities.

Rawlings and Carter (1977) suggest the following guidelines for nonsexist counseling:

1. The therapist is aware of his or her own values.

2. There are no prescribed sex-role behaviors.

3. Sex-role reversals in life-style are not labeled pathological.

4. Marriage is not regarded as any better an outcome of therapy for a female than for a male.

5. Females are expected to be as autonomous and assertive as males; males are expected to be as expressive and tender as females.

6. Theories of behavior based on anatomical differences are rejected.

7. The therapist does not use the power of his or her position to subtly reinforce or punish clients for exhibiting "appropriate" or "inappropriate" feminine or masculine behaviors.

8. Diagnoses are not based on a client's failure to achieve culturally prescribed sex-role behaviors.

9. Sex-biased testing instruments are not used. (pp. 51–53)

The counselor has the responsibility to help women understand their own values, abilities, aptitudes, and interests and to utilize these to develop their fullest potential. In so doing, the counselor must, as always, function as a nonbiased, nonstereotyping helper.

Ethnic Groups and Cross-Cultural Counseling

The United States has always been known as a country of great population diversity where many cultures have contributed to its greatness. Over the past 35 years, increasing attention has been given to the uniqueness and needs of these minority cultures, including through judicial decisions and legislative enactments. This increased national attention has also been reflected in the counseling profession, in which a noticeable increase in attention to the needs and issues of cross-cultural counseling has occurred over the past 20 years. Projected future increases in our cross-cultural diversity indicate a continuing and increasing need for counselors to become both cross-culturally conscious and competent.

Attending to these needs is further mandated by all the major associations that accredit the preparation of counselors (Council for the Accreditation of Counseling and Related Programs, Council on Rehabilitation Education, American Psychological Association, National Association for the Accreditation of Teacher Education, and all the regional accreditation associations).

Certainly, our often stated philosophical assumptions of the inherent worth and dignity of the individual, respect for the individual's uniqueness, the right of the individual to self-actualization, and so forth, would indicate our commitment to effective cross-cultural counseling. However, as a number of authoritative (usually minority) writers have noted, commitment, while important, does not in and of itself assure effectiveness in the counseling of minority clients. It is equally important that counselors be sensitive to and respectful of the uniqueness of these various populations as well and to recognize that these groups do not want to be mainstreamed, develop middle-class values, or be robbed of their individuality and dignity (Vacc & Wittmer, 1980).

In this same sense, Sue and Sue (1972), cited in Sue (1981), note that many of the traditional characteristics of counseling, such as client openness, verbal and emotional expressiveness, discussion of intimate aspects of their lives, and the counselor's unwillingness to take charge of the dialogue or decision-making process, are inconsistent with the expectancies and values of many minority groups.

Hall and Maloney (1983) ascribe much of the failure and ineffectiveness of mental health programs to the lack of recognition given to the needs of minority groups. Their review of the literature and conclusions pertaining to treatment of minority populations, as cited in Kottler and Brown (1985), are the following:

1. Minority clients are diagnosed as having more severe disturbances and pathological conditions than White persons—a not surprising finding, considering that most tests of mental illness are culturally biased and most diagnosticians are not members of minority groups.

2. Minority clients will tend to use mental health services only in cases of emergency or severe psychopathology, again skewing the perceptions of clinicians, who may be used to working with normal or neurotic Whites but only very disturbed minorities. It is a cultural norm, for instance, among South American populations to handle most psychological problems through the resources of the family and church, relying on counselors or therapists only in extreme cases.

3. Minority clients more often drop out of treatment prematurely, usually within the first six sessions (Sue, 1977). Whether this tendency is a function of poor motivation or a difference in how they are treated is not clear.

4. In inpatient settings, evidence does indicate that Black clients are treated differently from Whites, more often receiving stronger medication, seclusion, restraints, and other punitive "therapies" and less often receiving recreational or occupational therapy (Flaherty & Meagher, 1980).

5. The minority group attitudes toward psychological disturbances are markedly different from those of Whites, more often stressing the roles of organic factors. Hispanics have more faith in the power of prayer than in psychotherapy for healing what they believe are inherited illnesses (Edgerton & Karno, 1971). The expectations of minority clients are thus not conducive to success, since so often the faith and hope that are so important are not operating at high levels.

6. Many people feel more comfortable and prefer working with others whom they perceive as similar (particularly with regard to race or ethnic background). Yet there are relatively few trained minority counselors who are available to serve this need.

7. With minority clients, and particularly with those of the lower class, it is important that counselors adapt their strategies and interventions to cultural differences. Eye contact and attention patterns can be interpreted variously as resistance, passivity, or aggression, depending on the client's culture (Hall, 1976).

8. Counseling can be viewed as one form of social control because its goals are most often to help deviants better adjust to the cultural norms of the majority. For the minority client this sort of adjustment presents special problems, since more conflict can result from the clash between sub-cultural values and those of the majority. (pp. 260–261)

Broadly defined, multicultural counseling is a helping process that places the emphasis for counseling theory and practice equally on the cultural impressions of both the counselor and the client (Axelson, 1985). Within this context, counseling professionals must consider language differences that may exist between themselves and their culturally different clients (Lee, 1991).

> Multiculturalism is a pervasive force in modern society that acknowledges the complexity of culture. During the last 20 years, multiculturalism has become recognized as a powerful force, not just for understanding "exotic" groups but also for understanding ourselves and those with whom we work in a complicated social context. Multiculturalism has gained the status of a general theory, complementing other scientific theories to explain human behavior. (Pedersen, 1991, p. 6)
>
> Whether or not multiculturalism emerges as a truly generic approach to counseling and whether or not it emerges as a fourth force with an articulated impact on counseling equivalent to behaviorism, psychodynamics, and humanism, culture does provide a valuable metaphor for understanding ourselves and others. It is no longer possible for counselors to ignore their own culture or the culture of their clients. Until the multicultural perspective is understood as making the counselor's job easier instead of harder and increasing rather than decreasing the quality of a counselor's life, however, little real change is likely to happen. (Pedersen, 1991, p. 11)

It is especially important that counselors in schools be sensitive to the differing cultures represented there. This not only increases their effectiveness as professional counselors and makes them more acceptable and approachable to their minority students, but it also enables them to serve as adults modeling appropriate behaviors and attitudes toward all ethnic, cultural, and minority groups.

Further, school counselors in particular must be aware that minority children and adolescents are the most rapidly growing segment of the youth population but that there is little information available about their problems or needs (Gibbs, Huang, & Associates,

1989). Counselors who work with children have an added responsibility because children cannot control their environment. The understanding or lack of understanding demonstrated by others about cultural differences can influence the core of the child's developing personality. Children are in the early stages of cultural awareness and may not recognize that their experiences differ from others and that forms of discrimination may exist.

A major developmental task is to discover and integrate one's ethnicity, culture, and race as these affect oneself and others (Christensen, 1989). Children may internalize the beliefs of the majority about their own cultural group. One of the goals of culturally sensitive counselors is to foster the child's environment so that the emphasis is on the child's uniqueness and not on conformity with the norm (Anderson & Cranston-Gingras, 1991, p. 91).

Pedersen (1988) recommends that students in counselor preparation programs need to develop awareness that would require an individual to have

- ❖ ability to recognize direct and indirect communication styles;
- ❖ sensitivity to nonverbal cues;
- ❖ awareness of cultural and linguistic differences;
- ❖ interest in the culture;
- ❖ sensitivity to the myths and stereotypes of the culture;
- ❖ concern for the welfare of persons from another culture;
- ❖ ability to articulate elements of his or her own culture;
- ❖ appreciation of the importance of multicultural teaching;
- ❖ awareness of the relationships between cultural groups; and
- ❖ accurate criteria for objectively judging "goodness" and "badness" in the other culture. (p. 9)

The question must also be raised, What can practicing counselors do to interact effectively in the counseling relationship with minority counselees (assuming that the counselor is not a minority member)? Belkin (1981) suggests that counselors' understanding of nine special situations that he found commonly expressed by minority group members in a New York City school system will enable them to understand better and interact more effectively with the minority group client. These nine needs are as follows:

1. The Minority Group Client (MGC) needs to feel that he is perceived as an individual, rather than only as a member of a group.

2. The MGC wants to be able to retain his own identity as well as to function within the context of the larger society.

3. The MGC may tend to perceive the white counselor as being white above all other perceptions. This implies that whatever general stereotypical feelings about whites he has will be projected onto the counselor.

4. The MGC needs a sense of social mobility; he wants to be able to feel that he has an opportunity to rise above his present station in life. Often this hope has been tempered by the realization of the severe restraints that poverty imposes upon social advancement.

5. The MGC wants the emotional freedom to be able to express his own prejudices toward white people. He wants to be able to feel that the white counselor will not be overly threatened by this expression.

TABLE 5–6 Generic Characteristics of Counseling

Language	Middle Class	Culture
Standard English Verbal Communication	Standard English Verbal communication Adherence to time schedules (50-minute session) Long-range goals Ambiguity	Standard English Verbal communication Individual centered Verbal/emotional/behavioral expressiveness Client-counselor communication Openness and intimacy Cause-effect orientation Clear distinction between physical and mental well-being

Source: From D. W. Sue, *Counseling the Culturally Different: Theory and Practice*, p. 30. Copyright © 1981 John Wiley & Sons, Inc. Reprinted by permission of John Wiley & Sons, Inc.

6. The MGC wants the school, through its curriculum, its teachers, and its rules to relate to his world rather than to the world of "whitey."

7. The MGC sees things happening around him over which he feels no control. He wants to be better able to control his world, and thus his own destiny, but he is lacking many of the educational and psychological tools necessary for doing so.

8. The MGC often has less opportunity than his white counterpart to discuss home and family life problems. His loyalty to his family may deter him from discussing these with an outsider.

9. The MGC may see the school as the primary social institution (which he considers oppressive and non-responsive) and be inclined to act out his rage and anger within the school environment.* (pp. 455–456)

Sue (1981) presents sources of conflict and misinterpretation in cross-cultural counseling, as noted in Tables 5-6 and 5-7.

Sue (1978) also proposes a list of characteristics that distinguish culturally effective counselors:

1. Culturally effective counselors understand their own values and assumptions of human behavior and recognize that those held by others may differ.

2. Culturally effective counselors realize that "no theory of counseling is politically or morally neutral."

3. Culturally effective counselors understand that external sociopolitical forces may have influenced and shaped culturally different groups.

*From Gary S. Belkin, *Practical Counseling in the Schools,* 2nd ed. Copyright © 1981 Wm. C. Brown Communications, Inc., Dubuque, Iowa. All rights reserved. Reprinted by permission.

TABLE 5–7   Third World Group Variables

Language	Lower Class	Culture
	Asian Americans	
Bilingual background	Nonstandard English Action oriented Different time perspective Immediate, short-range goals Concrete, tangible, struc- tured approach	Asian language Family centered Restraint of feelings One-way communication from authority figure to person Silence is respect Advice seeking Well-defined patterns of interaction (concrete structured) Private versus public display (shame/disgrace/pride) Physical and mental well- being defined differently.
	Blacks	
Black language	Nonstandard English Action oriented Different time perspective Immediate, short-range goals Concrete, tangible, struc- tured approach	Black language Sense of "peoplehood" Action oriented Paranorm due to oppression Importance placed on non- verbal behavior
	Hispanics	
Bilingual background	Nonstandard English Action oriented Different time perspective Immediate, short-range goals Concrete, tangible, struc- tured approach	Spanish speaking Group-centered cooperation Temporal difference Family orientation Different pattern of commu- nication A religious distinction between mind/body
	American Indians	
Bilingual background	Nonstandard English Action oriented Different time perspective Immediate, short-range goals Concrete, tangible, struc- tured approach	Tribal dialects Cooperative not competitive individualism Present-time orientation Creative/experiential/ intuitive/nonverbal Satisfy present needs Use of folk or supernatural explanations

Source: From D. W. Sue, *Counseling the Culturally Different: Theory and Practice*, p. 30. Copyright ©
1981 John Wiley & Sons, Inc. Reprinted by permission of John Wiley & Sons, Inc.

4. Culturally effective counselors are able to share the world-view of their clients rather than being culturally encapsulated.

5. Culturally effective counselors are truly eclectic in their counseling, using counseling skills because of their appropriateness to the experiences and lifestyles of the culturally different.

"Minorities," as a label, implies less than full-time or "majority" membership in a society. It is important that counselors convey through their attitudes and actions that these populations are full, equal members of society. Because understanding alone will not accomplish the task, it is vitally important that counselors educate themselves about different ethnic peoples. The counselor must learn to communicate both verbally and nonverbally in a manner and style that is recognizable and comfortable for the client. The counselor must convey his or her own attitude of acceptance and respect for the ethnic client, and the counselor must genuinely feel this respect if he or she is to convey it successfully.

Older Adults

In the 1980s we became increasingly aware that our population was growing older, living longer and more actively, and becoming another special population for counseling services. Although in the past the elderly were in a sense often "out of sight, out of mind," it is clear that in the 1990s they are increasingly in the mainstream of public thought and activity. Popular books like *Old Friends* by Tracy Kielder (1993) and *The Fountain of Age* by Betty Friedan (1993) remind us of the increasing age of our population and awareness of this aging. (In the latter publication, it is noted that life expectancy in the United States has increased 30 years in this century and that in 1970–1985, the number of people over 65 increased by 30%!) As we approach the turn of the century, we can anticipate an elderly population (65 and older) of over 31 million. Further, this population will live and work longer and place greater demands on our health care system, including mental health needs.

The counseling needs of the elderly have been described by Blake and Peterson (1979), who draw the following conclusions:

1. Since the older old people (those over 75 years of age) are the fastest increasing part of the 65+ population, the demands for physical health services will be very great. These are the most expensive services, and the bulk of available funds for older people is most likely to go in that direction, rather than for retirement adjustment or other such programs oriented more toward the younger old. Since the physical needs are more obvious, counseling-type needs may require more action from counseling organizations if they are to be recognized and counselors' potential contributions better known.

2. When facts about the geographical distribution of older people are considered, we can see that all communities will have some older residents. (Even if there is an apartment building or block that has no older residents, there are almost certain to be many sons and daughters of older people. Some of these sons and daughters have concerns for their parents and often are involved in very serious problems related to them.) Demographic data or living patterns also suggest that some areas have proportionately more older people than other areas and have different demographic trends. This suggests a need for identifi-

cation of local data for planning in relation to local situations; over-reliance on national data or trends may be quite inappropriate.

3. Since the life expectancy of men is less than that of women, the potential clientele, generally speaking, will be women. The concerns of older women need special emphasis in the training of counselors and the design of service delivery. The greater number of older women may make it relatively easy to obtain funding for women-oriented programs. On the other hand, there is a considerable number of older men, and counseling as well as other service groups should guard against the neglect of these persons who might otherwise become a forgotten minority within a minority.

4. Services for "lonely" persons, or those living alone, are especially likely to have female clientele. There are more older women than men, but more of the older men are married than older women. This is because men tend to marry younger women, and more older men remarry than do older women. Proportionately, there are more older single women than men.

5. Most counseling for older people will be through public rather than private fee services. This is even more true of the older population than it is for the rest of the adult population and results from the substantially worsened financial condition of older people in general.

6. Existing counseling services such as the employment service or vocational rehabilitation can expect their client populations to be increasingly older. This suggests the possible need for additional aging-specific training of counselors in these programs. Such training may be needed for increased self-awareness of beliefs and values, possible special counseling techniques, referral sources, and possibly other factors particular to working with older people.

7. Counseling programs aimed at serving the general population of older persons can expect most potential clients to be physically able to travel to the service. But no program for older people can be truly inclusive unless it also has a capacity for having home delivery of service and a capacity for providing transportation assistance for those who require it. Five percent of the non-institutionalized older population is homebound and another 14 percent needs some human or mechanical aid in getting about.

8. The age to which older persons, on the average, can expect to live is greater than that for persons just born or that of the population in general. Data on life expectancy at birth are not appropriate for use with older persons. Counselors can better assist middle-aged or older clients in life planning by using the most relevant demographic data available. Counselors can help allay the mistaken beliefs about life expectancy that some older clients or their families may have.

9. Demographic data differ substantially between sexes and among racial groups. This implies that at least in some instances sex- and race-specific data are more helpful for clear understanding than general data. General demographic data are not always accurate in reflecting the condition of specific subgroups within the population, and counselors sometimes need group-specific data.

10. In all respects except age itself, older people are as different from each other as from any other group. In fact, the differences between people may be accentuated with age and the indicators of central tendency less meaningful. In wealth and health, for example, the differences among the old are the most extreme of any age group. Only among the old are found both newlyweds and couples who have been married for 60 years. Counselors are accustomed to viewing people as individuals, but there is no group for which this is more essential than for the extremely diverse older population.

11. Mental health problems of older adults are of such magnitude that the best hope for substantial improvement is to change the general psychosocial milieu in which we age. This suggests that counselors should be social activists working against factors such as ageism that mitigate against mental health. It also suggests a training role for professional counselors fostering an improved quality of relationships between older persons and those with whom they are in contact: children, friends, neighbors, and providers of all kinds of services. The level of self-help within the community of older persons can be raised by using appropriately prepared counselors as trainers for large numbers of peer counselors.* (pp. 223–224)

For most older Americans, one of the significant transitions of that period of their life is the move from work to retirement. For many retirees, adjusting to life without work is difficult because they feel a loss of status; workers are more valued in our society than nonworkers; for many it means a loss of planned involvement with other people; and some have developed so few supplemental leisure time/recreational activities that life suddenly becomes boring or meaningless because they have excess time on their hands. But there is promise of a better transition for these older adults, and this promise appears to rely heavily on counseling.

As employee assistance programs (EAPs) are increasingly helping older workers plan for their retirements and make psychological adjustments, such assistance is becoming an increasingly significant employee benefit.

In general, most older adults face a series of major and traumatic changes in their twilight years, including these:

❖ Retirement from work and the status, relationships, and motivations associated with one's job

❖ The loss of one's spouse

❖ The decline of physical and often mental capacity and well-being

❖ A decline in financial security

❖ A decline in mobility—not just their own physical ability but also a time when they can no longer drive, which in itself may increase one's isolation

Schlossberg (1984), in discussing adults (including retirees) in transition, depicts the process in Figure 5–4. She then describes a detailed look at the process as outlined in Table 5–8.

In their discussion of counseling with the elderly living in public housing, Leung and Eargle (1980) conclude:

Counselors who work with the elderly must (a) be aware of specific circumstances in the living environment of the elderly, (b) be aware of the particular psychological factors of anxiety, loss, and interpersonal struggles of the elderly client, (c) be aware of the need to carefully build a trusting relationship, and (d) be able to adapt general counseling techniques to specific concerns important to the elderly. With an increasing population of elderly persons, there will be

---

*Reprinted from R. Blake and D. Peterson, "*Module I: Demographic Aspects of Aging: Implications for Counseling*" in M. L. Ganikos, *Counseling the Aged: A Training Syllabus for Educators,* 1979, pp. 223–224. © American Counseling Association. Reprinted with permission. No further reproduction authorized without written permission of the American Counseling Association.

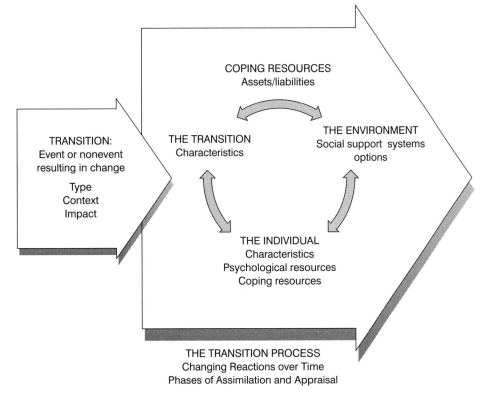

FIGURE 5–4 The Individual in Transition
Source: From Schlossberg, N. K. *Counseling Adults in Transition,* p. 68. Copyright © 1984 Springer Publishing Company, Inc., New York 10012. Used by permission.

an increasing need for counselors who are able to work with the elderly. Counselors need to become sensitive to the needs of the elderly and prepare themselves to serve this important segment of today's society. (p. 445)

Counselors will thus have the opportunities to meet, primarily through community services, the needs of another distinct and worthy segment of our population. Counselors working with older clients must again exhibit acceptance, openness, and respect of clients and their values. Even the oldest client must be permitted to look ahead and plan for a different future if this is the client's desire. If a lack of awareness and attitudes is not inhibiting, counselors can help older clients find new meanings and roles in life.

Business and Industry

The 1970s and 1980s witnessed a steady broadening of the opportunities for counselors to function in a variety of settings. This pattern is due in part to organizations, agencies, and special populations recognizing that they share needs and concerns in common with other

TABLE 5–8 The Individual in Transition: A Detailed Look

The Transition (Event or Nonevent Resulting in Change)	Coping Resources (Balance of Assets and Liabilities)			The Transition Process (Reactions over Time for Better or for Worse)
	Variables Characterizing the Transition	Variables Characterizing the Individual	Variables Characterizing the Environment	
Type Anticipated Unanticipated Nonevent Chronic hassle	*Event or nonevent characteristics* Trigger Timing	Personal and demographic characteristics Socioeconomic status Sex role	Social support Types: intimate, family unit, friendship network, institution	**Phases of Assimilation** Pervasiveness Disruptions Integration, for better or for worse
Context Relationship of person to transition Setting in which transition occurs	Source Role change Duration Previous experience with a similar transition Concurrent stress	Age and stage of life State of health Psychological resources Ego development Personality Outlook	Functions: affect, affirmation, aid, feedback Measurement: convoy Options Actual Perceived	**Appraisal** Of transition, resources, results Of preoccupation vs. life satisfaction
Impact Relationships Routines Assumptions Roles	*Assessment*	Commitments and values Coping responses Functions: Controlling situation, meaning, or stress Strategies: Information seeking, direct action, inhibition of action, intrapsychic behavior	Utilized Created	

Source: From Schlossberg, N. K. *Counseling Adults in Transition*, p. 108. Copyright © 1984 Springer Publishing Company, Inc. New York 10012. Used by permission.

populations and settings where these needs and concerns are recognized and dealt with. Increasingly, business and industrial organizations, and their work forces, have realized that they may benefit, from both a corporate and individual viewpoint, from programs of counseling assistance. Certainly, the development of EAPs has provided increased opportunities for counselors and other helping professionals to assist individuals in their work settings.

Brammer et al. (1989) indicate:

> Although EAPS focus primarily on alcoholism and chemical dependency, the primary purpose of many programs is to provide assistance with psychological, family, legal, and financial difficulties. The key functions of EAPs are prevention as well as early identification and treatment of employee problems. Corporate motivation to establish such programs is economic as well as humane in that employee problems impact on safety, performance, waste, medical, absenteeism, and replacement training costs. (p. 321)

Toomer (1982) reports a survey of the primary work settings of 1,000 counseling psychologists in which 2.94% were employed in manufacturing (business settings). An additional 7.84% were employed in consulting (individual or firms). Forrest (1983) also notes that EAPs in business and industry are increasing, transforming, and offering new and expanded work opportunities for counselors. He adds that the essential components for an effective EAP program as described in the literature by Busch (1981), Dickman and Emener (1982), and Good (1982) include these:

1. Early intervention and crisis assistance
2. Self-referral, peer referral, supervisory referral
3. Confidentiality and easy access
4. Management/leadership/union support
5. Supervisor and union representative training
6. Written policies distributed to all participants
7. Insurance involvement
8. Treatment separated from work evaluation
9. Staffing by trained helping professionals
10. Breadth of service components
11. Follow-up and evaluation (p. 106)

Forest (1983) adds that for counselors in all work settings, the immediate implications pertain to employment opportunity, availability of treatment, and issues related to territoriality.

Certainly counselors can provide worthwhile programs to facilitate the career development and placement or replacement of workers and management personnel. Personnel training, especially in human relationship and communications skills, is another area of promise. Retirement counseling is also an area of potential counseling service.

Toomer (1982) suggests possible roles and functions in business and industry, as outlined in Figure 5–5.

Cristiani and Cristiani (1979) feel that it is apparent that counselors could become a vital part of many business and industrial organizations. The problem seems to be one of lack of information and resources. Should this be the case, here are a few additional sug-

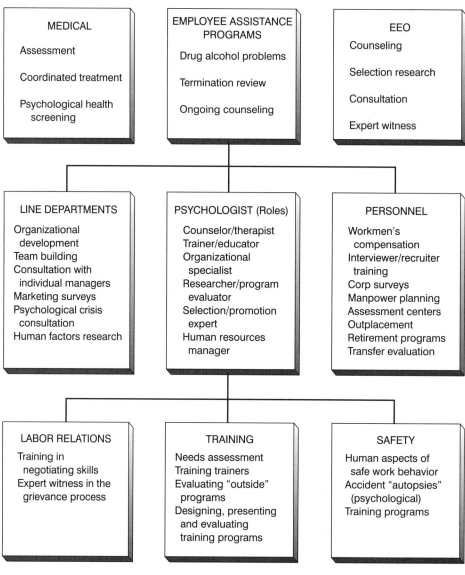

FIGURE 5–5 Counseling Psychologists in Business and Industry:
Roles and Relationships
Source: From J. E. Toomer, *Counseling Psychologists in Business and Industry,* p. 13, 1982. Copyright © 1984 Sage Publications. Reprinted by permission from Sage Publications and author.

gestions to those with counseling backgrounds for approaching jobs in the industrial or business setting:

1. Become familiar with the American Society for Training and Development (ASTD); read the ASTD Journal and attend meetings of local chapters. This is an excellent way to meet those people who have interests similar to yours and who are working in the field. They may be able to give you specific suggestions about approaching the job market in your location, possibly providing leads and contacts in your area.

2. Conduct library research in the area of training and development; become familiar with readings by major business authors.

3. Take business courses in industrial psychology and management. Strengthen your background in the behavioral sciences if needed.

4. Do not be intimidated by employers who try to discourage you because of your lack of experience in the business world. You have the essential skills and expertise that are part of training and development in the business community. The first person to convince is yourself! (p. 169)

AIDS Patients

Acquired immunodeficiency syndrome (AIDS) was recognized and labeled a little more than a decade ago. Since that time it has become one of the most feared of diseases and health epidemics. The rapid spread of AIDS, as cases double every 10–12 months (Mason, 1985), and its incurability and rapid fatality rate have caused widespread public concern. In 1991 the Centers for Disease Control reported 161,073 cases of AIDS in the United States and estimated 450,000 Americans would be diagnosed with AIDS in 1993. The distribution of those affected by this disease is noted in Table 5–9.

AIDS is also a disease of the young, with 22% of the victims in their twenties, 47% in their thirties, and 22% in their forties.

As noted by Hoffman (1991):

Although a number of promising treatments have been developed and life spans have been increased due to these interventions, at present there is no cure and no way to restore the immune systems of those infected. Consequently, HIV infection can be viewed as a debilitating, progressive disease with widespread and devastating effects. (p. 468)

Hoffman (1991) goes on to point out:

Statistics can only hint at the enormity of this crisis and its consequences. Every aspect of a person's life is affected. The progression of HIV infection is associated with deterioration (physical and neurological), changes in day-to-day functioning, loss of employment, stigma, and in many cases, exposure of one's life-style around the issues of sexuality and/or drug use. At its simplest, AIDS is about loss. It is about the loss of one's health, vitality, sensuality, and career—and most profoundly, the letting go of the future as one had envisioned it. (p. 468)

As patients and their close friends and relatives increasingly seek counseling to help them cope with the emotional stresses resulting from AIDS, counselors must become more knowledgeable about the disease and the psychological reactions most likely to occur. Initial shock and panic are typical reactions of those learning they have contracted AIDS.

TABLE 5–9 Distribution of AIDS Cases by Risk Group

Group	Percentage of Diagnosed AIDS Cases
Homosexual/bisexual contact	59
Intravenous drug use (heterosexual males/females)	22
Male homosexual/bisexual and IV drug users	7
Heterosexual contact	5
Blood transfusions	2
Other	5

Source: U.S. Centers for Disease Control (1991).

Price, Omizo, and Hammett (1986) suggest that counselors working with AIDS clients should also be aware of (a) the victim's extreme sense of isolation and alienation, (b) the severe drop in self-esteem that accompanies this condition, (c) the use of denial, permitted as a coping strategy as long as medical treatment is not compromised, and (d) the pitfalls of personalization and the tendency to overidentify with the client.

In addition to victims of AIDS as clients, a second population of clients from high-risk groups often seek counseling. Risk reduction counseling has three phases according to Mejta (1987): "(a) risk assessment, (b) education about AIDS, risk behaviors, and "safer" behaviors, and (c) learning and maintaining new behavior patterns" (p. 10).

> The objectives of psychological interventions with AIDS clients, as outlined by Namir (1986), should include: (a) to help these clients come to terms with the diagnosis and its meaning; (b) to improve the person's quality of life—to focus on life and living, not only on death and dying; and (c) to help the person feel more in control of his or her life and illness. Psychological interventions should be sensitive to the individual's feelings, reactions, and experiences related to the AIDS diagnosis, the process of adjusting to it, and self-reported concerns and needs. Typically, both emotional and practical support is needed. (Mejta, 1987, p. 5)

Abuse Victims

Domestic violence characterized by spouse abuse and/or child abuse is rampant in the United States, and the personal, social, and economic costs are inestimable. Reports indicate that one-third of all married people engage in spouse abuse, while approximately 1 million children are annually abused by their parents (Hershenson & Power, 1987). As public awareness of the extent of the problem has increased, so have efforts to provide assistance and refuge for the victims.

Spouse abuse is frequently associated with poverty, substance abuse, and career disappointments. For abused spouses, the most popular response has been providing shelters and crisis lines. Most of the personnel for these settings are drawn from the ranks of paraprofessionals and volunteer workers, although Roberts (1984) notes that approximately 44% did employ such helping professionals as counselors, social workers, and/or psychologists on their staffs.

In recent years the public has become more aware of the nature and extent of child abuse in the United States. Even so, we suspect the real extent of this national tragedy is largely unreported. Not only does child abuse destroy the joys and memories of youth, but its damaging aftereffects can cause psychological problems throughout the victim's adult life. The federal government and all states have passed legislation to stop child abuse. School counselors are mandated reporters of suspected child abuse in most states and, as a result, can be penalized for failing to report such cases.

Baker (1992) suggests steps as follows in reporting child abuse as a school system employee:

1. Report suspected cases of child abuse to the building principal immediately; that is, children under age eighteen who exhibit evidence of serious physical or mental injury not explained by the available medical history as being accidental; sexual abuse or serious physical neglect, if injury, abuse, or neglect has been caused by the acts or omissions of the child's parents or by a person responsible for the child's welfare.

2. Each building principal will designate a person to act in his or her stead when unavailable.

3. The principal may wish to form a team of consultants with whom to confer (e.g., school nurse, home and school visitor, counselor) before making an oral report to public welfare service representatives. This should be done within twenty-four hours of the first report.

4. It is not the responsibility of the reporter to prove abuse or neglect. Reports must be made in good faith, however.

5. Any person willfully failing to report suspected abuse may be subject to school board disciplinary action. (p. 222)

Additionally:

school counselors are the central helpers in any school system's child abuse prevention efforts. They must recognize the symptoms of possible abuse and their legal reporting responsibilities. They must also recognize their responsibility to take a leadership role in developing and implementing an effective program of child abuse prevention. Allsopp and Prosen (1988) emphasize the increasing need for counselors to provide appropriate training and information for school personnel who might be involved in cases of suspected child abuse. They discuss a model program which has been successfully implemented in the training of over 2,000 teachers and administrators to deal with sexual abuse cases. The program consisted of: (a) information related to offenders, victims, and non-offending family members; (b) present laws and proposed legislation; (c) requirements and procedures for school systems in reporting suspected child sexual abuse; and (d) available community resources for victim's use. Ninety-eight percent of teachers reported that the program increased their awareness of victims and offenders; 92 percent stated that the program provided them with a clearer understanding of the school system's procedures for reporting child sexual abuse; 93 percent expressed they had increased their knowledge of county services currently available to victims; and 98 percent reported that as a result of participation in the program, they felt more adequately prepared to deal with a situation in which a child was sexually abused.* (Gibson et al., 1993, p. 109)

*From Gibson, Robert L., Mitchell, Marianne H., and Basile, Sherry K., *Counseling in the Elementary School: A Comprehensive Approach.* Copyright © 1993 by Allyn and Bacon. Reprinted by permission.

Further, the American School Counselor Association (1988) encourages its members to participate in the implementation of the following guidance and counseling activities:

❖ Coordinate team efforts involving the principal, teacher, counselor, school nurse, protective services workers, and the child.

❖ Serve as a support to teachers, and other school personnel, especially if the child was abused as a result of a report sent home about the child from school.

❖ Emphasize the non-punitive role of protective services and allay fears that the child will be removed immediately from the home.

❖ Facilitate the contact between the child and the social worker. The issue of confidentiality and re-establishing the trust of the child after the report is made is critical to the child-counselor relationship.

❖ Provide ongoing counseling services to the child and/or family after the crisis is over, or refer to an appropriate community agency.

❖ Provide programs designed to help prevent child abuse. Counselors can help children with coping skills and ways to prevent their own abuse by improving their self-concepts, being able to recognize stress in their parents, and being sensitive to cues that abuse may occur if their own behavior is not changed.

❖ Help teachers and administrators in understanding the dynamics of abuse and abusive parents, and in developing a nonjudgmental attitude so they can react more appropriately in crisis situations.

❖ Provide developmental workshops and/or support groups for parents focusing upon alternative methods of discipline, handling anger and frustration, and enhancing parenting skills. (p. 263)

In recent years we have also been made much more aware of the incidence of sexual abuse as the victims come forward and discuss the harmful effects of their experiences. A statistical summary by Finkelhor (1984) makes the following points:

❖ Incidence research shows that between 8% to 38% of women and 5% to 9% of men in the United States have been victimized.

❖ Sexual abuse is an international concern, although specific statistics are not available.

❖ Sexual abuse is committed primarily by men (Finkelhor, 1979; Bell & Weinberg, 1978). Among victims, 95% of women and 80% of men are abused by men.

❖ Sexual abuse essentially, by definition, is harmful.

❖ The most common ages of victims are 8 through 12, with many cases outside of that span.

❖ Stepfathers may be five times as likely to victimize a daughter sexually than fathers are, although other family members (brothers, uncles, grandfathers) could be offenders.

❖ Most female victimization occurs within the family.

❖ Boys are more likely to be abused outside the family than are girls. (Rencken, 1989, p. 3)

We can only assume that the extent of reported sexual abuse is minimal and that because of guilt, stigma, and fear, many, many incidents continue to go unreported.

Regardless, the effect can be traumatic. Cooney (1991) indicates that the emotional effects of childhood sexual abuse include the *loss of childhood* since those who have been abused experience the adult world of sexuality; *guilt* and a sense of being responsible for the abuse; *low self-esteem* and the feeling that they are not as good as their peers; many kinds of *fear; confusion; depression; anger; inability to trust others; helplessness;* and *altered attitudes toward sexuality.*

Again, it is important to note the role of prevention programs. Such programs require careful planning and a coordinated effort involving school and community agency counselors, social workers, school teachers, administrators, nurses, and significant community groups. Parents obviously should be involved and educated regarding their responsibilities. Children themselves need to be educated and informed regarding sources of help if needed. The local media should also be requested to fully publicize the efforts to prevent child sexual abuse.

Sexual abuse is, of course, not limited to children. Adolescents are also frequently victimized, and rape, including date rape, is being increasingly reported. While prevention is the desired antidote, we must still be prepared to assist the victims through crisis lines, crisis centers, and specialized rape assistance programs.

The victims of child abuse may be placed in temporary shelters or, in extreme cases, foster homes. The current trend, however, is to hold the family together if at all possible. An effort is made to give the parents

> the support they need to become adequate parents. Rather than punish the parents, the goal is to help them break the cycle of abuse. One approach is to use groups to teach effective parenting to those whose own parents were usually disastrous role models. The abusing parents are encouraged to call staff of the mental health agency when they feel the impulse to hurt their children. It must be understood by all concerned that effective parenting does not come naturally but must be learned in a step-by-step fashion. (Schmolling, Youkeles, & Burger, 1985, pp. 47–48)

Counselors functioning in those settings serving abused spouses or children need special skills in individual and group counseling and crisis and short-time interventions, plus a knowledge of marriage and family dynamics.

Gays and Lesbians

In recent generations the counseling profession has become more aware of issues relating to the counseling of lesbian women and gay men. Too, as many of this population are now readily acknowledging their sexual orientations and moving more openly into the public mainstream, more members of this group can be expected to seek assistance from counseling professionals.

Given that the research on the lesbian and gay populations to date is complex, often contradictory, and, in some cases, biased as well, counselors may find it confusing to find agreed-upon guidelines for providing effective counseling. However, in practice, many of the profession's proven approaches would appear to provide a basis for assistance inasmuch as many of the common problems faced by gays and lesbians are not unique to this population. These include the problems of (a) societal prejudice, (b) family conflict, (c) peer ridicule and rejection, and (d) health fears (especially AIDS).

In counseling, then, we would assume that awareness, acceptance, and understanding would provide a basic foundation. Going beyond these basics, in assisting adolescent gays and lesbians, Teague (1992) points out that

> homosexuality as a life-style can be many things to many people. For the gay or lesbian adolescent, it can lead to confusion, isolation, or a number of other serious problems such as attempted suicide. As a means of finding support and accurate information, these teens may seek out a mental health professional. (p. 422)

He concludes that

> effective intervention with gay and lesbian adolescents requires that mental health counselors take a positive approach that entails more than a simple acceptance of homoerotic people and life-styles. It requires a willingness to work with clients in accordance with the realities of a gay life-style rather than non-gay interpretations of those realities. It is a time to move beyond merely helping gays cope and adjust. As mental health counselors, we need to help them develop innovative and satisfying ways to grow as gay people. (Moses & Hawkins, 1982, as seen in Teague, 1992, p. 422)

In assisting gay and lesbian clients across a range of ages, Fassinger (1991) suggests

> a variety of theoretical approaches and techniques may be effective with gay and lesbian clients. Cognitive approaches, for example, may be useful in overcoming negative thinking and self-talk about gayness, whereas client-centered approaches may have great utility in encouraging expression of repressed affect. Gestalt "empty chair" techniques may be particularly effective in bringing into awareness all sides of the ambivalence and confusion about gay and non-gay affiliation, as well as helping individuals vicariously confront family, friends, co-workers and others about their identity. Feminist approaches are empowering in their examination of oppression and sex-role socialization, as well as their emphasis on equality in relationships (including the therapeutic alliance). Bibliotherapy is particularly important for this population, because so little is known about healthy gay people and life-styles due to societal invisibility and the lack of diverse role models. Family/systems approaches and couples counseling are important for working with relationship issues, and group therapy is an effective means for reducing shame and alienation and developing social support. Cross-cultural approaches provide an important foundation for work with culturally diverse gay and lesbian clients. Overall, any theoretical approach or intervention should be carefully examined and reexamined throughout implementation for inherent bias and should be applied with sensitivity and professional self-awareness. (pp. 171–172)

Counselors should anticipate gays and lesbians among their clientele at all ages, and be comfortable as well as knowledgeable in working with this population. The latter includes understanding the lifestyle- and gender-specific issues common at different stages across the life span of gays and lesbians. In some settings and situations, counselors may find it useful to identify therapists who are themselves gays or lesbians for referral or consultative purposes.

SUMMARY

Counseling is the heart of the counselor's activity. Although there is general agreement in broadly defining counseling, a variety of theoretical concepts have emerged over the years. Traditional approaches such as psychoanalytic and client-centered theories are still popular, but in recent generations, the behavioral theory, the rational-emotive therapy theory, the reality therapy theory, and the integrative theory have attracted followers. However, as noted in concluding our discussion of theory, counselors may still opt for the eclectic approach, one that gives the option of selecting from any and all the existing theories.

The counseling process initially focuses on relationship establishment, then seeks to identify and explore the client's problem, with the objective of establishing client goals. The process then proceeds to the planning and problem-solving stage and, finally, to the applying of the solution and termination of the counseling relationship. Although these stages tend to blend into each other, they serve as a guide to a logical sequence of events for the counseling process. The effective application of the process is dependent on the basic counseling skills required of the counselor.

More and more attention has been given to the counselor's responsibility and need for special preparation in dealing with our population's diversity and a range of special problems. Recent generations have also noted increased usage of group counseling and other group techniques by counselors. These will be discussed in the next chapter.

DISCUSSION QUESTIONS

1. What theoretical orientation would you prefer for your own counselor?

2. How can counseling help improve the quality of life for (a) children of elementary school age and (b) the elderly of postretirement age?

3. When, or under what circumstances, would you encourage a friend to see a counselor?

4. How do you interact in establishing a relationship when you meet someone for the first time? What impresses you most about an individual when you meet them for the first time?

5. What are the differences and similarities among advising, providing guidance, and/or counseling an individual?

6. Discuss counseling as a growth enhancement and/or development activity.

7. Discuss "preventive counseling."

CLASS ACTIVITIES

1. Interview a practicing counselor regarding his or her theoretical orientation and how he or she determined that this theory was the most appropriate.

2. Identify the counseling theory that at this early point in your training, you feel would be most appropriate for you. Share your rationale with others in the class who have selected the same theory.

3. Conscientiously practice the basic counseling skills of attending behavior in your interactions with others for a week. Report your reactions and/or results.

4. Keep a log noting the effectiveness of your communication skills with others over a 3-day period. What are the implications of your findings?

5. Organize the class into groups of three. Each individual in the triad is to alternate role-playing the part of counselor, client, and observer. The client is to role-play a client with a problem; each of the three role-playing counselors is to practice, in the first round, the skill of attending behavior;

in the second round, attending behavior plus reflection of feelings; in the third round, attending behavior, reflection of feeling, and facilitative communications. The observer, in addition to observing the process, is to evaluate the effectiveness of the counselor in practicing the basic skill or skills, in addition to being the time keeper for each session (approximately 5–7 minutes for the first round, 10 minutes for the second and third rounds). After the conclusion of each counseling "session," counselor and client should also assess the process (allow about 15–20 minutes after each session for this activity).

SELECTED READINGS

Atkinson, D. R. (1985). A meta-review of research on cross-cultural counseling and psychotherapy. *Journal of Multicultural Counseling and Development, 13*, 138–153.

Atkinson, D., Morteu, G., and Sue, D. (1983). *Counseling American minorities: a cross-cultural perspective* (2nd ed.). Dubuque, IA: Brown.

Brammer, L. (1988). *The helping relationship* (4th ed.). Englewood Cliffs, NJ: Prentice-Hall.

Claibourne, C., & Ibrahim, F. (Eds.). (1987). Counseling and violence [Special issue]. *Journal of Counseling and Development, 65*, 338–390.

Cooney, J. (1988). Child abuse: A developmental perspective. *Counseling and Human Development, 20*, 1–10.

Dworkin, S. H., & Gutierrez, F. J. (1992). *Counseling gay men & lesbians: Journey to the end of the rainbow*. Alexandria, VA.: American Association for Counseling and Development.

Dworkin, S. H., & Pincu, L. (1993). Counseling in the era of AIDS. *Journal of Counseling and Development, 71*, 275–281.

Erickson, S. H. (1990). Counseling the irresponsible AIDS client: Guidelines for decision-making. *Journal of Counseling and Development, 68*, 454–455.

Hill, C., Helmer, J., Tichenor, V., Spiegel, S., O'Grady, K., & Perry, E. (1988). Effects of therapist response made in brief psychotherapy. *Journal of Counseling Psychology, 35*, 222–233.

Ivey, A., & Goncalves, O. (1986). Developmental therapy: Integrating developmental processes into the clinical practice. *Journal of Counseling and Development, 66*, 406–413.

Keeling, R. P. (1993). HIV-disease: Current concepts. *Journal of Counseling and Development, 71*, 261–274.

LaFromboise, T. (1988). American Indian mental health policy. *American Psychologist, 33*, 388–397.

Okun, B. (1987). *Effective helping: Interviewing and counseling techniques* (3rd ed.). Monterey, CA: Brooks/Cole.

Romano, J. L. (1992). Psychoeducational interventions for stress management and well-being. *Journal of Counseling and Development, 71*, 199–202.

Shaikur, B. (1988). The measurement and treatment of client anger in counseling. *Journal of Counseling and Development, 66*, 361–365.

Smith, E., & Vasquez, M. (Eds.). Cross-cultural counseling. *The Counseling Psychologist, 13*, 531–720.

Tracey, T., & Dundon, M. (1988). Role anticipation and preparations over the course of counseling. *Journal of Counseling Psychology, 35*, 3–14.

Weinrach, S. (1987). Microcounseling and beyond: A dialogue with Allen Ivey. *Journal of Counseling and Development, 65*, 532–537.

Ybarra, S. (1991). Women and AIDS: Implications for counseling. *Journal of Counseling and Development, 69*, 285–287.

RESEARCH OF INTEREST

Atkinson, D. R. (1985). A meta-review of research on cross-cultural counseling and psychotherapy. *Journal of Multicultural Counseling and Development, 13,* 138–153.

Abstract

    Analyzes four major reviews of the research on the effects of race on counseling and psychotherapy.

Ford, D. Y., Harris, J. J., III, & Schuerger, J. M. (1993). Racial identity development among gifted black students: Counseling issues and concerns. *Journal of Counseling and Development, 71,* 409–417.

Abstract

    Discusses a review of the literature regarding the paucity of information pertaining to culture-specific issues of being African American and gifted. Psychological issues of being African American and gifted and perspectives on racial identity development are presented. Components of counseling interventions are indicated.

Haines, A. (1992). Comparison of cognitive-behavioral stress management techniques with adolescent boys. *Journal of Counseling and Development, 70,* 600–605.

Abstract

    Explores the effectiveness of two cognitive-behavioral interventions in helping adolescent boys cope with stress and other types of negative emotions. Reductions in anxiety, anger, anger expression, and depression are reported.

Holloway, E. L., & Wampold, B. E. (1986). Relation between conceptual level and counseling-related tasks: A meta-analysis. *Journal of Counseling Psychology, 33,* 310–319.

Abstract

    Uses meta-analysis to review 24 studies that applied conceptual systems theory (CST) (a) to investigate the effect of counselor's conceptual level (CL) on the counselor's performance and (b) to investigate the matching of CL and environmental structure. Results corroborate the predictive power of CST in the context of the counseling situation. The prediction that counselors who were matched with a compatible environment (i.e., low CLs with high structure and high CLs with low structure) would perform better than those who were mismatched is corroborated. Low CLs generally performed significantly better in more highly structured environments, whereas high CLs showed only a slight improvement in their matched low-CL environment. Due to the lack of standardization in the task stimulus, it was unclear whether higher CLs generally performed better than low CLs. Methodological, conceptual, and training issues are discussed.

Neimeyer, G. J., & Gonzales, M. (1982, August). *Duration, satisfaction, and perceived effectiveness of cross-cultural counseling.* Paper presented at the Annual Convention of the American Psychological Association, Washington, DC.

Abstract

    It is generally acknowledged that racial groups differ in their values, beliefs, and behaviors as well as counseling needs, but evidence is mixed as to the effects of racial differences in the counseling process. A sample of 70 clients participated in a study to examine the differences in the duration, satisfaction, and effectiveness resulting from combinations of white and nonwhite counselors and clients. Results indicate that white counselors provided fewer sessions, and nonwhite clients expressed lower levels of overall satisfaction with counseling regardless of counselor race. No differences in counseling effectiveness were observed. White clients seeing white counselors attributed their change more to counseling than to other outside factors. The results suggest that racial factors may be associated with the duration, satisfaction, and attribution of perceived change in counseling, but not with perceived effectiveness.

Warren, R., Smith, G., & Velten, E. (1984). Rational-emotive therapy and the reduction of interpersonal anxiety in junior high school students. *Adolescence, 19*, 893–902.

Abstract

Evaluates the effectiveness of rational-emotive therapy and rational-emotive imagery in 59 junior high school students assigned to rational-emotive therapy without imagery (RET), rational-emotive therapy with imagery (REI), relationship-oriented counseling (ROC), and control (WLC) groups. The RET and REI groups are rated on sociometric measures as significantly less interpersonally anxious.

Weisz, J. R., Weiss, B., Alicke, M. D., & Klotz, M. L. (1987). Effectiveness of psychotherapy with children and adolescents: A meta-analysis for clinicians. *Journal of Consulting and Clinical Psychology, 55*, 542–549.

Abstract

Conducts meta-analysis of 108 well-designed outcome studies using 4- through 18-year-old subjects to examine effectiveness of psychotherapy with children and adolescents. Overall, findings reveal significant, durable effects of treatment that differ somewhat with client age and treatment method but are reliably greater than zero for most groups, most problems, and most methods.

Chapter 6

Group Techniques
for Counselors

The rugged individualist has been extolled over the years in U.S. history. The sagas and accomplishments of Daniel Boone, Davey Crockett, "Wild Bill" Hickok, Wyatt Earp, Buffalo Bill, Susan B. Anthony, Charles Lindbergh, and others have been told and retold. We still pay certain homage today to the "lone wolf" who can make it alone, ignore the system, or shun the spotlight. Perhaps one of the reasons we so admire this rugged individualist is that we recognize it is almost impossible to go it alone in today's group-oriented, group-dominated, and group-processed society. In fact, today, to be well adjusted in a given society usually means that the individual has mastered the society's norms of social interaction—of functioning appropriately in groups.

The objectives of this chapter are therefore to (a) identify the various types of group settings used by counselors to assist their clients and (b) introduce the process and values of group counseling, group guidance, and values clarification techniques.

Suggestions of the influence and dependence on groups result from an examination of the individual's functioning in today's society. Such an examination leads to the following conclusions:

1. Humans are group oriented. People are meant to complement, assist, and enjoy each other. Groups are natural for these processes to occur.

2. Humans seek to meet most of their basic and personal-social needs through groups, including the need to know and grow mentally; thus, groups are a most natural and expeditious way to learn.

3. Consequently, groups are most influential in how a person grows, learns, and develops behavioral patterns, coping styles, values, career potentials, and adjustment techniques.

For counselors, teachers, and others who work with groups in leadership, facilitative, and teaching capacities, the following additional assumptions can be made:

1. An understanding of the influences and dynamics of groups can help further assessments and understandings of the individuals.

2. An understanding of the organization and utilization of groups can help in the teaching and guidance of others.

3. Group counseling may be more effective for some people and some situations than individual counseling.

4. Special populations can benefit from groups specially designed to recognize their uniqueness and/or their needs.

DEFINITIONS AND EXPLANATIONS

In any study of groups, particularly of an introductory nature, it is important at the onset to clarify the various labels in group counseling and guidance, including a definition of *group*. Webster's *Third New World International Dictionary* (unabridged) defines a group as "a number of individuals bound together by a community of interest, purpose, or function." However, within and across the professional disciplines engaged in the study and practice of groups, there are wide variations in defining a group. To narrow the definition of *group* for discussion here, it should be noted that counseling groups are characterized by interaction. They are functional or goal-oriented groups. Aggregate groups without interaction of the members are not functioning groups.

Counselors may view various group activities as occurring at three levels: the guidance level, the counseling level, and the therapy level. In brief, the levels may be defined as follows.

Group Guidance

Group guidance refers to group activities that focus on providing information or experiences through a planned and organized group activity. Examples of group guidance activities are orientation groups, career exploration groups, college visitation days, and classroom guidance (discussed later in this chapter). Group guidance is also organized to prevent the development of problems. The content could include educational, vocational, personal, or social information, with a goal of providing students with accurate information that will help them make more appropriate plans and life decisions.

Group Counseling

Group counseling is the routine adjustment or developmental experiences provided in a group setting. Group counseling focuses on assisting counselees to cope with their day-to-day adjustment and development concerns. Examples might focus on behavior modification, developing personal relationship skills, concerns of human sexuality, values or attitudes, or career decision making.

Gazda (1989) suggests that group counseling can be growth engendering insofar as it provides participation incentives and motivation to make changes that are in the clients' best interests. On the other hand, it is remedial for those persons who have entered into a spiral of self-defeating behavior but who are, nevertheless, capable of reversing the spiral with counseling intervention.

Group Therapy

Group therapy provides intense experiences for people with serious adjustment, emotional, or developmental needs. Therapy groups are usually distinguished from counseling groups by both the length of time and the depth of the experience for those involved.

Ohlsen (1977) notes that whereas counselors devote most of their time to helping clients learn to recognize and cope early with self-defeating behaviors and to master developmental tasks, psychotherapists devote most of their time to remediation for emotionally disturbed persons.

Gazda's (1989) continuum, describing relationships among the group processes, is presented in Figure 6–1.

T-Groups

T-groups are derivatives of training groups. They represent the application of laboratory training methods to group work. T-groups represent an effort to create a society in miniature in which an environment is created for learning.

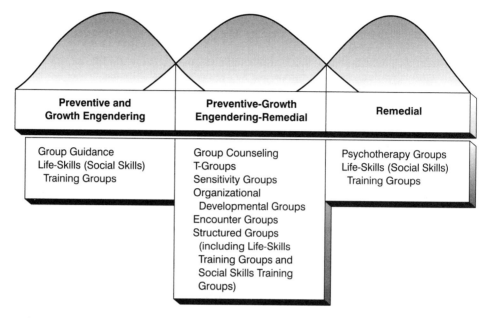

FIGURE 6–1   Relationships Among Group Processes
Source: From Gazda, George M., *Group Counseling,* p. 9. Copyright © 1989 by Allyn and Bacon.
Reprinted by permission.

T-groups are relatively unstructured groups in which the participants become responsible for what they learn and how they learn it. This learning experience also usually includes learning about how people function in groups and about one's own behavior in groups. A basic assumption appropriate to T-groups is that learning is more effective when the individual establishes authentic relationships with others.

Sensitivity Groups

In actual practice, the label *sensitivity groups* appears to be applied so frequently and broadly as to be almost meaningless. In a more technical sense, however, a sensitivity group is a form of T-group that focuses on personal and interpersonal issues and on the personal growth of the individual. There is an emphasis in sensitivity groups on self-insight, which means that the central focus is not the group and its progress but rather the individual member.

Encounter Groups

Encounter groups are also in the T-group family, although they are more therapy oriented. Rogers (1967) defines an encounter group as a group that stresses personal growth through the development and improvement of interpersonal relationships via an experiential group process. Such groups seek to release the potential of the participant:

In an intensive group, with much freedom and little structure, the individual will gradually feel safe enough to drop some of his defenses and facades; he will relate more directly on the feeling basis (come into a basic encounter) with other members of the group; he will come to understand himself and his relationship to others more accurately; he will change in his personal attitudes and behavior; and he will subsequently relate more effectively to others in his everyday life situation. (Rogers, 1967, p. 262)

Extended encounter groups are often referred to as *marathon groups*. The marathon encounter group uses an extended block of time in which massed experience and accompanying fatigue are used to break through the participants' defenses.

Although encounter groups offer great potential for the group members' increased self-awareness and sensitivity to others, such groups can also create high levels of anxiety and frustration. It is, therefore, obvious that if encounter groups are to have maximum potential and minimal risk, they must be conducted by highly skilled and experienced counselor leaders.

Minigroups

Although technically two or more people can constitute a group, the use of the term *minigroup* has become increasingly popular in recent years to denote a counseling group that is smaller than usual. A minigroup usually consists of one counselor and a maximum of four clients. Because of the smaller number of participants, the potential exists for certain advantages resulting from the more frequent and direct interaction of its members. Mercurio and Weiner (1975) indicate that

because of the increased dynamics that seem to occur in a group of this limited size, members of the mini group are less able to withdraw or hide, and interaction seems to be more complete and responses fuller. . . . Mini-groups may either function as the singular treatment focus or be used in conjunction with individual counseling. (p. 227)

Group Process and Group Dynamics

Two terms commonly used in describing group activities are *process* and *dynamics*. Although often used interchangeably, they do have different meanings when used to describe group counseling activities. The beginning counseling student should note that group process is the continuous, ongoing movement of the group toward achievement of its goals. It represents the flow of the group from its starting point to its termination. It is a means of identifying or describing the stages through which the group passes.

Group dynamics, on the other hand, refers to the social forces and interplay operative within the group at any given time. It describes the interaction of a group, which may include a focus on the impact of leadership, group roles, and membership participation in groups. It is a means of analyzing the interaction between and among the individuals within a group. Group dynamics is also used on occasion to refer to certain group techniques such as role playing, decision making, "rap" sessions, and observation.

In-Groups and Out-Groups

While these are not groups organized or overseen by counselors, they are often important in understanding influences on client behaviors. These groups can be based on almost any criteria, such as socioeconomic status, athletic or artistic accomplishments (in schools especially), a particular ability, racial-cultural origins, and so forth. In-groups are characterized by associations largely limited with peers of like characteristics, while out-groups consist of those excluded from in-groups. For example, these are nonparticipants in athletics or drama and/or have not been invited to participate in such things as social clubs. In many counseling situations, it is important for counselors to understand how clients see themselves and others in terms of "in" or "out."

Social Networks

While not a group in a formal sense, social networks result from the choices that individuals make in becoming members of various groups. As counselors we may be concerned with how these choices are made and their impacts on individuals. Sociologists engage in social network analyses to determine how the interconnectedness of certain individuals in a society can produce interaction patterns influencing others both within and without the network.

PROFESSIONAL STANDARDS FOR THE TRAINING OF GROUP WORKERS

The Association for Specialists in Group Work (ASGW) advocates for the incorporation of core group competencies as part of the master's level training required in all counselor education programs. It also supports preparation of group work specialists at the master's level and the continued preparation of group work specialists at the post-master's level (Ed.S. or certificate, doctoral, continuing education, etc.), recognizing that recommended levels of group work specialty training in many programs will need to be accomplished following completion of the master's degree.

The 1990 revision of the *Professional Standards for Training of Group Workers* contains two levels of competencies and related training that have been identified by the ASGW Standards Committee:

1. *Core Group Competencies:* The minimum core of group worker competencies and related training necessary for all counselors, including knowledge, skills, and practice (minimum: 10 clock hours; recommended: 20 clock hours)

2. *Group Work Specialists:* Advanced competencies that build on the generalist core in the four identified group work specialties of

   - Task/work groups, including knowledge, skills, and supervised practice beyond core group training (additional minimum: 30 clock hours; recommended: 45 clock hours);
   - Guidance/psychoeducation groups, including knowledge, skills, and supervised practice beyond core group training (additional minimum: 30 clock hours; recommended: 45 clock hours);
   - Counseling/interpersonal problem-solving groups, including knowledge, skills, and supervised practice beyond core group training (additional minimum: 45 clock hours; recommended: 60 clock hours);
   - Psychotherapy/personality reconstruction groups, including knowledge, skills, and supervised practice beyond core group training (additional minimum: 45 clock hours; recommended: 60 clock hours). (Association for Specialists in Group Work, 1990, p. 13)

GROUP COUNSELING

More than 100 years ago, the psychologist William James (1890) wrote:

> We are not only gregarious animals liking to be in sight of our fellows, but we have an innate propensity to get ourselves noticed and noticed favorably, by our kind. No more fiendish punishment could be devised, were such a thing physically possible, than that one should be turned loose in society and remain absolutely unnoticed by all the members thereof. (p. 293)

James, as well as others, have noted over the years the importance of human relationships in meeting basic needs and influencing the personal development and adjustment of persons. For most people, the vast majority of these relationships are established and maintained in a group setting, and for many, daily routine adjustment problems and developmental needs also have their origins in groups. Interest has increased in group social skills development in the elementary grades and in the development of group relationships and communications skills across all ages of the adult population.

Counseling, as a facilitative science, has a helping relationship base, which must also be a human relationship. Because the most frequent and common human relationship experiences occur in groups, groups also hold the potential to provide positive developmental and adjustment experiences for many people. The following sections examine some of the potential values of group counseling and how these values are realized. The careful selection of participants and formations of groups and the skillful utilization by the counselor of appropriate group techniques are also discussed.

Theoretical Considerations

In the previous chapter, the important rationale base that theory provides for good counseling practice was discussed, as were popular theoretical orientations. As in individual counseling, effective group counseling emanates from a sound theoretical base. Therefore, let us briefly reexamine the popular counseling theories in the context of their application to group rather than individual counseling settings.

In groups led by counselors with a *psychoanalytic* theoretical orientation, the counselor interprets transference and resistances in order to free the unconscious. The analysis may focus on the behavior of individual members of the group and/or the behavior of the group as a whole.

Individual or *Adlerian* group leaders are somewhat direct and active in the group process while recognizing that the group members can decide what to do for themselves. The group setting is viewed as a safe opportunity for members to examine themselves, develop self-respect, and improve their social interactions as they strive to develop their potential.

Client-centered counselors have always had an active interest in group counseling. Carl Rogers coupled his beliefs of human behavior with his observations of therapeutic groups to formulate his ideas of group counseling and therapy, labeled a *basic encounter group*. The client-centered approach assumes that people have a natural tendency to grow and improve themselves. Group counseling can provide an atmosphere within which members feel safe to reveal their needs and ultimately to improve their lives.

The leader sets an example for group members by providing facilitative conditions such as empathy, respect, and positive regard for others. This therapeutic climate brings about self-exploration, revelation of past and current feelings, and self-acceptance. The group atmosphere is one of acceptance and sensitivity. (Vander Kolk, 1985, p. 99)

The *behavioral* counselor in the group setting proceeds to systematically identify the members' problems in behavioral terms. Behavioral objectives are established for members, and the counselor reinforces those behaviors clients wish to acquire.

In group counseling, the *rational-emotive* therapist, not the environment, is prominent in promoting client change. He or she does this through reason, persuasion, role playing, and so forth. The counselor seeks to bring about cognitive and rational behavior change. Within the group, members help each other in identifying illogical, emotionally driven behaviors.

Reality-oriented groups provide a caring environment in which clients can feel worthwhile and secure enough to explore more satisfying behavior. The counselor may function as teacher in order to lead the group members to adapt more appropriate behaviors and make more realistic choices.

As noted in Chapter 5, *transactional analysis* (TA) is essentially a process for counseling individuals within the group setting. TA counselors usually feel that the first step in establishing a TA group is the teaching of the recognition of ego stages.

Gestalt therapists focus on the integration of the person—"getting it all together"—with counselor-client interaction a key. This focus does not change in the group setting, as may be noticed in the goals of such groups as are identified in Table 6–1.

Eclectic counselors will, in group counseling situations, as in individual counseling, utilize a variety of theoretical perspectives to respond to the variety of clients, interactions, and problems.

Values of Group Counseling

Group counseling is not a team sport. The goal is not to have a winning group. The goal of group counseling is the achievement of the goals, the meeting of needs, and the providing of an experience of value to the individual members who constitute the group. The following are some of the opportunities that may be provided by group counseling:

1. *Exploration, with the reinforcement of a support group, of one's developmental and adjustment needs, concerns, and problems, may be possible.* Groups can provide a realistic social setting in which the client can interact with peers who not only are likely to have some understanding of the problem or concern that the client brings to the group but who will, in many instances, also be sharing the same or a similar concern. The counseling group can provide the sense of security needed by the group members to interact spontaneously and freely and take risks, thus promoting the likelihood that the needs of each of the members will be touched on and that the resources of peers will be utilized. The old saying that "misery loves company" may in fact provide a rationale for group counseling. One is more comfortable in sharing a problem with others who have similar experiences and may also be more motivated to change under these conditions.

TABLE 6–1   Comparative Overview of Group Goals

Model	Goals
Psychoanalytic	To provide a climate that helps clients reexperience early family relationships. To uncover buried feelings associated with past events that carry over into current behavior. To facilitate insight into the origins of faulty psychological development and stimulate a corrective emotional experience.
Adlerian	To create a therapeutic relationship that encourages participants to explore their basic life assumptions and to achieve a broader understanding of lifestyles. To help clients recognize their strengths and their power to change. To encourage them to accept full responsibility for their chosen lifestyle and for any changes they want to make.
Psychodrama	To facilitate the release of pent-up feelings, provide insight, and help clients develop new and more effective behaviors. To open up unexplored possibilities for solving conflicts and experiencing dominant sides of oneself.
Existential	To provide conditions that maximize self-awareness and reduce blocks to growth. To help clients discover and use freedom of choice and assume responsibility for their own choices.
Person-centered	To provide a safe climate in which members can explore the full range of their feelings. To help members become increasingly open to new experiences and develop confidence in themselves and their own judgments. To encourage clients to live in the present. To develop openness, honesty, and spontaneity. To make it possible for clients to encounter others in the here and now and to use the group as a place to overcome feelings of alienation.
Gestalt	To enable members to pay close attention to their moment-to-moment experiencing, so they can recognize and integrate disowned aspects of themselves.
Transactional analysis	To assist clients in becoming free of scripts and games in their interactions. To challenge members to reexamine early decisions and make new ones based on awareness.
Behavior therapy	To help group members eliminate maladaptive behaviors and learn new and more effective behavioral patterns. (Broad goals are broken down into precise subgoals.)
Rational-emotive therapy	To teach group members that they are responsible for their own disturbances and to help them identify and abandon the process of self-indoctrination by which they keep their disturbances alive. To eliminate the clients' irrational and self-defeating outlook on life and replace it with a more tolerant and rational one.
Reality therapy	To guide members toward learning realistic and responsible behavior and developing a "success identity." To assist group members in making value judgments about their behaviors and in deciding on a plan of action for change.

Source: From *Theory and Practice of Group Counseling,* Third Edition, p. 53, by Gerald Corey. Copyright © 1990, 1985, 1981 by Wadsworth, Inc. Reprinted by permission of Brooks/Cole Publishing Company, Pacific Grove, CA 93950.

2. *Group counseling may give the client an opportunity to gain insights into his or her own feelings and behavior.* Yalom (1985), in discussing the group as a social microcosm, states that "a freely interactive group, with few structural restrictions, will, in time, develop into a social microcosm of the participant members" (p. 30). He also points out that, given enough time in the group setting, clients will begin to be themselves, interact with others, and create the same interpersonal universe they have experienced, including the display of maladaptive, interpersonal behavior to the group. Yalom also states that corrective emotional experiences in groups may have several components, including these:

   a. A strong expression of emotion which is interpersonally directed and which represents a risk taking on the part of the patient

   b. A group supportive enough to permit this risk taking

   c. Reality testing which allows the patient to examine the incident with the aid of consensual validation from the other members

   d. A recognition of the inappropriateness of certain interpersonal feelings and behavior or of the inappropriateness of certain avoided interpersonal behaviors

   e. The ultimate facilitation of the individual's ability to interact with others more deeply and honestly.* (p. 28)

As the client gains new insights into behaviors and feelings as a result of interactions with members of the counseling group, influences on self-concept formation may also occur. Because of the significant influence of self-concept on one's personal-social adjustment, perception of school and career decision making, the opportunity to bring about positive change in self-concept through new insights provided by the group counseling experience is a value not to be overlooked.

3. *Group counseling provides clients with an opportunity to develop positive, natural relationships with others.* The personal interactions that take place within the group counseling structure provide an excellent and continuous opportunity for the group member to experiment with and learn to manage interpersonal relations. This includes developing sensitivities to others, their needs, and feelings. It also provides opportunities to learn of the impact one's behavior has on others. Thus, through the group process and its interactions and sharing of experiences, the client may learn to modify earlier behavior patterns and seek new, more appropriate behaviors in situations that require interpersonal skills.

4. *Group counseling offers opportunities for the client to learn responsibility to self and others.* Becoming a member of a counseling group implies the assumption of responsibilities. Even when there are initial tendencies to avoid assuming responsibility for one's behavior, contributing to the group's interactions, or accepting one's "assignment" within the group, these avoidance techniques will usually fade away as group relationships develop and group goals are established.

Selection of Group Members

All of us have had experience in organizing groups. When deciding on group members for a social occasion we select good old Charlie because he is a laugh a minute; Diane, because she gets along with everybody; Harry, in case we need some serious conversation; and Olga, because she is a good listener. On the other hand, if the purpose of the group is a more serious one, such as planning a neighborhood park, we might choose Rosalie, because of her know-how with flowers and shrubbery; Jim, because he is a landscaping expert; Jane, because of her architectural skills; and Jerry, because of his proven fund-raising abilities. In each instance, people are usually selected because they can contribute something to the group and its interaction. Although group counseling focuses on the needs of the individual, the importance of group membership to the achievement and adjustments of individuals in the group cannot be overestimated. Group member selection is one key to a successful counseling group.

The following are possible criteria for the selection of group members: (a) common interest, (b) volunteer or self-referred, (c) willingness to participate in the group process, and (d) ability to participate in the group process. A popular criterion for group selection also may be a common interest of the potential members in a similar problem, concern, or issue.

Many group specialists believe that the best group member is a self-referred group member. Group counseling should be an option chosen by the group participants. Choice guarantees the protection of the client's rights. It also further enhances the motivation for counseling should the client decide to be in a counseling group.

Corey (1990) notes that

> screening should be a two-way process. Therefore, the potential members should have an opportunity at the private screening interview to ask questions to determine whether the group is right for them. Group leaders should encourage prospective members to be involved in the decision concerning the appropriateness of their participation in the group. (p. 89)

In the selection of potential group participants, Corey (1990) states that

> careful screening will lessen the psychological risks of inappropriate participation in a group. During the screening session the leader can spend some time exploring with potential members any fears or concerns they have about participating in a group. The leader can help them make an assessment of their readiness for a group and discuss the potential life changes that might come about. (p. 88)

In some instances, potential group members may lack the ability or desire to communicate with others or to relate to and assist others. From a temperament viewpoint, not everyone will be a suitable group member. In short, a person must possess certain abilities or aptitudes if he or she is to profit from and contribute to the group experience. Thus, while there are any number of procedures that may be used by counselors to form a group, inviting clients to participate once the counselor has become familiar with the individual and his or her concerns is a procedure that is the most realistic and professionally sound.

Hardy and Cull (1974) add that by using the interview invitation approach:

> the counselor has (1) made an assessment of the probable needs of the clients who comprise the group; (2) assessed the probable contributions the client will make to the group; (3) set the

parameters with respect to the personality composition of the group; (4) ascertained the probable extent to which each would benefit from the group experience; and (5) established in his mind the probable goals for the group. (p. 10)

During the process of screening interviews for possible group membership, the counselor may want to specify the "ground rules" group members are expected to follow. Gazda (1989) presents the following example:

1. Set a goal or goals for yourself before you enter the group, or at the very latest, as early as you can isolate and define your direction of change. Revise these goals as clarification and/or experience dictates.

2. Discuss as honestly and concretely as you can the nature of your trouble, including the successful and unsuccessful coping behaviors you have employed.

3. When you are not discussing your own difficulties, listen intently to the other group members and try to help them say what they are trying to say and to communicate your understanding, caring, and empathy for them.

4. Maintain the confidentiality of all that is discussed in the group. (There are no exceptions to this rule other than those things that pertain to you only.)

5. Be on time and attend regularly until termination of the group (if a closed group) and until you have met your goals (if the group is open ended).

6. Give the counselor the privilege of removing you from the group if the counselor deems it necessary for your health and for the overall benefit of the group.

7. Concur that all decisions affecting the group as a whole will be made by consensus only.

8. Inform the group counselor in private, before the group is constituted, of individuals who would for various reasons constitute a serious impediment to your group participation. (I feel that the "cards should be stacked in the counselee's favor" as much as possible; therefore those individuals who could inhibit the counselee should be excluded from the group if at all possible.)

9. You may request individual counseling interviews, but what is discussed in these interviews should be shared with the group at the appropriate time and at the discretion of the counselor and yourself.

10. When fees are involved, concurrence on amounts and payment schedules is made with the counselor before counseling begins.* (pp. 37–38)

Another consideration in the formation of the counseling group is "What should the size of the group be to get the best results?" Yalom (1985) notes that his own experience and a consensus of the clinical literature implies that the

ideal size of an interactional therapy group is approximately seven or eight, with an acceptable range of five to ten members. The lower limit of the group is determined by the fact that a critical mass is required for an aggregation of individuals to become an interacting group. When a group is reduced to a size of four or three, it often ceases to operate as a group; member interaction diminishes, and therapists often find themselves engaged in individual therapy within the group. Many of the advantages of a group—the opportunity for broad consensual validation, the opportunity to interact and to analyze one's interaction with a large variety of individuals—are compromised as the group size diminishes. (p. 283)

*From Gazda, George M., *Group Counseling*. Copyright © 1989 by Allyn and Bacon. Reprinted by permission.

The upper limit is determined by sheer economic principles; as the group increases in size, less and less time is available for the working through of any individual's problems. (Yalom, 1985 p. 284)

Luft (1984) also writes:

The influence of the sheer number of persons contained in a group is entangled with other variables such as the purpose of the group and the composition of the membership. A few generalizations can be made on the basis of specific studies. Cohesion tends to be weaker and morale tends to be lower in larger groups than in comparable smaller ones. How often groups meet varies inversely with size and duration and directly with closeness of feelings (Coleman & James, 1961; Fischer, 1953; Tannenbaum, 1962).

Two- and three-person groups have unique characteristics with reference to closeness of feeling and power as interaction factors (see especially Theodore Caplow's *Two against One: Coalitions in Triad*). Thomas and Fink (1961) also report that, for most kinds of tasks or problems in which group discussion is desirable, a five-person group appears to be an optimal size. Hare (1976) presents a summary of research bearing on group size, referring to work by Bales and Borgatta (1965):

As size increases, there is a tendency toward a more mechanical method of introducing information (by round robin procedure, for example), a less sensitive exploration of the point of view of the other, and a more direct attempt to control others and reach a solution whether or not all group members indicate agreement. (p. 226)

Consistent with these findings is Simmel's (1955) observation:

A group upon reaching a certain size must develop forms and organs which serve its maintenance and promotion, but which a smaller group does not need. On the other hand . . . smaller groups have qualities, including types of interaction among their members, which inevitably disappear when the groups grow larger. (in Nixon, 1979, p. 23)

Meeting time for groups in nonschool settings should be based on predetermined or mutually convenient times. In schools, however, Stockton and Toth (1993) note:

It is important to involve teachers in the group planning process (i.e., how many times, and when, will students be called out of class?). Some counselors have found it effective, at the middle or high school level, to schedule the group during different class periods each meeting time so as not to have a student miss the same class time over and over again. (p. 74)

GROUP LEADERSHIP

In his book *Leadership*, James M. Burns (1978, p. 2) refers to the activity of leadership as "that most observed and least understood phenomenon," a viewpoint that few would dispute. The nature and quest for leadership at all levels and across all settings has been a continuing challenge to humankind. However, Burns's suggestion that "true leaders emerge from, and always return to, the wants and needs of their followers" (cited in Goodwin, 1978, p. 48) appears to have some relevance for leaders of counseling groups.

In discussing the personal characteristics of the effective group leader, George and Dustin (1988) note that

> there is general agreement as to the characteristics of an effective leader. Honesty and openness are important in that they imply a willingness to accept feedback and a willingness for the leader to self-examine needs and values to determine their impact on the group. These qualities suggest the leader's interest in personal and professional growth as well as the personal growth of the group members. Such a leader can be nonjudgmental and accepting, can value personal relationships, and can have positive relationships. Without narrow or rigid behavior patterns the effective group counselor takes risks, is flexible and spontaneous, and has a healthy degree of self-confidence and enthusiasm. (p. 37)

Within this framework of the group counselor as a leader-member nourisher, what are the leadership responsibilities or functions? Helen Driver (1958), an early leader in the group counseling movement, identifies leadership techniques for the group counselor:

1. Support: giving commendation; showing appreciation.
2. Reflection: mirroring feelings.
3. Clarification: making meanings clear, showing implications of an idea.
4. Questioning: bringing out deeper feelings, inviting further response.
5. Information: providing data for examination, serving as a resource person, teaching.
6. Interpretation: explaining the significance of data, using analogy.
7. Summary: asking for client summary first, pointing out progress, alternatives. (pp. 100–102)

In preparation for group leadership responsibility, Stockton (1980) reviews the importance of training in four areas:

> (1) didactic knowledge (e.g., potential group leaders should understand theories of group counseling, ethical principles, research); (2) individual clinical skills such as those involving assessment, interpreting nonverbal behaviors, ability to use self-disclosure, confrontation and other standard therapeutic tools; (3) knowledge of group dynamics, most particularly developing a keen sense of the importance of timing and knowing how to pace a variety of specific group leader techniques and interventions; and (4) achieving a healthy personality oneself. (p. 57)

Bates, Johnson, and Blaker (1982) specify four responsibilities of leadership as (a) directing traffic (helping members become aware of behaviors that facilitate or inhibit open communications), (b) modeling, (c) acting as an interaction catalyst, and (d) facilitating communications (pp. 95–117).

Stockton and Morran (1982) surveyed the group leadership research and report that the results are inconclusive: "There is very little research that provides clear evidence for a particular style of leadership as being most effective" (p. 48). Some of the more significant results from their survey is that leadership is multidimensional, which thus makes it difficult to control for unidimensional examination. Stockton and Toth also conclude that the Lieberman, Yalom, and Miles (1973) study of encounter groups comes closest to supporting a specific style of leadership. This study's results are summarized as follows:

> The most effective encounter group leaders (a) were moderate in amount of emotional stimulation (emphasizing disclosure of feelings, challenging, confronting, etc.), (b) were high in car-

ing (offering support, encouragement, protection, etc.), (c) had meaning-attribution utilization (providing concepts for how to understand, clarifying, interpreting, etc.), and (d) were moderate in expression of executive functions (setting rules, limits, norms, time management, etc.). (Stockton & Morran, 1982, pp. 70–71)

Corey (1990) points out that

group counseling techniques cannot be divorced from the leader's personal characteristics and behaviors. Group leaders can acquire extensive theoretical and practical knowledge of group dynamics and be skilled in diagnostic and technical procedures yet be ineffective in stimulating growth and change in the members of their groups. Leaders bring to every group their personal qualities, values, and life experiences. In order to promote growth in the members' lives, leaders need to live growth-oriented lives themselves. In order to foster honest self-investigation in others, leaders need to have the courage to engage in self-appraisal themselves. In order to inspire others to break away from deadening ways of being, leaders need to be willing to seek new experiences themselves. In short, the most effective group direction is found in the kind of life the group members see the leader demonstrating and not in the words they hear the leader saying. (pp. 52–53)

An examination of these suggestions for group leadership indicates the group counselor's responsibility for the structure, conduct, and general overseeing of the group sessions. It should also be mentioned that conscientious group leaders do not become involved in group activities beyond their depth of professional preparation. Group counseling emphasizes factors of associations rather than deep emotional disturbances. The counselor's depth of psychological understanding and skill in group dynamics are individual considerations in the level of group counseling that he or she undertakes. For those counseling groups that focus on specific and narrow concerns, such as family relations, human sexuality, or substance abuse, it is obviously desirable that the counselor-leader have some special understanding of the topic.

GROUP PROCESS

The elements of the group counseling process share much in common with those identified with individual counseling. These may be separated into their logical sequence of occurrence.

The Establishment of the Group

The initial group time is used to acquaint the new group membership with the format and processes of the group, to orient them to such practical considerations as frequency of meetings, duration of group, and length of group meeting time. Additionally, the beginning session is used to initiate relationships and open communications among the participants. The counselor also may use beginning sessions to answer questions that clarify the purpose and processes of the group. The establishment of the group is a time to further prepare members for meaningful group participation and set a positive, promising group climate.

The group counselor must remember that in the initial group sessions the general climate of the group may be a mixture of uncertainty, anxiety, and awkwardness. It is not uncommon for group members to be unfamiliar with one another and uncertain regarding the process and expectancies of the group regardless of previous explanations or the establishing of "ground rules."

Gladding (1991) notes that

group leaders and group members have tasks to accomplish during the first sessions of a group. These tasks include:

1. dealing with apprehension

2. reviewing members' goals and contracts

3. specifying more clearly or reiterating group rules

4. setting limits

5. promoting a positive interchange among members so they will want to continue (Weiner, 1984). (p. 181)

George and Dustin (1988) point out that

writers have emphasized that one important aspect of the first counseling group meeting is the clarification of member expectations (Corey, 1981). Most writers stress that the first meeting of a counseling group provides an opportunity for the group leader to deal with such issues as member expectations, purposes of the group, and norms. The strategy for the group leader will indicate whether early in this first session the group leader plans time for disclosures about hopes for the group and leader expectations or the delivery of a succinct list of group member expectations. It has been emphasized that early in a counseling group, members can benefit from the chance to exchange expectations as well as individual objectives they would envision for the group (Johnson & Johnson, 1982). (p. 93)

Identification: Group Role and Goal

Once an appropriate climate has been established that at least facilitates a level of discussion, the group may then move toward a second, distinct stage—that of identification. In this stage, a group identity should unfold, the identification of individual roles should emerge, and group and individual goals should be established. These may all develop simultaneously or at different paces. They are, however, significant at this stage of the group counseling process. It is also important to make operational the group counseling goals.

Most of us have few undirected, non-goal-oriented activities in our typical everyday plan of action. Those who work with groups frequently, whether in teaching or other capacities, can well predict the outcome if they were to ask, "How would you like to spend your time today?" At worst, chaos would result, and at best, considerable time would be lost before determining how the group could best utilize the time available.

Goal setting is no less important in group counseling than in any other activity that seeks to be meaningful. The early identification of goals in group counseling will facilitate the group's movement toward a meaningful process and outcomes. These goals are most readily identified and implemented when they are specified in behavioral terms.

Hansen, Warner, and Smith (1980) also believe that it is important to make operational the group counseling goals:

Group goals are operationalized when broad statements of intent for the group are analyzed into cognitive, affective, and behavioral dimensions, which in turn can be described as behavioral objectives for individual members. Behavioral objectives include specific, pertinent, obtainable, measurable, and observable behavior that will result from planned intervention. She [referring to T. A. Ryan] suggests that operationalizing group goals has four advantages that increase the likelihood of counseling success: (1) operationalized goals produce more homogeneity in the group's shared interest; (2) operationalized goals contribute to more realistic expectations; (3) operationalized goals lead to more highly motivated members because they know what they are working for; (4) operationalized goals make the group members more interdependent as they are able to see how goals for other members fit into their objectives as well. . . .

[T]here are certain problems in the process of goal setting for a group. The importance of a particular group goal for any individual in the group may be influenced by his individual needs. Obviously, goal setting is a part of the counseling process which must be accomplished jointly by the counselor and the group members. If a counselor establishes the goals for the group, he may not be aware of the individual sub-goals. Other members in the group may not be aware of each other's individual goals underneath the umbrella goal for the group. The extent to which group goals implement personal goals will vary from time to time throughout the group. Despite these difficulties involved in the goal setting process, however, it is one of the most important aspects to success in group counseling.* (pp. 490–491)

It is important for counselors to be aware of the probable, or at least possible, conflict and confrontation during this stage of the group's development. Yalom (1985) labels this second phase as "the conflict, dominance/rebellion stage." He adds that it is a time when

the group shifts from preoccupation with acceptance, approval, commitment to the group, definitions of accepted behavior, and the search for orientation, structure, and meaning to a preoccupation with dominance, control, and power. The conflict characteristic of this phase is between members or between members and the leader. Each member attempts to establish for himself his preferred amount of initiative and power, and gradually a control hierarchy, a social pecking order, emerges. (p. 304)

Hansen et al. (1980) describe this second stage as one in which the group members manifest their dissatisfaction with the operation of the group. It is a time following the initial acquaintance period when

members are frequently frustrated in their attempts to evolve new patterns of behavior through which to work toward group goals. The discrepancy between individuals' real selves and their stereotyped images of the group may lead to conflict. Group members may challenge others' reactions to them and insist on their own rights. Some conflict may erupt when certain issues are discovered to be more complex than the group members originally perceived. The process of conflict and confrontation also occurs as group members begin to perceive and experience difficulty implementing changes in behavior.† (p. 502)

They further note that

---

*From James C. Hansen, Richard W. Warner, and Elsie J. Smith, *Group Counseling: Theory and Process,* Second Edition. Copyright © 1980 by Rand McNally College Publishing Company. Used by permission of Houghton Mifflin Company.

†From James C. Hansen, Richard W. Warner, and Elsie J. Smith, *Group Counseling: Theory and Process,* Second Edition. Copyright © 1980 by Rand McNally College Publishing Company. Used by permission of Houghton Mifflin Company.

in many counseling groups Stage Two may not emerge early or may be avoided completely unless there is enough commitment to the group so that the members will risk open confrontation. In fact, the conflict may not be expressed openly but through passive resistance. The members may remain silent rather than confront each other or the counselor. Open conflict and confrontation is not often seen in group counseling conducted in school settings or other short-term counseling situations in which the counselor is perceived as an authority figure.

Without working through this phase and establishing appropriate norms of behavior, only a superficial level of cohesiveness can develop. As the group members work through their differences of opinions about appropriate behavior for each other and the counselor, they are able to accept the real person rather than the stereotyped image. This can lead to a greater feeling of identity with the group. It is important to recall that even when the group moves into a cohesive stage, it may regress to periods of conflict and confrontation.

The necessity for working through the stage of conflict and confrontation cannot be emphasized too strongly. For groups to evolve from a superficial to a more truly effective level of functioning, this painful and difficult period must be experienced and dealt with successfully.* (pp. 391–392)

When conflicts and confrontations, as previously described, do occur, a more cohesive group usually emerges, with resulting increased openness in communication, consensual group action and cooperation, and mutual support among the members. A concern at this point may also be the tendency of some group members to withdraw. Stockton, Barr, and Klein (1981) warned that not only does the group member lose, but premature termination can result in negative effects on the group from which the member has dropped. Initial work stages of the group require membership stability in order to develop therapeutic potential from group treatment, and loss of members makes this task more difficult.

Productivity

In the third stage of the group's development, a clear progression toward productivity is noted. As the group has achieved some degree of stability in its pattern of behaving, the productivity process can begin. Also, because the members are now more deeply committed to the group, they may be ready to reveal more of themselves and their problems.

This is the period of problem clarification and exploration, usually followed by an examination of possible alternate solutions.

The emphasis of this stage is on recognizable progress toward the group's and individual members' goals. In this process, however, each group member is exploring and seeking an understanding of self, situation, and problem or concern, and each member develops a personal plan integrating these understandings. The three subphases of this stage may be (a) assessment, (b) understanding, and (c) planning. The group structure tends to be functional.

In group counseling, productivity can be frequently translated as successful problem solving. Group counseling thus often becomes a process seeking to promote change. Johnson and Johnson (1982) specify four concerns in problem solving:

*From James C. Hansen, Richard W. Warner, and Elsie J. Smith, *Group Counseling: Theory and Process,* Second Edition. Copyright © 1980 by Rand McNally College Publishing Company. Used by permission of Houghton Mifflin Company.

(1) determining the actual or current state of affairs; (2) specifying the desired state of affairs; (3) determining the best means of moving the group from the actual to the desired state of affairs; and (4) doing so. Problem solving requires both an idea about where the group should be and correct information about where it is now. Every group, furthermore, can be evaluated on the basis of its problem-solving adequacy. Problem-solving adequacy has four elements: (1) general agreement about the desired state of affairs; (2) structures and procedures for producing, understanding, and using relevant information about the actual state of affairs; (3) structures and procedures for inventing possible solutions, for deciding upon and implementing the best solutions, and for evaluating its effectiveness in having permanently eliminated the problem; and (4) accomplishing these three activities without deteriorating—preferably while augmenting—the effectiveness of the group's problem-solving capabilities. (p. 401)

Although group strategies may be selected by the group for any or all of these phases, it is important that they make sense to each member in terms of their individual needs. The counselor may note that progress is being made when progress can be seen. Of course, progress is not always constant during this time, and occasionally regression, stagnation, or even confusion may occur. Certainly it is appropriate that

whenever the group does not know what it is doing, it ought to stop and find out. This does not mean that the group ought to argue over its objectives, but rather, that it ought to describe to itself what it is doing. In unclear situations, there is actually discrimination against the participation of some members. When a person knows what the group is doing, then he also knows how to participate, and if he does not participate, it is reasonable to assume that he has nothing to contribute. But when a person does not know what the group is doing, he does not know how to participate, and he is blocked. Therefore, with every change in the nature of the group's activity it is well to be sure the member roles are redefined. (Thelen, 1954, p. 288)

It is also on these occasions that the counselor is alert to prevent process problems from handicapping progress and group achievement. Often, a simple reminder by the counselor of the stated goals or objectives of the group can prevent activities or discussions that tend to sidetrack members or the group as a whole from maintaining progress. However, because of the relationships and the group climate previously established, groups should overcome these difficulties and regain their productivity.

During this phase, the problem or concern should be clarified to everyone's satisfaction and ownership should be verified. This clarification includes a thorough understanding of the nature of the problem and its causes. It is only when this has been achieved that resources for problem solutions can be realistically examined. This phase may be successfully concluded when all possible solutions have been considered and examined in terms of their consequences. These solutions should be practical or capable of being realized (obtainable), and the final choice of a solution should be made only after appropriate considerations and discussion. It should be emphasized that this is not the time for snap judgments and hurried commitments. At this point, then, the group members have examined themselves and the problem as it applies to them and have explored these considerations in considerable depth; have looked at possible solutions and their consequences; have determined the course of action that appears most appropriate; and are ready to move into the next stage, one in which they will try out or experiment with their chosen solution. In this process, they have, by making their own decisions, also established their ownership of the problem and the chosen solution.

Realization

When members of the group recognize the inappropriateness of past behaviors and begin to try out their selected solutions or new behaviors to implement in practice their decisions, progress is being made toward realization of their individual goals. At this time, responsibility has been established with the individual members to act on their own decisions. The counselor encourages the sharing of individual experiences and goal achievement both within and outside the group. Although general success with the new behaviors may provide sufficient reinforcement for many members to continue, for others a support base of "significant others" outside the group should now be developed to facilitate a maintenance of the change once the counseling group is terminated. In school settings, counselors might, for example, consult with parents and teachers to implement this strategy.

Termination

Most of us have experienced occasions of regret and even sorrow when temporary groups to which we have belonged reach the break-up point. Regardless of the purpose for which the group is organized, we may try to prolong its eventual dissolution by promising get-togethers, planning social activities, and in general agreeing that "this has been too much fun to let it end." On many such occasions, casual strangers have become the best of friends in relatively short periods of time, and the threatened termination of the relationships is at least psychologically resisted.

For these same reasons, members may resist the break-up of a counseling group. The very nature of counseling groups, with their emphasis on interpersonal relationships, open communication, trust, and support, promises the development of a group that the membership may want to continue indefinitely. It is therefore important from the very beginning that the group counselor emphasize the temporary nature of the group and establish, if appropriate, specific time limitations. The counselor also reminds the group, as the time approaches, of the impending termination. This does not mean that the counselor alone is responsible for determining the termination point of a group. Although the counselor may, of course, assume this responsibility, termination may also be determined by the group members or the group members and counselor together.

Termination, like all other phases or stages of the group counseling experience, also requires skill and planning on the part of the counselor. Termination is obviously most appropriate when the group goals and the goals of the individual members have been achieved, and new behaviors or learnings have been put into practice in everyday life outside the group. The group will also be ready to terminate when, in a positive sense, it has ceased to serve a meaningful purpose for the members. Under less favorable circumstances, groups may be terminated when their continuation promises to be nonproductive or harmful or when group progress is slow, and long-term continuation might create overdependency on the group by its members.

Members may be terminated from a group at any time during the group's existence. Members who are disruptive, seriously handicap the other members, may be more effectively assisted through individual counseling, or personally desire to terminate are not uncommon subjects for individual terminations. Group counselors should be aware that this is a regular happening, especially in the beginning stages of a group, when several members may voluntarily terminate. It is important that the counselor accept this as a matter of course and refrain from exerting pressure on such persons to remain in the group. At the same time, however, the counselor may indicate a willingness to see the person(s) on an individual basis.

The point of termination is a time for review and summary by both counselor and clients. With some groups, time will be needed to work through the feelings of the members regarding termination. Even though strong ties may have developed and there are pressures from the group to extend the termination time, those pressures must be resisted, and the group must be firmly, though gently, moved toward the inevitable termination.

An excellent summary of essential counseling skills related to stages of the group process is presented by Gill and Barry (1982) in Table 6–2.

GROUP GUIDANCE ACTIVITIES

In a broad, general context, group guidance is probably as old as formal schooling. Good teachers through the years have used groups for what today would be called pupil guidance purposes. In schools group guidance activities have been designed to provide information to students in groups or experiences beyond those associated with the day-to-day learning activities in the classroom. In nonschool settings, group activities have been planned to provide information, skill building, opportunities for personal growth and development, orientation, and assistance in decision making.

Values

Over the years certain values have been attributed to group activities of a guidance nature. Some of these will be discussed in the following sections.

Facilitating Personal Development

Certain experiences that lead to personal development can take place only in the group setting. These include the opportunity to learn and play certain roles, such as group leader, group follower, or member; the development of patterns of cooperation with others; and the learning of group communication skills.

Stimulation of Learning and Understanding

In group settings people can be provided with opportunities to learn more about and understand themselves and their relations with others better. They can also acquire information about the external world. In this context group guidance activities are important in providing learning and understanding—relevant to career and educational decision making and making personal-social adjustments. Care must be taken in how the information is presented and perceived. Clients must feel that the information is important to them if they are to assimilate it.

TABLE 6–2 Classification System for Group-Focused Counseling Skills

Stage I	Stage II	Stage III
Group Formation: Facilitating cooperation toward common goals through development of group identity	*Group Awareness:* Facilitating a shared understanding of the group's behavior	*Group Action:* Facilitating cooperative decision-making and problem-solving
1. *Norming* Stating explicitly the expected group behavior	1. *Labeling Group Behavior* Identifying and describing group feelings and performance	1. *Identifying Group Needs* Asking questions and making statements that clarify the want and needs of the group
2. *Eliciting Group Responses* Inquiries or invitation to members that encourage comments, questions, or observations	2. *Implicit Norming* Describing behavior that has become typical of the group through common practice	2. *Identifying Group Goals* Asking questions and making statements that clarify group objectives
3. *Eliciting Sympatic Reactions* Inquiries or invitations to members that encourage disclosure of experiences or feelings similar to those being expressed	3. *Eliciting Group Observations* Inquiries or invitation to members that encourage observations about group process	3. *Attributing Meaning* Providing concepts for understanding group thought, feelings, and behavior
4. *Identifying Commonalities and Differences* Describing comparative characteristics of participants	4. *Eliciting Mutual Feedback* Inquiries or invitations to members that encourage sharing of perceptions about each other's behavior	4. *Eliciting Alternatives* Providing descriptions of possible courses of action and inviting members to contribute alternatives
5. *Eliciting Empathic Reactions* Inquiries or invitations to members that encourage reflection of one member's expressed content or feeling	5. *Identifying Conflict* Labeling discordant elements of communication between members	5. *Exploring Consequences* Inquiries or invitations to the group that evaluate actions and potential outcomes
6. *Task Focusing* Redirecting conversation to immediate objectives; restating themes being expressed by more than one member	6. *Identifying Nonverbal Behavior* Labeling unspoken communications between members (facial expression, posture, hand gestures, voice tone and intensity)	6. *Consensus Testing* Requesting group agreement on a decision or course of action
	7. *Validating* Requesting group confirmation of the accuracy of leader or members' perceptions	
	8. *Transitioning* Changing the group's focus on content or feelings being expressed	
	9. *Connecting* Relating material from group events at a particular time or session to current situation	
	10. *Extinguishing* Ignoring, cutting off, diverting members' inappropriate talk/actions	

Source: From S. J. Gill and R. A. Barry (1982), "Group-Focused Counseling: Classifying the Essential Skills," *Personnel and Guidance Journal, 60,* 304. © American Counseling Association. No further reproduction without written permission of the American Counseling Association. Reprinted with permission.

Advantages of Group Interaction

By actively participating in groups organized for guidance purposes, members have the opportunity to broaden their scope of understanding regarding the subject or purpose for which the group is organized. Additionally, participants should grow in their understanding of group interactions and dynamics as well as understanding their own behavior in groups.

Economy

Groups should not be organized for guidance purposes solely on the basis of economy. However, when effectiveness in terms of outcome is not lessened, the saving of both the counselor's and clients' time through the use of groups can be of considerable value.

Organizing Group Guidance Activities

All of us have experienced being participants in some type of group activity, social or otherwise, that has been organized on the spur of the moment. Occasionally these unanticipated activities have been enjoyable or worthwhile, but probably more often, they have resulted in confusion, uncertainty, perhaps even frustration, and have been considered a waste of time. The popularity of group activities has, in some instances, led to their scheduling without appropriate preparation, but that is not and should not be the pattern. If group guidance activities are to achieve their potential, a great deal of consideration and organization must go into their planning, conducting, and evaluation. Although the organization process is very similar to group counseling, discussed earlier in this chapter, the differences, though often subtle, should be noted and the similarities should be reemphasized. The following guidelines therefore may be helpful.

Determining That There Is a Need for Group Guidance

All too often group guidance activities are simply scheduled. On occasion, the scheduled activities may be responding to an actual need. If we are to ensure their success, it must be determined beforehand that there is a need that a group shares in common and for which a group guidance response is appropriate. Questionnaires, problem surveys, or checklists administered to specific populations often will provide a factual basis for determining possible group guidance activities.

Determining That Group Guidance Is the Most Appropriate or Effective Response

Once needs have been determined, the counseling staff must identify those for which a group guidance activity would be appropriate, in contrast to group counseling or individual counseling, or perhaps even some form of instruction. Group guidance activities are those that may be useful to nearly everyone in a specific population or setting; hence the total group would experience the activity. Examples might be a stress management program for employees in an industrial setting, a behavior workshop for public relations workers, or a career day for high school students.

Small-group guidance activities, in broad general terms, are those designed for specific outcomes which cater to the needs of smaller subgroups within the total population served by the school or agency counseling and guidance program. These activities may focus on providing information for decision-making and planning purposes, activities for personal development purposes, and assistance for educational adjustments. Small-group guidance activities can emphasize smaller components or follow-up activities for the larger college, career, or orientation programs. Other specific examples are guidance groups organized to develop job-seeking and interviewing skills, how-to-study techniques, assertiveness training, career education, values clarification activities, discussion groups, and experiences in nonverbal communications.

Determining the Characteristics of the Group

Once the nature of the group guidance activity has been established, certain group characteristics must be determined. Obviously, size of the group must be one consideration. Here, the counselor must determine what size group will be most appropriate for the activities planned and outcomes anticipated. Size will also have an influence on the operational format of the group. Format planning includes determining the types of activities of the group, the length of time allotted for each group session, the number of sessions, and the setting.

A final consideration affecting the group characteristics will be the role of the counselor. Will the counselor be an active participant or an inactive observer who remains in the background once the group's activities are under way? Will the counselor direct the group? Will the counselor be a group arbitrator? What information will the leader provide the group? Will roles be assigned, or will roles evolve as the group progresses?

Establishing the Group

Once the characteristics of the group have been determined, members may be selected. They may volunteer, or they may be invited to participate. Invitation includes the right of the persons to refuse participation. In establishing the membership of the group, it must be verified that the planned activity will respond to the needs of the individual member and that the structure or operational format will be comfortable for the group member. In large groups, such as those organized for orientation purposes, career needs, or other special information purposes, this is not necessarily essential, but for smaller, intimate groups, it is an important consideration.

Monitoring the Ongoing Activities

Once the group has been established and the members oriented to its purpose and processes, the counselor or facilitator assumes the responsibility for keeping the group "on track." It is relatively easy, especially considering the participants' lack of experience and understanding of the group process, to deviate from the purposes of the group, become bogged down in irrelevant discussions and activities, or encounter personal factors that inhibit or impede the functioning of the group. The counselor must, therefore, be constantly on the alert to detect such symptoms and to use his or her skills to minimize these effects. The ongoing activities of the group are meaningful only as long as they promote the progress of the group and its members toward their goals.

Evaluating Outcomes

The importance of evaluation in assessing the outcomes of groups cannot be overemphasized, and evaluation and the accountability process will be discussed in greater detail in Chapter 12. The goals or projected outcomes of the group must be stated in clear, objective, and measurable terms. The criteria for measuring goal achievement must be identified and stated, and data then collected that, when analyzed, will present an objective evaluation of outcomes. Such evaluations can assist counselors and others involved to determine which group guidance activities are most effective and which techniques within groups are most and least effective. Implications for group memberships, roles, and leadership may also result.

Classroom Guidance Activities

Classroom guidance is a planned process for assisting school populations in acquiring useful and needed information, skills, and/or experiences. It is also determined that the classroom is the most effective setting for carrying out the designated program and that the program will not detract from but, in fact, may even enhance the regular ongoing curricular offerings.

Classroom guidance activities are characterized by being (a) developmental, (b) ongoing, and (c) having counselors as instructors (but they may be planned with faculty assistance). The substance of the instruction is based on specific needs of the population for which the program is designed to serve. This provides a rationale for the program, which in turn is translated into program goals. Program procedures (including timetables), feedback, and evaluation planning follow. In this context, school counselors will have responsibility for developing a communications plan for orienting all interested parties to their role and function. They will also be responsible for identifying the topics needing attention, gathering resource materials, and preparing handouts.

School counselors will note that programs of classroom guidance help ally them with the teaching faculty. Classroom guidance provides additional opportunities for student interactions and natural settings for identifying and reacting to student needs.

VALUES CLARIFICATION TECHNIQUES FOR GROUPS: AN OVERVIEW

When we state that we believe in free speech, freedom of the press, equal rights for women, and access to education for all, we are, in effect, expressing values. Those values might appropriately reflect the consensual values of our society. Each society is characterized by well-defined, articulated values that are passed on to and practiced by the members of the society. On the other hand, when we extol the pleasures of travel abroad, the virtues of exercise and careful diets, and the inspiration of a specific religious faith, we may, in effect, be expressing our personal values. Thus, values also represent what a person considers important in life, and these ideas of what is good or worthwhile are acquired through the modeling of the society and the personal experiences of the individual.

A discussion of values is basically a discussion of what people believe in, what they stand for, and what is important in life. In recent years we have seen a dramatic increase in public and political attention to "values" in relationship to violence and other crimes, political and corporate scandals, the decline in morality, and disrespect for laws and rights. There has also been much discussion regarding who is responsible for imparting desirable values.

We do know that values are the reasons people behave and even think the way they do. They motivate one to plan and act and serve as a standard for judging the worth of activities, achievements, things, and places. In short, it has been claimed that values give direction to one's life and, hence, one's behavior. On the other hand, people who do not know what they value often engage in meaningless, nonproductive, and usually frustrating behavior. In both individual and group counseling, an understanding of the client's values can facilitate the counselor's understanding of the client's behavior, goals or lack of goals, and what is or has been of significance in the client's life.

Values Defined

The proliferation of values clarification techniques and the increasing examination of values education in the school curriculum, as with any popular movement, have clouded traditional definitions and brought forth complex explanations of what is meant by values. We do not propose to add to this confusion but rather to present several of the more popular definitions appropriate to those engaged in counseling.

First, the dictionary defines *values* as ideals, customs, and institutions that arouse an emotional response, for or against them in a given society or a given person—a simple, straightforward, and, we think, acceptable definition. Another equally clear definition is that proposed by Smith and Peterson (1977): Values "are those elements that show how a person has decided to use his or her life" (p. 228). Another relatively simplistic definition is presented by Ziegler (1972), who describes values as "symbolic categories—ideas, notions, articulated feelings, if you will—which enable us to rank behaviors and events and discover which we prefer and which we don't" (p. 18).

Kalish and Collier (1981) describe the values clarification process:

> Values clarification involves trying on various values to see how they fit. The process proceeds on two fronts. First, it points out that, according to a given set of values, certain things are desirable. Second, it requires you to consider whether or not you agree that these things really are valuable. Thus, you might be invited to imagine yourself caught up in some situation. Then you'd be asked to think through the implications of certain values, always keeping in mind your own feelings about these implications.
>
> Notice something very important about this process. It is not concerned with discovering what absolute values there may or may not be. Instead, it is designed to help you clarify what values you actually hold, whether or not these values are absolute or relative, right or wrong. This means that values clarification does not replace such philosophical disciplines as ethics, aesthetics, and political theory. It is, however, what might be called "applied philosophy"—that is, the application of philosophy to real people's real problems. (p. 3)

Values Theory and Process

In the development of values theory, no individual has made a greater contribution than that of Lawrence Kohlberg. His research was significant in formulating a theoretical viewpoint on moral (or values) development. Kohlberg's early conclusions were that children go through six stages of moral development:

1. Heteronomous morality—Obeying the rules to avoid punishment.

2. Individualism, instrumental—purpose and change—Following rules when it is in one's best interest. Serving one's own interests.

3. Mutual interpersonal expectations, relationships and interpersonal conformity—Living up to what is expected of you by others. Being a good person in your own eyes.

4. Social system and conscience—Fulfilling duties, contributing to the group and society. Satisfying your conscience.

5. Social contract or utility and individual rights—Obligation to the law—commitment to family, friends, work.

6. Universal ethical principles—Follows universal principles of morality. (McCandless & Coop, 1979, pp. 163–164)

Kohlberg believed that the individual's development could become fixed at any one of the six stages. He

> proposed a moral education program centered around discussions of real and hypothetical dilemmas. The ultimate goal of the program was the moral maturity of the student with moral maturity being defined as "the principled sense of justice." Realizing there might be a disparity between the values the schools said they wished to foster and those they exemplified in their hidden curriculum, he insisted that the hidden curriculum be made "explicit in intellectual and verbal discussions of justice and morality." (Pyszkowski, 1986, p. 22)

A major hypothesis of values clarification that has significant implications for counselors utilizing these techniques suggests that the skillful and consistent use of the valuing process by an individual increases the likelihood that the individual will make appropriate decisions that will be satisfying both to the individual and to society. Raths, Harmin, and Simon (1978) translated this theory into a process consisting of seven subprocesses grouped under three categories. They then suggested that a value in one's life must meet the following criteria:

Choosing

1. freely
2. from alternatives
3. after thoughtful consideration of each alternative

Prizing

4. cherishing, being happy with the choice
5. willing to affirm the choice publicly

Acting

6. doing something with the choice
7. repeatedly, in some pattern of life. (p. 28)

Howe and Howe (1975) suggest a process that seems particularly adaptable to counseling strategies:

1. Developing a climate of acceptance, trust, and open communication
2. Building self-concepts
3. Creating awareness of prizing and publicly affirming values
4. Helping individuals choose freely from alternatives after weighing the consequences
5. Helping individuals learn to set goals and take actions on their values

This process is applicable in both individual and group counseling settings.

Having broadly viewed values and their impact on behavior, noted a basis for values theory, and described similarities between valuing and counseling process, let us examine further some of the relationships between values and counseling.

VALUES AND COUNSELING

Historic Concerns

Rockwell and Rothney (1961) indicate that from the very beginning of the counseling and guidance movement in the United States, leaders in this movement have expressed concern with values. The "father" of this movement, Frank Parsons, has been described as a "utopian social reformer," believing in the perfectibility of humanity. He viewed guidance as a means to a mutualistic society and the counselor's role as one leading to social goals by offering prescriptive advice. Jessie Davis preached the moral values of hard work, ambition, honesty, and the development of good character as assets in the business world.

Later, Carl Rogers stated his beliefs in the goodness and worthwhileness of people and their abilities to chart their own destiny. C. Gilbert Wrenn, in *The Counselor in a Changing World* (1962) and *The World of the Contemporary Counselor* (1973), discussed the values of the counselor and his or her clients. In the former book he writes:

> It has become increasingly clear that the counselor cannot and does not remain neutral in the face of the student's value conflicts. Even the counselors who believe most strongly in letting the student work out his own solutions have firm values of their own and cannot help communicating them. They communicate their values in what they do and don't do even if they never mention their beliefs verbally. Furthermore, we expect more and more of the counselor with reference to the needs of society. Just to accept the need for the full development of abilities in the interest of a stronger nation as well as the interest of the individual is a manifest expression of a social value. Because the counselor cannot escape dealing with values and expressing values in his own behavior, he must be clear about the nature of his own values and how they influence his relationships with other people.
>
> A second developing conviction about values is that they are now seen by some psychologists as the central difficulty for many troubled people. Fifty years ago values were clearly defined, and acute maladjustment seemed to result from a willful violation of them. Psychological treatment consisted primarily of freeing the individual from an overwhelming sense of guilt over his transgression against his parents and other representatives of society. But today the picture seems almost the reverse of what it was. The maladjusted person feels himself more lost than guilty. Social expectations have become more diverse, less well defined, less insistent. The

social processes of inculcating strong values are less effective today, in part because family and community are less cohesive.

As a consequence the individual feels a lack of purpose and direction. He feels less estranged from others and even from himself; he feels worthless and unsure of his identity. He must discover character in himself for himself. Values strongly felt are the foundation upon which he can build an increasingly satisfying personal existence. Thus, clarifying values and perhaps acquiring new values becomes a major task for the individual in counseling, as in education generally.* (pp. 62–63)

In the later publication, *The World of the Contemporary Counselor*, Wrenn discusses the counselor's and client's values:

The Counselor's Values

A first concern is that the counselor examine his own hierarchy of values and check it against the contemporary scene. I do not suggest that the counselor must change his values to meet changing assumptions, but rather that he attempt to increase his openness to the intrusions of change. A feeling of great certainty that what he now thinks is right and is right for all time can become a simple rigidity. It is too easy to retreat into a secure castle of one's own construction and close the gates to all that might disturb. It is healthy to be disturbed, for this means that one is required to think, to test assumptions, to question thoughtfully the bases for conduct. It is more realistic to confess confusion than to parade conviction.

On the other hand, admitting confusion could be interpreted as justifying having no convictions, no assurances of vital values. I must anticipate at this point what I want to discuss more carefully later, that one can be committed to values and goals even though they are tentative. In fact, one must be committed to be real, but the commitment may be to values which are seen as subject to modification, as changing with experience. "Tentativeness and commitment" paralleling each other are powerful principles.

The Client's Values

The second area of concern is the acceptance of the client's right to be different in his values. This difference between the values of the client and those of the counselor is often a difference between generations or between cultures. Always, of course, the values of the client are the product of his life experience, unique to him and often markedly different from the experience of the counselor. The 30-year-old, middle-class, socially accepted, college-educated counselor cannot be expected to understand in all cases the values of a 16-year-old, ghetto-reared, socially rejected boy or girl or those of an affluent, socially amoral, parentally rejected youth. In fact, experiential understanding of another is rare. What is most important, however, is that the counselor accept the client's values as being as real and as "right" for him as the counselor's values are for the counselor. There is too frequently a tendency to protest inwardly, "He can't really mean that," when the value expressed by the client is in sharp contrast to a related value held by the counselor. The point is that the client does mean that; his value assumption is as justifiable to him as yours is to you.

So far I have said nothing about the counselor's responsibility for helping the client to examine a given value assumption, particularly if the value is likely to result in behavior harmful to another or to society. He has such a responsibility, I am sure, differing widely from client to client and varying often with the client's psychological readiness to examine values. Basic to

---

*From C. Gilbert Wrenn, *The Counselor in a Changing World*. Copyright © 1962 by Houghton Mifflin Company. Used with permission.

the success of any such confrontation, however, is the counselor's acceptance of the "right" of the client to have different values. If a counselor enters into a discussion of another's point of view with the implicit assumption that he is "right" and the other is "wrong," failure is assured.* (pp. 34–35)

Relationship to Counseling Theory

As we proceed to examine values or moral education and values clarification and its relationship and potential usefulness for counselors and other helping professionals, let us examine its relationship to some of the traditional, theoretical approaches to counseling. For example, Simon and deSherbinin (1975) note that values clarification skills were natural companions of other skills that help people to develop their potential and live life more fully. Values clarification skills, it was suggested, go hand in hand with the work of Carl R. Rogers, emphasizing warmth and genuineness among people. Simon and deSherbinin go on to state:

> Values clarification can borrow something from Harvey Jackin's re-evaluation counseling model, in which people make commitments to help each other grow. Generally, people divide the time they have for each other into two equal segments during which each works as both client and counselor. This reciprocity generates power that penetrates deeply into people's lives; values clarification techniques can be used in exactly the same way.
>
> More and more, people working in T-groups are also coming to see that values clarification exercises rapidly advance their aims of getting people close to others' thoughts and feelings.
>
> It has also found its way into the training of Gestalt therapists. Gestalt teachers have sensed that its various strategies are useful in clarifying the way people respond to each other's problems.
>
> Other counselors simply fit a values clarification exercise into a transactional analysis technique. One way that transactional analysis workers have used values clarification is to ask a client to respond to a values question as if the child inside of him or her is speaking, then the parent inside, and then the adult. (p. 683)

Smith and Peterson (1977) note the relationship between counseling theory and values as the common ground for "teaching human beings how to live meaningfully with self and with one another" (p. 230). They then point out that a number of theoretical approaches to counseling and psychotherapy have long advocated this. For example, "All counseling and psychotherapy teaches values either directly (knowingly) or indirectly (unknowingly)" (p. 230). Smith and Peterson conclude that the actualization of consensual values in human affairs is an enormous task that requires the involvement of all persons who render guidance services.

Another concern for counselors using values clarification techniques was the criticism of these techniques in the early 1980s. These criticisms, frequently expressed on behalf of religious groups, often portray values clarification techniques as encouraging permissiveness, associated with secular humanism, and detracting from the role of the home and church in teaching values.

---

*From C. Gilbert Wrenn, *The World of the Contemporary Counselor.* Copyright © 1973 by Houghton Mifflin Company. Used with permission.

TABLE 6–3 Similarities Between Values Clarification and Counseling Processes

Stage	Values Clarification	Counseling
1	Getting acquainted Develops a climate of • Trust • Acceptance • Open communication	1. Relationship establishment Developing a helping relationship that facilitates the client's communication of his or her reasons for seeking counseling assistance
2	Builds an individual's self-concept	2. Identification and exploration of client's concern
3	Helps an individual become aware of his or her values	3. Awareness and examination of options available to client
4	Helps individuals choose and affirm their values freely from alternatives after weighing the consequences	4. Client makes decisions after weighing consequences of each option
5	Helps individuals set goals and take action on their values	5. Implementation of decision Goals are set and client takes action

VALUES CLARIFICATION TECHNIQUES AND COUNSELING PRACTICE

The process of counseling and the processes of values clarification share much in common. As depicted in Table 6–3, both depend heavily on relationship establishment and maintenance; both seek to identify and explore the consequences of appropriate options; both emphasize that choices or decisions are made by the client; and both processes recognize the importance of carrying out decisions through action.

Most values clarification techniques appear to emphasize group participation—and although this is true, it does not necessarily limit their utilization or inclusion in the process of individual counseling. Many of the techniques can be completed by an individual client and then shared and examined within the framework of the counseling process. Such exercises (some of which will be described in more detail later in exercises at the end of this chapter) as drawing a hobby plaque, listing 20 things you like to do, selecting from alternatives, and discussing situational anecdotes are examples of those that can be satisfactorily completed by the client, then discussed and examined with the counselor. They may in turn help the client confirm and practice more appropriate and satisfying behavior.

THE COUNSELOR AND VALUES CLARIFICATION TECHNIQUES

Values clarification theory and practice has much in common with counseling theory and practice. In theory, both are seeking to assist individuals in realizing their fullest potential. In practice, both values clarification and counseling seek to assist the individual in developing better self-understanding and a positive self-concept, making appropriate decisions and meaningful choices, and satisfactorily adjusting to the demands of everyday living.

Because values clarification techniques are popularly practiced in groups, their potential for group counseling and guidance is considerable. For example, numerous values clarification techniques designed to promote getting acquainted and developing interpersonal relationship and communication skills would have their appropriate moments in group counseling and guidance. Group values exercises designed to facilitate self-assessment, self-concept clarification, and reinforcement for change would have their usefulness for the group counselor. Exercises that give a person the opportunity to compare, examine, and defend his or her behavior, values, and interests against the norms of others can also be useful in group counseling.

SUMMARY

Today's society is group oriented, and each person belongs to many groups. These groups serve a variety of purposes, and in them one plays a variety of roles. Because of this group orientation, group counseling and guidance have become increasingly recognized as a means of assisting individuals in meeting their adjustment and developmental needs in both school and non-school settings. These group activities are distinguished by the nature of their concern and the type of group experience provided. Group guidance activities are primarily confined to school settings with an emphasis on providing information or experiences helpful in decision making. Group counseling tends to focus on routine adjustments and developmental needs or problems of individuals, whereas group therapy provides an intense experience that may last for a considerable length of time for individuals with serious adjustment, emotional, or developmental needs. The counselor's role and leadership are important to the success and accomplishment of both guidance and counseling groups. The group counselor must also be skillful and aware of the steps through which the group process moves. This process begins with the selection of members and the initial establishment of the group as a group, the identification of group goals, the clarification and exploration of the group's and its individual members' problems and/or concerns, the exploration of solutions and consequences, decision making regarding solutions, implementation of the decision, and, finally, termination and evaluation.

In recent years much media attention has been given to the values of youths, the shifting values of the adult world, and the significance of personal values for satisfaction in the world of work. Values have also become increasingly important to professional counselors. Values clarification techniques can provide a helpful and nonthreatening approach for assisting clients in groups and appraising individuals. In a planned program of values clarification and development, the individual initially engages in exercises designed to identify his or her values, then shares them; next, examines them; confirms them, and finally, practices values. Varied group exercises are available for utilization by counselors.

Of course, for counseling—whether group or individual—to be maximally effective, it is important to know the client as well as possible. Assessment techniques that counselors may utilize for this purpose are discussed in the next two chapters.

DISCUSSION QUESTIONS

1.   In how many different groups do you actively participate during a typical day? How does your role and function differ across groups?

2. What are the differences among group counseling, group guidance, and group therapy?

3. What are some typical guidance needs of school-aged youth that can be dealt with effectively in groups? What are some typical guidance needs of adult populations that can be dealt with effectively in groups?

4. Identify counseling situations in which you believe group counseling might be more effective than individual counseling.

5. How do you account for the popularity of sensitivity, T-, and encounter groups in recent years? Do you see any potential dangers in the popularity of these groups?

6. Can individuals with differing personality traits be equally effective as group leaders?

7. Discuss differences in the values generally held by three different client populations: adolescents, working, middle-aged adults, and older Americans approaching retirement.

8. Are there any general societal values that ought to be taught to all youth through a deliberate program of values education?

CLASS ACTIVITIES

1. Divide into small groups, with the goal of each group member to be the identification of a new behavior that he or she would like to develop. The group then works together to write a contract to be used by all group members. Reconvene in 1 week to discuss progress/setbacks as well as possible changes in the contract.

2. In small groups, discuss in which situations you would like to improve your communication skills with others. Include both in-school and career settings.

3. Organize the class into small groups. Each group identifies a growth or learning activity agreed on by the group members and proceeds to accomplish the goal of their group (insofar as

time will permit). Each group then analyzes the dynamics and varying roles of members in the group.

4. Organize the class into small groups. Groups are to assume they are being exiled to an island for 1 week. Transportation to the island will be furnished by a rowboat. In addition to normal clothing for mild, but rainy, fall weather, each member of the group may bring six items (not to exceed 20 pounds) for the group's survival. These items should include the necessary foodstuffs and liquids for the group's nourishment during their period of internment. Following the conclusion of the exercise and the reporting of it to the class, each group should reconvene to analyze the dynamics of the group experience, noting the various roles played by members of the group.

5. Organize the class into small groups. Each group will design a meaningful group activity and demonstrate this activity. (You may use another classroom group for the demonstration if this would be more meaningful.)

6. Observe the dynamics of a group outside this class and report your observations.

SELECTED READINGS

The following special issues of *The Journal for Specialists in Group Work:* "Critical Issues in Group Work: Now and 2001," *10*(1); and "Support Groups," *11*(2).

Bretzing, B. H., & Caterino, L. C. (1984). Group counseling with elementary students. *School Psychology Review, 3*, 515–518.

Kalra, S. K. (1980). Development of achievement values during childhood: Nonfamily members' influence. *Journal of Social Work, 41*, 235–239.

Karniauski, C. (1988). Using group development theory in business and industry. *The Journal for Specialists in Group Work, 13*, 30–43.

Morganett, R. S. (1990). *Skills for living: Group counseling activities for young adolescents.* Champaign, IL: Research Press.

Riordan, R. J., Beggs, M. S., & Karniauski, C. (1988). Some critical differences between self-help and therapy groups. *The Journal for Specialists in Group Work, 13,* 24–29.

Stockton, R., & Morran, K. (1985). Perceptions on group research programs. *Journal for Specialists in Group Work, 10,* 186–191.

Tedeschi, R. G., & Calhoun, L. G. (1993). Using the support group to respond to the isolation of bereavement. *Journal of Mental Health Counseling, 15,* 47–54.

RESEARCH OF INTEREST

Bundy, M. L., & Boser, J. (1987). Helping latch-key children: A group guidance approach. *School Counselor, 35,* 58–65.

Abstract

Develops a curriculum to give latchkey children more comprehensive instruction in survival skills. Field tests were conducted to determine the effectiveness of the program with 15 participants. Children who participated in the program became more knowledgeable about the procedures they should use when home alone.

Elliot, T. R. (1990). Training vocational rehabilitation counselors in group dynamics: A psychoeducational model. *Journal of Counseling and Development, 68,* 696–698.

Abstract

Describes a psychoeducational program for training vocational rehabilitation counselors in group dynamics. Emphasizes that training programs may be effective in providing vocational rehabilitation counselors with information to understand team dynamics and skill to competently work with group issues. Favorable reactions of participants to the program support its utility with vocational rehabilitation counselors.

Graff, R. W., Whitehead, G. I., III, & LeCompte, M. (1986). Group treatment with divorced women using cognitive behavioral and supportive-insight methods. *Journal of Counseling Psychology, 33,* 276–281.

Abstract

Compares the effectiveness of two kinds of group counseling with divorced woman: cognitive behavioral and supportive insight. On the posttest, both cognitive-behavioral-and supportive-insight-oriented treatments were more effective on most criteria. At follow-up, cognitive-behavioral counseling continued to be beneficial.

Morran, D. K., & Stockton, R. (1991). Delivery of positive and corrective feedback in counseling groups. *Journal of Counseling Psychology, 38,* 410–414.

Abstract

Data are analyzed for 48 group members, each participating in one of six personal growth groups. Members compose, rate, and deliver items of positive and corrective feedback. Each feedback item is rated by the deliverer on four dependent measures related to fears of giving feedback to another group member. Findings indicate that group members are more reluctant to give corrective feedback than positive feedback. Follow-up analyses of this significant effect reveal that group members feared that their corrective feedback would be regarded as harmful by the recipient and other group members. However, group members' strongest fears are related to being rejected by other group members as a result of having delivered corrective feedback. Implications are discussed, and suggestions for future research are provided.

Omizo, M. M., Cubberly, W. E., & Longaro, D. M. (1984). The effects of group counseling on self-concept and locus of control among learning disabled children. *Journal of Humanistic Education and Development, 23,* 69–79.

Abstract

Examines the effectiveness of group counseling, focusing on elimination of self-defeating behaviors in 60 children with learning disabilities. Results of pre- and posttest measures indicate that compared to controls, children in the counseling group have higher aspirations, lower anxiety, and significantly higher internal locus-of-control scores.

Omizo, M. M., & Omizo, S. A. (1987). Group counseling with children of divorce: New findings. *Elementary School Guidance and Counseling, 22,* 46–52.

Abstract

Assigns 60 children of divorce to experimental or control conditions, with experimental subjects participating in group counseling intervention. Comparison of two groups reveals that participation in group counseling appears beneficial for enhancing self-concept and internal locus of control among elementary school children experiencing parental divorce.

Omizo, M., & Omizo, S. A. (1988). Group counseling's effects on self-concept and social behavior among children with learning disabilities. *Journal of Humanistic Education and Development, 26,* 109–117.

Abstract

Examines the efficacy of 10 weekly group counseling sessions on the self-concept and social behavior among 62 fourth, fifth, and sixth grade children with learning disabilities from various ethnic backgrounds. Participation in the group sessions is found to be beneficial to the self-concept and specific areas of social behavior among the children with learning disabilities. Recommends that the study be replicated with other populations who are having similar difficulties and the long-term efficacy of the intervention strategy be done.

Oppenheimer, B. T. (1984). Short-term small group intervention for college freshmen. *Journal of Counseling Psychology, 31,* 45–53.

Abstract

Examines the effectiveness of a short-term small-group intervention in facilitating the social adjustment of 99 college freshmen. The social adjustment of vulnerable subjects was significantly enhanced by group participation, whereas nonvulnerable subjects were unaffected, which demonstrates the value of a small-group experience in facilitating the transition to college.

Rohde, R. I., & Stockton, R. (1992). The effect of structured feedback on goal attainment, attraction to the group, and satisfaction with the group in small group counseling. *Journal of Group Psychotherapy, Psychodrama, & Sociometry, 44,* 172–180.

Abstract

Recent literature examines the effects of goal attainment, cohesion, and feedback in group counseling, but relatively little work examines the direct effects of structured feedback on goal attainment. Fifty-one clients participated in a 6-week small-group counseling experience. Clients in the experimental condition set goals and participated in structured feedback exercises at the end of each session. Clients in the control condition set goals but did not participate in structured feedback exercises. At the last session, members completed the attraction scale and the reflective questionnaire and assessed their own and other members' level of goal attainment. The results indicate a significant relationship between participation in structured feedback exercises and goal attainment.

Wantz, R. A., & Recor, R. D. (1984). Simultaneous parent-child group intervention. *Elementary School Guidance and Counseling, 19,* 126–131.

Abstract

Investigates the effects of a 6-week parent training program and parallel children's group on parent participation ($N = 11$) and child behavior ($N = 9$). Pretest and posttest results indicate the children's behavior improved significantly, parents' attendance increased, and parents felt they perceived their identified child more favorably.

Chapter 7

Standardized Testing and Human Assessment

This chapter will acquaint you with the role of standardized testing in assessment for counseling purposes. We will begin by acknowledging some of the controversies attending standardized testing, then move to a brief overview of test interpretation. Criteria for test selection and the different kinds of standardized tests will also be presented.

Few activities in education and psychology have remained as consistent an issue over the past 60 years or have been subject to the controversy and debate that has accompanied the standardized testing movement, not only in schools but in government agencies and business and industry as well. From statements in Cubberly's (1934) *Public Education in the United States* (1934) and Gross's (1963) *The Brain Watchers*, to "Use and Misuse of Tests in Education: Legal Implications" (Nolte, 1975), "IQ Tests and Culture Issue" (Ornstein, 1976), and "Standardized Tests: Are They Worth the Cost?" (Herndon, 1976), through Robinson's (1983) "Nader versus ETS [Educational Testing Services]" and more recently "America's Test Mania" (Fiske, 1988), the pros and cons of standardized test usage have been publicly dissected.

Social issues have been raised, and legal implications have been tested. Prominent psychologists and educators have also expressed concern over the continued uses and abuses of standardized testing. Many authorities have cautioned counselors and other users of the risks of clients drawing unwarranted conclusions from test results, while others have lamented the overemphasis on test scores by individuals, school systems, government agencies and many businesses and industries. In addition, tests are also misused because of

> the too human desire for shortcuts, quick solutions, and clear-cut answers to our questions. This common human weakness has been capitalized on by soothsayers over the centuries, from phrenologists to astrologers and other self-styled expert advisers. People seeking guidance are often attracted by the facile promises of charlatans, in contrast to the slower, deliberate considerations and the carefully qualified suggestions of the scientifically trained professional. Similarly, if one or two short tests—whatever their technical limitations and defects—seem to offer a simple answer to questions about career choice, interpersonal difficulties, emotional problems, or learning deficiencies, many test takers will be temporarily satisfied. At another level, some misuse of tests by a counselor or other test user may arise from time pressure or work overload, which renders shortcuts attractive. (Anastasi, 1992, p. 610)

Albert Shanker, president of the American Federation of Teachers, writes that "exams fail the test" (1988), for the following reasons:

> ❖ Since the reputation of a school, its principal, its teachers and the school board and superintendent depends largely on these test scores, schools are devoting less time to reading real books, writing essays, and discussing current events and more and more time teaching kids strategies for filling in blanks and choosing the answers to multiple-choice questions. This destroys much of the value of these tests, which only tell you something if they are an independent measure of what the student knows. School districts are now engaged in a process called "curriculum alignment." That means that course content, textbooks, lesson plans, etc. are all being geared to items that will be on the test. These tests only tap a sample of skills, so it's possible for kids to do well and still not be able to understand real books. But since there's only so much time, schools now minimize or totally leave out those things that are not on these tests. This is the tail wagging the dog. Schools and teachers should not be pressured to drop content they believe to be valuable just because it won't be on the test.

✦ The tests are very costly in terms of both time and money. Coaching and testing time has increased so much that it is significantly taking away blocks of time from teaching and learning.

✦ The test scores published by schools and districts are misleading if not downright fraudulent.

✦ Students who take these tests are not being measured against their peers, but against norm groups who took the test as much as 3 to 10 years earlier.* (p. E7)

A nationwide survey of test usage in grades 7 through 12 by Engen, Lamb, and Prediger (1982) confirmed that testing still was playing an integral role in most schools. The data indicated that 9 out of 10 schools provide career guidance tests, 3 out of 4 administer achievement tests, and 2 out of 3 use aptitude tests. The majority of the 547 schools administered each of these three categories of tests to all students in one or more grades.

Anne Anastasi (1982), an internationally recognized expert on psychological and educational testing, notes:

Even well-educated laypersons have been known to confuse percentiles with percentage scores, percentiles with IQs, norms with standards, and interest ratings with aptitude scores. But a more serious misinterpretation pertains to the conclusions drawn from test scores, even when their technical meaning is correctly understood. (p. 55)

In 1983 the popular report of the National Commission on Excellence in Education entitled *A Nation at Risk* based much of its negative findings on standardized test results, fueling once again the controversies over the role of testing in educational evaluation. In the 1990s the continued impact of the accountability movement plus demands that schools "measure up" have resulted in the continued and, yes, increased use of standardized tests despite the controversies.

Although critics of standardized testing abound, and standardized measurement continues to be criticized, much of the criticism may be as appropriately directed at the misuse and misinterpretation of the instruments as at the tests themselves. The misuse of tests in schools, especially, appears to stem from test users who are inadequately prepared in administering and interpreting standardized tests. At the same time, however, in many schools and school systems, as well as a wide variety of agency settings, tests are used with prudence and caution by adequately trained counselors and psychologists. In most institutional or agency settings where counseling takes place, including schools, standardized tests have been the counselor's basic instrument for objective assessment of the personality traits, aptitudes, interests, and other characteristics of individuals. Clearly, individual counseling demands a knowledge and recognition of the individuality of clients. Measurement of individual differences is a part of the mainstream of personnel psychology.

It therefore is most appropriate to introduce potential counselors to this important area of counselor understanding and skill, recognizing the continuing debates and issues. Such knowledge plus a basic understanding of these areas of testing will enable you to more effectively discriminate between uses and abuses and retain in your counseling repertoire a useful analytical tool.

---

*From A. Shanker, "Where We Stand: Time for Truth in Testing: Exams Fail the Test," *New York Times*, April 24, 1988. Used by permission.

Standardized assessment is largely represented in the processes and practice of standardized testing. The term *standardized* is derived from the application of standards to (a) prescribed conditions and procedures to be uniformly utilized in administering, scoring, and interpreting the assessment instrument and (b) the measurement by the instrument of performance through the creation of norms or expected patterns of performance by specific populations.

STANDARDIZED TEST SCORES—WHAT DO THEY MEAN?

Whenever we evaluate someone, we do it in terms of some kind of comparison or point of reference. For instance, we may refer to Paul as the most handsome one in the group, Kathy as the best student in the class, and Nancy as the hardest worker in the bookstore. Here, we are comparing Paul to all others in the group, Kathy to the other students in the class, and Nancy to the other workers in the bookstore. Although we might attempt to make some predictions or deduce some other traits for Paul, Kathy, and Nancy from our observation, these would amount to nothing more than speculations, and we could justifiably be accused of unreliable procedures and data. If Paul, Kathy, and Nancy were to seek counseling, their counselor would want more objective and valid data before attempting to describe their traits and performances against the average traits and performances of others with comparable characteristics and experiences. An elementary understanding of statistics and statistically based tests, however, would enable the counselor to do this.

These basic understandings of educational and psychological statistics enable the counselor to (a) describe the characteristics of an individual or group in comparison with a specific group or population, (b) predict the probability of future success or failure in a given area on the basis of present or past behavior, and (c) infer the characteristics of a population from a sample of that population. It therefore follows that a good working knowledge of elementary statistical concepts is important for anyone who uses the various techniques of individual analysis and mandatory for all who use tests and other tools of measurement. This section offers a brief overview of descriptive statistics, the basic statistical terms, and essential computational procedures, beginning with perhaps the most common—and most commonly misunderstood—of all statistical terms, average.

Averages

When Linda reports to her parents that she scored "70" on her history test, should they be pleased, satisfied, disappointed, or what? Until they have more information, they cannot be sure how to react, because 70 could represent 70% of the questions answered correctly, 70 answered correctly out of 75 asked, a formula score of 70 (i.e., rights minus wrongs), or 70th in a class of 120 taking the examination. In this example, you may note that a score in and of itself is of little value. A score only becomes meaningful when it provides an index of how well or how poorly one performed in comparison with others taking the same test and, knowing that, what other significance can be interpreted from the results. Linda's parents might be asking what an average performance is on this test and how she differs from the average. Also, one might ask to what does her score relate— what does it mean? Let us begin then by reviewing what is meant by averages.

Most educational and psychological evaluation is based on a person's position in a group compared with others who constitute the group. The average position in a group becomes an important point of mathematical reference in standardized testing for human assessment. There are three distinct statistical types of averages, known as *measures of central tendency:* the mean, the median, and the mode. For most nonstatisticians, the definition of the mean is commonly associated with the term *average,* for the *mean* is defined as the mathematical average of a group of scores. The *median* is the midpoint of a set of scores with 50% of the scores being distributed above and 50% below that point. The *mode* represents the most frequent score in a set of scores. Of these three averages, the mean is the most useful and popular, and the mode, having little statistical value, is the least popular.

Variations from the Average

Once we have determined what is average, we must utilize a statistical methodology to measure the degree to which each person varies from this established average, or *point of central tendency.* Such statistical measures are called *measures of variability.* Two common measures of variability are the range and the standard deviation. The *range* is the spread from the lowest score to the highest score in a distribution. The actual statistical formula is the highest score in a group, minus the lowest score plus one. (The plus one in this formula extends the range to its real limits, which are one-half of a score unit below the lowest.) The range is a relatively simple measurement device with limited descriptive value. The *standard deviation,* on the other hand, is a statistical process that allows for an exact determination of distances of scores from the mean.

The mean and the standard deviation, when computed for a specific set of test scores, enable a counselor to determine how well an individual performed in relation to the group. This interpretation is made by specifying standard deviation distance from the mean and determining the proportion of the population that will be beyond or deviate from it, assuming that the scores are normally distributed. This normally distributed population is most popularly viewed as a normal curve, as shown in Figure 7–1. (Note: Rarely are the mean, median, and mode the same.)

FIGURE 7–1
The Normal Curve

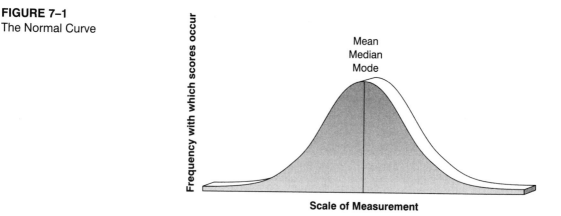

FIGURE 7–2 Scores in a
Normal Distribution

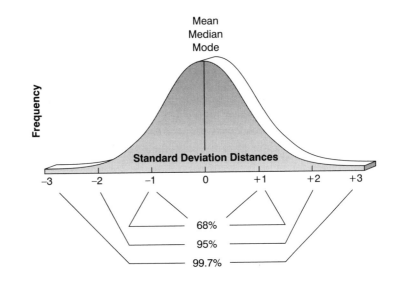

In Figure 7–2, the normal curve is, in effect, sliced into bands, one standard deviation wide, with a fixed percentage of cases always falling in each band. Figure 7–2 then illustrates a significant fact: The mean plus and minus one standard deviation encompasses approximately 68% of a normally distributed population; the mean plus and minus two standard deviations encompasses approximately 95% of that population; and the mean plus and minus three standard deviations encompasses 99.74% of that population. This information, which remains constant for any normally distributed set of scores or values, makes possible a meaningful interpretation of any score in a group. As you view the normal curve and its segmentation into standard deviations, note that these facts are handy for interpreting standard scores. Furthermore, whenever you can assume a normal distribution, you can convert standard scores to percentile scores, and vice versa. Thus, three basic facts for deriving a statistical evaluation of a person's performance on a psychological test are the person's raw score, mean, and standard deviation for the group with which the individual is being compared.

Relationships

Once you have determined the meaning of an individual's score in relation to others who have been administered the same measure, you must ask what are the other relationships or meanings of this score. The score and its comparative standing will take on meaning when it can be related to some meaningful purpose. For example, if students who score high on a college entrance examination actually perform at a high academic level in college, then one can assume that there is a relationship between scores on the examination and performance in college. The test score then becomes meaningful in terms of its prediction of college success, a meaningful purpose.

When you look for a statistical method to express relationships between two variables such as test scores and academic performance, you can compute a *correlation coefficient*.

Correlation coefficients range from plus one through zero to minus one. A plus one indicates a perfect positive correlation; that is, the rank order of those taking the college entrance examination and their academic rank order in the college program are identical. On the other hand, a correlation of minus one means that the scores go in exactly the reverse direction. Thus, a correlation of minus one would indicate that persons who score highest on the entrance examination achieve the lowest in college. A zero correlation would represent a complete lack of relationship between two sets of data. A frequently computed coefficient of correlation is the Pearson product-moment coefficient.

Statistical Symbols

The counselor, teacher, or others who read test manuals, interpret test data, or in other ways seek to interpret simple statistical data should be familiar with basic statistical symbols. Although there is no "universal statistical language," the following are some of the more commonly recognized symbols and their meanings:

M	Mean
Σ	Sum of
SD (or S)	Standard deviation for a particular set of scores
X	Actual or "raw" scores obtained
MD	Median
x	Distance (or score difference) of a score from the mean
N	Number of cases
i	Size of a class interval in scale units
M'	Assumed mean
r	Coefficient of correlation
z	Scale value of the standard normal distribution; the standard deviation of distance of a given score from the mean
f	Frequency; the number of times a particular score occurs
p	Percentage of persons getting a test item correct
q	Percentage of persons getting a test item wrong ($p + q = 100$)

Presenting Test Scores

Inasmuch as raw test scores are in themselves meaningless, they have little value for the reporting of individual test results. As previously indicated, a raw score becomes meaningful only when it can be converted into some type of comparative score—one that enables an individual to be compared against others of a group. Most standardized tests, therefore, utilize one or more of the following methods of converting raw scores into a more meaningful method of presenting an individual's test results.

Percentiles

A percentile score represents the percentage of persons in the standardized sample for a given test who fall below a given raw score. A person's percentile ranking indicates his or her relative position in a normative sample. For example, if 60% of the students answer fewer than 30 problems correctly on an English usage test, then a raw score of 30 corresponds to the 60th percentile.

Percentiles are probably the most common method of presenting scores and are relatively easy to interpret. Due to their relative ease of interpretation, however, several cautions should be noted. In working with non-test-sophisticated groups, such as parents, students, and most general populations, it is important to emphasize that percentiles do not represent percentages. Because percentiles represent comparison scores, it is also important to note the population with which an individual is being compared and the valid purposes for which comparisons can be made. It should also be noted that there are inequalities in percentile units.

The reason such distortion occurs is quite simple. When a raw-score distribution approximates the normal curve, there are many more moderate scores, which fall in the middle of the distribution, than either high or low scores, which occur at the ends. Since percentiles are based on the raw-score distance encompassed by a specified percentage of the total group, percentile distances near the median with its high concentration of cases will encompass a much smaller raw-score difference than the same percentile distance farther from the median. Hence the 15 points of raw-score difference between the 5th and 10th percentiles may shrink to 5 points of difference between the 40th and 45th.

These distortions make it difficult to use percentiles for profiling and other comparisons of a student's performance on two or more tests. To overcome the limitations in test interpretation resulting from the inequality of percentiles, more and more test publishers are turning to some type of standard score for norming.

Computing Percentiles. To expedite test interpretation, one may want to compute percentiles for a given group. Their computation is almost identical with the procedures for computing the median (which is the 50th percentile).

The formula for computing percentiles from a grouped frequency distribution is

$$P_x = l + \left(\frac{P_r N - \Sigma fb}{fw} \right) i$$

Thus if the 75th percentile is desired, $P_x = 0.75$; if the 40th percentile is desired, $P_x = 0.40$. The other symbols have the same meaning as in the formula for the median.

As noted earlier, a grouped frequency table—once it is properly prepared—can be used for computing most of the elementary statistics a counselor might need for that set of scores. However, the computation of percentiles is made easier by adding to the table a column showing progressive accumulation of frequencies. This is called a *cf* (cumulative frequency) column; it is shown at the left in Table 7–1, which uses the hypothetical Oakwood High School data.

The following steps show how one would go about finding the 25th percentile for the Oakwood High School data given in Table 7–1.

1. Multiply N by the desired percentile (converted to a decimal) to determine the class in which this percentile falls. For the Oakwood group, N is 250 and the desired percentile is 25. The product of 0.25×250 is 62.5; the *cf* column indicates that the score value of the individual ranking 62.5 from the bottom is found within the class 50–54, so it is established that P_{25} lies between 49.5 and 54.5.

TABLE 7–1 Computation of percentiles

cf	X	f	d	fd
250	95–99	2	7	14
248	90–94	3	6	18
245	85–89	5	5	25
240	80–84	10	4	40
230	75–79	15	3	45
215	70–74	22	2	44
193	65–69	38	1	38
155	60–64	55	0	0
100	55–59	32	−1	−32
68	50–54	28	−2	−56
40	45–49	17	−3	−51
23	40–44	14	−4	−56
9	35–39	5	−5	−25
4	30–34	4	−6	−24
		$N = 250$		$\sum fd = -20$

2. Determine the necessary values for the formula:
$$P_{25}N = 62.5$$
$$\sum fb = 40$$
$$fw = 28$$
$$i = 5$$

3. Insert the values in the formula and perform the indicated computations:
$$P_{25} = 49.5 + \left(\frac{62.5 - 40}{28}\right) 5$$
$$= 49.5 + \frac{22.5 \times 5}{28}$$
$$= 49.5 + 4.02$$
$$= 53.52 \text{ or, rounded, } 54$$

Deciles and Quartiles

Chase (1984) describes deciles and quartiles as follows:

> Two kinds of figures besides percentiles are also frequently used to show relative standing in a group. These are *deciles* and *quartiles,* both of which are similar to, and indeed can be read from, percentile tables. Deciles are points that divide the distribution of raw scores into segments of 10 percent each. Thus, the first decile D_1 would be that point on the distribution below which 10 percent of the cases fall, D_2 the point below which 20 percent of the cases fall, etc. Deciles can be computed in the same manner as percentiles, since D_1 is P_{10}, D_2 is P_{20}, etc.

Deciles, like percentiles, are points on a scale. Therefore, a score can be between the third and the fourth deciles, i.e., in the fourth lowest 10 percent of the group, but it cannot be in the third decile, since that decile is only a point on the scale.

Quartiles divide the distribution of raw scores into segments of 25 percent each. Thus, the first quartile, Q_1 is the point that cuts off the lowest 25 percent, Q_2 the lowest 50 percent of the group (what is another name for this point?), and Q_3 the lowest 75 percent of the distribution.

It should be emphasized, however, that deciles and quartiles, like percentiles, are points along the scale. They are not segments of that scale. It is wrong to say that case X *is in the third quartile* or something similar. This is an error because the third quartile is only a point on the scale. (p. 77)

Standard Scores

Standard scores have become increasingly popular with standardized test developers. A standard score expresses a person's distance from the mean in terms of the standardized deviation of the distribution. For example, let us return to Kathy, Paul, and Nancy and their scores on a test:

Mean of the test takers	75
Standard deviation	15
Kathy's score	90
Paul's score	65
Nancy's score	45

Using the formula $\dfrac{X(\text{raw score}) - M(\text{mean})}{SD(\text{standard deviation})}$, the following standard scores are obtained:

$$\text{Kathy:} \quad \frac{90 - 75}{15} = +1.0$$

$$\text{Paul:} \quad \frac{65 - 75}{15} = -0.7$$

$$\text{Nancy:} \quad \frac{45 - 75}{15} = -2.0$$

Because both decimal points and plus and minus signs may be confusing or easily misplaced, they can be transformed into a more convenient form by multiplying each standard score with some constant. For example, if we multiply these scores by 10, we have +10, −7, and −20. We can then eliminate the plus and minuses by adding a constant of 100. Thus, Kathy's score becomes 110, Paul's 93, and Nancy's 80.

Stanines

Another variation for normalizing standard scores was developed by the United States Air Force in World War II. The name *stanine* is a contraction of standard nine, a nine-point scale having a mean of five and a standard deviation of two. The percentages of a normal distribution that fall within each of the nine stanines are as follows:

Stanine	1	2	3	4	5	6	7	8	9
Percentage	4	7	12	17	20	17	12	7	4

Relationships among various types of test scores and the normal curve may be noted in Figure 7–3.

A favorite expression of soldiers in the ranks is *snafu* (situation normal—all fouled up). We label persons as normal or abnormal if they deviate from our concept of normalcy, and we use such expressions as "He would normally do this" or "Under normal conditions you can expect that." The term *norm* or *normal* is a popular one that most persons use frequently to denote the expected or that which can be reasonably anticipated. The concept of normal or norm as utilized in standardized testing terminology also implies normal or average performance on a given test. Norms are derived during the process of standardizing a test. As a basis for determining the norms, a test is administered to a sample (usually large) that is representative of the population for whom the test is designed. This group then comprises the standardization sample to establish the norms for the test. These norms reflect not only the average performances but also the relative frequency of the varying degrees of deviation below and above the average.

Age Norms

The use of age norms or standards is a fairly popular one in the nonscientific sense. We often suggest that Joey is as big as a 10-year-old or Janie has the vocabulary of a 6-year-old. The use of this concept in reporting standardized testing results became popular when the term *mental age* was used during the translations and adaptations of the original Binet scales. From this initial usage, age norms were frequently used to measure any trait that showed progressive change with age. For example, in physical development, it would be relatively simple to prepare norms for the height or weight of growing children by years. In testing, age norms represent the test performance of persons grouped and normed according to their chronological age. This type of score is more likely to be noted in the reporting of achievement tests, especially in the elementary school grades.

There are two shortcomings to this concept of scoring and reporting results. First, there is a lack of agreement regarding when children should be introduced to certain basic academic subjects, at what rates, and what comprehension level should normally be expected in these subjects. Also, age norms assume uniform growth from year to year, an assumption of questionable validity.

Grade Norms

Grade norms are similar to age norms inasmuch as they are based on the average score earned by students at a specific grade level. Again, grade norms are popular for reporting achievement test results in terms of grade equivalents. This method of reporting standardized test results, however, suffers from the same shortcomings as do age norms, but is more readily viewed as suggesting standards to which teachers should aspire. Table 7–2 contrasts the main type of norms for educational and psychological tests.

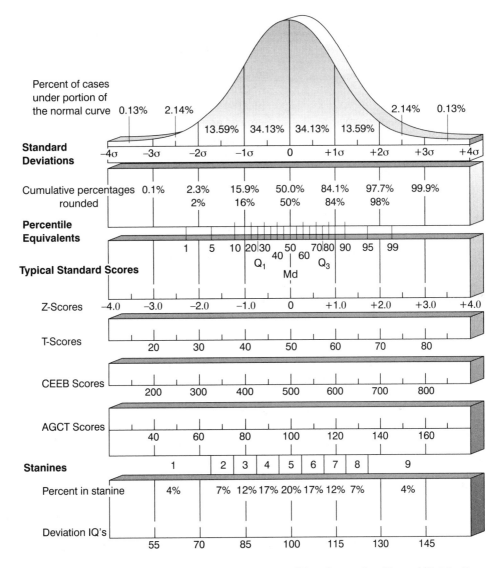

FIGURE 7–3 Relationships Among Different Types of Test Scores in a Normal Distribution
Source: Reprinted with the permission of Macmillan College Publishing Company from *Measurement and Evaluation in Psychology and Education,* 4th ed., by Robert M. Thorndike and Elizabeth P. Hagen (New York: Macmillan College Publishing Company, 1977), p. 133. All rights reserved.

TABLE 7–2 Main Types of Norms for Educational and Psychological Tests

Type of Norm	Type of Comparison	Type of Group
Age norms	Individual matched to groups whose performance he [or she] equals	Successive age groups
Grade norms	Same as above	Successive grade groups
Percentile norms	Percent of group surpassed by individual	Single age or grade group to which individual belongs
Standard score norms	Number of standard deviations individual falls above or below average of group	Same as above

Source: Reprinted with the permission of Macmillan College Publishing Company from *Measurement and Evaluation in Psychology and Education,* 4th ed., by Robert M. Thorndike and Elizabeth P. Hagen (New York: Macmillan College Publishing Company, 1977), p. 117. All rights reserved.

SELECTING A TEST—WHAT CRITERIA?

The numbers and variety of standardized tests available to counselors and other users today require a recognition and application of appropriate criteria in test selection. Furthermore, much of the criticism of standardized testing over the years has focused on poorly designed instruments and poorly prepared users, which implies the need of criteria for both. Certainly, there are clinical as well as research-based reasons for concern with the trustworthiness of the data produced by assessment devices.

For obvious reasons, counselors should not use standardized tests that do not give accurate measures or that they (the counselors) are not competent to interpret. An error in measurement and/or interpretation can lead to an error in client decision making.

Validity

Validity is traditionally defined as the degree to which an instrument measures what it claims to measure or is used to measure. For example, does the Whiffenpoof Mechanical Aptitude Test really measure one's aptitude for mechanical activities, as claimed, or does it simply reflect one's previous experiences in the areas being tested? Or, to raise a question of traditional controversy, do IQ tests really measure basic or native intelligence, or do they more appropriately reflect one's cultural and educational experiences? In establishing validity, one must note the appropriateness of test or interview questions and situational samples to the evaluation objectives. Since it is impossible to include all possible questions or situations in an evaluation tool, those selected for inclusion must be representative of the content areas or behavioral patterns being assessed and appropriate for the individual under study and the given circumstances. When an instrument meets these conditions, it is said to have *content validity*.

When the foregoing types of validity do not or cannot provide sufficient evidence of a test's validity, its construct validity may be cited. *Construct validity* pertains to the adequacy of the theory or concept underlying a specific instrument. In other words, it involves logically ascertaining the psychological attributes that account for variations in test scores or other derived data. Construct validity is reported in terms of the kinds of responses the test should elicit and the ways in which those responses should be interpreted on the basis of logical inferences about the behavior the test is designed to appraise.

Reliability

The second major criterion to be applied in standardized test selection is reliability. *Reliability* represents the consistency with which a test will obtain the same results from the same population but on different occasions. An instrument's reliability enables a counselor or other user to determine the degrees to which predictions based on the established consistency of the test can be made.

Two techniques are popularly used to establish reliability. One is the *test-retest method*. When this method is used, timing between the tests is crucial because growth or decline in performance could occur if the interval is too long, whereas recall of original test items might occur if the interval is too short. A second approach for determining reliability is by establishing an instrument's *internal consistency*. This consistency is established by comparing persons' responses to the odd-numbered questions with the consistency of their responses to the even-numbered questions.

Practicality

A third important, but often overlooked, criterion in the selection of a standardized instrument is that of practicality. First and foremost of the practical considerations is whether trained personnel are available to administer, score (if necessary), and interpret the particular standardized test under consideration. The importance of users' understanding the fine points of interpretation cannot be overemphasized.

A second and important practical consideration is the cost of the instrument and accompanying materials. The expense of scoring is included in this consideration. Additionally, many standardized tests can be used only for one testing, so replacement costs may become another factor. Time required for administration is also a practical consideration, especially, but not exclusively, in school settings.

TYPES OF STANDARDIZED TESTS

Having briefly examined statistical concepts, methods of scoring, and criteria for the selection of standardized tests, let us now consider the specific areas for which standardized tests are available. These include aptitude, achievement, interest, and personality testing. There is admittedly some overlap in these categories, especially in interest and personality, but we will examine them as discrete, though not exclusive, areas for the classification of standardized tests. This discussion will focus on group standardized tests. Although recognizing the value of individual tests and that counselors and psychologists in a variety of nonschool settings frequently use individual tests, beginning counselors, especially in educational settings, work almost exclusively with group tests.

Intelligence or Aptitude?

The terms *aptitude* and *intelligence* are often used synonymously. However, in the discussion of standardized tests, one should examine the subtle differences that distinguish measures of intelligence from measures of aptitude. One distinction is that intelligence tests tend to provide a broad measure of overall or general ability, primarily related to one's potential for learning, whereas aptitude measures tend to focus more narrowly on specific factors. Mehrens and Lehmann (1984) note:

> The distinction between the terms "aptitude" and "intelligence" is not at all clear, but some distinctions have been made on two separate bases. One distinction that has been made is whether the measure we obtain is considered a general measure. If so, the test is frequently called an intelligence test. If the test measures multiple or specific factors, it is termed an aptitude test. Thus, we might conceptualize different measures of intelligence (aptitude) as lying on a continuum, with global measures falling at one end and specific measures at the other. At some point along the continuum we could arbitrarily change the label of the construct we are measuring, from intelligence to aptitude. Although this schema has been suggested by some, it certainly is not universally followed. It does present some difficulties, because some tests are considered measures of a general factor, yet report subscores.
>
> Another distinction between the meaning of the two terms has an historical basis. During the time intelligence tests were first being developed, psychologists thought of intelligence as being an innate characteristic not subject to change. This assumption is invalid. However, the term "intelligence" unfortunately still connotes complete innateness to some people. To avoid the implications of innateness, many test makers prefer to use the term "aptitude." Because these aptitude tests are most useful in predicting future school success, some have suggested that the phrase scholastic aptitude tests is the most honest and descriptive. Others prefer to refer to all such tests as measures of learning ability.* (p. 372)

Intelligence Testing

The most popular area of aptitude or ability testing is the category that includes tests purporting to evaluate general academic ability, mental ability, and intelligence. Of these subsets, intelligence or IQ testing is the oldest and most controversial. Much of this controversy has centered around the various views of what constitutes intelligence, what influences it—heredity versus environment—and whether intelligence changes. These controversies have led to some renaming with more popularly accepted labels such as *academic ability, mental maturity, scholastic ability,* or *academic aptitude tests.* Some of these latter labels are probably more appropriate inasmuch as many of the earlier "IQ" tests were largely normed on school populations and developed to predict performance in school.

Other shortcomings of general intelligence assessment are that different people arrive at the same end by different intellectual means. The reading level of the test taker can bias the results. Judgments about intelligence can be linked with judgments about the "worth" of the individual. Finally, there has been a strong tendency to overlook the cultural and value relativity of intelligence judgments.

The first intelligence tests were designed for individual administering by a Frenchman, Alfred Binet, and in the early 1900s several American versions were developed.

---

*From *Measurement and Evaluation in Education and Psychology,* Third Edition, by William A. Mehrens and Irvin J. Lehmann, copyright © 1984 by Holt, Rinehart and Winston, Inc. Reprinted by permission of the publisher.

The most popular of these, the Stanford-Binet, based on the work of Lewis Terman at Stanford University, was published in 1916. This test has remained popular, with the most recent revisions reflected in the fourth edition (1986, Riverdale Publishing Company). The other popular individually administered intelligence tests are the various Wechsler scales.

One of the most popular group intelligence tests over the years has been the Otis, or, as currently labeled, the Otis-Lennon School Abilities Test (Harcourt Brace Jovanovich, 1989). The first Otis test appeared in 1918 as the Otis Group Intelligence Scale and later achieved great popularity in both industry and education as the Otis-Quick Scoring Mental Abilities Tests. The current (1989) edition has five levels ranging from grades 1–12, with working times of 60 or 75 minutes, depending on the level.

Two other popular group intelligence tests are the Lorge-Thorndike and the Henmon-Nelson Tests of Mental Ability. The Lorge-Thorndike intelligence test is available in two forms for grades 3–13. It provides both verbal and nonverbal batteries for those grades in a single reusable booklet. The verbal battery is made up of five subtests, using only verbal items: vocabulary, verbal classification, sentence completion, arithmetic reasoning, and verbal analogy. The nonverbal battery uses items that are either pictorial or numerical. The three subtests involved are pictorial classification, pictorial analogy, and numerical relationships. The tests in this battery yield an estimate of scholastic aptitude that is not dependent on an ability to read. The working times are verbal battery, 35 minutes; nonverbal battery, 27 minutes.

The Henmon-Nelson Test of Mental Ability is available in two editions: Form 1 for grades 3–12, and a primary battery for kindergarten–grade 2. The primary battery is normatively integrated with Form 1, which permits school systems to use the Henmon-Nelson tests throughout the entire kindergarten–grade 12 range.

Form 1 for grades 3–12 has three levels (3–6, 6–9, and 9–12), consisting of 90 items presented in order of increasing difficulty. Form 1 of the Henmon-Nelson Tests of Mental Ability was standardized in the fall of 1972 on a national sample of 35,000 subjects in grades 3–12.

The primary battery for kindergarten–grade 2 consists of three separate subtests: a listening test (general information, 30 items); a picture vocabulary test (33 items); and a size and number test (23 items). These short subtests measure simple verbal and quantitative skills considered important in assessing readiness for schoolwork.

Standardization in grade 2 was carried out concurrently with the norming of the Henmon-Nelson in grades 3–12 during the fall of 1972. For kindergarten and grade 1, standardization was done in early 1973 on a sample of approximately 5,000 pupils drawn from the same schools that participated in the grades 2–12 norming program.

Counselors should also be aware that many IQ tests have for years been suspected of cultural bias—a bias that would discriminate against minorities and populations in special environments. The use of intelligence tests should therefore be approached with extreme caution, if in fact they are to be used at all.

Aptitude Tests

Aptitude may be defined as a trait that characterizes an individual's ability to perform in a given area or to acquire the learning necessary for performance in a given area. It presumes an inherent or native ability that can be developed to its maximum through learn-ing or other experiences. However, it cannot be expanded beyond this certain point, even by learning. Although that may be a debatable concept, it is stated here as a basis on which aptitude tests are developed. In theory, then, an aptitude test measures the poten-tial of one to achieve in a given activity or learn to achieve in that activity.

Aptitude tests may potentially be used by counselors and others because they may (a) identify potential abilities of which the person is not aware, (b) encourage the develop-ment of special or potential abilities of a given person, (c) provide information to assist a person in making educational and career decisions or other choices between competing alternatives, (d) help predict the level of academic or vocational success a person might anticipate, and (e) be useful in grouping persons with similar aptitudes for developmental and other educational purposes. It should be emphasized that these are *potential* advan-tages only and will accrue only under optimal conditions, which include initially the use of appropriate and proper measurement instruments relevant to the client's needs.

While we usually anticipate that a person is likely to demonstrate considerable differ-ences across a range of aptitudes, we should also be alert to the possibility that a person will not demonstrate or "measure" at the same level for a given aptitude every time. In other words, a track star may run the 100-yard dash in 10 seconds one day and the same distance under the same conditions in 10.4 seconds the next day. Aptitude measures are thus actuarial rather than absolute.

Special Aptitude Tests

Special aptitude tests usually refer to those tests that seek to measure a person's potential ability to perform or acquire proficiency in a specific occupation or other type of activity. Tests that measure special aptitudes are sometimes referred to as *single-aptitude tests* or *component ability tests* because they only secure a measure for one specific aptitude or a single special ability. Tests of special aptitude have generally declined in popularity as apti-tude batteries have increased in popularity. Counselors must frequently use standardized tests to measure a single aptitude in areas of mechanical, clerical, or artistic abilities. Sin-gle-aptitude tests have also been developed for use in various graduate and professional schools. Aptitude tests are also available for particular school subjects, especially in the areas of mathematics and foreign languages.

Vocational Aptitude Batteries

Aptitude batteries are developed on the assumption that different career fields have their own set of unique criteria. Further, being able to profile and contrast results for differing careers is an advantage.

Multiple-aptitude tests are an outgrowth of factorial studies of intelligence. Anastasi (1988) discusses the objective of factor analysis:

> The principal objective of factor analysis is to simplify the description of data by reducing the number of necessary variables, or dimensions. Thus, if we find that five factors are sufficient to account for all the common variance in a battery of 20 tests, we can for most purposes substi-tute five scores for the original 20 without sacrificing any essential information. The usual

practice is to retain from among the original tests those providing the best measures of each of the factors.* (pp. 374–375)

These batteries typically consist of a series of subtests related in varying combinations to a series of occupations or occupationally related activities. The major advantages of batteries over single-aptitude tests are (a) convenience in administration as a result of having in one package a test that can be used to measure potential in a variety of activities; (b) the norming of all the battery's subtests on the same population, which thus yields comparable subtest norms; and (c) the opportunity to compare potential in a wide variety of areas with one test.

The oldest and most widely used of these multiple-aptitude batteries are the General Aptitude Test Battery (GATB), used by the United States Employment Services, and the Differential Aptitude Battery (DAT). The Flanigan Aptitude Classification Test (FACT), the Academic Promise Test (APT), and the Armed Services Vocational Aptitude Battery (ASVAB) are also extensively used. A brief examination of the characteristics of these tests may help you further understand the nature of aptitude batteries.

General Aptitude Test Battery (GATB). The General Aptitude Test Battery is administered through the United States Employment Service. However, it is available to non-profit institutions such as schools for counseling purposes. This battery has 12 subtests, which yield 9 scores (see Figure 7–4). It should also be noted that these aptitudes are not all independent, as some of the subtests are used in determining more than one aptitude score. As might be anticipated, this battery is primarily used in career counseling for job placement for individuals 16 years of age or older.

Differential Aptitude Test. The Differential Aptitude Test consists of a battery of eight subtests. The current (1990) edition features two levels. Level 1 is primarily for students in grades 7–9 and level 2, for those in grades 10–12. Both versions may be appropriate to older populations as well. The subtests are verbal reasoning, numerical ability, abstract reasoning, clerical speed and accuracy, mechanical reasoning, clerical speed and accuracy, mechanical reasoning, space relations, language usage—spelling, and language usage—grammar. This battery has for many years been one of the most popular in common use in schools as a means of assisting counseling for vocational and educational decision making.

Flanigan Aptitude Classification Test. The Flanigan Aptitude Classification Test is one of the more time-consuming multiple-aptitude tests, requiring approximately 8 hours to administer. This comprehensive aptitude test battery was based on the job elements approach basic to performance in a wide range of job classifications. The battery consists of 19 subtests:

1. Inspection
2. Mechanics
3. Tables
4. Reasoning
5. Vocabulary
6. Assembly

*Reprinted with the permission of Macmillan College Publishing Company from *Psychological Testing*, 6th ed., by Anne Anastasi. Copyright © 1988 by Anne Anastasi.

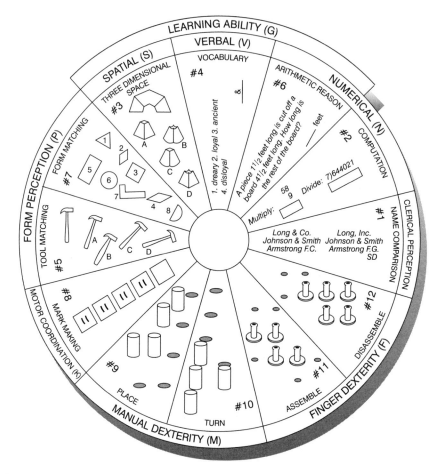

FIGURE 7–4   Nine Aptitudes Measured by 12 Tests in the General Aptitude Test Battery B1002

7. Judgment and Comprehension

8. Components

9. Planning

10. Memory

11. Arithmetic

12. Ingenuity

13. Scales

14. Expression

15. Precision

16. Alertness

17. Coordination

18. Patterns

19. Coding

The results of these tests are profiled for various occupational areas. Counselors may use these results as an aid in job placement or career and educational planning.

The Armed Services Vocational Aptitude Battery (ASVAB). Since 1972 approximately 1 million high school students per year have taken the ASVAB, a service that is available to local high schools at no cost or obligation to either the school or student. This battery, also used throughout the military services and the Department of Defense, consists of 10 tests, namely arithmetic reasoning, numerical operations, paragraph comprehension, work knowledge, coding speed, general science, mathematics knowledge, electronics information, mechanical comprehension, and automotive and shop information. Approximately 3 hours' administration time is needed for the current edition of the battery.

Scholastic Aptitude Tests

Scholastic or academic aptitude tests propose to measure a person's potential for performing in academic situations. Such tests as those that constitute the SCAT and SAT batteries have much merit insofar as predicting academic performance at higher educational levels. However, more appropriate labels would be academic achievement or academic predictions, because they tend to predict future academic achievement on the basis of past learning rather than native ability.

A popular academic aptitude test for the high school level is the advanced level of the School and College Ability Tests (SCAT III), designed for grades 9–12. This test, which requires 40 minutes' testing time, yields a verbal, quantitative, and total score. In line with trends in testing theory, Anastasi (1988) notes:

> SCAT undertakes to measure developed abilities. This is simply an explicit admission of what is more or less true of all intelligence tests, namely that test scores reflect the nature and amount of schooling the individual has received rather than measuring "capacity" independently of relevant prior experiences. Accordingly, SCAT draws freely on work knowledge and arithmetic processes learned in the appropriate school grades. In this respect, SCAT does not really differ from other academic intelligence tests, especially those designed for the high school and college levels; it only makes overt a condition sometimes unrecognized in other tests.* (p. 238)

Two popular tests used for the admission, placement, and counseling of college students are the Scholastic Aptitude Test (SAT) of the College Entrance Examinations Board and the American College Testing Program (ACT), introduced in 1959, which is also used by many institutions of higher education. The ACT consists of four tests: English usage, mathematical usage, social studies reading, and natural sciences reading.

Anastasi (1988) makes a point frequently stated by experienced high school and college admissions counselors, noting that tests such as the SAT and the ACT

> are not intended as substitutes for high school grades in the prediction of college achievement. High school grades can predict college grades as well as most tests or slightly better. When test scores are combined with high school grades, however, the prediction of college performance is

significantly improved. In part, this improvement stems from the fact that a uniform, objective test serves as a corrective for the variability in grading standards among different high schools. Moreover, such tests are not subject to the influence of irrelevant variables and possible personal biases that may enter into the assignment of course grades.* (p. 331)

Achievement Tests

Achievement measurement is an area of standardized testing to which most students have been subject, not on just a single occasion or two but probably numerous times during their educational programs. Of all the areas of standardized testing, achievement tests are the most popular in terms of numbers administered to numbers of different individuals.

> Hundreds of thousands of achievement tests are administered each year primarily in educational institutions ranging from kindergarten through graduate and professional schools. Some are administered for licensing and certification in trades and professions, or in medical specialties, or for the selection and promotion of postal workers. Achievement tests differ from aptitude tests in that they attempt to assess the results of some relatively standardized or specific set of experiences. (Hood & Johnson, 1991, p. 78)

The emphasis on achievement testing as indexes of educational excellence in school reform movements of the late 1980s has stimulated both the use of achievement tests and attention to their results. Despite the widespread popularity of achievement tests, they are frequently confused with other measures, especially aptitude tests.

Drummond (1988) identifies the various types of achievement tests as follows:

1. *Survey achievement batteries.* Partially norm-referenced and partially criterion-referenced tests that measure knowledge and skill in reading, mathematics, language arts, social studies, and science

2. *Subject area tests.* Achievement tests in a single subject area, such as math or spelling

3. *Criterion-referenced tests.* Tests that measure knowledge and comprehension of a specific skill or competency, for example, the ability to draw specified inferences from pictorial or written content or the ability to read a metric scale and give the weight of an object in metric and English units of weight

4. *Minimum level skills tests.* Tests that measure objectives or skills identified as the minimum skills to be achieved in order to pass from one level or grade to another

5. *Individual achievement tests.* Tests that measure objectives or skills identified as the minimum skills to be achieved in order to pass from one level or grade to another

6. *Individual achievement tests.* Tests that are administered individually across a wide age or grade range to measure achievement

7. *Diagnostic tests.* Tests that are used to assess the strengths and weaknesses of individuals in a given subject area by measuring a limited number of skills thoroughly (p. 117)

Achievement tests are used to provide measures of (a) the amount of learning, (b) the rate of learning, (c) comparisons with others or with achievement of self in other

---

*Reprinted with the permission of Macmillan College Publishing Company from *Psychological Testing,* 6th ed., by Anne Anastasi. Copyright © 1988 by Anne Anastasi.

areas, (d) level of learning in subareas, (e) strengths and weaknesses in a subject matter area, and, in some instances, (f) predictions of future learning. Because of their extensive use and the relatively easy task of identifying appropriate content measures, achievement tests are among the best designed standardized measures available to counselors. There are, however, certain considerations that users of achievement tests must keep in mind if such instruments are to be used appropriately.

First, it is important that the content of the test is relevant to the subject matter content the student has experienced. In other words, the test should measure what the student has had the opportunity to learn. Further, it is important that the emphasis within the test, in terms of topics covered, is appropriate for the emphasis the student has experienced in the subject matter class. Additionally, the level of difficulty of the test items must be appropriate for the age/grade level being tested. A final consideration, one that bears repeating, is the norming sample on which the test has been standardized.

If this sample is representative of the general population appropriate to the age/grade level being tested, comparison with this general population may be appropriate. If the population of the sample is similar to the population being tested, that would usually be desirable. On the other hand, if the norming population is considerably dissimilar, it may not be an appropriate group against which to compare the group being tested.

Although achievement tests that measure only a single subject matter are available, batteries that measure and compare across a series of subject matter areas are far more popular. Kubiszyn and Borich (1987) point out:

> The most frequently used type of achievement test is the achievement test battery, or survey battery. Such batteries are widely used, often beginning in the first grade and administered each year thereafter. There are several reasons survey batteries are more popular than single-subject achievement tests. The major advantages of survey batteries over single-subject achievement tests are identified here:
>
> 1. Each subtest is coordinated with every other subtest resulting in common administration and scoring procedures, common format, and minimum redundancy.
> 2. Batteries are less expensive and less time consuming to administer than several single-subject tests.
> 3. Each subtest is normed on the same sample, making comparison across subtests, both within and between individuals, easier and more valid. (p. 358)

One of the popular achievement test batteries is the Iowa Test of Basic Skills. This series is available in two forms for grades K–8. Depending on which level and form are used, testing time is 60–80 minutes. The five major areas tested by this battery are vocabulary, reading comprehension, language skills, work-study skills, and mathematical skills. The test developers point out that this battery measures pupils' abilities to use and acquire skills, for no test or subtest is concerned with only the repetition or identification of facts.

The Iowa Tests of Educational Development are normed for grades 9–12 and consist of seven subtests measuring subject matter areas appropriate for secondary school curricula. Standard scores, grade-equivalent scores, national percentile ranks, normal curve-equivalent scores, stanines, and large-city norms are available for all tests and for the composites. Local norms are available from the Riverside Scoring Service and the Riverside Publishing Company in Chicago.

The Metropolitan Achievement Test consists of eight battery levels for measuring performance from the beginning of kindergarten–grade 12. This battery consists of single tests for reading comprehension, mathematics, language, social studies, and science. The basic battery consists of the first three tests. The complete battery utilizes all five tests. This battery is available from the Psychological Corporation, a subsidiary of Harcourt Brace Jovanovich, Inc., New York.

Interest Inventories

In a discussion on career planning, one might hear such statements as "I've always been interested in nursing," "The thought of teaching really turns me off," "I know I'd enjoy selling cars," or "Being a flight attendant would be the most exciting career I could imagine!"

Such pronouncements of career interests are common among adolescents and young adults. Equally common are statements of uncertainty and frustration regarding career choices, such as "I wish somebody would just tell me what career I should enter," "I can't make up my mind between engineering or coaching," or "I'm really upset because I can't think of any job I'm interested in."

Although interest testing has, for many years, been a popular psychometric aid to adolescents and young adults in career planning, recently it has been increasingly used for older populations considering midlife or other career changes.

Discussions and other explorations of interest are valuable aids for career planning and related career counseling and guidance; even a simple listing in hierarchical order of possible careers may be as valid in some instances as standardized, inventoried interests.

However, certain values may result from the use of standardized interest inventories of which counselors, teachers, and others who assist youth and adults in career and related decision making should be aware. Such potential values are these:

1. A comparative and contrasting inventory of a person's interests
2. Verification of a person's claimed interest or tentative choice
3. Identification of previously unrecognized interests
4. Identification of the possible level of interests for various (usually career) activities
5. Contrast of interest with abilities and achievements
6. Identification of problems associated with career decision making (no areas of adequate interest; high stated interest versus low inventoried interest in a career field)
7. A stimulus for career exploration or career counseling

If, however, these values are to be realized, certain guidelines should be followed in deciding when to use interest tests. Hood and Johnson (1991) suggest the following guidelines:

> First, counselors should keep in mind that interest inventories measure likes and dislikes, *not* abilities. . . .
>
> Second, clients should be positively motivated to participate in the assessment process. . . .
>
> Third, general interest inventories are of limited value for people who must make rather fine distinctions, such as choosing between civil and electrical engineering. . . .

Fourth, interest inventories may be inappropriate for people with emotional problems (Brandt & Hood, 1968). Disturbed people make more negative responses and endorse more passive interests than do people who are not disturbed (Dragow & Carkhuff, 1964). Personal issues can interfere with decision making. Counselors usually must address the emotional difficulties before career planning can take place.

Fifth, scores on interest inventories can show significant changes for clients who are young or after long time periods (Johansson & Campbell, 1971). . . .

Sixth, interest scores should be particularly helpful for clients who are undecided about their career plans. . . .

Finally, counselors may wish to use an interest card sort instead of an interest inventory if they are interested in the underlying reasons for the client's choices (Dolliver, 1982). (pp. 108–109)

The popular development of interest tests evolved from studies indicating that people in a given occupation seemed to be characterized by a cluster of common interests that distinguish them from people in other occupations. It was also noted that these differences in interests extended beyond those associated with job performance and that persons in a given occupation also had different nonvocational interests—hobbies and recreational activities that could distinguish them from those in other occupations. Thus, interest inventories could be designed to assess one's interests and relate them to those of various occupational areas. Two of the earlier and more popular of these inventories, still extensively used today, are the Kuder Preference Record and the Strong Vocational Interest Blanks, currently designated as the Strong-Campbell Interest Inventories.

The Kuder Preference Record is the original and most popular of the various Kuder interest inventories. It provides a series of interest items arranged in triads, from which the respondents choose the one they would like most and the one they would like least. The results are scored and profiled for the occupational areas of outdoor, mechanical, computational, scientific, persuasive, artistic, literary, music, social service, and clerical activities. Revision of the original preference record, the Kuder General Interest Survey, extends the use downward to the sixth grade by employing a simpler vocabulary that requires only a sixth-grade reading ability (the original version was usually considered appropriate for use in grades 9–12). The Kuder Occupational Interest Survey is still another version that provides scores showing similarities with occupational and college-level areas. This form differs from previous Kuder tests in expressing a person's score on each occupational scale as a correlation between his or her interest pattern and the pattern of a particular occupational group.

The Strong-Campbell Interest Inventory is a revision of the earlier forms of the Strong Vocational Interest Blank, which was first published in 1933. Its latest edition was published in 1985.

The SVIB introduced two principal procedures in the measurement of occupational interest. First, the items dealt with the respondent's liking or dislike for a wide variety of specific activities, objects, or types of persons that he or she commonly encountered in daily living. Second, the responses were empirically keyed for different occupations. (Anastasi, 1988, p. 564)

The various interest inventories have been suggested as usable with older adolescents and adults who may be considering higher-level professional or skilled occupations. The

Strong-Campbell Interest Inventory (SCII) can be scored only by computer. This later version contains 325 items grouped according to occupations, school subjects, activities, amusements, types of people, preference between activities, and personal characteristics. Results are displayed on a variety of scales. For example, the six general occupational theme scales provide scores for realistic, investigative, artistic, social, enterprising, and conventional categories. The major and most popular scales for the Strong Vocational Interest series are the 207 occupational scales. The Strong-Campbell Interest Inventory is published by the Stanford University Press, Stanford, California and distributed by Consulting Psychologists Press.

The Ohio Vocational Interest Survey (OVIS) is one of a number of somewhat newer interest inventories developed for use with high school students and adults. It was developed after the model on which the Dictionary of Occupational Titles is based (a cubistic model of data, people, and things). The OVIS is separated into three parts: (a) a questionnaire, (b) a local information survey, and (c) the interest inventory. The OVIS reports its results on 25 scales and is available through Harcourt Brace Jovanovich, Inc., New York.

Another approach to the assessment of career interests is the Self-Directed Search (SDS). This instrument was developed by John Holland, whose hexagonal model of six occupational themes is represented in the six summary scores of Realistic, Investigative, Artistic, Social, Enterprising, and Conventional. The SDS is designed to be self-administered, self-scored, and self-interpreted. When an individual completes the SDS, he or she uses a summary code comprising the types that rank first and second across all the subtests. Utilizing this code, he or she refers to a Job Finder, which presents information about 456 jobs listed in terms of two-letter SDS codes. Once a person gets his or her lists of careers that match a summary code, suggested next steps are listed for his or her organized career planning. The Self-Directed Search is marketed by Consulting Psychologists Press, Palo Alto, California.

The Career Maturity Inventory, although not precisely an interest inventory, has been designed to measure the maturity of attitudes and competencies that are involved in career decision making. The attitude scale surveys five attitudinal clusters: (a) involvement in the career choice process, (b) orientation toward work, (c) independence in decision making, (d) preference for career choice factors, and (e) conceptions of the career choice process. In contrast, the competency test measures the more cognitive variables involved in choosing an occupation. The five parts of the competency test are (a) self-appraisal, (b) occupational information, (c) goal selection, (d) planning, and (e) problem solving. The Career Maturity Inventory is available from McGraw-Hill Book Company, New York.

Personality Tests

Of all the areas of standardized testing, none is more intriguing to the general public, and perhaps to the counseling profession as well, as personality assessment. From the do-it-yourself personality test in the daily newspaper to sophisticated, projective techniques requiring highly specialized psychological training, personality testing represents a universal quest to understand what makes human beings "tick." But personality testing is as complex as what it seeks to measure. Let us examine some of the questions or concerns that must be considered.

What Is Personality?

Aiken (1988) notes that

> the term *personality* has many different meanings. To some, it refers to a mysterious charisma possessed by Hollywood stars and other popular, influential people but not by everyone. To others, personality is the same as temperament, a natural, genetically based predisposition to think, feel, and act in a particular way. To still others, personality consists of a person's unique mixture of emotional, intellectual, and character (honesty, courage, and so forth) traits. And to more behaviorally oriented psychologists, personality is not something internal but rather the externally observable pattern of organized behavior typical of an individual. (p. 321)

You can readily discern the wide variations in viewpoints regarding this topic by asking a group, "What is personality?" and noting the wide range of responses. The concept of personality is a difficult one to treat with the precision usually associated with standardized tests. Thus, constructors of personality tests face the challenge of determining what workable definition of personality they will use and what aspect or aspects of that definition they will measure. Generally speaking, however, in conventional psychometric terminology, "personality tests are instruments for the measurement of emotional, motivational, interpersonal, and attitudinal characteristics, as distinguished from abilities" (Anastasi, 1988, p. 523).

What Is "Normal" Personality?

This question would probably also elicit a variety of answers from the public. Most persons tend to view "normal" in terms of their own behavioral personality traits and values. Thus, an extremely extroverted person, viewed as normal by one group, may be viewed as "abnormal" by another group. Even if one is able to identify norms objectively for specific behavioral responses, one still must determine at what point the deviations from those norms become "abnormal."

Can Personality Be Measured?

This question has objectively been answered affirmatively by many authors of standardized personality measures and has further been affirmed by many practicing counselors, psychologists, and psychiatrists utilizing observation and other nonstandardized techniques. Some of the difficulties involved in obtaining accurate assessments are client based and must be the concern of the test interpreter:

1. The capability of a person to accurately analyze many aspects of his or her own personality is questionable. In some instances, the client may not possess the insight to respond accurately. Although the client's view of self is important, it may not be appropriate to the intent of the measuring instrument. In other instances, one must recognize that the individual's view of self can be distorted, differ from the perceptions of others, and be misleading to the test interpreter.

2. Some persons may deliberately falsify their responses. Most often, deception occurs when a person responds in a manner that he or she views as more socially acceptable than perhaps his or her true response might be. For example, little children almost inevitably

respond that they love their parents, even when they do not know them or when they actively dislike them. Also, one can anticipate that some respondents will project an ideal self rather than the real self in their answers. Some persons may respond as the friendly and popular person they wish they were, rather than the withdrawn individual with few friends they recognize themselves to be. The intimate nature of a question may dissuade the respondent from answering accurately. Most notable examples in this category are questions dealing with a person's sexual activities, beliefs, and values.

Several of the more popular personality inventories or standardized personality assessment instruments are the Mooney Problem Checklist, the Edwards Personal Preference Schedule, and the Minnesota Multiphasic Personality Inventory. The latter two instruments require special training and supervised experience before their use in school or clinical settings.

The Mooney Problem Checklist consists of a series of problems to which the client reacts by underlining the problems that are of some concern, circling the problems that are of the most concern, and then writing a summary in his or her own words. It is obviously not standardized in a psychometric sense since it is designed to identify problems for group or individual counseling.

In this sense, the Mooney Problem Checklist is useful for conducting group surveys and identifying persons who want or need counseling assistance with personal problems. Cohen, Montague, Nathanson, and Swerdlik (1988) state:

> Some personality tests are closely tied to a particular theory of personality, and all of the items on such a test are designed to measure traits or states presumed to exist on the basis of that theory. For example, a personality test constructed within a psychoanalytic framework might have items on it designed to assess id, ego, and super-ego functioning. (p. 307)

The Edwards Personal Preference Schedule (EPPS) is a personality inventory based on the theory of personality presented by Henry Murray (Murray, Barrett, & Honburger, 1938). The Edwards Personal Preference Schedule is designed to show the relative importance to the individual of 15 key needs or motives:

Achievement	Affiliation	Nurturance
Deference	Intraception	Change
Order	Succorance	Endurance
Exhibition	Dominance	Heterosexuality
Autonomy	Abasement	Aggression

Another clinically oriented instrument is the Minnesota Multiphasic Personality Inventory (MMPI). This is the most widely used of the personality assessment tests. It is constructed entirely on the basis of clinical criteria and contains 566 statements covering a wide range of subject matters related to the instrument's 10 scales (16 of the items are repeats for scoring purposes):

Hypochondriasis	Paranoia
Depression	Psychasthenia

Hysteria	Schizophrenia
Psychopathic deviate	Hypomania
Masculinity-femininity	Social introversion

In addition to the 10 clinical scales, the MMPI contains three "validity scales." These are an L or the Lie score; an F score, which may indicate the seriousness with which the individual responded to the test items; and the K score, a suppressor variable refining the discrimination of five of the clinical variables. As mentioned earlier, the MMPI requires special training and supervised experience.

CRITERION-REFERENCED TESTING

One of the most frequently raised issues in the 1970s and 1980s was that of criterion-referenced testing versus norm-referenced testing. Many educators will suggest that it is not a case of either/or—that, in fact, criterion-referenced testing complements norm-referenced testing and vice versa. The inference cannot be ignored, however, when in many school systems criterion-referenced testing has increased as norm-referenced testing has decreased. One cannot deny the rapid gains in popularity that criterion-referenced testing, aided by the accountability movement, has made in recent years.

A criterion-referenced test measures whether a person has attained the desired or maximum goal in a learning experience. If we were to contrast criterion-referenced testing with norm-referenced testing by using a practical example, we might note that a sixth-grade class could achieve an average score ahead of 52% of other sixth-grade classes in a representative nationwide sample. This information, however, might not tell those interested, such as teachers, parents, and students, more specifically how well this sixth-grade class reads or what they have learned to read. On the other hand, a typical criterion-referenced test result would indicate how many pupils in this sixth-grade class can read at a certain rate of reading, comprehend at a certain level of comprehension, and recall with reasonable accuracy what they have read after passage of a specific period of time. In the first instance, a class is competing against other classes to demonstrate to what degree pupils have learned or not learned to read. In the latter case, however, pupils are competing against a locally established standard, a learning objective, a criterion.

The big debate (Rowntree, 1987, p. 178) in the professional literature appears to be split between the following questions:

1. How well has the individual done compared with norms established by his peer groups (norm referenced)?

versus

2. How well has the individual done by comparison with some predetermined criteria (criteria referenced)?

These questions seem to omit one very important possibility:

3. How well has the individual done by comparison with him- or herself?

Rather than noting the range of individual differences in test scores, criterion-referenced tests place persons in one of two groups: those who have attained the criterion and those who have not.

Perhaps Hawes (1973) best expressed the popularity of criterion-referenced testing by entitling his article "Criterion-Referenced Testing—No More Losers, No More Norms, No More Parents Raising Storms."

COMPUTERIZED ADAPTIVE TESTING

Another popular as well as innovative movement in testing is computerized adaptive testing. In this approach a computer selects different questions from an item pool to administer to different students. Worthen, White, and Borg (1993) describe the process:

> The computer selects each question from a pool of items of known difficulty. The question is displayed on a TV screen, and the student either types the letter of the correct multiple-choice response or touches the screen at the location of the correct response. The computer records whether the response is correct or incorrect and selects the next question, based on the student's response to the previous question. If the student's response is correct, the next item selected will be more difficult; if the student's response is incorrect, the next item selected will be easier. As more items are administered, the computer considers the student's performance on all previous items in estimating his mastery level and selecting the next item to be administered. As a result, the items are adapted to the level of the student. That is, on the whole they will be neither too easy nor too difficult for the individual. The main advantage of this method over conventional testing is that in *computerized adaptive testing,* because each student is administered a different combination of items, the teacher cannot teach to the test, and the student cannot help his peers by passing on the test items he remembers, because most of the items administered to other students will be different.* (p. 212)

Since each student responds to different sets of questions, their resulting scores are not comparable.

DEVELOPING A TESTING PROGRAM

In many school settings, testing programs may be mandated by state legislative bodies or agencies or set by local school boards with limited input from schools and their counselors. In nonschool settings, counselors may find that organizational policies dictate, at least in part, the nature of the organization's utilization of standardized tests. However, in those more ideal circumstances where counselors and their fellow helping professionals can determine the nature of the organization's standardized assessment program, it is

*From *Measurement and Evaluation in the Schools* by Blaine R. Worthen, Karl R. White, and Walter R. Borg. Copyright © 1993 by Longman Publishers USAQ. Reprinted with permission.

obviously desirable to develop a logical, sequential approach that provides for account-ability. The following steps present one such procedure that, while appropriate perhaps to school settings, may also be suitable for some community and business and industrial set-tings as well:

1. *Determine the needs.* This is obviously the initial and critical step that defines the degree to which the testing program will be relevant. Here the key question is "What new information do we need to provide good (not just adequate) service to the organization's target population?" The word *new* implies that a specific type of test data should not be a priority if it duplicates information already available through other sources. In other words, priority goes to that needed data not already available. Second priority would be for that information that tests can provide for supplementing already existing data.

2. *Determine the program's objectives.* Once the testing needs have been identified, these needs should be translated into the testing program's objectives. For accountability pur-poses, these objectives should be stated in concise, measurable terms.

3. *Select the appropriate instruments.* In determining which tests are "best" to serve the program's objectives, obviously the basic criteria of validity, reliability, norming appropriate-ness, and administrative practicality are applied. In addition, the skills needed to adminis-ter and interpret the tests must be available. Costs are always an important consideration.

4. *Determine the testing schedule.* Tests should be scheduled for specific dates to provide data at the time it is most needed or most appropriate. Spacing is also important to avoid testing overload for both those administering and those taking the tests.

5. *Evaluate the outcomes.* Data indicating the degree to which the objectives have been achieved should be collected and utilized. Appropriateness of the instruments should be examined. Results should lead to continuous program improvement.

In testing program planning one must always bear in mind that testing is not an end in itself but rather an opportunity to develop a more complete picture of the client—a picture mutually shared by both the client and the counselor.

SUMMARY

Standardized testing and computerized testing programs have become popular benchmarks for measuring educational attainment of individuals and schools. Most of us have experienced at least the "receiving end" of this phenomenon. Stan-dardized testing is also a traditional and impor-tant tool in the counselor's array of techniques for understanding the client. Despite the historic and extensive use of standardized tests, coun-selors and other users must be aware of the many criticisms and concerns that have been voiced regarding their use for diagnostic purposes. An understanding of these criticisms and concerns and the degree to which they are valid will enable users to administer standardized tests effectively but safely in their practices.

The importance of comprehending basic sta-tistical processes should not be underestimated. An understanding of averages and variations from the average, as expressed in statistical ter-minology, and relationships as computed math-ematically is basic to the interpretation of stan-dardized tests. The user of standardized tests also must be aware of and able to apply the criteria for test selection. These basic criteria are the validity, reliability, and practical characteristics of the test under consideration. Strengths and weaknesses of the common areas of standardized testing should be understood. It is also important that the user recognize the limitations as well as the strengths of a given instrument if it is to be intelligently used in practice. Counselors and others may also want to consider criterion-referenced tests as a substitute or supplement to their programs of standardized testing. Counselors should also be aware of the contributions other disciplines make to the understanding of human behavior. In addition, a wide variety of nonstandardized techniques for human assessment, utilized across many disciplines, is available to the counselor who is knowledgeable in their construction and usage. The next chapter will provide an overview of these possibilities.

DISCUSSION QUESTIONS

1. What standardized tests have you taken? (Poll the class.) Did the results ever influence your planning or decision making?

2. How do you feel about being "measured" by standardized tests? How do you feel about the use of standardized tests to "measure" traits of your clients?

3. Under what circumstances would you recommend standardized (norm-referenced) testing over criterion-referenced testing and vice versa?

4. Are you aware of or have you been involved in public controversies regarding standardized testing? If so, describe and analyze the situation.

5. What standardized tests would you recommend, if any, to screen potential candidates seeking admission to a counselor training program? Defend your answer.

6. Are there any measurement voids (areas of performances, behaviors, circumstances, etc.) in

which it would be helpful to have standardized tests developed?

7. What would you do in the following situations?

  a. An "honor" student makes a score of 90 on a group intelligence test.

  b. A problem and failing student makes scores at the 95th percentile on an achievement battery.

  c. A client breaks his or her pencil in the middle of a standardized test.

  d. An African-American client asks you whether standardized tests are culture-fair. How would you respond?

CLASS ACTIVITIES

1. Develop a profile of the "normal" personality.

2. Develop an interest checklist that might distinguish potential counselors from those who would not enjoy careers as counselors.

3. Develop test items for a standardized test designed to measure an individual's potential for entering a counselor preparation program.

4. Administer the test to students, score in class, and discuss the process.

SELECTED READINGS

Anastasi, A. (1992). What counselors should know about the use and interpretation of psychological tests. *Journal of Counseling and Development, 70,* 610–615.

Campbell, V. (1987). Strong-Campbell Interest Inventory (4th ed.). *Journal of Counseling and Development, 66,* 53–56.

Eaves, R. C. (1985). Educational assessment in the United States. *Diagnostique, 10,* 5-39. [Theme issue: Assessment in Special Education.]

Gottfredson, L. S., & Crouse, J. (1986). Validity versus utility of mental tests: Example of the SAT. *Journal of Vocational Behavior, 29,* 363–378.

Healey, C. C., & Mourton, D. L. (1984). The Self-Directed Search personality scales and career maturity. *Measurement and Evaluation in Guidance, 17,* 3-13.

Lynch, A. Q. (1985). The Myers-Briggs Type Indicator: A tool for appreciating employee and client diversity. *Journal of Employment Counseling, 22,* 104–109.

Wainer, H. (1988). How accurately can we assess changes in minority performance on the SAT? *American Psychologist, 43,* 774–778.

Wiggins, G. (1993). Assessment: Authenticity, context and validity. *Phi Delta Kappan, 75,* 200–214.

RESEARCH OF INTEREST

Crouse, J. (1985). Does the SAT help colleges make better selection decisions? *Harvard Educational Review, 55,* 195–219.

Abstract

Using data from the National Longitudinal Survey of high school students to calculate the actual improvement in freshmen grade point average, college completion, and total years of schooling from colleges' use of the Scholastic Aptitude Test (SAT), Crouse compares predictions based on high school rank to argue that the SAT's costs do not justify its limited predictive ability.

Grougeon, D. (1985). CEEB SAT mathematics scores and their correlation with college performance in math. *Educational Research Quarterly, 9,* 8–11.

Abstract

Investigates whether the constant decline in SAT mathematics scores since 1963 reflected a decrease in student mathematical ability or the SAT's inadequacy in measuring mathematical ability. Findings indicate a very low correlation between SAT math scores and overall college math grades of six graduating classes at one university.

Kerr, B. A. (1986). Career counseling for the gifted: Assessments and interventions. *Journal of Counseling and Development, 64,* 602–604.

Abstract

Compares (a) three vocational assessment batteries, (b) structured individual counseling, and (c) mixed-sex versus same-sex career groups in terms of their usefulness, educational value, and enjoyability as perceived by gifted adolescents. Students preferred a test battery consisting of the Self-Directed Search and the Edwards Personal Preference Schedule.

Krug, S. E. (1991). The adult personality inventory. *Journal of Counseling and Development, 69,* 266–271.

Abstract

Describes the historic perspective, development, and design of the Adult Personality Inventory (API). Discusses the primary application areas of the API in individual and family counseling, employee selection and placement, and personal development programs. Considers counseling uses and implications.

Lambert, M. J., Benjamin, M. O., & Masters, K. S. (1992). Choosing outcome assessment devices: An organizational and conceptual scheme. *Journal of Counseling and Development, 70,* 527–534.

Abstract

Suggests an organizational and conceptual scheme consisting of content, source, technology, and time orientation dimensions in assessing counseling outcome. Discusses a review of the scheme as applied to outcome studies over a 3-year period. Concludes that by using an organizational and conceptual scheme investigators can collect results regarding counseling intervention effectiveness that can be more easily summarized in larger literature reviews.

Randahl, G. J., Hansen, J. C., & Haverkamp, B. E. (1993). Instrumental behaviors following test administration and interpretation: Exploration validity of the Strong Interest Inventory. *Journal of Counseling and Development, 71,* 435–439.

Abstract

Explores the exploration validity of the 1985 Strong Campbell Interest Inventory (SCII) with 157 college students. Results demonstrate that students in the experimental group who participated in the SCII testing and a group interpretation reported significantly more instrumental career exploration behaviors at a 1-year follow-up than participants in the control group.

Watkins, E. O., & Wiebe, M. J. (1984). Factorial validity of the Stanford Achievement Test for first-grade children. *Educational and Psychological Measurement, 44,* 951–954.

Abstract

The factorial validity of the Stanford Achievement Test (SAT) was investigated with a sample of first-graders ($N = 393$). Although eight areas are proposed from the SAT, this analysis produced only one general factor. Results suggest limiting SAT interpretation for first graders to a total score approach.

Chapter 8

Nonstandardized Techniques for Human Assessment

Sometimes we are called on to explain, even justify, why one of our close friends acts the way he or she does. The reply may, at least subconsciously, draw on our knowledge of our friend's home and family background; the environment in which he or she grew up or now lives; the cultural background; the physical and psychological characteristics, as we perceive them; or the experiences of the friend. In these instances, a wealth of background information provides insights into the behavior of those we know well. Nor is this knowledge limited by our own particular occupation or discipline. Some of what we know might be classified as cultural or anthropological, some as environmental or sociological, and some as psychological.

In a similar vein, most of us feel more confident with a family physician who has looked after our ailments for years, who knows us from a broader standpoint than what we are as a physical specimen, who understands us totally. It is a situation that an equally competent but "newcomer" physician cannot duplicate.

In the world of sporting competition there are frequent references to "psyching out the opponent." This "psyching out" attempts to go beyond understanding the athletic skills of the opponent appropriate to the contest, to imply that the better we know our competition, the better we can play them.

These examples suggest the objective of this chapter, namely, to describe nonstandardized assessment techniques for increasing and broadening our understanding of our client population. Thorough assessment increases the potential for maximum treatment efficacy. Interdisciplinary concepts of human assessment are presented, followed by some suggested guidelines or principles of human assessment. We then focus on the nonstandardized techniques commonly employed for individual analysis by counselors in various settings. It should be noted that standardized techniques, such as psychological testing, are those with a precise and fixed format, set of procedures, and method of scoring that enable the instrument to be used for the same purpose in a variety of settings and times. Standardization suggests uniformity and objectivity. Nonstandardization suggests a broader, variable, and more subjective approach to gathering and interpreting data for human assessment.

CONCEPTS OF HUMAN ASSESSMENT

The most intelligent yet most complicated and difficult to understand living organization known to civilization today is the human being. When we place human beings in their environment, a rapidly changing and complex society, we cannot help but recognize the enormity of the task of those who seek to understand, predict, and assist the development of human behavior. In undertaking this responsibility, we are quick to recognize that no one discipline or area of expertise alone possesses the theoretical or technical basis for a comprehensive understanding of modern people in modern society. To this end, then, those who study human behavior—whether from an individual or societal viewpoint; whether from the viewpoint of an anthropologist, sociologist, or psychologist; whether from the viewpoint of an American, Japanese, or German—must be willing to both learn and share with those who have this common interest. It is in this context that we suggest that counselors, regardless of the setting in which they function, can better understand their clients' behavior through the insights gained by studying behavior in the context of other disciplines and cultures. The following is not intended to substitute for such study but only to examine briefly these other perspectives and their implications for counselors.

Sociology

Sociology is a social and behavioral science that focuses on the study of individuals and groups in society and how they behave and interact with one another. The science of sociology contributes to an understanding of the social networks and their impact on individuals, individual roles, and relationships within those networks. Furthermore, sociology is concerned with the study of socialization agents or institutions. These institutions, such as the family, church, school, and government, assume the responsibility of teaching people within that environment what constitutes normal and abnormal behavior for the society. These patterns of normal and abnormal behavior are further shaped by customs, folkways, mores, and laws. Sociology also helps in understanding behavior that deviates from the norms of a group or society. The study of social deviance helps in understanding behaviors, including alcoholism and crime, that are defined as social problems. Such study also helps us recognize that what is considered "normal" behavior in one group may be defined as deviant behavior in another group. Furthermore, study in this area can help the counselor recognize the influence of social controls or pressures on the behavior of clients, students, and others. For counselors, it is also important to keep in mind that human beings are social beings, affected by the society of which they are members and, at the same time, expected to contribute to that society.

Counselors will find that sociological understandings contribute to their understanding of the groups and structures within the society of which they are a part. It is particularly important to understand the significance of the groupings and roles of clients, the influences on client behavior of the various groups of which they are members, the roles and relationships that are most significant to clients, and the restriction on clients' behavior and behavior change of the social system of which they are a part. The counselor must understand the various roles of people and the behavior that occurs or is anticipated as a result of these roles. That also includes an understanding of the significance of status, as already noted in many psychological studies. Some suggest that perhaps there has never been a more status-conscious society than our own. Sociologists help us understand status and its implications through the study of social stratification, which involves social classes, social mobilities, social structures, and, in general, the ranking of social positions within society.

The sociologist, like the psychologist, is also concerned with the study of the development of a person's self-concept. Sociological study focuses on self-concept development through the socialization process and its influence by others. It is especially important for counselors to recognize the impact of "significant others" and reference groups (both within the domain of sociological study) on the development of a person's self-concept. Who are the people whose judgments, imagined or otherwise, are significant to one's self-concept, and what are the groups that one uses to develop and test attitudes, beliefs, and so forth?

Psychology

As we examine the various scientific disciplines, we should note that psychology has been the one most closely associated with the profession of counseling. Over the years, psychology has made numerous significant contributions to the development and practice of counseling, including counseling theory and processes, individual and group counseling, standardized assessment, and career development and decision-making theories.

Traditionally the discipline of psychology has been closely related to the study of school-aged groups and their education. Such fields as educational psychology and human development have been offsprings of these interests. Learning theory has also been extended through work by psychologists. Developmental theorists have assisted counselors and others in understanding why and how humans grow and develop over the life span. Social psychology has provided counselors with insight into the socialization process and social influences, attitudes, attribution, group dynamics and interpersonal interactions. Ecological theorists have alerted us to the importance of the environment and how it influences individuals and their behavior.

Anthropology

Anthropology is the study of the culture of a society and the characteristics of its social behavior. It involves the recording, describing, and analyzing of the cultures of humankind throughout the world and throughout history. In these studies, anthropology identifies the traditions, norms, patterns of learning, coping styles, and other behaviors, from both current and historic perspectives. Among the understandings that the study of anthropology can provide for counselors are recognizing (a) that different cultures have different and similar concepts, (b) the importance of the ethnic and cultural background of the client, (c) the importance of the ethnic and cultural background of the counselor, and (d) the significance of subcultures within the larger societal or cultural context. The application aspects of anthropology are suggested by James Clifton (1970) when he states that "a description of culture is a statement of what one has to know in order to understand events in a community as its members understand them and to conduct oneself in a way that they will accept as meeting their standards for themselves" (p. 221).

In this context, culture is viewed as the beliefs and practices of people within a society, including guidelines for their behavior in given situations (such as religious ceremonies, funerals, weddings, the attainment of puberty, maturity, etc.). Human development is dependent on environmental characteristics. The characteristics of the environment that have been developed by the past inhabitants of the environment constitute the culture with which a person interacts. That culture provides people with their initial values, behavioral guidelines, and expectancies for the future. As just noted, the self-concept is central to the study of personality and behavior by psychologists and sociologists, and the study of anthropology contributes through an understanding of the nature of self as culturally defined. We also view ourselves as influenced by the perspective we have of self in relation to culture. The study of anthropology alerts us to the fact that personality, as it develops, seeks to prepare the individual for living in his or her culture and, by the same token, that a culture functions only through the personalities of those who constitute it, which thus enables predictions regarding overt behavior on the basis of a knowledge of a culture and its traditions.

Today, we are aware that different subcultures often have different values and lifestyles. For example, counselors should be able to understand the lifestyles and values of such populations as African Americans, Native Americans, Asians, Hispanics, Jews, Poles, and others. It is helpful not only to be able to function free of ignorance in helping relationships with clients from various backgrounds but also to interact without prejudice and bias.

Finally, and related to the study of both anthropology and sociology, we note an increased interest in the field of counseling on cultural and environmental influences on events. In this regard, Blocher and Biggs (1983) have described the movement beyond the traditional community mental health approaches to one that examines relationships between human beings and their environment. They suggest that (a) human beings are characterized by a basic and inherent drive toward competence or mastery of an environment, and (b) the development of competence needs to be studied as it occurs in natural settings.

Conyne (1985) discusses a counseling ecology model for helping improve both people and their environments and in which help-giving is defined in an ecological context.

Economics

Economics is a science that studies human production, consumption, and distribution. Its significance in the creation of status and influences on our wants shapes many of our behaviors.

Economics is another social science concerned with individual behavior and human relationships. Economists' concern is with people living in various types of economic systems. Economists, like sociologists, are concerned with one's economic position, the socioeconomic status of people in a society. Economic attainment interacts with other factors in a culture to determine "status." This socioeconomic status can be significant as a determinant of client feelings, attitudes, behavior, and so forth.

Three major socioeconomic strata have been identified: upper, middle, and lower class. Within each of these levels are three sublevels of upper, middle, and lower (e.g., lower middle class). The most reliable indicators of assignment to a status are income, education, occupation, and geographic location. Since the economic environment in which people live is so closely interwoven with nearly every activity in which counselors engage, we cannot be uninvolved in this area.

C. Gilbert Wrenn (1962) notes the importance of economic learning to counselors when he comments that "the school counselor cannot afford to be a graduate student in psychology and a second-grader in economics" (p. 42). For the counselor, understanding the influences on career choices of economic systems and theories can be meaningful. In addition, the impact of economic systems on human behavior should not go unnoticed by counselors who propose to assess human behavior. The influence of the socioeconomic level of the home on the self-concept of the developing child is also of concern to the counselor.

Interdisciplinary Implications for Counselors

The preceding sections presented a brief overview of perspectives from other disciplines. From these perspectives, implications can be drawn that have relevance to counselors and their functioning in a variety of settings:

1. Counselors must reflect a greater awareness of the various cultures that may be represented within the client population they are hoping to serve.

2. To be effective and relevant, counselors must increase their understanding of the language that is vital to communicating with different cultures, which results from living in one culture and learning in another, the role expectancies of cultures, and cultural biases in schools and other basic institutions that create tensions, hostilities, and distrust among subcultures.

3. Counselors must have an understanding of the social structures of the communities and institutions within which they function. They must also recognize the impact of these and other social structures on how a person views him- or herself, his or her work, education, and other experiences.

4. Counselors must recognize that behavior is a function of an individual's interaction with his or her environment.

5. Counselors must recognize the potential relationships between clients' socioeconomic characteristics and their behaviors and concerns.

6. Counselors should acquire a deeper understanding of the various societal influences on behavior, growth, and development of the individual based on an interdisciplinary approach.

7. Counselors must function more effectively as consultants. In this capacity, the counselor has the opportunity to interpret the social and cultural characteristics of clients and their implications for specific programs and settings.

Guidelines for Human Assessment

As we move toward the examination of specific tools and techniques available to counselors for assessing human characteristics, it is important next to recognize some basic principles or guidelines. These guidelines provide a framework for effectively and professionally functioning in the sometimes delicate task of individual assessment.

1. *Each individual human being is unique, and this uniqueness is to be valued.* Although the principle of individual differences has been eulogized throughout educational and societal circles the better part of this century, in practice, constant pressures encourage conformity and standardization. Counselors must not enlarge this gap between principle and practice but should stress the principle that assessment is a means of increasing understanding of the uniqueness of the individual, a uniqueness that sets one apart from all other people, that provides each person with the basis for his or her own personal worth. That uniqueness is to be valued, not standardized.

2. *Variations exist within individuals.* Each person is unique as well as distinct from others. This principle notes that individual assessment seeks to identify, for example, the special talents, skills, and interests of a person and, at the same time, forestall tendencies to generalize from a single or several characteristics of a person, such as "Anyone who excels in math can excel in anything," or "You give me an 'All-American' in one sport and I'll make them 'All-American' in another." Nor do we overlook the shortcomings. Although the emphasis on assessment is on the strengths and positive attributes of a person, all of us have our weaknesses—shortcomings that we must recognize if we are to overcome, bypass, or compensate for them.

3. *Human assessment presumes the direct participation of the person in his or her own assessment.* For human assessment to be as meaningful and accurate as possible, the person must be willingly and directly involved. This involvement includes input by the client, feedback, clarification, and interpretation, as appropriate, by both the client and counselor, and evaluation by the client. This principle presumes more than the client's one-way feeding in of data, such as taking a standardized test or completing a questionnaire. It assumes his or her right to interpretation and response to that interpretation. It presumes the client's right to clarify and expand his or her response and, as others come to know the client better, to gain better understandings of him- or herself as well.

4. *Accurate human assessment is limited by instruments and personnel.* The effective utilization of assessment techniques is dependent on a recognition of the limitations of instruments and personnel as well as acceptance of their potential. These limitations begin with the human element—ourselves, our knowledge and skill in the techniques we would use. Counselors should not under any circumstances use assessment techniques, including standardized tests, in which they have not been thoroughly trained. Additionally, the limitations of clients in responding to individual items as well as instruments must be taken into account. These limitations may include an unwillingness as well as an inability to respond. In addition to these human elements, there are the limitations of the instruments themselves to consider. These include an awareness of the particular shortcomings unique to a given instrument or technique and the general recognition that any of these provide at best only a "sample," only clues, not absolutes, and results that may vary among similar instruments and techniques.

5. *Human assessment accepts the positive.* A goal of human resource assessment is the identification of the potential of each person. It is a positive process that, as noted earlier, seeks to identify the unique worth of each person. Assessment can lead to the identification of worthwhile goals and positive planning. It should be a process clothed in optimism rather than, as is so often the case, fear of outcomes and predictions of doom. The counselor's own attitude becomes important in the establishment of the positive environment for assessment and in utilization of results for the best interests of clients.

6. *Human assessment follows established professional guidelines.* It is important for counselors, and all other helping professionals who use human assessment techniques, to be aware of the relevant ethical guidelines established by their professional organizations. These guidelines are aimed at protecting both the client and the professional practitioner. Ethical standards for counselors, which address assessment as well as other aspects of practice, are presented in Appendices B, C, G and H.

DOING WHAT COMES NATURALLY—OBSERVATION

On any given day most of us are the subjects of informal analysis by others, and vice versa. These "analysts" are not among the handful of psychiatrists, psychologists, or counselors with whom we may be acquainted but are amateurs doing what comes naturally: observing their fellow human beings, both friend and stranger, and drawing some conclusions about the kind of persons they are based on what is observed. Depending on what we see and how we interpret it, we may variously categorize people as executive types, models, drifters, untrustworthy, fun-loving, and so on. Furthermore, we are often prone to defend or "validate" our observations by noting, "I knew there was something that just didn't look right about her" or "You could tell he was a real athlete by the way he walked" and, on other occasions, calling on old clichés (many of which are sexist) as back-up evidence, such as "Just another dumb blonde" or "Watch out for those fiery redheads."

When we make observations "au naturel," we are, in effect, studying behavior as it is occurring in "real life." Although we must recognize (and we will help you do this) the weakness of the uncontrolled observation method, we must at the same time recognize that many important questions about a person's natural social behavior cannot be determined through a controlled or clinical approach, much less be measured by standardized instruments. As noted earlier in this chapter, counselors are also being encouraged to adopt an ecological perspective that suggests the study of behavior "intact" within the natural setting of the person being observed.

As we begin an examination of the various techniques counselors use for gaining a better understanding of their clients, let us begin with the most natural and popular of all these techniques: observation. As previously noted, we all employ this technique to varying degrees in drawing conclusions about others, but this is not to suggest that all observations are equally useful for human assessment. As a basis for classifying the differing approaches to observation, we make the following points.

Forms of Observation

Blocher (1987) suggests that systematic observation takes one of three basic forms: (a) naturalistic observation, when we might observe clients or subjects in a natural setting; (b) the survey method, when we survey (observe) particular samples of individuals' behavior we wish to assess; and (c) experimentation, when we not only observe but impose specific conditions on those being observed.

Observations may also be classified by the level of sophistication and training required, as noted here:

> *First Level: Casual Information Observation.* The daily, unstructured, and usually unplanned observations that provide casual impressions; engaged in daily by nearly everyone. No training or instrumentation expected or required.
>
> *Second Level: Guided Observation.* Planned, directed observations for a purpose. Observation at this level is usually facilitated by simple instruments such as checklists and rating scales. Some training desired.

Third Level: Clinical Level. Observations, often prolonged, and frequently with controlled conditions. Sophisticated techniques and instruments used with training, usually at a doctoral level.

At this level and in many clinical settings, the counselor may need to make a diagnosis of mental disorders or may receive a client case history with psychiatric diagnostic nomenclature. The American Psychiatric Association's most recent effort to categorize mental disorders, *The Diagnostic and Statistical Manual of Mental Disorders* (*DSM-III-R*) is generally used for this purpose (APA, 1987).* (Hansen et al., 1986, p. 388)

The Diagnostic and Statistical Manual of Mental Disorders [*DSM-IV*] (American Psychiatric Association, 1994) contains authoritative information and "official opinions" about the range of mental problems. Counselors rely on the [*DSM-IV*] (1) as a source of standardized terminology in which to communicate with other mental health specialists, (2) to satisfy the record-keeping requirements of insurance companies or credentialing agencies like the Joint Commission on Accreditation of Hospitals, (3) for classifying clientele in statistical categories, as is necessary for research and accountability, (4) to predict the course of a disorder and the progress of treatment based on available evidence, and (5) to construct a treatment plan that will guide interventions (Seligman, 1983). The actual process of differential diagnosis with the [*DSM-IV*] is complex, and mastery of the system requires considerable study. (Kottler & Brown, 1985, p. 161)

Common Weaknesses of Observation

Because observation is a technique we all use and use frequently, it is only natural that we assume we are reasonably accurate in our observations. However, this is a misleading assumption. Observation can be one of the most abused techniques in human assessment. Let us therefore proceed to examine some of these abuses or common weaknesses, followed by suggestions for increasing the effectiveness of this valuable assessment technique.

One of the popular questions on the written examinations for drivers' licenses in many states is to ask the applicant to identify, by shape only, the meaning of the various traffic signs. Perhaps you would like to pause and test your recall of these signs, which all of us see every day:

Now compare your responses to the following answers: stop, yield, warning, information, railroad. How did you do? For many at least, this points up one of the glaring weaknesses in undirected observation:

Casual observations do not lend themselves to consistent accurate recall.

---

*From J. C. Hansen, R. R. Stevic, and W. R. Warner, *Counseling: Theory and Process* (4th ed.). Copyright © 1986 by Allyn and Bacon. Used with permission of James Hansen.

Envision yourself on the witness stand in the classical courtroom scene in which you are matching wits with the prosecuting attorney. In a fine "You are guilty" voice, the prosecutor asks, "Who were the first three people you observed on the morning of October 13 a year ago?" Some witnesses might have their recall saved by habit (the wife and kids) or a special event (the minister, a best friend, or a future in-law), but most would have difficulty recalling with accuracy and certainty the first three people they observed on that fateful day and even more difficulty in accurately describing what they were wearing. Although most of us have confidence in our ability to recall accurately what we have observed in the past, courtroom witnesses, witnesses to accidents, observers of historic or sensational events, and even news reporters are so frequently wrong as definitely to suggest that we are not so accurate in our recall of the past, especially the details, as we often assume. Another weakness of undirected observations, then, would be this:

> Complete and accurate recall of undirected or casual observations tends to decrease with the passage of time.

Now assume that you are a devout sports fan. Your favorite team is involved in a close game in the final minutes when an official calls a penalty that could conceivably cost your team the game. Regardless of how flagrant that offense or the call, it would be highly predictable that you, and those supporting your team, would have "observed" the call differently from the officials and the supporters of the other team. An impartial witness would note that different observers were viewing the same situation differently. Similar illustrations may occur when two different observers describe the same western desert scene as "a beautiful blending by nature of sand, greenery, and beautiful hills" and "a wasteland of sand and drab plants running into bleak mountains." All of us have experienced the discrepancies that often occur as someone describes a boyfriend or girlfriend and as the same person appears to us. The point is that people differ in how they view the same event, person, or place, and also in the details they observe. We would note this as another weakness in casual and informal observations for assessment purposes:

> Similar observations will be viewed differently because each person has his or her own unique frame of reference for interpreting what he or she sees.

These and other shortcomings suggest that undirected and casual observations of our clients may result in incomplete, misleading, or erroneous assessments. The values and opportunities of observation in client analysis are recognized, but some guidelines and instruments must be developed for increasing the accuracy and effectiveness of this technique. Here are some guiding principles for client analysis through observation, followed by a discussion of some useful instruments for reporting and recording our observations of others.

Guidelines for Client Analysis Through Observation

1. *Observe one client at a time.* Observation for individual analysis is just that; it focuses on the person. We are intent on noticing every observable detail of client behavior that may be meaningful in the counseling context. This is just as desirable an objective for observations of people in external group settings as in the more restricted setting of the counseling office.

2. Have specific criteria for making observations. We observe our clients for a purpose. We are observing for characteristics of the person appropriate to this purpose. These provide a basis for the identification of specific criteria, which in effect tell us "what to look for." For example, if we are observing young persons for the purpose of determining their relationships with adults, we might decide that two criteria or characteristics of this relationship that we would specifically observe would be interactions with teachers and interactions with parents. Of course, it is important that the criteria we use be appropriate to our observational objectives.

3. Observations should be made over a period of time. Although there is no specific time span formula for conducting observations, they should take place over a period of time that is long and frequent enough to establish the reliability of our observation. A single sample of behavior is seldom enough for us to say with certainty that this is characteristic of the person. An illustration of this principle is to recall how your later impressions of people often differ from your first impressions, once you have had the opportunity to observe them over a period of time. Also, although concentrated periods of observation may be appropriate, the amount of observational time should not be confused with the span of time over which observations take place.

4. The client should be observed in differing and natural situations. Natural behavior is most likely to occur in natural situations. Although these situations vary somewhat among persons, for most youth, the school, home, neighborhood, and favorite recreational locales will be natural; with adults, the place one works will replace the school. Even within these natural settings, people will behave differently but naturally in different locales. For example, a student in school may behave differently in the classroom, the cafeteria, the gym, the hallways, and on the playground. If possible, therefore, clients should be observed in those settings and situations that are typical for them. Furthermore, this means a reasonable variety of those settings. For example, a school-aged youth may exhibit different behavior in one class at school than in others and completely different behavior in social-recreational settings. An adult may behave differently on the job than at home and differently again in other social settings. Observing in these different settings may help us determine whether some behaviors are limited to or conditioned by specific environments or situations.

5. Observe the client in the context of the total situation. In observation for human analysis, it is important to avoid a "tunnel vision" approach, or one in which we are so visually intent on observing just the client that we may miss noting those interactions and other factors in the setting that cause the person to behave the way he or she does. An example might be a classroom situation in which we observe that at the conclusion of nearly every math class, Nancy always leaves in tears, but we fail to observe that her classroom "neighbors" Joe and Jay appear to tease her throughout the class every day. We have observed the results but not the cause.

6. Data from observations should be integrated with other data. In individual analysis it is important to bring together all that we know about our client. Because we are seeking to see the client as a whole person, we would combine the impressions we gained from our observations with all other pertinent information available to us. The case study technique used by most helping professionals illustrates this point of integrating and relating data before interpretation.

7. *Observations should be made under favorable conditions.* Anyone who has tried to witness a parade three rows back or watch a key play at a game when the crowd jumps up in front can bear witness to the importance of favorable conditions for making observations. In planned observation it is desirable that we are in a position to clearly view what we are planning to report. Ideally, we should be able to conduct our observation for a sufficient period of time without either obstructions or distractions. There are also attitudinal considerations in creating favorable conditions for observation. These include an approach that is free from bias toward the client, any projections of expected behavior, or permitting one trait to predict another. It is just as important to have a clear psychological viewing point as a physical viewing point for observation for individual analysis. We should also be alert to another form of bias that may occur when the person being observed modifies his or her behavior because he or she is aware of being observed.

It has been said, "Anticipation is a wonderful thing. It often ensures that we will see what we want to see whether it is there or not."

OBSERVATION INSTRUMENTS

A variety of instruments are available to counselors for use in recording their observations. Most are designed to eliminate one or more of the common weaknesses of undirected or casual observation. They provide a means of recording and preserving an impression of what was observed—an impression that is as accurate a year later as when it was initially recorded. Additionally, many instruments for reporting observations (checklists, rating scales, observation guides) provide specific directions or traits to guide the observer. Some instruments such as rating scales also provide for some degree of discrimination among the traits observed. Because many of these instruments also include definitions or descriptions of their items that users are to accept and follow, they can also form a "mutual frame of reference" that can promote some consistency among observers viewing the same subject. The most popular of these instruments are rating scales, checklists, and observation and anecdotal reports.

Rating Scales

Rating scales, as the name implies, are scales for rating each of the characteristics or activities one is seeking to observe or assess. They enable an observer to observe a person systematically and objectively and record those observations. Although such scales are not limited to the recording and evaluating of observations, those are the common and popular uses of the instrument.

Rating scales have long been valued as an observation instrument by counselors. They are useful as a means of focusing on specific characteristics, increasing the objectivity of the rater, and providing for comparability of observations among observers; and they are easy to use.

Designing a Rating Scale

Although commercially designed rating scales are available, counselors may find it more desirable under most circumstances to design their own. A good self-designed scale will be

---

Example 8–1   DEVELOPING THE RATING SCALE

The Beatty-Tingley Secondary School has a history of high incidence of pupil dropout before graduation. The problem has become particularly severe in the past 3 years, and various remedial efforts have had little effect. The school board has therefore determined that a concerted effort will be made to identify potential early leavers and then to design possible preventive measures. The counseling staff has been requested to design an instrument that will lead to the identification of these potential early leavers through the observation of certain behavioral traits. They proceeded to develop a rating scale by first stating the purpose as follows:

Purpose

    1. To identify potential dropouts

Following a review of relevant research, the counselors agreed on four possible criteria of potential school leavers:

    1. Interest in school
    2. Relations with peers
    3. Relations with teachers
    4. Coping styles

Having identified criteria, they next had to agree on descriptors appropriate for the designing of items on the rating scale. These were determined to be as follows:

    1. *Interest in school:* attention in class, participation in class activities, preparation for class
    2. *Relations with peers:* frequency of interaction with peers, nature of interaction with peers, attitude of peers, friendships with peers
    3. *Relations with teachers:* frequency and nature of interaction with teachers, attitudes toward teachers, attitudes of teachers
    4. *Coping styles:* problem-solving skills, dealing with frustration and failure, work habits

---

more appropriate for both the situation and the rater or raters, can be revised if needed, and, of course, is economical. The potential of any rating scale, however, is first determined by its design. There are five steps in designing a rating scale.

Determine the Purpose(s).   An obvious initial step is to determine the potential population and the purpose of the observations or ratings. Usually, the purposes or objectives of such an instrument should be limited in both number and scope. This tends to prohibit the development of scales that are too lengthy and overlapping and that discourage user completion. Scales that are clear and concise and directed toward limited and precise objectives also increase the likelihood of accurate responses.

Identify the Items.   Once the purposes or objectives of the scale have been established, the developer next identifies appropriate criteria or items to be rated. These items should

---

Example 8–1

(continued)

They then began designing the rating scale. The first items were designed to assess the interest of students in their classes.

Interest in School (check most appropriate category)

Class attention:
Consistent and general alertness to ongoing activities in the subject matter class

| Never | Rarely | Sometimes | Usually | Always |

Comments:

Class participation:
Quality of participation: knowedgeable and appropriate contributions and interactions

| Poor | Below Average | Average | Superior | Excellent |

Comments:

Frequency of participation:

| Never | Seldom | Occasionally | Often | Always |

Comments:

Preparation for class:
Readiness in terms of reading and other assignments for meaningful participation in class

| Never | Seldom | Occasionally | Usually | Always |

Comments:

---

be clearly and directly related to the objectives of the observation. Also, they should be clearly understood, easily observed, and assessed.

Identify the Descriptors.   Although there is often a subtle difference between items and descriptors, it is important to honor this difference. Items may not be ratable, so descriptors are used to effect a transition between an "identifying item or statement" and an "objective description."

Example 8–1 is a rating scale for identifying potential school dropouts.

Identify Evaluators.   As the label implies, evaluations or ratings in some kind of a scale are an anticipated characteristic of this particular technique for making and reporting observations. There are a variety of options for this purpose, such as the number of intervals or points on the scale, the defining of the evaluators, and deciding whether to provide space for comments.

Determine the Format.   A part of the format will be determined by the identification of evaluators, as described in the previous step. Additionally, the organization usually relates items together; the length—not too long—and the directions for completion will all be items to attend to in determining the final format for the instrument.

Limitations of the Rating Scale

Limitations in using rating scales are basically those to which all instruments administered and developed by humans are subject: the limitations of the instrument and the limitations imposed by the user. The most common instrument limitations are (a) the result of poor and unclear directions for the scales' use, (b) a failure to define terms adequately, (c) limited scales for rating, (d) items that tend to prejudice how one responds, (e) overlapping items, and (f) excessive length.

The limitations that raters impose are equally prevalent and can be even more serious, because they can distort or misrepresent the characteristics of a person. The following are common examples:

1. *Ratings made without sufficient observations.* Many raters have an apparent need to complete all the items on a scale and, as a result, will "take a stab" at items with which they are unfamiliar. Others, in their haste to complete the scale, will make a rating on the basis of limited observation.

2. *Overrating.* There is a growing conviction among those who frequently use rating scales that overrating is a common practice among raters. For example, a recent review of rating scales used in conjunction with admissions to graduate work in a Big Ten university revealed that all 324 candidates were rated "considerably above average" or higher in three categories: appearance, social skills, and leadership.

3. *Middle rating.* Another group of raters appears to play it safe by using only the average or middle categories on a scale, thus avoiding either extremes of high or low assessments. Such ratings tend to misrepresent everyone as being just about average in everything.

4. *Biased ratings.* In addition to personal bias, bias may occur in ratings when raters permit one item that they particularly value or emphasize to set a pattern for the rating of other items.

Although the focus of this discussion has centered on the utilization of rating scales in reporting observations, this instrument is not limited in use to only the reporting of observations. Rating scales are also used extensively by counselors and others for performance ratings, evaluations (both personal and institutional), and measurement of attitudes, aspirations, and experiences.

Checklists

Another instrument that may be used for recording observations is the observer checklist. This instrument is typically designed to direct the observer's attention to specific, observable personality traits and characteristics. It is relatively easy to use inasmuch as it not only directs the observer's attention to certain specific traits but provides a simple means of indicating whether those traits are characteristic to the person being observed. Unlike the rating scale, the observer checklist does not require the observer to indicate the degree or extent to which a characteristic is present. Figure 8–1 shows an example of a simple form of a checklist.

Observation Checklist

Personal characteristics of _____
                                              (name of student)
Observed by (name or code) _____
Periods (dates of observation): from_____ to _____
Conditions under which student was observed: _____
_____

Instructions: Place a check mark in the blanks to the left of any of the following traits you believe to be characteristic of the student.

Positive Traits	Negative Traits
_____ 1. Neat in appearance	_____ 16. Unreliable
_____ 2. Enjoys good health	_____ 17. Uncooperative
_____ 3. Regular in attendance	_____ 18. Domineering
_____ 4. Courteous	_____ 19. Self-centered
_____ 5. Concerned for others	_____ 20. Rude
_____ 6. Popular with other students	_____ 21. Sarcastic
_____ 7. Displays leadership ability	_____ 22. Boastful
_____ 8. Has a good sense of humor	_____ 23. Dishonest
_____ 9. Shows initiative	_____ 24. Resists authority
_____ 10. Industrious	_____ 25. A bully
_____ 11. Has a pleasant disposition	_____ 26. Overly aggressive
_____ 12. Mature	_____ 27. Shy and withdrawn
_____ 13. Respects property of others	_____ 28. Cries easily
_____ 14. Nearly always does his/her best	_____ 29. Deceitful
_____ 15. Adjusts easily to different situations	_____ 30. Oversolicitous

Comments: _____
_____
_____
_____

FIGURE 8–1   Observation Checklist

Anecdotal Report Form
Henry H. Higgins High School

Name _____   Observed by _____

Where observed _____   When: Date _____

                                            Time _____ to _____

Description:

Comments:

FIGURE 8–2   Anecdotal Record: Form A

Inventories

Self-report inventories typically consist of structured questions or statements to which the respondent answers "yes" or "no," or "yes," "?," or "no" (Hopkins & Stanley, 1981). Like rating scales, they use objective statements and responses in eliciting a person's view of self in regard to the listed items. Self-report inventories are often used to assess self-concept, study habits, and attitudes.

Anecdotal Reports

Anecdotal reports, as the label implies, are descriptions of a client's behavior in a given situation or event. Such reports are subjective and descriptive in nature and recorded in a

Anecdote

Return to:
Guidance Offices
Nelson Elementary
School

Student's name

Description of incident observed	Comments:

Observed by _____

Time _____   Place _____

FIGURE 8–3   Anecdotal Record: Form B

```
┌──────────────────────────────────────────────────────────────────────┐
│  Anecdotal report for                                                  │
│    Name                                  Date                           │
│                                                                        │
│    Situation                                                           │
├──────────────────────────────────────────────────────────────────────┤
│  Description                                                           │
│                                                                        │
│                                                                        │
│  - - - - - - - - - - - - - - - - - - - - - - - - - - - - - - - - - - - │
│  Comments:                                                             │
│                                                                        │
│  Observer:                                                             │
│  - - - - - - - - - - - - - - - - - - - - - - - - - - - - - - - - - - - │
│  Comments:                                                             │
│                                                                        │
│  Observer:                                                             │
│                                                                        │
└──────────────────────────────────────────────────────────────────────┘
```

FIGURE 8–4   Anecdotal Record: Form C

narrative form. Often a counselor will collect several of these reports, which then become an anecdotal record of a client's behavior over a period of time or situations.

Design of Anecdotal Records

The format for anecdotal records usually consists of three parts: (a) recording identifying data, (b) reporting of the observations, and (c) comments of the observer. This format has several variations, as may be noted by examining three different designs for anecdotal records. Figure 8–2 presents a format that follows in sequence the three parts previously identified. Figure 8–3 alters this format to provide space for comments alongside that are appropriate to particular statements of the anecdotal description. Figure 8–4 has space for comments of additional observers, if desired.

Using the Anecdotal Reporting Method

The first consideration in anecdotal reporting is the selection of incidents that may be significant to report. There may be incidents that are typical of a client's behavior and are relevant for the counselor's or client's better understanding of the client. They may also be incidents so atypical of the client's behavior that their reporting and understanding may be advisable. In some situations, a series of anecdotes reporting similar behaviors over a period of time would increasingly suggest that the observed characteristics are typical of the client's behavior. Different observers making similar observations of a client's behavior on a specific occasion, or over a period of time, would have similar implications. Also, anecdotal reporting covering a period of time may identify trends or changes in client behaviors.

In school settings, teachers may be encouraged to use anecdotal reports in calling counselor attention to students who may need their assistance or in contributing to case studies or just a better understanding of individual students. Example 8–2 illustrates uses of anecdotal reporting in school settings, as well as the counselor's interpretations of these reports.

Example 8–2   USES OF ANECDOTAL REPORTING IN SCHOOL

Student's Name:	Therese
Incident 1:	Mr. Michael
Reported by:	History teacher
Date:	January 16 (Monday)

Therese was not herself in class today. She usually is very active in the class discussions and always responds to questions when no one else seems to have the answer. However, today she sat quietly in her seat. At one point, when the discussion was bogging down, I called on Therese as always, asking her, "What were some of the factors that kept the United States from joining the League of Nations after World War I?" I could barely hear her response, but I thought she said, "Who cares?" and then in a louder voice that bordered on breaking into tears, "I'm sorry, I don't know the answer."

Teacher's Comments: Therese is one of my more mature and capable students. Something is upsetting her, and it would be helpful if a counselor could talk with her.

Student's Name:	Therese
Incident 2:	Ms. Atwood
Reported by:	Chemistry teacher
Date:	January 18 (Wednesday)

For the first time in the 2 years I have known Therese as a student, she has fallen behind in her work in my class. Furthermore, her behavior has been almost disruptive. For example, today, when one of her best friends, Ann, asked her if she could borrow a test tube from her, Therese snapped back at her, saying, "Don't you ever have enough stuff to do your own assignments? No, I'm not lending you anything anymore!" The exchange obviously was unexpected to Ann, who didn't exchange another word with Therese for the rest of the period, while Therese seemed to spend most of the period simply staring at her lab book.

Teacher's Comments: Something is clearly wrong with this girl. This behavior is not typical at all. She needs to see a counselor.

Student's Name:	Therese
Incident 3:	Mrs. Kemp
Reported by:	Physical education teacher
Date:	January 19 (Thursday)

Example 8–1

(continued)

	Today, Therese approached me before my fifth period in which she is enrolled and said, "Ms. Findley, I am quitting the gymnastics team and I don't want to talk about it." When I put my arm around her and said, "That's OK, Therese, I hope you're all right," she broke into tears and said, "I'll never be all right again!" and then ran into the locker room. I decided to leave her alone and didn't follow up on our conversation at this time.
Teacher's Comments:	I have noted for the past couple of weeks that Therese hasn't seemed to be herself, but today things seemed to explode. I don't know what the difficulty is, but I do intend to follow up on her problem, whatever it may be, when I see her next week. Do you have any suggestions?

In this situation it is obvious that the school counselor, by the end of the week, is able to put together a picture of a young lady who is clearly upset. Although there are no indications of cause in the incidents described, the counselor has sufficient reason to either call in Therese or, through consultation with Mrs. Kemp, attempt to provide her with appropriate help.

The previous discussion illustrates how a series of anecdotes can lead to the identification of a student in need of counseling assistance. In some situations, however, even a single anecdote is enough to alert the counselor to a person in need of assistance.

Student's Name:	Leonard
Reported by:	Mr. Peters, history teacher
Date:	April 8
	Leonard's behavior in class today was most unusual. For example, every time a door slammed or there was any unexpected noise, he would jump as though suddenly startled. On one occasion, Sue accidentally knocked her textbook on the floor, and Leonard grabbed his desk tightly and exclaimed, "My God!" Most of the period he was continuously looking around the room as if expecting to be hit from all sides, and I noticed that he was in a cold sweat when he left the classroom at the end of the period. When I asked him, as he was leaving, "Leonard, are you feeling OK?" he replied, "We are all going to get it . . . you just wait and see."
Teacher's Comments:	Leonard is usually so unobtrusive in class that he attracts little attention to himself. Today, however, everyone noticed his unusual behavior.

Advantages versus Disadvantages

Because anecdotal reports are designed to subjectively describe what has been observed, they become more lifelike than more objective measures. They present a broader, more complete viewpoint of a situation, which at the same time avoids the bleakness of the more quantitative or objective methods of reporting.

The major limitations of anecdotal reporting are those imposed by the observer-reporter. Most common of these are the reporting of "feelings about" rather than actual "behavior of" the person observed. The tendency to "read in" biases or expectancies can result in misleading reports. Overinterpretation or misinterpretation by inexperienced observers are not uncommon. The reporting of insignificant, rather than meaningful, behavior can also limit the usefulness of anecdotal reporting.

Time-Based Observations

Observations of behavior based on units or periods of time may be useful. One strategy of measuring behavior is based on units of time rather than discrete response units. Kazdin (1981) describes this as follows:

> Behavior is recorded during short time intervals for the total time that it is observed. With interval recording, behavior is observed for a single block of time (e.g., 30 minutes) once per day. A block of time is divided into a series of short intervals (10 or 15 seconds), and the behavior of the client is observed during each of them. The target behavior is scored as having occurred or not occurred during each interval. If a discrete behavior, such as hitting someone, occurs one or more times in a single interval, the response is scored as having occurred. Several response occurrences within an interval are not counted separately. If the behavior is ongoing with an unclear beginning or end, such as talking, playing, or sitting, or occurs for a long period of time, it is scored during each interval in which it is occurring.
>
> A variety of interval recording is referred to as *time sampling*. This variation uses the interval method but the observations are conducted for brief periods at different times, rather than in a single block of time.* (p. 107)

Another time-based method of observation is the amount of time, or duration of a particular response. Kazdin (1981) indicates:

> This method is particularly useful for ongoing responses that are continuous rather than discrete acts or responses of extremely short duration. Programs that attempt to increase or decrease the length of time a response is performed might profit from a duration method. For example, duration has been used to assess the amount of time that a claustrophobic patient spent sitting voluntarily in a small room (Leitenberg, Agras, Thompson, & Wright, 1968) and the time delinquent boys spent returning from school and errands (Phillips, 1968).
>
> Another measure based upon duration is not how long the response is performed, but how long it takes for the client to begin the response. The amount of elapsed time between a cue and the response is referred to as *latency*. (p. 108)

---

*From Kazdin, A. E., "Behavioral Observation" in Bellack, Alan S. and Hersen, Michael, *Behavioral Assessment: A Practical Handbook.* Copyright © 1988 by Allyn and Bacon. Reprinted by permission.

Instrument Selection

The preceding paragraphs have discussed a variety of observation techniques and instruments. In many situations, counselors and other observers will make a decision about which instrument or instruments are most appropriate for the observation task at hand. They may be aided in determining which types of instruments to use by considering the following:

1. Is some direction for recording observation(s) for individual analysis desired? (The answer to this is usually yes, or should be.)
2. Is a descriptive or objective report more appropriate?
3. Will more than one observer be reporting observations of the client (or potential client)?
4. Are assessments or evaluations of what has been observed desired?
5. Are comparisons among different clients or between clients and other populations likely to be made?
6. Are opinions or impressions—not necessarily facts or factually based information—desired?
7. Does the instrument avoid complex observations and recording methods?
8. Will the instrument make it relatively easy to complete a report in a short period of time, even if some accuracy or depth of observation may be sacrificed?
9. Will instruments be used by counselors or others who are experienced or trained in their use?

DSM-III-R/DSM-IV

The most popular diagnostic system in the United States is the *Diagnostic and Statistical Manual of Mental Disorders* (revised), published by the American Psychiatric Association. While the manual itself presents a standardized system of recording, the judgments on which these entries are often made will be subjective.

According to the *DSM-III-R*, a mental disorder is characterized by distress, disability, and/or risk. At least one of these features must be present in order for a client to be diagnosed as having a mental disorder (Capuzzi & Gross, 1991). These features also are often present in combination. Whether or not clients who present themselves for counseling have mental disorders, the multiaxial diagnosis of the *DSM-III-R* offers counselors a way to organize the information they have on clients' symptoms, their physical conditions, their levels of coping, and the stressors they are experiencing (Capuzzi & Gross, 1991).

The *DSM-III-R* is divided into 18 broad categories of mental disorders, with many specific mental disorders under each category. A new edition entitled *DSM-IV* was released in 1994. This edition retains the definition of a mental disorder previously noted and the multiaxial diagnosis of the *DSM-III-R*, as well as the 18 broad categories of mental disorders. Counselors planning to use this resource should take special course work or training prior to using it.

SELF-REPORTING: THE AUTOBIOGRAPHY AND OTHER TECHNIQUES

Up to this point we have been discussing observation and observation techniques for client assessment. In such techniques clients may be aware of their being observed, but rarely are they direct participants in the process.

Some of the most valuable techniques of human assessment for counseling purposes are those that call for the active involvement of the client. These techniques not only provide special insights for the counselor but also can be valuable to the clients as they engage in a process of guided self-assessment. The use of such techniques as autobiographies, self-expression essays, structured interviews, and questionnaires can facilitate both counselor and client understanding of the client's strengths, weaknesses, and uniqueness.

The Autobiography: A Popular Technique

The autobiography has been one of the most popular forms of literature throughout the ages. Humankind has consistently been interested in the personal view people have of their own life experiences. Additionally, almost everyone, famous or obscure, has at one time jotted down a personal view of life's experiences. Some hope for publication, whereas others only write for their own personal satisfaction. For the majority of those feeling compelled to examine and set down in writing life's experiences, it is unlikely that the desire will coincide with a need for counseling. Nonetheless, the autobiography, even when it represents a nonvoluntary effort, can be a useful source of information to the skilled counselor. Let us briefly examine its use as a nonstandardized technique in human assessment.

Autobiography: A Different Technique

At this point it is probably appropriate to indicate that counselors should avoid the use of overlapping or similar techniques. For example, there is little to be gained in using both rating scales and observation checklists to report observations of the same type of behavior or in using three different achievement tests to measure the same area of achievement. A feature of the autobiography is that it is different from any other technique available to the counselor, for it provides clients (or students) with the opportunity to describe their own life as they have experienced it and view it.

The autobiography lets a person express what has been important in his or her life, emphasize likes and dislikes, identify values, describe interests and aspirations, acknowledge successes and failures, and recall meaningful personal relationships. Such an experience, especially for the mature client, can be thought-provoking, insightful, and a stimulus for action. On occasion, the experience can also relieve tension.

The Autobiography as an Assignment

As previously indicated, there are times in most people's lives when they reach a state of psychological readiness for writing their own life story. However, because this is unlikely to occur at the time such information may be needed by a counselor, some attention should be paid to the autobiography as a client or student assignment. If the autobiography is to be requested and used solely by the counselor, the suggestion should be presented as naturally and straightforwardly as possible, with an indication of how it will be helpful to both the counselor and the client in the counseling process. It should also be emphasized that the contents of the autobiography will at all times (within legal limits) be treated as confidential information. The counselor should also indicate possible content and approaches for preparing this assignment. Written guidelines may also be prepared for use in such a situation. Example 8–3 is one such set of guidelines that provides the client three possible options for preparing an autobiography.

In a school setting, the autobiography is often collected through a subject-matter classroom. It is most frequently a written assignment in an English class at the secondary school level, and in the elementary school, as a language assignment or an assignment related to the study of famous historic figures. As a classroom assignment, the autobiography should be treated in such a way that the student will regard it as a worthwhile educational experience. This suggests that it is treated as a regular assignment for a grade, although, if grades are assigned, the teacher must emphasize that one is not receiving an A or F for his or her life thus far but rather for the technical manner in which he or she described it in relation to the assignment.

Limitations

The autobiography has a number of potential limitations that counselors and other users must take into consideration. For instance, many people may find the writing of an autobiography a chore; thus, it will become a brief, bleak, and usually boring document that contributes little to a better understanding of the writer. The writing ability of the author as well as the conditions under which it is written will influence the potential usefulness of this technique. Also, as with any recall-based instrument, the ability of the writer to recall past experiences accurately and in considerable detail is important. Self-insight is another important factor. The reader must also be aware of distortions that overemphasize insignificant happenings or ignore those that are important, or inject falsehoods or fantasies, which very often are descriptive of the ideal or hoped-for life experiences of a writer. Current values may also influence how an author views past experiences and associations, and these may not be consistent with how they are viewed at the time.

Interpretation

With both the possible advantages and limitations of the autobiography in mind, let us note possible analyses by the counselor. The counselor-reader may first of all prepare a checklist or summary form for those items that would be particularly relevant to the counseling needs of the client. In other situations, the counselor may simply summarize at the conclusion of the reading the most relevant aspects or, assuming that the copy will be for the counselor's viewing only, may underline or make appropriate notes in the margins. In a general reading one might use the format depicted in Figure 8–5 for analyzing an autobiography.

Autobiographical Excerpts

Two brief excerpts are presented as examples of significant statements that are often found in student autobiographies.

Example 8–3   GUIDELINES FOR PREPARING AN AUTOBIOGRAPHY

Purpose

1. To provide you with an opportunity to experience the planning, organizing, and writing of your autobiography
2. To provide you, the writer, and me, the reader, with opportunities for increased understanding, insights, and appreciations of you, the writer

Each writer may develop and work to an outline that suits his or her own style. The emphasis and detail that you give any period, event, or person will be whatever you determine as appropriate. The following are *examples only* of outlines and topics that might be appropriate for inclusion in an autobiography. (Note: I will be the only reader of your autobiography and will, of course, regard its contents as confidential.)

Example A

Part I	My preschool years
	My family, where I lived, early memories, friends, likes and dislikes
Part II	My school years
	Elementary, junior, senior high school, college, teachers, friends, subjects liked and disliked, activities, significant events, experiences, travels, concerns, and decisions
Part III	My adult years
	Where I lived, work experience, friends and family, travels, hobbies, continued education, concerns, and decisions
Part IV	The current me
Part V	My future plans

Example B

1. Significant people in my life
2. Significant events and experiences in my life
3. Significant places in my life

Example C

Start your autobiography as far back as you can remember—your earliest childhood memories. Tell about those things that really made an impression on you, that stood out in your memory, whether happy or sad. Try to include those events that you believe have affected your life, such as moving to another city or entering junior high school. As you write about the event, try to show how the event affected you, what people have truly influenced your life the most, and how they affected the way you feel and act today. Mention your hopes and plans for the future—what you hope to be doing 10 years from now, for example.

When a counselor desires that a client emphasize a certain aspect of his or her life's experiences, that should be indicated to the writer.

I	Significant incidents

II	Organization–length, language (choice of vocabulary, depth of expression)

III	Omissions, glossing over, inaccuracies

IV	Points to check further

V	Summary comments

FIGURE 8–5 Analyzing an Autobiography

Source: From M. A. Kiley, *Personal and Interpersonal Appraisal Techniques*, 1975, p. 66. Courtesy of Charles C. Thomas, Publisher, Springfield, Illinois.

When I moved from East Park High School to Newry High School I guess I had assumed that things would go on as usual. I had been a big wheel at East Park—you know what I mean— member of the Student Council, president of the "Jokers"—most popular boys' club in school, king of the Sophomore Stomp, member of about half a dozen other clubs, invites to all the parties and social activities that were of any importance. But at Newry, many of the clubs I had belonged to before didn't exist. There were no boys' social clubs and, try as I might, I couldn't seem to make friends that moved in the "popular" circles. A lot of the kids spoke to me and were pleasant enough, but they never thought of me at party time. I found as time went on I missed East Park more and more, and I even began cutting school so I could drive back and visit East Park while school was in session. I had been a "B" student before at East Park, but my grades really took a beating at Newry. In fact, some of the kids at Newry began thinking of me as a "dum-dum" and I know many of the teachers did.

The counselor in this instance found a significant clue in this portion of the client's autobiography to explain his poor grades and the subsequent difficulty he was having in securing college admission.

I guess I felt like a nobody as far back as I can remember. I think maybe my mother resented me because I wasn't a girl, because when I was born she already had five boys. I know as a kid I could never seem to do anything right, and my mother used to say I couldn't do anything right because I was a nobody. I remember that she and my Dad both began calling me "ole nobody." Then my oldest brother, the one with the sense of humor, started calling me "N.B." (for *nobody*). The rest of the family thought that was real "cute" and so when I started school, and all through school, I have been called N.B. Actually, my name is James Lucifer Laswich. But I often have to stop to think what my real name is, I'm so used to N.B. I guess one reason I am so used to it is that I just seem to fit the name "Ole Nobody" so well. I sometimes don't think there is a single teacher in this school who remembers me once I leave the class, and I know most of the kids don't. I must be the only kid in school who doesn't have a "best friend."

The case of "Ole Nobody" is another example of a significant statement in a person's autobiography that provides the counselor with clues to his client's seemingly withdrawn behavior and poor self-concept.

Autobiographical Tapes

In recent years, an innovative deviation from the usual written autobiography—the autobiographical tape—has been found useful by counselors with some clients. The autobiographical tape presents the client an opportunity orally to describe and discuss one's life. In utilizing this technique, the counselor may first determine whether it is more likely to be useful than the written autobiography. Once the counselor has determined that the tape approach is more appropriate, the counselor may then decide whether to provide the client with a structured outline to respond to or simply to describe the client's life as it comes to him or her.

There may be some advantages to the autobiographical tape that will determine the circumstances under which it will be used. For example, some persons can express themselves better orally than in writing. Furthermore, because this method requires less preparation and effort on the part of the client, he or she may more freely present details that would otherwise be omitted. In addition, some clients may feel that there is less likelihood that the contents of a tape "give away one's secrets" than a written document. Voice tone on a taped autobiography may also reveal feelings and emotions of the client and, because of the nature of recording, the autobiography by tape is less likely to be subject to client editing or censoring. Finally, the taping of an autobiography for some clients is a more fascinating or innovative approach than the traditional writing experience.

There are, of course, disadvantages as well to taping one's autobiography. The usual shortcomings of the written autobiography, such as lack of recall, exaggeration, and fantasy, are every bit as probable in this approach. In addition, some clients lack the ability to express themselves clearly orally. Also, for some, the "unnaturalness" of this approach will be an inhibitor. Nonetheless, the taped autobiography is a tool that the counselor may wish to consider for certain clients under certain circumstances.

Self-Expression Essays

Another useful technique that counselors may want to employ on occasion is the self-expression essay. This technique seeks to solicit the client's response, usually in a short, written essay form, to a particular question or concern. The objective of this technique is to elicit spontaneous, uncensored responses to a topic or topics relevant to the counseling needs of the client. Examples of appropriate topics would include these:

Example 8–4   A SELF-EXPRESSION ESSAY: MY SCHOOL PROBLEM

My school problem is that I have no problem! Look at us! We have a beautiful school and, just my luck, a great faculty. We can't seem to lose more than once or twice a year in any sport. The greatest gang of kids go here and the crowning blow—even the food in the cafeteria is edible. So I have a problem because I'm a natural born griper—I'm at my best when I can complain—I have a feeling of accomplishment when I can point out the weaknesses of others. I used to have a field day before I came to Lee Street High. Now I'm dejected because I'm not rejected.

To help solve my problem I suggest that:

1. The students get busy and deface the school, mark up the restrooms, pull out the shrubbery, and all the other things that make a school more homelike.
2. The faculty get busy telling us how stupid we are, that they quit treating us like humans (I actually feel superior to my dog now), and that they get back in the old game of teacher versus student to the bitter end.
3. Our teams lose a few more games, and that our coaches get rid of their coats and ties and wear baggy sweatshirts and swear loudly at the officials so they won't be mistaken for ladies and gentlemen, and that our student body do something pronto to get rid of that disgraceful "good sportsmanship" trophy.
4. The students start forming cliques, avoid welcoming newcomers, and in general act more like adolescents than young adults. Oh, yes, we need a few more "kookie" dressers also.
5. Finally, the school cafeteria manager go copy the menus and recipes from some other schools (mashed potatoes should always be served cold, and lumpy gravy should taste like glue, and fried chicken served stringy and dried out).

My biggest concern is . . .
I'll bet you don't know that . . .
I value . . .
My future plans are . . .
My job is. . .

It should be emphasized that such documents can elicit positive responses as well as descriptions of possible problems or concerns. Example 8–4 illustrates a positive response.

The Self-Description

The self-description is another client-participation tool that enables the counselor to see the client as he or she sees him- or herself. The client is requested to "paint a picture of yourself in words," in one page, if desired.

Such a portrait may share whatever aspects the client wishes to have the reader know. It is usually desirable to do this in the early stages of counseling to give the counselor an additional means of getting to know the client. This differs from the self-expression essay because the self-description is one's view of one's self, as indicated in Example 8–5, whereas the self-expression essay may describe one's attitudes toward activities, events, and beliefs.

Example 8–5   EXCERPTS FROM SELF-DESCRIPTION ESSAYS

Sample 1

I would describe myself as a pleasant and amiable person. Others remark about my easygoing manner and happy-go-lucky personality. Honesty is a virtue I hold very dearly, and I perhaps trust others equally, thinking that they have my virtues.

My mother had always taught me that I should be conscious of others' feelings and do my best to please them. I went for many years applying this philosophy, yet found that others were not as conscious of my feelings. This led me to be hurt and used by others emotionally and mentally. I had to almost retrain myself to believe that thinking of myself was not altogether selfish and at times is the only way to think in order to lead a happy life.

Counselor's Notations: The counselor would no doubt notice the section of this self-description that indicates the client has been hurt and used by others emotionally and mentally. Also of interest to the counselor is the client's statement, "I had to almost retrain myself to believe that thinking of myself was not altogether selfish."

Sample 2

I believe that a person should not be too overtly predictable but should possess a consistency of covert thought and feeling. I do not mean to say that I delight in the misconceptions of those who wish to categorize or predict the responses of others. I am not one to purposely masquerade, or, for some reason, to mislead those I work or come in contact with. But oftentimes an unpredictable action, comment, or response will reveal or trigger a surprising reaction on the part of an eager conversationalist. I do not become close to many, and am not always patient enough to seek out the best points of my peers or colleagues. My point of view has been said to be too sensitive at times, but I like to think that my increased sensitivity allows me to take a deeper breath of life and enjoy what beauty I may sense.

I am idealistic, serious, extremely concerned about those who need help, and a good listener.

Counselor's Notations: The counselor reading this self-description might note the fact that the client keeps his or her distance from colleagues and is considered at times to be overly sensitive. This self-description is of interest, too, for the writer's description of interactions with his or her peers.

Self-Awareness Exercises

Many persons pride themselves on their self-control, their ability "to put their feelings aside and deal in a practical manner with the situation at hand." Others simply find it difficult to express their feelings openly to others, as, for example, the often dramatized shy young man who never can work up the courage to tell his true love that he cares for her. At the other extreme, we can identify persons who may express their feelings openly in such a way as to be harmful to their personal relationships with others. Even in these extremes, persons are often unaware of how their expressions of feelings and emotions may be handicapping rather than helping their relationships with others.

Self-awareness exercises are designed to help people become more aware of their feelings, emotions, and values as a step toward more effectively expressing their emotions, feelings, and values. Egan's (1977) chart of difficulty in expressing emotion (Figure 8–6) says that in many (if not most) cases it becomes more and more difficult to express feelings and emotions the farther down the chart you go. Therefore, it is relatively easy to express a positive feeling about a past situation when the feeling is directed toward a person who is absent.

Examples of self-awareness exercises are Exercises 8–1 and 8–2.

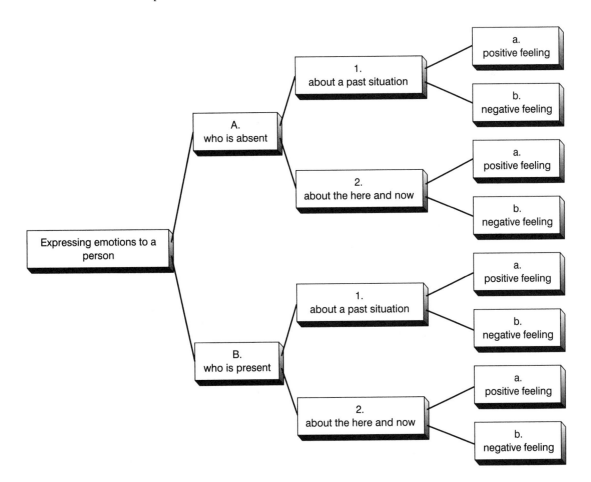

FIGURE 8–6 Difficulty in Expressing Emotion
Source: From *You and Me: The Skills of Communicating and Relating to Others,* p. 81, by G. Egan. Copyright © 1977 by Wadsworth, Inc. Reprinted by permission of Brooks/Cole Publishing Company, Pacific Grove, CA 93950.

Exercise 8–1

This exercise is designed to help you increase your awareness of how the expression of feelings/emotions affects your relationships with others. There are no right or wrong answers, so you should react to each statement as honestly as you can, recognizing that "who" and circumstances might alter your response in actual situations.

Use the following scale:

1 = Very annoying
2 = Somewhat bothersome
3 = Doesn't usually bother me
4 = Feel OK
5 = Will probably feel very positive

Indicate in general how you feel about persons who

1. Shout at you in anger   ____
2. Slap you on the back in greeting you   ____
3. Cry in your presence when reading a "sad" book or newspaper item   ____
4. Talk in a very loud voice when they are frustrated or upset   ____
5. Laugh easily and often   ____
6. Are silent and moody when they are mad   ____
7. Are silent and moody when they are sad   ____
8. Are silent when they are disappointed   ____
9. Become emotional whenever things go wrong   ____
10. Become emotional whenever something nice happens to them   ____
11. Never show any emotions   ____
12. Are inconsistent in their open displays of emotion   ____

Daily Schedules and Diaries

As with the autobiography, many of us have kept a diary from time to time. We may recall how we bared our soul in those secret pages, often protected with a little tin lock, that if reread today might help us better understand some of our present behavior and attitudes. Probably today's clients are no more willing than their predecessors to share such recordings, but when a client willingly maintains and shares diary entries with the counselor, they can provide valuable insights into understanding the client and his or her problem. Some clients will find it easier to present some aspects of their behavior and experiences in writing than in oral communication, and, if so, the counselor may decide to suggest the keeping of a diary for a period of time.

Another technique for systematically recording the client's daily activities is the daily schedule. This is a simple listing, usually an hour-by-hour accounting of a client's daily activities. This technique can be useful in helping the counselor and client understand

---

Exercise 8–2

Indicate how you usually manage your emotions using the following scale:

> 1 = Express my feelings openly
> 2 = May express my feelings openly to close friends or family
> 3 = Would modify my expression of feelings so that they would not convey the real intensity of the emotion I'm feeling
> 4 = Would keep my feelings to myself

1. I think something is funny but I doubt that others may see it that way. ____
2. I am very disappointed at not achieving a level or a goal I had hoped to. ____
3. I am very angry as a result of a great inconvenience caused me by the actions of another person. ____
4. I am frustrated by unnecessary delays and "red tape" in completing an assigned task. ____
5. I am awarded a great and unexpected honor. ____
6. I am saddened by a close personal loss. ____
7. I am a participant in an exciting event or activity. ____

In reviewing your responses to the items indicated in Exercise 8–1 and 8–2, can you identify circumstances under which emotional expressions directed at you by others or your own emotions affect how you interact with others?

---

how the latter is organizing and using his or her time. Whereas the diary is usually a summary of the day's activities, often with feelings and interpretations, the daily schedule is a more objective presentation or listing of the day's activities. Figure 8–7 presents an example of the less familiar of these two instruments, the daily schedule.

Questionnaire

An extremely popular nonstandardized instrument with which all of us have had many encounters is the questionnaire. Questionnaires today appear to be a part of the American way of life, since they are constantly used to inventory public reactions, solicit opinions, predict needs, and evaluate a wide range of commodities, services, and activities. This popularity does not, however, belittle their importance as an instrument for the economical collection of data from individual clients or groups of clients.

The questionnaire has a variety of uses for the counselor. In a broad, general way, it obviously provides an opportunity to easily collect a great deal of information that may be useful in further understanding the client. Also, the questionnaire is a client-participation technique that promises opportunities to advance the self-understanding, at least under some circumstances, of those completing it. More specifically, questionnaires may be designed in such a way as to collect specific types of information related to specific needs of the counseling clientele. Questionnaires may also seek information for the purpose of validating other data already available to the counselor. Additionally, questionnaires can

Diary for _____ Week of _____

Morning	Afternoon	Evening
Monday	12:15–1:00 Lunch in school	6:00–7:00 Dinner
6:45 Get up	cafeteria	7:00–8:00 Watch TV
8:00 Leave for school	1:00–3:30 More school	8:00–9:30 Study English
8:15–12:15 School	4:00 Get home	and history
	4:00–5:00 Loaf around with	9:30–9:45 Take dog
	friends	for walk
	5:00–5:30 Go to store for	9:45–10:15 Study French
	Mom	10:45 Bed
	5:30–6:00 Read evening	
	paper, mostly sports	
Tuesday:	12:15–12:45 Lunch in school	6:00–7:00 Dinner
Same as Monday	cafeteria	7:00–8:00 Watch TV
	12:45–1:00 Talk to	8:00–8:30 Study English
	Mr. Leonard	and chemistry
	1:00–3:30 Classes	8:30–9:00 Watch favorite
	3:30–4:30 Work on	TV program
	chemistry experiment	9:00–9:30 Study English
	4:45–6:00 Get home, read	and chemistry
	paper, listen to CDs	9:30–9:45 Phone call
		9:45–10:15 Study French
		10:15 Bed
Wednesday:	12:15–1:00 Bring lunch;	6:00–6:30 Dinner
Same as Monday	eat in Mr. Leonard's class	6:30–8:00 Study for history
	and watch experiment	test
	1:00–3:30 Classes	8:00–8:30 Watch TV
	4:00 Get home	8:30–9:45 Study for history
	4:00–4:45 Study trig	test
	4:45–5:30 Loaf around with	9:45–10:00 Walk dog
	guys who come by	10:00–10:30 Study French
		10:50 Bed

FIGURE 8–7   Daily Schedule

be useful in identifying problems of individuals or groups, as well as their opinions, attitudes, or values. Questionnaires can also be valuable in collecting needs assessment data as a basis for establishing program objectives and evaluation data as a basis for program improvement.

The usefulness of the instrument, however, will be determined, at least in part, by the kind of information it seeks to collect, the appropriateness of the questionnaire's design, and the skill of the person who administers it.

In questionnaire design there are certain basic considerations to keep in mind:

1. *Directions:* Indicate the purpose of the instrument and give clear, concise directions for its completion.

2. *Item design:* Design items that are clear, concise, and uncomplicated. Items should solicit only one response and should be stated in such a way that the responder will not be biased or influenced in how he or she responds. Questionnaire items should also reflect the language level of the anticipated respondents.

3. *Item content:* Questions should be designed to collect the kinds of information appropriate to the assessment purpose of the instrument. However, caution must be taken in eliciting socially sensitive, culturally restricted, or other personal-private information. Even a few such items (e.g., "Would you engage in sexual activity outside of marriage?" "Have you ever thought of committing a crime?") can arouse resentment or suspicions of some respondents that will affect their response to the total questionnaire as well. Although unsigned questionnaires may secure reasonably accurate group responses to a sensitive topic, the counselor will find such unidentified responses of considerably less value in individual counseling.

4. *Length:* A final consideration, obvious but important, is the length of the questionnaire. Often, we receive questionnaires of such length that we are discouraged from even beginning them. Clients and student populations are no exceptions in their reactions to lengthy questionnaires. Such instruments must be of reasonable length if they are to facilitate the data collection for which they are designed.

Structured Interviews

Another basic and popular technique for increasing a counselor's understanding of the client is the structured interview. This approach not only provides opportunities for client observation under certain controlled conditions but, equally important, enables the counselor to obtain specific information and to explore in-depth behavior or responses. Interviews that are structured are usually planned to serve a particular purpose. Once the purpose has been clearly specified, questions are designed that are suitable to achieve the goal or purpose of the interview. These questions are usually arranged in some sort of a logical sequence, although the interviewer must be flexible to alter both the nature and sequence of the questions as circumstances suggest.

Although the basic principles of counseling are appropriate for the one-to-one interview (see Chapter 5), it is appropriate at this point to note that the interviewing process and setting, to be successful, should be as natural as possible, not anxiety producing. Because the interviewing setting and process may be natural and comfortable to counselors, they may, on occasion, forget that for the interviewee unfamiliar with either, it can be a frightening experience. Perhaps if you recall your own experiences when called in for an income tax audit by the Internal Revenue Service or when interviewed for a first job, you can appreciate a client's wariness. One must also recognize the possible existence of such human qualities as client forgetfulness, exaggeration, or trying too hard to give the "right" answer as limitations in some structured interviews.

For an example of a structured interview, let us go again to the Beatty-Tingley High School and its high school dropout problem. Once potential dropouts had been identified through combining the rating scale with other data, the counseling staff decided to conduct structured interviews with those students who were willing to do so. The purpose of these interviews was to further explore each individual student's views and attitudes about school in relation to their educational and career planning. They then proceeded to structure the interview as follows:

Structured Interview

1. Introduction and explanation of the purpose of the interview, how we will proceed, and the answering of any questions.
2. First, tell me how it has been going for you in school this year.
3. What have been the best things about school this year?
4. What have you disliked the most about school?
5. How do you spend your time when you're not in school?
6. Have you ever thought of dropping out? If so, what would you plan to do then?
7. How could school be made more enjoyable for you?
8. Let's talk a little about your future—what are your job or career plans? (Follow up with questions regarding reasons of choice: long-range goals and further education.)
9. Are there any questions you'd like to ask me? Anything else you'd like to say?
10. Conclude.

You will note that an initial explanation is made of the purpose and procedures of the interview. Also, the questions are structured in such a way as to elicit discussion rather than a "yes" or "no" response. Of course, the interviewee is given the opportunity to ask questions or make additional comments before the interview is terminated.

In many agency or clinical settings this process may be referred to as a *diagnostic interview*. In these settings the large number of individuals served often necessitates some form of diagnostic workup. Many agencies will use a separate diagnostic interview, separating the diagnostic from the counseling process. As noted earlier in this chapter, clinical guidelines such as the *Diagnostic and Statistical Manual of Mental Disorders III-R* may be used for this purpose.

Intake Interviews

Initial interviews with clients in agency and most other counselor settings too, are usually referred to as "intake interviews"—or sometimes history interviews. (History interviews are designed to collect facts about the client's life in a systematic way.) This, the intake interview, is a part of the assessment process, when the counselor is seeking information regarding the client's concerns, current status, and perhaps certain personal traits. An assumption behind the intake interview, according to Cormier and Hackney (1993)

is that the client is coming to counseling for more than one interview and intends to address problems or concerns that involve other people, other settings, and the future, as well as the present. Most counselors try to limit intake interviews to an hour. In order to do this, the counselor must assume responsibility and control over the interview. No attempt is made to make it a "therapeutic session" for the client. The second session can begin to meet those needs. . . .

Because the intake session is different from a regular counseling session, it is helpful if the counselor gives the client an explanation about the purpose and nature of the initial session. You might say something like: "Marie, before counseling gets started, it is helpful if I have some preliminary background information about you. So this time, I'd like to spend the hour getting to know you and asking you some questions about your school, work and family background, and so on. Then at the next session, you will be able to start discussing and working on the specific concerns that brought you to counseling. Do you have any questions about this?"*
(pp. 80–81)

GROUP ASSESSMENT TECHNIQUES

Group guidance and counseling techniques are discussed in greater detail in Chapter 6, but it is appropriate in this chapter dealing with nonstandardized assessment techniques to review briefly techniques for assessing the roles and relationships of individuals in groups. The understanding of our clients as total beings is heavily dependent on understanding their group associations. Groups are a natural form of human association. In today's world, the hermit is an almost extinct species; persons are no longer rugged individualists, going it alone. Group associations are natural, and all of us belong to many different and diverse groups. For example, some of us may, within a brief period of 24 hours, associate with our family group, our work group, our social recreation group, a civic group, political group, and church group. In each of these several different settings, the roles and relationships are significant in shaping our behavior, both within and without the group.

Also, in many of these groups, an outsider would find it difficult to assess roles and relationships accurately by only a casual observation of the group. Probably you have experienced going to a party, a class, or some activity in which there are in-group jokes, a history of previous group activities that precluded you, and apparent roles and relationships that you did not understand.

Even experienced group observers such as teachers and counselors find it helpful to use structured assessment instruments on occasion to facilitate accurate understandings of persons in the group setting as well as group interactions themselves. The more popular of these techniques include sociograms, "Guess Who," communigrams, and social distance scales.

Sociometric Techniques

Sociometric techniques are basic approaches for the study of social relationships, such as degrees of acceptance, roles, and interactions within groups. Sociometric instruments provide a means for assessing and displaying such information as interpersonal choices made by group members.

Although sociometric devices appear to be relatively easy to devise, administer, and interpret, these impressions are deceiving. In fact, extreme caution and careful planning

---

*From Cormier, L. Sherilyn, and Hackney, Harold, *The Professional Counselor*. Copyright © 1993 by Allyn and Bacon. Reprinted by permission.

and analysis should be prerequisites to the use of these methods. In determining the appropriateness of conditions for using sociometric analyses, the following must be considered:

1. *The length of time the group has been together.* The longer the group has existed, the more likely that the data collected will be meaningful.

2. *The age level of the group.* A general rule of thumb is that the older the participants, the more likely that the information provided will be reliable. J. L. Moreno, the acknowledged founder of modern sociometry, hypothesized that social cohesion develops with age (Moreno, 1960). He reports the cohesion of children's groups up to the age of 6 or 7 to be poor and weak, the cohesion of groups formed by children from 7 to 8 years to age 14 to be relatively high, and the cohesion of groups formed by youths between the ages of 14 and 18 to have become stabilized.

3. *The size of the group.* Groups that are too large or too small will provide less valid information. It is also important to remember that all members of a group must be included in any sociometric studies.

4. *The activity provides a natural opportunity to secure responses.* In order for group members to participate willingly and honestly in sociometric analysis, the group activities for this purpose should appear logical and meaningful to the members. "What gives every sociometrically defined group its momentum is the 'criterion,' the common motive that draws persons together spontaneously, for a certain end" (Moreno, 1960, p. 97).

5. *The group chosen for study should be appropriate to the informational needs of the counselor.* For example, if it is a school counselor seeking to identify the causes of behavior problems in a given classroom, the observation of this same group of students in, for example, a recreational setting outside the classroom would not be as appropriate.

Constructing and Administering the Sociometric Test

From a construction standpoint, the sociometric test or inventory is a very simple instrument. The basic and most important aspect of its construction is the nature of the grouping situation, or criterion, on which it is based; unless the criterion is appropriate to the participants' ages, activities, and actual opportunities for association, the elicited responses will have little sociometric value. More specifically, a criterion or situation must be selected to elicit participants' choices that, when applied, will have practical significance; and to maintain the confidence of those participating, as previously noted, the results must be applied. Examples of school situations that lend themselves well to sociometric studies include assigning students to various committees, setting up small study groups, and organizing class projects. In these cases, and in many others, the selection of associates could appropriately be made by the participants themselves.

When the criterion has been determined, attention must next be directed to the number of choices the participant should make. Although the optimum number of choices has not been determined, it would appear that too few choices would not have the practical values of five or six where, for example, group assignments are to follow. It is recommended that sociometric techniques to be used with school groups contain only "positive" choices.

Much of the success of a sociometric test hinges on how well it is administered. The person administering it must be respected and be on good terms with the group members. The actual administration of a sociometric test should be kept highly informal; any resemblance to a typical test situation should be avoided. The instrument itself should never be referred to as a test, nor should the group members be forewarned of its administration (in keeping with sociometric theory, which emphasizes spontaneity as an important aspect of response). For example, in a school setting, sociometric studies are more effective when the teacher merely states without prior or subsequent discussion that the class is going to engage in an activity (e.g., forming committees to give special reports) that requires small groups to be established and that students' choice of associates are to be used as much as possible as a basis for grouping. The teacher then adds a statement about confidentiality and about the impossibility of honoring every choice of every student. Finally, the students are instructed to write their name at the top of the blank paper or card they will be given, number their paper from one to five, and list in order of preference the names of the students with whom they would like to work.

Cautions in Interpretation

The responses to sociometric questions first should be tabulated and then used to construct a *sociogram*—a graphic depiction of the interpersonal relationship existing in a group at the time a sociometric test is given to its members. A sociometric analysis of group structure requires that a sociogram be constructed. However, if each participant's relative degree of social acceptance is all that is desired, a simple count of the total responses each one receives is sufficient.

As previously noted, sociometric data must be interpreted with a great deal of caution. Sociometric techniques do not analyze or provide interpretations in themselves but rather initiate or contribute to the assessment or understanding of persons. It is also important to remember that in many group settings the choices of group members may say more about the chooser than the chosen. Finally, we should recognize that some group members may not want to be chosen; they may prefer to be alone or with a few friends in certain group settings.

Perhaps the easiest of the different kinds of sociograms to make is that shown in Figure 8–8. This sociogram uses concentric circles in a targetlike pattern, with each student represented by a number. Only mutual positive choices are shown, and preferential rank is not considered. The highly chosen individuals, or sociometric stars, are placed in the small center circle; the sociometric isolates, students not chosen and who choose no one, are placed in the large outer circle; and all other students are placed in the area between the inner and outer circles, those more frequently chosen being placed closer to the inner circle. Sex is indicated by different geometric designs: the males' numbers are placed within a triangle; the females' numbers are encircled. For even clearer differentiation, males are confined to one side of the figure, females to the other.

The "Guess Who?" Technique

Another useful sociometric technique is the "Guess Who?" questionnaire. This technique is best used with relatively well-established groups in which members have had the oppor-

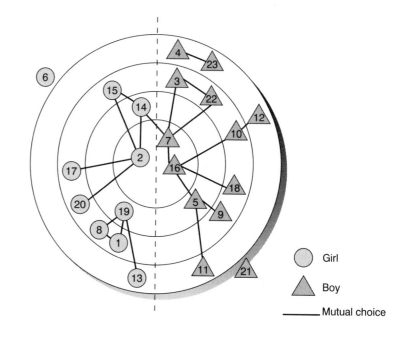

FIGURE 8–8 Sociogram Depicting Mutual Choices

tunity to become reasonably well acquainted. It is also most effective when the questions are positive in nature rather than negative. For example, "Who is most friendly?" is a better "Guess Who?" than "Who is the least friendly?" The "Guess Who" questionnaire provides for the association of characteristics or activities with individuals. It can help us understand why some members of the group receive attention, behave in certain ways, or function in certain roles. We may also be able to identify those who are "popular" with group members and those who receive little, if any, recognition. The "Guess Who?" instrument is usually designed to collect specific information that counselors, teachers, or other group observers believe would be helpful in working with the group and its individual members. Figure 8–9 presents an example of a short "Guess Who?" instrument.

The directions for this technique may be altered to permit persons to list all group members they believe are, for example, funny, friendly, helpful, and so on. The teachers or other group observers may use a simple tally system that notes the total number of times each group member was mentioned for each item. A popular variation in school settings is one in which pupils are asked to assume that the class is going to put on a play. They are provided with a list of characters and asked to nominate classmates that could best portray the roles described. Examples of such characters might be as follow:

> This person is known as "the arbitrator." They are always ready to try and prevent arguments from growing serious by suggesting compromises. They usually can see both sides of an argument and as a result rarely take sides.
>
> This person is known as "the good humor person." They are always pleasant and good-natured. They smile a lot and laugh easily. They rarely show anger.

One other variation is to tell a story or describe a situation, real or fictional, in which group members are asked to assign to their peers the different characters. Consider Example 8–6.

Group_____ Date _____

Directions: Write the name of at least one but no more than two persons whom you
would identify as most outstanding in your group for the trait or activity listed.
Your teacher (counselor, group leader) will use the results from your responses for
planning group activities. If you cannot identify a group member for an item, you
may leave it blank. It is not necessary to sign your name.

1. Tells the funniest jokes or stories _____
2. Enjoys funny jokes and stories the most _____
3. Is the most friendly _____
4. Is the most helpful _____
5. Is the most sincere _____
6. Can always be depended on _____
7. Has the best imagination _____
8. Is a good organizer _____
9. Is optimistic _____
10. Is a good leader _____
11. Has special talents _____
12. Is generous _____

FIGURE 8–9 "Guess Who?" Example

Example 8–6 THE "GUESS-WHO?" TECHNIQUE

Ron Bakersfield is a new student who has just enrolled in Snow Deep High School. In his
previous school, Ron was an outstanding and all-round athlete, a good student, and popular with his fellow students. He is a handsome young man who dresses neatly and
cleanly, but on this day he is a bit unsure of himself. He wonders whether his new school-
mates will accept him, how long it will take him to get acquainted, who his new friends will
be, what his new teachers will be like, and whether he will make the teams.

The school counselor, recognizing Ron as a new student, has called in two of the
more popular students in the school to meet Ron and show him around. The first to arrive
is Marie Shafer, an attractive, personable girl, who greets Ron with a handshake and a big
smile. The counselor suggests to Ron that Marie is known as the sunshine girl in the
school because she is always smiling and has a friendly word for everyone. The next
arrival is Craig Brewer, whom the counselor introduces as one of the most popular students in the school and whose hobby is photography. Craig appears also to be pleasant
but a bit more reserved than Marie. With an assurance that "We'll see that Ron gets
around," Craig and Marie usher him out of the counselor's office.

On the way to his first class, Ron is introduced in quick succession to Darlene, whom
they refer to as "Miss Energy"; Tom, a serious student who is taking pilot lessons; Rex,
who was introduced as the most interesting storyteller in the school; and Dave, to whom
they gave the label, "Mr. Reliable." At this point, Ron is beginning to feel more at home
and more welcome in his new school and already sees the prospect of making some
good friends with fine qualities.

After reading this brief scenario, to whom would you assign the roles of Ron, Marie,
Craig, Darlene, Rex, Dave, and Tom?

FIGURE 8–10 Communigram:
Participation of Individuals

> Maria TᕼᕼL III   Heather TᕼᕼL
>
> Bill   II
>
> Amy   I   Eduardo III

As you may have noted, the "Guess Who?" technique is relatively easy to use. Scoring is not complicated since a simple counting of the number of nominations received for each description will suffice. If both positive and negative descriptors are used, you may subtract the number of negatives from the number of positives received for each characteristic.

Communigrams

Another aspect of observation of persons in a group setting and the group process is an assessment of the verbal participation of its members. This is perhaps the easiest communication pattern to observe and record because, in its simplest form, we are recording who talks and how often they talk over a given period of time. Figure 8–10 shows a chart in which the number of participations of each member of the group is noted with a tally mark. Each mark represents one communication, usually defined as an uninterrupted statement.

Figure 8–11 illustrates an alternative that uses the same form but indicates positions of members within the group to each other and to the group leader. Such reportings not only will identify those who frequently participate versus those who do not but may also, for example, indicate the amount of discussion generated by certain topics and how members individually react to one topic and not another; enable comparisons between groups in terms of their frequency of communication; and, if carried one step further, as noted in Figure 8–12, will also indicate the direction of communication among members.

Social Distance Scales

Another client participation technique that counselors may find useful is social distance scales. Most of the existing social distance or social acceptance scales devised for use with

FIGURE 8–11 Communigram:
Communication of Group Position
Source: From G. E. Myers and M. T.
Myers, *The Dynamics of Human
Communication,* p. 135. Copyright ©
1973. Used with permission of
McGraw-Hill, Inc.

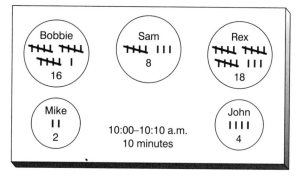

FIGURE 8–12 Communigram: Direction of Communication Among Members
Source: From G. E. Myers and M. T. Myers, *The Dynamics of Human Communication,* p. 137. Copyright © 1973. Used with permission of McGraw-Hill, Inc.

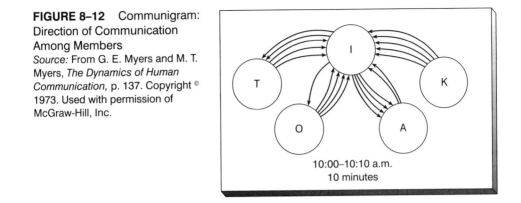

10:00–10:10 a.m.
10 minutes

classroom or other school groups are patterned after the scale devised in 1925 by E. S. Bogardus. The Bogardus scale was designed for measuring and comparing attitudes toward different nationalities—specifically, to determine the degree to which various racial and nationality groups were accepted or rejected. Thus, social distance is usually defined by social psychologists as that distance a person indicates exists between other persons and him- or herself. This distance is usually identified through the reaction to statements that measure and compare attitudes of acceptance or rejection of other people. An example of a social distance item might be the following:

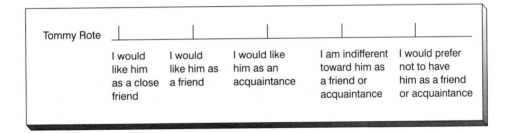

Tommy Rote

I would like him as a close friend

I would like him as a friend

I would like him as an acquaintance

I am indifferent toward him as a friend or acquaintance

I would prefer not to have him as a friend or acquaintance

Other social distance items may be built around choices such as with whom one would like to take trips, study, or go to a dance. The results from social distance scales may indicate a self social distance and group social distance. The degree of acceptance of the group by a person may be an index of "self score" and the degree of acceptance of the person by the group would be the "group score." Many studies of social distance scales in classrooms have tended to lead to the conclusion that the greatest contribution of social distance scales is in revealing the wide range of acceptance and rejection of any one student in a group. Again, as with many other client participation techniques, there is frequently a tendency to overuse or misinterpret them because of their simplicity of administration. Counselors and other users should be aware that such information does not reveal the "why" of a person's acceptance or rejection of others. Furthermore, the users of this instrument must determine how they can use negative data such as indicated group rejection to the client's advantage.

ECOLOGICAL ASSESSMENT

In recent generations many people have become environmentally conscious. We are concerned with the preservation of our natural resources and environments, the air we breathe, the water we drink, the fruit and vegetables we eat, and so forth. Too, we note the frequency of publications suggesting the best communities in which to live, the best retirement areas, and the most healthy states. All these examples suggest what we already know: that there is an ongoing relationship between individuals and their environments. As early as 1936 Kurt Lewin, in his *Principles of Topological Psychology*, presented the field of psychology with his mathematical formula of $B = F(PXE)$, or behavior is a result of persons interacting with their environment. While this formula would seem to be beyond question, it is only in the 1980s and 1990s that we have noted significant attention being given in counseling literature to this concept and the growing importance of ecological psychology.

Thus, while our traditional models of assessment have led us to focus primarily and only on people, we are now recognizing that people cannot be studied as complete entities outside their environments. As Lewin suggested, behavior always occurs in a specific setting. It is in this context then, and in this chapter discussing nonstandardized assessment, that we examine ecological assessment.

Ecological assessment is concerned with assessing how individuals orient to, operate in, and evaluate their environments. It is concerned with how the individual perceives, shapes, is shaped by and views his or her environments. In this process, counselors would seek to understand the characteristics of such significant settings as the home, school, community, and workplace and their impact on the individual, and for certain purposes (i.e., prevention programs, minority relationships, etc.), groups of individuals.

All of us seek to optimize our environmental experiences—to achieve optimal environments that maximize the fulfilling of our needs and enable us to achieve our goals. The degree to which we fail to do this will, of course, influence our satisfaction with our lives and mental health. Counselors must become aware of the aspirations of their clients and the degree to which their environments are facilitating or handicapping their achievement.

In assessing an environment, counselors should note such ecological variables as the physical, geographic, and meteorological characteristics. They should become aware of the characteristics of the general population as reflected in its norms, values, attitudes, relationships, traditions, and other personal traits.

Counselors should also understand those behavior settings (institutions and agencies) that have control over the behavior occurring within them as well as those that influence external behavior.

Ecological assessment would seem to stress the importance of the counselor getting out of the office and into the physical community. This will facilitate an understanding of the environments—the people, agencies, and institutions—with which his or her clients interact.

RECORDS

It has often been suggested that the first slabs of stone that our prehistoric ancestors carved out of the mountains were for the purpose of setting up personnel files. It appears that systems of recording are as old as civilization and that the primary object of much that has been recorded over the ages has been the individual. Record keeping is a reflection of humans' historic curiosity to understand to the fullest extent possible their fellow humans (and just so we will not forget what we have already learned, we record it). Records are important to counselors and other helping professionals in understanding and working effectively and efficiently with their clients.

Basic Considerations

If records or a record system are to serve their potential for client understanding and assistance, certain basic considerations need to be examined before determining the nature and characteristics of the record and its attending system. These include the following.

The Extent of Record Keeping

The ever-increasing and seemingly never-ending preoccupation with record keeping may give all of us cause to wonder how many records we actually have in our name, where they are located, for what purposes, and so on. Extensive records have been maintained by the educational institutions that we attended, for even as students we become aware of the extensive and varied record data that the school maintains "to understand us better." Figure 8–13 rather accurately (but not too seriously) depicts the varying views to which the many records or types of data might, on occasion, seem to lend themselves.

In a more serious vein, Hummel and Humes (1984) point out that

> one of the dramatic developments in recent decades was the attention paid to student records. As class action suits developed during the 1960s, there was concern on the part of parents with regard to the use and misuse of pupil records and interpretation. This resulted in legislation in several of the state jurisdictions and culminated in the passage of federal legislation, namely, the Family Rights and Privacy Act (commonly referred to as the Buckley Amendment). Almost immediately the schools had to change their way of doing business. With the passage of this legislation, not only were parents permitted full access to pupil records and the privilege of denying access to them, but they now had the right to challenge the content of the pupil's record. Accordingly, cumulative records were purged and federal, state, and local guidelines were established for subsequent collection and use.

As seen by his health record

As seen by his attendance record

As seen by his activity record

As seen by his academic record

As seen by his discipline record

As seen by his book report record

As seen by his guidance testing record

FIGURE 8–13   "Harry High School" as Seen Through a Multirecord System

The new approach to record keeping posed many problems for pupil services. School psychologists, social workers, and school counselors had traditionally been prime contributors to the cumulative record through psychological reports, social case histories, and counselor notations. They now not only had to review the records for appropriateness, but also had to change ways of reporting results and contacts. Perhaps hardest hit were school psychologists who had been accustomed to writing clinical reports designed only for professional view and scrutiny. Reports now had to be written that could be also shared with parents and, at age eighteen, with students. There developed much "tooth gnashing" over watered-down reports that would contribute but little to the presenting problem. This difficulty was finally resolved through the medium of detailed oral reports, usually at team meetings, to be followed by more general written reports. (pp. 358–359)

The advent of the computer and other technological advances have, if anything, seemed to stimulate a challenge to gather and record data in a manner befitting these new developments in data storage, manipulation, and retrieval. Nor can school counselors belittle the importance of the decisions made on the basis of such recorded data—decisions that most frequently influence career directions and educational opportunities. Counselors working with school-aged clients through community agencies and other non-school settings must also be aware of the extent and impact of school-maintained records.

Who Will Use the Client's Record?

The answer to this question varies across the many places in which counselors function. For example, counselors in private practice may, subject to legal limitations, have exclusive access to a client's records, whereas, at the other end of the continuum, many school counselors may be expected to share client records with school administrative and supervisory personnel, teachers, parents, and, of course, the client. Counselors, ever concerned with client confidentiality, must, at the outset, determine who legally and ethically will have access to any data recorded in a systematic or institutional manner.

The use of student and client records also raises the question of record security. The increased utilization of computerized record systems requires the exercise of appropriate precautions and restrictions to safeguard client data. Although students and parents may exercise the right to examine their records, that does not lessen the counselor's responsibility in the school, or any setting, to provide proper security for those records that are the responsibility of the counseling program. These responsibilities include provisions for the "lock and key" security of client records at all times, instructions and policies for nonprofessional (clerical) handling of data, and stated policies including ethical and legal guidelines for access to and review of data by clients, parents, and others. In determining "access" to school records, it must be noted that certain records of students are at least quasi-public in nature. The questions that arise are, Who may inspect such records, for what purposes, and when?

What Are Other Legal and Ethical Considerations?

Practicing counselors, as well as those in preparation, may be confused somewhat by the apparent proliferation of statements by professional organizations providing ethical guidelines for the maintenance and use of client records. However, an examination of statements by the American Counseling Association (formerly called the American Association for Counseling and Development) and the American Psychological Association would indicate little that is in conflict and much in general agreement. These standards are presented in Appendices B and C.

The primary legal concerns of counselors insofar as records and recording are concerned continue to focus on the confidentiality of the counseling records and the right of privileged communications. Although attorneys have possessed this right by common law over the centuries and statutory law has extended this privilege to physicians, clergy, and sometimes psychologists, counselors have limited legal guarantee in terms of statutory provisions.

School counselors must be particularly aware of the provisions of the Family Educational Rights and Privacy Act of 1974. Key statements from this act presented by Flygare (1975) point out the following:

❖ A student (or his parents) must be given access to his records within 45 days from the time a request is made.

❖ A student (or his parents) must be granted a hearing by the institution upon request to determine the validity of any document in the student's file.

❖ Confidential letters or statements placed in the file prior to January 1, 1975, need not be disclosed under the law.

❖ A student may waive his right of access to confidential letters regarding admissions, honors, or employment.

❖ An educational institution cannot, with certain exceptions, release personally identifiable information about students.

❖ Educational institutions must notify students and parents of their rights under the law. (p. 15)

The detailed provisions of this act are presented in Appendix D.

Furthermore, as Wilhelm and Case (1975) emphasize, counselors must be aware of the implications of Title IX of the Education Amendments of 1972, effective July, 1975, which provides that

no person . . . shall on the basis of sex be excluded from participation in, be denied the benefits of, or be subjected to discrimination under any education program receiving federal financial assistance. (p. 85)

The implications for record keeping are clear; sexual discrimination must not be maintained. That includes standardized test results based on male/female norms, and career exploration activities and counseling that reflect sex-role stereotyping.

School counselors should also be aware of other kinds of unacceptable statements often found in student records. Wilhelm and Case (1975) note these frequent examples:

1. Libelous, unverified statements regarding the student.
2. Unverified statements regarding parents, family, or home.
3. Ambiguous, opinionated, subjective descriptions of the student, "glop" statements.
4. Factual but biased statements with negative implications.
5. Factual but inconsequential statements that add nothing to understanding the student.
6. Inferential statements with negative implications that may or may not be verifiable. (p. 85)

Counselors must bear in mind that "privileged communication" is for the benefit of the client. Thus, only the client has the option to waive that right and he or she may do so if he or she chooses, even if protected legally. It should also be noted that privileged communications and confidentiality are not "one and the same" (Hummel & Humes, 1984).

We would point out that *privileged communication* and *confidentiality* have often been used interchangeably, even though there is a significant distinction between the two terms. Privileged communication refers to the right of the counselor to refuse to divulge confidential information in a court of law. Confidentiality represents an ethical guideline in terms of counselor decisions that they should not and will not divulge what has been revealed to them in contacts with their clients.

What Purposes Will the Client's Record Serve?

The use of the client's records will, of course, be determined to a large extent by the answer to the question previously raised: Who are the users? There are certain traditional uses appropriate for almost all types of personnel records:

1. They provide an available pool of basic information about the person.

   a. They provide a means for recording and preserving meaningful information about the person for later use.

   b. They assist the users of the information in gaining a better understanding of the person with whom they will be interacting.

   c. They assist the person on whom the record is maintained to gain new insights and perspectives.

2. In addition, counselors use records in

   a. preparation for the counseling interview;

   b. the development of case studies;

   c. client placement or referral;

   d. consultation with other therapists, medical personnel, parents; and

   e. follow-up and research studies.

3. School counselors also use records for the following purposes:

   a. Identifying students who may be in need of counseling assistance

   b. Identifying students who possess special talents or interests

   c. Identifying students who may have special needs because of physical disabilities, for example

   d. Assisting faculty and parents in gaining a better understanding of the individual student, which, it is hoped, may contribute to positive student-parent and student-teacher relationships

   e. Assisting the individual student to gain self-understanding

   f. Contributing to school and community needs assessments of school-aged populations

   g. Facilitating the orientation of new pupils

These listings are meant to be illustrative only and not exclusive, since any practicing counselor could readily expand on them.

Record Interpretation

The interpretation of any kind of counseling or personnel record will obviously be limited by the data recorded, and the skill and understanding of the user. Some guidelines or safeguards include the following:

❖ Records provide only clues to behavior—no more, and some clues are relevant whereas others are not.

❖ Does the present (the time at which you are examining the record data) compare to the past (the time when the data are originally recorded)?

❖ Look for trends or significant changes, but beware of the fact that many people have unique patterns of growth and development.

❖ Feelings, attitudes, and intensity of emotions seldom show in recorded information.

❖ Distinguish between symptoms and causes.

❖ Determine whether record data are based on substantial facts or merely represent opinions.

❖ Remember that records present only a small sample of the client's behavior.

❖ School records, especially, can also provide opportunities to examine certain habitual performance measures, such as attendance, grades, and health.

SUMMARY

This chapter has presented an overview of non-standardized techniques that may be used in human assessment. Although many nonstandardized techniques cannot lay claim to either the validity or reliability of standardized instruments, they nonetheless provide the counselor with a wide range of data collection options from which to choose, according to the dictates of the counseling situation and the assessment needs of one's clients.

Observation was noted as the most popular of the techniques usually used to assess others; however, in order that it be as accurate and meaningful as possible, we suggested that some forms for recording observation such as anecdotal records and forms for further directing observations toward specific characteristics such as rating scales and checklists might be used. In this regard, the popularity (and sophistication) of the *DSM-IV* in clinical settings was noted.

Questionnaires and autobiographies were suggested as techniques in which useful information can be collected. Assessing behavior and roles in groups by techniques such as sociograms, communigrams, social distance scales, and role-playing were suggested. The growing interest in ecological assessment was also discussed. There followed an examination of the role of records in

human assessment and some of the legal and ethical considerations in record keeping. Assessment, both standardized and nonstandardized, can play an important role in career planning and decision making. Chapter 9 examines this important activity.

DISCUSSION QUESTIONS

1. Have you taken courses in sociology, anthropology, economics, political science, and the like, that helped you understand others better? What were these courses? How were they helpful?

2. Have you ever found your observations of a situation, scene, or person differing from other observers present at the same time? How do you account for these differences?

3. When you meet someone for the first time, what do you "look for" or observe that influences your initial impressions?

4. What autobiographies have you read by famous people? Did any of these provide you with special insights into the writer? How?

5. Have you ever kept a diary? What prompted you to keep one? Did it help you understand yourself better in any way? Discuss your responses.

6. In assessment, would you prefer to have your own traits assessed by standardized tests or rating scales? Why?

7. What environmental factors are important to you in considering a community as your possible place of residence?

8. What are examples of customs, folkways, mores, and laws that influence patterns of normal and abnormal behavior?

9. If you were to write your autobiography for publication, what title would you use?

CLASS ACTIVITIES

1. Identify someone in the class that you are barely acquainted with. Design an observation instrument to guide your observations for the next week. At the end of the week, discuss how your instrument has increased your understanding of the individual.

2. In small groups, develop a checklist that might be used to evaluate candidates applying for admission to a master's level counselor preparation program. Share and discuss with the class.

3. Also in small groups, design a rating scale to assess individual personal relationship skills. Share and discuss.

4. In small groups, members are instructed to share learnings from working with, living near, and other contacts with people from different cultures.

SELECTED READINGS

Cone, J. D. (1982). Validity of direct observation assessment procedures. *New Directions for Methodology of Social and Behavioral Science, 14,* 67–79.

Goldman, L. (1982). Assessment in counseling: A better way. *Measurement and Evaluation in Guidance, 15*(1), 70–73.

Goldman, L. (1992). Qualitative assessment: An approach for counselors. *Journal of Counseling and Development, 70,* 616–621.

RESEARCH OF INTEREST

Galassi, J. P. (1992). What one should know about behavioral assessment. *Journal of Counseling and Development, 70,* 624–631.

Abstract

Introduces the components of behavioral assessment in terms of assumptions and methods as compared and contrasted with traditional assessment procedures. Illustrates two case studies in which the principles and methods of behavioral assessment are discussed.

Haase, R. F., Strohmer, D. C., Biggs, D. A., & Keller, K. E. (1983). Mediational inferences in the process of counselor judgment. *Journal of Counseling Psychology, 30,* 275–278.

Abstract

Replicates research on the process of moving from observations to clinical judgments. Counselors ($N = 20$) made status inferences, attributional inferences, and diagnostic classifications of clients based on case folders. Results suggest the clinical judgment process was stagewise mediated, and attributional inferences had little direct impact on final diagnostic classification.

Lambert, M. J., Hatch, D. R., Kingston, M. D., & Edwards, B. C. (1986). Zung, Beck, and Hamilton Rating Scales as measures of treatment outcome: A meta-analytic comparison. *Journal of Consulting and Clinical Psychology, 54,* 54–59.

Abstract

Treatment studies using the Zung Self-Rating Scale, the Beck Depression Inventory, and the Hamilton Rating Scale for Depression as dependent measures are viewed to determine whether these scales provide comparable data for assessing treatment effects. Results indicate that the Zung and the Beck show less change in depression following treatment than does the Hamilton.

Lopez, F. G., & Gover, M. R. (1993). Self-report measures of parent-adolescent attachment and separation-individuation: A selective review. *Journal of Counseling and Development, 71,* 560–569.

Abstract

Reviews and critiques the three self-report measures of parent-adolescent attachment: Parental Bonding Instrument, Parental Attachment Questionnaire, and Inventory of Parent and Peer Attachment. Also reviews and critiques the three self-report measures of parent-adolescent separation-individuation: the Psychological Separation Inventory, the Personal Authority in the Family System Questionnaire, and the Multigenerational Interconnectedness Scales and Family Intrusiveness Scale. Pertinent issues in conceptualizing and measuring attachment and separation individuation constructs are discussed.

Merluzi, T. V. (1993). Cognitive assessment: Clinical applications of self-statement assessment. *Journal of Counseling and Development, 71,* 539–545.

Abstract

Provides an overview of cognitive assessment which focuses on assessment of self-talk. Reviews clinical methods of cognitive assessment, the balance between positive and negative thoughts, and provides examples of case studies illustrating the use of self-statement methods in a clinical setting. Concludes that the study of cognitive products might prove most fruitful for clinical practice and research.

Chapter 9

Counseling for Career Planning and Decision Making

As noted in Chapter 1, the counseling movement in the United States has had a long association with and concern for career development and decision making. This chapter will introduce you to this traditional area of counselor activity. The objectives of the chapter are to (a) describe specific interests in and influences on career planning, (b) present popular theories of career decision making, and (c) examine career planning and counseling in various settings.

During its early years, organized counseling efforts consisted primarily of vocational guidance. This early interest, originating with Parsons, was an outgrowth of a concern for the complexity of the world of work and the resultant difficulty in career planning, a concept that is still viable today. As originally practiced by Parsons and his associates, the concept of matching youths with jobs, based on the characteristics of both, has also had a long and traditional association with the counseling movement.

As this concept was broadened and other basic activities were added in the 1920s and 1930s, vocational guidance became a service activity most frequently identified with the provision of occupational and educational information. In the late 1950s and 1960s, with the original impetus from the National Defense Education Act of 1958, placement and follow-up also became significant activities of the vocational or career guidance phase of counseling programs. Thus, for nearly 60 years the counseling movement had been the caretaker for career planning in U.S. schools and agencies.

In 1971, however, the U.S. Office of Education, through the commissioner of education at that time, Sidney P. Marland, Jr., committed more than $9 million of discretionary funds to research and development projects focusing on the establishment of comprehensive career education models. With this act, the concept of career education as an all-school responsibility was launched, and counselors were no longer the sole designated professionals for providing career counseling and guidance for students in schools.

In the 1990s, however, a trend has emerged toward once again recognizing counselors as the priority professionals in the providing of career guidance and counseling. This trend has included the development and recognition of career counseling specialists and the establishment of career centers serving special populations such as college students, women, minorities, and retirees. As previously noted, projected changes in the workplace in the immediate future will bring about further demands for career counseling, not just in schools but in nonschool settings as well.

DEFINITIONS AND CLARIFICATIONS

An outgrowth of the increased attention to career needs and the attending emphasis on career counseling and guidance has been a proliferation of definitions, with attending confusion, seeking to differentiate among such terms as *career education, career development, career guidance, vocational education,* and *human development.* In this chapter and elsewhere in this text, the following definitions apply:

> *Career:* "The totality of work one experiences in a lifetime" (Hoyt, 1974, p. 6). A more limited definition would view a career as the sum total of one's work expe-

riences in a general occupational category such as teaching, accounting, medicine, or sales.

Occupation: A specific job or work activity.

Career development: That aspect of one's total development that emphasizes learning about, preparation for, entry into, and progression in the world of work.

Career education: Those planned-for educational experiences that facilitate a person's career development and preparation for the world of work. The totality of experiences through which one learns about and prepares for engaging in work as part of a way of living. A primary responsibility of the school with an emphasis on learning about, planning for, and preparing to enter a career.

Career guidance: Those activities that are carried out by counselors in a variety of settings for the purpose of stimulating and facilitating career development in persons over their working lifetimes. These activities include assistance in career planning, decision making, and adjustment.

Occupational information: Data concerning training and related educational programs, careers, career patterns, and employment trends and opportunities.

Vocation: A trade or occupation.

Vocational education: Education that is preparatory for a career in a vocational or technical field.

These rather limited definitions are perhaps at one end of the continuum. For example, a career is sometimes defined as the sum total of a person's life experiences and lifestyles, whereas career education is frequently viewed as consisting of all activities and experiences, planned or otherwise, that prepare the person for work. However, straightforward and concise, although limited, definitions are most practical in specific planning for programs of career counseling development, or education.

It should also be noted that, though differing in definition, career development, career education, and career counseling are interwoven and interrelated. One without the other is ineffective and meaningless. As career education stimulates career development, career counseling provides direction for career education and development.

Counselors must also recognize that career education and complementary programs of career counseling should be developmental in nature and thus not limited to a particular age group. Career development across the life span is the appropriate theme for now and the foreseeable future.

CURRENT INTERESTS IN CAREER PLANNING

As previously noted, the present high level of interest in career planning was initially stimulated when Sidney Marland made his plea for "career education now" in a speech to the National Association of Secondary School Principals at its convention in Houston in 1971. Since then, the concept has swept the educational establishment in the United States. Educators from every field and discipline have been involved in the movement.

Additionally, many state legislatures passed career education legislation, and career education became a mandate of the Congress of the United States when Public Law 93-380 was signed by former President Ford in August 1974. In less than a decade, more than 10 major national associations endorsed career education, hundreds of publications on career education were published and distributed, and an astounding array of proponents and interpreters of the career education concept emerged.

Continued interest in career guidance and counseling programs was reflected in the Carl D. Perkins Vocational Education Act (Public Law 98-524) of 1984, which mandated programs designed to assist individuals in developing self-assessment, career-planning, career decision-making, and employability skills. Significant national conferences attracting professional counselors such as the 20/20 Conference: Building Strong School Counseling Programs, held in Washington, DC, in 1987; The National Career Development Association's Diamond Jubilee Conference, Orlando, Florida, in January 1988; and the first Association for Counselor Education and Supervision national conference in St. Louis in October 1988, which established three national task forces, including one chaired by Dr. Kenneth Hoyt, to examine national concerns in the world of work, reflect the interest and commitment of the counseling profession in a continued and major involvement in career development, counseling, and guidance.

In addition, the need for this assistance became increasingly apparent in the late 1980s and early 1990s as career-related problems such as youth unemployment, underemployment, midlife career changes, discrimination in the work place, and so forth, became major societal issues. Further reflecting the need for planned programs of career assistance for all ages has been the establishment of career counseling centers on many campuses, women's (career) centers, and other community centers focusing on the special career assistance needs of individuals as we move towards a new century.

Too, career development has moved from the stage theories of the 1940s, 1950s, 1960s and early 1970s in which individuals explored, made decisions about, prepared for, and entered into careers by early adulthood and stayed until retirement, to the concept of recent decades: "career development across the life span." The current and projected demands of the workplace, plus the life-long working potential of the worker, have established new career variables that include workers experiencing a variety of jobs and related educational experiences, across an increasingly healthier and longer lifetime. The career development of the individual promises to be continuous and ongoing; thus, career counseling and assistance programs must be available to all ages from elementary school to the elderly. By the same token, counselors may assist client populations in settings ranging from elementary schools to senior citizen centers to meet the needs of career development across the life span.

THE CHANGING NATURE OF THE WORLD OF WORK

In addition to the needs that prompted the career education movement and have more recently created a renewed interest in career counseling and guidance, other needs also have been generated by significant changes in some of our traditional concepts of careers and work. Symptomatic of these changes are the following points.

No longer one world–one career.

Whereas our ancestors, perhaps even our parents, could, on identifying their life's work, enter into their own little world and career for life, more and more persons entering the work force in the 1990s will have, at the very least, three different and significant careers over the span of their life's work. From a career standpoint, we are now living in an age in which the rapidity of technological development can affect what we do and how we do it almost literally overnight. Counselors are being more frequently reminded that such changes can result in increasing numbers of adults who, either by choice or necessity, will be making career decisions throughout their working life span.

No longer is the concept "Men only–Women only" appropriate for career planning.

The influx of women into the workplace since World War II has changed "who" is working. "Where" they are working has also changed as recent generations have witnessed the elimination of many barriers to career entry, which in the past limited certain professions and occupations exclusively to certain populations or sexes. Career exclusiveness, for example, excluded women from traditional male professions and occupations such as engineering, airline piloting, and taxicab and truck driving, to mention but a few. These once male-dominated careers and some for women, such as nursing, have been effectively challenged not only in the courts but, more importantly, in the world of work.

Additionally, the antipoverty and antidiscrimination movements have further challenged the exclusiveness of certain careers that were once limited to only racial majority members of upper socioeconomic income populations. Hoyt (1988) presents a research-based overview of problems and needs as follows:

1. The rate of job growth between 1986 and the year 2000 will be only about half as great as it was during the 1972–1986 period (Kutscher, 1987a).

2. The percent of 16–24 year olds in the total labor force will decline from 20% in 1986 to 16% in 2000 while the percent of 25–54 year old workers will increase from 67% in 1986 to 73% in the year 2000 (Fullerton, 1987).

3. Skill levels required for occupational success will increase with both the content and complexity of jobs being modified by technological change (Kutscher, 1987b; Johnston & Packer, 1987; Mark, 1987).

4. When compared to current jobs, a higher percent of the new jobs to be created during the 1986–2000 period will demand some form of post-secondary education while a sharp decline will occur in the percent of new jobs requiring less than a high school education (Silvestri & Lukasiewicz, 1987).

5. Almost five in six of the 21 million new labor market entrants will be minority persons, women, and/or immigrants (Johnston & Packer, 1987; Kutscher, 1987a). Only 8% of this 1986–2000 increase will be non-minority white men—down from 18% of labor force growth during the 1976–1986 period (Fullerton, 1987). Birth rate statistics make it likely this trend will accelerate in the future (Hodgkinson, 1985).

6. Women, minority persons, and immigrants in today's labor force are underrepresented in those occupational areas experiencing the greatest job growth and overrepresented in those areas experiencing the least amount of job growth (Ehrhart & Sandler, 1987; Johnston & Packer, 1987; National Alliance of Business, 1986).

7. Women and minority persons are currently less well prepared for occupational success by the existing education system than are non-Hispanic white males (Garrett Park Press, 1987; Astin, 1982, Ehrhart & Sandler, 1987; National Governor's Association, 1986a, b; National Education Association, 1987; Wetzel, 1987).

8. Blacks, Hispanics, and Asians account for a rising proportion of the school population and twenty-three of the twenty-five largest city school systems enroll more minority than non-minority pupils (*A Nation Prepared*, 1986).

9. Minority youth and family households headed by women under age 25 are likely to find employment problems greatly compounded by the fact they are poor (Wetzel, 1987).

10. Both Black and Hispanic youth have higher dropout rates than non-minority youth and this contributes to their difficulties in career development (Research and Policy Committee, CED, 1987a; Wetzel, 1987). (Hoyt, 1988, p. 2)

No longer the old college try and tie.

Much has also been written in recent years regarding the decline of demand in the job market for the college graduate. Although this is not necessarily a rationale for declining college enrollments in some fields, as some claim, it indicates that career opportunities are no longer tied directly to the level and locale of educational preparation but may be more appropriately linked to the career relevancy of one's educational preparation and the opportunities available in a constantly shifting job market.

Hoyt (1988) also notes:

> The fact that 37.8% of the projected 21 million new jobs to be created between 1986–2000 will require some form of postsecondary education does not mean they will require a baccalaureate degree. On the contrary, the fastest growing category within the BLS "some college" classification is "technicians and related support workers" which is predicted to grow by 38%—twice as fast as total employment. Persons in this category will require postsecondary education at the sub-baccalaureate degree level (Silvestri & Lukasiewicz, 1987). The surplus of college graduates that began in the early 1970s is expected to continue through the year 2000 (Kutscher, 1987a). The prime challenge to career development professionals is not to contribute even more to this surplus. (p. 3)

No longer can the future be predicted by the present.

In other times people interested in charting their future could make many appropriate preparations and predictions based on their knowledge of the present, even the past. However, changing technology affecting the workplace, plus drastic changes in the international marketplace, and changes in the makeup of our work force have made it increasingly difficult, if not almost impossible, in recent years to adequately predict the future by examining only the present and the past. The accelerated rate of change in modern society prevents us from assuming, as we might have in the past, that the future will be similar to the present. In fact, we must recognize that much present planning is being based on what is anticipated in the future. Furthermore, this science of future predicting has become an increasingly precise and accurate one. Even without the scientific evidence, the one certainty we can predict for the future is that it will be different.

No longer is one in charge of one's own destiny.

It is clear that the day of the rugged individualist—one who would achieve his or her own destiny—is but a memory. In today's complicated society with its many interacting forces, many variables affect the destiny of people over which they have little or no control and of which many are unaware. Although people can plan and chart their futures, they must also consider alternatives and adjustments. Finally, it is evident that individual entrepreneurship and "locally owned" have given way to corporate conglomerates with absentee ownership so that a person may be known more by the group's achievements than by his or her own individual efforts. Herr and Cramer (1988) contrast changes in the work ethic in the 1960s and 1980s as noted in Table 9–1.

THEORIES OF CAREER DEVELOPMENT AND DECISION MAKING

One of the more fascinating aspects of the study of careers, both formally and informally, is the never-ending attempt to identify why people end up in certain careers. In history we may read about the factors that resulted in a lifetime of politics for Franklin D. Roosevelt; the multicareer talents of Benjamin Franklin, Thomas Jefferson, or George Washington Carver; the cowboy who became O. Henry, the famous author; Elizabeth Cady Stanton, who became a dazzling patriot and activist; and more recently, the actor who became president of the United States, Ronald Reagan. At one time or another we have probably been curious about the career decisions of friends and acquaintances. But to become more personal, why are you in your present career? What influenced your career planning and decision making?

You probably have been asked this question before, and as you reflected and responded, you may have analyzed a set of facts or reasons that appeared relevant to your decisions. You presented some plausible explanation. Many of us have also offered career advice to others, based on our own personal career experiences or personal "theory" of career development. Even so, one must recognize the biases and limitations of one's own experiences. To develop a theory to a usable state, it is necessary to gather data that are relevant, study the relationships between the data, and finally, speculate on what these mean. One's speculations are stated as hypotheses, explanations, or predictions, which can be tested. If a theory proves to have some validity, it will be built on and developed further through research and application activities.

Counselors and others who work as helping professionals with youth and adults for their career development, planning, and adjustment must have some understanding of the better recognized and researched theories of career development that have emerged in the last half of this century. An understanding of such theories gives the practicing counselor a knowledge of the studies of others, usually specialists in the field. They provide a rationale for counselor action that goes beyond personal experience and intuition.

Because many disciplines (education, economics, psychology, sociology) are interested in and actively engaged in investigating various career questions, a multitude of theories have emerged. Both the numbers of theories and the extensiveness of investigation of some preclude any attempt here to analyze the various major theories in detail. Also, it

TABLE 9–1 Trends in the Work Ethic in the 1960s and 1980s

1960s	1980s
The Good Provider Theme The breadwinner—the man who provides for his family—is the real man. *The Independence Theme* To make a living by working is to "stand on one's own two feet and avoid dependence on others." *The Success Theme* Hard work always pays off. *The Self-Respect Theme* Hard work of any type has dignity whether it be menial or exalted. A man's inherent worth is reflected in the act of working.	*Reduced Fear of Economic Insecurity* For most people economic security continues to dominate their lives. But today people take some economic security for granted. A substantial minority say that they are now prepared to take certain risks with their own economic security for the sake of enhancing the quality of life. *Economic Division of Labor between the Sexes* The economic discipline that maintained the rigidity of sex roles in the past has weakened. The idea of women working for purposes of self-fulfillment rather than economic motives gains wider acceptance all the time. *The Psychology of Entitlement* A broad new agenda of social rights is growing and a psychological process is developing whereby a person's wants and desires become converted into a set of presumed rights. *The Adversary Culture Challenges the Cult of Efficiency* The average American has begun to wonder whether too great a concern with efficiency and rationalization is not robbing life of the excitement and pleasure desired. *The Changing Meaning of Success* An increasing number of people are coming to feel that there is such a thing as enough money. A "big earner" who has settled for an unpleasant life-style is no longer considered more successful than someone with less money who has created an agreeable life style. People are no longer as ready to make sacrifices for economic success as they were in the past.

Source: From E. L. Herr and S. H. Cramer, *Career Guidance and Counseling Through the Lifespan: Systematic Approaches* (3rd ed.), p. 48. Copyright © 1988 Scott, Foresman, and Co. Reprinted by permission of HarperCollins College Publishers.

is appropriate to point out that "all theory is imperfect, a fact that is sometimes overlooked by zealous psychologists seeking to 'prove' theories. It should properly be assumed that theories will eventually die and be replaced by newer theories that deal with observed events in a more general and useful way than their predecessors" (Osipow, 1983, p. 3).

In this regard, we would note that in recent years the relevancy of many of the traditional theories of career choice have been examined for their appropriateness for the high-tech information-processing work world of the 1990s and 2000s and for a work force with a significant female and minority population. Further, as noted earlier, the drastic changes in career stability for the future generations will continually challenge the traditional career theories. However, we suggest that proven theories, though in need of updating, can still provide us with some appropriate guidelines. With these limitations in mind, let us explore several of the more popular categories for illustrative purposes only, without any intent to suggest or recommend a particular theoretical approach.

The Process Theories

The process theories state, in effect, that occupational choice and eventual entry is a process consisting of stages or steps that the individual will go through. For example, over 40 years ago Ginzberg, Ginsburg, Axelrod, and Herma (1951) analyzed the process of occupational decision making in terms of three periods: fantasy choices, tentative choices, and realistic choices. This theory suggests a process that moves increasingly toward realism in career decision making as one becomes older.

In 1972, Ginzberg modified the original theory to suggest that the process of vocational choice and development is lifelong and open-ended. In the process, achieving the optimum is more appropriate to describe the ongoing efforts of persons as they seek to find the most suitable job. Originally, Ginzberg and colleagues suggested that the crystallization of occupational choice inevitably had the quality of compromise. Ginzberg's revised theory also places considerable weight on constraints such as family income and situation, parental attitudes and values, opportunities in the world of work, and value orientations. Both the early theory and Ginzberg's later revision suggest the importance of the early school years in influencing later career planning.

Osipow (1983) notes:

> The authors of the theory conclude that four important ingredients contribute to the adequacy of an individual's occupational choice process during adolescence. These are reality testing, the development of a suitable time perspective, the ability to defer gratifications, and the ability to accept and implement compromises in vocational plans. Should too many of these ingredients fail to develop properly, a deviant vocational pattern is likely to emerge. It further seems reasonable that should these four traits fail to develop adequately, the youth's overall emotional adjustment is not likely to be effective. Thus, a tie between emotional stability and vocational deviancy seems to exist, but whether of a casual or correlate nature is not clear. (p. 199)

Blau, Gustad, Jessor, Parnes, and Wilcock (1956) conceive of occupational choice as a process of compromise, continually modified, between preferences for and expectations of being able to get into various occupations. They identify eight factors determining entry into an occupation. Four of these characterize the occupation: demand, technical (functional) qualifications, personal (nonfunctional) qualifications, and rewards. Those characterizing the person were information about an occupation, technical skills, social characteristics, and value orientations.

Herr and Cramer (1988) point out:

> Blau et al. (1956) suggest that geography, the historic moment in time, occupational character-istics, political factors, and the occupational possibility structure and its requirements affect anyone's career development. Stopping there, however, understates situational effects on choice, because while interacting with such external circumstances, the individual has also incorporated and will act on the belief system held by family, peers, neighborhood, ethnic, and religious groups that also define his or her "situation."* (p. 123)

The Developmental Theories

The developmental theories relevant to career planning view career development as one aspect of a person's total development. Donald Super, a leading researcher in career or vocational development theory since the 1950s, formulated a theory of vocational devel-opment in 1953 that became a basis for later research and theory.

Super (1975) states that like other aspects of development, vocational development may be conceived of as beginning early in life and proceeding along a continuum until late in life, passing through the stages of growth, exploration, establishment, maintenance, and decline. At each of these stages the person must master increasingly difficult tasks. Such a concept of vocational development leads logically, according to Super, to that of vocational maturity as denoting the degree of development reached on such a continuum.

In revisions to Super's original theory, Super, Starishevsky, Matlin, and Jordaan (1963) point out that one's occupation makes possible the playing of a role appropriate to the self-concept of the person. This process "requires a person to recognize himself as a distinctive individual, yet at the same time to be aware of the similarities between himself and others" (Osipow, 1983, p. 154). Role playing, stimulated by the process of identifica-tion, further facilitates the development of the vocational self-concept among youth. This does not suggest, however, that a person's characteristics or traits are so unique that only a specific "type" of person would qualify. To the contrary, Super suggests that the range of individual abilities and the latitude within occupational areas result in a multipotential of appropriate opportunities for most people.

More recently, Super (1990) has presented a life span development theory based on 14 propositions, as follow:

1. People differ in their abilities and personalities, needs, values, interests, traits, and self-concepts.
2. People are qualified, by virtue of these characteristics, each for a number of occupations.
3. Each occupation requires a characteristic pattern of abilities and personality traits—with tolerances wide enough to allow both some variety of occupations for each individual and some variety of individuals in each occupation.

4. Vocational preferences and competencies, the situations in which people live and work, and, hence, their self-concepts, change with time and experience, although self-concepts, as products of social learning, are increasingly stable from late adolescence until late maturity, providing some continuity in choice and adjustment.

5. This process of change may be summed up in a series of life stages (a "maxicycle") characterized as a sequence of growth, exploration, establishment, maintenance, and decline, and these stages may in turn be subdivided into (a) the fantasy, tentative, and realistic phases of the exploratory stage and (b) the trial and stable phases of the establishment stage. A small (mini) cycle takes place in transitions from one stage to the next or each time an individual is destabilized by a reduction in force, changes in type of personnel needs, illness or injury, or other socioeconomic or personal events. Such unstable or multiple-trial careers involve new growth, re-exploration, and reestablishment (recycling).

6. The nature of the career pattern—that is, the occupational level attained and the sequence, frequency, and duration of trial and stable jobs—is determined by the individual's parental socioeconomic level, mental ability, education, skills, personality characteristics (needs, values, interests, traits, and self-concepts), and career maturity and by the opportunities to which he or she is exposed.

7. Success in coping with the demands of the environment and of the organism in that context at any given life-career stage depends on the readiness of the individual to cope with these demands (that is, on his or her career maturity).

8. Career maturity is a hypothetical construct. Its operational definition is perhaps as difficult to formulate as is that of intelligence, but its history is much briefer and its achievements even less definite.

9. Development through the life stages can be guided partly by facilitating the maturing of abilities and interests and partly by aiding in reality testing and in the development of self-concepts.

10. The process of career development is essentially that of developing and implementing occupational self-concepts. It is a synthesizing and compromising process in which the self-concept is a product of the interaction of inherited aptitudes, physical makeup, opportunity to observe and play various roles, and evaluations of the extent to which the results of role playing meet the approval of superiors and fellows (interactive learning).

11. The process of synthesis of or compromise between individual and social factors, between self-concepts and reality, is one of role playing and of learning from feedback, whether the role is played in fantasy, in the counseling interview, or in such real-life activities as classes, clubs, part-time work, and entry jobs.

12. Work satisfactions and life satisfactions depend on the extent to which the individual finds adequate outlets for abilities, needs, values, interests, personality traits, and self-concepts. They depend on establishment in a type of work, a work situation, and a way of life in which one can play the kind of role that growth and exploratory experiences have led one to consider congenial and appropriate.

13. The degree of satisfaction people attain from work is proportional to the degree to which they have been able to implement self-concepts.

14. Work and occupation provide a focus for personality organization for most men and women, although for some persons this focus is peripheral, incidental, or even nonexistent. Then other foci, such as leisure activities and homemaking, may be central. (Social traditions, such as gender-role stereotyping and modeling, racial and ethnic biases, and

TABLE 9–2 Vocational Development: A Lifelong Process

Stages of Vocational Development	Age
I. Identification with a worker Father, mother, other significant persons. The concept of Working becomes an essential part of the ego-ideal.	5–10
II. Acquiring the basic habits of industry Learning to organize one's time and energy to get a piece of work done. School work, chores. Learning to put work ahead of play in appropriate situations.	10–15
III. Acquiring identity as a worker in the occupational structure Choosing and preparing for an occupation. Getting work experience as a basis for occupational choice and for assurance of economic independence.	15–25
IV. Becoming a productive person Mastering the skills of one's occupation. Moving up the ladder with one's occupation.	25–40
V. Maintaining a productive society Emphasis shifts toward the societal and away from the individual aspect of the worker's role. The individual sees himself as a responsible citizen in a productive society. He pays attention to the civic responsibility attached to his job. The individual is at the peak of his occupational career and has time and energy to adorn it with broader types of activity. He pays attention to inducting younger people into stages III and IV.	40–70
VI. Contemplating a productive and responsible life This person is retired from work or is in the process of withdrawing from the worker's role. He looks back over his work life with satisfaction, sees that a personal social contribution has been made, and is pleased with it. While he may not have achieved all of his ambitions, he accepts life and believes in himself as a productive person.	70–+

Source: Reprinted from R. J. Havighurst, *Youth in Exploration and Man Emergent* (1964), p. 216. © American Counseling Association. No further reproduction authorized without written permission of the American Counseling Association.

the opportunity structure, as well as individual differences, are important determinants of preferences for such roles as worker, student, leisurite, homemaker, and citizen.)* (Super, 1990, pp. 206–208)

Another early and continuing popular theory was Havighurst's "developmental tasks theory." Havighurst (1964) discusses vocational development as a lifelong process consisting of six stages from childhood to old age. Each age period has characteristic tasks that must be successfully achieved if a person is to attain happiness and success with tasks appropriate to the vocational stages that follow. The developmental stages are outlined in Table 9–2.

*Reprinted with permission of Jossey-Bass from "A Life-Span, Life-Space Approach to Career Development" by D. E. Super in D. Brown and L. Brooks, *Career Choice and Development: Applying Contemporary Theories to Practice* (San Francisco: Jossey-Bass, 1990). All rights reserved.

Personality Theories

Personality theories view vocational preferences as expressions of personality. They suggest that much career-seeking behavior is an outgrowth of efforts to, in effect, match one's individual characteristics with those of a specific occupational field. As one example, Holland's theory of personality types and environmental models may be noted. This theory is based on major assumptions regarding personality types, their determination, and relation to various outcomes and vocational choices. In other words, individuals express themselves, their values and interests, and so forth, through their career choices—their work environments. The concepts and assumptions that underlie the theory are as follow:

1. The choice of vocation is an expression of personality.

2. Interest inventories are personality inventories.

3. Vocational stereotypes have reliable and important psychological and sociological meanings.

4. The members of a vocation have similar personalities and similar histories of personal development.

5. Because people in a vocational group have similar personalities, they will respond to many situations and problems in similar ways, and they will create characteristic interpersonal environments.

6. Vocational satisfaction, stability, and achievement depend on the congruence between one's personality and environment (composed largely of other people) in which one works.

The following statements summarize the major assumptions of Holland's (1966, 1973, 1985a) theory:

1. In our culture, most persons can be categorized as one of six types: realistic, intellectual, social, conventional, enterprising, and artistic.

2. There are six kinds of environments: realistic, intellectual, social, conventional, enterprising, and artistic.

3. People search for environments and vocations that will permit them to exercise their skills and abilities, to express their attitudes and values, to take on agreeable problems and roles, and to avoid disagreeable ones.

4. A person's behavior can be explained by the interaction of his personality and his environment. (Holland, 1966, pp. 8–12)

Table 9–3 summarizes Holland's (1985b) theory, describing the personality characteristics of the six categories and the work environments related to each. Holland has developed a popular assessment instrument based on his theory, *The Self-Directed Search*, accompanied by an *Occupational Finder*. Holland does not suggest his categories as mutually exclusive, as noted in the *Occupational Finder*, which suggests a work setting would be a combination of three environments. It is also equally rare for an individual to fit into only one of the six psychological types.

TABLE 9–3   Holland's Personality Types

The **Realistic** type likes realistic jobs such as automobile mechanic, aircraft controller, surveyor, farmer, electrician. Has mechanical abilities, but may lack social skills. Is described as:

Asocial	Inflexible	Practical
Conforming	Materialistic	Self-effacing
Frank	Natural	Thrifty
Genuine	Normal	Uninsightful
Hardheaded	Persistent	Uninvolved

The **Investigative** type likes investigative jobs such as biologist, chemist, physicist, anthropologist, geologist, medical technologist. Has mathematical and scientific ability but often lacks leadership ability. Is described as:

Analytical	Independent	Rational
Cautious	Intellectual	Reserved
Critical	Introspective	Retiring
Complex	Pessimistic	Unassuming
Curious	Precise	Unpopular

The **Artistic** type likes artistic jobs such as composer, musician, stage director, writer, interior decorator, actor/actress. Artistic abilities: writing, musical, or artistic, but often lacks clerical skills. Is described as:

Complicated	Imaginative	Intuitive
Disorderly	Impractical	Nonconforming
Emotional	Impulsive	Open
Expressive	Independent	Original
Idealistic	Introspective	Sensitive

The **Social** type likes social jobs such as teacher, religious worker, counselor, clinical psychiatric case worker, speech therapist. Has social skills and talents, but often lacks mechanical and scientific ability. Is described as:

Ascendant	Helpful	Responsible
Cooperative	Idealistic	Sociable
Empathic	Kind	Tactful
Friendly	Patient	Understanding
Generous	Persuasive	Warm

The **Enterprising** type likes enterprising jobs such as salesperson, manager, business executive, television producer, sports promoter, buyer. Has leadership and speaking abilities but often lacks scientific ability. Is described as:

Acquisitive	Energetic	Flirtatious
Adventurous	Excitement-	Optimistic
Agreeable	seeking	Self-confident
Ambitious	Exhibitionistic	Sociable
Domineering	Extroverted	Talkative

The **Conventional** type likes conventional jobs such as bookkeeper, stenographer, financial analyst, banker, cost estimator, tax expert. Has clerical and arithmetic ability, but often lacks artistic abilities. Is described as:

Careful	Inflexible	Persistent
Conforming	Inhibited	Practical
Conscientious	Methodical	Prudish
Defensive	Obedient	Thrifty
Efficient	Orderly	Unimaginative

Source: Adapted and reproduced by special permission of the Publisher, Psychological Assessment Resources, Inc., 16204 North Florida Avenue, Lutz, FL 33549, from "The Self-Directed Search Professional Manual," by John L. Holland, Ph.D. Copyright 1985 by PAR, Inc. Further reproduction is prohibited without permission from PAR, Inc.

Another personality theory developed by Roe (1956) and more recently modified by Roe and Lunneborg (1984) suggests that

> there are relationships between the psychic energy, genetic propensities, and childhood experiences that shape individual styles of behavior, and that the impulse to acquire opportunities to express these individual styles is inherent in the choices made and the ensuing career behavior. Thus, the strength of a particular need, the delay between the arousal of the need and its satisfaction, and the value that the satisfaction has in the individual's environment are the conditions—shaped by early childhood experiences—that influence career development. (Herr & Cramer, 1988, p. 127)

Sociological Theories

Popular among the sociological views of careers is one that suggests that people arrive at a particular occupation destiny more by chance than through deliberate planning or steady progress toward an earlier defined goal. Newspapers and television reports constantly remind us of persons who seem to be "at the right place at the right time" and for no other reason end up in an unanticipated career. In a broad sense, we might include the "chance" one has for career choice as influenced by the environment, social class, culture, and other conditions one is born into or raised in; opportunities for education; observation of role models; and so forth. More narrowly we may note that chance factors result in occupational choice by an impulse or sudden emotional reaction in which unconscious forces appear to determine a person's behavior and occupation choice. Consider, for example, the person who on apparent impulse walks out of a good office job to work as a missionary in an African jungle. As described by Caplow (1954), evidence such as this indicates that occupational choice may result from an accidental or unforeseen factor or factors. Accident theory, then, contends that because people may make decisions or be influenced by unforeseen or accidental circumstances, it is not possible to evaluate the decisive factors in their choices.

Bandura (1982) has expressed the view that chance encounters play a prominent role in changing the course of the lives of many of us. Herr and Cramer (1988) synthesize Bandura's perspectives (see Table 9–4).

Sociological theory also notes the influences of home, school, social class, communities, and peer groups. Hotchkiss and Borow (1984) identify four

> ways in which social institutions influence career activity: (a) socializing the individual as a member of the work force, (b) determining interpersonal affiliations, (c) permitting pursuit of certain material and social lifestyles, and (d) giving direction to the career pattern via mobility and advancement. (Isaacson & Brown, 1993, p. 44)

Economic Theories

Economic theories suggest the importance of economic factors in career choice. Prominent among these are the availability of types of jobs versus the availability of qualified workers for these jobs. Too, as many studies have indicated, a major factor in career choice is "What kind of job can I get?" In these instances, the most important consideration is being able to provide at least the basic necessities for oneself and family. Job security has also become an important consideration in career choice in the 1990s, and worker

TABLE 9–4   A Synthesis of Bandura's Perspectives of Factors Influencing Chance Encounters

Personal Determinants of the Effect of Chance Encounters	Social Determinants of the Effect of Chance Encounters
Entry Skills Interest, skills, personal knowledge likely to gain acceptance or sustain contact with another	*Milieu Rewards* The types of rewards and sanctions an individual or group provides if a chance encounter alters a life path
Emotional Ties Interpersonal attractiveness tending to sustain chance encounters so that certain social determinants might operate	*Symbolic Environment and Information* Images of reality provided by other than direct experience; different individuals or groups furnish different symbolic environments
Values and Personal Standards Unintended influences more likely to be important if persons involved share similar standards and value systems	*Milieu Reach and Closedness* Chance encounters with a relatively closed milieu—e.g., cults, communal groups—have the greatest potential for abruptly reordering life paths
	Psychological Closedness Belief systems provide structure, directions, and purpose in life. Once persons, through chance encounter, get caught up in the belief system of a particular group, it can exert selective influence on the course of development and erect a psychological closedness to outside influence. Beliefs channel social interactions in ways that create their own validating realities

Source: From E. L. Herr and S. H. Cramer (1988), *Career Guidance and Counseling Through the Lifespan: Systematic Approaches* (3rd ed.), p. 120. Copyright © 1988 by Scott, Foresman, and Co. Reprinted by permission of HarperCollins College Publishers.

benefits, especially medical insurance and retirement plans, can also be factors in where one seeks employment.

Decision-making theory has its origins in the field of economics and implies that careers are selected from alternatives on the basis of which choice promises to be the most "rewarding" or of value to the individual (and not necessarily in a monetary sense).

Other Theories

A number of other perspectives further broaden the concepts of influences on career development and decision making. For example,

> a social learning theory approach to career selection has been proposed by Krumboltz, Mitchell, and Gelatt (1975). The theory is an attempt to simplify the process of career selection and is primarily based on life events that are influential in determining career selection. In this theory, the process of career development involves four factors: (1) genetic endowments and special abilities, (2) environmental conditions and events, (3) learning experiences, and (4) task approach skills. (Zunker, 1990, p. 48)

Learning theory suggests that career development is a learning process in which academic experiences influence career decisions. Isaacson (1985) suggests an "eclectic" theory, drawing from the prominent theories of occupational choice. The eight major points of his summary are as follow:

1. The career development process is an ongoing, lifelong aspect of human existence.

2. Since the process is essentially developmental in nature, it is generally predictable but also can be modified by changing circumstances, even to the point of being reversible as the individual attempts to optimize the benefits and satisfactions derived from the worker-job relationship.

3. Individuals have differing patterns of abilities, interests, and personality as a result of the interaction of genetic inheritance and environmental factors.

4. Occupations also have differing patterns of characteristics required or expected of successful workers.

5. The extent to which a person develops and applies his or her unique pattern of individual characteristics depends on attitudes, motivations, and values. These patterns can be approached from either the basis of psychological need or the development of self-concept.

6. The individual learns about jobs and their relationship to the individual specifically and to society generally from many sources, including the family, peer groups, community, school, media, and the planned and unplanned experiences of everyday life. The attitudes toward and knowledge of work developed in the growth, exploration, and crystallization periods of childhood and adolescence will have lasting influence on the worker-job relationship of the adult years.

7. The optimization that the individual seeks in the worker-job relationship is the product of the interaction between the individual and the realities of his or her situation. The ability and desire of the individual to capitalize on these interactions influence the level of optimization.

8. The degree of satisfaction experienced by the worker is largely determined by the extent to which the potential for optimization is apparent to the individual and is viewed as agreeable and acceptable.* (pp. 76–77)

IMPLICATIONS OF CAREER THEORIES FOR COUNSELORS

A review of the various theories can lead to the conclusions that career development is a process that leads to a decision, there are stages through which one passes en route to vocational maturity and decision making, one must accomplish certain tasks at each stage, and personality traits are related to career decision making. Furthermore, there are environmental constraints on the careers to which one may aspire or recognize, and the best-laid career plans may be altered by chance or accident.

The characteristics of these theories have certain implications for counseling clients with career development or adjustment needs:

*From Isaacson, Lee E., *Basics of Career Counseling*. Copyright © 1985 by Allyn and Bacon. Reprinted by permission.

1. Counselors must understand the process and characteristics of human development, including readiness to learn and successfully complete particular tasks at certain developmental stages.

2. Counselors must understand the basic human needs as well as the special needs of persons and their relationship to career development and decision making.

3. Counselors must be able to assess and interpret individual traits and characteristics and to apply these assessments to a variety of counselee career-related needs.

4. Counselors must recognize and assist clients to recognize that unforeseen or chance factors may, on occasion, alter career planning.

5. Counselors must recognize that the rapid changes constantly occurring in the way people work and live in this high-tech era require a constant examination and "updating" of the theory and research we use as a basis for our career counseling efforts.

CAREER COUNSELING AND THE DEVELOPMENT OF HUMAN POTENTIAL

Beyond the various career choice theories is the recognition that all aspects of human development, whether they be social, physical, emotional, or educational, are but parts of one's total development—parts that are usually interwoven and often difficult to separate and distinguish from the other aspects of human development. Career development is, of course, no exception. A recognition of these relationships and the application of certain basic principles of human development are significant in the design and implementation of programs providing counseling over the life span for the development of human potential. Seven of these developmental dimensions were discussed in a publication of the National Vocational Guidance Association (1973) (which is now the National Career Development Association):

1. Development occurs during the life time of an individual. It can be described in maturational terms denoting progression through life stages and the mastery of developmental tasks at each stage. Although research evidence is lacking, it seems unlikely that intervention can substantially shorten this maturational process.

2. Individual development is influenced by both heredity and environment. Psychological, sociological, educational, political, economic, and physical factors affect development. Appropriate intervention strategies which focus upon these factors can influence the quality of individual development.

3. Development is a continuous process. Individual development can best be facilitated by intervention strategies that begin in the early years and continue throughout the life of the person. Programs which focus only at certain points or at certain stages in the individual's life will have limited effectiveness.

4. Although development is continuous, certain aspects are dominant at various periods of the life span. Programs designed to facilitate career development should account for the dominant aspects at given stages.

5. Individual development involves a progressive differentiation and integration of the person's self and his perceived world. Intervention strategies need to be designed to assist individuals during normal maturational stages of career development rather than to provide remedial assistance to individuals whose development has been damaged or retarded.

6. While common developmental stages can be observed and described during childhood and adult life, individual differences in progressing through these stages can be expected. Intervention programs should provide for these differences, making no assumption that something is wrong with those who progress at atypical rates.

7. Excessive deprivation with respect to any single aspect of human development can retard optimal development in other areas. Optimal human development programs are comprehensive in nature, not limited to any single facet. It is recognized that those who suffer from deprivation may require special and intensive assistance. Where deprivation is long-term, short-term intervention is not likely to be sufficient. (pp. 3–4)

Of course, we do not have to examine developmental theory to understand the potential that exists within the human being. The achievements of humankind from the discovery of fire to walking on the moon are testimony to the ever-present undetermined potential of human beings. While we must presume that the multiple potentials of most people will never be fully exploited, the challenge nonetheless remains to achieve and develop to the optimum possible. Selecting and functioning in a career may offer the greatest opportunity for a person to achieve much of his or her potential.

Career counseling for the development of human potential may include a focus on encouraging clients to challenge the limitations of their present self-concept; to, in a manner of speaking, redefine their potential and stimulate their vitality.

Let us next examine groups that traditionally represent populations in our society with underdeveloped human potential: women, minorities, the poor, people with disabilities, and dual-career couples.

Women

A prime example of the development of human potential through the world of work is the large-scale movement of women into the work force during and since World War II. Not only are more women entering the work force, but they are entering a wide range of occupations far beyond such traditional women's careers as nursing, teaching, waitressing, and clerical work that represented the limits of their realistic aspirations in the first generation of this century. Today, women seek careers in the medical, legal, law enforcement, military, construction, sales, and transportation fields, to name but a few heretofore bastions of male employment. Further, women are being increasingly appointed to managerial and supervisory positions and high judicial offices, elected to governorships and legislative bodies, and, in general, are making significant advances up the career ladder in all areas. All this is happening as we note projections that anticipate nearly as high a percentage of adult women in the work force as adult men by the year 2000.

Despite the previous optimistic note on progress in developing women's career potential, we must recognize that many barriers to women achieving their full potential still persist. High among these "restrictors" is the age-old problem of prejudice. Prejudice is reflected in numerous ways, but two specific examples might be salaries and opportunities.

TABLE 9–5 Mean Annual Earnings by Gender and Educational Attainment, Full-Time Year-Round Workers, 1986

	Earnings ($)	
Level of Educational Attainment	**Female Workers**	**Male Workers**
Less than 8 years	10,706	15,593
1–3 years of high school	12,496	19,923
Graduated high school	15,402	23,759
1–3 years of college	17,937	28,114
Graduated college	22,943	37,538
1 or more years of postgraduate training	28,629	46,286

Source: U.S. Department of Commerce (1989), p. 450, as cited in Curran and Renzetti (1990), p. 258.

As noted in Table 9–5, a U.S. Chamber of Commerce study in 1989 compared mean annual earnings by sex by educational attainment and found women earned significantly less at every level.

In noting opportunities, the Chamber of Commerce report points out that while the number of female lawyers had increased by over 900% between 1970 and 1985, they still made up only 13% of the total number of lawyers in this country. Further,

> occupational sex segregation is especially acute for minority women. African American, Hispanic, Asian, and Native American women are most likely to be employed in clerical, operative, and domestic and nonhousehold service occupations. These jobs obviously have low prestige and generate low incomes. Hispanic women, for instance, are concentrated in the poorly paying, female-dominated jobs of food processing, electronics, and garment manufacturing (stitching and sewing), although their numbers have increased in female-dominated white collar work, especially clerical (Zavella, 1987). Seventy percent of Asian women are employed in clerical, service, and blue-collar jobs, even though they have a higher level of educational attainment than other women. The greatest shift for African American women workers has been from domestic labor to clerical work. Between 1940 and 1987, the percentage of African American women working as domestics declined from 70 percent to 3.6 percent, while those in clerical jobs increased from 1 percent to 26.4 percent. However, minority women have been less successful than white women in moving into the prestigious and high-paying male professions. African American women, for example, are just 1.5 percent of lawyers and judges, 1.1 percent of college teachers, and 3.8 percent of managers and business executives (Edwards, 1987; Jones, 1986; Taeuber and Valdisera, 1986). (Curran & Renzetti, 1990, pp. 256–257)

Additionally, we have noted increased media attention in recent years to the old problem of sexual harassment of the female worker, homemaking as well as workplace demands on the dual-career couple's working females as males fail to be equal partners on the home front, and increasing numbers of females as single parents. Thus, while laudable progress has been made in developing women's potential, much remains to be done. Career counselors have the opportunity to facilitate this development. The female client must be aided in looking beyond stereotypes and other imagined restrictions. Some may need assistance in appropriately balancing family life and work and accepting their rights to be both a mother and a worker. Counselors must also help female clients recognize educational opportunities that may increase their opportunities and enhance their earning power. With some, assertiveness training, job search skills, and positive self-concept development may also be helpful.

Minorities

Minorities in the United States have, throughout the country's history, represented a tragic loss of human potential. Although progress has been made in recent generations to eliminate barriers and open opportunities to minority populations, much remains to be done. The nation's shortcomings are recognizable in the underrepresentation of minorities in professions, managerial and supervisory positions, government offices of leadership, and preparatory programs in higher education. At the opposite end of the career ladder, minorities are overrepresented in lower-paying and lower-prestige jobs, underemployment and unemployment, school attrition, and the criminal justice system. They truly have been neglected and underserved.

Clearly, attention and effort must be invested in developing the potential of minorities. The urgency of this mission is underscored when we note that it is projected

> that a third of the new entrants into the work force between now and the year 2000 will be minority group members (Johnston & Packer, 1987). Those future workers are today's minority children, more than half of whom are being raised in poverty (Horowitz & O'Brien, 1989). As a result, the ranks of new workers in the future will be dominated by those who have traditionally been ill-served by the nation's school system—the poor, minorities, and immigrants (Hamilton, 1988). One societal effect of this trend has been to increase the focus of corporate executives, legislators, and educators on poverty as an economic issue affecting national productivity rather than exclusively as a social issue (Rauch, 1989). It is hoped that this broader view will widen support for poverty reduction and early educational intervention programs. (Offermann & Gowing, 1990, p. 97)

From a similar viewpoint, Sue and Sue (1989) comment:

> in California, nonwhite youths now account for over half of the student population in the schools. By the year 2000, half of the working-age population in the state will be Hispanic, Asian, Native American or Black. By the year 2003, it is estimated that minorities will constitute the majority population in California. And the rapid increase in minority population is not just a one-state phenomenon. The United States is becoming increasingly heterogeneous in ethnic characteristic. Twenty percent of children in the U.S. are nonwhite, and by 2020, this will increase to 38 percent (U.S. Bureau of Census, 1980). The rapid increase in the nonwhite population increases the urgency for counselors to develop the multicultural knowledge and skills necessary to deal with a much more diverse clientele. (p. 1)

Counselors and counseling programs clearly have both a significant challenge and a significant opportunity to assist minority populations in achieving career equity and developing their individual human potential. To even entertain the promise of effectiveness in this regard, counselors must be sure that they themselves do not hold or reinforce educational or career stereotypes for minorities, do not use biased assessment instruments, and are at all times culturally aware and sensitive.

What do counselors need to consider when designing career interventions for ethnic minorities? From a sociological perspective, Hotchkiss and Borow (1990) noted that the counselor should be involved in the following tasks. First, they must inform clients about potential barriers to ethnic minorities in the labor market, and help them develop strategies to meet them. Second, counselors must provide direct advocacy (e.g., help in completing applications for programs or jobs). Third, they should work to reduce racial and ethnic barriers to success whenever possible (e.g., by assisting in school-to-work transitions). Finally, they should help raise clients' educational aspirations as a way of expanding vocational opportunities. Hawks and Muha (1991) added that counselors should emphasize student-generated versus counselor-generated knowledge, and should incorporate the student's language and culture into programs. They also stated that the minority community, especially parents, should be included in career programs. Finally, they suggested that counselors view problems as external or systemic problems instead of flaws within the student, then use that viewpoint to challenge students to overcome those problems. (Bowman, 1993, p. 18)

The Poor

Although we are frequently reminded that the United States is the richest country on earth, not all of our population is involved in the sharing of the wealth. Certainly, a glaring tarnish on our image is the significant numbers of our population who exist in poverty. Of all Americans, 14.5% live below the poverty line, and 11.7% of all families live below the poverty line. The figures are even more despairing for minority populations. Often overlooked or uncountable are the estimated 1 million-plus homeless, a group that represents the ultimate in underdeveloped human potential. The challenges presented to counseling and the other helping professions are complex and difficult.

From a programmatic standpoint, three concerns must be addressed. First, schools in poverty areas *must* have *good* counseling programs, staffed by competent, caring and environmentally aware counselors. Second, community career assistance programs must be located in those areas where the need is greatest—where the poor reside. Finally, adult education programs with strong counseling components must be made much more accessible and convenient to these populations.

In terms of individual counseling, Isaacson and Brown (1993) point out:

Personal counseling may be needed by disadvantaged individuals to clarify self-concept as well as to understand their circumstances. Several authors have emphasized the devastating impact that job loss has on feelings of self-worth. The chronically poor are likely to carry an even heavier feeling of worthlessness. The so-called American dream suggests that one's success in life is the product of hard work—the harder one works, the more one reaps in material rewards, status, and self-satisfaction. One frequent product is the feeling of guilt and failure by those without jobs or with only marginal jobs. Marshall (1983) and Shifron, Dye, and Shifron (1983) describe ways to help such clients deal with feelings and values that may interfere with everyday life and often result from forces outside the individual's control.

Realistic and practical information about the world of work can be used to help the disadvantaged to see potential opportunities to break out of what is frequently viewed as a hopeless morass. Interviews with workers, work samples, plant visits, and synthetic work situations may help the person to understand the job, to relate that job to self, to see attainable goals, and perhaps to acquire usable role models. (pp. 314–315)

The homeless poor are the most challenging of all. Responding to the diverse needs of homeless people calls for the emergence of a counseling professional who is both client sensitive and a skilled enabling model of helping. Therefore, the helping professional's intervention strategies should begin with focusing on the immediate needs and concerns of the homeless client: providing transportation, locating a safe place to sleep for the night, completing forms, arranging a meeting with school officials, providing support by going to a scheduled appointment with the client, and identifying the local soup kitchens and facilities for taking a shower. In addition, case management is highlighted as perhaps the most effective intervention for providing comprehensive, continuous, and coordinated services for homeless people. The basic functions of the case management system include client identification and outreach, individual assessment, service planning, linkage with requisite services, monitoring of service delivery, and client advocacy. (Solomon & Jackson-Jobe, 1992, p. 104)

People with Disabilities

Another population whose human potential is often underdeveloped is individuals with disabilities. While the terms *disability* and *handicapped* are often used interchangeably, state rehabilitation agencies make an important distinction between the terms:

A *disability* is an impairment or functional limitation in one or more bodily systems. A *handicap* refers to an inability to perform work required by a particular job or to function in a work environment (Daniels, 1981). (as cited in Zunker, 1990, p. 448)

Herr and Cramer (1988) define *the disabled* as

a population that has a disability or several disabilities that may or may not be a vocational handicap. The disability may be *physical* (such as amputations, birth defects, cancer, heart problems, burns, deafness, blindness, multiple sclerosis, muscular dystrophy, orthopedic, spinal injury), *intellectual* (mental retardation, learning disability, brain damage, speech and language disorders), *emotional* (mental illness, substance abuse, alcoholism, obesity and other eating disorders), or *sociocultural*. In any case, best estimates are that in the United States over ten percent of the population have chronic physical, mental, or emotional conditions that limit their activity sufficiently to make a substantial career difference. (pp. 162–163)

In educational settings, the term *handicap* is used to identify individuals who have a physical or mental condition or limitation that prevents them from succeeding in a regular school program. More specifically, individuals who are mentally retarded, learning disabled, emotionally disturbed, orthopedically or visually handicapped, and hearing, speech, or health impaired (with chronic problems such as diabetes or heart condition) are classified as handicapped. (Zunker, 1990, p. 448).

State rehabilitation agencies provide individual counseling and other services to individuals who meet two eligibility requirements: (a) the person must have a disability that results in a substantial handicap to employment and (b) vocational rehabilitation services must reasonably be expected to benefit the person in terms of employability (Texas Rehabilitation Commission, 1984).

In counseling clients with disabilities for career assistance, counselors must (a) have an understanding of various disabilities and their career implications; (b) be knowledgeable regarding appropriate resources, training, and career opportunities; and (c) be sensitive, supportive, and, at the same time, realistic. Counselors must be prepared to assist clients with disabilities in personal adjustment, self-concept development, career development, and job placement. Counselors may also play the role of advocates for such clients seeking access to education or other training or the workplace itself. In other instances, counselors may find themselves facilitating family support for the efforts of people with disabilities. The family support system is important at all ages, of course, and with children it is important in many ways, not the least of which is the influencing of how they feel about themselves. Gilbride (1993, p. 149) reports the results of a study that suggests that parent's attitudes, apart from their actual instrumental capacity, may influence attitudes and expectations of their child's success.

Counselors also assist these clients' placement in peer support groups with other individuals with disabilities. As with so many other services, minorities have not proportionally availed themselves of rehabilitation counseling. Dziekan and Okocha (1993) comment:

> It is only possible to speculate about reasons for lower acceptance rates for minority clients, and a number of factors might have contributed. Lower proportions of minority individuals applying for services may have actually met agency eligibility criteria. Lower proportions of minority clients may have chosen not to follow through with the acceptance process because of their frustrations with the steps and delays involved. Alternatively, biases in the perceptions of rehabilitation counselors determining eligibility for services may have resulted in inaccurate assessments and underestimations of rehabilitation potential. (p. 187)

While much progress has been made through legislative enactments and increased public awareness, counselors can play a vital role in the still-needed advancements of people with disabilities toward the development of their potential.

Dual-Career Couples

Dual-career couples have become increasingly the norm rather than the exception in the last quarter century. However, the question has frequently been raised as to whether one or both partners will fail to develop their full career potential in such relationships.

This question becomes increasingly significant when we note that couples in which both partners

> are employed represent the largest segments of workers at all major corporations. Estimates show that these couples represent 60% to 70% of current employees and it is expected that this percentage will rise to 80% within the next decade (Johnson, 1990). Their needs and lifestyles will affect future corporate development. Members of dual career couples are highly committed to their careers and are productive members of their institutions; however, their achievements are associated with individual and couple stresses, role conflicts and challenges. (Stoltz-Loike, 1992, p. 3)
>
> Stoltz-Loike (1992) presents

> five major career dilemmas (Rapoport & Rapoport, 1976; Sekaran, 1986): (1) role overload from multiple roles, (2) identity confusion between socially learned roles, (3) role-cycling dilemmas between family and career roles, each receiving priority at different points in time, (4) social network dilemmas because of limited discretionary time, and (5) normative dilemmas that result from environmental sanctions. (p. 14)

The continued growth of dual-career couples has presented counselors with relatively new and unexplored challenges in career, and marriage and family counseling. Certainly, the traditional theories of career counseling were not developed with the dual-career couple in mind. New conceptual frameworks must be researched and developed. Individual counseling must be interspersed with co-joint counseling. Too, open communications and compromise must be encouraged. A multitude of issues regarding the shared responsibilities of child rearing should be explored before they become major issues.

A code or credo of couple equity, either written or verbally discussed, is suggested by Stoltz-Loike (1992) consisting of six elements:

> (1) personal needs, (2) preferences for balance, (3) gender issues, (4) life-span issues, (5) balance of career concerns, and (6) commitment to redeveloping the credo. This credo will direct individual performance and couple balance, and result in greater satisfaction with the couple relationship. Moreover, it can specify functional ways to deal with the normal stresses and strains of the relationship over time.
>
> The rewards of couple growth associated with negotiated equity will enhance both individual and family functioning and lead to richer dimensions in the couple relationship. Moreover, equitable couples will be able to pursue a greater variety of challenging business and personal roles. This balance will be attained through discussion of, commitment to, and concern with family and career achievements. Family and career equity may be quite difficult to negotiate, but when it exists, it represents life-span success. (p. 245)

Since schools are looked on as an agency of society for developing youths' potential, let us examine, in the next section, how career programs providing for career planning and decision making in schools contribute to the development of human potential.

CAREER PLANNING AND DECISION MAKING IN SCHOOLS

Nearly all human beings can anticipate three common experiences. The first of these, development or growth, begins at birth and is especially attended to through much of one's youth. Second is education, which, in an informal sense, also starts at birth and continues throughout life, with a special societal emphasis during most of one's youth when formal schooling is provided. The third common experience is work, beginning in one's youth and continuing through most of adulthood.

These three experiences are significantly shaped by one common setting—the school. It is here that a person's development is stimulated and shaped for the three great experiences of his or her life: learning, living with others, and working. Thus, the role of the school in what the person may become and, in turn, what society itself may become is critical. Counselors in any setting have an interest in the impact the school experience has on their clients.

The counseling program's role in the school setting must be one of facilitating and enhancing the school's contributions to young people's learning, growth and development, and preparation for work. In this chapter we are particularly concerned with the latter—preparation for the world of work, including attending to a person's career development, planning, and decision making within the educational context.

In order to emphasize the opportunities for the student's career development, certain guiding principles are suggested as appropriate objectives for the school counseling program in general and the career guidance phase in particular. The following principles are stated within a developmental framework:

1. *All students should be provided with an opportunity to develop an unbiased base from which they can make their career decisions.* The shrinking of the pupil's occupational choice field as one proceeds through the school years is an educational tragedy. The first grader seems to regard most familiar occupations in a positive light. By the time they reach the seventh or eighth grade, pupils have begun to make decisions based on at least some general occupational considerations. Many have developed or have been educated toward biases that automatically eliminate many possibilities from further consideration. The large percentage of students who enter college preparatory courses at the ninth-grade level and never enter college or even fail to complete their secondary schooling is but one evidence of this fact. In this regard, then, the school counseling program seeks, in effective cooperation with the classroom teacher, to develop in each pupil positive attitudes and respect for all honest work. This is a formidable task, for many students are almost constantly bombarded with the biases of the adult world surrounding them. If these students are to benefit from a true freedom of choice, the career counseling and guidance program has a vital mission in the schools.

2. *The early and continuous development of positive pupil attitudes toward education is critical.* The deterioration of the elementary pupil's occupational choice field is unfortunate, but the failure to maintain the pupil's continuing interest in an optimum educational development is disastrous. For objective evidence, one need only turn to the various dropout studies and the equally countless studies concerning the lack of pupil motivation and achievement commensurate with ability. In short, career development has limited meaning without parallel educational development. Any program of pupil career counseling and guidance must have as a major objective the stimulation of the student's educational development.

3. *As a corollary to these previous points, the student must be taught to view a career as a way of life and an education as a preparation for life.* Frequently pupils arrive at the educational decision-making stage of life viewing careers only in terms of job descriptions. At all educational levels the opportunity exists to develop, not only widen, occupational horizons. This broader approach to the eventual career choice is based on the realization that one's way of work is one's way of life. Similarly, there must be attention to the concept of education itself, keeping in mind the idea of education for life rather than education only for one's eventual career. This approach—one of education for a fuller life—also has obvious implications for education's continuing efforts to reduce the number of school dropouts.

4. *Students must be assisted in developing adequate understanding of themselves and must be prepared to relate this understanding to both social-personal development and career-educational planning.* These understandings are significant in the fulfillment of the individual's need for self-actualization. In this context, both career guidance and pupil appraisal seek to further enrich their meaning and value to students by preparing them to look at themselves realistically in terms of continuing educational opportunities, career requirements, and the demands and relationships of society.

5. *Students at all levels must be provided with an understanding of the relationship between education and careers.* If pupils are to develop an attitude and belief that education is relevant, they must understand how it is relevant. Pupils need an awareness of the relationships between levels of education and related career possibilities. They should also be made aware of both the vocations and avocations that stem directly from certain subjects.

6. *Pupils need an understanding of both where and why they are at a given point on the educational continuum at a given time.* It is not enough for pupils to know they will be in the third grade this year and in the fourth grade next year if all goes well. If they are to gain an increased appreciation of current educational programs as well as future educational possibilities, pupils must be provided specific opportunities to gain insights into the educational process, its sequence, and its integration of knowledge.

7. *Pupils at every stage of their educational program should have career-oriented experiences that are appropriate for their levels of readiness and simultaneously meaningful and realistic.* This means that opportunities for participation and observation will frequently take precedence over discussions and teacher or counselor lectures.

8. *Students must have opportunities to test concepts, skills, and roles to develop values that may have future career application.* The school career counseling and guidance program takes advantage of natural school groupings in providing "secure" opportunities for the pupil to experience and develop human relationships and other skills, a variety of roles, and a system of values and concepts that are related to everyday living.

9. *The school career counseling and guidance program is centered in the classroom, with coordination and consultation by the school counselor, participation by parents, and resource contributions from the community.* The pupil's career counseling and guidance team needs the involvement of all those concerned with his or her development, with the teacher, counselor, and parent playing key roles.

10. *The school's program of career counseling and guidance is integrated into the functioning counseling and guidance and total educational programs of the institution.* The complete development of the individual is vital; therefore, the career aspects should not be separated from the whole. In fact, it is only within the total educational program framework that each segment can be strengthened by and in turn strengthen every other segment.

The School Counselor's Role in Student Career Development

As has been noted, the need for career guidance and counseling is increasingly evident in the mass of data pointing to difficulties in career decision making, the underutilization of human resources, dissatisfaction with chosen careers, and such perennial problems as the hard-core unemployed. Career guidance programs are designed, in cooperation with programs of career education, to cope with such needs. To satisfactorily plan such programs, which will increase students' planning and decision-making skills, counselors must understand how career decisions are made and the possible consequences of certain decisions. This approach implies an understanding of theories and related research in career decision making and the counselor's potential role in youths' career development.

Since the career movement in schools has been viewed as primarily a developmental and educational process, the school counselor has, at last, the opportunity to function in a developmental and, in a sense, preventive capacity. Although the teacher is clearly the key person on the career education team, the school counselor, by virtue of special understandings and skills, can make a valuable contribution to the school's total effort. These contributions may be categorized under the following activities.

Career Counseling

Programs of career education are designed to prepare persons for the eventual selection of a career, but many adolescents and young adults will be unable to adequately cope with this critical decision making without the assistance of a professional counselor. Parental counseling, group counseling, and group guidance activities represent contributions of the counselor to the career development of the individual and the school's career education program.

Career Assessment

An important aspect of the career education program provides students the opportunities to assess their personal characteristics in relation to career planning and decision making. The counselor can make a significant contribution to the development of appropriate self-understandings of youth through the employment of both standardized and nonstandardized assessment techniques. However, it is important that these instruments are free of gender or cultural biases.

Resource Person and Consultant

The school counselor has been traditionally active in acquiring materials appropriate to career decision making and planning. The counselor is also aware of computerized information programs and media aids such as films, filmstrips, and audio- and videotapes. Although the counselor cannot collect all materials, it is reasonable to expect that the counselor will be aware of the sources from which such materials may be obtained. In this capacity, the counselor serves as a resource person to the individual teachers involved in the career education program.

The counselor also serves in a consulting capacity, utilizing his or her understanding of the pupil population and career development resources and opportunities to complement the career education program.

Linkage Agent

Increasingly, the counselor will be active in collaborative efforts, not only with teachers and others in the school setting but with community agencies and employers. Local government employment counselors and their agencies are especially important contacts.

The counselor has an important role to play in implementing and strengthening career education programs. This role does not, however, diminish the importance of the career guidance function in career planning and decision making. Let us, therefore, move on to examine some techniques for this activity.

Techniques for Career Planning and Decision Making

In counseling youths for their career development and eventual placement, counselors may employ a variety of facilitative techniques to assist persons in

- ❖ self-awareness,
- ❖ educational awareness,
- ❖ career awareness,
- ❖ career exploration, and
- ❖ career planning and decision making.

Self-Awareness

From a very early age onward people must become aware of and respect their uniqueness as human beings. Learning about one's aptitudes, interests, values, personality traits, and so forth, is important in the development of concepts related to self and the utilization of these concepts in career exploration. Counselors may use such techniques as values clarification exercises, group guidance activities, written assignments (such as autobiographies), films and videotapes, and standardized tests. Individual or group counseling should follow if circumstances warrant.

Educational Awareness

Awareness of the relationships between self, educational opportunities, and the world of work is an important aspect of career planning. Counselors may use films as well as printed materials for this purpose. Group guidance activities (such as orientation days), presentations by school alumni, and the use of educational awareness inventories can be useful. Games that relate hobbies and recreational activities to courses and careers can be stimulating for grade school and middle school pupils. Guided activities can also educate school-aged youth to the relationships between desirable school habits (i.e., responsibility, punctuality, effort, positive human relationships) and good worker traits.

Career Awareness

Counselors and counseling programs in schools should, at all educational levels, assist the pupil in the continuous expansion of knowledge and awareness of the world of work. This must include a developing recognition of the relationships between values, lifestyles, and careers. Many excellent films and printed materials are available for this purpose, but, of course, these must be integrated into a planned, developmental program appropriate to the student's age or grade level. Specialized programs (i.e., career days, career shadowing, junior partners, closed circuit television "trips," and actual field trips) are useful if well planned. Excellent computer programs (noted later in this chapter) are available, and with secondary school students, standardized interest inventories can increase a student's career awareness.

Career Exploration

Career exploration represents a movement toward a systematic, planned inquiry and analysis of careers that are of interest. Comparisons, reality testing, and standardized testing may be useful. Computerized programs, to be discussed later, can also be helpful. Classes in career exploration and decision making are not uncommon.

A variety of techniques are available for career exploration in schools. The integrating of career information into classroom instruction enhances the meaning of both as the relationship between learning in school and living out of school becomes more evident to the pupil. The relation of subject matter to careers, hobbies, everyday living needs, and the accomplishments of well-known personalities exemplifies accomplishing this integration. Many excellent published materials are also available for facilitating career exploration.

Career Planning and Decision Making

Students eventually need to narrow their career or career planning possibilities and then proceed to examine and test these options as critically as possible. Here again, such established techniques as values clarification activities, standardized testing, job shadowing, career days, and other group guidance activities are helpful. Many students will need to learn the process of decision making, including choosing between competing alternatives, examining the consequences of specific choices, the value of compromise, and implementing a decision. At this point, students must recognize the impact of their current planning and decision making on their future life. It should also be a time when students are assisted to "take control" of their life and become an active agent for the shaping of their own future.

Placement and Follow-Up

Career placement and follow-up services are significant to the success of career counseling programs. The high rate of youth unemployment has highlighted the need for a greater emphasis on career placement for youth. Assistance to young people by both school and employment counselors is important if they are to avoid unnecessary difficulties and frustrations in their career search activities. Also, counselors are aware that unsatisfactory career entry can have long-term effects for youth. In this regard, it must be recognized that the current "TV generations" are often unrealistic in their expectations of career opportunities and their viewpoints of specific careers. Preemployment counseling may be necessary to assist these young people in obtaining a more realistic understanding of the world of work.

Earlier evidence of these problems is cited in the landmark *Nationwide Study of Student Career Development* by Prediger, Roth, and Noeth (1973), which reports a sharp contrast between the need for career planning and the help received by youth. This study confirms that youths are seriously deficient in knowledge about the world of work and career planning, and they are unable to cope with the career development tasks posed by society during the difficult high school–post high school transition and placement period. The study recommends the reorientation of the traditional school counseling model to provide increased and more realistic assistance in career placement and initiate significant changes that would, in effect, increase the effectiveness of counseling youth for today's world of work.

In another historic national study focusing on career placement in schools only, Gibson and Mitchell (1976) note:

Of all the guidance placement activities, none is more important or has the potential for assisting more youth in the school setting than the job placement service. Such a service can be designed to assist both in-school and out-of-school youth, both school dropouts and school graduates. Such programs are typically involved in:

1. Assessing the needs of students regarding part-time and full-time employment, training, employability skills, and further educational desires.

2. Establishing a working relationship with business, industry, and labor representatives in order to facilitate effective cooperation and communication between these groups and educators.

3. Providing avenues and assistance to students seeking part-time or full-time employment that are compatible with their abilities and interests.

4. Establishing an efficient, participatory communication-feedback network among all involved—students, business, industry, and labor personnel, community leaders, parents, media, and school personnel. (p. 1)

With many school guidance programs currently in the process of developing or expanding the placement function, it might be helpful to note the procedural steps developed in the Indiana Model Career Placement Project for developing or expanding this phase of the school guidance program (see Figure 9–1).

In considering placement program development, the existence in many communities of well-established local governmental employment programs that often give special attention to the needs of local youth should be recognized. In such settings, the school guidance program seeks to work cooperatively and complementarily with local government employment personnel to provide the best possible assistance for young job seekers. Even under such ideal conditions, however, it must be remembered that the important developmental aspects of school placement programs are not the responsibility of other agencies or institutions. School placement programs, therefore, must include activities that develop or enhance the student's skills, attitudes, and knowledge needed for job acquisition and retention.

Placement program activities may be viewed as three-dimensional. The primary activity, of course, is student development; however, this will obviously be handicapped if job development is not also a planned program activity, and both of these activities will be less than effective without plans for program maintenance and operation.

Since placement in its broader context includes the placement of clients in a variety of settings (i.e., work, educational, environmental) for a variety of reasons and benefits, let us now proceed to examine educational and environmental placement.

Educational Placement

In general, educational placement differs little from other forms of placement inasmuch as it represents an organized effort to match the qualifications of individuals plus personal interests and resources with the requirements of institutions and programs. Typically, school counselors, with responsibilities for college and other postsecondary educational placement, provide information to students regarding institutional entrance requirements, expenses, characteristics of the institution, and program content. They also frequently will

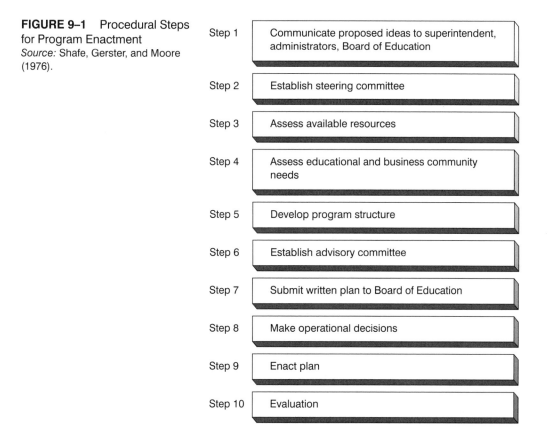

FIGURE 9–1 Procedural Steps for Program Enactment
Source: Shafe, Gerster, and Moore (1976).

Step 1　Communicate proposed ideas to superintendent, administrators, Board of Education

Step 2　Establish steering committee

Step 3　Assess available resources

Step 4　Assess educational and business community needs

Step 5　Develop program structure

Step 6　Establish advisory committee

Step 7　Submit written plan to Board of Education

Step 8　Make operational decisions

Step 9　Enact plan

Step 10　Evaluation

assist students in completing the necessary application forms. An example of a form that counselors may use with high school students interested in college placement is the college checklist (see Figure 9–2).

Many school counselors are also involved in educational placement within their schools. In this capacity they are concerned with placing students in appropriate curricula and specific courses. However, scheduling activities that consist largely of a mechanical process designed to get all pupils into all slots at a given time, with a total disregard of individual differences, is not considered a guidance responsibility, even though counselors report that they spend many hours doing such tasks.

In the literature, at least, if not always in practice, placement within educational institutions has been viewed as more than just career, college, and educational placement. In its broadest sense, placement is an activity that places or facilitates the self-placement of persons in settings that will enable them to benefit from needed experiences, make satisfactory adjustments, gain useful information, and, in general, contribute to their total development. As an example of this broader concept of placement, let us look at placement that focuses on giving a person experiences in different roles and environments.

	Name of College		Name of College		Name of College	
I. *Entrance Requirements and General Information*						
1. Does this college offer major preparation in the field of _____ (student's planned major)?	Yes	No	Yes	No	Yes	No
2. Will I be eligible for admission upon completion of my currently planned program for high school graduation?						
3. Are entrance examinations required?						
4. Must I take a physical examination?						
5. Are there other entrance requirements? (If so, list in Section VII, under Notes and Comments.)						
6. Is this a coeducational college?						
7. Is this a state- or city-supported college?						
8. Are the offerings of this college accredited by the accrediting association?						
9. Does this college have an ROTC program?						
10. What is the average enrollment?						
II. *Expenses (per school year)*						
11. Room						
12. Board						
13. Tuition						
14. Activity fees						
15. Any other special expenses:						
(item) _____						
(item) _____						
16. Total basic cost per year	$		$		$	
III. *Room and Board*						
17. Are dormitory facilities available for men and women?						
18. Are noncommuting freshmen required to live in the dormitory?						
19. May you select your own roommate if you desire?						
20. Are dining facilities available (three meals per day) for students?						

FIGURE 9–2 College Checklist

Role placement assumes that experiencing different and significant roles is important for all developing pupils. Although many will experience some of these roles naturally and without planning, for the majority these developmental opportunities would be missed unless specific provisions are made. This is another opportunity for the school counselor and classroom teacher to work cooperatively in planning meaningful experiences that enhance both the instructional programs and the student's personal development. Significant role experiences would include opportunities to function periodically as a leader, a team member, an individual (isolated) worker, a teacher of others, an achiever, a responsi-

	Name of College		Name of College		Name of College	
	Yes	No	Yes	No	Yes	No
IV. *Student Services and Aids*						
21. Are scholarships available?	___	___	___	___	___	___
22. Are part-time jobs available?	___	___	___	___	___	___
23. Are guidance services provided?	___	___	___	___	___	___
24. Is there a freshman orientation program?	___	___	___	___	___	___
25. Are placement services available for						
(a) graduating seniors?	___	___	___	___	___	___
(b) summertime jobs?	___	___	___	___	___	___
26. Are health services provided?						
(a) Dispensary care?	___	___	___	___	___	___
(b) Dental care?	___	___	___	___	___	___
(c) Hospitalization plan?	___	___	___	___	___	___
27. Can I get special scholastic help (such as tutoring) if I need it?	___	___	___	___	___	___
V. *Student Activities*						
28. Fraternities and sororities?	___	___	___	___	___	___
29. Honorary organizations?	___	___	___	___	___	___
30. Social dancing permitted?	___	___	___	___	___	___
31. Are campus recreational facilities available?	___	___	___	___	___	___
32. Is there an intramural program?	___	___	___	___	___	___
33. Major varsity sports?	___	___	___	___	___	___
34. A convocation series?	___	___	___	___	___	___
35. Dramatic opportunities?	___	___	___	___	___	___
36. Music (band and glee club)?	___	___	___	___	___	___
37. Any others you are particularly interested in: (item) _____	___	___	___	___	___	___

VI. Any special questions you want to ask? _____

_____

VII. Notes and comments _____

_____

(Student's name)_____

FIGURE 9–2 *(continued)*

ble person, a social being, a person of authority and decision making, or one who serves others. A role assignment sheet, as illustrated in Figure 9–3, is a method of recording these experiences.

Environmental Assessment

Environmental placement can be another developmental activity. The major focus of this type of placement is to provide students with the opportunities to experience other signifi-

Grade _____ Class of _____ Period _____ to _____							
B. D. Lewis Elementary School							
Role Assignments	Leader	Team Member	Individual Worker	Achiever	Responsibility	Social Leader	Decision Maker	Server
Pupils' Names								
1. Marie Adams								
2. Alyssa Debrovitz								
3. Marc Collins								
4. Chester Dent								
5. Charles James								
6. Kathryn James								
7. Liona Chan								
8. Archie Leedy								
9. Paul Lewis								
10. Katherine Louise								
11. Daniel Kim								
12. Matt Nuzrem								
13. Jack Smith								
14. Alex Wagner								
15. Heather Watson								

* Dates are entered where role is assigned.
✓ indicates student has assumed or experienced this role and further assignment
is not needed at this time.

FIGURE 9–3   Role Assignments
Source: Gibson (1972), p. 60.

cant, yet distinctly different, environments from their own. An example is giving city youths opportunities to spend time in rural areas as part of farm days or "country cousins" programs. Urban youths may exchange places with rural youths for several days or weeks. Another example is a blend of educational preparation and environmental placement in which students spend some time in diverse collegiate settings.

Regardless of the nature of client placement, follow-up should also be planned. In the following section, reasons that clients are not placed and forgotten are set forth.

Follow-Up

Programs of placement activities, regardless of setting, must provide evidence of the effectiveness of their practices for both accountability and program improvement purposes. A large measure of supporting evidence for these purposes may be secured through carefully planned follow-up activities. As a complement to the guidance placement program, follow-up activities focus on effectiveness in placing persons for a variety of purposes and settings, as viewed not only by the clients but also by those to whom the client is responsible in such settings as job placement.

Follow-up data may be obtained through questionnaires, checklists, interviews, and phone calls. Placement follow-up with those placed usually focuses on how satisfied the persons are with their placement and the process, progress they believe they are making in their situation, adequacy of their previous preparation experience, and future plans and recommendations. Employers may be asked to respond concerning the adequacy of preparation and experience of the employee, adaptation to work, ability to work with others, progress anticipated by employee, and recommendations for improving the placement process.

In college placement, follow-up may seek to identify how adequately prepared for college the entering student is and areas of strength and weakness, the degree to which the student appears to be adjusting to college, and recommendations for improving the placement process. As follow-up data are collected, it is equally important to anticipate and plan for systematic utilization of the data.

In recognizing the importance of planning for career placement and follow-up, we would also be cognizant of the complexities and variables involved. In an effort to assist counselors and their clients to deal more effectively with those complexities and variables, computerized assistance systems have been and continue to be developed. Several of these systems will be described in the next section.

COMPUTERIZED CAREER ASSISTANCE SYSTEMS

The 1990s have witnessed the continued rapid development and public acceptance of the computer. Computers, already popular in business, industry, and higher education, are now becoming commonplace in schools at all levels, and the current boom in home computers appears likely to continue. Young people's fascination with this technological marvel is reflected not only in their patronage of video arcades and purchase of computerized video games but also in their quest for knowledge and use of even the most sophisticated of computers. In fact, it may be that youth have become one of the most computer-literate groups.

The attraction of students at all age levels to the computer has given schools unprecedented opportunities for its utilization in motivation and learning. This potential exists for school counseling programs as well, especially in providing career information and assistance.

While computer usage in counseling programs in educational settings is not new, having been around since the 1960s, the introduction of the microcomputer in the 1970s promoted major changes as well as opportunities for the utilization of computer-assisted career guidance systems. The economic and technical advantages of the microcomputer continue to be a major stimulus to their use in school settings for career counseling and guidance purposes.

Types of Systems

In this section two types of systems will be briefly described: (a) information systems and (b) guidance systems.

Information Systems

Information systems are generally designed to provide users with a structured search scheme for occupations and disseminate occupational and educational information to users. These procedural steps may be used separately or in sequence. In the former, the user may complete exercises or provide ratings, even test scores indicating interests and aptitudes as a basis for the computer's search for compatible occupations. In the latter, information accessing process, the user can access general information regarding specific occupations. The computer may also be programmed to respond to certain specific questions the user may ask about the occupation.

The development of information systems was greatly stimulated by grants provided by the Department of Labor and the National Occupational Information Coordinating Committee, which enabled states to develop statewide career information systems. Many of these, labeled career information systems (CISs), emphasize local and regional information. The components of the CIS systems include an initial questionnaire, labeled QUEST, for providing self-estimates of various areas including aptitudes, interests, physical limitations, and so forth. Users then receive a printout briefly describing occupations related to their QUEST's responses. Many CIS systems also use a file identifying ways to prepare for an occupation and a file identifying sources for additional information on each occupation.

Another information system, identified as the guidance information system (GIS), provides access to various kinds of national data regarding careers, educational opportunities, and the armed services. Several interest inventory systems are available as options. This system is marketed through the Educational Software Division of Houghton Mifflin Company, which reported use in 1990 at more than 4,500 locations. Information in this system is arranged according to groups of characteristics related to occupations and 4-year colleges.

Another popular system, the C-LECT, offers three modules: an occupational module, an educational module, and a financial aids–apprenticeship module. In addition, the system provides a report writer that allows the user to get a report on his or her inputs at any time during the session. C-LECT is marketed by Chronicle Guidance Publications, Inc.

Guidance Systems

Guidance systems are broader in scope and more instructional than information systems, providing in addition to the organized search and dissemination functions of information systems modules such as self-assessment, instruction in decision making, future planning, and so forth. The two most popular of these systems are the System of Interactive Guidance and Information (SIGI), now updated as SIGI PLUS, developed and marketed through the Educational Testing Service, Princeton, New Jersey, under the direction of Martin Katz, and the Discover System, developed by JoAnn Harris-Bowlsbey and marketed through Discover, Inc., Hunt Valley, Maryland, and the American College Testing Program.

The SIGI system was designed originally to assist college and college-bound students and out-of-school adults. It is now applied to 4-year schools and adults in a wide range of settings as well. SIGI PLUS consists of nine modules: (a) Introduction (orientation to the process), (b) Self-assessment, (c) Search (of possible preferred occupations), (d) Information (regarding possible occupations), (e) Skills, (f) Preparation, (g) Coping (can the individual do what is required), (h) Deciding (decision making), and (i) Next Steps (putting a plan into action).

The DISCOVER system offers different programs for junior/middle school, high school, adults in transition, employees and organizations, and those approaching retirement. The junior/middle school version consists of three modules: (a) You and the World of Work, (b) Exploratory Occupations, and (c) Planning for High School. The popular high school version has seven modules:

Module 1
Beginning the Career Journey
Administers and scores a career maturity inventory and suggests parts of DISCOVER to
be used.

Module 2
Learning About the World of Work
Helps users understand American College Testing's World-of-Work Map.

Module 3
Learning About Yourself
Administers and scores on-line assessment and inventories and accepts results of paper
and pencil versions.

Module 4
Finding Occupations
Generates occupation lists from the results of Module 3.

Module 5
Learning About Occupations
Provides national details about hundreds of occupations and includes local or state infor-
mation if customized.

Module 6
Making Educational Choices
Helps users select a training pathway.

Module 7
Planning Next Steps
Provides details about educational opportunities and develops job-seeking skills. (pub-
lished by American College Testing)

The college versions add modules in career planning and transitions. The organizational and retirement versions consist of four modules, each unique to organizational settings or retirement planning.

In the mid-1990s the downsizing of the military and many of the industries supplying the military, the conversion of industries to new products and production methods and the creation of large pools of temporary or transitional employees have increased the need for adult career counseling and placement services.

Ethical Considerations

The rapid growth of computer usage in the field of counseling and its anticipated increased usage in the future have raised certain ethical questions related to the use of computers in counseling. Potential problems in client confidentiality, misinterpretation of test results and other data by clients, and lack of appropriate counselor interaction with clients are but a few examples. Sampson and Pyle (1983) suggest 14 principles in response to ethical issues involved with the use of computer-assisted counseling, testing, and guidance systems:

1. Ensure that confidential data maintained on a computer are limited to information that is appropriate and necessary for the services being provided.

2. Ensure that confidential data maintained on a computer are destroyed after it is determined that the information is no longer of any value in providing services.

3. Ensure that confidential data maintained on a computer are accurate and complete.

4. Ensure that access to confidential data is restricted to appropriate professionals by using the best computer security methods available ("appropriate professionals" are described in existing ethical standards).

5. Ensure that it is not possible to identify, with any particular individual, confidential data maintained in a computerized data bank that is accessible through a computer network.

6. Ensure that research participation release forms are completed by an individual who has automatically collected individually identifiable data as a result of using a computer-assisted counseling, testing, or guidance system.

7. Ensure that computer-controlled test scoring equipment and programs function properly thereby providing individuals with accurate test results.

8. Ensure that generalized interpretations of test results presented by microcomputer-controlled audiovisual devices accurately reflect the intention of the test author.

9. Ensure that a client's needs are assessed to determine if using a particular system is appropriate before using a computer-assisted counseling, testing, or guidance system.

10. Ensure that an introduction to using a computer-assisted counseling, testing, and guidance system is available to reduce possible anxiety concerning the system, misconceptions about the role of the computer, and misunderstandings about basic concepts or the operation of the system.

11. Ensure that a follow-up activity to using a computer-assisted counseling, testing, and guidance system is available to correct possible misconceptions, misunderstandings, or inappropriate use as well as assess subsequent needs of the client.

12. Ensure that the information contained in a computer-assisted career counseling and guidance system is accurate and up-to-date.

13. Ensure that the equipment and programs that operate a computer-assisted counseling, testing, and guidance system function properly.

14. Determining the need for counselor intervention depends on the likelihood that the client would experience difficulties that would in turn limit the effectiveness of the system

or otherwise exacerbate the client's problem. It is the counselor's responsibility to decide whether the best approach to avoiding the above problems for a specific client population is direct intervention or indirect intervention through the use of workbooks, self-help guides, or other exercises. (pp. 285–286)

Certainly, we must hope that rapid developments in computer technology will not "outrun" careful consideration of the ethical issues involved.

CAREER COUNSELING IN NONSCHOOL SETTINGS

The initial out-of-school career contacts of many youths will be made through the assistance of their state employment services. In these offices, career guidance activities may be based on a review and discussion of the applicant's qualifications and interests in relation to available employment opportunities. Appraisal instruments, such as the General Aptitude Classification Battery, may be used to further assist the client and the counselor in career planning. Counselors in these settings are usually especially well versed in their knowledge of local job opportunities and characteristics and usually have access to computerized job bank systems. These employment office counselors often work closely with high school counselors in facilitating the career planning and transitions of youths from school to work.

Career counseling and placement, however, can no longer be considered an activity that focuses on youth alone. A variety of factors have resulted in significant changes in the career "habitats" of adult populations. Those changes, some of which were noted earlier in this chapter, in turn have influenced the career counseling and placement efforts in governmental and business settings. Contributing factors to this change include the impact of technological and social change, shifts in societal and consumer values, a population that is growing older and capable of working longer, economic necessity, and international market influences.

Moreover, technological change has resulted in related societal changes such as population shifts, altered consumer demands, and major new government policies regarding health, education, and welfare. These changes have had an impact on other occupations not directly affected by changing technologies. Human service occupations are a good example. Thousands of young adults entered educational programs in these fields. When they graduated several years later, they frequently found the labor market quite different from what it was when they began their schooling. Many could not find jobs in their career areas; other took jobs for which they were overqualified and underpaid.

Americans preparing for jobs in several other occupations have encountered similar difficulties. As technological and social changes become more rapid, predicting the state of the work force becomes increasingly difficult.

During recent generations, social and cultural changes have also resulted in the alteration of traditional concepts and expectations that resulted in sex-role stereotyping in the world of work. As noted earlier in this chapter, this situation has led to not only more female engineers, construction workers, airplane pilots, and more male nurses and elementary school teachers but also increasing numbers of women who, in the process of combining careers and marriage, interrupt their careers for child rearing before returning to the labor force.

In short, midlife career changes and entries are becoming commonplace for both men and women.

> Every occupation is represented, but some are more visible than others. Classic cases of midlife career change can be found in the ranks of those who put in twenty years or so in the military or in municipal activities, such as fire and police protection and then retire at a relatively young age, free to pursue a second career. In the 1970s, thousands of engineers and scientists became unemployed because of substantial cuts in space and defense spending; these workers in declining industries were often forced to seek unrelated types of employment, or to take lesser paying jobs in the same occupation. More recently, the field of education has experienced cutbacks, causing teachers and other educational personnel to switch career paths. Whether voluntary or involuntary, it is clear that midlife career change is a visible phenomenon and that a significant proportion of workers will not fit the one life–one occupation mode. (Herr & Cramer, 1988, p. 360)

Even though midlife career changes may be commonplace, even anticipated by many workers, such changes can prompt adjustment as well as decision-making difficulties. Some adjustments will be the result of adapting to a new work routine with new skills, new work associates, and possible movement to a new environment and new way of life. Also, some will view the necessity or desirability of career change as a reflection on their status as valued workers and an indication that they have erred in their earlier career planning. Marital relationships can be threatened, even when one of the spouses is not facing career change, and existing problems are usually agitated further.

In counseling this more mature and work-experienced group, the career counselor will want to consider the following counseling goals outlined by Herr and Cramer (1988):

1. Assist the individual to explore, specify, and evaluate the clarity of the reasons for a career shift. Is the individual confused and anxious as a result of an involuntary career shift, secure and optimistic because of the prospects of a voluntary career shift, or some combination of both? Are stress factors with which an individual has difficulty coping in a current job likely to be present in an intended job? Does the individual appear distressed, depressed, or dysfunctional? How carefully has the individual planned? These and other questions relate to the goal of shift clarification.

2. Assist the individual to acquire all necessary information relevant to a career shift. Does the individual recognize the relationship between education or training and the proposed work shift? What steps are necessary to effect the change? Where and how does one get the necessary information? One comprehensive review of the literature (Pascal, Elmore, Endo, & McClusky, 1975) concluded that redirection schemes usually emphasize aptitude diagnosis, provision of realistic job information, on-the-job instruction, and placement assistance.

3. Help the individual to envision the possible effects of a career shift. Will there be financial ramifications? Will family life be affected? Will life style change appreciably? Will geographical relocation be required? What will be the immediate, intermediate, and long-range consequences?

4. Aid the individual to develop appropriate job-seeking or education-seeking behaviors. Can the person write an effective resume? Does the individual have good skills as an

interviewee? Has he or she narrowed down to manageable proportions the education or training universe? Does the person have adequate information?

5. Assist the individual to clarify abilities, interests, and personal characteristics. Will the attributes of the person facilitate or impede the transition to a different career, occupation, or job? Are these characteristics germane to the person that would make his or her functioning dissatisfying in any job? Are there any physical, mental, or emotional problems to be considered?

6. Assist, if appropriate, to place the individual in a job. Certain settings wherein counselors work with midcareer shifters will have placement as a goal (such as the Employment Service or Outplacement Counseling). Other agencies that do not perform a brokerage role may well consider performing this function if no alternative is readily available.

7. Gauge the extent of the individual's support network. Are social support and financial support adequate to meet the demands of the career change? What buffers exist to assuage the sometimes painful effects of a significant life change? (Entine, 1984).* (p. 361)

Many of those seeking new careers will probably again seek the assistance of counselors in the Employment Security Division of the U.S. Department of Labor. The Comprehensive Employment and Training Act of 1982 is an example of federal assistance to state and local governments for the purpose of developing training programs to meet local job needs. This program has a wide range of training activities aimed at economically disadvantaged youth and adults. Other state and/or federal government programs include provisions for school-to-work transition programs, senior community service employment, job corps, and work incentive programs. State rehabilitation agencies provide career counseling and other services to those eligible.

While, ideally, much midlife career change and career retirement counseling would take place in the workplace, some obstacles still impede this development. However, career development and change programs that provide supporting counseling services are also emerging in business and industry.

Moving along the maturity continuum, the "aging of America" is another phenomenon that is increasingly challenging those responsible for providing career counseling in institutional and agency settings. As people marvel at the artistic accomplishments of Grandma Moses at 100 and Pablo Picasso at 90, George Burns's Academy Award-winning performance in *The Sunshine Boys,* or the political activities of Ronald Reagan, the oldest president of the United States, one must be aware that age is not an inevitable barrier to career accomplishments. Coupled with this is also an awareness that life expectancy is increasing at the same time that human physical well-being and vigor are steadily improving for all age groups. It can be anticipated that increasing numbers of older and healthier citizens will be capable and desirous of work.

For many older Americans, retirement will mean a search for another career. Others may seek part-time employment. Many will simply be looking for ways to remain active and in touch with people. Volunteer work and leisure-time activities may be important to this group. Counselors working with senior citizens must help them plan an appropriate distribution of their time among any work activities, leisure/recreational pursuits, and retirement living.

SUMMARY

Dramatic changes in the world of work and the increased need for career assistance among all ages has resulted in career counseling and placement receiving a new impetus in both school and agency settings in recent decades. In the past, career counseling was a recognized activity of most school counseling programs, but it received little curricular emphasis and, as a result, was less than effective in many settings. The career education movement of the 1970s, however, led schools to recognize the inseparability of career education and career counseling and guidance. Career counseling programs were also encouraged to provide increased attention to placement and follow-up as a planned program activity. This emphasis has been prompted by legislative funding and recognition that career development without placement is an incomplete process. In this area, significant developments in computerized career assistance programs have been noted.

The concern over career planning and decision making has focused attention on why people make the decisions they do and with what results. To help develop an understanding of these issues, we reviewed a number of the traditional theories in this chapter. Some investigators are challenging these theories as inappropriate for today's populations and careers.

Agencies and other noneducational institutions that in the past were primarily concerned with career placement of first-time job seekers are now recognizing the probability and importance of midlife career changes, the possibility of employment in a new field after retirement, and the elimination of many traditional barriers to the employment of women, minorities, and older adults. Additionally, attention is being focused on increased recognition of the career needs of workers with disabilities and the career concerns of dual-career couples. These and other factors have led to a renewed interest in and examination of influences on career planning and decision making of adults. Also, the unique career assistance needs of older, retiring Americans is receiving increased attention. Career counseling across the lifetime is becoming a reality.

While, as previously noted, career counseling has been a historic traditional concern and activity of counselors, the next chapter will discuss a comparatively recent development in our profession—the counselor's role as a developmental and educational consultant.

DISCUSSION QUESTIONS

1. What are the differences among career education, vocational education, and business education?

2. If we anticipate that many adults will have as many as five major career changes during their working lifetimes, what are the implications for counseling in all settings? Identify five different careers you might consider.

3. Discuss this multipotentiality of individuals and its implications for career planning and decision making.

4. What significant changes have occurred in careers and the world of work as you have observed it in recent generations? What changes may be anticipated in the remainder of this century?

5. Discuss a career in counseling as "a way of life."

6. Why have you decided to enter the career that you are in? What do you expect to give to this career? What do you anticipate that you will receive from it?

7. Discuss the impact of significant career development experiences in your life.

8. How are technological developments affecting the way we work?

9. Discuss relationships between leisure time and work time.

10. Identify and discuss the relationship between basic needs and career decisions.

CLASS ACTIVITIES

1. Have each member of the class identify the significant influences on his or her career planning and decision making. Following a discussion of these with other members (in small groups), have each individual identify the theory of career choice that seems most appropriate for his or her career development. Place individuals in groups according to the theories they have identified, and compare influencing factors among group members.

2. Draw a career map (using newsprint and felt-tip pens, with stick figures and simple drawings going from lower left to upper right) that depicts significant events and influencing factors in your career development and experiences.

3. Organize small groups to investigate career-oriented societal problems of a career nature and recommend national and/or local solutions. Problems might include concerns such as unemployment for a special population (i.e., minorities, youth, women), underemployment for a special population, substance abuse in the workplace, dual-career families and latchkey children, and school dropouts and career failures.

4. Discuss your personal experiences with career assessment instruments, and/or take a career interest or aptitude test and report your impressions of the results.

5. Interview individuals either entering the work force for the first time or approaching retirement regarding their experiences for the coming year.

6. If you had to identify an alternate career, indicate what that career might be and why.

SELECTED READINGS

Bundy, M., & Boser, J. (1987). Helping latchkey children: A group guidance approach. *School Counselor, 35,* 58–65.

Borders, L. D., & Archadel, K. A. (1987). Self-beliefs and career counseling. *Journal of Career Development, 14,* 69–79.

Brown, D. (1987). The status of Holland's theory of vocational choice. *Career Development Quarterly, 36,* 13–23.

Feller, R., & Gluckman, N. (1986). The unemployed and counselors: An analysis of responses to a complex social issue. *Counseling and Human Development, 18,* 1–11.

Gerstein, L., & Bayer, G. (1988). Employee assistance programs: A system's investigation of their use. *Journal of Counseling and Development, 66,* 294–297.

Gilbert, L. A. (Ed.). (1987) Special edition: Dual-career families in perspective. *The Counseling Psychologist, 15,* 31–45.

Herr, E. (1987). Comprehensive career guidance and vocational education: Natural allies. *Vocational Education Journal, 62,* 30–33.

Holland, J. (1987). Current status of Holland's theory of careers: Another perspective. *Career Development Quarterly, 36,* 24–30.

Johnson, R. (1985). Microcomputer-assisted career exploration. *The Vocational Guidance Quarterly, 33*(4), 296–304.

Levinson, E. (1987). Vocational assessment and programming of students with handicaps: A need for school counselor involvement. *School Counselor, 35,* 6–8.

Lopez, F., & Andrews, S. (1987). Career indecision: A family systems perspective. *Journal of Counseling and Development, 65,* 304–307.

Myers, S. L., Jr. (1986). Black unemployment and its link to crime. *Urban League Review, 10,* 98–105.

Perosa, S. L., & Perosa, L. M. (1987). Strategies for counseling midcareer changers: A conceptual framework. *Journal of Counseling and Development, 65,* 558–561.

Prediger, D. J., & Sawyer, R. L. (1986). Ten years of career development: A nationwide study of high school students. *Journal of Counseling & Development, 65,* 45–49.

Wrenn, C. G. (1988). The person in career counseling. *Career Development Quarterly, 36,* 337–342.

RESEARCH OF INTEREST

Apostal, R. A. (1985). Expressed inventoried interest agreement and type of Strong/Campbell Interest Inventory Scale. *Journal of Counseling Psychology, 32,* 634–636.

Abstract

Examines expressed inventoried interest agreement for each type of Strong-Campbell Interest Inventory scale in a sample of female college students. Three levels of agreement are established: low, statistical, and high. Findings reveal statistical and high levels of agreement across occupations, in addition to differences in agreement level across scale types.

Brown, D., Ware, W. B., & Brown, S. T. (1985). A predictive validation of the Career Decision-Making System. *Measurement and Evaluation in Counseling and Development, 18,* 81–85.

Abstract

A predictive validation study of the Career Decision-Making (CDM) System, using as criteria the stated career choices and expected postsecondary majors of high school seniors ($N = 164$), yields support for the instrument.

Cooper, S. E. (1986). The effects of group and individual vocational counseling on career indecision and personal indecisiveness. *Journal of College Student Personnel, 27,* 39–42.

Abstract

A sample of 24 students, in both group and individual vocational counseling, show decreases in career indecision and personal indecision.

Fernandez, E., Brechtel, M., & Mercer, A. (1986). Personal and simulated computer aided counseling: Perceived versus measured counseling outcomes for college students. *Journal of College Student Personnel, 27,* 224–228.

Abstract

Examines computer-aided counseling, using a simulated computer-aided model of cognitive counseling and clients' perceived outcomes. Results indicate a group that received counseling using computers view their experience as less effective than did a group counseled personally; however, no differences were found on outcome measures.

Fleenor, J. (1986). The personal career development profile: Using the 16 PF for vocational exploration. *Measurement and Evaluation in Counseling and Development, 18*, 185–189.

Abstract

Reviews the Sixteen Personality Factor Questionnaire and the Personal Career Development Profile as tools for vocational exploration and career development. Reliability and validity problems are reported, followed by a recommendation to use the Strong-Campbell Interest Inventory instead.

Haviland, M. G., & Hansen, J. C. (1987). Criterion validity of the Strong-Campbell Interest Inventory for American Indian college students. *Measurement and Evaluation in Counseling and Development, 19*, 196–201.

Abstract

Assesses criterion validity of the Strong Vocational Interest Blank–Strong-Campbell Interest Inventory for a heterogeneous sample of American Indian college students ($N = 49$). For the analysis of the concurrent validity between major and Occupational Scale score, the excellent and moderate concurrent hit rate for women in the direct relationship category is 64%; for men it is 44%.

Kinnier, R. T., Katz, E. C., & Berry, M. A. (1991). Successful resolutions to the career-versus-family conflict. *Journal of Counseling and Development, 69*, 439–444.

Abstract

Examines how resolved husbands and wives ($N = 60$ couples) are regarding career-versus-family conflict in their lives. Results indicate that high self-esteem and life satisfaction best predict being resolved about the conflict and that wives are more rationally resolved about the conflict than their husbands.

Kivlighan, D. M., Jr., & Shapiro, R. M. (1987). Holland Type as a predictor of benefit from self-help career counseling. *Journal of Counseling Psychology, 34*, 326–329.

Abstract

Uses Holland high-point code and Self-Directed search scale scores to predict the benefit from a self-help career counseling intervention for 52 students undecided about career. Participants with realistic, investigative, or conventional high-point codes show greater changes in vocational identity when compared with participants with artistic, social, or enterprising high-point codes.

Mitchell, L. K., & Krumboltz, J. D. (1987). The effects of cognitive restructuring and decision-making training on career indecision. *Journal of Counseling and Development, 66*, 171–174.

Abstract

Develops a cognitive restructuring intervention for individuals having difficulty with career decision making, which proves more effective than decision-making training and a no-treatment control condition in reducing anxiety about career decision making and encouraging vocational exploratory behavior. Cognitive-restructuring clients use skills learned more and are more satisfied with their decisions.

Prediger, D. J. (1987). Validity of the new Armed Services Vocational Aptitude Battery job cluster scores in career planning. *Career Development Quarterly, 36*, 113–125.

Abstract

Examines the validity of the Armed Services Vocational Aptitude Battery Form 14 (ASVAB-14) composites as well as the validity of new ASVAB-14 Job Cluster scales as developed by the American College Testing Program.

Shahnasarian, M., & Peterson, G. W. (1988). The effect of a prior cognitive structuring intervention with computer-assisted career guidance. *Computers in Human Behavior, 4*, 125–131.

Abstract

A 10-minute videotape demonstrating Holland's (1985) model of the world of work was utilized in an attempt at cognitive structuring. Subjects viewed the videotape prior to using the DISCOVER computer-assisted guidance system. Results demonstrate that the use of cognitive structuring and DISCOVER may prove useful in vocational counseling activities with adults.

Sherry, P., & Staley, K. (1984). Career exploration groups: An outcome study. *Journal of College Student Personnel, 25,* 155–159.

Abstract

Examines the differential impact of an experimental program in group career counseling and a control group of undergraduate students ($N = 30$) on a measure of career development. Results indicate that career exploration groups may facilitate the career development of undergraduates.

Wrenn, R. (1985). The evolution of Anne Roe. *Journal of Counseling and Development, 63,* 267–275.

Abstract

Provides an interview with and biographical sketch of Anne Roe as she describes her research efforts and views as related to occupational and counseling psychology. Focuses on her work with her husband, her experience as a woman in a male-dominated field, and her appointment at Harvard University.

Chapter 10

The Counselor as Developmental and Educational Consultant

A network television news program on February 13, 1979, carried a report that a group of big business executives were going to offer their consulting services to small businesses to aid their survival chances. These businesspeople were referred to as "consultants"—a term so common even then that the newscaster did not bother to define it. A *consultant* is usually an expert in a field who consults with or offers professional expertise to others both within and outside the profession. In fact, the activity is so common in the business world that we frequently hear humorous definitions of a consultant, such as "anyone 50 miles from home with a briefcase" or "one who pulls in, pops off, and pulls out."

Consultation as a mental health and educational activity is less well recognized and understood, although mental health consultation has a long tradition in the healing arts. The objective of this chapter is to introduce and describe the activity of consulting and the counselor's role as a consultant.

Although consultation is similar to counseling in emphasizing the importance of building and maintaining relationships, it differs in other dimensions. As Lewis, Hayes, and Lewis (1986) note:

> Although the relationship principles of consultation are similar to counseling, the context, role, and functions are different for consulting. One difference is that most consultation occurs in work-related situations. Counselors, psychologists, and members of other professions who value helping people are becoming increasingly more active as consultants to individuals, groups, and total organizations. When consulting with individuals, there is considerable similarity to counseling individuals. As in team building in system and organization consulting, respect, trust, competence, and other skills are just as important as in counseling. (p. 122)

The consultant is the helper in a triad that includes a consultee and the objective of the consultation. For example, a school counselor may serve as a consultant to parents who want to improve their children's social skills; unlike counseling, this is not a therapeutic relationship. It is also important to keep in mind that the consultant's role is an advising or enhancing one, not a supervisory one. Remember, too, that these distinctive roles are maintained throughout the consultation experience and that their identities are not blurred or distorted in any way.

Lewis and Lewis (1983) suggest:

> Consultation in the human services involves helping individuals or organizations improve their effectiveness. Usually, the process has a dual aim: assisting consultees as they deal with immediate problems and helping them enhance their long-term capabilities for problem solving. Consultation may focus either on service delivery or on organizational issues. In either instance, it is characterized by a relationship that is voluntary, professional, and essentially egalitarian. (p. 173)

Woody, Hansen, and Rossberg (1989), in noting the growth of consultation in one field of counseling psychology, comment that

> during the past 20 years the development of consultation has been the major addition to the practice of a counseling psychologist. Although psychologists continue to perform traditional activities, consultation has become an increasing part of their professional role. Consultation has long been used in other professions. It generally refers to an interaction between two professionals in which one provides expertise to the other—for example, a medical specialist giving a consultation to another physician. (p. 171)

Consultation in its application to counseling as a mental health activity in schools has been even less widely recognized and defined. Most of the attention given to consultation as a school counseling activity before the 1970s seemed to suggest that it was primarily appropriate for the elementary school only. Articles such as Abbe's (1961) "Consultation to a School Guidance Program, Crocker's (1964) "Depth Consultation with Parents," Eckerson and Smith's (1962) "Elementary School Guidance: The Consultant," and Faust's (1967) "The Counselor as a Consultant to Teachers" dealt with consultation in elementary school guidance programs. Some of the popular basic guidance texts of the 1950s and 1960s—such as Jones's (1963) *Principles of Guidance,* Hutson's (1958) *The Guidance Function in Education,* Crow and Crow's (1960) *An Introduction to Guidance,* Ohlsen's (1955) *Guidance: An Introduction,* and Froehlich's (1958) *Guidance Services in Schools*— made no mention of consultation as a school counseling activity.

In discussing consultation in his early landmark publication *The Counselor-Consultant in the Elementary School,* Faust (1967) notes:

> Although counseling has been described and researched for many years, this is not true of consultation. The latter has been practiced for as many years as counseling, if not longer, but the literature is strangely sparse in its treatment of this role. (p. 32)

Although these early discussions focused on consultation in community agencies, industrial settings, and the elementary school, in the past decade consultation as an appropriate counselor activity in any setting, including secondary schools and higher education institutions, has developed rapidly. For example, two consecutive special issues of the American Counseling Association's (then called the American Personnel and Guidance Association) journal, the *Personnel and Guidance Journal* (February and March 1978; Kurpius & Robinson, 1978; Kurpius, 1978) and the special issue of *The Counseling Psychologist* (Volume 13[3], July 1985; Brown & Kurpius, 1985) consider the counselor's role and function as a consultant at all educational levels as well as in community and other mental health settings. An increasing number of textbooks also deal with the topic. The Association for Counselor Education and Supervision published two monographs in 1988 (Kurpius & Brown, 1988; Brown, Kurpius, & Morris, 1988) focusing on consultation, and then, in 1993, the American Counseling Association (formerly named the American Association for Counseling and Development) again devoted two special issues of its journal, *Journal of Counseling and Development* (July-August [Kurpius & Fuqua, 1993a] and November–December [Kurpius & Fuqua, 1993c]) to consultation. Let us, therefore, proceed to examine some of the roles and models for consultation.

MODELS FOR CONSULTATION

The increase in popularity and demand for consultation services has resulted in the development or identification of a variety of models or styles appropriate to the consultation process. Although differences exist among authorities in the area of consultation in terms of the organization or categorization of theories or systems for providing consultation services, similarities are far more prevalent than differences.

The traditional historic model that highlights the basic consultation process is a triadic model, as suggested by Tharp and Wetzel (1969). In this model, consultation services are offered indirectly through an intermediary to a target client or clients. The model illustrated in Figure 10–1 is described as a consultative triad, in which all effects proceed to the target via the mediator, none directly from consultant to target. This analysis describes functional positions, not the people who occupy those positions. For example, any number of individuals in any number of social roles might serve as mediator: "father, teacher, sister, minister, mother, employer, friend, and psychotherapist. Indeed, the same is true of the functions of either consultant or target" (Parker, 1975, p. 137).

Four popular consultation models, as identified by Kurpius (1978), suggest the counselor-consultant can function effectively by providing a direct service to a client identified by another party, prescribing a solution to a specific problem identified by a consultee, assisting others in developing a plan for problem solution, and taking direct responsibility for defining a problem and proposing a solution. Kurpius (1978; Kurpius & Fuqua, 1993b) organizes these functions into four consulting modalities as follows:

Provision Mode

The provision mode of consultation is commonly used when a potential consultee finds himself confronted with a problem for which he or she may not have the time, interest, or competence to define objectively, to identify possible solutions, or to implement and evaluate the problem-solving strategy. Consequently, a consultant is requested to provide a direct service to the client, with little or no intervention by the consultee after the referral is accepted.

Prescriptive Mode

Sometimes consultees experience unusual work-related problems for which they request special help. Even though competent and motivated to solve the problem directly, the consultees may lack confidence in their own intervention strategy or may lack certain specific knowledge and skills for carrying out a given problem-solving plan.

In these situations, the consultee is often in need of a resource person (consultant) to support the diagnosis and treatment plan already developed by the consultee or to explore additional alternatives for defining and solving a specific problem.

There are other times, however, when a consultee is looking for an exact "prescription" to ameliorate a specific problem. While the prescriptive mode is quite appropriate for many situations, there are four questions that should be answered jointly by the consultant and consultee: (a) Has all the information needed to define and solve the problem been shared and is [it] accurate? (b) Has the plan prescribed by the consultant been accepted by the consultee and will it be implemented as designed? (c) Who will evaluate the "process" and "outcomes" associated with the prescriptive plan—the consultant, the consultee, or both? (d) Will adjustments in the prescription, if needed, be requested by the consultee?

FIGURE 10–1 The Consultative Triad
Source: From R. G. Tharp and R. Wetzel, *Behavioral Modification in the Natural Environment* (1969), p. 47. Copyright © 1969. Used with permission of Academic Press and Ralph J. Wetzel.

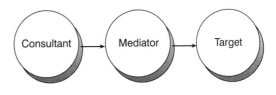

Collaboration Mode

When following the collaboration mode the consultant's goal is to facilitate the consultee's self-direction and innate capacity to solve problems. As a result, the consultant serves more as a generalist than a technical expert. His major efforts are directed toward helping people develop a plan for solving problems. Hence he acts as a catalyst and "reality tapper," helping consultees to share observations, concepts, and proven practices. He also helps consultees examine forces that are facilitative or debilitative in both the immediate and larger environments.

Mediation Mode

Mediation is uniquely different from the other three modes of consultation in which the consultee initiates the contact and requests help for solving a problem. In mediation, it is the consultant who recognizes a persisting problem, gathers, analyzes, and synthesizes existing information, defines the problem, decides on the most appropriate intervention, and then calls together the persons who have direct contact with the problem and have the greatest potential to influence a desired change. (Kurpius, 1978, p. 335)

Schein (1978, 1991) organizes the consultation process into three models. The assumptions of these models are as follows:

Model I: Purchase of Expertise

The core characteristic of this model is that the client has made up his or her mind on what the problem is, what kinds of help are needed, and to whom to go for this help. The client expects expert help and expects to pay for it, but not to get involved in the process of consultation itself.

In order for this model to work successfully, the following assumptions have to be met, however.

1. That the client has made a correct diagnosis of his or her own problem.
2. That the client has correctly identified the consultant's capabilities to solve the problem.
3. That the client has correctly communicated the problem.
4. That the client has thought through and accepted the potential consequences of the help that will be received.

In summary, this model of consultation is appropriate when clients have diagnosed their needs correctly, have correctly identified consultant capabilities, have done a good job of communicating what problem they are actually trying to solve, and have thought through the consequences of the help they have sought. As can be seen, this model is "client intensive," in that it puts a tremendous load on the client to do things correctly if the problem is to be solved. If problems are complex and difficult to diagnose, it is highly likely that this model will not prove helpful.

Model 2: Doctor-Patient

The core of this model is that the client experiences some symptoms that something is wrong but does not have a clue as to how to go about figuring out what is wrong or how to fix it. The diagnostic process itself is delegated completely to the consultant along with the obligation to come up with a remedy. The client becomes dependent upon the consultant until such time as the consultant makes a prescription, unless the consultant engages the client in becoming more active on his or her own behalf. Several implicit assumptions are the key to whether or not the doctor-patient model will in fact provide help to the client.

1. That the client has correctly interpreted the symptoms and the sick "area."

2. That the client can trust the diagnostic information that is provided by the consultant.

3. That the "sick" person or group will reveal the correct information necessary to arrive at a diagnosis and cure, i.e., will trust the doctor enough to "level" with him or her.

4. That the client has thought through the consequences, i.e., is willing to accept and implement whatever prescription is given.

5. That the patient/client will be able to remain healthy after the doctor/consultant leaves.

In summary, the doctor-patient model of consultation highlights the dependence of the client on the consultant both for diagnosis and prescription and thus puts a great burden on the client to correctly identify sick areas, accurately communicate symptoms, and think through the consequences of being given a prescription.

Model 3: Process Consultation
The core of this model is the assumption that for many kinds of problems that clients face, the only way to locate a workable solution, one that the client will accept and implement, is to involve the client in the diagnosis of the problem and the generating of that solution. The focus shifts from the content of the problem to the process by which problems are solved, and the consultant offers "process expertise" in how to help and how to solve problems, not expertise on the particular content of the client's problem. The consultant does not take the problem onto his or her own shoulders in this model. The "monkey always remains on the client's back," but the consultant offers to become jointly involved with the client in figuring out what is the problem, why it is a problem, why it is a problem right now, and what might be done about it. This consulting model is not a panacea appropriate to all problems and all situations. It also rests on some specific assumptions that have to be met if the model is to be viewed as the appropriate way to work with a client.

1. That the nature of the problem is such that the client not only needs help in making an initial diagnosis but would benefit from participation in the process of making that diagnosis.

2. That the client has constructive intent and some problem-solving ability.

3. That the client is ultimately the only one who knows what form of solution or intervention will work in his or her own situation.

4. That if the client selects and implements his or her own solution, the client's problem-solving skills for future problems will increase.

How does the consultant implement the process consultation model? The basic principle is to get into the client's world and see it initially from the client's perspective. This usually means paying attention to the "task process—and how the problem is defined, how the agenda is set, how information is gathered, how decisions are made, all the activities that make up the "problem-solving process."* (Schein, 1978, pp. 340–342)

It has become a principle in education and psychology that it is far better in the long run to teach others to be effective problem solvers than it is merely to solve a given problem for them. Thus, the more effective organizational consultants will leave the organization with a model that has been learned and can be independently implemented. (Fuqua & Kurpius, 1993, p. 607)

---

*Reprinted from E. H. Schein, "The Role of the Consultant: Content Expert or Process Facilitator?" *Personnel and Guidance Journal, 56,* 1978. © American Counseling Association. Reprinted with permission. No further reproduction authorized without written permission of the American Counseling Association.

Fuqua and Kurpius (1993) then go on to discuss five conceptual models and conclude by presenting them in a table (see Table 10–1).

Blocher (1987) identifies seven models of consultation as follow:

1. *Triadic consultation*—three distinct roles characterize this model. They are the consultant who provides the expertise, the mediator who applies what he or she receives from the consultant and the client who is the object or recipient of the service.

2. *Technical consultation*—a more narrow and focused intervention in which a consultant's expertise is sought in relation to a specific situation or problem.

3. *Collaborative consultation*—suggests a cooperative relationship in which information and resources are pooled and the consultant and consultee work together as equal partners in the process.

4. *Facilitative consultation*—the consultant facilitates the consultee's access to a variety of new resources. In this model both parties recognize the consultant's legitimate interest in the broad aspects of the functioning of the consultee system.

5. *Mental health consultation*—the consultant assists a consultee (therapist) to gain a better understanding of one's interaction with a client through such means as analyzing the treatment approach, consideration of their (consultee's) responses to their client and in general, providing support to the consultee.

6. *Behavioral consultation*—focused on the use of behavioral management techniques as suggested or taught by the consultant to a consultee in order to influence or shape the behavior of the consultee's clients in a systematic way.

7. *Process consultation*—the consultant delivers services to an organization in order to increase the effectiveness of a work group in reaching its goals. This consultation addresses the interactions among groups of individuals who work with each other in face-to-face relationships. (pp. 264–270)

Regardless of one's choice of consultation models, Gallessich (1982) suggests certain common characteristics that apply to most consultation:

1. Consultants are professionals who are experts in specialized bodies of knowledge. Many are also experts in the process of helping peers (other professionals) solve problems.

2. Consultants work with consultees, staff members of human service organizations, to help them with their work-related concerns. Consultants do not focus on consultees' personal concerns except as they relate directly to the work situation.

3. Consultation is an indirect service. In working with an agency's staff, consultants serve a third party, the agency's clients, indirectly. Exceptions may occur, however; for example, a consulting clinician may, at times, directly examine the consultees' clients. Further client contact ordinarily moves the consultant into direct services and outside the consultant role.

4. Consultants are outsiders. The consultation relationship is a temporary one. Consultants come from external bases, such as private practice or agendas that are independent of the consultee. Sometimes, however, consultants belong to the same agency as their consultees; in these situations, the consultant role is significantly modified by the consultant's membership in the agency's authority structure and social life.

5. The consultation relationship is between peers whose areas of responsibility and expertise differ. The relationship is voluntary for both parties, and each maintains control over her or his involvement. When the agency and the consultant agree to a contract, the consul-

TABLE 10–1 Integrating Conceptual Models

Conceptual Model	Operating Frames			
	Reactive	**Responsive**	**Proactive**	**High Performing**
Systems Theory	Where is the breakdown? What subsystem is causing the problem?	Who's responsible for what?	How do we refine our system for the long term?	How does a system achieve flexibility?
Organizational Culture	Who is causing us pain and why?	How do we resolve conflict?	How is our culture affecting us?	How do we manage our culture for improving the quality of life?
Strategic Planning	How do we alleviate the pain in the short term?	What needs to work better? How do we correct it?	How do we develop a plan for moving forward?	How does strategic planning become part of our system?
Organizational Change Cycles	How did we "bottom out" developmentally?	How do we cope with these circumstances?	How do we get to the developmental phase?	How do we monitor and influence normal developmental cycles?
Paradigm Shift Thinking	How can we relieve stress without changing our thinking?	What thoughts need to be adjusted?	Is our thinking congruent with our purposes?	How can we continually update our knowledge and our thinking in a changing world?

Source: Reprinted from D. R. Fuqua & D. K. Kurpius, "Conceptual Models in Organizational Consultation," *Journal of Counseling and Development, 71,* 1993, p. 617. © American Counseling Association. Reprinted with permission. No further reproduction authorized without written permission of the American Counseling Association.

tant is authorized to enter the consultee's work domain; barring a binding contractual provision, the consultee may withdraw this permission at any time. Similarly, the consultant may elect to terminate the relationship. Consultees determine the concerns to be discussed. Both consultant and consultee may introduce ideas or questions they perceive to be important and screen out irrelevant or inappropriate topics. To illustrate, a consultee might decline to discuss certain work topics even though the consultant perceived them to be related to the focal problem; or a consultant might decline to discuss a consultee's family problems. A consultant might also choose either to introduce or to withhold theories, research findings, or principles pertinent to the problem under discussion.

6. The consultee retains responsibility and authority for any action and is free to accept or reject the consultant's advice. However, two assumptions underlying the relationship are that consultees (1) will seriously consider the input of the consultant and (2) have the power to mobilize resources to effect improvements in their work situation.* (pp. 11–12)

THE CONSULTATION PROCESS

The counselor functioning as a consultant recognizes certain basic assumptions:

1. The existing need cannot be satisfactorily met by the primary helper (parent, teacher, etc.).

2. The consultant (in this instance, the counselor) possesses the special knowledge or expertise to be able to assist the consultee in dealing more effectively with the need.

3. The consultee is willing and able to implement the consultant's suggestions.

4. The counselor-consultant is aware of the organization involved and its potential influences.

Woody et al. (1989), after reviewing several writers, consolidated their conceptualizations of the consultation process into five stages as follows: "(1) pre-entry, (2) initial contact and establishment of a relationship, (3) assessment and diagnosis, (4) intervention, and (5) termination" (p. 179).

Even though the process of consultation is initiated by the consultee in need of assistance, the consultant must keep in mind that consultation is not primarily therapeutic in nature. In other words, those seeking consultative assistance do not usually come to the counselor-consultant for personal counseling; rather, they come for assistance with a usually well-defined professional problem.

GOALS OF CONSULTATION

Turner (1982) discusses a hierarchy of consulting goals that, though focusing on business and industrial settings, have some relevancy for counselors functioning as consultants in many settings. These are presented in Figure 10–2.

*Reprinted with permission of Jossey-Bass from *The Profession and Practice of Consultation: A Handbook for Consultants, Trainers of Consultants, and Consumers of Consultation Services* by J. Gallessich (San Francisco: Jossey-Bass, 1982). All rights reserved.

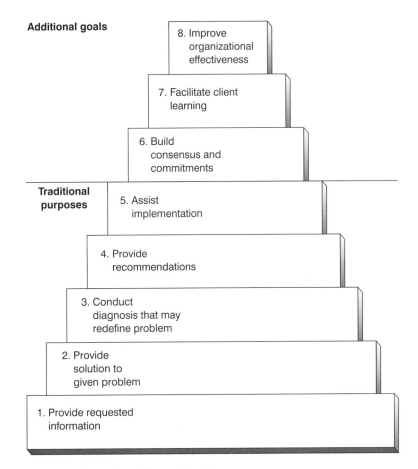

Additional goals

8. Improve organizational effectiveness

7. Facilitate client learning

6. Build consensus and commitments

Traditional purposes

5. Assist implementation

4. Provide recommendations

3. Conduct diagnosis that may redefine problem

2. Provide solution to given problem

1. Provide requested information

FIGURE 10–2   A Hierarchy of Consulting Purposes
Source: Reprinted by permission of *Harvard Business Review.* An exhibit from "Consulting Is More Than Giving Advice" by Arthur N. Turner, September–October 1982, p. 122. Copyright © 1982 by the President and Fellows of Harvard College; all rights reserved.

SKILLS FOR CONSULTATION

As with all counseling and guidance activities, certain special skills are needed if the counselor is to function effectively as a consultant in either school or agency settings. According to Zins and Curtis (1984):

> Consultation is a complex process that requires in-depth examination and practice in order to achieve significant skill development. Perhaps many of the confusions about the process would not be so commonplace if more practitioners and trainers themselves had received formalized training.
>
> It is also important that the person who provides consultative services have a strong background in some content area (e.g., behavioral interventions, learning disabilities, interpersonal relations). It is not always enough to be a good facilitator in order to be an effective consultant.

In addition to being well trained in consultative theory and techniques, a potential consultant must have an understanding of systems theory and change strategies. Certain organizational factors may enhance or impede efforts to develop consultative services. The fact is that not all consultee organizations are equally receptive or willing to change. (p. 221)

Of course, the counselor who is functioning in a consultation role should possess and employ those skills essential in the counseling process. Certainly communication and other interpersonal skills such as attending, listening, questioning, and feedback are critical. Respect and understanding should be exhibited. Also, consultants should possess expertise in systematic problem-solving techniques and evaluation procedures.

CONSULTATION ROLES

According to Lewis and Lewis (1983):

The human service professional, especially when he or she has moved into an administrative role, finds that consultation with others becomes a major area of involvement. In human service settings, the consultant is most likely to provide assistance through internal consultation, within his or her own work setting; through networking, or collaboration with helpers in other settings; and through community organization, or enhancement of the problem-solving capacities of community groups. (p. 184)

Kurpius and Lewis (1988) state that consultants focus on multiple roles of collaborators, mediators, facilitators, and liaisons. They also suggest that consultants are in an excellent position to act as advocates, especially when advocacy may be hidden from or ignored by those closest to the problem. Earlier, Kurpius (1985) had also discussed the consultant's functioning as a human resource developer, organizational culture builder, strategic planner, job designer and enricher, survey researcher, and manager by objectives.

CONSULTATION IN SCHOOL SETTINGS

In school settings, counselors who function in a consulting role are in effect giving their special expertise to teachers, school administrators, and other appropriate personnel. In this role, they become a resource professional for the developmental or adjustment needs involving third parties, usually students. For the counselor to function effectively as a consultant in the educational setting, he or she must possess, as noted earlier in this chapter, special knowledge or skills appropriate to the consulting need. Among the relevant skills the counselor can bring to consulting with teachers and other educational providers and planners are the following:

1. An understanding of human growth and development, the problems and processes of adjustment, and the needs of the individual as one goes through those processes.
2. An understanding of psychological or affective education in the classroom, and a concern for its importance.

3. An understanding of and skills in promoting communications and other desirable human relationship skills.

4. Training in the assessment of individual characteristics and skills in relating these assessments to the development of the individuals' potential.

5. Special knowledge of educational and career development and opportunities.

6. An ability to communicate, counsel, and consult with parents, fellow educators, and the community.

7. An understanding of group processes and skills useful in facilitating group motivation and change. (p. 51)

In addition, to function effectively as a consultant, the counselor must have a background of understanding of the person or group with whom he or she is consulting, the target population for the consulting, and the characteristics of the school in which the consulting is taking place. The counselor-consultant should also be knowledgeable regarding contributing external environmental factors.

As a consultant, the school counselor has the potential to engage in a wide range of activities or roles, which we will look at next.

Consulting with Teachers

As mentioned previously, the teacher is the key person in school settings at any level. In consultation in schools, then, the counselor must assume that he or she will most frequently consult with teachers individually or in groups. This probability is further highlighted by the facts that teachers have the most frequent contacts with pupils and that the developmental and adjustment needs of their pupils are often expressed in classroom groups. Counselors may effectively assist teachers as consultants to individualize classroom instruction.

School counselors are also experienced in collecting, organizing, and synthesizing data on individual students and in interpreting this information to identify individual differences. Through these activities, they sharpen their own understanding of the individual and share these insights in consultation with the classroom teacher.

Additionally, the counselor's expertise in human behavior and development theory combined with the teacher's knowledge of instructional methods and materials is the basis for an excellent team effort in the crucial task of planning and establishing a productive learning environment.

The classroom teacher is obviously the most knowledgeable about resources appropriate to his or her subject matter, but the counselor can nonetheless be profitably consulted on those occasions when specialized career and educational information is needed to make a class more meaningful. He or she can also be consulted to identify out-of-school resources and experiences relevant to students' learning needs. The counselor's insights can be helpful in the development of materials and methodologies that will enable counselors and teachers to work together in special educational activities with vocational students.

Further, the effects of Public Law 94-142, requiring all children categorized as disabled to be placed in regular educational programs to the fullest extent possible, has resulted in a wider diversity in the characteristics and abilities of classroom groups. Too, the counselor has an important role to function as a guidance curriculum consultant. Schmidt (1993) suggests that

> guidance is the responsibility of everyone and is best implemented when it is integrated as an essential part of the school curriculum. Guidance does not occur at a single moment or as a solitary event with a teacher saying "Students put your books away; it is time for guidance!" Rather, it is infused with all subjects, and in all daily instruction. For this infusion to happen successfully, teachers and counselors plan appropriate activities for classroom instruction.
>
> In elementary and middle schools where teachers team by grade levels or subject areas to plan instructional programs, counselors consult with these groups to share guidance objectives and offer suggestions of activities to use in classroom instruction. In high schools, counselors meet with departments to achieve a similar purpose. This process of planning together allows teachers to use counselors as resources while maintaining their leadership role in the instructional program. These consultations also allow counselors and teachers to share information about particular students who are struggling and in need of additional services beyond classroom guidance. (p. 85)

Counselors will continue to play a significant consultant role in assisting teachers specifically and the educational system generally in implementing this act.

Again, a basic principle of effective consultation is that the recipients must believe that they need it. Teachers and others will neither seek out nor be receptive to the counselor as a consultant if they see no value or rationale for such assistance. In each situation, therefore, the counselor must communicate and demonstrate his or her role as an effective consultant.

The Counselor as a Consultant to the School Administrator

The school counselor can also make significant consultation contributions to the educational leadership of the school and the school system. The counselor has the capacity to gather data descriptive of the characteristics of the student population and their needs, which, in turn, can provide useful information for educational planning and management. The counselor's understanding of the process and characteristics of human growth and development enables him or her to relate and provide special counsel regarding the special needs of individuals and groups of pupils.

The counselor can also provide valuable consulting experience to the school administrator on the school climate or environment. A mentally healthy school environment facilitates not only learning but also positive social interactions and good citizenship. Since this aspect of school life seems often overlooked (or ignored, as accountability models stress standardized measured academic achievements), counselors may have to become advocates for a healthy school environment with their school administrators. In this capacity, counselors may help administrators understand the counselor's role in planning and implementing schoolwide programs that have a good impact on the school's psychological environment. Finally, the counselor does not overlook the morale needs of his or her colleagues—the teachers. Stress management workshops, working to establish better and more open communications between teachers and administrators, and "jelly bean" days (i.e., special compliment-giving times) are all helpful ways counselors can, through consultation, assist school administrators and the school environment.

TABLE 10–2 Steps of Parental Consultation and Counselor Functions

Step	Functions
Establishing a working relationship	Structure Active listening
Define concern	Mutual agreement Identify causal factors
Define goal	Mutual agreement Realistic expectations
Intervention	Explore alternatives Plan of action Role-play
Continued support	Evaluate effectiveness Modifications Monitor progress

Source: Reprinted from M. H. Ritchie (1982), "Parental Consultation: Practical Considerations," *School Counselor, 29,* p. 405. © American Counseling Association. Reprinted with permission. No further reproduction authorized without written permission of the American Counseling Association.

Consulting with Parents

The counselor can effectively consult with parents on various occasions to promote understanding of pupil characteristics and their relationships to pupil behavior. Consultation can assist parents in coping with or modifying student behaviors, improving interpersonal relationship skills, and adjusting attitudes. Parents may also consult with the school counselor in regard to their children's academic planning, progress, or problems. High school parents will frequently consult with school counselors about their child's career-planning needs. The counselor may also serve as a consultant to interpret school programs to parents and in the mainstreaming of students with disabilities.

Most parents expect and want to be informed by the school regarding their child's needs and accomplishments. The school's public relations program in general and its counseling program in particular will be enhanced by an active program of consultation with parents. Ritchie (1982) outlines a step-by-step process as presented in Table 10–2.

The Counselor as a Curriculum Consultant

As noted when discussing the counselor's consulting role with the classroom teacher, the counselor can play an important role in curriculum consultation. Additionally, federal legislation specifies the counselor's importance in implementing programs of career education and education of children with disabilities. In an instructional sense, the school counselor is not, of course, a curriculum specialist. However, when the curriculum is viewed as the sum of educational experiences the school proposes to provide, it follows that the counselor, because of his or her professional commitment to each student's total development, should be actively involved, regardless of legislative mandates, in curriculum planning.

As a consultant in matters related to the career interests and concerns of students, a counselor may conduct comprehensive assessments of student career interests to provide a basis for expanded and relevant curriculum offerings. Nor should the important area of avocational interests be overlooked. A combination of educational and avocational opportunities often serves to maintain student interest and motivation. The counselor should assume major responsibility to identify and interpret these interests and concerns to all educators involved. Assessment of student interest must be translated into action, however, and it is at that point that many opportunities for curriculum development are left to flounder in the sea of academic indifference.

School counselors and curriculum planners have a joint responsibility to see that these important aspects of the student's total development are not left to chance. In this regard, it should be noted that curricular consultation frequently points out the need for curricular change. Because the school counselor's responsibilities involve him or her with both teachers and administrators, the counselor is in a position to facilitate their cooperation and interaction in promoting curricular change. Such change usually involves the prerequisites of (a) identification of the need for change, (b) a willingness on the part of those involved to consider change, and (c) the development and acceptance of a plan for change.

CONSULTATION IN COMMUNITY MENTAL HEALTH SETTINGS

Consultation has emerged, since the 1970s, as a well-established activity and specialty in mental health agencies. The general purpose

> of the consultation mandate in community mental health is for professionals to provide "indirect" services that will expand mental health personpower. In general, consultation efforts are directed to schools, clergy, criminal justice settings, industry, and other human service agencies. . . . The classic typology of so-called mental health consultation was offered by one of its founders, Gerald Caplan (1963, 1970). He divides consultation activities in community agencies into four major categories: (1) client-centered case consultation, in which the focus is on helping the consultee deal with a particular case or client; (2) program-centered administrative consultation, in which the major aim is to help the consultee in administering a treatment or prevention program; (3) consultee-centered case consultation, in which the primary goal is to help the consultees with problems in working with clients in general; and (4) consultee-centered administrative consultation, in which the goal of the consultant is to aid the consultee or consultee agency in planning, implementing, and maintaining mental health programs. (Jeger & Slotnick, 1982, p. 141)

Bloom (1984) believes, "Mental health consultation is the major form of indirect service associated with the community mental health movement" (p. 155). He distinguishes consultation

> from other mental health activities with which it is sometimes confused and with which it has some overlapping characteristics. Consultation can be distinguished from supervision on the grounds that (1) the consultant may not be of the same professional specialty as the consultee, (2) the consultant has no administrative responsibility for the work of the consultee. Consultation can be distinguished from education on the basis of (1) the relative freedom of the consul-

tee to accept or reject the consultant's ideas, (2) the lack of a planned curriculum, and (3) the absence of any evaluation or assessment of the consultee's progress by the consultant. Consultation also needs to be differentiated from psychotherapy. In psychotherapy, there is a clear contractual relationship between an individual designated as a patient and another individual designated as a therapist. In this relationship, the patient acknowledges the existence of personal problems and allows the invasion of his or her privacy in order to resolve these problems. No such contractual relationship exists between consultant and consultee. The goal of consultation is improved work performance rather than improved personal adjustment. The consultant and consultee are in a peer relationship, and each expects his or her privacy to be honored. Consultation should, finally, be distinguished from collaboration. Consultation carries no implication that the consultant will participate with the consultee in the implementation of any plans. The task of the consultant is to assist the consultee in meeting his or her work responsibilities more effectively. (p. 156)

Bloom (1984) also notes:

To assist community mental health centers in evaluating their consultation programs, Mannino and MacLennan (1978) reviewed how consultation services were monitored and evaluated in nearly 80 settings. They found that information being collected could be grouped into three categories: (1) information on the community being served, such as assessment of needs, survey of available resources, or characteristics of the population, (2) characteristics of the consultation program, such as target groups, frequency of contacts, financing, program descriptions, progress reports or use of staff, and (3) outcome data, such as measures of consultee satisfaction, subjective judgments by consultants, or goal attainment measures. (p. 177)

Bloom (1984) concludes:

The usefulness of consultation as a community mental health technique is being increasingly supported. Consultation has enormous appeal among mental health professionals, and substantial time is currently allocated to the activity by mental health professionals working in community health centers.* (pp. 186–187)

Blocher (1987) draws attention to the suggestion that

[l]ike other forms of consultation, mental health consultation is not seen as the taking over of a case by a more highly trained or specialized professional. The primary purpose of such consultation is to help the consultee or therapist to understand better his or her own interaction with the client. The consultant helps the consultee analyze the approach to treatment, consider his or her own responses to the client, and also provides a supporting relationship to the consultee in coping with stress and tension. The nature of the consultant/consultee interaction in mental health consultation is heavily dependent on the theoretical orientation of the consultant. (p. 268)

In discussing community-based interventions, Werner and Tyler (1993) project that

community mental health centers can play a large role in helping communities solve their social problems by working to create an interdependent service delivery system through consultation and education. Jemerin and Philips (1988) note that this coordination effort is essential for the success of our interventions with children. Furthermore, it is recommended that this coordination emanate from a single, central location, which can ensure both vertical integration, moving the child into the least restrictive therapeutic environment, as well as horizontal integration, allowing the breadth of services the child is entitled to.

In the role of community consultant, the community mental health center can have a broader impact on the community structure than would be possible through direct services alone. (p. 690)

Contracts between consultants and consultees have become increasingly popular in recent years. Such agreements can benefit both the consultant and the consultee. Remley (1993) notes:

Consultants enter into legal contracts each time they agree to a consultation arrangement outside of their regular work setting. They need to understand the legal context of contracts within which they perform their services and recognize the benefits a written agreement provides. Counselors often provide consultation services as a regular part of their job responsibilities. In such situations, a separate legal contract is not formed when a consultation relationship is created. A written understanding of the consultation arrangement, however, can be beneficial to the consultant and consultee even though a legal contract does not exist. (p. 157)

SUMMARY

In almost any Sunday issue of a major metropolitan newspaper, such as the *New York Times* or the *Chicago Tribune,* the classified business section advertises either to employ consultants or utilize their consulting services. Usually, these consulting services focus on planning and strategies, economic and technical reviews, marketing assistance, material development, and evaluations. Certainly the business and industrial world has used consulting services for generations.

Consultation has also been a recognized mental health activity for a number of years, although not nearly as well publicized as its business counterpart. There are consulting firms that specialize in educational matters, and consultation contracts are also becoming increasingly popular.

However, consultation as an activity of counselors has led to an examination of various models appropriate to the consultation process and their adaptation to counselor use. Kurpius (1978)

describes these as four modalities of provision, prescription, collaboration, and remediation. Schein (1978) organizes the process into three models: purchase of expertise, doctor-patient, and process consultation. Werner (1978) describes six possible agency models as client-centered case consultation, consultee-centered case consultation, program-centered administration consultation, consultee-centered administrative consultation, community-centered ad hoc consultation, and consultee-centered ad hoc consultation.

Regardless of model choice, counselor-consultants must recognize that they are involved in a process that provides structure and direction for their consultation efforts. It is naive to think that knowledge or experience in itself qualifies one to consult. An understanding of the process of consultation and the acquisition of the skills for consultation are prerequisites to success as a consultant. These are usually acquired through special courses in consultation.

The qualified counselor will have opportunities to consult. It is important to keep in mind, however, that consultation must be wanted—

must be requested—if it is to take place. Even when requested, the counselor-consultant should proceed with tact and understanding. After all, no one likes to be told off, even by experts!

Counselors have utilized consultation more and more to enhance the delivery of their services. The 1990s will see yet another trend increasingly emphasized in our profession. Prevention and wellness have caught the public's fancy, and serious efforts to prevent many of the disorders that have handicapped individuals and society are under way. The helping professions are responding, and the next chapter discusses how the counseling profession is doing just that.

DISCUSSION QUESTIONS

1. In your opinion how is the title "consultant" generally viewed by the public?

2. Discuss any experience that you, your family, or a close friend has had involving a consultant. What were the circumstances leading to the use of the consultant? What were his or her special skills or knowledge? How had he or she acquired these special skills or knowledge? Describe the consultation process.

3. Describe circumstances in which you as a practitioner-counselor might call on the services of a consultant. Describe the setting of your envisioned employment and how you might utilize consultation assistance.

4. What is the consultation expertise that a counselor can offer to

   a. schools,

   b. business or industry, and

   c. other settings.

5. Give examples in which each of the following models of consultation might be used:

   a. Purchase of expertise

   b. Doctor-patient

   c. Process consultation

6. Envision and discuss situations in which you might be employed as a consultant.

CLASS ACTIVITIES

1. Organize the class into small groups of three or four people, then discuss the following situation. Assume that you are the newly hired counseling staff of North Rogerian High School. Your predecessors were terminated because, in the words of the school principal, "they were too much into therapy—spent all their time in one-to-one!" You have been advised to avoid even a hint of this image in your first year on the job. The director of pupil services for the school system has suggested the consultation approach for this coming year. Discuss and outline a consultation approach for this 3-year high school of 57 teachers and 1,400 students in an affluent midwestern setting. What would be your rationale, and how would you describe your model in a presentation to the school's faculty meeting? To the school's parents' association? Compare and discuss the differing approaches among the small groups.

2. Organize the class into three groups (one group per each of three topics). Groups are to develop a rationale for one of the following topics:

   a. A major role for consultation in community mental health agencies

   b. Consultation on the college campus

   c. A private practice mental health consulting firm

3. Organize into groups of three or four. Assess the strengths of your group from the perspective of a consultation team. Report to the class the special consultation expertise (counseling or noncounseling) of your group.

4. Identify several consultants or consulting firms in your community and invite them to participate on a class panel discussing their qualifications, role, and function as consultants.

SELECTED READINGS

Aplin, J. (1985). Business realities and organizational consultation. *The Counseling Psychologist, 13*, 396–402.

Fuqua, D., & Newman, J. (1985). Individual consultation. *The Counseling Psychologist, 13*, 390–395.

Goodman, R., & Sonaas, D. (1984). Elementary school family counseling: A pilot project. *Journal of Counseling and Development, 63*, 255.

Heller, K. (1985). Consultation to community groups: Some useful discussions between social regulators and indigenous citizen groups. *The Counseling Psychologist, 13*, 403–409.

Kurpius, D., & Brown, D. (Eds.). (1985). Consultation [Special issue]. *The Counseling Psychologist, 13*, 333–476.

Martin, R. (1983). Consultant, consultee, and client explanations of each other's behavior in consultation. *School Psychology Review, 12*, 35–41.

Schmidt, J. J., & Medl, W. A. (1983). Six magic steps of consulting. *The School Counselor, 30*, 212–216.

Turner, A. (1982). Consulting is more than advice giving. *Harvard Business Review, 60*, 120–129.

Ulmansky, D. L., & Holloway, E. L. (1984). The counselor as consultant: From model to practice. *School Counselor, 31*, 329–338.

RESEARCH OF INTEREST

Chusmir, L. H. (1990). Men who make nontraditional career choices. *Journal of Counseling and Development, 68*, 11–16.

Abstract

Reviews the professional literature as well as framework for understanding of the men's nontraditional career choice process. Implications for professional counselors and organizations are discussed.

Gresham, F. M., & Kendell, G. K. (1987). School consultation research: Methodological critique and future research. *School Psychology Review, 16*, 306–316.

Abstract

Reviews the current status of school consultation research and critiques the research methodologies used in consultation research. Major theoretical models in which consultation research has been conducted are briefly described. Consultation research is reviewed in three primary areas of investigation: (a) outcome research, (b) process research, and (c) practitioner utilization research.

Horton, G. E., & Brown, E. (1990). The importance of interpersonal skills in consultee-centered consultation: A review. *Journal of Counseling and Development, 68*, 423–426.

Abstract

Literature review that examines empirical research pertaining to the significance of interpersonal communication skills in the consultation process. Studies point to consultants' facilitative characteristics and use of appropriate verbal and nonverbal skills as important. Implications for research, counselor education, and practitioners are discussed.

Petipas, A., Danish, S., McKelvain, R., & Murphy, S. (1992). A career assistance program for elite athletes. *Journal of Counseling and Development, 70*, 383–386.

Abstract

Describes a career assistance program for athletes (CAPA) to assist Olympic athletes ($n = 142$) in making the transition out of active sports participation. An outline and evaluation of the program is presented, with implications for counselors.

Pryzwansky, W. B. (1986). Indirect service delivery: Considerations for future research in consultation. *School Psychology Review, 15,* 479–488.

Abstract

This article considers trends in recent consultation research from the standpoint of themes or emphases that are emerging rather than from a methodological perspective. The effect of those patterns is considered on future research and practice. Some directions for enhancing the database of consultation are presented for trainers and practitioners.

Chapter 11

Prevention and Wellness

Although the old saying "An ounce of prevention is worth a pound of cure" would seem to be particularly appropriate to the health professions, the fact is that until recently, these professions, including the mental health professions, have given little more than lip service to prevention. However, recent generations have witnessed the pursuit of wellness by millions of Americans with near revolutionary zeal. At times, our whole country seems to be waking up to "jazzercise," washing down vitamin pills with instant "stay trim" break-fasts, practicing relaxation techniques on the job, jogging after work, attending stress management workshops, following the Pritikin diet, and so forth. These signs of the times point to our growing concern with the prevention of health disorders, including mental health. It represents, if not a shift in emphases, a sharing of emphasis between remediation and prevention. The objectives of this chapter are, therefore, to (a) present the role of prevention in counseling programs and (b) introduce prevention through stress management, attention to nutrition, and the wise use of recreation and leisure time.

PREVENTION

In the field of mental health, a substantial increase in reported prevention activities, research, and professional literature appropriate for counselors is evident. These include a broad range of studies reported in publications such as *Preventive Psychology* (Felner, Jason, Moritsugu, & Farber, 1983); special issues of *The Personnel and Guidance Journal* (Barclay, 1984a, 1984b), now entitled *The Journal for Counseling and Development*, focusing on primary prevention in schools, on college campuses, and in the community; and more recently, special issues of *The Journal of Counseling and Development* (November/December 1992), focusing on "wellness throughout the lifespan," and the *Journal of Mental Health Counseling* (Robinson & Roth, 1992) special issue on women and health.

The model of prevention adopted by counselors and other mental health workers is in large part the model of prevention adopted by psychology, which in turn was borrowed from the field of public health. Prevention may be viewed as an effort that seeks to avoid the occurrence of something undesirable. Within this definition, three levels of prevention are identified as primary, secondary and tertiary. "*Primary prevention* refers to intentional programs that target groups of currently unaffected people for purposes of helping them to continue functioning in healthy ways, free from disturbance" (Conyne, 1987, p. 6).

Secondary prevention efforts are characterized by attempts at early identification and intervention with individuals who are displaying initial signs of disorder but for whom it is not yet ingrained (Felner et al., 1983).

Tertiary prevention closely parallels traditional approaches. The focus is on the individual who has an established disorder, and the goals are to reduce the residual effects of it and rehabilitate the individual to a level where he or she may readjust to community life (Felner et al., 1983).

Recognizing that prevention is the effort to avoid the undesirable, we would recognize that the priority prevention activities of societies have been on (a) prevention of that which threatens life and/or healthy living—hence immunizations against killing or disabling diseases, treaties to avoid war, diets and exercise, and so forth, to promote our health; and (b) prevention of that which threatens our security—hence insurance against financial loss, contracts for job security, concern about law enforcement to prevent crime, and so forth.

In these instances, individuals do not want to spend time in the "best" hospital or the "best" jail or have the "best" artificial tooth. Prevention is clearly preferred in instances such as these when the alternative is clearly recognized as undesirable; hence, we work at it and are willing to pay for it. Thus, prevention programs are in demand when life or security is threatened. These demands are further underlined when large numbers are victims or potential victims of the threat. Such current social problems as substance abuse, people abuse, AIDS, crime and delinquency, teen pregnancies, and school dropouts clearly meet the criteria of affecting or threatening large numbers. The helping professions, especially counseling, must respond with programs of primary prevention.

Schmolling, Youkeles, and Burger (1989) give four reasons why an emphasis on primary prevention is critical:

1. There has never been a major disease or disorder eliminated through treatment alone.
2. There are not enough human services personnel to treat or rehabilitate all those in need.
3. Society pays a high financial cost for disorders that are not prevented.
4. Emotional and behavioral disorders exact an enormous human cost in terms of personal pain and suffering. (pp. 238–239)

Of course, conditions must be met for programs to be effective. Cowen (1982) suggests three conditions for an effective prevention program:

1. It must be group- or mass-, rather than individually oriented (even though some of its activities may involve individual contacts).
2. It must have a before-the-fact quality, i.e., be targeted to groups not yet experiencing significant maladjustment (even though they may, because of their life situations or recent experiences, be at risk for such outcomes).
3. It must be intentional, i.e., rest on a solid knowledge-base suggesting that the program holds potential for either improving psychological health or preventing maladaptation. (p. 444)

In planning for prevention, some obvious needs may exist. Preventive programs in substance abuse are popular in schools. Premarital counseling is commonplace. Also, many counseling agencies have programs to help married couples avoid some of the anticipated problems and adjustments of marriage. In general, however, prevention has not reached the level of sophistication or popularity attained by remediation.

In the area of physical health, prevention has always been recognized by the public and the medical professions as the most valued approach. Millions of dollars have been spent on the development of vaccines and other preventive measures. In the field of mental health, however, the public (and often the profession itself) has, until recently, appeared to give a higher priority to remediation and treatment. For example, the public seems to consistently support the building of bigger and better jails, substance abuse treatment programs, and rape crisis centers, and at the same time, in many locales, it has opposed such preventive efforts by schools as sex education and values clarification techniques.

Despite the obstacles that must be overcome, counselors and other mental health professionals are being urged, even mandated by legislation in some instances, to broaden the scope of their prevention activities in order to identify and thus intervene with even larger populations at risk. This approach recognizes the importance of significant settings and experiences that influence individual adjustment and development. The home, school, workplace, church, and community are obviously relatively stable settings over periods of time that have a significant impact on large numbers of people. It is in these settings that prevention programs should flourish.

Of course, prevention planning must be based on some systematic approach for identifying the needs of specific client populations. This involves the study of

1. factors associated with adjustments,

2. characteristics of particularly susceptible people,

3. interrelationships between 1 and 2 above,

4. examination of how people adapt in a given environment, and

5. identification of significant events in the environment that signify success or growth outcomes.

Prevention program development should follow certain principles. Drum (1984) suggests the following as key principles:

1. Prevention programs should be designed to go beyond informing to transforming. Too often, prevention efforts rely largely on didactic presentations that fail to enable the individual to translate the information into a strategy for change. We "must transform general information into personal information for decision making" (Schinke, Gilchrist, & Small, 1979, p. 84).

2. Design of such programs must take into account the psyche of the consumer—his or her motivation, sense of urgency, feeling of susceptibility, and so forth. Interventions built on misappraisal of the target group's readiness for and investment in change are likely to fail.

3. Preventive programs must be goal-focused in order to give coherence to the effort. Program design must accurately reflect the sequence in which information, activities, exercises, and media should be employed to help achieve the purpose of the intervention. Much like structured groups, the preparation time required to design an intervention far exceeds the time required to execute it successfully. Successful active prevention programs are probably four-fifths preparation and one-fifth implementation.

4. The problem to be addressed must be preventable. Not all problems can be anticipated prior to their being experienced.

5. The intervention must be appropriately timed. Bloom (1981) suggested that "a preventive program . . . should occur before the problem is manifested . . . but not so long before as to diffuse the effort." (p. 25) Timing the intervention to occur as close as possible to the individual's awareness of the need for change will likely ensure better results. An aversive conditioning program for teenagers enrolled in a driver education course may have more impact on changing driving habits than the same program offered several years earlier or later.

6. The intervention must be targeted to people who are susceptible (at risk) to the problem being addressed. If the consumer fully believes himself or herself to be immune to the

problem, most efforts to inform, raise consciousness, and create change will be counter-productive. For example, a workshop on the art of building friendships may have more impact and be better attended by freshmen students eight weeks into the semester than during summer orientation, when they are perhaps still hoping that fortuitous circumstances will provide new relationships.

7. Once a person believes that preventive action is desirable, the intervention offered must be able to reinforce a sense of hope and movement toward the desired outcome. Far too many prevention efforts are better at raising desire for change than they are at fostering lasting change, and thus they frustrate and discourage participants even further. Many of the ills addressed by preventive programs are not solvable in any final sense, and progress is measured by positive movement or approach to complete resolution. Awakening the person to a potential or emerging problem should be followed quickly by tactics that foster risk reduction and movement toward problem solution.

8. Many prevention programs must go beyond intrapsychic solutions to include removal of environmental hazards or barriers. Person-environment interaction models are important in the construction of high-impact interventions. Problems are seldom exclusively a function of the individual or of the environment.

9. The environment in which the program is offered must be conducive to the changes being sought. In the campus environment, special attention needs to be paid to the social structure of the groups in which the intervention is being conducted. In particular, existing relationships among potential participants must be considered carefully in planning the program format (exercises, activities, self-disclosure, etc.).

10. Materials, information, exercises, problem-solving strategies, and decision-making components of a program need to be paced according to the participant's motivation, coping skills, tolerance for disclosure, ability to absorb and personalize information, and other key process variables. If guidelines involving careful planning and timing have been observed, the pace of events in the change strategy should be less problematic. The pace of the material should not preclude the participant's being able to identify with it or with the presenter.

11. Change involves resistance and ambivalence, which, if not carefully attended to, will frustrate and stall change efforts. Careful planning decreases the likelihood that participants will be unnecessarily resistant. It is necessary to relate decision-making and problem-solving processes to the strategies used; one-shot, short intervention efforts are likely to be ineffective in creating or maintaining change, as resistance often runs deep.

12. A well-designed preventive effort reflects a delicate balance between the challenges such programs pose to participants and the supports each participant has at his or her disposal to cope with the challenges presented. Preventive programs encourage people to adopt more functional behaviors and to eliminate maladaptive coping styles. In the process, participants often face having to let go of current semi-functional mechanisms (supports) in order to incorporate what should prove, in the long run, more effective ways of being. Therefore, it is important to avoid overwhelming participants with challenges that outstrip their supportive resources for incorporating the desired change.

13. The change technique or tactic should be well-suited to the setting (location, number of participants, demographics) of the program. Techniques such as consultation, peer or paraprofessional networks, environmental assessment, counterconditioning, and cognitive restructuring are just a few of the many options available to the design of preventive programs for instigating change. Some techniques are ideally matched to certain types of

problems and participants. For example, in a program with 300 participants, use of positive reinforcement as a change technique may prove more difficult than the use of aversive conditioning techniques.

14. Regardless of how well-planned a prevention intervention may be, it is still necessary to have legitimate access to those to be served. Points of access are often created after someone in an at-risk group has developed a problem that causes others to become aware of their own susceptibility to or complicity in the problem. For example, shortly after someone in a sorority, fraternity, or campus residence hall attempts suicide, others closely involved usually welcome the opportunity to talk as a group with a counselor or crisis intervenor about a variety of issues. What should they have done before this happened? What can be done now? Why would anyone try to kill themselves? And so on. Prior to the crisis, these same students would have had little interest in the subject. It is ironic that "postventions" are often more productive than work performed before the crisis existed. Avenues of legitimate contact with the target group often involve use of nonprofessionals in the development of interventions, especially where those in the target group perceive susceptibility to be lower than it is in reality. Use of multiple avenues of access, such as programs, brochures, peers, student affairs professionals, workshops, and media is also important.

15. Evaluation design should allow feedback about the impact of the intervention (outcome), processes used, and leadership style. Each of these three types of feedback is a necessary ingredient for refinement of future efforts.* (pp. 511–512)

Prevention programs are unusually complex since they must be designed to deal with multiple factors. Some disorders are associated with many risk factors, and some risk factors are also selected with many disorders. Additionally, some risk factors appear to vary in their impact at different stages of the individual's development. Too, certain disorders may result from a specific chain of events.

In prevention, individuals' transactions with their environments may provide critical clues for successful programs. The consensus of experts seems to suggest that environmental assessment using the field survey method is the most reliable technique, and Public Law 88-169 has mandated needs assessments for community mental health centers. In examining environments and their impacts on populations, special attention should be given to (a) high-impact environments such as the home, school, and workplace; (b) how normal developmental tasks are facilitated or impeded by the environment; (c) "what is important?"—significant life events in the environment; and (d) the quality of everyday life for the inhabitants of the environment. An environmental needs assessment also gives counselors the opportunity to assess the readiness of a population for a given type or types of prevention programs.

As an obvious and crucial starting point, the elementary school can play a significant role in any community or school system's preventive efforts, and evidence indicates that schools are responding to this challenge. A study by Gibson (1989) indicates that prevention was a major emphasis of elementary school counseling and guidance programs in 85% of the 114 elementary programs surveyed. The primary objectives of these programs are noted in Table 11–1.

*Reprinted from D. J. Drum (1984), "Implementing Theme Focused Prevention: Challenge of the 1980's," *Personnel and Guidance Journal, 62.* © American Counseling Association. Reprinted with permission. No further reproduction authorized without written permission of the American Counseling Association.

TABLE 11–1 Prevention Objectives of Elementary School Counseling and Guidance Programs

Prevention Objectives	Percentage
1. To prevent child and/or sexual abuse	69.7
2. To prevent substance abuse	64.9
3. To promote self-concept development	35.8
4. To promote personal safety	17.6
5. To promote social-skills development	15.0
6. To prevent teenage pregnancy	6.3
7. To prevent premature school leaving	4.4
8. To prevent school vandalism	2.1

Source: From R. L. Gibson (1989), "Prevention and the Elementary School Counselor," *Journal of Elementary School Guidance and Counseling, 24,* p. 34. © 1989 by the American Counseling Association. Reprinted by permission. No further reproduction authorized without written permission of the American Counseling Association.

Among the popular activities used in elementary school prevention programs were group counseling for self-concept improvement, a guidance curriculum for the classroom to develop interpersonal and social relationship skills and avoid personal conflicts, and facilitation of problem solving and decision making. Self-concept development was also facilitated through consultation and training with parents. Attendance was improved and dropouts prevented through tutoring, career guidance, and group guidance activities. Substance abuse prevention was initiated through a wide range of activities including "Just Say No" clubs, peer intervention, behavioral self-management groups, drug education, and use of local celebrities as advisors. Many schools have successfully initiated comprehensive safety programs for the prevention of sexual abuse and child abuse and the promotion of personal safety using drama, games, films, and classroom guidance programs.

A variety of studies have reported successful prevention programs in schools.

A number of these (Cobb & Richards, 1983; Myrick & Dixon, 1985; Myrick, Merbell, & Swanson, 1986) reported programs for the prevention of maladaptive social behavior, which resulted in improved attitudes and behaviors as the result of classroom guidance activities, including small-group sessions. Chandler, Weissberg, Cowen, and Guarez (1984) reported positive results for fourth-grade children who had been seen 2–5 years earlier in a prevention intervention program for children who were experiencing school adjustment problems. Bleck and Bleck (1982) reported that third-grade pupils who participated in a series of group counseling sessions for 5 weeks showed significant improvement in both self-concept scores and the disrespect defiance factor, when compared to the control group. Anderson and Lemoncelli (1982) used assessment data as a basis for identifying pupils when behavior would place them at risk and then designed strategies for behavior improvement. Results indicated success of these programs. (Gibson, 1989, pp. 30–31)

Early intervention with low-achieving elementary school students was effective in preventing their continued underachievement in studies reported by Jackson, Cleveland, and Merander (1975) and Esters and Levant (1983). The former study provided the experimental group with 2.5 years of counseling and consultation directed primarily at parents and teachers. This study found differences in favor of the counseled students over those in the control group. The Esters and Levant study used parent training for parents and self-esteem groups for students (Gibson, 1989, p. 31).

Wirth-Bond, Coyne, and Adams (1991) describe a successful dropout prevention study in which high-risk students stayed in school because they had a significant other adult in the school setting who understood them well and supported them, and a high availability of counselors.

Schmolling et al. (1989) note a study by Lodish (1985) of a program to prevent smoking among adolescents:

> Twelve hundred fifth- and sixth-grade students from six different public schools were divided into three groups. One group received skills training and instruction on attitude change. The second group only received instruction on attitude change, and the third group was the control group. (A control group is one that receives no service or training so that it can be compared with the groups that had service or training). The skills training group were taught adolescent basic life skills aimed at helping the students resist peer and social pressures to smoke. Some of the skills taught were self-praise and assertiveness, problem solving, and decision making. This group also received the same information given to the students in the attitude modification group. The information included data on smoking and its effects on health and costs to society. The control group were only pretested and post-tested regarding smoking. Results indicated that the students in the first group, those who received both skills training and information, showed a stronger determination not to smoke than the students in the other two groups. (p. 242)

Prevention programs are usually complex, since they must be designed to deal with multiple factors. As an example, Table 11–2 represents a comprehensive primary prevention model for a campus alcohol education project on the University of Cincinnati campus.

Gelso and Fretz (1992) report some evaluative studies of selected prevention programs. Sprinthall (1990) notes

> the evidence for both primary prevention and developmental interventions has been remarkable. Baker, Swisher, Nadenichak, and Popowicz (1984) reviewed a large number of empirical evaluations of prevention strategies and, using meta-analytic techniques to combine the results of these studies, concluded that the treatment effect size was larger for such interventions than that found in meta-analytic analyses of the results of psychotherapy. In addition to such research on primary prevention strategies, there are now an ever increasing number of studies of all sorts of outreach endeavors which continue to yield significant results for their target populations. For two very different examples, consider the work of Taylor and colleagues (1986) showing that social support groups for persons suffering from cancer led to significantly decreased depression and the work of Burnette, Williams, and Law (1987) suggesting that, for Vietnam veterans who participated in discussion groups, self-management effectiveness increased and expression of anger scores decreased. (p. 506)

Shaw (1986) also suggests that prevention activities in schools could be divided into two categories: direct and indirect. Direct services are those provided to children by counselors, psychologists, or teachers. Indirect services are those provided to adults by counselors or psychologists with the anticipation that improved adult functioning will result in improved child functioning. Table 11–3 is an outline of some of the types of direct and indirect services that might be included in a primary prevention program in schools. A program of primary prevention in a school will require active planning and participation by behavioral specialists, instead of the passive role taken by many.

TABLE 11–2 The University of Cincinnati Alcohol Education Project Design for Primary Prevention

Primary Prevention Level	Primary Prevention Scope					
	Extensive			Intensive		
	Method	Target	Strategy	Method	Target	Strategy
	Research findings	University community	Newspapers, campus, and city	Research findings	Student gov't. student orgs., Faculty Senate, campus admin., Board of Trustees	Presentation and discussion
Environmental	New alcohol policy	(Cell A)	Campus media; distribution	New alcohol policy	Student gov't. student orgs., Faculty Senate, campus admin., Board of Trustees (Cell C)	Presentation, discussion, and acceptance
	Multilevel mass media education campaign	University student population (Cell B)	Multisession education	Selected fraternities	Ongoing structured group experience aimed at normative change	
Personal	Students helping students	University student population (Cell B)	Establish local "BACCHUS" chapter	One-session education	Requesting groups (Cell D)	Short workshop aimed at knowledge and certain skills

Source: From R. K. Conyne (1984), "Primary Prevention Through a Campus Alcohol Education Project," *Personnel and Guidance Journal, 62,* 526. © 1984 by the American Counseling Association. Reprinted by permission. No further reproduction authorized without written permission of the American Counseling Association.

TABLE 11–3 Examples of Different Types of Primary Preventive Activities

Direct	Indirect	
Children	Teachers	Parents
Interpersonal skills	Classroom management	Behavior management skills
Communication skills	Communication skills	Communication skills
Relaxation training	Behavior conferencing	Child-rearing skills
Study skills	Parent conferencing skills	Support/information
Racism/sexism/ageism training	Curriculum development skills	Support/information
Career/life-style development		

Source: From M. C. Shaw (1986), "The Prevention of Learning and Interpersonal Problems," *Journal of Counseling and Development, 64,* p. 626. © 1986 by the American Counseling Association. Reprinted by permission. No further reproduction authorized without written permission of the American Counseling Association.

STRESS MANAGEMENT

The U.S. work force has become aware that millions of its members are "going up in smoke," that their effectiveness is handicapped by the psychological symptom labeled "burnout." Although we must assume that many workers across all careers have felt that their job is getting them down, the pressures are getting to them, the boss is driving them to drink, and so forth, it was not until the 1970s that a popular label, *burnout,* was commonly used to describe various psychological conditions associated with stress and adjustment needs. In fact, today, we recognize that the term *burnout* can refer to one or a combination of factors that psychologists say contribute to a person's inability to cope with the expectancies and demands of everyday living. Counselors in all settings must be prepared to prevent or intervene with clients threatened by or actually under stress.

Matheny, Aycock, Pugh, Curlette, and Cannella (1986) suggest

> that high stress levels, if chronically sustained, may contribute significantly to a lowering of one's energy levels, ineffective cognitive processes, performance failures, ruptures in interpersonal relationships, flattened affect, a weakened immune system, and degenerative diseases of various kinds. Quite understandably a phenomenon with such pervasive effects on human functioning holds great interest for health service providers. Stress coping is of particular concern to counseling psychology with its emphases on such matters as the person-environment fit, personal growth and wellness. (p. 500)

Synonymous with the labeling of the disorder was the increasing awareness at management and supervisory levels that employee health is as important as other job-related concerns to the effectiveness of the organization and a further recognition that employee illness can be psychological as well as physical. As a result, one of the large-scale preventive efforts of the 1980s was the "stress management" movement. Not unexpectedly, counselors have been increasingly called on to develop prevention and early intervention programs in stress prevention and management. Counselors involved in these efforts have been quick to recognize the value of such prevention efforts because of the dangerously cumulative phenomenon of psychosocial stress.

Although the causes for burnout or stress may vary significantly from person to person, counselors need to be cognizant of the more common factors, such as the following:

- ❖ Too many demanding, frustrating, or otherwise stressful situations
- ❖ Constant pressure to do more than can be done
- ❖ Too much time-consuming but not rewarding work (i.e., paperwork)
- ❖ Constant conflicts between competing alternatives for time and effort (i.e., home and work)
- ❖ Persistent demands for skills or knowledge that appear beyond that possessed by the individual
- ❖ Constant interference or interruptions of planned or anticipated activities
- ❖ Lack of positive feedback, recognition, reward, or notice of efforts or accomplishments
- ❖ Lack of clarity or direction regarding work expectancies
- ❖ Depressing work environment
- ❖ Poor interpersonal relationships
- ❖ Constant disillusions or disappointments
- ❖ All work and no play, failure to lead a "balanced" lifestyle

Counselors may also recognize that candidates for burnout may be identified by the level, stage, or degree of burnout. For example, Veninga and Spradley (1981) identify five stages of job burnout:

Stage 1: The Honeymoon: A period of enthusiasm and job satisfaction that nevertheless begins to use up valuable energy reserves

Stage 2: Fuel Shortage: Job dissatisfaction and inefficiency; fatigue coupled with sleep disturbances; escape activities such as smoking, drinking, drugs, shopping sprees

Stage 3: Chronic Symptoms: Chronic exhaustion, physical illness; acute anger and depression

Stage 4: Crisis: Deep pessimism and self-doubt; obsession with problems; physical illness grows from discomfort to incapacity; development of an escape mentality: the "flight response"

Stage 5: Hitting the Wall: Career, and life, are endangered

Another view of this sequence to burnout is presented here:

1	2	3	4	5
Environmental demands are challenging	→ Demands are more than can be handled	→ Physical and psychological alarm	→ Frantic attempts to cope, resist, or ignore	→ Burnout

---

- Emotional problems are responsible for 20–30% of absenteeism

- Personal factors cause 80–90% of industrial accidents

- Of a large workforce 25–30% have serious needs for professional mental health services

- Of people who are fired 65–80% are terminated due to personal rather than technical factors

- Substance abuse (drugs and alcohol) is an increasing problem

- Sick leave and low productivity are major costs to American industry

- Troubled employees cost a company 25% of their total annual salaries

- Of the population over 13 years of age 7% are "at risk" for alcoholism

- Four persons are affected by each problem drinker

- In the oil-rich Permian Basin of West Texas (Midland-Odessa) 15.5 thousand persons are potential problem drinkers and 62 thousand persons could benefit from counseling services (Texas Commission on Alcoholism estimates); 21.3 million dollars was lost during 1976 in business due to alcoholics

- The annual drain in the nation's economy attributed to problem drinking may be as high as 42 billion dollars

---

FIGURE 11–1 Stress-Related Problems in Business and Industry
Source: General data secured from Weiner, Akabas, and Sommer (1973). Alcohol abuse statistics are from the Texas Commission on Alcoholism included in the Permian Basin Regional Planning Commission (1980) Report. Cited in S. Southern and C. Hannaford (1981), "Health Counseling: An Emergent Specialization," *Counselor Education and Supervision, 20,* p. 258. © 1981 by the American Counseling Association. Reprinted by permission. No further reproduction authorized without written permission of the American Counseling Association.

Counselors working in business and industrial settings should be aware of the extent and impact of stress in these settings. Southern and Hannaford (1981) identify stress-related problems in business and industry as indicated in Figure 11–1.

A study by Tableman, Marceniak, Johnson, and Rodgers (1982) describes a pilot program of stress management training involving women on public assistance who were generally isolated and subjected to more than average stress in their lives.

> None of the women were in crisis, nor did they display maladaptive behaviors that required treatment. The women took part in ten sessions during which they learned skills and methods of reducing stress that helped them change their perceptions of their situations. The program resulted in significant change in the lives of the participants. They were no longer isolated and were able to function more effectively with stress, thus preventing the kinds of behavioral disorders discussed earlier. The program has been further tested and used with different populations living under stressful conditions. (Schmolling et al., 1989, pp. 242–243)

Fong and Amatea (1992) discuss stress and the single, professional woman. They report that studies of the work stress of women have conceptualized stress as stemming from multiple role issues, ignoring other potential stressors and the fact that many women are single. This study of 141 academic women explored levels of stress, career satisfaction, career commitment, personal resources, and coping strategies among four role groups: single, single-parent, married, and married-parent women. Although all groups of women had high levels of career commitment, career satisfaction, and personal resources, the single women had significantly higher ($p = .01$) levels of stress symptoms than did the married-parent women. A near significant association ($p = .07$) was found between typical coping strategy and role group, with single women using passive coping strategies more often. (p. 20)

In working for stress prevention or reduction, initially the counselor and client need to identify the stressors in the client's situation, their relative significance, whether they can be dealt with or not, and possible preventive or coping strategies. Among the general strategies that may be helpful to clients (and even yourself on occasion) are the following:

1. Bring burnout into the open—talk about it, especially with others sharing the same situation and concerns.

2. Build a support system with a small group of colleagues (including at least one optimist); help others in stress; be positive; be mutually supportive.

3. Practice time management; organize your time and stick with it. This includes planning for and protecting of your free time on and off the job.

4. Develop leisure-time pursuits or hobbies.

5. Get away from it all, especially when you feel the pressure beginning to build. Take real vacations regularly.

6. Shape up, both physically and psychologically; feel good about yourself!

The last point, shaping up, brings us to an important concept in prevention—the belief that psychological prevention is enhanced by one's physical well-being. This emerging area of interest to counselors is briefly examined in the next section.

WELLNESS

Nowhere has the craze for wellness and prevention manifested itself more than in the growth in popularity of health foods and healthy eating plans, exercise books, fitness equipment, and clubs. The United States is jogging its way through the 1990s, munching alfalfa sprouts, and drinking mineral water. The concern of the individual for his or her well-being cannot and should not be ignored by today's counselor. Counselors must be aware of the relationship between individual experiences and individual health, both mental and physical. Counselors need to be aware of the psychological consequences of illness and accidents.

A special issue of *The Journal of Counseling and Development* (Myers, Emmerling, & Leafgren, 1992) focused on the theme of "Wellness Throughout the Life Span." In this issue, one of the editors, Myers (1992) indicates that

Remley (1991) noted that the counseling profession has rejected the medical-illness-oriented model as the basis for our services. In defining what differentiates us as a separate and distinct mental health profession, he stated, "We do not believe that people must first be diagnosed with an illness before they can be treated with counseling services. Instead, we believe that all people can benefit from counseling. . . . Fully functioning people who experience everyday stress in their lives and those who are seriously mentally ill can benefit from a counseling philosophy that offers hope for a better tomorrow." The philosophy described by Remley is grounded in a developmental approach that focuses on prevention and wellness. (p. 138)

Counselors in community, school, business, and industrial settings are being increasingly involved in programs promoting lifestyle change for healthy living. These efforts have focused on health concerns such as smoking, alcohol and drug abuse, eating disorders, and sexually transmitted diseases.

Nor should this concern be limited to our clients. As fully functioning counselors, we must also be concerned with our own physical well-being. The advantages of a holistic health program for both clients and counselors include the following:

1. It teaches clients a total sense of personal responsibility.
2. Its effects are immediate and create a better sense of well-being.
3. Wellness rather than the absence of symptoms is the main goal of therapy.
4. All modalities of healing are used.
5. The client's inner capacity for change has a distinct and clear direction to better health and well-being.
6. Clients can continue patterns that are healthy and significantly decrease problem reoccurrence.
7. Self-discipline is learned and appreciated.
8. Disease prevention is enhanced for clients.
9. Counselors can benefit from all these aspects and be a significant model for clients. (Martin & Martin, 1982, p. 22)

A popular phrase is that "you are what you eat." Now, scientific inquiry seems to be further emphasizing this point as research has increasingly highlighted the relationships between nutrition and behavior, between our emotions and our diet. While counselors are not expected to be experts in nutrition, dieting, and exercise, they should be aware of basic factors and their possible linkage with the client's mental health.

Witmer and Sweeney (1992) identify a landmark study

that showed the significant relationship between health habits, health, and life expectancy [and] was conducted with approximately 7,000 adults in Alameda County, California (Belloc, 1973; Belloc & Breslow, 1972). Seven factors were found to be significantly related to health and life expectancy:

1. three meals a day at regular times and no snacking
2. breakfast every day
3. moderate exercise two or three times a week
4. adequate sleep (7 or 8 hours a night)

5. no smoking

6. moderate weight

7. no alcohol or only in moderation (p. 143)

Omizo, Omizo, and D'Andrea (1992) report a program promoting wellness among elementary school children. The results of the study

> seem to support the use of classroom guidance activities in promoting wellness among elementary school children. Children who participated in the guidance activities had significantly higher levels of self-esteem and knowledge of wellness information than did children who did not participate in the guidance activities. Although the anxiety measure did not reach a level of significance, children in the experimental group had lower levels of stress subsequent to the treatment. The class allowed the children to participate in the activities that focused on prevention as opposed to remediation. They had opportunities to share, receive and give feedback, receive guidance and information, and apply what they had learned. The teacher was an excellent role model and practiced good health habits. She also incorporated the material into other areas of the curricula. (p. 197)

Nelson (1992), a choice-awareness counseling theorist, suggests that there are three levels of counseling: spa, learning, and relearning.

> A place may be made in nearly every counseling session for *spa:* uplifting, positive experiences in which the focus is placed directly on helping clients feel good about themselves. With many clients, a few minutes at the end of each interview may be saved for these positive experiences; with some clients the entire effort of an individual session may be that of spa. The simplest of the several examples of spa in counseling offered in Nelson's article is the activity "Things I Can Do," in which the counselor helps the client focus on and savor some of the most often-repeated actions of which he or she is capable: breathe, walk, talk, eat, sleep, think, and so on. All counseling clients can benefit from the emerging sense of wellness that can come from spa in counseling. (p. 214)

Ponzo (1992) encourages counselors to become more active in promoting successful aging. He stresses that

> prime-time living is possible to the end. People need to know and believe this. So imbued, and given the skills to translate vision into reality, we should find larger numbers of people dying at the prime of their life. Consequently, there will be reductions in health care costs and increases in the productivity of elderly persons. Accomplishing this, the huge waves of people soon to be old need not be seen as a potentially destructive force, but as a dynamically productive opportunity for society. These people can view their elder years as a time for continued growth and fulfillment. Counselors can play a key role in helping people better prepare for living out a long and vital life. As many have said, "If I knew I was going to live this long, I would have prepared better." Regardless of how good the preparation, it will not restore Woody Allen's desired immortality, but it will assure mortal beings of more prime-time living. Promoting successful aging is a lifetime process. The time to start is now. (p. 213)

Appropriate exercise, a good diet, and a stress-free lifestyle are recognized important considerations in any program of client wellness. Perhaps not so well recognized is the importance of wise and enjoyable leisure and recreational activities in prevention and wellness.

RECREATION AND LEISURE

If you could spend three days doing whatever you wished, how would you choose to spend your time? What do you plan to do with your vacation time this year? Chances are, your answers to these questions indicate what recreational and leisure-time activities are important to you. We may also be reminded of how important this time is to us and that recreation and leisure are important activities in U.S. society. We need but pause to consider the amount of time, money, and effort we expend in these pursuits to recognize their significance in our lives. Furthermore, as the work week continues to shrink, more and more people will find that they have additional time on their hands, time that can be expended in meaningless ways or in ways that bring pleasure, relaxation, and improved well-being for the individual except in cases where they opt for a second job. The interrelationships between a "career" and a "way of life" cannot ignore the role of recreation and leisure in the latter. Counselors concerned with the total well-being of their clients must therefore become more sensitive to the role and potential of leisure-time activities for enhancing their clients' quality of life and meeting their unmet or partially fulfilled needs.

Tinsley, Hinson, Tinsley, and Holt (1993) report an earlier (Tinsley & Tinsley, 1986, 1988) proposed theory of leisure that

> focuses on the individual's subjective experience. They viewed leisure experiences as characterized by both cognitive (i.e., concentration on the ongoing experience, forgetting of self, and decreased awareness of time) and affective (i.e., feelings of freedom, enriched perception of objects and events, and increased intensity of emotions and sensitivity to bodily sensations) attributes. Leisure can vary in intensity, but four conditions are necessary for this experience to occur. The individual must perceive the activity as (a) freely chosen, (b) intrinsically satisfying, (c) optimally arousing, and (d) requiring a sense of commitment. Leisure experiences are thought to occur in all aspects of life, including work, but they are most likely to occur during leisure activity because of the importance of the perception of freedom of choice. (p. 447)

At this point, it may be helpful to distinguish between "free time" and "leisure time." We might define free time as unencumbered time that the individual can use or not use in any way he or she may decide. Leisure time is that time spent in the pursuit of specific activities anticipated to be enjoyable. While some "free" or unencumbered time is desirable, large amounts of free time can result in boredom, frustration, anger, low self-esteem, anxiety, and stress. Enjoyable leisure time, however, has a number of potential benefits such as stimulation and motivation (which often carries over into work), feelings of rejuvenation (also important to work), relaxation and stress reduction, personal growth, opportunities for exploration, and the development of new horizons.

Bloland and Edwards (1981) suggest that two themes, need deprivation and compensatory leisure, provide a useful theoretical foundation for integrating career and leisure counseling. They present this four-step model:

Step 1. Identify client needs   WHY?
    a. Survey client's past and current interests and activities
    b. Clarify client values
    c. Determine potential need-satisfying interest and activities.

Step 2. Identify activities to meet needs   WHAT?
   a. Ascertain needs fulfilled and not fulfilled by activities and
       interests already experienced
   b. Determine needs likely to be fulfilled by activities and interests
       not yet experienced
   c. Clarify client assets and limitations.

Step 3. Differentiate work and leisure activities   WHICH?
   a. List interest and activities to be investigated for need-satisfying
       potential
   b. Conduct field research on selected activities
   c. Divide activities into work and leisure

Step 4. Facilitate client's participation in selected activities   WHERE?
   a. Assist client to find places and ways in which to engage in chosen
       activities, some in work and others in leisure. (p. 105)

A rationale for leisure counseling may be based on the following list:

1. The amount of time available for leisure pursuits for many individuals is increasing.

2. The interactions between an individual's work experiences and his or her leisure and recreational experiences clearly impact his or her mental health.

3. Self-fulfillment includes the development of all the individual's potentials, including those that might be labeled avocational or recreational.

4. Therefore, planning for the wise and fulfilling use of leisure time is essential if the individual is to use his or her time in rewarding, enriching, and stress-reducing ways.

5. Leisure counseling can facilitate this planning by assisting individuals in identifying possible options consistent with their lifestyles and interests, making appropriate choices, and, when needed, securing the necessary education.

We have become increasingly aware of the lack of recreational facilities and positive leisure-time activities for large segments of our youth population today, especially among the poor, inner-city, and rural youth. We are also aware that the resulting time on their hands frequently leads to youth gangs, substance abuse, delinquency, and crime. Perhaps school counselors should develop programs to assist youth in exploring and developing avocational interests as well as vocational interests.

Much of the adult population also needs assistance in expanding their leisure-time activities beyond visiting relatives and watching television. Growth groups focusing on the discovery of meaningful recreational pursuits can be helpful. Special-interest groups in which individuals can explore and learn more about specific leisure activities (e.g., travel, ballroom dancing, square dancing, eating out, bowling, playing tennis, swimming, etc.) can arouse interests, as can "play" fairs.

As counselors we are seeking to assist our clients in improving their quality of life—to live life to the fullest—to optimize their human potential. In this context, then, the professional counselor is sensitive to the potential contributions that leisure counseling may make to their clientele in achieving these outcomes.

In concluding this brief examination of leisure counseling, we would suggest that the demands for counseling in this area will increase rapidly in the years ahead. We also believe that continued research into the role of leisure and its relationship to work will increase our knowledge and skills not only for life adjustment counseling but, perhaps more importantly, for preventive and developmental purposes as well.

SUMMARY

This chapter has presented, in a sense, a beginning to important new directions for counselors and the counseling profession that promise to raise the profession to heretofore unanticipated heights of societal service. To what more lofty goals can counselors aspire than the prevention of mental illness and the promotion of a happy productive life through wellness and wise, enjoyable use of leisure time?

Whereas other helping professions may concentrate on the remedial or, at best, the restoration of the client to a previous "status quo," counseling, of all the helping professions, has the prospects to advance clients to the level of the best they can become. This potential does not mean a deemphasis on the traditional skills and knowledge discussed in earlier chapters (i.e., counseling, assessment, career development, etc.) but rather suggests applying these skills to new opportunities that optimistically view the positive, the possible.

The effectiveness of prevention and the other activities of counseling programs will be influenced to a large degree by how effectively programs are planned, managed, and led. The next chapter will discuss this important contribution to the delivery of counseling services.

DISCUSSION QUESTIONS

1. What major societal/mental health concerns would appear to most effectively be treatable by prevention programs?

2. What can be done nationally, that may not be currently undertaken, to more effectively prevent such social ills as substance abuse, child and spouse abuse, AIDS, homelessness, and teen pregnancies? What can counselors do at the local community level?

3. What are the implications of the current interest in health and wellness for the counseling profession?

4. How important is leisure time in your life? Explain. How do you like to spend your leisure time? Discuss and compare.

5. Discuss the importance and problems of counselor wellness.

6. Discuss ways in which you have personally adapted to your environment.

CLASS ACTIVITIES

1. In small groups, discuss and compare the healthy living efforts of class members. Each group will identify a member to briefly report their discussion to the class.

2. Each class member shares (a) two or three favorite recreational or leisure-time activities with the class, (b) their favorite vacation, and/or (c) a new leisure activity they would like to explore.

3. In small groups, identify a mental health problem, and design a prevention program or activity for a specific organizational setting. Share with the group.

4. Read one prevention article in a professional journal. Summarize this article in an oral presentation to the class.

SELECTED READINGS

Backer, C. (1988). Health professionals and mass media's campaigns to prevent AIDS and drug abuse. *Counseling and Human Development, 20,* 1–10.

Backer, T., Batchelor, W., Jones, J., & Mays, V. (1988). Psychology and AIDS [Special issue]. *American Psychologist, 43,* 835–987.

Coie, J. D., Watt, N. F., West, S. G., Hawkins, J. D., Asarnow, J. R., Markman, H. J., Ramey, S. L., Shure, M. B., & Long, B. (1993). The science of prevention: A conceptual framework and some directions for a national research program. *American Psychologist, 48,* 1013–1022.

House, R. M., & Walker, C. M. (1993). Preventing AIDS via education. *Journal of Counseling and Development, 71,* 282–289.

Myers, J. E. (1991). Wellness as the paradigm for counseling and development: The possible future. *Counselor Education and Supervision, 63,* 3–10.

Meyers, J. E. (1992). Wellness, prevention, development: The cornerstone of the profession. *Journal of Counseling and Development, 71,* 136–139.

Nicholson, J. (1986). Risk recreation: A context for developing client potential. *Journal of Counseling and Development, 64,* 528–530.

Paisley, P. (1987). Prevention of child abuse and neglect: A legislative response. *School Counselor, 24,* 226–228.

Panterotto, J. (1985). A counselor's guide to psychopharmacology. *Journal of Counseling and Development, 64,* 109–115.

School, M., & Johnson, J. (1988). Keeping pregnant teens in school. *Vocational Education Journal, 63,* 42–43.

Shaw, M. (1986). The prevention of learning and interpersonal problems. *Journal of Counseling and Development, 64,* 624–627.

United States Department of Health and Human Services. (1990). *Healthy people 2000: National health promotion and disease prevention objectives.* Washington, DC: U.S. Government Printing Office.

Weber, J. (1988). The relevance of vocational education to dropout prevention. *Vocational Education Journal, 63,* 36–38.

Witmer, J. M., & Sweeney, T. J. (1992). A holistic model for wellness and prevention over the life span. *Journal of Counseling and Development, 71,* 140–148.

Zarski, J., Bubeuzer, D., & West, J. (1986). Social interest, stress, and the prediction of health status. *Journal of Counseling and Development, 64,* 386–389.

RESEARCH OF INTEREST

Baker, S. B., Swisher, J. D., Nadenichek, R. E., & Popowicz, C. L. (1984). Measured effects of primary prevention strategies. *Personnel and Guidance Journal, 62,* 459–464.

Abstract

Uses a meta-analysis of over 40 primary prevention studies to investigate the measured effects of primary prevention strategies. Studies selected are those that were controlled experiments with empirical comparisons between treatment and controlled conditions and studies in which the treatment conditions had goals and involved participants, which allows the studies to be classified as primary prevention. Fifteen of the studies utilized or included elementary school populations. Considering the difficulties that limit opportunities to conduct successful primary prevention programs in the school, the results are encouraging.

Blount, W. R., & Dembo, R. (1984). Personal drug use and attitudes toward prevention among youth living in a high-risk environment. *Journal of Drug Use, 14,* 207–224.

Abstract

Nonusers, users of alcohol, and users of both alcohol and marijuana are identified coexisting in the same neighborhoods. (Sample selection also includes a procedure guaranteeing at least part of each group saw themselves as "at risk.") Separate subcultures for each of the three populations are strongly indicated. Differences are found in terms of behavior, attitudes, peer groups (including a distinct rejection of hard-drug users), and significant adults in the environment, especially those felt to possess accurate information about drugs and to whom they would go for help with a drug problem. Almost any activity is seen as appropriate for a drug use prevention program, although there are strong differences in terms of desirability. How users can be differentiated from nonusers in the same population is discussed along with additional implications of prevention programming.

Chandler, C. L., Weissberg, R. P., Cowen, E. L., & Guarez, J. (1984). Long-term effects of a school-based secondary prevention program for maladapting children. *Journal of Consulting and Clinical Psychology, 52,* 165–170.

Abstract

Assesses the current status of 61 fourth–sixth graders, seen 2–5 years earlier in an intervention program for children experiencing school adjustment problems. Based on comparisons of teacher ratings of children's problems and competencies at three time points (referral, termination, and follow-up), program children are found to have maintained initial intervention gains. At follow-up, they were significantly better adjusted than a demographically comparable, teacher-identified group of current problem children but not as well adjusted as a randomly selected, demographically matched "never-seen" group. The three groups do not differ systematically on measures of self-esteem or academic achievement. The absolute placement of the seen sample on those measures is at the midpoint of normal range. Thus, the immediate gains shown by young, maladjusted children seen through the early intervention program endured over time.

Hitchcock, R. A., & Young, D. (1986). Prevention of sexual assault: A curriculum for elementary school counselors. *Journal of Elementary School Guidance and Counseling, 20,* 201–207.

Abstract

Emphasizes the unique position elementary school counselors are in to develop and provide programs regarding the prevention of sexual assault of children. Also discusses such a program that was implemented with 3,500 schoolchildren during the 1984–85 school year. Counselor responses to the program are reported as positive, while parental support of the program is described as substantial.

Omizo, M. M., Omizo, S. A., & D'Andrea, M. J. (1992). Promoting wellness among elementary school children. *Journal of Counseling and Development, 71,* 194–198.

Abstract

Describes a developmental perspective in promoting wellness in children, wellness activities for promoting physical development, and children's psychological needs. Also discusses a study involving wellness promotion guidance activities with fifth-grade students ($n = 62$). Emphasizes the need to develop more effective wellness promotion for children.

Palombi, B. J. (1992). Psychometric properties of wellness instruments. *Journal of Counseling and Development, 71, 221–225.*

Abstract

Examines the Wellness Inventory, the Life Assessment Questionnaire–Wellness Assessment Questionnaire, and the Lifestyle Coping Inventory. Results indicate that wellness is an observable and measurable behavior and that wellness instruments provide users with information related to their level of wellness and areas in which improvements might be necessary.

Chapter 12

Program Management, Development, and Leadership

Prospective counselors should be aware of the probabilities and significance of program management, development, and leadership. The objective of this chapter is to provide an introduction to the significance, principles, and practices of counseling program development, management, and leadership.

Through the centuries, a great deal has been written about the importance of management, leadership, and development to success in the worlds of business and government. The business world has long studied the successes and failures of corporations large and small and the styles of management that have accounted for their achievements or lack of them. Leadership has played a major role in the rise and fall of nations, management is important in government effectiveness and fiscal soundness, and development is crucial in many countries.

In this century, school administration in education, hospital administration in medicine, and personnel administration in business and the armed services have become areas for specialization. In the 1980s, books such as *In Search of Excellence* by Peters and Waterman (1982), *The One-Minute Manager* by Blanchard (1982), and *Iacocca: An Autobiography* by Iacocca and Novack (1984) are examples of publications in this area that appeared with regularity on the best-seller lists.

Additionally, the tax-paying public has become increasingly interested in how efficiently and effectively human service organizations are serving their designated publics. As inflation deflated personal incomes, as well as real dollars available to tax-supported organizations, including school systems and mental health agencies, these organizations were called upon to give "good value." This good value in turn meant that counseling programs were expected to be responding to client needs in an effective (proven results) and efficient (maximizing services, minimizing costs) manner.

Lewis, Lewis, and Souflee, Jr. (1993), state that

> given the turbulent environments in which most of today's human service organizations find themselves—environments characterized by scarcity, ambiguity, and uncertainty—one of the issues revealed to the manager in the move up the managerial tiers is that of organizational survival. Demands for accountability, demands to do more with less, shifting political and economic priorities—all of these factors constitute an additional challenge to management and to contemporary human service organizations. (p. 21)

Thus, despite a general recognition of the importance of management, leadership, and development to any organized enterprise, little attention has been given (in terms of formal preparation, at least) to the "art" of developing and managing counseling programs in various settings. In an editorial commentary in *Education Week*, Hartman (1988) states that few counselors are prepared by their training programs in strategies for handling groups or managing broad programs. He writes that because counselors rarely receive training in program development and organizational management, they tend to deal with major issues in a case-by-case manner.

The complex, multiple goals required of most public agencies, institutions, and schools and school systems emphasize the need for development and management of counselor programs and accountability to the public. *Accountability* means the provision of objective evidence to prove that counselors are successfully responding to identified needs. Such evidence requires recording and writing, and, perhaps, computations and tables. However, all too often those preparing to enter the profession and practice of counseling naively assume that the practice of therapy precludes any involvement with mundane matters such as program management, including administration. This is not to suggest that paperwork should replace people work or that it should be an equal priority. However, prospective counselors should be aware of the prospects and significance of their "other" responsibilities as well. Let us first define these terms:

> *Management:* Those activities that facilitate and complement the daily, ongoing functions of the counseling staff. These include such administrative activities as recording and reporting, budgetary planning and control, facility management, and provisions for support personnel resources.
>
> *Development:* Includes needs assessment for program planning, research, evaluation, and the establishment of program accountability. Also presumes planning for program improvement.
>
> *Leadership:* The providing of positive direction and motivation for personnel and program improvement. Primarily, but not exclusively, the responsibility of the professional designated as the chief management person for a specified unit (program, office, department, clinic).

UNDERSTANDING PROGRAM MANAGEMENT AND DEVELOPMENT

Beginning counselors might view the prospects of program management and development responsibilities and the likelihood of being involved in administering an ongoing program as not only remote but also potentially undesirable. Let us therefore advance some of the reasons why counselors should possess a minimal understanding of management, development, and leadership.

Administration and Your Job

A common complaint throughout all organizations today and perhaps throughout history concerns the inroads made on professional time by nonprofessional or administrative activities. Administrative responsibilities, however, are a fact of life for all functioning professionals, including counselors in all settings. Because one cannot avoid all responsibilities for program administration, management, and development at any level, it will be beneficial if, from the beginning of your professional activities as a counselor, you have some minimal understandings of these matters and how you may best respond.

Recognizing the inevitability of administrative responsibilities, what can one do to discharge these responsibilities as expeditiously and effectively as possible? The following are suggestions gleaned from informal interviews with successful program managers and administrators in various settings.

1. *Be organized.* To be organized means, among other things, having a place for everything and everything in its place. This keeps you from wasting time in search-and-find operations. Being organized also means planning the use of your time. This includes the maintaining of a daily calendar that allows sufficient time for each task for which you are

responsible. Because it is not always possible to estimate the exact amount of time a counseling interview may consume, it is better to allocate too much rather than too little time on one's calendar. Implicit in organization is an efficient filing and record-keeping system that allows ready access of items as needed. Files should contain all necessary and relevant information but should be periodically purged of outdated and nonuseful materials. Although neatness is not necessarily a guarantee of organization, there appears to be a relationship between a neat office and a well-organized office.

2. *Do it right the first time.* Much administration seems to focus on preparing reports, maintaining records, and organizing data. As previously indicated, increasing emphasis on accountability, plus requirements mandated by state or federal statutes, has further accentuated the necessity of gathering objective data supporting the counseling enterprise. It is important to take time to understand exactly what it is you have to report and how it is to be reported. If you do not understand it, do not hesitate to ask for help if you need it. Do not waste your time and someone else's by doing it wrong the first time. You must also demand accuracy of yourself in the completing of any report or record and in the organizing of data. Long, cumbersome documents encourage guessing on the part of respondents. Other reports, especially those of an evaluative nature, may tempt one to fake or "fudge" a bit on the responses; the single word of advice is *don't*. In addition to the risk of being embarrassed by someone noting your inaccuracies, you risk the more dangerous possibility of important decisions being made on the basis of inaccurate and irresponsible data.

3. *Do it on time.* Assuming that you have been convinced to do your reporting and recording accurately, do not detract from your administrative responsibilities by being late. Usually, there is a reason that certain data are required at certain times for certain decisions. Your delays can handicap this process, especially when your colleagues have all responded on time. On those rare occasions when an emergency prevents the completion of a responsibility on time, it is important to give it the most immediate priority for completion at the earliest opportunity to avoid a domino effect in which every activity down the line will also be subject to tardiness.

4. *Plan your own time.* All of us on occasion will come up against constraints on our time. Walking down the halls in almost any setting, we can hear comments such as "All I ever do is go to meetings," or "All I get done is answer the phone," or "If people would just stop dropping in unannounced," or "I don't seem to have any time to myself any more." Time frustration seems to occur with all of us. Thus, the use and control of time are critical in one's efficient functioning, in both administration and counseling; they also have an impact on one's morale. The objective of planning your time is to make the most of it and, at the same time, leave you enough freedom and flexibility so you do not feel that the clock is your boss. In order to do this, there are several considerations. One is to do the things you do at the times when you do them best. For example, some may find they prepare reports most efficiently if they do so first thing in the morning. Others may find it desirable to use the first hour or so at work to complete the waking-up process with a second cup of coffee. It is also important to do the things we do where we do them best, perhaps getting away to some private little corner where we are uninterrupted for certain administrative responsibilities. On the other hand, we may wish an informal setting for conferences with colleagues. In planning the use of time, it is important that we under-

stand ourselves in relationship to where and how we function best. We adapt our time commitment to our working style.

5. *Do it neatly.* The effects of doing it right and doing it on time may still be lost if an interpreter is needed to translate what you have done. If your handwriting is sloppy, try typing or printing written reports for others. Lack of neatness can also detract from the impressions or impact of reports. A report that looks as if it had been done and redone a dozen times may also be more subject to scrutiny and questioning by superiors.

Suggestions for functioning effectively also include the following "don'ts":

1. *Don't let it spoil your day.* Although not everyone may enjoy the challenges of recording and reporting, such tasks should be accepted as inevitable responsibilities that will not be facilitated by constant complaints. The frequent suggestions of many administrators is that you do it and forget it.

2. *Don't expect to understand the need for every report.* Frustrations frequently occur when one fails to see a rationale for the kind of data that are needed. Allied with this is the fact that we may also not understand why it has to be done "their" way instead of our "better" way. When something is requested by your immediate supervisor, you are more likely to understand the need than if it is requested by the upper management, several layers removed. However, there will inevitably be occasions when reports are requested from afar that will challenge all that is rational. Again, do it and forget it.

3. *Don't be tempted to become an administrator.* In some settings, counselors appear to receive their largest number of "brownie points" from their superiors by meeting their administrative responsibilities. It therefore becomes a natural temptation to overemphasize that aspect of the job. A common complaint of many counselors is that they spend too much time in administrative activities; even many program administrators agree. The major responsibility of a counselor in any setting, with the possible exception of a program director, is to counsel. This should be the counselor's major time-consuming activity. Although it is important to meet one's administrative responsibilities efficiently and effectively, that does not imply they overshadow in importance or time the primary reason for which one is hired as a counselor.

As an aid to help those who may be reluctant to move from disorganization to organization, the score pad in Table 12–1 will enable you to play the time game. It may help persons develop an awareness of their personal time management styles.

Program Management

Kotter (1988), writing from a business school perspective, states:

> Modern management, as it has evolved over the past five decades, can be described in any number of different ways. But at the heart of virtually all such descriptions, one always finds four or five key processes:
>
> 1. Planning. Planning is the science of logically deducing means to achieve given ends. A variety of techniques have been developed to aid in this process.
> 2. Budgeting. Budgeting is that part of the planning process associated with an organization's finances.

TABLE 12–1

The Time Game Score Pad (Object: To Improve Your Score on a Daily, Weekly, or Monthly Basis)

Hour	What Did I do?	Had I Planned to Do It?[a]	How Well Did I Do It?[b]	Did I Do It with a Positive Attitude?[c]	Comments to Self[d]
8 A.M.					
9 A.M.					
10 A.M.					
11 A.M.					
12 noon					
1 P.M.					
2 P.M.					
3 P.M.					
4 P.M.					
5 P.M.					

[a] 5 points if you had planned to do it.
3 points if you had planned to do it because was overdue.
0 points if you hadn't planned to do it.
−3 points if you hadn't planned to do it but it was an unexpected requirement that had a higher priority than what you had planned.

[b] Score yourself on a scale of 0 to 5.

[c] 3 points if you did it with enthusiasm.
2 points if you did it with a positive attitude.
1 point if you did it and then forgot about it.
0 points if you did it and then worried about it.
−1 point if you did it with frustration and/or anger.
−5 points if you did it and it drove you to drink.

[d] 1 point for each constructive suggestion.
−1 point for statements using profanity.

Totals:
1. Subtotal A + B + C + D.
2. Subtract 5 points if you didn't take a lunch break.
3. Subtract 10 points if you didn't take a lunch break for a second day in a row.

3. Organizing. Organizing means creating a formal structure that can accomplish the plans, staffing it with qualified people, defining clearly what each person's role is, providing them with appropriate financial and career incentives, and then delegating appropriate authority to those people. Again, a variety of techniques have been created to aid these processes.

4. Controlling. Controlling involves looking constantly for deviations from plan ("Problems"), and then using formal authority to "solve" them. This often takes place via "review" meetings. For the financial part of plans, this means using management control systems and the like. (pp. 21–22)

Program management as a process seeks to provide structure, order, and coordination of those activities for which it is responsible. This information, of course, will function at varying levels. For example, in educational systems, the board of education, the school superintendent, and the assistant principals can be viewed as middle management, and program directors, such as the director of counseling, represent component or lower management. Figure 12–1 depicts this concept.

Regardless of the levels of management, however, the overall objective remains the same: the facilitation of the goal achievement of the organization. It is important for

FIGURE 12–1 Levels of Educational Management

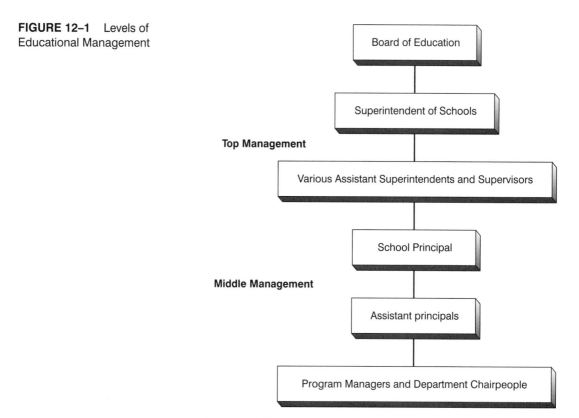

Board of Education

Superintendent of Schools

Top Management

Various Assistant Superintendents and Supervisors

School Principal

Middle Management

Assistant principals

Program Managers and Department Chairpeople

Component Management

counselors in various settings to note that the objectives of the counseling program must be consistent with and contribute to the achievement of the objectives of the institution of which it is a part. For example, in recent years, counselors working in school settings have been called upon to indicate the contributions they are making to the education of school-aged youth. Although education may be viewed broadly as all growth and development, it may be more difficult for counselors to respond in those settings when education is viewed as a learning activity only. As noted by Gibson, Mitchell, and Higgins (1983):

> Helping "Harry High School" become a happy, well-adjusted (whatever this means) individual may be a commendable outcome of counseling; however, if, in the process or as a result, he does not become better educated or more effective as a student, the counseling program may be viewed by many as of questionable value to the educational institution. (p. 145)

The responsibilities and activities of program management may vary according to levels and settings, but it is possible to identify two basic areas of functioning. The first deals with the managing of basic resources, such as personnel, budget, and facilities. The second focuses on organizing and facilitating such basic activities as coordination, communication, cooperation, decision making, and evaluation. The emphasis of discussions here will be on what is involved rather than on how one should do it. Following are some suggestions appropriate for entry-level counselors, who should also be aware that as one moves into management responsibilities, one's own style and techniques tend to emerge.

MANAGING RESOURCES

Of all the resources that a program manager is called upon to use, the human resource is by far the most important. The manner in which this resource is managed will largely determine the success or failure of the program and also whether the manager is a program leader or simply a program administrator. The program manager's initial responsibility in many instances will begin with staffing, which will be a consistent consideration as long as there is staff turnover. Staff selection should minimally involve four factors, which are discussed next.

Qualifications

These are primarily but not exclusively based on training and experience in relation to the expectancies of the position. In viewing one's training background, consideration should be given not only to the content of the training program but also to when, where, and areas of specialization. Although academic achievements in themselves are not the sole criterion for performance on the job, one's academic achievements should not be completely ignored. There may be little difference in performance between the A and B student, but one should not anticipate that the C student will perform as well on the job as the A student.

When examining experience, program managers usually compare the type, amount, and success of previous experiences. Experience may not always be a factor, for many program managers are anxious to hire recent graduates who can bring new ideas, more up-to-date concepts, and, perhaps, needed youthful enthusiasm to their programs.

Staff Versatility

When the program manager has a staff of at least one to manage, providing for program versatility enters into staff selection. Differing backgrounds should provide a wider range of specialty skills. Also, it has frequently been noted that staffs of two or more should include one member of each sex and minority or cultural representation, as appropriate. Some range in age representation is important, especially in institutional and community settings, and the old schoolboy network (hire all graduates from the same school) should not be perpetuated at the expense of program versatility.

Adaptability

Another consideration often overlooked in staffing is the adaptability of a staff member to both the job setting and the community or area environment. Not only must the person like the job, but the job must like the person. A staff member will function more effectively when there are congenial relationships among the staff as well as those with whom they come in frequent contact. This, of course, would include the clients that the staff is serving. It is not suggested that one form friendships with clients, but it is important to be able to relate to the client population, whether it is inner-city, suburban society, Appalachian poor, or Alaskan Eskimo.

Staff members must also be able to adapt to the community or area environment that supports the job setting. It is highly unlikely that people can be unhappy in their community-home life and happy in their work life. The inability to adapt to a community environment can also have adverse effects on the public relations aspect of the counseling program.

Once staffing decisions have been made and personnel are functioning on a job, management's responsibilities continue to be important. These include the following:

1. *The assignment of responsibility.* Each staff member should have specific activities for which they are responsible and for which the staff member knows they are responsible. In assigning these responsibilities, the program manager seeks to capitalize on the staff member's special skills, experience, and personal characteristics. In some instances this process will involve delegating some undesirable or less-favored tasks. Staff members must anticipate these as well as their share of the more rewarding activities. A good program manager will not delegate all the "donkey work" and keep only the "goodies" for him- or herself.

2. *Provisions for staff development.* The fact that counselors are providing helping services and human support to others does not mean that counselors should or can function without the support of others. A program manager must see that staff members help and support each other and, additionally, receive help and support from beyond the counseling offices. Ways in which this may be accomplished include meaningful group work or committee assignments in which members share interest in a common problem or topic with other personnel outside the counseling staff. Obviously, part of this human support system is the program manager's personal interaction with each staff member.

Budget

The importance of budget and budget management in any setting can hardly be overemphasized. A budget's significance in any system of accountability is paramount. In effect, it enables the supporting public, whether they are taxpayers or donators, to see what they are paying for or whether they are getting their money's worth. To the individual staff member, budgeting is often a mysterious, misunderstood, maddening, and far-removed process that has a direct and undeniable relationship to staff morale. It is, therefore, important that staff members recognize the level at which their immediate program manager is involved and the extent of that involvement.

It is also helpful to understand the level at which budgeting decisions, especially those affecting staff members, are made. In many settings, lower-level managers may be limited in their budget responsibilities to recommending or requisitioning from budgets established elsewhere. Crucial budget decisions, such as salaries and salary increments, staffing additions, and equipment purchases, tend to be made at middle- and upper-management levels. These real budget managers are usually involved in budgeting for personnel, including both professional and support staff; and services, such as consultants, communications, supplies, equipment, and travel. Budget decisions for capital improvements, such as new buildings or significant remodeling, are usually made at only the highest level of management.

One form of budgeting that has become increasingly prevalent at even the lower levels of management involves program activities supported by federal or state grants. These are usually developed in response to mandated federal or state programs. These programs have specific objectives and procedures and a budget that is directly related and accountable to those procedures and objectives.

Beginning counselors are unlikely to be involved in budget management, but they probably will be involved in budget expenditures. Because mismanagement or misspent monies may become your personal expense, the following suggestions are pertinent:

1. Each budget item is related to an activity, which in turn is related to a specific goal or objective of the organization. It is important to understand the reason for an expenditure, which also suggests spending only for those categories that are budgeted; for example, if professional travel is not provided for in a budget, you do not travel professionally by taking $500 from the supply item in the budget even if it is not being spent and even if the travel is to a professional meeting.

2. Spend only what you have. Although you may occasionally overdraw a bank account, you are usually reminded quickly and make amends before it becomes a bankruptcy disaster. However, all too frequently, when spending someone else's money, there is an inclination to be less concerned until it is too late. Remember, any spending you do that is beyond the available budget will probably end up being your own personal expense.

3. Spend economically. The fact that you have a budget does not mean that the sky is the limit as long as you spend it for items in the budget and as long as you do not exceed the budget. Budget managers are expected to be good shoppers. This does not mean that you sacrifice quality for economy but that you get the most for your dollar. For example, on major purchases, such as typewriters, video equipment, and tape recorders, it is cus-

tomary to obtain two or three estimates including those provided by traditional discount houses before determining the place of purchase. If the expenditure is for travel, recipients are usually expected to be aware of the various bargain travel fares and travel regular or tourist class on common carriers. If private vehicles are used, mileage rates are usually established by federal, state, or local agencies.

4. Secure receipts. If you spend budgeted funds in any amount, you will be reimbursed only when you have proof of purchase. The only acceptable proof of purchase is a receipt for the goods or service obtained (showing the item, even if it is an elephant, is not considered proof of purchase).

5. Keep a running account. Anyone who has responsibility for any budget or segment of one must know exactly what has been expended and what remains at any given point during the duration of the budget. This means keeping a daily, if necessary, running account of debits, credits, and balances.

6. Be aware of any unusual (or usual) legal or contract restraints. This point is perhaps most appropriate when persons have budgetary responsibilities emanating from special contracts or grants. In such instances, budget managers, when in doubt, should consult the appropriate legal or contract authority before authorizing an expenditure.

Managing Facilities

The management of facilities takes on appropriate importance when one considers that persons spend more of their waking hours in their place of work than in their home or anywhere else. Facilities are important in determining whether persons will have the opportunity to do their job in a manner in which they are capable of doing it. In large, complex institutions, facilities are often viewed as symbols that reflect the importance with which the operation is viewed. (It is thus inevitable that a school principal's office will always be a shade larger, at least, than the school counselor's; that the college president's office and decor will be considerably larger and more luxurious than that of the institution's most distinguished professor, etc.) Facility concerns of program managers include the following:

❖ *Adequacy.* Size, furnishings, and general decor, cleanliness, and, above all for counselors, privacy are determinants of the adequacy of one's work space. These factors tend to determine the atmosphere in which one works. During a recent university visitation, a dean of students, showing the offices of the university counseling center, remarked that he had $30,000-a-year counselors in $10,000 offices turning in $5,000-a-year performances. Those who have ever worked in dingy, dreary, ill-equipped, or dirty facilities can recall the impact of these on their morale and subsequent performance. Yet, from time to time, high-level program managers seem to expect that as long as they are comfortable and their morale is good, it will spread to all levels regardless of working conditions.

❖ *Accessibility.* A person should not feel that he or she has already done a half day's work just by getting to his or her office. Accessibility is also important in terms of clients. Countless studies have noted that when university counseling centers or community agencies are situated in locations far from the main populations they are intended to serve, their clientele does not materialize.

❖ *Individuality.* Have you ever viewed the administrative offices of large-scale enterprises or business corporations, where dozens of employees have been provided identical cubicles and furnishings as so many similar mechanical parts in a precision machine? Such facilities provide little opportunity for the individual worker to assert any individuality. It would, therefore, seem inconsistent with that theoretical framework to suggest that individual counselors would not have enough flexibility in their personal office facilities to express this individuality.

❖ *Supplementary space.* Program managers also are responsible for securing and managing supplementary facilities, such as conference rooms, resource or staff rooms, filing areas (security can be important here), storage and supply areas, reception areas, and support-staff facilities.

Management by Objectives

Management by objectives (MBO) increased in popularity in the late 1960s. This system of management was first brought to public attention over 40 years ago by Drucker (1954) in *The Practice of Management,* which described it as an industrial system. It

is a system in which management attempts to aim all significant activities in an organization toward the achievement of specified, agreed-upon objectives. MBO is designed to promote goal attainment, organizational clarity of action, and increased satisfaction on the part of organizational members who benefit in an environment of achievement. Although it is fairly standardized in the literature as to its general parameters, the point is often made that the application of MBO varies with the characteristics of the organization involved.

According to Miringoff (1980), essentially MBO is summarized by the following characteristics:

a. Makes objectives explicit; recognizes multi-objective situations.

b. Identifies conflicting objectives; provides for participation management.

c. Ensures a control mechanism providing for feedback and measurement of accomplishment.

d. Fosters managerial acceptance of responsibility and evaluation of managers by results.

e. Encompasses little formal administrative machinery. (p. 123)

Organizing and Facilitating Basic Activities

The program manager must also initiate and guide the organization and facilitation of the basic activities of the counseling program. This does not mean the professional activities but rather the basic supporting activities that complement the professional services of the organization. These include the following:

❖ *Coordination.* In even less-than-complex organizations, some degree of coordination is necessary to prevent overlapping, conflicting, or duplicating of activities. Coordination is necessary among activities and programs, both internally and externally.

❖ *Cooperation.* Cooperation is a vital ingredient in both coordination and public relations. Program managers must encourage and demonstrate a willingness to work with others in such vital counselor activities as case studies, conferences, referrals, and consultation. As suggested previously, counselors should be willing to give help when called upon by fellow professional colleagues or support personnel in other fields as well. Cooperation is one of the basic functions in establishing and maintaining positive professional connections.

❖ *Effective communications.* Communications often determine whether a program is managed efficiently. Counselors are usually well trained in the art of personal communication, but it is surprising how frequently the communication process breaks down within a program as well as with higher-level management and external agencies and organizations. Guidelines for effective communication in management suggest care must be taken that the personal touch is not lost as a result of using impersonal means to communicate, such as memos, policy statements, and directives. When such impersonal means are necessary, there must be adequate personal follow-up to ensure that such communications are understood. In addition, communication must provide for some sort of feedback. Oral communication to large groups such as staff or faculty meetings must justify the time it consumes for the number of people present.

❖ *Evaluation.* A program manager is responsible for ensuring the gathering of data that provide for systematic, ongoing evaluation of the program's activities. A program manager also coordinates periodic and accreditation types of planning. At the individual staff member level, a program manager is responsible for evaluation of each member of the organization and communicating this evaluation to both the individual staff member and higher management.

❖ *Decision making.* Effective program management requires that someone be in charge. As the one in charge, a program manager must have decision-making authority commensurate with the responsibilities of the decision. Program managers can share the decision thinking, but they cannot be expected to share all the decision making.

Berk and Berk (1991) describe program management as

simultaneously an art and a science. The scientific aspects of the management discipline are fairly straightforward, and anyone with a reasonable degree of intelligence can learn the mechanics. You can't be successful as a manager if you are equipped only with the rules and procedures of the managerial business. You have to be adept at the artistic side of the managerial discipline. This is the part that requires an appreciation of the essence of the manager's job: understanding what it is you are responsible for doing, determining the best way to do it, recruiting and cultivating the right people, and helping these people to realize their full potential. (p. 9)

PROGRAM LEADERSHIP

Perhaps no single characteristic beyond the professional qualifications of the counseling staff is more significant to the success of the counseling operation than the quality of program leadership. It is desirable that counselors at least recognize those characteristics that tend to identify leaders and distinguish them from program administrators or managers. Most persons recognize the individual who is a true leader. A real leader is one who leads, not directs; real leadership gives priority to the benefit of the program and those who are led rather than to the leader. Some of the characteristics of program leadership include the following:

❖ *Has a record of success.* Program leaders have good track records. They justify the old concept that success breeds success. Included in the program leader's win column is previous recognition as a successful and resourceful counselor. Also, the program leader is an extracompetent professional. Program leadership for counseling programs can be provided only by professional counselors. Program leaders will contribute their competence and expert knowledge to the successful functioning of the counseling program, including an awareness of professional, ethical, and legal guidelines for the profession.

❖ *Inspires confidence.* A program leader inspires confidence in him- or herself and individual staff members. He or she does this by being supportive and also realistic. He or she expects the possible but not the impossible. He or she gives and shares credit publicly so that others know of the successes of individual staff members.

❖ *Shares.* The program leader shares the "ownership" of the operation and develops a feeling of "us" rather than "me and you." Active ownership does not mean that the staff runs the operation. It means that the staff shares in the running of it. Sharing the ownership of the operation creates a feeling of belonging, of being on the team. Real leadership sees that no one feels left out. There are no in-groups and out-groups.

❖ *Motivates.* All studies of leadership indicate that a common ingredient of leaders in nearly every setting is an ability to motivate others to achieve their potential and perhaps at times, even exceed it. Although each leader has a different and unique style, the evidence is present when one observes hard-working, achieving staff members.

❖ *Creates a positive atmosphere.* A leader understands what makes life at the office liveable or one happy in one's work by creating professional atmospheres conductive to accomplishment. This includes effective program organization, management, and administration. As Ailes (1988) points out, one of the secrets of successful leaders is being likeable.

❖ *Is visible.* One cannot lead in absentia. Successful program leaders at all levels are those who are frequently and clearly visible to and available for interaction with their supporting staff.

❖ *Is forward looking.* Leadership demands planning for the future. Program leaders are insightful and future-oriented in their planning.

❖ *Is a decision maker.* Effective leadership not only accepts the decision-making responsibility and will make the hard decisions but will also make the appropriate decision.

These characteristics can provide a checklist to identify potential counseling program leaders. As noted in Gibson, Mitchell, and Higgins (1983), program leaders are not likely to be chosen when the top management position is viewed as a consolation prize, a stepping stone for someone tagged to proceed up the organization, a political position to shore up support for top management, or proof that the "Peter Principle" (Peter & Hull, 1959) really operates. (This principle suggests that one is eventually promoted to his or her level of incompetence.)

CONTRIBUTING TO PROGRAM DEVELOPMENT AND IMPROVEMENT

All of us like to be members of "winning teams." We would also probably agree that talent alone is not enough, that winning teams require "teamwork" and a winning "game plan."

On joining a counseling staff, a counselor becomes not only a team member but also committed to and involved in the continuous process of program development and improvement—the implementation of a "game plan." The effective development of any counseling program, regardless of setting, is dependent first on an accurate and continuous assessment of the needs of the target population to be served. Such needs assessment is the key to successful planning for goals and objectives. The accurate assessment of potential client needs is critical in establishing and maintaining program relevance and fostering program accountability and evaluation. The needs assessment activity, which can range from a simple to a complex process, is concerned with two databases, as follows:

1. *Target population assessment.* This data gathering seeks to establish factually the needs of the target population that the counseling program has been established to serve. These data will also influence priorities among these needs.

2. *Environmental assessment.* This is the gathering of factual data that facilitate the counseling program's understanding of the setting from which the target population comes and within which the program functions. Also, as noted in Chapter 7, it is important that counselors understand the environment in which behavior occurs.

Target population assessment provides a factual basis for a program's goals and objectives, and environmental assessment provides a factual basis for the procedures by which a program achieves its goals and objectives. The personal needs are the internal factors that initiate, direct, and sustain the program's activities, whereas the environmental characteristics provide the depth of understanding for more effectively responding to the needs.

Lewis et al. (1991), writing from a community agency perspective, identify the generic planning process as one using the following basic steps: (a) needs assessment, (b) definition of goals and objectives, (c) identification of alternative methods for meeting goals, (d) decision making, and (e) development of plans for implementation and evaluation. "Each of these steps involves a major commitment both from agency personnel and from community members. Each step also depends on the effective completion of the previous task, beginning with the all-important process of needs assessment" (p. 35).

THE NEEDS ASSESSMENT SURVEY

The development of accountable and relevant programs begins with the assessment of the needs of the target population. This is the initial step in the sequence of six procedures for such program development (see Figure 12–2).

This process is not intended to identify problems only (Baruth & Robinson, 1987, p. 332). Thus, developmental, preventive, and enhancement needs of the population are considered as well as those that have intervention and remediation implications. This is a technique for factually establishing program goals and objectives. Such an assessment directly involves the target population or a sampling of it, as well as critical support populations. For example, a school guidance program would not only gather data from students but would also survey parents, teachers, and others who had frequent and direct contact with the student population. The direct involvement of these populations is usually secured through questionnaires or structured interviews. Figure 12–3 presents an example of a simple questionnaire used in student needs assessment and completed by not only students but support populations as well.

In addition to questionnaire and interview data, other sources such as school and community records will provide data that substantiate or identify the needs of potential clients. Environmental assessment seeks to establish the characteristics of program and population setting through identifying the characteristics of the environment's population, economics, and geography. Community assessment may be facilitated through the use and development of certain data-planning instruments, as may be noted in Figures 12–4 and 12–5. Typical sources from which the previously suggested data may be gathered are noted in Figure 12–4. Figure 12–4 is a checklist designed to guide the information seeker to common sources of community information. The form is not intended to record data but only to provide a guide to possible sources.

Step 1	Step 2	Step 3	Step 4	Step 5	Step 6
Assessment of Needs through Data Collection	Interpretation of Data	Priority Needs	Program Objectives	Program Procedures (activities developed based on program resources available)	Planning for Program Improvement (based on evaluation of outcomes and procedures)

FIGURE 12–2 Sequence of Procedures for Developing an Accountable Program of Counseling and Guidance
Source: From Gibson, Robert L., Mitchell, Marianne H., and Basile, Sherry K., *Counseling in the Elementary School: A Comprehensive Approach*, p. 272. Copyright © 1993 by Allyn and Bacon. Reprinted by permission.

Person filling out form:	Rankings: Check one for each question below					Additional Response
_____ Student _____ Parent _____ Teacher _____ Businessperson	Very Important	Quite Important	Moderately Important	Somewhat Important	Not Important At All	In your opinion is this service being provided? (check one)
1. How important is it for students to be able to discuss personal problems with the school counselor?						yes____ no ____
2. How important is it for the school counselor to provide career information?						yes____ no ____
3. How important is it for the school counselor to provide information concerning colleges, trade schools, or the armed services?						yes____ no ____
4. How important is it for the counselor to show the relationship between education and careers?						yes____ no ____
5. How important is it for the counselor to provide assistance to the student in job placement upon graduation?						yes____ no ____
6. How important is it for the counselor to discuss with students which courses they will take in school?						yes____ no ____
7. How important is it for the counselor to work with students who are failing or dropping out?						yes____ no ____
8. How important is it for the counselor to lead small-group discussions on current student problems?						yes____ no ____
9. How important is a counseling and guidance program in a high school?						yes____ no ____
10. What other services for students do you think the school counselor should provide? (Please write in the space below and on the back.)						yes____ no ____

FIGURE 12–3   Needs Identification Questionnaire

Community: _____

Survey dates: _____

Survey team: _____

_____

_____

_____ 1. Political leadership

_____

_____ 2. Governmental (nonpolitical) leadership

_____

_____ 3. Educational leadership

_____   (School board members, superintendents, principals,

_____   education association or union officials)

_____ 4. Major religious denominations

_____   (ministers, priests, rabbis)

_____ 5. Minority group (or groups) leadership

_____

_____

_____ 6. Judicial system

_____   (Chief of police, juvenile judge, lawyers,

_____   county sheriff, probationary officials)

_____ 7. Business/commercial/industrial leadership

_____   (Presidents [in residence] of local corporations,

_____   plant managers, owners of prominent local businesses)

_____ 8. Labor organization leadership

_____

_____ 9. Youth leadership

_____   (Student council members, athletic standouts,

_____   social club or gang leadership)

_____ 10. Civic leadership

_____   (Officials of civic clubs, volunteer organizations)

_____

_____ 11. Other (indicate status and representation)

_____   _____

_____   _____

_____   _____

Note: Be sure all interviewees meet the criteria for "significant contributors"
as indicated in interviewing instructions. Structured interview guides
should be adhered to insofar as possible. Exceptions should be noted
and reasons for deviations explained.

FIGURE 12–4 Community Survey Checklist: Interview Schedule

Community: _____

Survey dates: _____

Survey team: _____

_____

_____

_____	1.	Census data
_____	2.	News media analysis
_____	3.	Board of education (minutes of) meetings
_____	4.	Annual reports of schools
_____	5.	County government data
_____	6.	City government data
_____	7.	Employment agencies
_____	8.	Church board reports
_____	9.	Chamber of Commerce data
_____	10.	Geographic data
_____	11.	Ecological-environmental data
_____	12.	Other significant data (list sources)

_____

_____

_____

_____

_____

Note: If data are not available, place notation "NA" in blank at left of item. Otherwise, when data are collected, place a "✓".

FIGURE 12–5 Community Survey Checklist: Data Collection

Braucht and Weime (1990) describe a multiagency needs assessment in a rural setting with very limited financial resources. The school system networked with the Youth Services Planning Board established by the Illinois State Department of Children and Family Services in conducting a needs assessment using the key informant approach. This is an approach that involves selected community or area leaders to provide estimates of the needs and required services of a specific population. This results in a broad picture of these needs and services as perceived by community leaders. In Braucht and Weime's needs assessment, a questionnaire

was sent to the key informants to determine the problems they encountered in their contacts with youth. The questionnaire consisted of five items:

1. What problems or issues do adolescents face in your community?

2. If money were growing on trees, what services for adolescents would you like to see begun or improved in your community?

3. To which of the following sources have you referred adolescents in the past year? (Choices were churches, counseling agencies, investigating agencies, parents, school staff, self-help groups, significant adults, other—please specify.)

4. Please rank the top five referral sources from Question 3 according to frequency of referral, with 1 designating the most frequent and 5 the least.

5. Please feel free to share comments, concerns, or suggestions.

Follow-up telephone calls were made to encourage a higher response rate. (p. 179)

Identifying Priorities and Developing Program Relevancy

The needs assessment data that may be gathered through the previously described procedures provide direction for determining goals and priorities and the development of counseling program objectives that are relevant and meaningful to the target population and setting. The initial procedure is a simple listing of goals and priorities, first as perceived by the target population. These then may be slightly reordered, as verified by immediate support population, and then slightly reordered again, once these base data are supplemented by secondary populations and sources. In the school setting, the students would represent the target population, and teachers and parents, the immediate support population. Supplementary or secondary population would include community personnel and data from student and other relevant records. This process leads to a tentative prioritizing of needs. A final reordering is established by eliminating any needs that may not be the professional responsibility of the counseling program or may require resources beyond those available to the counseling program. The final outcome of this process is the establishment of working priorities in a hierarchical order, which are then translated into goals and objectives.

The translation of priorities into goals and objectives requires their being stated in written terms. The goals of a program are typically described in broad, general terms that may not be tied to specific time constraints. On the other hand, the program objectives must be stated in objective, measurable terms and related to a time frame. Objectives are designed to describe desired performances and should contribute to the achievement of a program goal and the meeting of one or more specifically identified needs. Of course, the assessment of needs and the establishment of related goals and objectives are not, in and of themselves, a guarantee of program relevancy. A needs assessment only establishes an awareness of what a counseling program should consider in planning the utilization of its resources. The real criteria of program relevancy will result from the degree of understanding and concern and the appropriateness of the plan of action developed and executed by the counseling staff. An effective plan of action will reflect many, if not all, of the following characteristics:

1. *It should be developmental.* Program planning should be developmental, indicating immediate, intermediate, and long-range program goals. As a starting point, it may be appropriate to envision an ultimate, utopian program for the setting for which it will be designed and, once having established these long-range goals, determine those priorities

that should be given immediate attention; those that may need attention within the next several years; and those that the program ultimately hopes to accomplish. Programs should never reach the point where they function simply to maintain the status quo. Programs should at all times be developmental, for development implies continuous growth and improvement.

2. *It should have a logical, sequential plan of development.* The development of any program usually proceeds from a foundation that seems appropriate to subsequent development. As previously suggested, the appropriate foundation from which planning proceeds are its needs and readiness assessment and their relationship to the resources at hand.

3. *It should be flexible.* Counseling programs must be flexible in order to meet the changing needs of youth and other client populations. This suggests also that initial planning for program development must be limited to that which can be reasonably achieved. Programs that are overly ambitious in their design allow little room for alternate or unexpected opportunities. A part of flexibility in planning should be the identification of possible problems and alternate procedures for goal achievement.

4. *It should give a high priority to communication, coordination, and cooperation.* Like the other components of program development, these activities should not be left to chance. It is important, for example, that there be a plan for communicating the development of the school guidance program to faculty members individually and in groups, as well as to students, parents, and others. Cooperation with other programs and persons is important if the program is to anticipate the need for reciprocal cooperation. In communicating with the various relevant groups and people in the community, different approaches must be used that recognize the uniqueness and differences of these individuals and groups. For example, techniques for communicating with youth would certainly be different in many ways than those that are effective with adults and related professionals. Often, counseling programs increasingly fail to communicate their mission clearly and effectively to others, which results in many questioning the need for such programs. Coordination and cooperation failures have also adversely affected the positive image that counseling programs seek to portray.

5. *It should provide a basis for resource employment.* An adequate plan for program development provides a logical basis for personnel assignment, budget development, and resource allocation and utilization. This means that the plan must be a clear and concise one in which the relationships between program goals, the activities for achieving these goals, and the personnel and other resources needed to accomplish them can be readily recognized. The program director must be a resource coordinator. Program planning must therefore take into account those resources that may be available for program development and goal accomplishment. An inventory of possible resources becomes, therefore, an important activity in planning for program development.

Any plan for program initiation and development must include provisions for program accountability or evaluation. The evaluation component of a developmental plan provides a built-in mechanism for program accountability, development, and improvement.

Gysbers and Henderson (1994) suggest four phases for program improvement and development with modified descriptors as follows:

1. *Planning:* This stage assumes the services provided must be organized into a program and that these services will be both developmental and comprehensive. It also includes planning to move from where the program is currently to the desired program plan.

2. *Designing:* "Once a comprehensive program model has been selected and data have been gathered that describe the current guidance program, the next phase of the program improvement process is to design the specific program that is desired for your school district or school building" (p. 135).

3. *Implementing:* "Having organized for change, adopted a comprehensive program model, assessed the current program, established the design for the desired program, and planned the transition, you, as the guidance program leader, are now ready to make the transition to an improved program. You also are ready to develop mechanisms to maintain the program once it is in operation. This is one of the most critical phases of the entire program improvement process. The questions to be answered include: How is the transition to a comprehensive program to be made? What new resources are needed to enhance the effectiveness and efficiency of the program? Are there special projects that will provide impetus to the needed changes in direction? How can we assist each building to improve its program?" (p. 209)

4. *Evaluating:* This process is described as ongoing, using specific and relevant criteria and as essential to continuous program improvement.

Gysbers and Henderson (1994) go on to say:

> Three kinds of systematic evaluation are required to achieve accountability for your guidance program. The first kind of evaluation—personnel evaluation—describes the procedures used by your district to evaluate school counselors and other personnel who may be assisting them in implementing the district's guidance program. Program evaluation, the second kind, examines your district's written guidance program using a process called an audit, to see if it is the district's implemented program. The third kind of evaluation, called results evaluation, focuses on the impact that the guidance and counseling activities in your district's program are having on students, the school, and the community (Gysbers, Hughey, Starr, & Lapan, 1992). (pp. 325–326)

Program relevance and, hence, development and improvement must, of course, consider previously mentioned priorities, including as appropriate

✤ career development and assistance needs of the population to be served;

✤ attention to preventive and developmental opportunities and needs of the target population; and

✤ recognition of special populations (i.e., minorities, poor and homeless, people with disabilities, etc.).

The Counselor's Professional Development

Much has been written in recent years regarding staff development, yet it is our observation that few counseling organizations have planned active programs for this purpose. However, it seems reasonable to assume that more programs will recognize the benefits that accrue, not only to the programs themselves but to their professional staffs as well, from active staff development programs that increase the skills and knowledge of their counselors.

> Staff development can encompass a wide variety of activity, including performance appraisal, continuing education, lectures, conferences, seminars, supervisory relationships, and numerous organizational relationships that allow staff members to enhance their possession of human service technology and skills (Miringoff, 1980, p. 147).

Other activities may include quality circles, research involvement, exchange programs, sabbatical leaves, and reviews of professional literature. Of course, practicing counselors must assume the primary responsibility for their own professional development, even when benefiting from well-planned organizational staff development programs. This means your career will be in your own hands, so to speak, and therefore you will be largely responsible for determining your professional goals, the accomplishments or procedures needed to achieve these goals, and the resources that must be used in the process. Your professional development, of course, can contribute to the further development of your organization and the counseling profession as well.

One of the first steps beginning counselors can take to ensure their professional development is to join appropriate professional organizations. Such organizations as the American Counseling Association and the American Psychological Association and their divisions provide excellent professional journals, newsletters, workshops, and conventions for the professional development of their members.

Beyond joining the appropriate professional organizations, counselors should be active participants in the development of the profession as well. This means participating and sharing through attendance at professional meetings and conference presentations and sharing one's ideas and findings through writing and research.

Finally, we would note that the counselor's professional development is not just about self-enhancement, although that is certainly one of the goals of professionalization. Nor is it just about contributing more to your organization and the profession of counseling, although these, too, are desirable outcomes. It is first and foremost being the best, the most up-to-date, the most relevant you can be for the benefits of your clients. Your clients have the right to expect this from you—as you in turn expect it of your physician, dentist, lawyer, and so forth. Thus, the true professional is one whose learning is continuous and ongoing, who steadily grows across his or her professional life span.

SUMMARY

Much of the success of any counseling program will depend on how the program is managed, developed, and led. As educational and community institutions have become more complex in their organizational and operational structure, the necessity for special preparation of program leaders in terms of managing resources, coordinating and facilitating activities, and providing personnel

motivation has become increasingly self-evident. Counselors, as organizational staff members, must also be aware of their responsibilities and be knowledgeable enough to carry them out.

The next chapter discusses an area to which counseling program leaders and their staffs are giving increased attention. Accountability and evaluation are being demanded of all programs, and counselors are being called on to advance "the frontiers of knowledge" of our profession.

DISCUSSION QUESTIONS

1.   Do you find activities such as writing letters, managing your finances, and handling such personal management items as insurance, food planning, and study planning challenging, boring, or something you put off?

2.   What differences do you see between the manager of a business (e.g., auto dealer, grocer, insurance agent) and the manager of a counseling program?

3.   Identify some well-known leaders (past or present) that you have admired. What is it that you have admired about them?

4.   What kind of a program leader would you like to work for?

5.   What is the relationship between needs assessment and program relevancy?

6.   Comment on the suggestions given when budgeting is of concern in program management.

7.   How can counseling programs protect themselves from budget and/or staff reductions?

CLASS ACTIVITIES

1.   Examine the leadership characteristics offered as being significant to the success of counseling and compare those to your personal characteristics. How do you size up?

2.   Compare the leadership qualities desired in counselors to leadership qualities typically identified with other fields (e.g., the military, business and industry, politics). Discuss in small groups and compare answers.

SELECTED READINGS

Ebert, M. K., Richardson, W. M., & Stevenson, J. W. (1985). *A study of the guidance program and its management in the Montgomery County Public Schools.* Rockville, MD: Montgomery County Public Schools, Department of Educational Accountability.

Gibson, R. L. (1990). Teachers' opinions of high school counseling and guidance programs: Then and now. *The School Counselor, 37,* 248–255.

Hannaford, M. J. (1987). Balancing the counseling program to meet school needs. *NASSP-Bulletin, 71, 34,* 69.

Lampe, R. E. (1985). Principals' training in counseling and development: A national survey. *Counselor Education and Supervision, 25,* 44–47.

MacDevitt, M., & MacDevitt, J. (1987). Low cost needs assessment for a rural mental health center. *Journal of Counseling and Development, 65,* 505–507.

Orzek, A. (1987). Innovations in ecological psychology: Conversations with Roger and Louise Baker. *Journal of Counseling and Development, 65,* 233–237.

The School Counselor, 39, January 1992 [Special issue].

Terril, J. L. (1987). Positive approaches strengthen school and counseling programs. *NASSP-Bulletin, 71,* 19–22.

Wilson, N. S., & Remley, T. P., Jr. (1987). Leadership in guidance: A survey of school counseling supervisors. *Counselor Education and Supervision, 26,* 213–230.

RESEARCH OF INTEREST

Peterson, S., & DeGracie, J. S. (1983). *Secondary counseling services as perceived by selected publics.* (Tech. Rep. N. RR-49). Mesa, AZ: Mesa Public Schools, Department of Research and Evaluation.

Abstract

In the spring of 1983, an evaluation of the junior and senior high guidance programs in the Mesa public schools was conducted. Surveys were developed to solicit opinions from parents, teachers, counselors, administrators, career specialists, and students as to how counselors actually spend their time versus how they should spend their time. Results were analyzed separately for each group of respondents and for the junior high and high school programs. Parents, teachers, counselors, career specialists, and students believed that junior high counselors devote the greatest amount of time on student registration, followed by registration and consultation with parents. All groups believed that counselors should spend most of their time on individual personal or academic/vocational counseling. Overall ratings of the junior high program varied by group; parent and student ratings were lowest. Results from the high school program evaluation were very similar, and recommendations cover both levels. Survey instruments were very similar, and recommendations cover both levels. Survey instruments and responses are included in the appendix.

Prout, H. T., & DeMartino, R. A. (1986). A meta-analysis technique to school-based studies of psychotherapy. *Journal of School Psychology, 24*, 285–292.

Abstract

The results indicate that psychotherapy in the schools is moderately effective. Evidence was also found of the greater efficacy of group and behavioral theory interventions that target observed behaviors and problem-solving abilities.

Warchal, P., & Southern, S. (1986). Perceived importance of counseling needs among adult students. *Journal of College Student Personnel, 27*, 43–48.

Abstract

This study fails to confirm the existence of major differences in the perceptions of counseling needs attributable to developmental period (age) and sex. Existing data on the nature of counseling needs of adult students are confirmed.

Chapter 13

Accountability, Evaluation, and Research

It is important for the beginning counselor to recognize that he or she alone is responsible—accountable—for being an effective and efficient counselor. The beginning counselor must also anticipate being the subject of professional evaluation as well as participating in organizational evaluation. Also, since both accountability and evaluation frequently imply research needs, it is important to understand basic research design and sources of research reports that may provide insights into local concerns or issues. Therefore, the objective of this chapter is to introduce concepts and guidelines for the beginning counselor's involvement in program accountability, evaluation, and research.

The mere mention of the activities of accountability, evaluation, and research is said frequently to strike fear into the hearts of many honest practitioners. Such concern includes (a) the fear of being held responsible, regardless of intervening variables, for one's activities; (b) the fear of being judged by criteria determined externally, over which one has no control; (c) the fear of being judged by unrealistic standards and expectancies; (d) the fear of being required, in the case of research, to master difficult mathematical formulas that one feels will never be used again; (e) the fear of being expected to understand and possibly even apply the results of research studies written by researchers to impress other researchers; and (f) the fear, or assumption, that evaluation is never intended to be positive.

Many of these fears will diminish to mere myths when one learns to appreciate the values and advantages of accountability, evaluation, and research for the practicing counselor.

DEFINITIONS

Although textbooks and many periodical articles have been published dealing with the separate topics of accountability, evaluation, and research, this chapter will present an overview that, while giving each area its just due, stresses the relationships among accountability, evaluation, and research. Let us then distinguish among these terms.

In discussing accountability, Blocher (1987) comments that

> the principle that users of resources should demonstrate the results they obtain with those resources is called *accountability*. Of course, truly professional counselors are always accountable to themselves, their clients, and their profession. However, organizational accountability often demands more specifically that counselors and their employing agencies demonstrate in formal ways that they are effective in advancing the goals for which their resources have been provided. (p. 387)

Leon Lessinger, who is often referred to as the "father of accountability" for the impetus given this movement during his tenure as commissioner of education, defines *accountability* as responsibility for something, to someone, with predictable consequences for the desirable and understandable performance of the responsibility (Lessinger, Cunningham, & Sabine, 1973). In effect, "accountability" is the holding of some one, group, or organization responsible for their planning, actions, and outcomes.

The term *evaluation* seems to take on many meanings depending on the definer. Certainly evaluation is both a term and a process, both suggesting a determination of the value or worth of the object of the process. Evaluations can be made of individual, group, organizational, or institutional performances. As Hershenson and Power (1987) note, "evaluation is an elastic word and the term *program evaluation* does not have a standardized, commonly accepted meaning" (p. 268).

A definition of *evaluation* from the National Institute of Mental Health suggests as a working definition the following:

> Program evaluation is a systematic set of data collection and analysis activities undertaken to determine the value of a program to aid management, program planning, staff training, public accountability, and promotion. Evaluation activities make reasonable judgments possible about the efforts, effectiveness, adequacy, efficiency, and comparative value of program options. (Hagedorn, Beck, Neubert, & Werlin, 1976, p. 3)

Another easily understood definition views

> evaluation as the determination of the worth of a thing. It includes obtaining information for use in judging the worth of a program, product, procedure, or objective, or the potential utility of alternative approaches designed to attain specific objectives. (Worthen & Sanders, 1973, p. 19)

We suggest that the process of evaluation seeks to provide objective evidence of a program's performance through an assessment of progress toward program objectives. The evidence collected through this process then becomes valuable as a basis for future program planning and decision making. As such, a planned and conscientious program evaluation is essential to the continuous improvement of counseling programs in any setting.

A common definition views *research* as organized scientific efforts that seek the advancement of knowledge. Galfo (1975) suggests that "research implies a systematic study of variables in order to determine if and/or how they may be related to one another" (p. 8). Research represents an effort and a way of establishing truths. It is a process for validating—or rejecting—theoretical assumptions and/or unsubstantiated claims or practices. According to Worthen and Sanders (1973):

> Research is the activity aimed at obtaining generalizable knowledge by contriving and testing claims about relationships among variables or describing generalizable phenomena. This knowledge, which may result in theoretical models, functional relationships, or descriptions, may be obtained by empirical or other systematic methods and may or may not have immediate application. (p. 1)

ACCOUNTABILITY

In the 1990s taxpayers, consumers, and organizational managements have demanded more and more that those offering goods and services provide some concrete evidence of their worthwhileness in return for the public's expenditures of monies, whether through taxation or purchases of goods or services. These demands have resulted from not only increased costs but also frequent failures to meet the public's expectations and/or lack of proof of accomplishments. The November 1993 issue of *Guidepost*, the official newspaper of the American Counseling Association, is headlined "Many school counseling programs cut when finances run low!" The article goes on to state that cuts are often made when school boards and the public perceive counseling as auxiliary services. Some examples are also noted of school systems retaining their counseling staffs thanks to public support. It might be concluded that accountability is an opportunity for counseling programs to prove themselves. It must not be neglected!

Although accountability first became a byword in education, its popularity has also spread to other tax-supported governmental institutions and agencies, including mental health agencies. Hershenson and Power (1987) point out:

> Much of the discussion of accountability in the mental health field assumes as an underlying premise that improved information and delivery structure can contribute to the productivity and efficiency of resource use. In other words, can greater benefits or effects be obtained at the same cost? (p. 270)

Thus, with the possible exception of private practice, the likelihood is great that counselors will be employed in settings in which they will be expected to be accountable—to provide factual evidence of their accomplishments related to their costs.

A Positive View of Accountability

Recognizing that many helping professionals have negative attitudes or, at the least, uneasy feelings about accountability, let us accentuate the positive. In his "An Argument for Constructive Accountability," Baker (1977) presents five positive aspects of accountability:

a. Skill acquisition: Whatever accountability system one uses, certain specific skills are required of the participants. Acquisition of such skills may increase one's satisfaction and confidence. Satisfaction with one's level of competence is associated with knowledge of specific skills possessed. Confidence in one's capacity to encounter new tasks, such as those related to an accountability system, increases with acquisition of new skills. Among those skills that may be acquired or improved through attention to an accountability system are the ability to envision and develop a system; developing data collection instruments; analyzing data; reporting results; making decisions based on acquired results; making plans for future actions based upon acquired results; and applying those plans to a real-life setting.

b. Program improvement: Conscientious counselors are constantly searching for ways to improve their services. Finding useful sources of evaluative information about the existing services is a universal problem for these people. An accountability system offers the solution of this universal need because data acquired from the accountability activities may be used as the basis for program improvement. As a result, data are used constructively.

c. Positive results: Results acquired through an accountability system may be complimentary. Prospects of acquiring complimentary outcomes from accountability studies need to be emphasized more than is presently the case.... Such results provide intrinsic rewards for the counselor because awareness of consumers' satisfaction or of successful program outcomes provides the counselor with a feeling of satisfaction and accomplishment.

d. A process rather than an event: A systematic ongoing model incorporates the accountability activities and other planned enterprises with a minimum amount of drudgery and maximum efficiency.

e. Rewards for a job well done: The ultimate outcome for an accountability system, it seems, is to reward intrinsically those who have demonstrated that their accomplishments are extraordinary. . . . The reward system is viewed as the ultimate outcome because it completes the unfinished accountability model. (pp. 53–55)

Krumboltz (1974) also notes:

The potential advantages warrant counselors' efforts to construct a sound accountability system for themselves. An accountability system would enable counselors to

❖ Obtain feedback on the results of their work.

❖ Select counseling methods on the basis of demonstrated success.

❖ Identify clients with unmet needs.

❖ Devise shortcuts for routine operations.

❖ Argue for increased staffing to reach attainable goals.

❖ Request training for problems requiring new competencies.

How would counselors benefit from a sensible accountability system? By learning how to help clients more effectively and efficiently, counselors would obtain:

❖ More recognition for accomplishments.

❖ Increased financial support.

❖ Better working relationships with other professionals.

❖ Acknowledged professional standing.

❖ The satisfaction of performing a constantly improving and valued service. (pp. 639–646)

It is clear from the statements of Baker, Krumboltz, and others that conscientious counselors, dedicated to improving their skills and serving their clientele as effectively and efficiently as possible, have little to fear and much to gain from a system that will be their ally. Accountability may, at last, provide the ultimate proof that counseling programs can make a positive difference.

Developing Accountability in Counseling Programs

Krumboltz (1974) identifies seven criteria to be met if an accountability system is to produce the desired results:

1. In order to define the domain of counselor responsibility, the general goals of counseling must be agreed to by all concerned parties.

2. Counselor accomplishments must be stated in terms of important observable behavior changes by clients.

3. Activities of the counselor must be stated as costs, not accomplishments.

4. The accountability system must be constructed to promote professional effectiveness and self-improvement, not to cast blame or punish poor performance.

5. In order to promote accurate reporting, reports of failures and unknown outcomes must be permitted and never be punished.

6. All users of the accountability system must be represented in designing it.

7. The accountability system itself must be subject to evaluation and modification. (pp. 640–641)

Biegel and Naparstek (1982) note:

Accountability is not a one-way street; that is, not only the public sector should determine what services are delivered to a neighborhood, and whether they are delivered appropriately and effectively. Procedures for insuring mutual accountability are necessary in which consumers are accountable to providers, and providers are accountable to consumers. In this way we can help ensure that the system remains relevant. Without procedures for mutual accountability, providers are often unable to identify the strengths and needs of individuals and their families. A delivery system cannot be effective if individuals are viewed only in relation to separate programs. By building mutual accountability procedures into the system, consumers will be assured an opportunity to make their views known and to make those views count. This implies, for example, citizen involvement in the development of a mental health service from planning to evaluation stages. (pp. 276–277)

Although there is no best single approach to developing an accountability model, most programs seem to focus on some form of needs assessment out of which program objectives are identified and perhaps arranged according to priorities that, in turn, lead to program activity planning and an accounting for and evaluation of the outcomes.

As we proceed from this section on accountability to the next section discussing evaluation, we would note the relationship of evaluation to accountability. According to Lewis and Lewis (1991):

Most human service programs are required to submit yearly evaluation reports for the scrutiny of funding sources or public agencies and many specially funded projects are required to spend set percentages of their total budgets on evaluation. Beyond this, however, agencies are also accountable to their communities. The "accountability model" Windle and Neigher (1978, p. 97) describe stresses this component of evaluation. The accountability model takes the position that a program should be evaluated by the public and/or those who support it. Such evaluation can have at least three purposes: (1) to let the public or other supporters make wise decisions concerning support, (2) to motivate the public and other supporters to greater program support by involving them in the goals and activities of the program, and (3) to motivate the program staff to greater public service and efficiency by their awareness that their activities are being monitored.

Dissemination of evaluation reports describing the agency's activities and their effects can help reinforce program accountability. People concerned with agency performance can gain knowledge about the results of services, and this information undoubtedly increases community members' impact on policies and programs. (p. 235)

EVALUATION

Everyone constantly seeks ways to improve many daily, routine chores, whether it is trying a new toothpaste or a different breakfast cereal or taking a new route to work. In a sense, people constantly evaluate many daily decisions and activities. People are also involved, usually unofficially, in many external evaluations such as of the local newspaper, a current

TV program, the decisions of Congress, and the teachers, courses, and textbooks with which children come in contact. Just as these evaluations are a part of the process of improving daily living or exercising a right to express one's opinions, the more formal, structured evaluations of one's professional activities and organizations should also receive daily and constant attention.

As the critics of counseling have so frequently and constantly pointed out in recent years, justifiably or not, evaluative evidence and activities appear, all too frequently, to be either missing or often misleading at best. In addition, Hershenson and Power (1987) have alerted us to the reality that counseling programs are under closer scrutiny and accountability from a variety of sources as our programs have expanded and the demands for our services have increased.

Evaluation: A Process for Professional and Program Improvement

One often reads or hears about a public-office holder, a salesperson, or a teacher with 30 years of experience but with no mention of the quality of that experience. Experience does not, in and of itself, guarantee improvement in quality. Professionals must have as their own personal-ethical goal the constant and critical evaluation of their professional performance. A lack of evaluation often leads to mediocrity or failure to reach one's full potential in terms of what professionals might accomplish for the clients they serve. Evaluation, then, for counselors in a variety of settings and for other professionals, is first and foremost a process for professional improvement, a process in which one gathers objective, performance-oriented data on a systematic and nonbiased basis. These data are then used as information that leads to constantly improving, upgrading, and updating one's professional performance.

Amid the changing concepts of evaluation in recent decades, one of the most popular among evaluation experts is the view of evaluation as a process for providing information for decision makers. Evaluation is viewed as a process that can provide decision makers at all levels with objective data that will assist them in determining the relative value of competing alternatives and that will immeasurably improve their probability of making the "right decisions" for program improvement.

In this context of evaluation as a process for program improvement, two distinctions in evaluation are important. The first—*formative evaluation*—focuses on the major purposes evaluation can serve. The second—*summative evaluation*—is concerned with the locus of the evaluator.

Worthen, White, and Borg (1993) note that

> formal evaluation studies can serve either a *formative* purpose (such as helping to improve a mathematics curriculum) or a *summative* purpose (such as deciding whether that curriculum should be continued). Although these distinctions may blur somewhat in practice, they are useful nonetheless.
>
> *Formative evaluation* is conducted during the planning and operation of a school program to provide those involved with evaluative information they can use in improving the program. For example, assume a school district is attempting to develop a local curriculum package on the history of their particular county. During development of the new curriculum unit, formative evaluation might involve content inspection by history experts' early tryouts with small

numbers of children in one school in the district, and so forth. Each step would provide immediate feedback to the curriculum developers, who could use such information to make necessary revisions.

Summative evaluation occurs after a curriculum or program is considered ready for regular use, and provides potential consumers evidence about the program's worth. In our example, after the local history program was developed, a summative evaluation might determine how effective the program was in teaching local history, using a broad sample of the schools, teachers, and students in the district for which it was developed. The findings of that summative evaluation could be made available to all schools in the district who could then better determine whether to use the history unit in their schools. Summative evaluation is also used to make "go/no go" decisions, such as whether to continue or terminate a particular curriculum.

Formative and summative evaluation are both essential because decisions are needed early in the development of a program, to improve it, as well as when it has stabilized, to judge its final worth.* (p. 625)

Evaluation: Other Functions

The wide range of evaluation purposes may seem to rival that of the political party platforms of "promising something for everybody." Although that is not the intent, it is important to recognize some of the values of this activity. Examples of these additional functions of evaluation are as follows:

❖ Verifies or rejects practices by providing evidence for what works and what does not, or the degree to which an activity seems to be effective. This also tends to lead to the avoidance of meaningless innovations and unproven fads.

❖ Measures improvement by providing evidence on a continuous basis so that both rate and level of progress may be ascertained.

❖ Enhances probability of growth by providing a basis for improvements in the operation and its activities.

❖ Builds credibility. By the very nature of the activity, evaluation suggests a continuous search for better ways of doing things; a constant quest for improvement; a willingness to put efforts on the line and take a look at "how we're doing."

❖ Provides for increased insights. By the fact of examining our own or an organization's functioning, we become more knowledgeable and understanding about this functioning, more aware of influencing factors and potential consequences.

❖ Increases and improves participating in decision making. Because evaluation involves everyone within the organizational structure, the process, by necessity, involves them in the outcomes, which in turn should bring about the participation of all such personnel in the planning of new directions and implementing the findings.

❖ Places responsibilities. By identifying who is responsible for what and when, evaluation stimulates linkages between specific persons and specific activities. It decreases the probability of everyone claiming responsibility for the successes and no one claiming the failures.

❖ Provides a rationality for the enterprise by improving overall accountability, including evidence of accomplishments and growth.

Lewis, Lewis, and Souflee (1993) state that evaluators may use

research techniques, but they apply them to the needs of specific agencies. Evaluation can be used to aid in administrative decision making, to improve currently operating programs, to provide for accountability, to build increased support for effective programs, and, in some instances, to make generalizations about the connections between specific activities and their effects. (p. 234)

Principles of Evaluation

Because evaluation is a process for appraising the value or effectiveness of a program or activity, it is most effective when conducted within a framework of guiding principles. Seven of these are discussed here.

1. *Effective evaluation requires a recognition of program goals.* Before any meaningful program of evaluation can be undertaken, it is essential that the goals or objectives of that program be clearly identified. These objectives provide indications of program intent, which form the basis for subsequent planning and procedures. The objectives of the program should be stated in clear and measurable terminology. This principle suggests that counseling programs be evaluated on the basis of "how well they are doing what they set out to do."

2. *Effective evaluation requires valid measuring criteria.* Once program goals are clearly defined, valid criteria for measuring progress toward those goals must be identified. The development of such criteria is crucial if the evaluation is to be both valid and meaningful. For example, if an annual program goal for a junior community college counseling program would be to provide each entering student with a series of three career interviews with a counselor, the measuring criteria could be a simple count indicating the percentage of students who did, in fact, have such an opportunity. If, on the other hand, the program goal was to provide each student with a "broadening of his or her career understanding," the measuring criteria would be less obvious and might depend on a further refinement of what is meant by "career understanding." In other words, vaguely stated goals and criteria lessen the effectiveness of program evaluation.

3. *Effective program evaluation is dependent on valid application of the measuring criteria.* As discussed in the previous paragraph, valid criteria for measuring progress toward the program's stated goals must be established. It is not sufficient, however, to merely establish criteria. Their ultimate validity will depend on their valid application. This implies that effective evaluation of all counseling programs should involve, in each instance, persons who are professionally competent in both evaluation techniques and understandings of such counseling programs. Too often, effective evaluation criteria are dissipated in the hands of evaluators who have, at best, only a superficial knowledge of the appropriate role and functions of counseling programs.

4. *Program evaluation should involve all who are affected.* Evaluation of a school counseling program, for example, should involve those who are participants in or who are affected by the program. This would include, in addition to the counseling staff, faculty members and administrators, students and their parents, and, on appropriate occasions, members of the community or supporting agencies. The major contribution to effective evaluation must come from those who have a firsthand knowledge or involvement in the program. External evaluators from governmental agencies, accrediting associations, or other educational institutions can, of course, be helpful, but those should not be the sole bases of evaluation.

5. *Meaningful evaluation requires feedback and follow-through.* The evaluation process and the evaluation report are not in and of themselves of great value. Only when the results are used for program improvement and development does the evaluation process take on meaning. This presumes, then, that the results of any program evaluation are made available to those concerned with the program management and development. It also presumes that the program manager and his or her staff will use these results for future program planning and decision making.

6. *Evaluation is most effective as a planned, continuous process.* This approach may enable the program staff to identify at any point in time weaknesses that need correcting immediately or accomplishments that should be capitalized on. This means that there are specific plans and designated responsibilities for both the ongoing evaluation of a program's progress and the more extensive annual or semiannual reviews.

7. *Evaluation emphasizes the positive.* Frequently, evaluation is viewed as a threatening process aimed at ferreting out hidden weaknesses and spotlighting "goofs." If program evaluation is to produce the most meaningful results possible, it must be conducted in a spirit that is positive, is aimed at facilitating program improvement, and emphasizes strengths as well as weaknesses.

Methods of Evaluation

Before-and-After Method

This method of evaluation seeks to identify the progress that takes place in a program's development as a result of specific program activities over a given period of time. For example, an objective of a school counseling program might be to provide each student with a weekend work experience during his or her junior year. At the beginning of the school year, before the program, it could be presumed that none had had this experience. At the end of the year, after the program, the number who actually participated would give some indication of goal achievement.

Comparison Methods

The "how do we compare" process makes evaluations on the basis of comparing one group against another or against the norm of a number of groups. Different techniques for achieving the same goal can also be evaluated by this comparative method. For example, a secondary school in Bloomington, Indiana, might note that it has a counselor-pupil ratio of 1 to 258, compared with the norm for 200 midwestern secondary schools of 1 to 418. Such a comparison would indicate, of course, that the Bloomington school system is making more adequate provisions for high school counseling personnel than most other school systems in the Midwest.

The "How Do We Stand" Method

This method is based on identifying desirable program outcomes and related characteristics and criteria. From these criteria, rating scales, checklists, and questionnaires may be developed and used to indicate the degree to which a program measures up. For example, evaluative criteria or checklists used by most accrediting associations and many state governmental agencies and departments reflect this approach. Although this method to evaluation may locally ignore appropriate objectives and sometimes unique and innovative practices, it does provide guidelines that enable programs to be compared with generally accepted standards.

Procedures for Evaluation

The evaluation process usually involves a series of activities in a sequence, which approximates the following.

1. *Identification of goals to be assessed.* The first step establishes the variables, or limits, for the evaluation. Evaluation can focus on the total counseling program or on only one or several particular objectives. These program objectives should be stated in clear, concise, specific, and measurable terms. Broadly stated goals (e.g., "to facilitate the adjustment of the student body of J. J. Jenkins High School") are much more difficult to measure than a specifically stated goal, such as "to provide each student in J. J. Jenkins High School with a yearly scheduled opportunity to discuss his or her career planning with a school counselor."

2. *Development of an evaluation plan.* Once the objectives for evaluation have been established, the identification and validation of criteria appropriate for measuring the program's progress toward these objectives follow. In the previous example, a simple yet valid criterion would be an indication of the percentage of the J. J. Jenkins High School students who actually did have a scheduled career-planning interview with a school counselor. This example illustrates the principle that measuring criteria should also be stated in specific and objective terms. The overall evaluation plan, in addition to specifying the kinds of data to be collected, should also describe how it will be collected, when, and by whom. This plan must also give attention to how the data will be organized and reported and to whom. Finally, such a plan should conclude with provisions for using the findings for future program development.

3. *Application of the evaluation plan.* After an acceptable evaluation plan has been designed, its validity is then dependent on the manner in which it is carried out. Once again, we stress the importance of adequate planning and a positive approach, utilizing evaluators who possess the necessary understanding and competency. Timing is also important because some aspects of a program can only be appropriately evaluated in a "longitudinal" sense, whereas other specific activities need an "immediately after" assessment.

4. *Utilization of the findings.* Evaluation as an activity is in itself of little value. It is in the application of the findings that the real worth of evaluation lies. Through the process of evaluation, programs can ascertain their strengths and weaknesses. The resulting insights may then provide directions for future program improvement. The utilization of these

findings, however, cannot be left to mere chance. There must be planning, with specific responsibilities for the utilization of the findings, and subsequent follow-up to establish the degree to which the evaluation recommendations have been fulfilled.

Worthen, White, and Borg (1993) state that

evaluations of school programs would improve if more people knew the importance of

❖ deciding *when* to evaluate

❖ deciding *what* precisely to evaluate

❖ deciding *whom* the evaluation is intended to serve

❖ deciding *who* should conduct the evaluation

❖ deciding *what* questions the evaluation should address

❖ planning the evaluation study

❖ deciding *how* to report the evaluation study

❖ dealing effectively with the political, ethical, and interpersonal issues in evaluation (p. 628)

Evaluation for Community Mental Health Counseling Programs

Community mental health center programs have also felt increased pressures to conduct systematic program evaluations, partly as the result of the rising demands of the federal government to verify program efficiency and effectiveness in community mental health centers. In this regard, Public Law 94-63, the Community Mental Health Centers Amendments of 1975, requires community mental health centers to allocate not less than 2% of their previous year's operating budgets to conducting program evaluation. The law mandates three general types of evaluation, as follow:

1. Quality assurance of clinical services. Each center is to establish an ongoing quality assurance of its clinical services.

2. Self-evaluation. Each center will collect data and evaluate its services in relation to program goals and values and to catchment area needs and resources. The data shall consist of (a) Cost of center operations; (b) Patterns of use of services; (c) Availability, awareness, acceptability, and accessibility of services; (d) Impact of services upon the mental health of residents of the catchment area; (e) Effectiveness of consultation and education services; (f) The impact of the Center on reducing inappropriate institutionalization.

3. Residents' review. Each center will at least annually publicize and make available all evaluation data of the type listed above to residents of the catchment area. In addition, it will organize and publicize an opportunity for citizens to review the Center's program of services in order to assure that services are responsive to the needs of residents of the catchment area. (Hagedorn, Beck, Neubert, & Werlin, 1976, pp. 6–7)

RESEARCH

Research does not always project a popular image, for some of the reasons listed here:

❖ Most research seems to ignore the common problems and everyday needs of practitioners.

❖ Most research reports are written in a manner that limits their interpretation and hence their application by practitioners.

❖ Research activities and resulting research reports rarely excite the imagination.

❖ The research monies made available by federal and state agencies are "cornered" by universities and private research and development corporations.

❖ Research is too time-consuming and has very few rewards for most practitioners.

All these concerns may have some basis in fact, as Goldman (1978), in his introduction to *Research Methods for Counselors*, writes:

> From 1969 to 1975 I was editor of the *Personnel and Guidance Journal* [currently entitled *The Journal of Counseling and Development*]. I resolved from the beginning that we would publish only those articles that had something to say to counseling practitioners, that we were a reader's not a writer's journal. We found almost no research manuscripts during those years that satisfied that criterion; quite a few research reports were received, especially in the earlier years, but almost every one of them either was so technical that it could not be truly understood except by very research-sophisticated people, or was so limited in its implications that it really had nothing to offer the practicing counselor. . . . I came to the realization that the problem was not "research" as a general idea but rather the kinds of research that have predominated in our field. I became convinced that the kinds of research methods and the kinds of research studies that prevail in the field are largely inappropriate or inadequate for most of the kinds of knowledge and insight counselors require in their daily work. (pp. 4–5)

Stockton and Hulse (1983) appropriately call attention to the fact that "[c]ounseling is an applied discipline with an emphasis on practice; yet, if the profession does not assume responsibility for intellectual inquiry which might provide answers to basic questions concerning effective practice, the field cannot advance" (p. 303). In joining those calling for more "useable" research in our field, we would emphasize that research can (a) provide positive outcomes, (b) be carried out by even beginning practitioners within a simple framework of research procedures, and (c) be interesting.

Positive Outcomes of Research

For general practitioners in counseling and other helping professions, the most positive general outcome of "practitioner research" is the improvement of one's professional skills and understanding. Research can answer professional questions, dilemmas, and failures. Research enables practitioners to become better at their "art." It can allow us to verify what works and what does not and, if pursued, why. It can eliminate much of the guesswork and uncertainty from practices. Engaging in practical research can increase our insights and deepen understandings of ourselves, the counseling profession, and the relationships between the two. Our own research can help us as individual professionals become better at what we do.

Also, practitioners' research tends to focus on "local" problems or concerns and may therefore have opportunities to provide results that are immediately applicable. The opportunities to "make a positive difference" in one's job environment can be challenging. Furthermore, even if practitioners tend to focus on local concerns in their research activities, that still gives them the opportunities to make contributions to their profession, to exchange their ideas and findings with other similar local settings and other interested professionals. Presentations and discussions at local, state, and national conferences give the researcher further opportunities to share findings, explore with other professionals the implications of the results, and possibly expand the interpretation of the research findings.

Finally, research can be interesting. Any new experience, learning of new knowledge or finding an answer to an old problem can be stimulating. Research only becomes dull and meaningless to researchers when they investigate topics or problems that are to them dull and meaningless. Identify a professional question (problem or concern) that you would personally like answered and set out to find the answer. You may find it a surprisingly exciting quest, and you may then agree that research can be one of the most rewarding professional activities.

Some Definitions

Basic Research

Basic research is concerned with or conducted solely for the purpose of theory development or the establishing of general principles. In educational and other settings, basic research provides the theory that, in turn, produces implications for solving problems.

Applied Research

Applied research provides data to support theory through applying or testing the theory and evaluating its usefulness in problem solving.

Action Research

Action research is designed to solve problems through the application of scientific method. For example:

> Action research provides a systematic framework in which the practicing counselor, therapist, or other professional in the helping field can solve problems and determine the effectiveness of his or her work. Action research provides a model for the evaluation of the effectiveness of an individual, a single program or a totality of guidance services. (Goldman, 1978; p. 80)

Historic Research

> Historical research involves studying, understanding, and explaining past events. The purpose of historical research is to arrive at conclusions concerning causes, effects, or trends of past occurrences which may help to explain present events and anticipate future events. (Gay, 1976, p. 9)

Galfo (1975) discusses four types of historic methods:

1. Crosschecking pieces of evidence against each other.
2. Establishing authorship of a document by comparative study.
3. Investigations of chronological events.
4. Word and language interpretation. (p. 15)

Descriptive Research

Descriptive research seeks to test hypotheses or answer questions concerning the present. There are two major classifications of descriptive research: qualitative and quantitative. In quantitative research the investigator

> either directly or through coding schemes observes events and then makes inductive inferences based on these observations. The qualitative researcher, rather than rely on outside observational schemes, tries to retain the perspective of the people being studied. This usually involves an analysis of field or observational notes or a study of audio or video recordings. Finally, quantitative and qualitative researchers usually address different research questions. According to Patton, the goal of quantitative research is to describe cause-and-effect relationships in the physical world. Qualitative researchers, on the other hand, attempt to describe and understand the ways that people give meaning to their own and others' behavior. (Patton, 1984, as cited in Heppner, Kivlighan, & Wampold, 1992, p. 195)

Experimental Research

This sort of research experiments with different variables in order to predict what will occur in the future under a given set of conditions.

> Experimental educational research has been derived from the laboratory method often used in the natural sciences. In its most elementary form, the experimental method of science is based on two assumptions regarding variables that may be identified in the phenomenon under investigation:
>
> 1. If two situations are equal in every respect except for a factor present in one of the situations, any difference which appears between the two situations can be attributed to the factor. This statement is referred to as the "law of the single variable."
>
> 2. If two situations are not equal but it can be demonstrated that none of the variables are significant in producing the phenomenon under investigation; or if significant variables are made equal, any difference occurring between the two situations after the introduction of a new variable to one of the systems can be attributed to the new variable. This statement is referred to as the "law of the only significant variable." The purpose of establishing experimental-control conditions, thus, is to create a situation in which the effect of a single variable can be studied. (Galfo, 1975, pp. 17–18)

Pilot Study

A pilot study is a preliminary trial of research methods and instruments before the development of the final research plan.

Hypotheses

Hypotheses are predictions regarding the probable outcome of a research study that, in turn, form a basis for goals and procedures to achieve these goals.

Sampling

Sampling is a research technique for selecting a specified number of people from a defined population as representative of that specific population.

The Research Process

Some research undoubtedly requires complex, sophisticated research skills. However, much valuable information can be obtained through research that meets the requirements of scientific inquiry but does not require a high level of research skill. In fact, "[e]legance of design is not the ultimate test of the adequacy of research. The test is whether the objectives of the researcher are furthered and whether these objectives turn out to be useful" (Cramer, Herr, Morris, & Frantz, 1970, p. 2).

Thus, the following examination of research procedures is not intended to provide a basis for undertaking research but rather to provide a better understanding of the basic factors involved in conducting research. It is hoped it will encourage practitioners to consider and become involved in relatively unsophisticated research investigations.

The first step in undertaking research is the identification of a researchable problem—a need for information. Whatever stimulates your interest or curiosity or arouses doubts in you may be a basis for the identification of a research problem. Most of us experience a constant and continuing need for information in our daily jobs. We wonder about the adequacy or effectiveness of our techniques, the various characteristics of our clients, and the nature of client needs. If we decide to initiate research in the area of techniques, we might simply seek to determine the kinds of information needed for justifying present practices or developing more effective and functional ones.

A second step in most research is to review or survey previous research and writings relevant to the possible research topic. The purposes of this review are to (a) see whether adequate answers have already been found to the questions the researcher has in mind, (b) gain a better understanding of the nature of the problem, and (c) gain insights regarding approaches that might be used to efficiently attain the outcomes desired. Although in the past this particular step may have been one that discouraged many from considering research activities, the computer capacities of libraries with various information retrieval systems enable even the neophyte researcher to have in hand, quickly, a computerized printout of relevant research and writings, usually summarized for convenience.

The third step is to identify specifically the nature of the information desired or formulate the specific research problem. The problem should be stated fully and precisely in objective terminology in a complete grammatical sentence. It should be written so that others can understand it without the prompting of the researcher.

The beginning researcher should also be aware that within the main problem there may be logical subcomponents, identified as subproblems:

> By being solved separately these subproblems resolve the main problem piecemeal. By looking at the main problem through its subproblems, the researcher frequently gets a more global view of the problem. Think of a problem, therefore, in terms of its component subproblems. Rather than make a frontal attack upon the entire problem, divide and conquer it in small segments. (Leedy, 1974, p. 51)

The fourth step in the research process is to determine the kinds of information needed to permit sound conclusions about the issue (or issues) in question. In this step, the previously stated problem and related subproblems are now viewed through questions or logical constructs, called *hypotheses*. Hypotheses are assumptions made regarding the problem or its solution that provide the researcher with some direction for the gathering of facts that will provide the most valid answers. For example, a research investigation may be attempting to determine why a school has an unusually high dropout rate. It could be hypothesized that there are several possibilities for this dropout rate: (a) students are not interested in school; (b) students lack the ability to continue in school; (c) students are under economic pressure to leave school and obtain a job. Each of these assumptions or hypotheses provides some direction or basis for identifying facts, which would enable the investigator to determine factually why the majority of students are leaving school.

Having identified the kinds of information needed, in the fifth step, the researcher determines what procedures are most appropriate for collecting and analyzing the data. In this stage, the population or sample to be used and the means by which it is to be selected are determined, as are instruments and other data-collecting tools appropriate for the questions or hypotheses that have been stated. In this step, the researcher seeks to determine the most appropriate sampling procedures and the most efficient, effective instruments or techniques for gathering the data needed in order to respond to the hypotheses as completely and validly as possible.

Once the types of information and the procedures and instruments needed for gathering this information have been determined, the sixth step is the actual collection of the data.

In the seventh step, the collected data are systematically organized and analyzed. The method of data analysis should be determined before collecting data in order to ensure that the suggested treatment is appropriate to the data collected and the manner in which it is organized. Depending on the research design developed in step 5 of this sequence, the analysis may be no more than a simple mathematical or elementary statistical one.

Beginning practitioners can still engage profitably in research activities by simply recognizing their limitations in the design of their study. In the final step, the research findings are interpreted and conclusions drawn, which may lead to resolving or answering the problems. Here the previously stated hypotheses are either confirmed or rejected and answers are provided to the questions that initiated the research activity. Figure 13–1 depicts the research process.

Utilizing Research Reports

Findings from research studies can be important to counselors in all settings. Research findings can provide factual data to reinforce or guide their professional judgment and improve their practice. Whether one is an active researcher or not, a counseling professional cannot afford to gloss over the important research in the field. We must, for example, be aware of both the reservoir of accumulated knowledge dealing with human behavior and the results of current research studies that broaden, deepen, or perhaps alter our understanding of this behavior. As research technology continues to improve, we can anticipate an increase in research studies, more sophistication in their methodology, and validity in their outcomes, as well as more relevance and application of the findings. Thus, all practicing counselors must not only recognize the importance of research but also be cognizant of what we might label "guidelines" for identifying research of potential significance. Gibson, Mitchell, and Higgins (1983) identify these as (on p. 440):

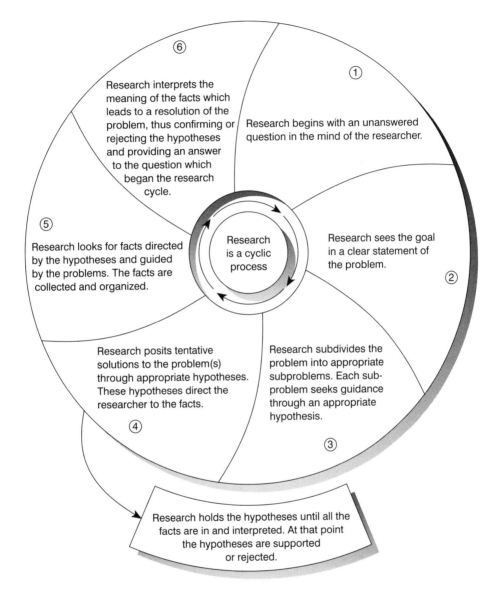

⑥ Research interprets the meaning of the facts which leads to a resolution of the problem, thus confirming or rejecting the hypotheses and providing an answer to the question which began the research cycle.

① Research begins with an unanswered question in the mind of the researcher.

Research is a cyclic process

Research sees the goal in a clear statement of the problem. ②

⑤ Research looks for facts directed by the hypotheses and guided by the problems. The facts are collected and organized.

④ Research posits tentative solutions to the problem(s) through appropriate hypotheses. These hypotheses direct the researcher to the facts.

Research subdivides the problem into appropriate subproblems. Each sub-problem seeks guidance through an appropriate hypothesis. ③

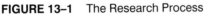

Research holds the hypotheses until all the facts are in and interpreted. At that point the hypotheses are supported or rejected.

FIGURE 13–1 The Research Process

Source: Reprinted with the permission of Macmillan College Publishing Company from *Practical Research: Planning and Design* by Paul D. Leedy, p. 8. Copyright © 1974 by Paul D. Leedy.

Be Aware of Common Sources of Research Reporting in Your Field

Some common indices and abstracts such as the *Review of Educational Research, The Education Index, Social Science Index, Sociology Index, Index Medicus, Psychological Abstracts,* and *Dissertation Abstracts* are good starting points to broadly identify reports of recent research investigations. Publications representing the professional organizations in counseling and related fields are rich sources of recent research studies in the field.

Identify Research Studies Which Appear to Be Relevant to Your Own Professional Needs

The abundance of reported research, past and present, is enough to overwhelm the most conscientious researcher. Any user of research findings must learn to be selective lest she or he drown in the ever growing tidal waves of research reporting. Therefore, it is important that we identify as specifically as possible the kind of knowledge we are seeking and focus our search on this topic.

Review the Studies You Have Selected in Terms of the Following:

a. The design of the study: (You may need the assistance of a competent researcher at this point. They are not too difficult to locate if you are close to a large school system, institution of higher education, large mental health agency, or state government office.) This is important in determining the probable accuracy of the findings, their generalizability to your situation, and the conclusions or implications which can be drawn from them.

b. Readability: Some research reports are technical reports written primarily for other researchers. Both the vocabulary and the statistical methods through which the data are presented may confuse, mislead, or simply confound the reader. Unsophisticated attempts to "figure out" what the report is saying should not be undertaken. If you cannot understand the report you should select a different report to study or you may again seek the help of a competent researcher who can interpret the study for you.

c. Originality of the research: A firsthand report of a study by the researcher(s) who was the principal investigator is more desirable than "second-hand" reporting, summaries, or citations by others. Whereas secondary sources can be useful, they are usually more brief than the original source and may inadvertently misrepresent the findings.

d. Reputation of the author/researcher may also be considered. Established researchers/authors have achieved their preeminence through previous studies that have been endorsed by their peers as sound in design, addressing important needs, and significant in their findings. (pp. 330–331)

Writing Research Grant Applications

Millions of dollars are made available to agencies, institutions, and school systems annually from federal and state agencies and private foundations. These monies, usually earmarked for specific purposes, are most frequently allocated or "awarded" on the basis of a competitive review of proposals or grant applications received. Since many funding opportunities are in the areas of counseling interest and expertise, counselors must possess the necessary "application skills" to competitively pursue such funding as may be of interest and appropriate for their organizations. The following general guidelines are suggested:

1. Read thoroughly the published announcements and/or other information that describes the guidelines to follow in preparing and submitting a grant application.

This will, among other things, help you determine the eligibility and appropriateness of a response from your organization.

2. Follow to the letter the guidelines for the preparation and submission of the grant proposal. The appropriate format is expected, and the dates or submission deadlines must be met.

3. Know, to the fullest extent possible, the funding agency or foundation.

Personal contacts by visit or phone are, of course, very useful in clarifying, explaining, or elaborating on purposes, procedures, and guidelines. Some agencies will provide, on request, examples of exemplary projects and lists of previous recipients. Foundations will send you their annual reports and publications such as the *Commerce Business Daily, Federal Register, The Education Daily,* and *Federal Grants and Contracts Weekly.* Descriptions of private foundations and their research priorities are indicated in *The Taft Foundation Reporter* (published by the Taft Group in Washington, DC) and *The Foundation Directory* (published by the Foundation Center, New York).

As Gibson et al. (1983) note:

All specified sections of a proposal format are important, but the four that are briefly explained in the following discussion require special attention.

Statement of the Problem
This section of the proposal should contain a well-defined, specific statement of the problem; the need for such a study (its educational significance); and concisely stated, measurable objectives. Conceptual and research literature should be cited to stress the significance of, or the need for, the study, but the literature cited should be specifically relevant to the proposed study.

Procedures
This section of the proposal must present the design of the study and a fully detailed description of the procedures to be utilized. It should be apparent to a reader that the stipulated procedures will enable the achievement of the project's stated objectives. It should describe the sample to be used and how the sample is to be selected, the instruments and other data-collecting tools or approaches to be utilized, the statistical treatments to be applied, and the evaluational procedures to be employed. If the objectives were definitely stated—as they should be—the evaluational procedures should evolve from them. Although this section must be concise, it must also be complete. A basic criterion for evaluating most proposals is the soundness of the methodology employed.

Personnel and Facilities
This, too, is a most important section, especially in proposals for federal funding. As the purpose of this section is to enable a determination of the research capabilities, care must be taken to identify the personnel involved and to show that by training and experience, these individuals have the research competencies required for the implementation of the proposed study. Similarly, the facilities required for the research endeavor should be described and their availability assured.

Budget
The cost estimates for the proposed project must be accurate, detailed, justifiable, and reasonable. It must be clearly evident how the anticipated expenditures relate to each of the specific procedural steps. (pp. 333–334)

Reporting Research Results

Obviously, conducting research is not enough—unless you intend to keep the results selfishly to yourself! Reporting your study enables you to advance not only yourself professionally but the profession as well. This reporting can either be done orally—through presentations at professional conferences, workshops, and such—or in writing, through reports in professional journals, newsletters, monographs, and so forth. Oral reports have the advantage of enabling the audience to directly question and interact with the presenter at the moment. Written reports have the advantage of reaching a wider audience. Heppner et al. (1992) present some general principles for writing research reports: "(1) be informative, (2) be forthright, (3) do not overstate or exaggerate, (4) be logical and organized, (5) have some style, (6) write and rewrite, and (7) if all else fails, just write!" (p. 376).

These authors go on to note that in writing for publication, the exact organization

of a research report varies depending on the publication for which it is intended and the nature of the study. Nevertheless, a perusal of counseling journals reveals a modal organization, roughly as follows:

Title

Abstract

Introduction

Method
- Subjects
- Measures (or Variables or Instruments)
- Materials
- Design (or Design and Analysis)
- Procedure

Results

Discussion (or Conclusions)

References

Tables

Figures

The nature of each of these components depends on the publication and the readership. Nevertheless, there are some aspects of each of these components that are critical to a well-written research report. (p. 376)

Ethical Issues in Human Research

By its very nature, counseling research, with rare exceptions, must involve human beings. Growing concern for the rights of human subjects has resulted in increased efforts on the part of professional organizations and research institutions and agencies, including the U.S. government, to safeguard the rights and dignity of individuals who are involved as subjects of research.

In this regard, attention must be given to protecting subjects' right to privacy, determining whether the research puts subjects at risk in any way, obtaining informed consent of subjects, and not involving subjects in research that challenges or threatens their morals or values.

SUMMARY

Accountability, evaluation, and research are all responsibilities of counseling programs and counselors in any setting. Although each is a distinct activity in its own right, the interrelationships are evident, since all can improve a program. Furthermore, all three activities hold promise for the advancement of the professional and the profession. Accountability provides a model or method for the assessment of professional achievements. Evaluation enables one to gather evidence regarding the quality of a program's performance. Research allows one to advance the scientific knowledge in a field. Counselors should therefore understand the research process, how to locate and read research reports, and how to compete for research monies.

DISCUSSION QUESTIONS

1. What is meant by the term *accountability?* Why has it become so popular in recent years?

2. How can counselors become more accountable?

3. What are the differences between accountability and evaluation?

4. Have you ever had an idea that you would have liked to research? If so, what did you do about it?

5. What are some of the relationships between evaluation and research?

6. What objective evidence could you provide to the general public that counseling "works"?

7. What difficulties do you envision in providing objective evidence that your counseling is effective?

CLASS ACTIVITIES

1. In small groups discuss the pros and cons of your experiences of being evaluated as a student over the years of your schooling.

2. Students are currently evaluated (graded) on certain performance criteria (i.e., tests, papers, projects, etc.). How might this change if students were asked to become "accountable"? Discuss in small groups.

3. Read a recent research report (periodical article) in the field of counseling. Report this research to the class, discussing its implications for practice.

SELECTED READINGS

Anderson, W., & Heppner, P. (1986). Counselor application of research findings to practice: Learning to stay current. *Journal of Counseling and Development, 65,* 152–155.

Brown, M. (1988). The mental health counselor and research: And never the twain shall meet? *Journal of Mental Health Counseling, 10,* 9–15.

Chamberlain, K., & Borrough, S. (1985). Techniques for teaching critical reading. *Teaching of Psychology, 12,* 213–215.

Conley, D. (1988). Critical attributes of effective evaluation systems. *Chronicle Guidance* (pp. 88–122). Monrovia, NY: CGP Professional.

Drott, M. C. (1984). How to read research: An approach to the literature for the practitioner. *School Library Media Quarterly, 12,* 445–449.

Fairchild, T. N. (1986). Time analysis: Accountability tool for counselors. *School Counselor, 34*(1) 36–43.

Fish, L. (1988). Why multivariate methods are unusually vital. *Measurement and Evaluation in Counseling and Development, 21,* 130–137.

Gillies, R. M. (1993). Action research in school counseling. *The School Counselor, 41*(2), 69–80.

Heaney, R. P., & Barger-Lux, M. J. (1986). Priming students to research critically. *Nursing and Health Care, 7,* 421–424.

Heppner, P. P., Gelso, C. J., & Dolliver, R. H. (1987). Three approaches to research training counseling. *Journal of Counseling and Development, 66,* 45–49.

Mancall, J. C. (1985). Evaluating research: A critical consumer approach. *Top of the News, 42,* 101–104.

Matthews, B., & Paradise, L. (1988). Toward methodological diversity: Qualitative research approaches. *Journal of Mental Health Counseling, 10,* 225–234.

Myrick, R. D. (1984). Beyond the issues of school counselor accountability. *Measurement and Evaluation in Guidance, 16,* 218–222.

Newman, J., & Scott, T. (1988). The construct problem in measuring counseling performance. *Counselor Education and Supervision, 28,* 71–79.

Ponterotta, J. (1988). Racial/ethnic minority research in the *Journal of Counseling Psychology:* A content analysis and methodological critique. *Journal of Counseling and Development, 35,* 410–418.

Robinson, S. E. (1986). Counseling research: Ethics and issues. *Journal of Counseling and Development, 64,* 331–333.

Stockton, R., & Hulse, D. (1983). The use of research teams to enhance competence in counseling research. *Counselor Education and Supervision, 22,* 303–310.

Tait, P. E. (1984). Do-it-yourself evaluation of experimental research. *Journal of Visual Impairment and Blindness, 78,* 356–363.

RESEARCH OF INTEREST

Boser, J. A., Poppen, W. A., & Thompson, C. L. (1988). Elementary school guidance program evaluation: A reflection of student-counselor ratio. *The School Counselor, 36,* 125–135.

Abstract

Examines the perceived effectiveness of guidance programs in Tennessee public schools representing the following three distinct student-to-counselor ratios: (a) one school, one counselor, fewer than 600 students; (b) one school, one counselor, 750–1,000 students; and (c) three to four schools, one counselor, 1,000 to more than 2,000 students per counselor. It was found that as the student-to-counselor ratios increase, the number of students who cannot be adequately served by the counselor also increases, which thus reduces the overall effectiveness of the counselor as perceived by students, parents, and school staff.

Gerler, E. R. (1985). Elementary school counseling research and the classroom learning environment. *Journal of Elementary School Guidance and Counseling, 20,* 39–48.

Abstract

Explores research evidence of elementary school counselors' effectiveness in helping children improve classroom behavior, explore feelings, improve socially, and enhance sensory awareness and mental imagery. Concludes that counselors should be able to use this evidence for demonstrating the importance of their work to school policymakers.

Hillenbrand, E., & Claiborn, C. D. (1990). Examining reasoning skill differences between expert and novice counselors. *Journal of Counseling and Development, 68,* 684–691.

Abstract

Examines the cognitive reasoning of expert and novice counselors involved in a diagnostic activity. Cases experienced variation according to the extent to which problem relevant information was clear and apparent. Concludes that the structure of the problem being diagnosed is likely to be a significant variable influencing reasoning.

Hinkle, J. S. (1992). Computer-assisted career guidance and single-subject research: A scientist-practitioner approach to accountability. *Journal of Counseling and Development, 70,* 391–395.

Abstract

Presents an overview of computer-assisted career guidance. Describes how use of intensive research designs can promote further accountability among computer-assisted career counselors. Describes applicable single-subject research, alternating treatment designs, and replication information.

Plake, B. S., Conoley, J. C., Kramer, J. J., & Murphy, L. U. (1991). The Buros Institute of Mental Measurements: Commitment to the tradition of excellence. *Journal of Counseling and Development, 69,* 449–455.

Abstract

Reviews the history of the Buros Institute of Mental Measurement by highlighting origins of the *Mental Measurements Yearbook.*

Bibliographic reference series, Tests in Print, and specialized monographed series are described through a historic perspective. Plans for the 1990s are discussed.

Sedlacek, W. E., & Adams-Gaston, J. (1992). Predicting the academic success of student-athletes using SAT and noncognitive variables. *Journal of Counseling and Development, 70,* 724–727.

Abstract

Compares the predictability of the Noncognitive Questionnaire (NCQ) and the Scholastic Aptitude Test (SAT) in predicting academic success for student-athletes at the collegiate level. Suggests that noncognitive variables are better predictors of grades and academic success for athletes than are SAT scores. Concludes that athletes need to be considered nontraditional student-athletes rather than student-athletes.

Segal, N. L. (1990). The importance of twin studies for individual differences research. *Journal of Counseling and Development, 68,* 612–622.

Abstract

Describes 10 research methodology designs related to twin research. Findings focus on personality and temperament issues, learning disabilities, attitudes, behavior disorders, and social behavior. Implications for mental health practitioners and counselors are discussed.

Seligman, L., & Kelly, S. C. (1990). Writing and publishing books in counseling: A survey of authors. *Journal of Counseling and Development, 68,* 42–45.

Abstract

Provides data from 74 authors of books published in the field of counseling. Reviews the process of writing and publishing books, and presents information regarding timetables, choosing publishers, and obtaining and negotiating contracts. Authors' suggestions for prospective authors are provided.

White A., & Hernandez, N. R. (1991). Trends in article citations in three counseling journals, 1952–1988. *Journal of Counseling and Development, 69,* 419–422.

Abstract

Examines article citations in the *Personnel and Guidance Journal, Journal of Counseling and Development, Journal of Counseling Psychology,* and *Counselor Education and Supervision Journal.* Results demonstrate that citations gradually became more numerous while also coming from increasingly distinct sources. The authors conclude also that the focus of each journal fills a special function while also contributing to the field of research as a whole.

Chapter 14

Ethical and Legal Guidelines

This final chapter focuses on the responsibilities that you incur as you enter the career world of the professional counselor. It emphasizes the importance of practicing within the ethical guidelines established by your professional associations and those legal guidelines established by law. In fact, the very labeling of counseling as a "helping profession" suggests that we have assumed the responsibilities of all professions in providing for our clientele and serving the public. These responsibilities include acceptable standards of performance or competence, accepted code of personal conduct in relationships with clients and the public, and a commitment to contribute to the public well-being that transcends monetary gain for the counselor.

A profession also takes responsibility for regulating or policing its membership to ensure that ethical and legal guidelines are adhered to and that legal enactments are sought where desirable to protect the public. A profession's commitment to appropriate ethical and legal standards is critical to the profession earning, maintaining, and deserving the public's trust. Without this trust, a profession ceases to be a profession. In addressing this point, Biggs and Blocher (1987) state:

> Ethical questions are rooted in the public trust that defines any profession, and that is the major reason that they are of central concern to all of the members of a professional group. Whenever the perceptions of the public are changed by the unethical, unprofessional, or irresponsible behavior of a member of the profession, all other members are harmed, and indeed their ability to function in professional ways is diminished or impaired.
>
> Professionals who deliver counseling services must be especially concerned with ethical problems because their clients are often very vulnerable to manipulation and exploitation. Clients disclose very intimate issues in their lives and should be assured that such risk-taking will be respected and dealt with in a professional manner. We believe that ethical counseling should involve an awareness of and a commitment to maintain this important responsibility to protect client trust. The ethical counselor must be keenly aware of the possible impact of his or her actions on a client's present and future status and must be able to make complex moral/ethical judgments (pp. 4–5)

THE NATURE OF ETHICS

A code of ethics represents the professional values of a profession translated into standards of conduct for the membership. Codes of ethics provide structure or guidelines for its membership to follow in their professional practice and also for the public to anticipate in their interactions with the profession and its membership.

For counselors at least two basic statements of ethical practice and behavior apply to work in the profession: (a) *Ethical Standards* of the American Counseling Association (see Appendix B), and (2) *Ethical Principles of Psychologists* (American Psychological Association, 1992) (see Appendix C). These codes of ethics and professional standards are expected to be followed by the members of these associations. Failure to abide by these standards may result in a member being expelled.

> The cited standards are basically concerned with counselor responsibilities, competence, client relationships and confidentiality. In addition, both the American Psychological Association (APA) and several divisions of the American Counseling Association (ACA) have adopted standards for measurement and evaluation. (Hummel & Humes, 1984, p. 382)

The primary types of items to be found in most codes are

✤ the specific duties or rights that differ from ordinary ethical requirements;

✤ the specific duties or rights that may simply be the application of general ethical principles in a particular professional area;

✤ a reiteration of certain ordinary ethical requirements that need emphasis for some reason;

✤ aims or general goals that the professional should aspire to realize;

✤ requirements that relate to coordinating or protecting the interest of members of the profession; and

✤ a statement of the responsibility of members of the profession for reporting code violations or other violations. (Mabe & Rollin, 1986, p. 294)

ETHICAL ISSUES

Competence

The ethical issue of competence begins when the counselor accepts a position as a professional counselor. The counselor must determine, along with the potential employer, whether she or he is qualified by virtue of training and, where appropriate, experience for the position. The counselor applicant must also indicate qualifications for licensure or certification where appropriate. It is also important to the prospective counselor-employee to indicate special interests and/or values that might influence on-the-job functioning. Obviously, from the outset, counselors should not apply for positions in which they are not interested or not competently qualified to fill.

On the job, the counselor is professionally responsible to practice within his or her limitations. Although "competence" is often difficult to determine, training and experience can provide useful guidelines for determining what we are qualified to do. Consultation with supervisors and/or more experienced professional colleagues can help identify the limits of one's professional competence.

Degrees, licenses, and certificates may convey to the public levels of competence, yet, in actuality, we must recognize variations in the competencies among practitioners with the same credentials. We would also again note the responsibility of the professional counselor to continuously "update" their competence through participation in various professional educational opportunities, reading the professional literature, and so forth.

When a counselor determines that a client's needs may be beyond his or her competencies, arrangements should be promptly made for an appropriate referral. This responsibility includes assisting the client in identifying and arranging an appropriate professional referral.

Confidentiality and Privileged Communication

Trust is an important cornerstone in the counseling relationship, and central to the development and maintenance of trust is the principle of confidentiality. The obligation of counselors to maintain confidentiality in their relationships with their clients is not absolute, however, and counselors need to be aware of both the ethical and legal guidelines that apply.

In distinguishing between "confidentiality" and "privileged communication," it is important to keep in mind that confidentiality is an *ethical* concept, whereas privileged communications is a *legal* concept.

Confidentiality is defined as

> an ethical responsibility and a professional duty that demands that information learned in private interaction with a client not be revealed to others. Professional ethical standards mandate this behavior except when the counselor's commitment to uphold client confidences must be set aside due to special and compelling circumstances or legal mandate.* (Arthur & Swanson, 1993, p. 3)

Sometimes counselors may be working with life-threatening clients involving child abuse, possible homicide, or suicide threats. In cases of known or suspected child abuse, in most states, state laws require that suspected cases be reported. Legally, counselors are also required to breach confidentiality to protect the life of a third party. The ethical codes of both the American Psychological Association and the American Counseling Association allow counselors to breach confidentiality if necessary to protect the life of a suicidal client. More on the legal aspects of privileged communications will be presented in the next section of this chapter.

Arthur and Swanson (1993) note exemptions cited by Bissell and Royce (1992) to the ethical principle of confidentiality:

1. The client is a danger to self or others. The law places physical safety above considerations of confidentiality or the right of privacy. Protection of the person takes precedence and includes the duty to warn.

2. The client requests the release of information. Privacy belongs to the client and may be waived. The counselor should release information as requested by the client.

3. A court orders release of information. The responsibility under the law for the counselor to maintain confidentiality is overridden when the court determines that the information is needed to serve the cause of justice.

4. The counselor is receiving systematic clinical supervision. The client gives up the right to confidentiality when it is known that session material will be used during supervision.

5. Clerical assistants process information and papers relating to the client. The client should be informed that office personnel will have access to the records for routine matters such as billing and record keeping.

6. Legal and clinical consultation are needed. Again, the client should be informed of the (ethical) right of the counselor to obtain other professional opinions about progress and the name(s) of those used as a consultant(s).

7. Clients raise the issue of their mental health in a legal proceeding. In a custody suit, for example, parents introduce their mental condition into the suit, whereupon they authorize release of the counselor's records.

8. A third party is present in the room. Clients are (presumably) aware a person other than the counselor is present and therefore waive their right of privacy in permitting the third person to be present.

*Reprinted from G. L. Arthur, Jr., and C. D. Swanson, "Confidentiality and Privileged Communication" in T. P. Remley, Jr. (Ed.), *ACA Legal Series, 6,* 1993. © American Counseling Association. Reprinted with permission. No further reproduction authorized without permission of the American Counseling Association.

9. Clients are below the age of 18. Parents or guardians have the legal right to communication between the minor and the counselor.

10. Intra-agency or institutional sharing of information is part of the treatment process. Otherwise confidential material may be shared among professional staff when it is in the interest of the client to do so. However, the client must be aware that this is being done.

11. Sharing of information is required within a penal system. Information obtained from prisoners that may otherwise be considered confidential may be shared within the system in the interest of the operation of the system and disposition of the case.

12. The client's purpose in disclosing information was to seek advice in the furtherance of a crime or fraud. The obligation here changes from one of maintaining confidentiality to one of protecting society from further criminal activity.

13. The counselor has reason to suspect child abuse. All states now legally require the reporting of suspected abuse.* (pp. 20–21)

Personal Relationships with Clients

In examining the personal relationships between counselors and their clients, professional organizations have sought to define the ethical limits of the professional relationship. A major concern of the mental health professions, in this regard, has been the sexual exploitation of clients by their therapists. Although the codes of ethics of all major professional organizations unequivocally condemn such activities, Herlihy, Healy, Cook, and Hudson (1987), among others, have specifically discussed the extent of this ethical violation. In this study, the authors state:

> The second most frequently claimed type of violation involved sexual relationships with clients. Although similar claims against psychiatrists and psychologists have received considerable publicity in the popular press, it is disturbing to learn that claims of sexual exploitation of clients by licensed counselors are reported with this frequency. (p. 75)

In their relationships with clients, counselors must, at all times, avoid exploiting the client's trust. This exploitation might be for financial gain, social status, research data, or other motives, as well as sexual favors. Hopkins and Anderson (1990) warn that

> a sexual relationship between a counselor and a client is clearly unethical, and may form the basis of an action for professional malpractice or negligence. In many states such conduct also constitutes a criminal offense, although a separate criminal suit must be prosecuted. The laws vary among the states in the requirements of this offense as well. In Minnesota, for example, sexual conduct with a patient is prohibited regardless of the client's consent. Some states also prosecute such relations as rape, or statutory rape in the case of a minor client. In each case specific penalties are prescribed as punishment, and in some states victim compensation may also be required. (p. 52)

In addition, relationships with clients that may impair the counselor's professional judgments or the client's responses must be avoided. This means avoiding counseling relationships with relatives, close friends, and employers, among others.

*Reprinted from G. L. Arthur, Jr., and C. D. Swanson, "Confidentiality and Privileged Communication" in T. P. Remley, Jr. (Ed.), *ACA Legal Series, 6,* 1993. © American Counseling Association. Reprinted with permission. No further reproduction authorized without permission of the American Counseling Association.

Finally, the counselor must at all times be aware of the "human rights" of clients. Even the severely mentally ill have legal and ethical rights that the counselor must be guided by in practice. This includes their right to participate in the decision making regarding their treatment, the use of psychological tests, and any participation in research studies.

THE COUNSELOR AND THE LAW

During recent decades few aspects of the counselor's role and function in any setting have remained untouched by judicial and legislative activities. For example, the Community Mental Health Centers Act of 1980 defined "community to be served" in terms of geographic and topographic characteristics. Of even greater consequence, however, is the effort

> to integrate mental health and general health services. In associating the community mental health center with physicians and hospitals, the current policy seems to assert that emotional disorders are primarily biological and require, among other responses, medical treatment, often including hospitalization. This assertion would seem inconsistent with the bulk of the evidence. At the same time, however, the policy recognizes the special role of the general hospital as the locus of what is ordinarily the highest quality community health care and serves to induce the general hospital to concern itself more with the treatment of emotionally disordered persons, even when such treatment is not medical in nature. In other words, the policy implied in the Act encourages the general hospital to broaden its view of its role in the community.*
> (Bloom, 1984, p. 33)

Many other services that counselors and their fellow helping professionals must provide in community agency settings are specified by law. These include drug abuse treatment as well as treatment for the chronically mentally ill and severely disturbed children and adolescents. Most states have enacted legislation that provides a legal basis for those who may practice or designate themselves as counselors, and social workers.

Increasingly, managers of counseling programs and counselors themselves have become aware of the legal implications of their activities, the legal restrictions, and even legal conflicts with their professional conscience. This increased legal intervention is an outgrowth of a dramatic increase in litigation and attending legislation during the past 25 years.

In performing their professional duties, counselors must not put themselves in jeopardy for either civil or criminal liability. Thus, counselors must exercise "due care,"

> or face liability in a civil suit for failing to perform their duties as required by law. Civil liability, stated simply, means that one can be sued for acting wrongly toward another, or for failing to act when there was a recognized duty to do so. Judicial relief is usually in the form of money damages awarded to the injured party. (Hopkins & Anderson, 1990, p. 23)

> Certainly few counselors ever anticipate that they might become defendants in a criminal action simply by practicing their profession. Fortunately, very few ever do. But counselors should be aware of certain occupational hazards that could lead to criminal liability. The ideal

for professional counselors is to maintain a certain distance between themselves and their clients so they may advise the clients in a professional way. Occasionally, however, situations arise that might lead counselors to go much further in protecting their clients, or to provide emotional support and comfort, than the law literally allows. In such cases, the counselor may unwittingly risk criminal liability.

Criminal liability resulting from the professional practice of counseling might result in a variety of criminal charges such as:

❖ accessory to a crime;

❖ failure to report suspected child abuse;

❖ contributing to the delinquency of a minor;

❖ sexual misconduct. (Hopkins & Anderson, 1990, p. 49)

Contributing to the delinquency of a minor is of special concern to school counselors and those whose practice includes children and families. However, counselors in all settings where the potential exists for juvenile clients should be aware of actions that could lead to prosecution for contributing to the delinquency of a minor. All states have enacted legislation designed to protect children from acts or relationships deemed injurious. However, as Hopkins and Anderson (1990) point out:

> Unfortunately, most state legislatures have not defined the specific conduct that constitutes the crime, and many jurisdictions leave it to the jury to determine whether a defendant's conduct was criminal. A broad definition of the offense might include any actions that tend to injure the health, morals, or welfare of juveniles, or that encourage juveniles to participate in such actions. There is no certainty as to what constitutes this immoral conduct from state to state, however. (p. 52)

Counselors in all settings cannot afford to be "legally ignorant." They must understand the law and its implications in arenas of counselor concern and function. These include acts or practices that might be viewed as discriminatory, compromising the constitutional and other legal rights of, and prejudicing the opportunities of individuals. In this regard, note some of the legal implications for counselors of Title IX, the Buckley Amendment, and the Education for All Handicapped Children Act.

The Counselor and Title IX

Title IX of the Education Amendments of 1972, which took effect in July, 1975, provides that

> no person . . . shall on the basis of sex, be excluded from participation in, be denied the benefits of, or be subjected to discrimination under any education program receiving federal financial assistance.

Some implications of this act for practicing counselors are as follows. First, adequate counseling services must not only provide for the needs, interests, and abilities of clients but also must consider the changing nature of society and how such changes affect working with students. Counselors must help students in self-understanding and sorting through varying options and what their decisions may imply.

Second, counselors must be aware that differential sex socialization is often subtly perpetuated in the language and impressions of the media (e.g., textbooks, newspapers, magazines, television). While not justifiable, it is not surprising that such biases appear in career and other counseling materials.

In *Cracking the Glass Slipper: PEER's Guide to Ending Sex Bias in Your Schools*, Knox (1977) discusses Title IX and many of its implications for counselors:

> Nearly half of all the girls now enrolled in vocational education are enrolled in consumer and homemaking courses which do not prepare them for employment. The courses of study which do train for employment and in which girls predominate offer training in only 33 different occupations. In contrast, courses of study in which boys predominate offer training for paid employment in 95 different occupations. When girls do enroll in programs leading to paid employment, it is most often in areas such as office education or health services which offer relatively poor pay and relatively poor prospects for advancement. Many girls limit their own opportunities because they and their parents often approach vocational education with a narrow vision of what is appropriate and many schools have reinforced these notions with their own discriminatory policies. Schools have barred girls from certain courses of study outright and guided them away from other traditionally male fields through recruitment, admission, and counseling practices which discouraged girls' enrollment when it did not directly forbid it. The major issue in vocational education is whether girls are going to be as capable of supporting themselves as boys with the same level of education. If this is to be accomplished, a lot of past practices need to be changed. ("Vocational Education," p. 1)

> Title IX requires the school to assure itself that any outside agencies, business organizations, or individuals with whom it cooperates do not discriminate against its students on the basis of sex. This might be in cooperative education, work-study programs, apprenticeships, or job placement. If the outside party refuses to give that assurance—or gives it but continues to discriminate—the school is required to end its cooperation. ("Vocational Education," p. 5)

> The counselor can no longer cooperate with an outside agency, organization, or individual that wishes to discriminate against students on the basis of sex. What that boils down to is that if an employer is seeking a boy for summer employment, the counselor may not refer only one sex. For a counselor to be genuinely effective in counteracting stereotypes, the counselor will need to do more than simply not discriminate. An active attempt to expand options and opportunities is required. While Title IX does not require this kind of activity from the counselor, it is the kind of help most girls need to get past their own built-in stereotypes. ("Counseling," p. 3)

> No club which is school sponsored can be limited to a single sex. Outside organizations which receive significant assistance from the school must also be nondiscriminatory UNLESS they meet very strict criteria set up by title IX to exempt youth service organizations such as the Girl Scouts and Campfire Girls. In order to be exempt the sponsoring organization must: be single sex; be a voluntary youth service organization; have a membership mostly under 19 years of age; and be tax exempt. ("Rules and Customs," p. 5)

> More than one million teenagers become pregnant each year. We will need to be concerned that in teenage pregnancy, which involved two sexes to begin with, discrimination is most often directed against just one sex. More than half of all female dropouts leave school because of pregnancy. Eighty percent of the young women who become pregnant for the first time at age 17 or younger NEVER complete high school. Teenage mothers are less likely than

other mothers to be working and more likely to be receiving Aid to Dependent Children. Their critical lack of education certainly plays a part in this. Under Title IX the pregnant student has the same rights and responsibilities as any other student. Solely because of pregnancy, she:

a. may not be expelled from school;

b. may not be required to attend a special school for pregnant students;

c. may not be barred from any program, course (including physical education), or extracurricular activity, including competing for, or receiving, any award, honor, or elective office;

d. may not be required to take special courses in child care or related topics unless those courses are required of every other student in the school;

e. may not be required to leave school at a certain time before the birth of the child or required to remain out of school for a certain length of time afterwards:

f. may not be required to furnish notes from her physician that she is able to continue or re-enter a course of study unless such notes are required of all students (e.g., to tell when they intend to leave for surgery; or after an illness, to say that they are strong enough to return).* (p. 5)

The Counselor and the Buckley Amendment

Few legislative actions have had a greater impact on the practice of counseling and attending record keeping than the Buckley Amendment. Before the passage in 1974 of the Family Educational Rights and Privacy Act (FERPA) as it is titled (or the Buckley Amendment, as it is commonly called), counselors derived most of their directions for their professional functioning from the ethical guidelines provided by their professional associations. In this regard, the American Counseling Association's (formerly the American Association for Counseling and Development) *Ethical Standards* (1988) suggest:

> Records of the counseling relationships, including interview notes, test data, correspondence, tape recordings, and other documents, are to be considered professional information for use in counseling and they should not be considered a part of the records of the institution or agency in which the counselor is employed unless specified by state statute or regulation. Revelation to others of counseling material must occur only upon the expressed consent of the client. (p. 1)

Although ethical standards were not in themselves legally binding, there are numerous instances, beginning with the case of *Cherry v. the Board of Regents of the State of New York* in 1942, that suggested courts might use professional ethical codes as guidelines for making judicial decisions. In the case of record keeping and confidentiality, however, the passage of the Buckley Amendment became the single most important guideline for professional conduct with regard to student records and related activities.

> The FERPA stipulates that the parents of unemancipated minor students have . . . the right to inspect and review any and all official records, files, and data directly related to their children, including all material that is incorporated into each student's cumulative record folder and intended for school use or to be available to parties outside the school or school system, and specifically including but not necessarily limited to identifying data, academic work

---

*From H. Knox, *Cracking the Glass Slipper: PEER's Guide to Ending Sex Bias in Your School.* © 1977. Reprinted by permission of the National Organization for Women Legal Defense and Education Fund.

completed, level of achievement (grades, standardized achievement scores), attendance data, scores of standardized intelligence, aptitude, and psychological tests, interest inventory results, health data, family background information, teacher or counselor ratings and observations, and verified reports of serious recurrent behavior patterns. (Getson & Schweid, 1976, p. 57)

Recognizing the conflict or, as they put it, ethical standards squeeze, Getson and Schweid (1976) suggest the following steps for school counselors to protect their counselees and students:

First, review all existing records to assure that there is no material that predates FERPA that would violate implied-to-stated guarantees of privacy to the child. Second, remove all material that, because of its technical nature or vocabulary, may be inappropriate for use by lay persons. Retain only materials that can be expressed in a form unlikely to be misinterpreted. Third, initiate a policy of maintaining only records that can be reviewed with parents without threat to the welfare of a counselee. Fourth, be sure that counselees understand the legal limitation of the privacy afforded the counseling relationship relative to the rights of parents to inspect official records. Fifth, initiate a study of the full implications of the conflict between the FERPA and ACA's Ethical Standards. There may be safeguards to the right to privacy of the student implicit in FERPA of which we who are not lawyers are not aware. Sixth, if there is a clear or probable conflict between the FERPA and ACA's Ethical Standards, initiate action to change the act, the standards, or both. It would seem that, as a minimum, a provision should exist within the act that withholds from anyone except public authorized investigative bodies information under study. (pp. 57–58)

Because school counselors as well as counselors in other educational settings are frequently called on to write letters of recommendation for college admissions or employment, it should be noted that the Buckley Amendment implications are clear that

unless the educator is specifically informed otherwise, he or she should assume that the student may have access to letters of recommendation. The student can be requested to sign a waiver, so that he or she will not have such access. However, unless such a waiver is signed, the student can be defended, both factually and professionally. In general educators are on relatively safe ground when writing letters of recommendation if the following conditions are met:

1. Letters of recommendation are an expected, normal, and integral part of one's duties and responsibilities.

2. Letters are sent only to second parties (not published), who can be expected to have a reasonable interest in and concern for the person in question.

3. Letters are factual, free of malice, and reasonably objective.

4. Letters are in response to a request. (St. John & Walden, 1976, p. 683)

St. John and Walden (1976) make three recommendations:

First, it is recommended that professional educators consult with an attorney, preferably one conversant with educational matters, or with the school district's legal counsel, on all matters regarding confidential communications. Second, it is recommended that school districts and state departments of education cooperatively develop detailed guidelines to assist all school personnel in protecting student confidences and to respect the confidentiality of communications consistent with state and federal statutes. Third, it is recommended that the various professional organizations develop specific and up-dated codes of ethics related to this area. (p. 683)

School Counselors and Public Law 94-142

Another act of importance to school counselors is the Education for All Handicapped Children Act (PL 94-142) of November 1975. This law guarantees the rights of all children, regardless of the severity of the disability, to a free, appropriate education. The law further establishes a formula for providing financial aid to states and local school districts, based on the number of children with disabilities receiving special education plus related services. It is this latter activity—related services—that provides for counseling by a certified counselor. In noting the implications of this act for counselors, Humes (1978) states that

> while the role of the counselor in the implementation of PL 94-142 will vary from district to district and in part will be contingent on the availability of other specialized personnel and whether the counselor has an elementary or secondary assignment, it is difficult to conceive of any situation in which a counselor will have no role to play. Some of the possible ranges of responsibility are
>
> 1. participation in team meetings.
> 2. development of the IEP (Individual Education Plan).
>
> (IEP—The core of the law is the concept of the IEP. An IEP, which is to be reviewed annually, must be developed for each handicapped child. The content of the IEP must include the present level of functioning, annual goals, short-term measurable objectives, and specific educational services required by the child.)
>
> 3. monitoring progress.
> 4. parental counseling.
>
> (A section of the law that is overlooked, partly because of its traditional neglect in American public education and partly because of the ambiguous nature of the language in the statute, is the requirement for parent counseling. Parent counseling may have a variety of meanings. Parent counseling suggests a possible range of services from psychiatric assistance to advice about academic offerings and may occur in an outside agency or within the school. A conservative approach would suggest that parent counseling should occur in the school setting and satisfy the definition of counseling as opposed to therapy. If we accept this assumption, the logical person to satisfy this need would be the counselor.)
>
> 5. extracurricular planning.
> 6. classroom consulting.
> 7. in-service training.
>
> (While it is reasonable to assume that in the early stages counselors will be the recipients of in-service training along with other pupil personnel services workers, it would be a reasonable assumption that in the middle-to-later stages of implementation the counselor will become one of the providers of in-service training.)
>
> 8. record keeping. (pp. 193–195)

Jenkins (1985) specifies skills for elementary school counselors involved in main-streaming as follows.

1. Working with nonhandicapped elementary school children to encourage acceptance of individual differences.

2. Helping handicapped children understand their strengths and weaknesses and make use of existing skills to function in an environment not equipped for handicapped persons.

3. Developing counseling activities for all elementary school children, including those with special needs.

4. Developing activities to assist the development of a positive self-concept in the child with special needs.

5. Formulating teacher, parent, and administrator counseling groups to discuss attitudes and feelings toward the student with special needs. (p. 203)

LEGAL CONCERNS OF COUNSELORS

Confidentiality

Earlier in this chapter we discussed the issue of confidentiality and privileged communication for counselors. This remains a paramount legal as well as ethical issue confronting the counseling profession. In a survey of existing privileged communications statutes and rules of evidence in the 50 states and the District of Columbia, Herlihy and Sheeley (1987) note that among helping professionals, psychologists are most frequently protected, followed by social workers. School counselors are granted the right to privileged communication, sometimes limited, in 27 states.

In a personal communication to the authors, Herlihy (1994) indicates the following:

At the present time, 39 states and Washington, DC, have some form of licensure, registration, or certification for counselors. A *preliminary* examination of the data from these states reveals that:

1. Some provision that establishes privileged communication between counselor and client exists in 27 states (AL, AZ, AK, DE, FL, ID, IL, KS, LA, ME, MA, MS, MO, MT, NE, NM, NC, OH, OK, OR, RI, SD, TX, VA, WA, WV, WY). No privileged communication provision was found in 12 states (CA, CO, GA, IA, MD, MI, NH, ND, SC, TN, VT, WI) or Washington, DC.

2. Although it has been suggested that attorney-client privilege has been used as a model for many licensure bills (Bloom et al., 1990), only four states (AL, AK, KS, LA) provide for privileged communication between counselor and client on the same basis as attorney and client.

3. Despite calls for uniformity in licensure laws, the privileged communication provisions in existing laws show considerable variation. Limitations and exceptions to privilege are spelled out in all but the four statutes noted above in 2., and include various combinations of the following:

   a. When the client or client's representative waives the privilege, or in family therapy when each family member agrees.

   b. When information is subpoenaed by a licensing board in connection with an investigation.

    c. When there is a duty to warn and protect.

    d. When minor children are involved.

    e. When a client brings a complaint or charges against the counselor.

    f. When the "umbrella" of privilege is extended to others who provide services (colleagues, superiors, clerical assistants, supervisees).

    g. When there are criminal law exceptions (violations or when the client was a crime victim).

    h. When a client voluntarily testifies.

    i. When the client's physical or mental condition is an issue in a court action.

    j. Other "catch-all" phrases such as "when disclosure is necessary for justice," "when court determines that information is not germance," and "as otherwise required by law."

Fischer and Sorenson (1991) cite Wigmore, the leading authority on the Anglo-American law of evidence, as indicating four requirements:

1. The communications must originate in confidence that they will not be disclosed.

2. The confidentiality must be essential to full and satisfactory maintenance of the relationship between the parties.

3. The relationship must be one which, in the opinion of the community, should be sedulously fostered.

4. The injury to that relation, caused by disclosure, would be greater than the benefit gained by the process of litigation.

These criteria are generally accepted by modern scholars of the law of evidence as the appropriate test for what qualifies as privileged communication.

    Judges have been very reluctant to grant or acknowledge such a privilege and more reluctant still to extend it to new relationships. Even with long-recognized exemptions, such as the lawyer-client relationship, courts have demanded that certain conditions be met. (p. 16)

Competence and Malpractice

As previously noted, counselors are expected to function within the limits of their professional expertise. This is not only ethically expected but also legally desirable. The dramatic increase in malpractice suits across all the helping professions indicates that our competence may be under legal scrutiny at any time. The governing legal principle in such cases is pointed out by Fischer and Sorenson (1985) as follows:

One who undertakes, gratuitously or for consideration, to render services to another which he should recognize as necessary for the protection of the other person or things, is subject to liability to the other for physical harm resulting from his failure to exercise reasonable care to perform his undertaking, if:

    a. His failure to exercise such care increases the risk of harm, or

    b. The harm is suffered because of the other's reliance upon the undertaking. (pp. 41–42)

They also note that the most common situations in which legal problems are most likely to occur are these:

❖ Prescribing or administering drugs

❖ Giving birth control advice

❖ Giving abortion-related advice

❖ Making statements that might be defamatory

❖ Assisting in searches of students' lockers

❖ Violating the privacy of records (Fischer & Sorenson, 1985, p. 50)

Counselors as Expert Witnesses

Counselors are increasingly making court appearances as "expert witnesses." Dependent on the counselor's work setting, she or he may be called on to testify in cases of child abuse and neglect, sexual abuse, child custody, divorce, and addictions, to name but a few. Being an expert witness and deporting oneself well as a professional counselor cannot be dealt with casually. We, therefore, recommend that practicing counselors review the American Counseling Association Legal Series monograph *The Counselor as an Expert Witness* (1993) by William Weikel and Paula Hughes, edited by Theodore P. Remley, Jr. In addition, if the counseling organization retains a lawyer for legal advice, it is also advisable to consult with this individual.

Third-Party Payments

A legal issue for many counselors, especially those in private practice or employed by agencies dependent on client payments, is the issue of third-party payments. This is the practice of reimbursement from a third party, usually an insurance company, for services that a counselor (the second party) renders to a client (the first party). "As of 1993, nine states mandated coverage for reimbursement for the services of professional counselors. These were California, Colorado, Connecticut, Florida, Maryland, New Hampshire, Mississippi, Texas, and Virginia" (Strosnider & Grad, 1993, p. 15).

However, there are some other circumstances under which counselors may receive third-party reimbursement. Counselors seeking third-party payments should be aware of the applicable state laws and regulations and policies of insurance companies and the policies of relevant federal legislation, such as that establishing Medicare/medical guidelines. In some circumstances, professional counselors may be eligible for reimbursement when they are providing services under the supervision of a recognized reimbursable practitioner.

SUMMARY

This chapter has reminded readers of ethical guidelines and expectancies for the profession of counseling. Special attention has been paid to the issues of competence, confidentiality, and personal relationships with clients.

This chapter has also noted the importance of counselors informing themselves of the legal implications and restrictions on their professional activities.

Whether our profession of counseling advances and achieves noble goals will depend very little on the writers of textbooks, past and present, but on *you*, our readers, who will represent our profession in the future. You are our future. We wish you well!

DISCUSSION QUESTIONS

1. Identify and discuss the lack of or questionable ethics in activities, such as sales, advertising, politics, and government.

2. What are the differences and similarities between ethics and values?

3. Why are codes of ethics important to the counseling profession?

4. Are warranties or guarantees for products indications that manufacturers want to treat customers ethically?

5. Are there any legal concerns you would have as a practicing counselor?

6. Are you aware of any recent court decisions or pending legislation that could have implications for counselors in schools? In nonschool settings?

7. How do you intend to keep abreast of legal enactments or court decisions affecting the counseling profession?

CLASS ACTIVITIES

1. Examine current newspapers and magazines for examples of ethical and legal violations that betray a "public trust." Share in class or small groups.

2. In small groups, share and discuss situations in which you feel you were treated unethically.

3. Ask a lawyer to address the class on the topic of professional malpractice.

4. In dyads, share your professional/personal ethical standards in the counseling position toward which your efforts are currently directed.

SELECTED READINGS

Aiello, H., & Humes, C. (1987). Counselor contact of the noncustodial parent: A point of law. *Elementary School Guidance and Counseling, 21,* 177–182.

Applebaum, P. (1993). Legal liability and managed care. *American Psychologist, 148,* 251–257.

Burn, D. (1992). Ethical implications in cross-cultural counseling and training. *Journal of Counseling and Development, 70,* 578–583.

Caublin, L., & Prout, H. (1983). School counselors and the reporting of child abuse: A survey of state laws and practices. *The School Counselor, 30,* 358–367.

Erickson, S. H. (1993). Ethics and confidentiality in AIDS counseling: A professional dilemma. *Journal of Mental Health Counseling, 15,* 118–131.

Ethics Committee of APA. (1988). Trends in ethics cases: Common pitfalls and published resources. *American Psychologist, 43,* 564–572.

Gilbert, S. P. (1992). Ethical issues in the treatment of severe psychopathology in university and college counseling centers. *Journal of Counseling and Development, 70,* 695–699.

Herlihy, B., Healy, M., Cook, E., & Hudson, P. (1987). Ethical practices of licensed professional counselors: A survey of state licensing boards. *Counselor Education and Supervision, 27,* 69–76.

Herlihy, B., & Sheeley, V. (1988). Counselor liability and the duty to warn: Selected cases, standards, trends, and implications for practice. *Counselor Education and Supervision, 27,* 203–215.

Hinkeldey, N., & Spokane, A. (1985). Effects of pressure and legal guideline clarity on counselor decision making in legal and ethical conflict situations. *Journal of Counseling and Development, 64,* 240–245.

Huey, W. (1987). Ethical standards for school counselors: Test your knowledge. *The School Counselor, 34,* 331–335.

Hummel, D. L. (1985). Law and ethics for practitioners in counseling and guidance. *Educational Perspectives, 23*, 3–12.

Kitchener, K. S. (Ed.). (1984). Ethical decision making in counseling psychology [Special issue]. *Counseling Psychologist, 12*, 19–98.

Krieshok, T. (1987). Psychologists and counselors in the legal system: A dialogue with Theodore Blau. *Journal of Counseling and Development, 66*, 69–72.

La Forge, J., & Henderson, P. (1990). Counselor competency in the courtroom. *Journal of Counseling and Development, 68*, 456–459.

Mabe, A. R., & Rollin, S. A. (1986). The role of a code of ethical standards in counseling. *Journal of Counseling and Development, 64*, 294–297.

Mappes, D., Robb, G., & Engels, D. (1985). Conflicts between ethics and law in counseling and psychotherapy. *Journal of Counseling and Development, 64*, 246–252.

Monahan, J., & Walker, L. (1988). Social science research in law: A new paradigm. *American Psychologist, 43*, 465–472.

Remley, T. (1988). More explanation needed in ethical and legal topics. *Mental Health Counseling, 10*, 167–170.

Robinson, S. (1988). Counselor competence and malpractice suits: Opposite sides of the same coin. *Counseling and Human Development, 20*(9), 1–7.

Sexton, T. L., Montgomery, D., Goff, K., Nugent, W. (1992). Ethical, therapeutic, and legal considerations in the use of paradoxical techniques: The emerging debate. *Journal of Mental Health Counseling, 15*, 260–277.

VanderCreek, L., & Knapp, S. (1984). Counselors, confidentiality and life-endangering clients. *Counselor Education and Supervision, 24*(1), 51–57.

Wilcoxon, S. A. (1987). Client consent in departures from customary and suggested treatment formats. *American Mental Health Counselors Association Journal, 9*(2), 77–83.

RESEARCH OF INTEREST

Chu, L., & Duling, J. (1987). Confidentiality and the university counseling center. *NASPA Journal, 24*(3), 50–56.

Abstract

Surveys 160 directors of college and university counseling centers to determine whether there is a consensus regarding confidentiality in terms of personal responsibilities and policies within their center. Results reveal a need for campus counseling centers to look at their policies regarding confidentiality and to keep current with legal implications of the limits of confidential communication.

Stadler, H., & Paul, R. D. (1986). Counselor-educators' preparation in ethics. *Journal of Counseling and Development, 64*, 328–330.

Abstract

The results of a national survey of department heads in counselor education and counseling psychology are reported. Conclusions are drawn regarding the respondents' training in professional ethics, their perceptions of the adequacy of this training, and their effectiveness in responding to ethical dilemmas.

Role Statement: The School Counselor

American School Counselor Association

The American School Counselor Association recognizes and supports the implementation of comprehensive developmental counseling programs at all educational levels. The programs are designed to help all students develop their educational, social, career, and personal strengths and to become responsible and productive citizens. School counselors help create and organize these programs, as well as provide appropriate counselor interventions.

School counseling programs are developmental by design, focusing on needs, interests, and issues related to the various stages of student growth. There are objectives, activities, special services and expected outcomes, with an emphasis on helping students to learn more effectively and efficiently. There is a commitment to individual uniqueness and the maximum development of human potential. A counseling program is an integral part of a school's total educational program.

THE SCHOOL COUNSELOR

The school counselor is a certified professional educator who assists students, teachers, parents, and administrators. Three generally recognized helping processes used by the counselor are counseling, consulting and coordinating: 1) Counseling is a complex helping process in which the counselor establishes a trusting and confidential working relationship. The focus is on problem-solving, decision-making, and discovering personal meaning related to learning and development; 2) Consultation is a cooperative process in which the counselor-consultant assists others to think through problems and to develop skills that make them more effective in working with students; 3) Coordination is a leadership process in which the counselor helps organize and manage a school's counseling program and related services.

School counselors are employed in elementary, middle/junior high, senior high, and postsecondary schools. Their work is differentiated by attention to age-specific developmental stages of growth and related interests, tasks, and challenges. School counselors are human behavior and relationship specialists who organize their work around fundamental interventions.

Counselor interventions have sometimes been referred to as functions, services, approaches, tasks, activities, or jobs. They have, at times, been viewed as roles themselves, helping to create the image of the counselor. In a comprehensive developmental counseling program, school counselors organize their work schedules around the following basic interventions:

Individual Counseling. Individual counseling is a personal and private interaction between a counselor and a student in which they work together on a problem or topic of interest. A face-to-face, one-to-one meeting with a counselor provides a student maximum privacy in which to freely explore ideas, feelings, and behaviors. School counselors establish trust and build a help-

SOURCE: From American Counseling Association (1990), *The Practice of Guidance and Counseling by School Counselors: ASCA Role Statement.* Copyright © 1990 American School Counselor Association. Reprinted with permission.

ing relationship. They respect the privacy of information, always considering actions in terms of the rights, integrity, and welfare of students. Counselors are obligated by law and ethical standards to report and to refer a case when a person's welfare is in jeopardy. It is a counselor's duty to inform an individual of the conditions and limitations under which assistance may be provided.

Small Group Counseling. Small group counseling involves a counselor working with two or more students together. Group size generally ranges from five to eight members. Group discussions may be relatively unstructured or may be based on structured learning activities. Group members have an opportunity to learn from each other. They can share ideas, give and receive feedback, increase their awareness, gain new knowledge, practice skills, and think about their goals and actions. Group discussions may be problem-centered, where attention is given to particular concerns or problems. Discussions may be growth-centered, where general topics are related to personal and academic development.

Large Group Guidance. Large group meetings offer the best opportunity to provide guidance to the largest number of students in a school. Counselors first work with students in large groups wherever appropriate because it is the most efficient use of time. Large group work involves cooperative learning methods, in which the larger group is divided into smaller working groups under the supervision of a counselor or teacher. The guidance and counseling curriculum, composed of organized objectives and activities, is delivered by teachers or counselors in classrooms or advisory groups. School counselors and teachers may co-lead some activities. Counselors develop and present special guidance units which give attention to particular developmental issues or areas of concern in their respective schools and they help prepare teachers to deliver part of the guidance and counseling curriculum.

Consultation. The counselor as a consultant helps people to be more effective in working with others. Consultation helps individuals think through problems and concerns, acquire more knowledge and skill, and become more objective and self-confident. This intervention can take place in individual or group conferences, or through staff-development activities.

Coordination. Coordination as a counselor intervention is the process of managing various indirect services which benefit students and being a liaison between school and community agencies. It may include organizing special events which involve parents or resource people in the community in guidance projects. It often entails collecting data and disseminating information. Counselors might coordinate a student needs assessment, the interpretation of standardized tests, a child study team, or a guidance related teacher or parent education program.

THE PREPARATION OF SCHOOL COUNSELORS

School counselors are prepared for their work through the study of interpersonal relationships and behavioral sciences in graduate education courses in accredited colleges and universities. Preparation involves special training in counseling theory and skills related to school settings. Particular attention is given to personality and human development theories and research, including career and life-skills development; learning theories, the nature of change and the helping process; theories and approaches to appraisal, multi-cultural and community awareness; educational environments; curriculum development; professional ethics; and program planning, management, and evaluation.

Counselors are prepared to use the basic interventions in a school setting, with special emphasis on the study of helping relationships, facilitative skills, brief counseling; group dynamics and group learning activities; family systems; peer helper programs, multicultural and cross-cultural helping approaches; and educational and community resources for special school populations.

School counselors are aware of their own professional competencies and responsibilities within the school setting. They know when and how to refer or involve other professionals. They are accountable for their actions and participate in appropriate studies and research related to their work.

RESPONSIBILITY TO THE PROFESSION

To assure high quality practice, counselors are committed to continued professional growth and personal development. They are active members of the American Counseling Association and the American School Counselor Association, as well as state and local professional associations which foster and promote school counseling. They also uphold the ethical and professional standards of these associations.

School counselors meet the state certification standards and abide by the laws in the states where they are working. Counselors work cooperatively with individuals and organizations to promote the overall development of children, youth, and families in their communities.

(Adopted July 1990)

Appendix B

Ethical Standards

American Counseling Association
Formerly the American Association for Counseling and Development
(As Revised by AACD Governing Council, March 1988)

PREAMBLE

The Association is an educational, scientific, and professional organization whose members are dedicated to the enhancement of the worth, dignity, potential, and uniqueness of each individual and this to the service of society.

The Association recognizes that the role definitions and work settings of its members include a wide variety of academic disciplines, levels of academic preparation, and agency services. This diversity reflects the breadth of the Association's interest and influence. It also poses challenging complexities in efforts to set standards for the performance of members, desired requisite preparation or practice, and supporting social, legal, and ethical controls.

The specification of ethical standards enables the Association to clarify to present and future members and to those served by members the nature of ethical responsibilities held in common by its members.

The existence of such standards serves to stimulate greater concern by members for their own professional functioning and for the conduct of fellow professionals such as counselors, guidance and student personnel workers, and others in the helping professions. As the ethical code of the Association, this document establishes principles that define the ethical behavior of Association members. Additional ethical guidelines developed by the Association's Divisions for their specialty areas may further define a member's ethical behavior.

SECTION A: GENERAL

1. The member influences the development of the profession by continuous efforts to improve professional practices, teaching, services, and research. Professional growth is continuous throughout the member's career and is exemplified by the development of a philosophy that explains why and how a member functions in the helping relationship. Members must gather data on their effectiveness and be guided by the findings. Members recognize the need for continuing education to ensure competent service.

2. The member has a responsibility both to the individual who is served and to the institution within which the service is performed to maintain high standards of professional conduct. The member strives to maintain the highest levels of professional services offered to the individuals to be served. The member also strives to assist the agency, organization, or institution in providing the highest caliber of professional services. The acceptance of employment in an institution implies that the member is in agreement with the general policies and principles of the institution. Therefore the professional activities of the member are also in accord with the objectives of the institution. If, despite concerted efforts, the member cannot reach agreement with the employer as to acceptable standards of conduct that allow for changes in institutional policy conducive to the positive growth and development of clients, then terminating the affiliation should be seriously considered.

3. Ethical behavior among professional associates, both members and nonmembers, must be expected at all times. When information is possessed that raises

doubt as to the ethical behavior of professional colleagues, whether Association members or not, the member must take action to attempt to rectify such a condition. Such action shall use the institution's channels first and then use procedures established by the Association.

4. The member neither claims nor implies professional qualifications exceeding those possessed and is responsible for correcting any misrepresentations of these qualifications by others.

5. In establishing fees for professional counseling services, members must consider the financial status of clients and locality. In the event that the established fee structure is inappropriate for a client, assistance must be provided in finding comparable services of acceptable cost.

6. When members provide information to the public or subordinates, peers, or supervisors, they have a responsibility to ensure that the content is general, unidentified client information that is accurate, unbiased, and consists of objective, factual data.

7. Members recognize their boundaries of competence and provide only those services and use only those techniques for which they are qualified by training or experience. Members should only accept those positions for which they are professionally qualified.

8. In the counseling relationship, the counselor is aware of the intimacy of the relationship and maintains respect for the client and avoids engaging in activities that seek to meet the counselor's personal needs at the expense of that client.

9. Members do not condone or engage in sexual harassment, which is defined as deliberate or repeated comments, gestures, or physical contacts of a sexual nature.

10. The member avoids bringing personal issues into the counseling relationship, especially if the potential for harm is present. Through awareness of the negative impact of both racial and sexual stereotyping and discrimination, the counselor guards the individual rights and personal dignity of the client in the counseling relationship.

11. Products or services provided by the member by means of classroom instruction, public lectures, demonstrations, written articles, radio or television programs, or other types of media must meet the criteria cited in these standards.

SECTION B: COUNSELING RELATIONSHIPS

This section refers to practices and procedures of individual and/or group counseling relationships.

The member must recognize the need for client freedom of choice. Under those circumstances where this is not possible, the member must apprise clients of restrictions that may limit their freedom of choice.

1. The member's primary obligation is to respect the integrity and promote the welfare of the client(s), whether the client(s) is (are) assisted individually or in a group relationship. In a group setting, the member is also responsible for taking reasonable precautions to protect individuals from physical and/or psychological trauma resulting from interaction within the group.

2. Members make provisions for maintaining confidentiality in the storage and disposal of records and follow an established record retention and disposition policy. The counseling relationship and information resulting therefrom must be kept confidential, consistent with the obligations of the member as a professional person. In a group counseling setting, the counselor must set a norm of confidentiality regarding all group participants' disclosures.

3. If an individual is already in a counseling relationship with another professional person, the member does not enter into a counseling relationship without first contacting and receiving the approval of that other professional. If the member discovers that the client is in another counseling relationship after the counseling relationship begins, the member must gain the consent of the other professional or terminate the relationship, unless the client elects to terminate the other relationship.

4. When the client's condition indicates that there is clear and imminent danger to the client or others, the member must take reasonable personal action or inform responsible authorities. Consultation with other professionals must be used where possible. The assumption of responsibility for the client's(s') behavior must be taken only after careful deliberation. The client must be involved in the resumption of responsibility as quickly as possible.

5. Records of the counseling relationship, including interview notes, test data, correspondence, tape recordings, electronic data storage, and other documents are to be considered professional information for use in counseling, and they should not be considered a

part of the records of the institution or agency in which the counselor is employed unless specified by state statue or regulation. Revelation to others of counseling material must occur only upon the expressed consent of the client.

6. In view of the extensive data storage and processing capacities of the computer, the member must ensure that data maintained on a computer is: (a) limited to information that is appropriate and necessary for the services being provided; (b) destroyed after it is determined that the information is no longer of any value in providing services; and (c) restricted in terms of access to appropriate staff members involved in the provision of services by using the best computer security methods available.

7. Use of data derived from a counseling relationship for purposes of counselor training or research shall be confined to content that can be disguised to ensure full protection of the identity of the subject client.

8. The member must inform the client of the purposes, goals, techniques, rules of procedure and limitations that may affect the relationship at or before the time that the counseling relationship is entered. When working with minors or persons who are unable to give consent, the member protects these clients' best interests.

9. In view of common misconceptions related to the perceived inherent validity of computer-generated data and narrative reports, the member must ensure that the client is provided with information as part of the counseling relationship that adequately explains the limitations of computer technology.

10. The member must screen prospective group participants, especially when the emphasis is on self-understanding and growth through self-disclosure. The member must maintain an awareness of the group participants' compatibility throughout the life of the group.

11. The member may choose to consult with any other professionally competent person about a client. In choosing a consultant, the member must avoid placing the consultant in a conflict of interest situation that would preclude the consultant's being a proper party to the member's efforts to help the client.

12. If the member determines an inability to be of professional assistance to the client, the member must either avoid initiating the counseling relationship or

immediately terminate that relationship. In either event, the member must suggest appropriate alternatives. (The member must be knowledgeable about referral resources so that a satisfactory referral can be initiated). In the event the client declines the suggested referral, the member is not obligated to continue the relationship.

13. When the member has other relationships, particularly of an administrative, supervisory, and/or evaluative nature, with an individual seeking counseling services, the member must not serve as the counselor but should refer the individual to another professional. Only in instances where such an alternative is unavailable and where the individual's situation warrants counseling intervention should that member enter into and/or maintain a counseling relationship. Dual relationships with clients that might impair the member's objectivity and professional judgement (e.g., as with close friends or relatives), must be avoided and/or the counseling relationship terminated through referral to another competent professional.

14. The member will avoid any type of sexual intimacies with clients. Sexual relationships with clients are unethical.

15. All experimental methods of treatment must be clearly indicated to prospective recipients, and safety precautions are to be adhered to by the member.

16. When computer applications are used as a component of counseling services, the member must ensure that: (a) the client is intellectually, emotionally, and physically capable of using the computer application; (b) the computer application is appropriate for the needs of the client; (c) the client understands the purpose and operation of the computer application; and (d) a followup of client use of a computer application is provided to both correct possible problems (misconceptions or inappropriate use) and assess subsequent needs.

17. When the member is engaged in short-term treatment/training programs (e.g., marathons and other encounter-type or growth groups), the member ensures that there is professional assistance available during and following the group experience.

18. Should the member be engaged in a work setting that calls for any variations from the above statements, the member is obligated to consult with other professionals whenever possible to consider justifiable alternatives.

19. The member must ensure that members of various ethnic, racial, religious, disability, and socioeconomic groups have equal access to computer applications used to support counseling services and that the content of available computer applications does not discriminate against the groups described above.

20. When computer applications are developed by the member for use by the general public as self-help/stand-alone computer software the member must ensure that: (a) self-help computer applications are designed from the beginning to function in a stand-alone manner, as opposed to modifying software that was originally designed to require support from a counselor; (b) self-help computer applications will include within the program statements regarding intended user outcomes, suggestions for using the software, a description of the conditions under which self-help computer applications might not be appropriate, and a description of when and how counseling services might be beneficial; and (c) the manual for such applications will include the qualifications of the developer, the development process, validation data, and operating procedures.

SECTION C: MEASUREMENT AND EVALUATION

The primary purpose of educational and psychological testing is to provide descriptive measures that are objective and interpretable in either comparative or absolute terms. The member must recognize the need to interpret the statements that follow as applying to the whole range of appraisal techniques including test and nontest data. Test results constitute only one of a variety of pertinent sources of information for personnel, guidance, and counseling decisions.

1. The member must provide specific orientation or information to the examinee(s) prior to and following the test administration so that the results of testing may be placed in proper perspective with other relevant factors. In so doing, the member must recognize the effects of socioeconomic, ethnic, and cultural factors on test scores. It is the member's professional responsibility to use additional unvalidated information carefully in modifying interpretation of the test results.

2. In selecting tests for use in a given situation or with a particular client, the member must consider carefully the specific validity, reliability, and appropri-

ateness of the test(s). General validity, reliability, and related issues may be questioned legally as well as ethically when tests are used for vocational and educational selection, placement, or counseling.

3. When making any statements to the public about tests and testing, the member must give accurate information and avoid false claims or misconceptions. Special efforts are often required to avoid unwarranted connotations of such terms as IQ and grade equivalent scores.

4. Different tests demand different levels of competence for administration scoring and interpretation. Members must recognize the limits of their competence and perform only those functions for which they are prepared. In particular, members using computer-based test interpretations must be trained in the construct being measured and the specific instrument being used prior to using this type of computer application.

5. In situations where a computer is used for test administration and scoring, the member is responsible for ensuring that administration and scoring programs function properly to provide clients with accurate test results.

6. Tests must be administered under the same conditions that were established in their standardization. When tests are not administered under standard conditions or when unusual behavior or irregularities occur during the testing session, those conditions must be noted and the results designated as invalid or of questionable validity. Unsupervised or inadequately supervised test-taking, such as the use of tests through the mails, is considered unethical. On the other hand, the use of instruments that are so designed or standardized to be self-administered and self-scored, such as interest inventories, is to be encouraged.

7. The meaningfulness of test results used in personnel, guidance, and counseling functions generally depends on the examinee's unfamiliarity with the specific items on the test. Any prior coaching or dissemination of test materials can invalidate test results. Therefore, test security is one of the professional obligations of the member. Conditions that produce most favorable test results must be made known to the examinee.

8. The purpose of testing and the explicit use of the results must be made known to the examinee prior to testing. The counselor must ensure that instrument lim-

itations are not exceeded and that periodic review and/or retesting are made to prevent client stereotyping.

9. The examinee's welfare and explicit prior understanding must be the criteria for determining the recipients of the test results. The member must see that specific interpretation accompanies any release of individual or group test data. The interpretation of test data must be related to the examinee's particular concerns.

10. Members responsible for making decisions based on test results have an understanding of educational and psychological measurement, validation criteria, and test research.

11. The member must be cautious when interpreting the results of research instruments possessing insufficient technical data. The specific purposes for the use of such instruments must be stated explicitly to examinees.

12. The member must proceed with caution when attempting to evaluate and interpret the performance of minority group members or other persons who are not represented in the norm group on which the instrument was standardized.

13. When computer-based test interpretations are developed by the member to support the assessment process, the member must ensure that the validity of such interpretations is established prior to the commercial distribution of such a computer application.

14. The member recognizes that test results may become obsolete. The member will avoid and prevent the misuse of obsolete test materials.

15. The member must guard against the appropriation, reproduction, or modification of published tests or parts thereof without acknowledgment and permission from the previous publisher.

16. Regarding the preparation, publication, and distribution of tests, reference should be made to:

    a. "Standards for Educational and Psychological Testing," revised edition, 1985, published by the American Psychological Association on behalf of itself, the American Educational Research Association and the National Council of Measurement in Education.

    b. "The Responsible Use of Tests: A Position Paper of AMEG, APGA, and NCME," *Measurement and Evaluation in Guidance*, 1972, 5, 385–388.

    c. "Responsibilities of Users of Standardized Tests," APGA, *Guidepost,* October 5, 1978, pp. 5–8.

SECTION D: RESEARCH AND PUBLICATION

1. Guidelines on research with human subjects should be adhered to, such as:

    a. *Ethical Principles in the Conduct of Research with Human Participants,* Washington, DC: American Psychological Association, Inc., 1982.

    b. Code of Federal Regulation, Title 45, Subtle A, Pan 46, as currently issued.

    c. *Ethical Principles of Psychologists,* American Psychological Association, Principle #9: Research with Human Participants.

    d. Family Educational Rights and Privacy Act (the Buckley Amendment).

    e. Current federal regulations and various state rights privacy acts.

2. In planning any research activity dealing with human subjects, the member must be aware of and responsive to all pertinent ethical principles and ensure that the research problem, design, and execution are in full compliance with them.

3. Responsibility for ethical research practice lies with the principal researcher while others involved in the research activities share ethical obligation and full responsibility for their own actions.

4. In research with human subjects, researchers are responsible for the subjects' welfare throughout the experiment, and they must take all reasonable precautions to avoid causing injurious psychological, physical, or social effects on their subjects.

5. All research subjects must be informed on the purpose of the study except when withholding information or providing misinformation to them is essential to the investigation. In such research the member must be responsible for corrective action as soon as possible following completion of the research.

6. Participation in research must be voluntary. Involuntary participation is appropriate only when it can be demonstrated that participation will have no

harmful effects on subjects and is essential to the investigation.

7. When reporting research results, explicit mention must be made of all variables and conditions known to the investigator that might affect the outcome of the investigation or the interpretation of the data.

8. The member must be responsible for conducting and reporting investigations in a manner that minimizes the possibility that results will be misleading.

9. The member has an obligation to make available sufficient original research data to qualified others who may wish to replicate the study.

10. When supplying data, aiding in the research of another person, reporting research results, or making original data available, due care must be taken to disguise the identity of the subjects in the absence of specific authorization from such subjects to do otherwise.

11. When conducting and reporting research, the member must be familiar with and give recognition to previous work on the topic, as well as to observe all copyright laws and follow the principles of giving full credit to all to whom credit is due.

12. The member must give due credit through joint authorship, acknowledgments, footnote statements, or other appropriate means to those who have contributed significantly to the research and/or publications, in accordance with such contributions.

13. The member must communicate to other members the results of any research judged to be of professional or scientific value. Results reflecting unfavorably on institutions, programs, services, or vested interests must not be withheld for such reasons.

14. If members agree to cooperate with another individual in research and/or publication, they incur an obligation to cooperate as promised in terms of punctuality of performance and with full regard to the completeness and accuracy of the information required.

15. Ethical practice requires that authors not submit the same manuscript or one essentially similar in content for simultaneous publication consideration by two or more journals. In addition, manuscripts published in who or in substantial part in another journal or published work should not be submitted for publication without acknowledgment and permission from the previous publication.

SECTION E: CONSULTING

Consultation refers to a voluntary relationship between a professional helper and a help-needing individual, group, or social unit in which the consultant is providing help to a client(s) in defining and solving a work-related problem or potential problem with a client or client system.

1. The member acting as consultant must have a high degree of self-awareness of his/her own values, knowledge, skills, limitations, and needs in entering a helping relationship that involves human and/or organizational change and the focus of the relationship must be on the issues to be resolved and not on the person(s) presenting the problem.

2. There must be understanding and agreement between member and client for the problem definition, change of goals, and prediction of consequences of interventions selected.

3. The member must be reasonably certain that she/he or the organization represented has the necessary competencies and resources for giving the kind of help that is needed now or may be needed later and that appropriate referral resources are available to the consultant.

4. The consulting relationship must be one in which client adaptability and growth toward self-direction are encouraged and cultivated. The member must maintain this role consistently and not become a decision maker for the client or create a future dependency on the consultant.

5. When announcing consultant availability for services, the member conscientiously adheres to the Association's Ethical Standards.

6. The member must refuse a private fee or other remuneration for consultation with persons who are entitled to these services through the member's employing institution or agency. The policies of a particular agency may make explicit provisions for private practice with agency clients by members of its staff. In such instances, the clients must be apprised of other options open to them should they seek private counseling services.

SECTION F: PRIVATE PRACTICE

1. The member should assist the profession by facilitating the availability of counseling services in private as well as public settings.

2. In advertising services as a private practitioner, the member must advertise the services in a manner that accurately informs the public of professional services, expertise and techniques of counseling available. A member who assumes an executive leadership role in the organization shall not permit his/her name to be used in professional notices during periods when he/she is not actively engaged in the private practice of counseling.

3. The member may list the following: highest relevant degree, type and level of certification and/or license, address, telephone number, office hours, type and/or description of services and other relevant information. Such information must not contain false, inaccurate, misleading, partial, out-of-context, or deceptive material or statements.

4. Members do not present their affiliation with any organization in such a way that would imply inaccurate sponsorship or certification by that organization.

5. Members may join in partnership/corporation with other members and/or other professionals provided that each member of the partnership or corporation makes clear the separate specialties by name in compliance with the regulations of the locality.

6. A member has an obligation to withdraw from a counseling relationship if it is believed that employment will result in violation of the Ethical Standards. If the mental or physical condition of the member renders it difficult to carry out an effective professional relationship or if the member is discharged by the client because the counseling relationship is no longer productive for the client, the member is obligated to terminate the counseling relationship.

7. A member must adhere to the regulations for private practice of the locality where the services are offered.

8. It is unethical to use one's institutional affiliation to recruit clients for one's private practice.

SECTION G: PERSONNEL ADMINISTRATION

It is recognized that most members are employed in public or quasi-public institutions. The functioning of a member within an institution must contribute to the goals of the institution and vice versa if either is to accomplish their respective goals or objectives. It is therefore essential that the member and the institution function in ways to: (a) make the institution goals specific, and public; (b) make the member's contribution to institutional goals specific; and (c) foster mutual accountability for goal achievement.

To accomplish these objectives, it is recognized that the member and the employer must share responsibilities in the formulation and implementation of personnel competency.

1. Members must define and describe the parameters and levels of their professional competency.

2. Members must establish interpersonal relations and working agreements with supervisors and subordinates regarding counseling or clinical relationships, confidentiality, distinction between public and private material, maintenance and dissemination of recorded information, work load, and accountability. Working agreements in each instance must be specified and made known to those concerned.

3. Members must alert their employers to conditions that may be potentially disruptive or damaging.

4. Members must inform employers of conditions that may limit their effectiveness.

5. Members must submit regularly to professional review and evaluation.

6. Members must be responsible for inservice development of self and/or staff.

7. Members must inform their staff of goals and programs.

8. Members must provide personnel practices that guarantee and enhance the right and welfare of each recipient of their service.

9. Members must select competent persons and assign responsibilities compatible with their skills and experiences.

10. The member, at the onset of a counseling relationship, will inform the client of the member's intended use of supervisors regarding the disclosure of information concerning this case. The member will clearly inform the client of the limits of confidentiality in the relationship.

11. Members, as either employers or employees, do not engage in or condone practices that are inhumane, illegal, or unjustifiable (such as considerations based on sex, handicap, age, race) in hiring, promotion or training.

SECTION H: PREPARATION STANDARDS

Members who are responsible for training others must be guided by the preparation standards of the Association and relevant Division(s). The member who functions in the capacity of trainer assumes unique ethical responsibilities that frequently go beyond those of the member who does not function in a training capacity. These ethical responsibilities are outlined as follows:

1. Members must orient students to program expectations, basic skills development, and employment prospects prior to admission to the program.

2. Members in charge of learning experiences must establish programs that integrate academic study and supervised practice.

3. Members must establish a program directed toward developing students' skills, knowledge, and self-understanding stated whenever possible in competency or performance terms.

4. Members must identify the levels of competencies of their students in compliance with relevant Division standards. These competencies must accommodate the paraprofessional as well as the professional.

5. Members, through continual student evaluation and appraisal, must be aware of the personal limitations of the learner that might impede future performance. The instructor must not only assist the learner in securing remedial assistance but also screen from the program those individuals who are unable to provide competent services.

6. Members must provide a program that includes training in research commensurate with levels of role functioning. Paraprofessional and technician-level personnel must be trained as consumers of research. In addition, personnel must learn how to evaluate their own and their program's effectiveness. Graduate training, especially at the doctoral level, would include preparation for original research by the member.

7. Members must make students aware of the ethical responsibilities and standards of the profession.

8. Preparatory programs must encourage students to value the ideals of service to individuals and to society. In this regard, direct financial remuneration or lack thereof must not be allowed to overshadow professional and humanitarian needs.

9. Members responsible for educational programs must be skilled as teachers and practitioners.

10. Members must present thoroughly varied theoretical positions so that students may make comparisons and have the opportunity to select a position.

11. Members must develop clear policies within their educational institutions regarding field placement and the roles of the student and the instructor in such placement.

12. Members must ensure that forms of learning focusing on self-understanding or growth are voluntary, or if required as part of the educational program, are made known to prospective students prior to entering the program. When the educational program offers a growth experience with an emphasis on self-disclosure or other relatively intimate or personal involvement, the member must have no administrative, supervisory, or evaluating authority regarding the participant.

13. The member will at all times provide students with clear and equally acceptable alternatives for self-understanding or growth experiences. The member will assure students that they have a right to accept these alternatives without prejudice or penalty.

14. Members must conduct an educational program in keeping with the current relevant guidelines of the Association.

Policies and Procedures for Processing Complaints of Ethical Violations

Approved March, 1990—Amended December, 1991

SECTION A: GENERAL

1. The American Counseling Association, hereinafter referred to as the "Association" or "ACA," as an educational, scientific, and charitable organization, is dedicated to enhancing the worth, dignity, potential, and uniqueness of each individual and rendering service to society.

2. The Association, in furthering its objectives, administers Ethical Standards that have been developed and approved by the ACA Governing Council.

3. The purpose of this document is to facilitate the work of the ACA Ethics Committee by specifying the procedures for processing cases of alleged violations of the ACA Ethical Standards, codifying options for sanctioning members, and stating appeal procedures. The intent of the Association is to monitor the professional conduct of its members to ensure sound ethical practices.

SECTION B: ETHICS COMMITTEE MEMBERS

1. The Ethics Committee is a standing committee of the Association. The Committee consists of six (6) appointed members, including the Chairperson. The editor of the *Ethical Standards Casebook* serves as an *ex officio* member of this Committee without vote. Two members are appointed annually for a three (3) year term by the President-Elect; appointments are subject to confirmation by the ACA Governing Council. Any vacancy occurring on the Committee will be filled by the President in the same manner, and the person appointed shall serve the unexpired term of the member whose place he or she took. Committee members may be reappointed to not more than one (1) additional consecutive term.

2. The Chairperson of the Committee is appointed annually by the incumbent President-Elect, subject to confirmation by the ACA Governing Council. A Chairperson may be reappointed to one additional term during any three (3) year period.

SECTION C: ROLE AND FUNCTION

1. The role of the Ethics Committee of the Association is to assist in the arbitration and conciliation of conflicts among members of the Association, except where appropriate client concerns may be expressed. The Committee is also responsible for:

   A. Educating the membership as to the Association's Ethical Standards,

   B. Periodically reviewing and recommending changes in the Ethical Standards of the Association as well as the Policies and Procedures for Processing Complaints of Ethical Violations,

   C. Receiving and processing complaints of alleged violations of the Ethical Standards of the Association, and

   D. Receiving and processing questions.

2. In processing complaints about alleged ethical misconduct, the Committee will compile an objective, factual account of the dispute in question and make the best possible recommendation for the resolution of the case. The Committee, in taking any action, shall

475

do so only for cause, shall only take the degree of disciplinary action that is reasonable, shall utilize these procedures with objectivity and fairness, and in general shall act only to further the interests and objectives of the Association and its membership.

3. The ACA Ethics Committee itself will not initiate any ethical violation charges against an ACA member.

4. Of the six (6) voting members of the Committee, a vote of four (4) is necessary to conduct business. In the event the Chair or any other member of the Committee has a personal interest in the case, he or she shall withdraw from reviewing the case. A unanimous vote of those members of the Committee who reviewed the case is necessary to expel a member from the Association.

5. The Chairperson of the ACA Ethics Committee and/or the ACA Executive Director (or his/her designee) may consult with ACA legal counsel at any time.

SECTION D: RESPONSIBILITIES OF COMMITTEE MEMBERS

1. The members of the Ethics Committee must be conscious that their position is extremely important and sensitive and that their decisions involve the rights of many individuals, the reputation of the counseling and human development community, and the careers of the members. The Committee members have an obligation to act in an unbiased manner, to work expeditiously, to safeguard the confidentiality of the Committee's activities, and to follow procedures that protect the rights of all individuals involved.

SECTION E: RESPONSIBILITIES OF THE CHAIRPERSON

1. In addition to the above guidelines for members of the Committee, the Chairperson, in conjunction with Headquarters staff, has the responsibilities of:

   A. Receiving (via ACA Headquarters) complaints that have been certified for membership status of the accused,

   B. Notifying the complainant and the accused of receipt of the case,

   C. Notifying the members of the Ethics Committee of the case,

   D. Presiding over the meetings of the Committee,

   E. Preparing and sending (by certified mail) communications to the complainant and accused member on the recommendations and decisions of the Committee, and

   F. Arranging for legal advice with assistance and financial approval of the ACA Executive Director.

SECTION F: COMPLAINTS

1. All correspondence, records, and activities of the ACA Ethics Committee will remain confidential.

2. The ACA Ethics Committee will not act on anonymous complaints, nor will it act on complaints currently under civil or criminal litigation.

3. The ACA Ethics Committee will act only on those cases where the accused is a current member of ACA or was a member of ACA at the time of the alleged violation. State Division and State Branch Ethics Committees may act only on those cases where the accused is a member of the State Division or State Branch and not a member of ACA.

SECTION G: SUBMITTING COMPLAINTS— PROCEDURES FOR ACA MEMBERS

1. The procedures for submission of complaints to the Ethics Committee are as follows:

   A. If feasible, the complainant should discuss with utmost confidentiality the nature of the complaint with a colleague to see if he or she views the situation as an ethical violation.

   B. Whenever feasible, the complainant is to approach the accused directly to discuss and resolve the complaint.

   C. In cases where a resolution is not forthcoming at the personal level, the complainant shall prepare a formal written statement of the complainant and shall submit it to the ACA Ethics Committee. Action or consideration by the ACA Ethics Committee may not be initiated until this requirement is satisfied.

   D. Formal written complaints must include a statement indicating the behavior(s) that constituted the alleged violation(s), and the date(s) of the alleged violation(s). The written statement must also contain the accused member's full name and complete address. Any relevant supporting documentation may be included with the complaint.

E. All complaints that are directed to the ACA Ethics Committee should be mailed to the Ethics Committee, c/o The Executive Director, American Counseling Association, 5999 Stevenson Avenue, Alexandria, Virginia 22304. The envelope must be marked "CONFIDENTIAL." This procedure is necessary to ensure the confidentiality of the person submitting the complaint and the person accused in the complaint.

SECTION H: SUBMITTING COMPLAINTS— PROCEDURES FOR NON-MEMBERS

1. The ACA Ethics Committee recognizes the rights of non-ACA members to file grievances concerning a member. Ordinarily this non-member will be a client or student of an ACA member who believes that the ACA member has acted unethically.

2. In such cases, the complainant shall contact the ACA Executive Director (or his/her designee) and outline, in writing, those behaviors he or she feels were unethical in nature. Headquarters staff will delineate the complaint process to the complainant.

SECTION I: PROCESSING COMPLAINTS

1. When complaints are received at Headquarters, the ACA Executive Director (or his/her designee) shall: (a) check on the membership status of the accused, (b) acknowledge receipt of the complaint within ten (10) working days after it is received in ACA Headquarters, and (c) consult with the Chairperson of the ACA Ethics Committee within ten (10) working days after the complaint is received in ACA Headquarters to determine whether it is appropriate to proceed with the complaint. If the Director (or designee) and Chairperson determine it is inappropriate to proceed, the complainant shall be so notified. If the Director (or designee) and Chairperson determine it is appropriate to proceed with the complaint, they will identify which Ethical Standard(s) that were allegedly violated will be forwarded to the complainant for his/her signature. This signed formal statement will then become part of the formal complaint.

2. Once the formal complaint has been compiled (as indicated above), the Chairperson of the ACA Ethics Committee shall do the following:

A. Inform the complainant in writing that the accused member has been notified of the charges,

B. Direct a letter to the accused member informing the member of accusations lodged against him or her, including copies of all materials submitted by the complainant, asking for a response, and requesting that relevant information be submitted to the Chairperson within thirty (30) working days.

3. The accused is under no duty to respond to the allegations, but the Committee will not be obligated to delay or postpone its review of the case unless the accused so requests, with good cause, in advance. Failure of the accused to respond should not be viewed by the Committee as sufficient ground for taking disciplinary action.

4. Once the Chairperson has received the accused member's response or the thirty (30) days have elapsed, then the Chairperson shall forward to the members of the ACA Ethics Committee legal counsel's opinion (if applicable), staff verification of membership status, allegations, and responses, and direct the Committee to review the case and make recommendations for its disposition within two (2) weeks of receipt of the case.

5. The ACA Ethics Committee will review the case and make recommendations for its disposition and/or resolution within two hundred (200) working days following its receipt.

6. The ACA Ethics Committee Chairperson may ask the President of ACA to appoint an investigating committee at the local or state level to gather and submit relevant information concerning the case to the Committee.

SECTION J: OPTIONS AVAILABLE TO THE ETHICS COMMITTEE

1. After reviewing the information forwarded by the Chairperson, the Ethics Committee shall have the power to:

A. Dismiss the charges, find that no violation has occurred, and dismiss the complaint, or

B. Find that the practice(s) in which the member engages that is (are) the subject of the complaint, is (are) unethical, notify the accused of this determination, and request the member to voluntarily cease and desist in the practice(s) without impositions of further sanctions, or

C. Find that the practice(s) in which the member engages, that is (are) the subject of the complaint, is (are) unethical, notify the accused of this determination, and impose sanctions.

SECTION K: APPROPRIATE SANCTIONS

1. The Committee may consider extenuating circumstances before deciding on the penalty to be imposed. If the Committee finds the accused has violated the Ethical Standards and decides to impose sanctions, the Committee may take any of the following actions:

A. Issue a reprimand with recommendations for corrective action, subject to review by the Committee, or

B. Place the member on probation for a specified period of time, subject to review by the Committee, or

C. Suspend eligibility for membership in ACA for a specified period of time, subject to review by the Committee, or

D. Expel the member from ACA permanently.

SECTION L: CONSEQUENCES OF SANCTIONS

1. Both a reprimand and probation carry with them no loss of membership rights or privileges.

2. A suspended member forfeits the rights and privileges of membership only for the period of his or her suspension.

3. In the event a member is expelled from ACA membership, he or she shall lose all rights and privileges of membership in ACA and its divisions permanently. The expelled member shall not be entitled to a refund of dues already paid.

4. If the member is suspended or expelled, and after any right to appeal has been exhausted, the Committee will notify the appropriate state licensing board(s) of the disciplined member's status with ACA.

Notice also will be given to the National Board for Certified Counselors, the ACA Divisions of which the disciplined party is a member, the State Branch of ACA in which the member resides, the members of ACA, the complainant, and other organizations as the Committee deems necessary. Such notice shall only state the sanctions imposed and the sections of the ACA Ethical Standards that were violated. Further elaboration shall not be disclosed.

5. Should a member resign from the Association after a complaint has been brought against him or her and before the Ethics Committee has completed its deliberations, that member is considered to have been expelled from the Association for failure to respond in a timely and complete manner to the Ethics Committee.

SECTION M: HEARINGS

1. At the discretion of the Ethics Committee, a hearing may be conducted when the results of the Ethics Committee's preliminary determination indicate that additional information is needed. The Chairperson shall schedule a formal hearing on the case and notify both the complainant and the accused of their right to attend.

2. The hearing will be held before a panel made up of Ethics Committee and, if the accused member chooses, a representative of the accused member's primary Division. This representative will be identified by the Division President and will have voting privileges.

SECTION N: RECOMMENDED HEARING PROCEDURES

1. Purposes of Hearings. The purposes for which hearings shall be conducted are: (a) to determine whether a breach of the Ethical Standards of ACA has occurred, and (b) if so, to determine what disciplinary action should be taken by the ACA. If a hearing is held, no disciplinary action will be taken by ACA until after the accused member has been given reasonable notice of the hearing and the specific charges raised against him or her and has had the opportunity to be heard and to present evidence on his or her behalf. The hearings will be formally conducted. The Committee will be guided in its deliberations by principles of basic fairness and professionalism, and will keep its

deliberations as confidential as possible, except as provided herein.

2. Notice. At least forty-five (45) working days before the hearing, the accused member should be advised in writing of the time and place of the hearing and of the charges involved. Notice shall be given either personally or by certified or registered mail and shall be signed by the Committee Chair. The notice should be addressed to the accused member at his or her address as it appears in the membership records of the ACA. The notice should include a brief statement of the complaints lodged against him or her, and should be supported by the evidence. The accused is under no duty to respond to the notice, but the Committee will not be obligated to delay or postpone its hearing unless the accused so requests in writing, with good cause, in advance. Failure of the accused to appear at the hearing should not be viewed by the Committee as sufficient ground for taking disciplinary action.

3. Conduct of the Hearing.

A. Accommodations. The hearing shall provide a private room to conduct the hearings, and no observers shall be permitted. The location of the hearing shall be determined at the discretion of the Committee, taking into consideration the convenience of the Committee and the parties involved.

B. Presiding Officer. The Chair of the Ethics Committee shall preside over the hearing and deliberations of the Committee. In the event the Chair or any other member of the Committee has a personal interest in the case, he or she shall withdraw from the hearing and deliberations and shall not participate therein. The Committee shall select from among its members a presiding officer for any case where the Chair has excused himself or herself. At the conclusion of the hearing and deliberation of the Committee, the Chair shall promptly notify the accused and complainant of the committee's decision in writing.

C. Record. A record of the hearing shall be made and preserved, together with any documents presented as evidence, at the ACA Headquarters for a period of three (3) years

following the hearing decision. The record may consist of a summary of testimony received, or a verbatim transcript, at the discretion of the Committee.

D. Right to Counsel. The parties shall be entitled to have counsel present to advise them throughout the hearing, but they may not participate beyond advising. Legal Counsel for ACA shall also be present at the hearing to advise the Committee and shall have the privilege of the floor.

E. Witnesses. Either party shall have the right to call witnesses to substantiate his or her version of the case. The Committee shall also have the right to call witnesses it believes may provide further insight into the matter before the Committee. Witnesses shall not be present during the hearings except when they are called upon to testify. The presiding officer shall allow questions to be asked of any witness by the opposition or members of the Committee and shall ensure that questions and testimony are relevant to the issues in the case. Should the hearing be disturbed by disparaging or irrelevant testimony or by the flareup of tempers, the presiding officer shall call a brief recess until order can be restored. Witnesses shall be excused upon completion of their testimony. All expenses associated with witnesses or counsel on behalf of the parties shall be borne by the respective parties.

F. Presentation of Evidence.

(1) A member of the Committee shall be called upon first to present the charge(s) made against the accused and to briefly describe the evidence supporting the charge(s).

(2) The complainant or a member of the Committee shall then be called upon to present the case against the accused. Witnesses who can substantiate the case shall be called upon to testify and answer questions of the accused and the Committee.

(3) If the accused has exercised the right to be present at the hearing, he or she shall

be called upon last to present any evidence which refutes the charges against him or her. This includes the presentation of witnesses as in Subsection (E) above. The accused member has the right to refuse to make a statement in his or her behalf. The accused will not be found guilty simply for refusing to testify. Once the accused chooses to testify, however, he or she may be cross-examined by members of the Committee or the complainant.

(4) The Committee will endeavor to conclude the hearing within a period of approximately three (3) hours. The parties will be requested to be considerate of this time frame in planning their testimony. Testimony that is merely cumulative or repetitious may, at the discretion of the presiding officer, be excluded.

(5) The accused has the right to be present at all times during the hearing and to challenge all of the evidence presented against him or her.

G. Relevancy of Evidence. The Hearing Committee is not a court of law and is not required to observe the rules of evidence that apply in the trial of lawsuits. Consequently, evidence that would be inadmissible in a court of law may be admissible in the hearing before the Committee, if it is relevant to the case. That is, if the evidence offered tends to explain, clarify, or refute any of the important facts of the case, it should generally be considered. The Committee will not receive evidence or testimony for the purpose of supporting any charge that was not set forth in the notice of the hearing or that is not relevant to the issues of the case.

4. Burden of Proof. The burden of proving a violation of the Ethical Standards is on the complainant and/or the Committee. It is not up to the accused to prove his or her innocence of any wrong-doing. Although the charge(s) need not be proved "beyond a reasonable doubt," the Committee will not find the accused guilty in the absence of substantial, objective, and believable evidence to sustain the charge(s).

5. Deliberation of the Committee. After the hearing with the parties is completed, the Committee shall meet in a closed session to review the evidence presented and reach a conclusion. The Committee shall be the sole trier of fact and shall weigh the evidence presented and judge the credibility of the witnesses. The act of a majority of the members of the Committee shall be the decision of the Committee and only those members of the Committee who were present throughout the entire hearing shall be eligible to vote.

6. Decision of the Committee. The committee will first resolve the issue of the guilt or innocence of the accused. Applying the burden of proof in paragraph 4 above, the Committee will vote by secret ballot, unless the members of the Committee consent to an oral vote. In the event a majority of the members of the Committee do not find the accused guilty, the charges shall be dismissed and the parties notified. If the Committee finds the accused has violated the Ethical Standards, it must then determine what sanctions to impose in accord with Section K: Appropriate Sanctions.

SECTION O: APPEAL PROCEDURES

1. Appeals will be heard only in such cases wherein the appellant presents evidence that the sanction imposed by the Committee has been arbitrary or capricious or that the procedures outlined in the "Policy Document" have not been followed.

2. The complainant and accused shall be advised of the appeal procedure by the Chairperson of the ACA Ethics Committee. The following procedures shall govern appeals:

A. A three (3) member review committee composed of the Executive Director of the ACA, the President of the ACA Division with which the accused member is most closely identified, and the immediate Past President of ACA. The ACA attorney shall serve as legal advisor and have the privilege of the floor.

B. The appeal with supporting documentation must be made in writing within sixty (60) working days by certified mail to the ACA Executive Director and indicate the basis upon which it is made. If the member requires a time extension, he or she must request it in writing by certified mail within thirty (30) working days of receiving the decision by the ACA Ethics Committee. The extension will consist of ninety (90) working days beginning from that request.

C. The review committee shall review all materials considered by the ACA Ethics Committee.

D. Within thirty (30) working days of this review, the members on the review committee shall submit to the President of the ACA a written statement giving their opinion regarding the decision of the Ethics Committee. Each member shall concur with or dissent from the decision of the Ethics Committee.

E. Within fifteen (15) working days of receiving this opinion, the President of ACA will reach a decision based on the considered opinions of the review committee from the following alternatives:

(1) support the decision of the Ethics Committee, or

(2) reverse the decision of the Ethics Committee.

3. The parties to the appeal shall be advised of the action in writing.

SECTION P: RECORDS

1. Records of the ACA Ethics Committee and the review committee shall remain at the ACA Headquarters.

SECTION Q: PROCEDURES FOR SUBMITTING AND INTERPRETING QUESTIONS OF ETHICAL CONDUCT

1. The procedures for submitting questions to the Ethics Committee are as follows:

A. Whenever possible, the questioner is first advised to consult other colleagues seeking interpretation of questions.

B. If a national level resolution is deemed appropriate, the questioner shall prepare a written statement, which details the conduct in question. Statements should include the section or sections of the Ethical Standards to be interpreted relative to the conduct in question. All questions that are directed to the Ethics Committee should be mailed to: Ethics Committee, c/o ACA Executive Director.

C. The ACA Ethics Committee Chairperson or his/her designee:

(1) may confer with legal counsel, and

(2) shall direct a letter to the questioner acknowledging receipt of the question, informing the member that the questions will be interpreted by the Committee, and outlining the procedures to be involved in the interpretation.

D. The Ethics Committee will review and interpret the question and, if requested by the questioner, make recommendations for conduct.

For further information write:
American Counseling Association
5999 Stevenson Avenue
Alexandria, Virginia 22304

Ethical Principles of Psychologists and Code of Conduct

American Psychological Association

CONTENTS

INTRODUCTION

PREAMBLE

GENERAL PRINCIPLES

ETHICAL STANDARDS

SOURCE: From American Psychological Association (1992), *Ethical Principles of Psychologists and Code of Conduct.* Copyright 1992 by the American Psychological Association. Reprinted by permission.

INTRODUCTION

The American Psychological Association's (APA's) Ethical Principles of Psychologists and Code of Conduct (hereinafter referred to as the Ethics Code) consists of an Introduction, a Preamble, six General Principles (A–F), and specific Ethical Standards. The Introduction discusses the intent, organization, procedural considerations, and scope of application of the Ethics Code. The Preamble and General Principles are *aspirational* goals to guide psychologists toward the highest ideals of psychology. Although the Preamble and General Principles are not themselves enforceable rules, they should be considered by psychologists in arriving at an ethical course of action and may be considered by ethics bodies in interpreting the Ethical Standards. The Ethical Standards set forth *enforceable* rules for conduct as psychologists. Most of the Ethical Standards are written broadly, in order to apply to psychologists in varied roles, although the application of an Ethical Standard may vary depending on the context. The Ethical Standards are not exhaustive. The fact that a given conduct is not specifically addressed by the Ethics Code does not mean that it is necessarily either ethical or unethical.

Membership in the APA commits members to adhere to the APA Ethics Code and to the rules and procedures used to implement it. Psychologists and students, whether or not they are APA members, should be aware that the Ethics Code may be applied to them by state psychology boards, courts, or other public bodies.

The Ethics Code applies only to psychologists' work-related activities, that is, activities that are part of the psychologists' scientific and professional functions or that are psychological in nature. It includes the clinical or counseling practice of psychology, research, teaching, supervision of trainees, development of assessment instruments, conducting assessments, educational counseling, organizational consulting, social intervention, administration, and other activities as well. These work-related activities can be distinguished from the purely private conduct of a psychologist, which ordinarily is not within the purview of the Ethics Code.

The Ethics Code is intended to provide standards of professional conduct that can be applied by the APA and by other bodies that choose to adopt them. Whether or not a psychologist has violated the Ethics Code does not by itself determine whether he or she is legally liable in a court action, whether a contract is enforceable, or whether other legal consequences occur. These results are based on legal rather than ethical rules. However, compliance with or violation of the Ethics Code may be admissible as evidence in some legal proceedings, depending on the circumstances.

In the process of making decisions regarding their professional behavior, psychologists must consider this Ethics Code, in addition to applicable laws and psychology board regulations. If the Ethics Code establishes a higher standard of conduct than is required by law, psychologists must meet the higher ethical standard. If the Ethics Code standard appears to conflict with the requirements of law, then psychologists make known their commitment to the Ethics Code and take steps to resolve the conflict in a responsible manner. If neither law nor the Ethics Code resolves an issue, psy-

chologists should consider other professional materials[1] and the dictates of their own conscience, as well as seek consultation with others within the field when this is practical.

The procedures for filing, investigating, and resolving complaints of unethical conduct are described in the current Rules and Procedures of the APA Ethics Committee. The actions that APA may take for violations of the Ethics Code include actions such as reprimand, censure, termination of APA membership, and referral of the matter to other bodies. Complainants who seek remedies such as monetary damages in alleging ethical violations by a psychologist must resort to private negotiation, administrative bodies, or the courts. Actions that violate the Ethics Code may lead to the imposition of sanctions on a psycholo-

---

This version of the APA Ethics Code was adopted by the American Psychological Association's Council of Representatives during its meeting, August 13 and 16, 1992, and is effective beginning December 1, 1992. Inquiries concerning the substance or interpretation of the APA Ethics Code should be addressed to the Director, Office of Ethics, American Psychological Association, 750 First Street, NE, Washington, DC 20002-4242.

This Code will be used to adjudicate complaints brought concerning alleged conduct occurring on or after the effective date. Complaints regarding conduct occurring prior to the effective date will be adjudicated on the basis of the version of the Code that was in effect at the time the conduct occurred, except that no provisions repealed in June 1989, will be enforced even if an earlier version contains the provision. The Ethics Code will undergo continuing review and study for future revisions; comments on the Code may be sent to the above address.

The APA has previously published its Ethical Standards as follows:

American Psychological Association. (1953). *Ethical Standards of Psychologists*. Washington, DC: Author.

American Psychological Association. (1958). Standards of Ethical behavior for psychologists. *American Psychologist, 13*, 268–271.

American Psychological Association. (1963). Ethical standards of psychologists. *American Psychologist, 18*, 56–60.

American Psychological Association. (1968). Ethical standards of psychologists. *American Psychologist, 23*, 357–361.

American Psychological Association. (1977, March). Ethical standards of psychologists. *APA Monitor*, pp. 22–23.

American Psychological Association. (1979). *Ethical standards of psychologists*. Washington, DC. Author.

gist by bodies other than APA, including state psychological associations, other professional groups, psychology boards, other state or federal agencies, and payors for health services. In addition to actions for violation of the Ethics Code, the APA Bylaws provide that APA may take action against a member after his or her conviction of a felony, expulsion or suspension from an affiliated state psychological association, or suspension or loss of licensure.

PREAMBLE

Psychologists work to develop a valid and reliable body of scientific knowledge based on research. They may apply that knowledge to human behavior in a variety of contexts. In doing so, they perform many roles, such

---

American Psychological Association. (1981). Ethical principles of psychologists. *American Psychologist, 36,* 633–638.

American Psychological Association. (1990). Ethical principles of psychologists (Amended June 2, 1989). *American Psychologist, 45,* 390–395.

SOURCE: Request copies of the APA's Ethical Principles of Psychologists and Code of Conduct from the APA Order Department, 750 First Street, NE, Washington, DC 20002-4242, or phone (202) 336-5510.

[1]Professional materials that are most helpful in this regard are guidelines and standards that have been adopted or endorsed by professional psychological organizations. Such guidelines and standards, whether adopted by the American Psychological Association (APA) or its Divisions, are not enforceable as such by this Ethics Code, but are of educative value to psychologists, courts, and professional bodies. Such materials include, but are not limited to, the APA's *General Guidelines for Providers of Psychological Services* (1987), *Specialty Guidelines for the Delivery of Services for Clinical Psychologists, Counseling Psychologists, Industrial/Organizational Psychologists, and School Psychologists* (1981), *Guidelines for Computer Based Tests and Interpretations* (1987), *Standards for Educational and Psychological Testing* (1985), *Ethical Principles in the Conduct of Research with Human Participants* (1982), *Guidelines for Ethical Conduct in the Care and Use of Animals* (1986), *Guidelines for Providers of Psychological Services to Ethnic, Linguistic, and Culturally Diverse Populations* (1990), and *Publication Manual of the American Psychological Association* (3rd ed., 1983). Materials not adopted by APA as a whole include the APA Division 41 (Forensic Psychology)/American Psychology—Law Society's *Specialty Guidelines for Forensic Psychologists* (1991).

as researcher, educator, diagnostician, therapist, supervisor, consultant, administrator, social interventionist, and expert witness. Their goal is to broaden knowledge of behavior and, where appropriate, to apply it pragmatically to improve the condition of both the individual and society. Psychologists respect the central importance of freedom of inquiry and expression in research, teaching, and publication. They also strive to help the public in developing informed judgments and choices concerning human behavior. This Ethics Code provides a common set of values upon which psychologists build their professional and scientific work.

The Code is intended to provide both the general principles and the decision rules to cover most situations encountered by psychologists. It has as its primary goal the welfare and protection of the individuals and groups with whom psychologists work. It is the individual responsibility of each psychologist to aspire to the highest possible standards of conduct. Psychologists respect and protect human and civil rights, and do not knowingly participate in or condone unfair discriminatory practices.

The development of a dynamic set of ethical standards for a psychologist's work-related conduct requires a personal commitment to a lifelong effort to act ethically; to encourage ethical behavior by students, supervisees, employees, and colleagues, as appropriate; and to consult with others, as needed, concerning ethical problems. Each psychologist supplements, but does not violate, the Ethics Code's values and rules on the basis of guidance drawn from personal values, culture, and experience.

GENERAL PRINCIPLES

Principle A: Competence

Psychologists strive to maintain high standards of competence in their work. They recognize the boundaries of their particular competencies and the limitations of their expertise. They provide only those services and use only those techniques for which they are qualified by education, training, or experience. Psychologists are cognizant of the fact that the competencies required in serving, teaching, and/or studying groups of people vary with the distinctive characteristics of those groups. In those areas in which recognized professional standards do not yet exist, psychologists exercise careful judgement and take appropriate precautions to protect the welfare of those with whom they work. They maintain knowledge of relevant scientific and professional information related to the services they render, and they recognize the need for ongoing education. Psychologists make appropriate use of scientific, professional, technical, and administrative resources.

Principle B: Integrity

Psychologists seek to promote integrity in the science, teaching, and practice of psychology. In these activities psychologists are honest, fair, and respectful of others. In describing or reporting their qualifications, services, products, fees, research, or teaching, they do not make statements that are false, misleading, or deceptive. Psychologists strive to be aware of their own belief systems, values, needs, and limitations and the effect of these on their work. To the extent feasible, they attempt to clarify for relevant parties the roles they are performing and to function appropriately in accordance with those roles. Psychologists avoid improper and potentially harmful dual relationships.

Principle C: Professional and Scientific Responsibility

Psychologists uphold professional standards of conduct, clarify their professional roles and obligations, accept appropriate responsibility for their behavior, and adapt their methods to the needs of different populations. Psychologists consult with, refer to, or cooperate with the other professionals and institutions to the extent needed to serve the best interests of their patients, clients, or other recipients of their services. Psychologists' moral standards and conduct are personal matters to the same degree as is true for any other person, except as psychologists' conduct may compromise their professional responsibilities or reduce the public's trust in psychology and psychologists. Psychologists are concerned about the ethical compliance of their colleagues' scientific and professional conduct. When appropriate, they consult with colleagues in order to prevent or avoid unethical conduct.

Principle D: Respect for People's Rights and Dignity

Psychologists accord appropriate respect to the fundamental rights, dignity, and worth of all people. They respect the rights of individuals to privacy, confidentiality, self-determination, and autonomy, mindful that legal and other obligations may lead to inconsistency and conflict with the exercise of these rights. Psychologists are aware of cultural, individual, and role differ-

ences, including those due to age, gender, race ethnicity, national origin, religion, sexual orientation, disability, language, and socioeconomic status. Psychologists try to eliminate the effect on their work of biases based on those factors, and they do not knowingly participate in or condone unfair discriminatory practices.

Principle E: Concern for Others' Welfare

Psychologists seek to contribute to the welfare of those with whom they interact professionally. In their professional actions, psychologists weigh the welfare and rights of their patients or clients, students, supervisees, human research participants, and other affected persons, and the welfare of animal subjects of research. When conflicts occur among psychologists' obligations or concerns, they attempt to resolve these conflicts and to perform their roles in a responsible fashion that avoids or minimizes harm. Psychologists are sensitive to real and ascribed differences in power between themselves and others, and they do not exploit or mislead other people during or after professional relationships.

Principle F: Social Responsibility

Psychologists are aware of their professional and scientific responsibilities to the community and the society in which they work and live. They apply and make public their knowledge of psychology in order to contribute to human welfare. Psychologists are concerned about and work to mitigate the causes of human suffering. When undertaking research, they strive to advance human welfare and the science of psychology. Psychologists try to avoid misuse of their work. Psychologists comply with the law and encourage the development of law and social policy that serve the interests of their patients and clients and the public. They are encouraged to contribute a portion of their professional time for little or no personal advantage.

ETHICAL STANDARDS

1.   *General Standards*

These General Standards are potentially applicable to the professional and scientific activities of all psychologists.

1.01 Applicability of the Ethics Code

The activity of a psychologist subject to the Ethics Code may be reviewed under these Ethical Standards only if the activity is part of his or her work-related functions or the activity is psychological in nature. Personal activities having no connection to or effect on psychological roles are not subject to the Ethics Code.

1.02 Relationship of Ethics and Law

If psychologists' ethical responsibilities conflict with law, psychologists make known their commitment to the Ethics Code and take steps to resolve the conflict in a responsible manner.

1.03 Professional and Scientific Relationship

Psychologists provide diagnostic, therapeutic, teaching, research, supervisory, consultative, or other psychological services only in the context of a defined professional or scientific relationship or role. (See also Standards 2.01, Evaluation, Diagnosis, and Interventions in Professional Context, and 7.02, Forensic Assessments.)

1.04 Boundaries of Competence

(a) Psychologists provide services, teach, and conduct research only with the boundaries of their competence, based on their education, training, supervised experience, or appropriate professional experience.

(b) Psychologists provide services, teach, or conduct research in new areas or involving new techniques only after first undertaking appropriate study, training, supervision, and/or consultation from persons who are competent in those areas or techniques.

(c) In those emerging areas in which generally recognized standards for preparatory training do not yet exist, psychologists nevertheless take reasonable steps to ensure the competence of their work and to protect patients, clients, students, research participants, and others from harm.

1.05 Maintaining Expertise

Psychologists who engage in assessment, therapy, teaching, research, organizational consulting, or other professional activities maintain a reasonable level of awareness of current scientific and professional information in their fields of activity, and undertake ongoing efforts to maintain competence in the skills they use.

1.06 Basis for Scientific and Professional Judgments

Psychologists rely on scientifically and professionally derived knowledge when making scientific or professional judgments or when engaging in scholarly or professional endeavors.

1.07 Describing the Nature and Results of Psychological Services

(a) When psychologists provide assessment, evaluation, treatment, counseling, supervision, teaching, consultation, research, or other psychological services to an individual, a group, or an organization, they provide, using language that is reasonably understandable to the recipient of those services, appropriate information beforehand about the nature of such services and appropriate information later about results and conclusions. (See also Standard 2.09, Explaining Assessment Results.)

(b) If psychologists will be precluded by law or by organizational roles from providing such information to particular individuals or groups, they so inform those individuals or groups at the outset of the service.

1.08 Human Differences

Where differences of age, gender, race, ethnicity, national origin, religion, sexual orientation, disability, language, or socioeconomic status significantly affect psychologists' work concerning particular individuals or groups, psychologists obtain the training, experience, consultation, or supervision necessary to ensure the competence of their services, or they make appropriate referrals.

1.09 Respecting Others

In their work-related activities, psychologists respect the rights of others to hold values, attitudes, and opinions that differ from their own.

1.10 Nondiscrimination

In their work-related activities, psychologists do not engage in unfair discrimination based on age, gender, race, ethnicity, national origin, religion, sexual orientation, disability, socioeconomic status, or any basis proscribed by law.

1.11 Sexual Harassment

(a) Psychologists do not engage in sexual harassment. Sexual harassment is sexual solicitation, physical advances, or verbal or nonverbal conduct that is sexual in nature, that occurs in connection with the psychologist's activities or roles as a psychologist, and that either: (1) is unwelcome, is offensive, or creates a hostile workplace environment, and the psychologist knows or is told this; or (2) is sufficiently severe or intense as to be abusive to a reasonable person in the context. Sexual harassment can consist of a single intense or severe act or of multiple persistent or pervasive acts.

(b) Psychologists accord sexual-harassment complainants and respondents dignity and respect. Psychologists do not participate in denying a person admittance or advancement, employment, tenure, or promotion, based solely upon their having made, or their being the subject of, sexual harassment charges. This does not preclude taking action based upon the outcome of such proceedings or consideration of other appropriate information.

1.12 Other Harassment

Psychologists do not knowingly engage in behavior that is harassing or demeaning to persons with whom they interact in their work based on factors such as those persons' age, gender, race, ethnicity, national origin, religion, sexual orientation, disability, language, or socioeconomic status.

1.13 Personal Problems and Conflicts

(a) Psychologists recognize that their personal problems and conflicts may interfere with their effectiveness. Accordingly, they refrain from undertaking an activity when they know or should know that their personal problems are likely to lead to harm to a patient, client, colleague, student, research participant, or other person to whom they may owe a professional or scientific obligation.

(b) In addition, psychologists have an obligation to be alert to signs of, and to obtain assistance for, their personal problems at an early stage, in order to prevent significantly impaired performance.

(c) When psychologists become aware of personal problems that may interfere with their performing work-related duties adequately, they take appropriate measures, such as obtaining professional consultation or assistance, and determine whether they should limit, suspend, or terminate their work-related duties.

1.14 Avoiding Harm

Psychologists take reasonable steps to avoid harming their patients or clients, research participants, students, and others with whom they work, and to minimize harm where it is foreseeable and unavoidable.

1.15 Misuse of Psychologists' Influence

Because psychologists' scientific and professional judgments and actions may affect the lives of others, they are alert to and guard against personal, financial, social, organizational, or political factors that might lead to misuse of their influence.

1.16 Misuse of Psychologists' Work

(a) Psychologists do not participate in activities in which it appears likely that their skills or data will be misused by others, unless corrective mechanisms are available. (See also Standard 7.04, Truthfulness and Candor.)

(b) If psychologists learn of misuse or misrepresentation of their work, they take reasonable steps to correct or minimize the misuse or misrepresentation.

1.17 Multiple Relationships

(a) In many communities and situations, it may not be feasible or reasonable for psychologists to avoid social or other nonprofessional contacts with persons such as patients, clients, students, supervisees, or research participants. Psychologists must always be sensitive to the potential harmful effects of other contacts on their work and on those persons with whom they deal. A psychologist refrains from entering into or promising another personal, scientific, professional, financial, or other relationship with such persons if it appears likely that such a relationship reasonably might impair the psychologist's objectivity or otherwise interfere with the psychologist's effectively performing his or her functions as a psychologist, or might harm or exploit the other party.

(b) Likewise, whenever feasible, a psychologist refrains from taking on professional or scientific obligations when preexisting relationships would create a risk of such harm.

(c) If a psychologist finds that, due to unforeseen factors, a potentially harmful multiple relationship has arisen, the psychologist attempts to resolve it with due regard for the best interests of the affected person and maximal compliance with the Ethics Code.

1.18 Barter (with Patients or Clients)

Psychologists ordinarily refrain from accepting goods, services, or other nonmonetary remuneration from patients or clients in return for psychological services because such arrangements create inherent potential for conflicts, exploitation, and distortion of the professional relationship. A psychologist may participate in bartering *only* if (1) it is not clinically contraindicated, *and* (2) the relationship is not exploitative. (See also

Standards 1.17, Multiple Relationships, and 1.25, Fees and Financial Arrangements.)

1.19 Exploitative Relationships

(a) Psychologists do not exploit persons over whom they have supervisory, evaluative, or other authority such as students, supervisors, employees, research participants, and clients or patients. (See also Standards 4.05–4.07 regarding sexual involvement with clients or patients.)

(b) Psychologists do not engage in sexual relationships with students or supervisees in training over whom the psychologist has evaluative or direct authority, because such relationships are so likely to impair judgment or be exploitative.

1.20 Consultations and Referrals

(a) Psychologists arrange for appropriate consultations and referrals based principally on the best interests of their patients or clients, with appropriate consent, and subject to other relevant considerations, including applicable law and contractual obligations. (See also Standards 5.01, Discussing the Limits of Confidentiality, and 5.06, Consultations.)

(b) When indicated and professionally appropriate, psychologists cooperate with other professionals in order to serve their patients or clients effectively and appropriately.

(c) Psychologists' referral practices are consistent with law.

1.21 Third-Party Requests for Services

(a) When a psychologist agrees to provide services to a person or entity at the request of a third party, the psychologist clarifies to the extent feasible, at the outset of the service, the nature of the relationship with each party. This clarification includes the role of the psychologist (such as therapist, organizational consultant, diagnostician, or expert witness), the probable uses of the services provided or the information obtained, and the fact that there may be limits to confidentiality.

(b) If there is a foreseeable risk of the psychologist's being called upon to perform conflicting roles because of the involvement of a third party, the psychologist clarifies the nature and direction of his or her responsibilities, keeps all parties appropriately informed as matters develop, and resolves the situation in accordance with this Ethics Code.

1.22 Delegation to and Supervision of Subordinates

(a) Psychologists delegate to their employees, supervisees, and research assistants only those responsibilities that such persons can reasonably be expected to perform competently, on the basis of their education, training, or experience, either independently or with the level of supervision being provided.

(b) Psychologists provide proper training and supervision to their employees or supervisees and take reasonable steps to see that such persons perform services responsibly, competently, and ethically.

(c) If institutional policies, procedures, or practices prevent fulfillment of this obligation, psychologists attempt to modify their role or to correct the situation to the extent feasible.

1.23 Documentation of Professional and Scientific Work

(a) Psychologists appropriately document their professional and scientific work in order to facilitate provision of services later by them or by other professionals, to ensure accountability, and to meet other requirements of institutions or the law.

(b) When psychologists have reason to believe that records of their professional services will be used in legal proceedings involving recipients of or participants in their work, they have a responsibility to create and maintain documentation in the kind of detail and quality that would be consistent with reasonable scrutiny in an adjudicative forum. (See also Standard 7.01, Professionalism, under Forensic Activities.)

1.24 Records and Data

Psychologists create, maintain, disseminate, store, retain, and dispose of records and data relating to their research, practice, and other work in accordance with law and in a manner that permits compliance with the requirements of this Ethics Code. (See also Standard 5.04, Maintenance of Records.)

1.25 Fees and Financial Arrangements

(a) As early as is feasible in a professional or scientific relationship, the psychologist and the patient, client, or other appropriate recipient of psychological services reach an agreement specifying the compensation and the billing arrangements.

(b) Psychologists do not exploit recipients of services or payors with respect to fees.

(c) Psychologists' fee practices are consistent with law.

(d) Psychologists do not misrepresent their fees.

(e) If limitations to services can be anticipated because of limitations in financing, this is discussed with the patient, client, or other appropriate recipient of services as early as is feasible. (See also Standard 4.08, Interruption of Services.)

(f) If the patient, client, or other recipient of services does not pay for services as agreed, and if the psychologist wishes to use collection agencies or legal measures to collect the fees, the psychologist first informs the person that such measures will be taken and provides that person an opportunity to make prompt payment. (See also Standard 5.11, Withholding Records for Nonpayment.)

1.26 Accuracy in Reports to Payors and Funding Sources

In their reports to payors for services or sources of research funding, psychologists accurately state the nature of the research or service provided, the fees or charges, and where applicable, the identity of the provider, the findings, and the diagnosis. (See also Standard 5.05, Disclosures.)

1.27 Referrals and Fees

When a psychologist pays, receives payment from, or divides fees with another professional other than in an employer-employee relationship, the payment to each is based on the services (clinical, consultative, administrative, or other) provided and is not based on the referral itself.

2. *Evaluation, Assessment, or Intervention*

2.01 Evaluation, Diagnosis, and Interventions in Professional Context

(a) Psychologists perform evaluations, diagnostic services, or interventions only within the context of a defined professional relationship. (See also Standard 1.03, Professional and Scientific Relationship.)

(b) Psychologists' assessments, recommendations, reports, and psychological diagnostic or evaluative statements are based on information and techniques (including personal interviews of the individual when appropriate) sufficient to provide appropriate substantiation for their findings. (See also Standard 7.02, Forensic Assessments.)

2.02 Competence and Appropriate Use of Assessments and Interventions

(a) Psychologists who develop, administer, score, interpret, or use psychological assessment techniques, interviews, tests, or instruments do so in a manner and for purposes that are appropriate in light of the research on or evidence of the usefulness and proper application of the techniques.

(b) Psychologists refrain from misuse of assessment techniques, interventions, results, and interpretations and take reasonable steps to prevent others from misusing the information these techniques provide. This includes refraining from releasing raw test results or raw data to persons, other than to patients or clients as appropriate, who are not qualified to use such information. (See also Standards 1.02, Relationship of Ethics and Law, and 1.04, Boundaries of Competence.)

2.03 Test Construction

Psychologists who develop and conduct research with tests and other assessment techniques use scientific procedures and current professional knowledge for test design, standardization, validation, reduction or elimination of bias, and recommendations for use.

2.04 Use of Assessment in General and with Special Populations

(a) Psychologists who perform interventions or administer, score, interpret, or use assessment techniques are familiar with the reliability, validation, and related standardization or outcome studies of, and proper applications and uses of, the techniques they use.

(b) Psychologists recognize limits to the certainty with which diagnoses, judgments, or predictions can be made about individuals.

(c) Psychologists attempt to identify situations in which particular interventions or assessment techniques or norms may not be applicable or may require adjustment in administration or interpretation because of factors such as individuals' gender, age, race, ethnicity, national origin, religion, sexual orientation, disability, language, or socioeconomic status.

2.05 Interpreting Assessment Results

When interpreting assessment results, including automated interpretations, psychologists take into account the various test factors and characteristics of the person being assessed that might affect psychologists' judgments or reduce the accuracy of their interpretations. They indicate any significant reservations they have about the accuracy or limitations of their interpretations.

2.06 Unqualified Persons

Psychologists do not promote the use of psychological assessment techniques by unqualified persons. (See also Standard 1.22, Delegation to and Supervision of Subordinates.)

2.07 Obsolete Tests and Outdated Test Results

(a) Psychologists do not base their assessment or intervention decisions or recommendations on data or test results that are outdated for the current purpose.

(b) Similarly, psychologists do not base such decisions or recommendations on tests and measures that are obsolete and not useful for the current purpose.

2.08 Test Scoring and Interpretation Services

(a) Psychologists who offer assessment or scoring procedures to other professionals accurately describe the purpose, norms, validity, reliability, and applications of the procedures and any special qualifications applicable to their use.

(b) Psychologists select scoring and interpretation services (including automated services) on the basis of evidence of the validity of the program and procedures as well as on other appropriate considerations.

(c) Psychologists retain appropriate responsibility for the appropriate application, interpretation, and use of assessment instruments, whether they score and interpret such tests themselves or use automated or other services.

2.09 Explaining Assessment Results

Unless the nature of the relationship is clearly explained to the person being assessed in advance and precludes provision of an explanation of results (such as in some organizational consulting, preemployment or security screenings, and forensic evaluations), psychologists ensure that an explanation of the results is provided using language that is reasonably understandable to the person assessed or to another legally authorized person on behalf of the client. Regardless of whether the scoring and interpretation are done by the psychologist, by assistants, or by automated or other outside

services, psychologists take reasonable steps to ensure that appropriate explanations of results are given.

2.10 Maintaining Test Security

Psychologists make reasonable efforts to maintain the integrity and security of tests and other assessment techniques consistent with law, contractual obligations, and in a manner that permits compliance with the requirements of this Ethics Code. (See also Standard 1.02, Relationship of Ethics and Law.)

3. *Advertising and Other Public Statements*

3.01 Definition of Public Statements

Psychologists comply with this Ethics Code in public statements relating to their professional services, products, or publications or to the field of psychology. Public statements include but are not limited to paid or unpaid advertising, brochures, printed matter, directory listings, personal resumes or curricula vitae, interviews or comments for use in media, statements in legal proceedings, lectures and public oral presentations, and published materials.

3.02 Statements by Others

(a) Psychologists who engage others to create or place public statements that promote their professional practice, products, or activities retain professional responsibility for such statements.

(b) In addition, psychologists make reasonable efforts to prevent others whom they do not control (such as employers, publishers, sponsors, organizational clients, and representatives of the print or broadcast media) from making deceptive statements concerning psychologists' practice or professional or scientific activities.

(c) If psychologists learn of deceptive statements about their work made by others, psychologists make reasonable efforts to correct such statements.

(d) Psychologists do not compensate employees of press, radio, television, or other communication media in return for publicity in a news item.

(e) A paid advertisement relating to the psychologist's activities must be identified as such, unless it is already apparent from the context.

3.03 Avoidance of False or Deceptive Statements

(a) Psychologists do not make public statements that are false, deceptive, misleading, or fraudulent, either because of what they state, convey, or suggest or because of what they omit, concerning their research, practice, or other work activities or those of persons or organizations with which they are affiliated. As examples (and not in limitation) of this standard, psychologists do not make false or deceptive statements concerning (1) their training, experience, or competence; (2) their academic degrees; (3) their credentials; (4) their institutional or association affiliations; (5) their services; (6) the scientific or clinical basis for, or results or degree of success of their services; (7) their fees; or (8) their publications or research findings. (See also Standards 6.15, Deception in Research, and 6.18, Providing Participants with Information about the Study.)

(b) Psychologists claim as credentials for their psychological work, only degrees that (1) were earned from a regionally accredited educational institution or (2) were the basis for psychology licensure by the state in which they practice.

3.04 Media Presentations

When psychologists provide advice or comment by means of public lectures, demonstrations, radio or television programs, prerecorded tapes, printed articles, mailed material, or other media, they take reasonable precautions to ensure that (1) the statements are based on appropriate psychological literature and practice, (2) the statements are otherwise consistent with this Ethics Code, and (3) the recipients of the information are not encouraged to infer that a relationship has been established with them personally.

3.05 Testimonials

Psychologists do not solicit testimonials from current psychotherapy clients or patients or other persons who because of their particular circumstances are vulnerable to undue influence.

3.06 In-Person Solicitation

Psychologists do not engage, directly or through agents, in uninvited in-person solicitation of business from actual or potential psychotherapy patients or clients or other persons who because of their particular circumstances are vulnerable to undue influence. However, this does not preclude attempting to implement appropriate collateral contacts with significant others for the purpose of benefiting an already engaged therapy patient.

4.   *Therapy*
4.01 Structuring the Relationship

(a) Psychologists discuss with clients or patients as early as is feasible in the therapeutic relationship appropriate issues, such as the nature and anticipated course of therapy, fees, and confidentiality. (See also Standards 1.25, Fees and Financial Arrangements, and 5.01, Discussing the Limits of Confidentiality.)

(b) When the psychologist's work with clients or patients will be supervised, the above discussion includes that fact, and the name of the supervisor, when the supervisor has legal responsibility for the case.

(c) When the therapist is a student intern, the client or patient is informed of that fact.

(d) Psychologists make reasonable efforts to answer patients' questions and to avoid apparent misunderstandings about therapy. Whenever possible, psychologists provide oral and/or written information, using language that is reasonably understandable to the patient or client.

4.02 Informed Consent to Therapy

(a) Psychologists obtain appropriate informed consent to therapy or related procedures, using language that is reasonably understandable to participants. The content of informed consent will vary depending on many circumstances; however, informed consent generally implies that the person (1) has the capacity to consent, (2) has been informed of significant information concerning the procedure, (3) has freely and without undue influence expressed consent, and (4) consent has been appropriately documented.

(b) When persons are legally incapable of giving informed consent, psychologists obtain informed permission from a legally authorized person, if such substitute consent is permitted by law.

(c) In addition, psychologists (1) inform those persons who are legally incapable of giving informed consent about the proposed interventions in a manner commensurate with the persons' psychological capacities, (2) seek their assent to those interventions, and (3) consider such persons' preferences and best interests.

4.03 Couple and Family Relationships

(a) When a psychologist agrees to provide services to several persons who have a relationship (such as husband and wife or parents and children), the psychologist attempts to clarify at the outset (1) which of the individuals are patients or clients and (2) the relationship the psychologist will have with each person. This clarification includes the role of the psychologist and the probable uses of the services provided or the information obtained. (See also Standard 5.01, Discussing the Limits of Confidentiality.)

(b) As soon as it becomes apparent that the psychologist may be called on to perform potentially conflicting roles (such as marital counselor to husband and wife, and then witness for one party in a divorce proceeding), the psychologist attempts to clarify and adjust, or withdraw from roles, appropriately. (See also Standard 7.03, Clarification of Role, under Forensic Activities.)

4.04 Providing Mental Health Services to Those Served by Others

In deciding whether to offer or provide services to those already receiving mental health services elsewhere, psychologists carefully consider the treatment issues and the potential patient's or client's welfare. The psychologist discusses these issues with the patient or client, or another legally authorized person on behalf of the client, in order to minimize the risk of confusion and conflict, consults with the service providers when appropriate, and proceeds with caution and sensitivity to the therapeutic issues.

4.05 Sexual Intimacies with Current Patients or Clients

Psychologists do not engage in sexual intimacies with current patients or clients.

4.06 Therapy with Former Sexual Partners

Psychologists do not accept as therapy patients or clients persons with whom they have engaged in sexual intimacies.

4.07 Sexual Intimacies with Former Therapy Patients

(a) Psychologists do not engage in sexual intimacies with a former therapy patient or client for at least two years after cessation or termination of professional services.

(b) Because sexual intimacies with a former therapy patient or client are so frequently harmful to the patient or client, and because such intimacies undermine public confidence in the psychology profession

and thereby deter the public's use of needed services, psychologists do not engage in sexual intimacies with former therapy patients and clients even after a two-year interval except in the most unusual circumstances. The psychologist who engages in such activity after the two years following cessation or termination of treatment bears the burden of demonstrating that there has been no exploitation, in light of all relevant factors, including (1) the amount of time that has passed since therapy terminated, (2) the nature and duration of the therapy, (3) the circumstances of termination, (4) the patient's or client's personal history, (5) the patient's or client's current mental status, (6) the likelihood of adverse impact on the patient or client or others, and (7) any statements or actions made by the therapist during the course of therapy suggesting or inviting the possibility of a posttermination sexual or romantic relationship with the patient or client. (See also Standard 1.17, Multiple Relationships.)

4.08 Interruption of Services

(a) Psychologists make reasonable efforts to plan for facilitating care in the event that psychological services are interrupted by factors such as the psychologist's illness, death, unavailability, or relocation or by the client's relocation or financial limitations. (See also Standard 5.09, Preserving Records and Data.)

(b) When entering into employment or contractual relationships, psychologists provide for orderly and appropriate resolution of responsibility for patient or client care in the event that the employment or contractual relationship ends, with paramount consideration given to the welfare of the patient or client.

4.09 Terminating the Professional Relationship

(a) Psychologists do not abandon patients or clients. (See also Standard 1.25e, under Fees and Financial Arrangements.)

(b) Psychologists terminate a professional relationship when it becomes reasonably clear that the patient or client no longer needs the service, is not benefiting, or is being harmed by continued service.

(c) Prior to termination for whatever reason, except where precluded by the patient's or client's conduct, the psychologist discusses the patient's or client's views and needs, provides appropriate pretermination counseling, suggests alternative service providers as appropriate, and takes other reasonable steps to facilitate transfer of responsibility to another provider if the patient or client needs one immediately.

5. *Privacy and Confidentiality*

These Standards are potentially applicable to the professional and scientific activities of all psychologists.

5.01 Discussing the Limits of Confidentiality

(a) Psychologists discuss with persons and organizations with whom they establish a scientific or professional relationship (including, to the extent feasible, minors and their legal representatives) (1) the relevant limitations on confidentiality, including limitations where applicable in group, marital, and family therapy or in organizational consulting, and (2) the foreseeable uses of the information generated through their services.

(b) Unless it is not feasible or is contraindicated, the discussion of confidentiality occurs at the outset of the relationship and thereafter as new circumstances may warrant.

(c) Permission for electronic recording of interviews is secured from clients and patients.

5.02 Maintaining Confidentiality

Psychologists have a primary obligation and take reasonable precautions to respect the confidentiality rights of those with whom they work or consult, recognizing that confidentiality may be established by law, institutional rules, or professional or scientific relationships. (See also Standard 6.26, Professional Reviewers.)

5.03 Minimizing Intrusions on Privacy

(a) In order to minimize intrusions on privacy, psychologists include in written and oral reports, consultations, and the like, only information germane to the purpose for which the communication is made.

(b) Psychologists discuss confidential information obtained in clinical or consulting relationships, or evaluative data concerning patients, individual or organizational clients, students, research participants, supervisees, and employees, only for appropriate scientific or professional purposes and only with persons clearly concerned with such matters.

5.04 Maintenance of Records

Psychologists maintain appropriate confidentiality in creating, storing, accessing, transferring, and disposing of records under their control, whether these are written, automated, or in any other medium. Psychologists maintain and dispose of records in accordance with law and in a manner that permits compliance with the requirements of this Ethics Code.

5.05 Disclosures

(a) Psychologists disclose confidential information without the consent of the individual only as mandated by law, or where permitted by law for a valid purpose, such as (1) to provide needed professional services to the patient or the individual or organizational client, (2) to obtain appropriate professional consultations, (3) to protect the patient or client or others from harm, or (4) to obtain payment for services, in which instance disclosure is limited to the minimum that is necessary to achieve the purpose.

(b) Psychologists also may disclose confidential information with the appropriate consent of the patient or the individual or organizational client (or of another legally authorized person on behalf of the patient or client), unless prohibited by law.

5.06 Consultations

When consulting with colleagues, (1) psychologists do not share confidential information that reasonably could lead to the identification of a patient, client, research participant, or other person or organization with whom they have a confidential relationship unless they have obtained the prior consent of the person or organization or the disclosure cannot be avoided, and (2) they share information only to the extent necessary to achieve the purposes of the consultation. (See also Standard 5.02, Maintaining Confidentiality.)

5.07 Confidential Information in Databases

(a) If confidential information concerning recipients of psychological services is to be entered into databases or systems of records available to persons whose access has not been consented to by the recipient, then psychologists use coding or other techniques to avoid the inclusion of personal identifiers.

(b) If a research protocol approved by an institutional review board or similar body requires the inclusion of personal identifiers, such identifiers are deleted before the information is made accessible to persons other than those of whom the subject was advised.

(c) If such deletion is not feasible, then before psychologists transfer such data to others or review such data collected by others, they take reasonable steps to determine that appropriate consent of personally identifiable individuals has been obtained.

5.08 Use of Confidential Information for Didactic or Other Purposes

(a) Psychologists do not disclose in their writings, lectures, or other public media, confidential, personally identifiable information concerning their patients, individual or organizational clients, students, research participants, or other recipients of their services that they obtained during the course of their work, unless the person or organization has consented in writing or unless there is other ethical or legal authorization for doing so.

(b) Ordinarily, in such scientific and professional presentations, psychologists disguise confidential information concerning such persons or organizations so that they are not individually identifiable to others and so that discussions do not cause harm to subjects who might identify themselves.

5.09 Preserving Records and Data

A psychologist makes plans in advance so that confidentiality of records and data is protected in the event of the psychologist's death, incapacity, or withdrawal from the position or practice.

5.10 Ownership of Records and Data

Recognizing that ownership of records and data is governed by legal principles, psychologists take reasonable and lawful steps so that records and data remain available to the extent needed to serve the best interests of patients, individual or organizational clients, research participants, or appropriate others.

5.11 Withholding Records for Nonpayment

Psychologists may not withhold records under their control that are requested and imminently needed for a patient's or client's treatment solely because payment has not been received, except as otherwise provided by law.

6. Teaching, Training Supervision, Research, and Publishing

6.01 Design of Education and Training Programs

Psychologists who are responsible for education and training programs seek to ensure that the programs are competently designed, provide the proper experiences, and meet the requirements for licensure, certification, or other goals for which claims are made by the program.

6.02 Descriptions of Education and Training Programs

(a) Psychologists responsible for education and training programs seek to ensure that there is a current and accurate description of the program content, training goals and objectives, and requirements that must be met for satisfactory completion of the program. This information must be made readily available to all interested parties.

(b) Psychologists seek to ensure that statements concerning their course outlines are accurate and not misleading, particularly regarding the subject matter to be covered, bases for evaluating progress, and the nature of course experiences. (See also Standard 3.03, Avoidance of False or Deceptive Statements.)

(c) To the degree to which they exercise control, psychologists responsible for announcements, catalogs, brochures, or advertisements describing workshops, seminars, or other non-degree-granting educational programs ensure that they accurately describe the audience for which the program is intended, the educational objectives, the presenters, and the fees involved.

6.03 Accuracy and Objectivity in Teaching

(a) When engaged in teaching or training, psychologists present psychological information accurately and with a reasonable degree of objectivity.

(b) When engaged in teaching or training, psychologists recognize the power they hold over students or supervisees and therefore make reasonable efforts to avoid engaging in conduct that is personally demeaning to students or supervisees. (See also Standards 1.09, Respecting Others, and 1.12, Other Harassment.)

6.04 Limitation on Teaching

Psychologists do not teach the use of techniques or procedures that require specialized training, licensure, or expertise, including but not limited to hypnosis, biofeedback, and projective techniques, to individuals who lack the prerequisite training, legal scope of practice, or expertise.

6.05 Assessing Student and Supervisee Performance

(a) In academic and supervisory relationships, psychologists establish an appropriate process for providing feedback to students and supervisees.

(b) Psychologists evaluate students and supervisees on the basis of their actual performance on relevant and established program requirements.

6.06 Planning Research

(a) Psychologists design, conduct, and report research in accordance with recognized standards of scientific competence and ethical research.

(b) Psychologists plan their research so as to minimize the possibility that results will be misleading.

(c) In planning research, psychologists consider its ethical acceptability under the Ethics Code. If an ethical issue is unclear, psychologists seek to resolve the issue through consultation with institutional review boards, animal care and use committees, peer consultations, or other proper mechanisms.

(d) Psychologists take reasonable steps to implement appropriate protections for the rights and welfare of human participants, other persons affected by the research, and the welfare of animal subjects.

6.07 Responsibility

(a) Psychologists conduct research competently and with due concern for the dignity and welfare of the participants.

(b) Psychologists are responsible for the ethical conduct of research conducted by them or by others under their supervision or control.

(c) Researchers and assistants are permitted to perform only those tasks for which they are appropriately trained and prepared.

(d) As part of the process of development and implementation of research projects, psychologists consult those with expertise concerning any special population under investigation or most likely to be affected.

6.08 Compliance with Law and Standards

Psychologists plan and conduct research in a manner consistent with federal and state law and regulations, as well as professional standards governing the conduct of research, and particularly those standards governing research with human participants and animal subjects.

6.09 Institutional Approval

Psychologists obtain from host institutions or organizations appropriate approval prior to conducting research, and they provide accurate information about their research proposals. They conduct the research in accordance with the approved research protocol.

6.10 Research Responsibilities

Prior to conducting research (except research involving only anonymous surveys, naturalistic observations, or similar research), psychologists enter into an agreement with participants that clarifies the nature of the research and the responsibilities of each party.

6.11 Informed Consent to Research

(a) Psychologists use language that is reasonably understandable to research participants in obtaining their appropriate informed consent (except as provided in Standard 6.12, Dispensing with Informed Consent). Such informed consent is appropriately documented.

(b) Using language that is reasonably understandable to participants, psychologists inform participants of the nature of the research; they inform participants that they are free to participate or to decline to participate or to withdraw from the research; they explain the foreseeable consequences of declining or withdrawing; they inform participants of significant factors that may be expected to influence their willingness to participate (such as risks, discomfort, adverse effects, or limitations on confidentiality, except as provided in Standard 6.15, Deception in Research); and they explain other aspects about which the prospective participants inquire.

(c) When psychologists conduct research with individuals such as students or subordinates, psychologists take special care to protect the prospective participants from adverse consequences of declining or withdrawing from participation.

(d) When research participation is a course requirement or opportunity for extra credit, the prospective participant is given the choice of equitable alternative activities.

(e) For persons who are legally incapable of giving informed consent, psychologists nevertheless (1) provide an appropriate explanation, (2) obtain the participant's assent, and (3) obtain appropriate permission from a legally authorized person, if such substitute consent is permitted by law.

6.12 Dispensing with Informed Consent

Before determining that planned research (such as research involving only anonymous questionnaires, naturalistic observations, or certain kinds of archival research) does not require the informed consent of research participants, psychologists consider applicable regulations and institutional review board requirements, and they consult with colleagues as appropriate.

6.13 Informed Consent in Research Filming or Recording

Psychologists obtain informed consent from research participants prior to filming or recording them in any form, unless the research involves simply naturalistic observations in public places and it is not anticipated that the recording will be used in a manner that could cause personal identification or harm.

6.14 Offering Inducements for Research Participants

(a) In offering professional services as an inducement to obtain research participants, psychologists make clear the nature of the services, as well as the risks, obligations, and limitations. (See also Standard 1.18, Barter [with Patients or Clients.])

(b) Psychologists do not offer excessive or inappropriate financial or other inducements to obtain research participants, particularly when it might tend to coerce participation.

6.15 Deception in Research

(a) Psychologists do not conduct a study involving deception unless they have determined that the use of deceptive techniques is justified by the study's prospective scientific, educational, or applied value and that equally effective alternative procedures that do not use deception are not feasible.

(b) Psychologists never deceive research participants about significant aspects that would affect their willingness to participate, such as physical risks, discomfort, or unpleasant emotional experiences.

(c) Any other deception that is an integral feature of the design and conduct of an experiment must be explained to participants as early as is feasible, preferably at the conclusion of their participation, but no later than at the conclusion of the research. (See also Standard 6.18, Providing Participants with Information about the Study.)

6.16 Sharing and Utilizing Data

Psychologists inform research participants of their anticipated sharing or further use of personally identifiable research data and of the possibility of unanticipated future uses.

6.17 Minimizing Invasiveness

In conducting research, psychologists interfere with the participants or milieu from which data are collected only in a manner that is warranted by an appropriate research design and that is consistent with psychologists' roles as scientific investigators.

6.18 Providing Participants with Information about the Study

(a) Psychologists provide a prompt opportunity for participants to obtain appropriate information about the nature, results, and conclusions of the research, and psychologists attempt to correct any misconceptions that participants may have.

(b) If scientific or humane values justify delaying or withholding this information, psychologists take reasonable measures to reduce the risk of harm.

6.19 Honoring Commitments

Psychologists take reasonable measures to honor all commitments they have made to research participants.

6.20 Care and Use of Animals in Research

(a) Psychologists who conduct research involving animals treat them humanely.

(b) Psychologists acquire, care for, use, and dispose of animals in compliance with current federal, state, and local laws and regulations, and with professional standards.

(c) Psychologists trained in research methods and experienced in the care of laboratory animals supervise all procedures involving animals and are responsible for ensuring appropriate consideration of their comfort, health, and humane treatment.

(d) Psychologists ensure that all individuals using animals under their supervision have received instruction in research methods and in the care, maintenance, and handling of the species being used, to the extent appropriate to their role.

(e) Responsibilities and activities of individuals assisting in a research project are consistent with their respective competencies.

(f) Psychologists make reasonable efforts to minimize the discomfort, infection, illness, and pain of animal subjects.

(g) A procedure subjecting animals to pain, stress, or privation is used only when an alternative procedure is unavailable and the goal is justified by its prospective scientific, education, or applied value.

(h) Surgical procedures are performed under appropriate anesthesia; techniques to avoid infection and minimize pain are followed during and after surgery.

(i) When it is appropriate that the animal's life be terminated, it is done rapidly, with an effort to minimize pain, and in accordance with accepted procedures.

6.21 Reporting of Results

(a) Psychologists do not fabricate data or falsify results in their publications.

(b) If psychologists discover significant errors in their published data, they take reasonable steps to correct such errors in a correction, retraction, erratum, or other appropriate publication means.

6.22 Plagiarism

Psychologists do not present substantial portions or elements of another's work or data as their own, even if the other work or data source is cited occasionally.

6.23 Publication Credit

(a) Psychologists take responsibility and credit, including authorship credit, only for work they have actually performed or to which they have contributed.

(b) Principal authorship and other publication credits accurately reflect the relative scientific or professional contributions of the individuals involved, regardless of their relative status. Mere possession of an institutional position, such as Department Chair, does not justify authorship credit. Minor contributions to the research or to the writing for publications are appropriately acknowledged, such as in footnotes or in an introductory statement.

(c) A student is usually listed as principal author on any multiple-authored article that is substantially based on the student's dissertation or thesis.

6.24 Duplicate Publication of Data

Psychologists do not publish, as original data, data that have been previously published. This does not preclude republishing data when they are accompanied by proper acknowledgment.

6.25 Sharing Data

After research results are published, psychologists do not withhold the data on which their conclusions are based from other competent professionals who seek to verify the substantive claims through reanalysis and who intend to use such data only for that purpose, provided that the confidentiality of the participants can be protected and unless legal rights concerning proprietary data preclude their release.

6.26 Professional Reviewers

Psychologists who review material submitted for publication, grant, or other research proposal review respect the confidentiality of and the proprietary rights in such information of those who submitted it.

7. *Forensic Activities*

7.01 Professionalism

Psychologists who perform forensic functions, such as assessments, interviews, consultations, reports, or expert testimony, must comply with all other provisions of this Ethics Code to the extent that they apply to such activities. In addition, psychologists base their forensic work on appropriate knowledge of and competence in the areas underlying such work, including specialized knowledge concerning special populations. (See also Standards 1.06, Basis for Scientific and Professional Judgments; 1.08, Human Differences; 1.15, Misuse of Psychologists' Influence; and 1.23, Documentation of Professional and Scientific Work.)

7.02 Forensic Assessments

(a) Psychologists' forensic assessments, recommendations, and reports are based on information and techniques (including personal interviews of the individual, when appropriate) sufficient to provide appropriate substantiation for their findings. (See also Standards 1.03, Professional and Scientific Relationship; 1.23, Documentation of Professional and Scientific

Work; 2.01, Evaluation, Diagnosis, and Interventions in Professional Context; and 2.05, Interpreting Assessment Results.)

(b) Except as noted in (c), below, psychologists provide written or oral forensic reports or testimony of the psychological characteristics of an individual only after they have conducted an examination of the individual adequate to support their statements or conclusions.

(c) When, despite reasonable efforts, such an examination is not feasible, psychologists clarify the impact of their limited information on the reliability and validity of their reports and testimony, and they appropriately limit the nature and extent of their conclusions or recommendations.

7.03 Clarification of Role

In most circumstances, psychologists avoid performing multiple and potentially conflicting roles in forensic matters. When psychologists may be called on to serve in more than one role in a legal proceeding—for example, as consultant or expert for one party or for the court and as a fact witness—they clarify role expectations and the extent of confidentiality in advance to the extent feasible, and thereafter as changes occur, in order to avoid compromising their professional judgment and objectivity and in order to avoid misleading others regarding their role.

7.04 Truthfulness and Candor

(a) In forensic testimony and reports, psychologists testify truthfully, honestly, and candidly and, consistent with applicable legal procedures, describe fairly the bases for their testimony and conclusions.

(b) Whenever necessary to avoid misleading, psychologists acknowledge the limits of their data or conclusions.

7.05 Prior Relationships

A prior professional relationship with a party does not preclude psychologists from testifying as fact witnesses or from testifying to their services to the extent permitted by applicable law. Psychologists appropriately take into account ways in which the prior relationship might affect their professional objectivity or opinions and disclose the potential conflict to the relevant parties.

7.06 Compliance with Law and Rules

In performing forensic roles, psychologists are reasonably familiar with the rules governing their roles. Psy-

chologists are aware of the occasionally competing demands placed upon them by these principles and the requirements of the court system, and attempt to resolve these conflicts by making known their commitment to this Ethics Code and taking steps to resolve the conflict in a responsible manner. (See also Standard 1.02, Relationship of Ethics and Law.)

8. Resolving Ethical Issues

8.01 Familiarity with Ethics Code

Psychologists have an obligation to be familiar with this Ethics Code, other applicable ethics codes, and their application to psychologists' work. Lack of awareness or misunderstanding of an ethical standard is not itself a defense to a charge of unethical conduct.

8.02 Confronting Ethical Issues

When a psychologist is uncertain whether a particular situation or course of action would violate this Ethics Code, the psychologist ordinarily consults with other psychologists knowledgeable about ethical issues, with state or national psychology ethics committees, or with other appropriate authorities in order to choose a proper response.

8.03 Conflicts Between Ethics and Organizational Demands

If the demands of an organization with which psychologists are affiliated conflict with this Ethics Code, psychologists clarify the nature of the conflict, make known their commitment to the Ethics Code, and to the extent feasible, seek to resolve the conflict in a way that permits the fullest adherence to the Ethics Code.

8.04 Informal Resolution of Ethical Violations

When psychologists believe that there may have been an ethical violation by another psychologist, they attempt to resolve the issue by bringing it to the attention of that individual if an informal resolution appears appropriate and the intervention does not violate any confidentiality rights that may be involved.

8.05 Reporting Ethical Violations

If an apparent ethical violation is not appropriate for informal resolution under Standard 8.04 or is not resolved properly in that fashion, psychologists take further action appropriate to the situation, unless such action conflicts with confidentiality rights in ways that cannot be resolved. Such action might include referral to state or national committees on professional ethics or to state licensing boards.

8.06 Cooperating with Ethics Committees

Psychologists cooperate in ethics investigations, proceedings, and resulting requirements of the APA or any affiliated state psychological association to which they belong. In doing so, they make reasonable efforts to resolve any issues as to confidentiality. Failure to cooperate is itself an ethics violation.

8.07 Improper Complaints

Psychologists do not file or encourage the filing of ethics complaints that are frivolous and are intended to harm the respondent rather than to protect the public.

Protection of the Rights and Privacy of Parents and Students— Family Educational Rights and Privacy Act of 1974

Public Law 93-380

Sec. 513.(a) Part C of the General Education Provisions Act is further amended by adding at the end thereof the following new section:

PROTECTION OF THE RIGHTS AND PRIVACY OF PARENTS AND STUDENTS

Sec. 438.(a)(1) No funds shall be made available under any applicable program to any State or local educational agency, any institution of higher education, any community college, any school, any agency offering a preschool program, or any other educational institution which has a policy of denying, or which effectively prevents, the parents of students attending any school of such agency, or attending such institution of higher education, community college, school, preschool, or other educational institution, the right to inspect and review any and all official records, files, and data directly related to their children, including all material that is incorporated into each student's cumulative record folder, and intended for school use or to be available to parties outside the school or school system, and specifically including, but not necessarily limited to, identifying data, academic work completed, level of achievement (grades, standardized achievement test scores), attendance data, scores on standardized intelligence, aptitude, and psychological tests, interest inventory results, health data, family background information, teacher or counselor ratings of serious or recurrent behavior patterns. Where such records or data include information on more than one student, the parents of any student shall be entitled to receive, or be informed of, that part of such record or data as pertains to their child. Each recipient shall establish appropriate procedures for the granting of a request by parents for access to their child's school records within a reasonable period of time, but in no case more than forty-five days after the request has been made.

(2) Parents shall have an opportunity for a hearing to challenge the content of their child's school records, to insure that the records are not inaccurate, misleading, or otherwise in violation of the privacy or other rights of students, and to provide an opportunity for the correction or deletion of any such inaccurate, misleading, or otherwise inappropriate data contained therein.

(b)(1) No funds shall be made available under any applicable program to any State or local educational agency, any institution of higher education, any community college, any school, any agency offering a preschool program, or any other educational institution which has a policy of permitting the release of personally identifiable records or files (or personal information contained therein) of students without the written consent of their parents to any individual, agency, or organization, other than to the following—

(A) other school officials, including teachers within the educational institution or local educational agency who have legitimate educational interests;

SOURCE: Reprinted with permission from *United States Code Congressional and Administrative News—1974*, Vol. 1, pp. 541–697. Copyright © 1975 by West Publishing Company.

(B) officials of other schools or school systems in which the student intends to enroll, upon condition that the student's parents be notified of the transfer, receive a copy of the record if desired, and have an opportunity for a hearing to challenge the content of the record;

(C) authorized representatives of (i) the Comptroller General of the United States, (ii) the Secretary, (iii) an administrative head of an educational agency (as defined in section 409 of this Act), or (iv) State educational authorities, under the conditions set forth in paragraph (3) of this subsection; and

(D) in connection with a student's application for, or receipt of, financial aid.

(2) No funds shall be made available under any applicable program to any State or local educational agency, any institution of higher education, any community college, any school, agency offering a preschool program, or any other educational institution which has a policy of practice of furnishing, in any form, any personally identifiable information contained in personal school records, to any persons other than those listed in subsection (b)(1) unless—

(A) there is written consent from the student's parents specifying records to be released, the reasons for such release, and to whom, and with a copy of the records to be released to the student's parents and the student if desired by the parents, or

(B) such information is furnished in compliance with judicial order, or pursuant to any lawfully issued subpoena, upon condition that parents and the student are notified of all such orders or subpoenas in advance of the compliance therewith by the educational institution or agency.

(3) Nothing contained in this section shall preclude authorized representatives of (A) the Comptroller General of the United States, (B) the Secretary, (C) an administrative head of an educational agency or (D) State educational authorities from having access to student or other records which may be necessary in connection with the audit and evaluation of Federally-supported education programs, or in connection with the enforcement of the Federal legal requirements which relate to such programs: *Provided* that, except when collection of personally identifiable data is specifically authorized by Federal law, any data collected by such officials with respect to individual students shall not include information (including social security numbers) which would permit the personal identification of such students or their parents after the data so obtained has been collected.

(4)(A) With respect to subsections (c)(1) and (c)(2) and (c)(3), all persons, agencies, or organizations desiring access to the records of a student shall be required to sign a written form which shall be kept permanently with the file of the student, but only for inspection by the parents or student, indicating specifically the legitimate educational or other interest that each person, agency, or organization has in seeking this information. Such form shall be available to parents and to the school official responsible for record maintenance as a means of auditing the operation of the system.

(B) With respect to this subsection, personal information shall only be transferred to a third party on the condition that such party will not permit any other party to have access to such information without the written consent of the parents of the student.

(c) The Secretary shall adopt appropriate regulations to protect the rights of privacy of students and their families in connection with any surveys or data-gathering activities conducted, assisted, or authorized by the Secretary or an administrative head of an education agency. Regulations established under this subsection shall include provisions controlling the use, dissemination, and protection of such data. No survey or data-gathering activities shall be conducted by the Secretary, or an administrative head of an education agency under an applicable program, unless such activities are authorized by law.

(d) For the purpose of this section, whenever a student has attained eighteen years of age, or is attending an institution of postsecondary education the permission or consent required of and the rights accorded to the parents of the student shall thereafter be required of and accorded to the student.

(e) No funds shall be made available under any applicable program unless the recipient of such funds informs the parents of students, or the students, if they are eighteen years of age or older, or are attending an institution of postsecondary education, of the rights accorded them by this section.

(f) The Secretary, or an administrative head of an education agency, shall take appropriate actions to enforce provisions of this section and to deal with violations of this section, according to the provisions of this Act, except that action to terminate assistance may be taken only if the Secretary finds that there has been a failure to comply with the provisions of this section, and he has determined that compliance cannot be secured by voluntary means.

(g) The secretary shall establish or designate an office and review board within the Department of Health, Education, and Welfare for the purpose of investigating, processing, reviewing, and adjusting violations of the provisions of this section and complaints which may be filed concerning alleged violations of this section, according to the procedures contained in sections 434 and 437 of this Act.

(b)(1)(i) The provisions of this section shall become effective ninety days after the date of enactment of section 438 of the General Education Provisions Act.

(2)(i) This section may be cited as the "Family Educational Rights and Privacy Act of 1974."

PROTECTION OF PUPIL RIGHTS

Sec. 514. (a) Part C of the General Education Provisions Act is further amended by adding after section 438 the following new section:

Protection of Pupil Rights

Sec. 439. All instructional material, including teacher's manuals, films, tapes, or other supplementary instructional material which will be used in connection with any research or experimentation program or project shall be available for inspection by the parents or guardians of the children engaged in such program or project. For the purpose of this section "research or experimentation program or project" means any program or project in any applicable program designed to explore or develop new or unproven teaching methods or techniques.

(b) The amendment made by subsection (a) shall be effective upon enactment of this Act.

The School Counselor in Career Guidance: Expectations and Responsibilities

ASCA Role Statement

INTRODUCTION

Career Guidance has consistently been seen as a high priority needed by youth, their parents, school boards, the private sector, and the general public. Such expectations are at an all time high. As these expectations have risen, so, too, has the difficulty of the task facing the professional school counselor. The certain rapidity of occupational change, coupled with the uncertain nature of the emerging service/information oriented high technology society, have combined to change career guidance practices in significant ways. This policy statement aims to recognize and react to some of these changes.

To do so demands that the professional school counselor recognize that the promise of high technology to increase both efficiency and effectiveness of operations applies to career guidance at least as much as to any other part of the formal education system. Thus, if the need for career guidance can be said to be greater than ever, so, too, is the potential for meeting this need. This potential can be recognized only if professional school counselors are willing to broaden their roles in ways that allow them to simultaneously take advantage of the promise and avoid the pitfalls implicit in a high technology approach to career guidance. The

promises and pitfalls to be recognized include but are not limited to:

- The **promise** through computer assisted management (CAM) to relieve professional school counselors of the need to spend long hours in maintaining student records coupled with the potential **pitfall** of violating student confidentiality.

- The **promise** of greatly expanding the nature, scope, and accessibility of educational/occupational information systems through the use of videodiscs and telecommunication coupled with the potential **pitfalls** associated with assuring the validity and lack of bias found in such materials.

- The **promise** of making computerized career decision-making systems available to students coupled with the plentiful **pitfalls** of failing to use the counselor/student relationship to move towards comprehensive career planning.

Thus, while high technology holds obvious promise for increasing both the efficiency and the effectiveness of career guidance, it simultaneously calls for a broadening of counselor expertise and counselor activity. The challenge to counselors for broadening their role in career guidance is fully as great as is the need to make career guidance a high priority item.

To make career guidance a high priority item for professional school counselors, several basic goals must be kept clearly in mind including:

- Delivering career guidance to each person in an **equitable** fashion that aims at **excellence** of **delivery** for each person.

- Taking advantage of the obvious opportunity of utilizing a wide variety of community resources in the delivery of effective career guidance.

- Protecting and enhancing individual freedom of career choices for every person served.

- Providing quality career guidance for **all** persons in the education system rather than limiting it to specific portions of the student population.

- Involving, to the greatest possible extent, all professional educators in the delivery of career guidance.

In order to address this need to designate our role in career guidance as a high priority, ASCA has prepared this policy statement.

Career guidance is a delivery system which systematically helps students reach the career development outcomes of self-awareness and assessment, career awareness and exploration, career decision making, career planning and placement. The school counselor's role covers many areas within a school setting and career guidance is one of the counselor's most important contributions to a student's lifelong development. Career guidance can best be conceptualized by the following basic concepts:

- Career development is a lifelong process.

- Career guidance is deeply rooted in the theory and research of the career development process.

- Career guidance is developmental in nature (K–post-secondary) moving from self and career awareness—to career exploration—to career decision-making—to career planning—to implementation of decisions and plans. The entire developmental process can be repeated more than once during the life span.

- Career guidance recognizes and emphasizes education/work relationships at all levels of education.

- Career guidance views the work values of persons as part of their total system of personal values—and so views work as an integral part of a person's total lifestyle.

- Career guidance recognizes the importance of both paid and unpaid work. In doing so, it recognizes that the human need to work, for any given person, can be met by either, or both, paid and unpaid work.

The School Counselor, as a Career guidance professional, is the person to assume leadership in the implementation of career development outcomes. Furthermore, indirect services to parents, staff and the greater community, as they relate to the career development outcomes for students, are also the school counselor's responsibility. Indirect services include but are not limited to staff development, parent and school board presentation, and the establishment of strong supportive linkages with business, industry and labor.

A FIVE-PHASED APPROACH TO CAREER GUIDANCE IN AN EDUCATION SYSTEM

Career guidance professionals are most needed and can gain greatest recognition through participation in process-oriented approaches to educational change. Of the several kinds of process-oriented approaches to educational change, career education represents the most logical and certainly the most ready one available for consideration by school counselors acting in their capacity as career guidance professionals.

Career guidance calls for educational change beginning no later than kindergarten and extending through all of publicly supported education. Concepts must be delivered in an equitable manner to all students in order to bring a sense of meaningfulness and purposefulness to both the curriculum and the services of the educational system.

Career guidance concepts have been influenced by the school counselor for many years but must now be broadened to invite support from faculty, staff, administration, students, parents and the very diverse segments of the broader community.

In order to broaden the support base, the person in authority must make clear to all school personnel that career guidance is everyone's responsibility. No one segment is in a position to deliver all of the concepts. However, one person must be appointed who will be held accountable and be given authority to develop, coordinate and monitor the total effort in order that a developmental delivery system is put in place and continues to function. The person responsible for this development and coordination should be a school counselor with management and organizational skills.

In order to implement a comprehensive career guidance program in an educational system, the initial emphasis must be on an effective process-oriented effort aimed at educational change. The following are considerations which are necessary but not sufficient to meet the needs for the educational change.

- School counselors, administrators and faculty members must become sensitized to the concepts of career guidance.
- School counselors, administrators and faculty members must become familiar with the concept that career infusion need not result in the loss of teaching or counseling time.
- Faculty members must be able to make the same kinds of connections between the subject(s) taught and the world of work that the students will make between the subject(s) learned and the world of work.
- Professional development and activities related to implementation of this process shall take place during the school day with appropriate or usual compensation provided participants.

Based on the philosophy and the practical outcomes listed above, the following five-phased approach to career guidance will allow the school counselor to utilize his/her training and expertise in facilitating groups, coordinating activities and identifying and developing community contacts and resources.

Phase I

The counselor as a career guidance professional develops a broad sense of understanding between the faculty members and the broader community. A series of inservice programs should be developed involving faculty members and significant members of both the private and public sectors of the community. The primary goals of these inservice programs include:

- Developing an understanding of career guidance.
- Developing a sensitivity to the concepts of race, sex and the exceptional student.
- Developing a "core committee" of persons representing all levels of the educational system with select representation from the private and public sectors.

Phase II

The counselor as a career guidance professional, with the "core committee," develops goals and objectives to form a skeleton around which the sub-committees will

add "flesh" in the form of faculty/counselor-developed lessons and activities.

Phase III

The counselor as a career guidance professional, utilizing the "core committee," coordinates the compilation of all the goals, objectives and activities (the product of Phase III) and a resource appendix into one infusion document. This document, developed with and delivered to the teachers, is to be used as a guide for infusion. Emphasis is placed on the interaction of faculty from all levels of the system working together to develop clearly articulated and developmentally sequenced activities.

Phase IV

The counselor as a career guidance professional, utilizing the "core committee," coordinates the compilation of all the goals, objectives and activities (the product of Phase III) and a resource appendix into one infusion document. This document, developed with and delivered to the teachers, is to be used as a guide for infusion. The document is disseminated to all faculty and administration as well as to those community members participating in an advisory manner to the core committee.

Phase V

The counselor as a career guidance professional will call upon the "core committed" whenever needed for the purposes of revising, updating, disseminating, and evaluating the career guidance program.

It should be noted that the role of the school counselor serving as a Career Guidance Professional is one of coordinating and facilitating not the writing or implementing of the career infusion plan for the classroom teacher.

These five phases, if implemented effectively, insure infusion of career guidance into all curriculum areas starting early in the educational process. The school counselor as a career guidance professional can then concentrate on the delivery of a series of common, core experiences leading to career maturity through awareness, exploration, decision making and planning. These experiences should be developmental in nature and serve as the link that ties together all of the infusion efforts and focuses on the student in relation to his/her future work experience.

The common core experiences should provide the following for all students:

- Individual and group counseling to clarify work values and develop coping and planning skills.

- Formal and informal assessment of abilities, personality traits and interest.

- Occupational/career information through community linkages such as field trips, speakers, shadowing experiences, internships.

- A career information center providing job hunting skills, interviewing skills, educational and training opportunities and financial aid possibilities.

Training, goal setting and decision making for the selection of tentative career paths based on the above.

- An opportunity for integration of academic and career planning leading to the selection of high school curriculum as it relates to the appropriate career clusters.

- An opportunity for continuous evaluation and revision of the goal setting process and action planning, including an annual review of all students' plan of study.

This policy statement presents a philosophy, some explanations and a prepared plan of action concerning the role of the school counselor as a career guidance professional. This is only a beginning—much more work needs to be done to implement a pro-active stance for school counselors to meet the career development needs for all students. Parents, school boards and the public and private sector are applying pressure on the educational system to meet these needs—we can avoid becoming victims of structural educational reform by participating in it.

Appendix F

Responsibilities of Users of Standardized Tests

RUST Statement Revised (AACD/AMECD Policy Statement)

I. INTRODUCTION

Background

At the 1976 AACD (then APGA) Convention, the Board of Directors requested the development of a statement on the responsible use of standardized tests to promote proper test use, reflecting the advantages of assessment along with concerns about negative effects, and to help its members employ safeguards against misuse of tests. A committee representing all AACD Divisions and Regions spent two years studying the issues and developed a statement, published in the October 1978, issue of *Guidepost,* entitled "Responsibilities of Users of Standardized Tests." The Association for Measurement and Evaluation in Counseling and Development was charged with maintaining ongoing review of the so-called RUST Statement. The present statement has grown out of that review.

Target Audience

The statement is intended to address the needs of the members of AACD and its Divisions, Branches, and Regions, including counselors and other human service workers. Although it may interest test developers, teachers, administrators, parents, the press, or the general public, it is not specifically designed for these audiences.

Organization and Focus

The statement is organized into eight sections: Introduction, Test Decisions, Qualification of Test Users, Test Selection, Test Administration, Test Scoring, Test Interpretation, and Communicating Test Results. Basic to the statement is the assumption that test data are merely numbers and that guidelines can help to promote their constructive use. The statement specifies general principles and activities which constitute responsible practice. These are grouped around similar issues and are indexed for ease of reference.

II. TEST DECISIONS

Decisions should be based on data. In general, test data improve the quality of decisions. However, deciding whether or not to test creates the possibility of three kinds of errors. First, a decision not to test can result in misjudgments that stem from inadequate or subjective data. Second, tests may produce data which could improve accuracy in decisions affecting the client, but which are not used in counseling. Third, tests may be misused. The responsible practitioner will determine, in advance, the purpose for administering a given test, considering protections and benefits for the client, practitioner, and agency.

A. Define purposes for testing by developing specific objectives and limits for the use of test data in relation to the particular assessment purpose:

   1. Placement: If the purpose is selection or placement, the test user should understand the programs or institutions into which the client may be placed and be able to judge the conse-

quences of inclusion or exclusion decisions for the client.

2. Prediction: If the purpose is prediction, the test user should understand the need for predictive data as well as possible negative consequences (e.g., stereotyping).

3. Description: If the purpose is diagnosis or description, the test user should understand the general domain being measured and be able to identify those aspects which are adequately measured and those which are not.

4. Growth: If the purpose is to examine growth or change, the test user should understand the practical and theoretical difficulties associated with such measurement.

5. Program Evaluation: If the purpose of assessment is the evaluation of an agency's programs, the test user should be aware of the various information needs for the evaluation and of the limitations of each instrument used to assess those needs, as well as how the evaluation will be used.

B. Determine Information Needs and Assessment Needs:

1. Determine whether testing is intended to assess individuals, groups, or both.

2. Identify the particular individual and/or group to be tested with regard to the agency's purposes and capabilities.

3. Determine the limitations to testing created by an individual's age; racial, sexual, ethnic, and cultural background; or other characteristics.

4. Avoid unnecessary testing by identifying decisions which can be made with existing information.

5. Assess the consequences for clients of deciding either to test or not to test.

6. Limit data gathering to the variables that are needed for the particular purpose.

7. Cross-validate test data using other available information whenever possible.

III. QUALIFICATIONS OF TEST USERS

While all professional counselors and personnel workers should have formal training in psychological and educational measurement and testing, this training does not necessarily make one an expert, and even an expert does not have all the knowledge and skills appropriate to some particular situations or instruments. Questions of user qualifications should always be addressed when testing is being considered.

Lack of proper qualifications can lead to errors and subsequent harm to clients. Each professional is responsible for making judgements on this in each situation and cannot leave that responsibility either to clients or to others in authority. It is incumbent upon the individual test user to obtain appropriate training or arrange for proper supervision and assistance when engaged in testing. Qualifications for test users depend on four factors:

A. Purposes of Testing: Technically proper testing for ill-understood purposes may constitute misuse. Because the purposes of testing dictate how the results are used, qualifications of test users are needed beyond general testing competencies to interpret and apply data.

B. Characteristics of Tests: Understanding the nature and limitations of each instrument used is needed by test users.

C. Settings and Conditions of Test Use: Assessment of the quality and relevance of test user knowledge and skill to the situation is needed before deciding to test or to participate in a testing program.

D. Roles of Test Selectors, Administrators, Scorers, and Interpreters: Test users must be engaged in only those testing activities for which their training and experience qualify them.

IV. TEST SELECTION

The selection of tests should be guided by information obtained from a careful analysis of the characteristics of the population to be tested; the knowledge, skills, abilities, or attitudes to be assessed; the purposes for testing; and the eventual use and interpretation of the test scores. Use of tests should also be guided by criteria for technical quality recommended by measurement professionals (i.e., the APA/AERA/NCME "Standards for Educational and Psychological Tests" and the APA/AERA/NCME/AACD/ASHA "Code of Fair Testing Practices in Education").

A. Relate Validity to Usage:

1. Determine the validity of a test (whether the test measures what is meant to be measured) through evidence of the constructs used in developing the test, the correlation of the test performance with other appraisals of the characteristics being measured, and/or the predictions of specified behaviors from the test performance.

2. Determine whether a test is congruent with the users' definition of the characteristics of human performance to be appraised.

3. Use tests for selection purposes only when they show predictive validity for the specific tasks or competencies needed in an educational or employment experience and when they maintain legal and ethical prescriptions for non-discriminatory practices in program selection, employment, or placement.

B. Use Appropriate Tests:

1. Document tests as appropriate for the characteristics of the population to be tested.

2. Only use tests within the level of skills of the practitioner.

3. Use tests consistent with local needs:

   a. Give attention to how the test is designed to handle variation of motivation, working speed, language facility, and experiential background among persons taking it; bias in response to its content; and effects of guessing in response to its questions.

   b. Determine whether a common test or different tests are required for accurate measurement of groups with special characteristics.

      i. Recognize that the use of different tests for cultural, ethnic, and racial groups may constitute ineffective means for making corrections for differences.

      ii. Determine whether persons or groups that use different languages should be tested in either or both languages and in some instances, tested first for bilingualism or language dominance.

C. Consider Technical Characteristics:

1. Select only tests that have documented evidence of reliability or consistency.

2. Select only tests that have adequate documented evidence of the effectiveness of the measure for the purpose to be served and justification of the inferences based on the results.

3. Scrutinize standardization and norming procedures for relevance to the local population and use of the data.

4. Use separate norms for men and women or other subgroups when empirical evidence indicates they are appropriate.

5. Determine the degree of technical quality demanded of a test on the basis of the nature of the decisions to be made.

6. Include ease and accuracy of the procedures for scoring, summarizing, and communicating test performance among the criteria for selecting a test.

7. Consider practical constraints of cost, conditions, and time for testing as secondary test selection criteria.

D. Employ User Participation in Test Selection: Actively involve everyone who will be using the assessments (administering, scoring, summarizing, interpreting, making decisions) as appropriate in the selection of tests so that they are congruent with local purposes, conditions, and uses.

V. TEST ADMINISTRATION

Test administration includes procedures to ensure that the test is used in the manner specified by the test developers and that the individuals being tested are working within conditions which maximize opportunity for optimum, comparable performance.

A. Provide Proper Orientation:

1. Inform testing candidates, parents, and institutions or agencies in the community as appropriate about the testing procedures. The orientation should make the test meaningful for the individual or group being tested, and should include the purposes of the test, the kinds of tasks it involves, how it is administered and how the scores will be reported and used.

2. Provide persons being tested sufficient practice experiences prior to the test.

3. Prior to testing, check all test takers' ability to record their responses adequately (e.g., in the use of machine-scorable answer sheets).

4. Provide periodic training by qualified personnel for test administrators within agencies or institutions using tests.

5. Review test materials and administration sites and procedures prior to the time for testing to ensure standardized conditions and appropriate response to any irregularities which may occur.

B. Use Qualified Test Administrators:

1. Acquire any training required to administer the test.

2. Ensure that individuals taking self-administered or self-scored instruments have the necessary understanding and competencies.

C. Provide Appropriate Testing Conditions:

1. Ensure that the testing environment (seating, work surfaces, lighting, heating, freedom from distractions, etc.) and psychological climate are conducive to the best possible performance of the test takers.

2. Carefully observe, record, and attach to the test record any deviation from prescribed test administration procedures.

3. Use a systematic and objective procedure for observing and recording environmental, health, or emotional factors, or other elements which may invalidate test performance. This record should be attached to the test scores of the persons tested.

4. Use sufficiently trained personnel to provide uniform conditions and to observe the conduct of the examinees when large groups of individuals are tested.

D. Give Proper Directions:

1. Present each test in the manner prescribed in the test manual to ensure that it is fair to each test taker.

2. Administer standardized tests with the verbatim instructions, exact sequence and timing, and identical materials that were used in the test standardization.

3. Demonstrate Professional Collaboration: In settings where skill and knowledge are pooled and responsibility shared, consider the qualifications of the testing team as a whole as more important than those of individuals. However, coordination and consistency of responsibilities with expertise must be maintained.

VI. TEST SCORING

Accurate measurement of human performance necessitates adequate procedures for scoring the responses of examinees. These procedures must be audited as necessary to ensure consistency and accuracy of application.

A. Consider Accuracy and Interpretability: Select a test scoring process that maximizes accuracy and interpretability.

B. Rescore Samples: Routinely rescore samples of examinee responses to monitor the accuracy of the scoring process.

C. Screen Test Results: Screen reports of test results using personnel competent to recognize unreasonable or impossible scores.

D. Verify Scores and Norms: Verify the accuracy of computation of raw scores and conversion to normative scales prior to release of such information to examinees or users of test results.

E. Communicative Deviations: Report as part of the official record any deviation from normal conditions and examinee behaviors.

F. Label Results: Clearly label the date of test administration along with the scores.

VII. TEST INTERPRETATION

Test interpretation encompasses all the ways that meaning is assigned to the scores. Proper interpretation requires knowledge about the test which can be obtained by studying its manual and other materials along with current research literature with respect to its use; no one should undertake the interpretation of scores on any test without such study.

A. Consider Reliability: Reliability is important because it is a prerequisite to validity and because the degree to which a score may vary due to measurement error is an important factor in its interpretation.

1. Estimate test stability using a reliability (or other appropriate) coefficient.

2. Use the standard error of measurement to estimate the amount of variation due to random error in individual scores and to evaluate the precision of cut-scores in selection decisions.

3. Consider, in relationship to the uses being made of the scores, variance components attributed to error in the reliability index.

4. Evaluate reliability estimates with regard to factors that may have artificially raised or lowered them (e.g., test speededness, biases in population sampling).

5. Distinguish indices of objectivity (i.e., scorer reliability) from rest reliability.

B. Consider Validity: Proper test interpretation requires knowledge of the validity evidence available for the intended use of the test. Its validity for other uses is not relevant. Indeed, use of a measure for a purpose for which it was not designed may constitute misuse. The nature of the validity evidence required for a test depends upon its use.

1. Use for Placement: Predictive validity is the usual basis for valid placement.

   a. Obtain adequate information about the programs or institutions in which the client may be placed to judge the consequences of such placement.

   b. Use all available evidence to infer the validity of an individual's score. A single test score should not be the sole basis for a placement or selection recommendation. Other items of information about an individual (e.g., teacher report, counselor opinion) frequently improve the likelihood that proper judgements and decisions will be made.

   c. Consider validity for each alternative (i.e., each placement option) when interpreting test scores and other evidence.

   d. Examine the possibility that a client's group membership (socioeconomic status, gender, subculture, etc.) may affect test performance and, consequently, validity.

   e. Estimate the probability of favorable outcomes for each possible placement before making recommendations.

   f. Consider the possibility that outcomes favorable from an institutional point of view may differ from those that are favorable from the individual's point of view.

2. Use for Prediction: The relationship of the test scores to an independently developed criterion measure is the basis for predictive validity.

   a. Consider the reliability and validity of the criterion measure(s) used.

   b. Consider the validity of a measure in the context of other predictors available (i.e., does the test make a valid contribution to prediction beyond that provided by other measures).

   c. Use cross-validation to judge the validity of prediction processes.

   d. Consider the effects of labeling, stereotyping, and prejudging people (e.g., self-fulfilling prophecies that may result from labeling are usually undesirable).

   e. If a statistically valid predictor lacks both construct and content validity, analyze the mechanism by which it operates to determine whether or not its predictive validity is spurious.

3. Use for Description: Comprehensiveness of information is fundamental to effective description, since no set of test scores completely describes an individual.

   a. Clearly identify the domain assessed by any measure and the adequacy of the content sampling procedures used in developing items.

   b. Clarify the dimensions being measured when multiple scores from a battery or inventory are used for description.

      i. Examine the content and/or construct validity of each score separately.

      ii. Consider the relative importance of each of the separate elements for interpretation.

iii. Give appropriate weights to reflect the variabilities (e.g., standard deviations) and relationships (e.g., correlations) of scores which are to be combined.

c. Distinguish characteristics that can be validated only empirically and those for which content specifications exist.

4. Use for Assessment of Growth: Assessment of growth or change requires valid tests as well as a valid procedure for combining them.

a. Specifically evaluate the reliability of differences between scores as measures of change.

b. Establish the validities of the measures used to establish change in relation to one another as well as individually.

c. Consider comparability of intervals in scales used to assess change.

i. Evaluate derived or extrapolated scores (e.g., grade equivalents) for possible different meanings at different score levels.

ii. Consider problems in interpretation and comparability of tests (e.g., floor or ceiling effects, content changes from level to level, poor articulation in multilevel tests, lack of comparability of alternate forms, inadequacy of score-equating across forms, and differences in administration and timing of tests from that of their norming).

d. Assess potential for undesirable correlations of difference scores with the measures entering into their calculations (e.g., regression toward the mean).

e. Recognize the potential lack of comparability between norms for differences derived from norms and norms for differences derived from differences (i.e., mathematically derived norms for differences are not necessarily equivalent to norms based on distributions of actual differences).

5. Use for Program Evaluation: Assessments of group differences (between groups or within groups over time) are based on research designs which to varying degrees admit competing interpretations of the results.

a. Use procedures in the evaluation which ensure that no factors other than those being studied have major influence on the results (i.e., internal validity).

b. Use statistical procedures which are appropriate and have all assumptions met by the data being analyzed.

c. Evaluate the generalizability (external validity) of the results for different individuals, settings, tests, and variables.

C. Scores, Norms, and Related Technical Features: The result of scoring a test or subtest is usually a number called a raw score which by itself is not interpretable. Additional steps are needed to translate the number directly into either a verbal description (e.g., pass or fail) or into a derived score (e.g., a standard score). Less than full understanding of these procedures is likely to produce errors in interpretation and ultimately in counseling or other uses.

1. Examine appropriate test materials (e.g., manuals, handbooks, users' guides, and technical reports) to identify the descriptions or derived scores produced and their unique characteristics.

a. Know the operational procedures for translating raw scores into descriptions or derived scores.

b. Know specific psychological or educational concepts or theories before interpreting the scores of tests based on them.

c. Consider differential validity along with equating error when different tests, different test forms, or scores on the same test administered at different times are compared.

2. Clarify arbitrary standards used in interpretation (e.g., mastery or nonmastery for criterion-referenced tests).

a. Recognize that when a score is interpreted based on a proportion score (e.g., percent correct), its elements are being given arbitrary weights.

b. Recognize that the difficulty of a fixed standard (e.g., 80 percent right) varies widely and thus does not have the same meaning for different content areas and for different assessment methods.

c. Report the number (or percentage) of items right in addition to the interpretation when it will help others understand the quality of the examinees' performance.

3. Employ derived scores based on norms which fit the needs of the current use of the test.

a. Evaluate whether available norm groups are appropriate as part of the process of interpreting the scores of clients.

i. Use norms for the group to which the client belongs.

ii. Recognize that derived scores based on different norm groups may not be comparable.

iii. Use local norms and derived scores based on them whenever possible.

b. Choose a score based on its intended use.

i. Consider relative standing scores (e.g., percentile ranks) for comparison of individuals to the norm or reference group.

ii. Consider standard or scaled scores whenever means and variances or other arithmetic operations are appropriate.

iii. When using a statistical technique, use the test's derived score which best meets the assumptions of the analysis.

D. Administration and Scoring Variation: Stated criteria for score interpretation assume standard procedures for administering and scoring the test. Departures from standard conditions and procedures modify and often invalidate these criteria.

1. Evaluate unusual circumstances peculiar to the administration and scoring of the test.

a. Examine reports from administrators, proctors, and scorers concerning irregularities or unusual conditions (e.g., excessive anxiety) for possible effects on test performance.

b. Consider potential effects of examiner-examinee differences in ethnic and cultural background, attitudes, and values based on available relevant research.

c. Consider any reports of examinee behavior indicating the responses were made on some basis other than that intended.

d. Consider differences among clients in their reaction to instructions about guessing and scoring.

2. Evaluate scoring irregularities (e.g., machine scoring errors) and bias and judgment effects when subjective elements enter into scoring.

VIII. COMMUNICATING TEST RESULTS

The responsible counselor or other practitioner reports test data with a concern for the individual's need for information and the purposes of the information. There must also be protection of the right of the person tested to be informed about how the results will be used and what safeguards exist to prevent misuse (right to information) and about who will have access to the results (right to privacy).

A. Decisions about Individuals: Where test data are used to enhance decisions about an individual, the practitioner's responsibilities include:

1. Limitations on Communication:

a. Inform the examinee of possible actions that may be taken by any person or agency who will be using the results.

b. Limit access to users specifically authorized by the law or by the client.

c. Obtain the consent of the examinee before using test results for any purpose other than those advanced prior to testing.

2. Practitioner Communication Skills:

a. Develop the ability to interpret test results accurately before attempting to communicate them.

b. Develop appropriate communication skills, particularly with respect to concepts that are commonly misunderstood by the intended audience, before attempting to explain test results to clients, the public, or other recipients of the information.

3. Communication of Limitations of the Assessment:

a. Inform persons receiving test information that scores are not perfectly accurate and indicate the degree of inaccuracy in some way, such as by reporting score intervals.

b. Inform persons receiving test information of any circumstances that could have affected the validity or reliability of the results.

c. Inform persons receiving test information of any factors necessary to understand potential sources of bias for a given test result.

d. Communicate clearly that test data represent just one source of information and should rarely, if ever, be used alone for decision making.

4. Communication of Client Rights:

a. Provide test takers or their parents or guardians with information about any rights they may have to obtain test copies and/or their completed answer sheets, to retake tests, to have tests rescored, or to cancel test scores.

b. Inform test takers or their parents or guardians, about how long the test scores will remain on file along with the person to whom, and circumstances under which, they may be released.

c. Describe the procedures test takers or their parents or guardians may use to register complaints or have problems resolved.

B. Decisions About Groups: Where standardized test data are being used to describe groups for the purpose of evaluation, the practitioner's responsibilities include:

1. Background Information:

a. Identify the purposes for which the reported data are appropriate.

b. Include additional information (e.g., population characteristics) if it can improve accuracy of understanding.

2. Averages and Norms:

a. Clarify the amount of meaning that can be attached to differences between groups (e.g., statistical significance should not be taken as a judgement of importance).

b. Qualify norms based on their appropriateness for the group being tested.

3. Use obsolescence schedules so that stored data are systematically relocated to historic files or destroyed.

4. Process data used for research or program evaluation to assure individual anonymity (e.g., released only in aggregated form).

5. Political Usage:

a. Emphasize that test data should be used only for the test's stated purposes.

b. Public release of test information provides data for many purposes. Take steps to minimize those which may be adverse to the interests of those tested.

6. Agency Policies:

a. Advocate agency test-reporting policies designed to benefit the groups being measured.

b. Advocate the establishment of procedures for periodic review of test use.

IX. EXTENSIONS OF THESE PRINCIPLES

This statement is intended to address current and emerging problems and concerns that are generic to all AACD divisions, branches, and regions by formulating principles that are specific enough to serve as a template for more closely focused statements addressed to specific situations. Individual divisions, branches, and regions are encouraged to elaborate upon this statement to reflect principles, procedures, and examples appropriate to their members.

This revision of the 1978 RUST Statement was prepared by a standing committee of AMECD chaired by William D. Schafer. Participating in the revision were Esther E. Diamond, Charles G. Eberly, Patricia B. Elmore, Jo-Ida C. Hansen, William A. Mehrens, Jane E. Myers, Larry Rawlins, and Alan G. Robertson.

Additional copies of the RUST Statement may be obtained from the American Association for Counseling and Development, 5999 Stevenson Avenue, Alexandria, VA 22304. Single copies are free.

Appendix G

AMHCA Code of Ethics

American Mental Health Counselors Association

PREAMBLE

Mental health counselors believe in the dignity and worth of the individual. They are committed to increasing knowledge of human behavior and understanding of themselves and others. While pursuing these endeavors, they make every reasonable effort to protect the welfare of those who seek their services or of any subject that may be the object of study. They use their skills only for purposes consistent with these values and do not knowingly permit their misuse by others. While demanding for themselves freedom of inquiry and community, mental health counselors accept the responsibility this freedom confers: competence, objectivity in the application of skills and concern for the best interests of clients, colleagues, and society in general. In the pursuit of these ideals, mental health counselors subscribe to the following principles:

Principle 1.   Responsibility

In their commitment to the understanding of human behavior, mental health counselors value objectivity and integrity, and in providing services they maintain the highest standards. They accept responsibility for the consequences of their work and make every effort to insure that their services are used appropriately.

---

a. Mental health counselors accept ultimate responsibility for selecting appropriate areas for investigation and the methods relevant to minimize the possibility that their findings will be misleading. They provide thorough discussion of the limitations of their data and alternative hypotheses, especially where their work touches on social policy or might be misconstrued to the detriment of specific age, sex, ethnic, socio-economic, or other social categories. In publishing reports of their work, they never discard observations that may modify the interpretation of results. Mental health counselors take credit only for the work they have actually done. In pursuing research, mental health counselors ascertain that their efforts will not lead to changes in individuals or organizations unless such changes are part of the agreement at the time of obtaining informal consent. Mental health counselors clarify in advance the expectations for sharing and utilizing research data. They avoid dual relationships which may limit objectivity, whether theoretical, political, or monetary, so that interference with data, subjects, and milieu is kept to a minimum.

b. As employees of an institution or agency, mental health counselors have the responsibility of remaining alert to institutional pressures which may distort reports of counseling findings or use them in ways counter to the promotion of human welfare.

c. When serving as members of governmental or other organizational bodies, mental health counselors remain accountable as individuals to the Code of Ethics of the American Mental Health Counselors Association (AMHCA).

d. As teachers, mental health counselors recognize their primary obligation to help others acquire knowledge and skill. They maintain high standards of scholarship and objectivity by presenting counseling information fully and accurately, and by giving appropriate recognition to alternative viewpoints.

e. As practitioners, mental health counselors know that they bear a heavy social responsibility because their recommendations and professional actions may alter the lives of others. They, therefore, remain fully cognizant of their impact and alert to personal, social, organizational, financial or political situations or pressures which might lead to misuse of their influence.

f. Mental health counselors provide reasonable and timely feedback to employees, trainees, supervisors, students, clients, and others whose work they may evaluate.

Principle 2.   Competence

The maintenance of high standards of professional competence is a responsibility shared by all mental health counselors in the interest of the public and the profession as a whole. Mental health counselors recognize the boundaries of their competence and the limitations of their techniques and only provide services, use techniques, or offer opinions as professionals that meet recognized standards. Throughout their careers, mental health counselors maintain knowledge of professional information related to the services they render.

a. Mental health counselors accurately represent their competence, education, training and experience.

b. As teachers, mental health counselors perform their duties based on careful preparation so that their instruction is accurate, up-to-date and scholarly.

c. Mental health counselors recognize the need for continuing training to prepare themselves to serve persons of all ages and cultural backgrounds. They are open to new procedures and sensitive to differences between groups of people and changes in expectations and values over time.

d. Mental health counselors with the responsibility for decisions involving individuals or policies based on test results should know and understand literature relevant to the tests used and testing problems with which they deal.

e. Mental health counselors and practitioners recognize that their effectiveness depends in part upon their ability to maintain sound interpersonal relations, that temporary or more enduring aberrations on their part may interfere with their abilities or distort their appraisals of others. Therefore, they refrain from undertaking any activity in which their personal problems are likely to lead to inadequate professional services or harm to a client, or, if they are already engaged in such activity when they become aware of their personal problems, they would seek competent professional assistance to determine whether they should suspend or terminate services to one or all of their clients.

f. The mental health counselor has a responsibility both to the individual who is served and to the institution with which the service is performed to maintain high standards of professional conduct. The mental health counselor strives to maintain the highest levels of professional services offered to the individuals to be served. The mental health counselor also strives to assist the agency, organization or institution in providing the highest caliber of professional services. The acceptance of employment in an institution implies that the mental health counselor is in substantial agreement with the general policies and principles of the institution. If, despite concerted efforts, the member cannot reach agreement with the employer as to acceptable standards of conduct that allow for changes in institutional policy conducive to the positive growth and development of counselees, then terminating the affiliation should be seriously considered.

g. Ethical behavior among professional associates, mental health counselors and non-mental health counselors is expected at all times. When information is possessed which raises serious doubt as to the ethical behavior of professional colleagues, whether Association members or not, the mental health counselor is obligated to take action to attempt to rectify such a condition. Such action shall utilize the institution's channels first and then utilize procedures established by the state, division, or Association.

h. The mental health counselor is aware of the intimacy of the counseling relationship and maintains a healthy respect for the personhood of the client and avoids engaging in activities that seek to meet the mental health counselor's personal needs at the expense of the client. Through awareness of the negative impact of both racial and sexual stereotyping and discrimination, the member strives to ensure the individual rights and personal dignity of the client in the counseling relationship.

Principle 3.   Moral and Legal Standards

Mental health counselors' moral, ethical and legal standards of behavior are a personal matter to the same degree as they are for any other citizen, except as these may compromise the fulfillment of their professional responsibilities, or reduce the trust in counseling or counselors held by the general public. Regarding their own behavior, mental health counselors should be aware of the prevailing community standards and of the possible impact upon the quality of professional services provided by their conformance to or deviation from these standards. Mental health counselors should also be aware of the possible impact of their public behavior upon the ability of colleagues to perform their professional duties.

a. To protect public confidence in the profession of counseling, mental health counselors will avoid public behavior that is clearly in violation of accepted moral and legal standards.

b. To protect students, mental health counselors/ teachers will be aware of the diverse backgrounds of students and, when dealing with topics that may give offense, will see that the material is treated objectively, that it is clearly relevant to the course, and that is treated in a manner for which the student is prepared.

c. Providers of counseling services conform to the statutes relating to such services as established by their state and its regulating professional board(s).

d. As employees, mental health counselors refuse to participate in employer's practices which are inconsistent with the moral and legal standards established by federal or state legislation regarding the treatment of employees or of the public. In particular and for example, mental health counselors will not condone practices which result in illegal or otherwise unjustifiable discrimination on the basis of race, sex, religion or national origin in hiring, promotion or training.

e. In providing counseling services to clients mental health counselors avoid any action that will violate or diminish the legal and civil rights of clients or of others who may be affected by the action.

f. Sexual conduct, not limited to sexual intercourse, between mental health counselors and clients is specifically in violation of this code of ethics. This does not, however, prohibit the use of explicit instructional aids including films and video tapes. Such use is within accepted practices of trained and competent sex therapists.

Principle 4.   Public Statements

Mental health counselors in their professional roles may be expected or required to make public statements providing counseling information, professional opinions, or supply information about the availability of counseling products and services. In making such statements, mental health counselors take full account of the limits and uncertainties of present counseling knowledge and techniques. They represent, as objectively as possible, their professional qualifications, affiliations, and functions, as well as those of the institutions or organizations with which the statements may be associated. All public statements, announcements of services, and promotional activities should serve the purpose of providing sufficient information to aid the consumer public in making informed judgements and choices on matters that concern it.

a. When announcing professional counseling services, mental health counselors limit the information to: name, highest relevant degree conferred, certification or licensure, address, telephone number, office hours, cost of services, and a brief explanation of the other types of services offered but not evaluative as to their quality or uniqueness. They will not contain testimonials by implication. They will not claim uniqueness of skill or methods beyond those acceptable and public scientific evidence.

b. In announcing the availability of counseling services or products, mental health counselors will not display their affiliations with organizations or agencies in a manner that implies the sponsorship or certification of the organization or agency. They will not name their employer or professional associations unless the services are in fact to be provided by or under the responsible, direct supervision and continuing control of such organizations or agencies.

c. Mental health counselors associated with the development of promotion of counseling devices, books, or other products offered for commercial sale will make every effort to insure that announcements and advertisements are presented in a professional and factually informative manner without unsupported claims of superiority and must be supported by scientifically acceptable evidence or by willingness to aid and encourage independent professional scrutiny or scientific tests.

d. Mental health counselors engaged in radio, television or other public media activities will not participate in commercial announcements recommending to the general public the purchase or use of any proprietary or single-source product or service.

e. Mental health counselors who describe counseling or the services of professional counselors to the general public accept the obligation to present the material fairly and accurately, avoiding misrepresentation through sensationalism, exaggeration or superficiality. Mental health counselors will be guided by the primary obligation to aid the public in forming their own informed judgements, opinions and choices.

f. As teachers, mental health counselors ensure their statements in catalogs and course outlines are accurate, particularly in terms of subject matter to be covered, bases for grading, and nature of classroom experiences.

g. Mental health counselors accept the obligation to correct others who may represent their professional qualifications or associations with products or services in a manner incompatible with these guidelines.

h. Mental health counselors providing consultation, workshops, training, and other technical services may refer to previous satisfied clients in their advertising, provided there is no implication that such advertising refers to counseling services.

Principle 5. Confidentiality

Mental health counselors have a primary obligation to safeguard information about individuals obtained in the course of teaching, practice, or research. Personal information is communicated to others only with the person's written consent or in those circumstances where there is clear and imminent danger to the client, to others or to society. Disclosures of counseling information are restricted to what is necessary, relevant, and verifiable.

a. All materials in the official record shall be shared with the client, who shall have the right to decide what information may be shared with anyone beyond the immediate provider of service and to be informed of the implications of the materials to be shared.

b. The anonymity of clients served in public and other agencies is preserved, if at all possible, by withholding names and personal identifying data. If external conditions require reporting such information, the client shall be so informed.

c. Information received in confidence by one agency or person shall not be forwarded to another person or agency without the client's written permission.

d. Service providers have a responsibility to insure the accuracy and to indicate the validity of data shared with their parties.

e. Case reports presented in classes, professional meetings, or in publications shall be so disguised that no identification is possible unless the client or responsible authority has read the report and agreed in writing to its presentation or publication.

f. Counseling reports and records are maintained under conditions of security and provisions are made for their destruction when they have outlived their usefulness. Mental health counselors insure that privacy and confidentiality are maintained by all persons in the employ or volunteers, and community aides.

g. Mental health counselors who ask that an individual reveal personal information in the course of interviewing, testing or evaluation, or who allow such information to be divulged, do so only after making certain that the person or authorized representative is fully aware of the purposes of the interview, testing or evaluation and of the ways in which the information will be used.

h. Sessions with clients are taped or otherwise recorded only with their written permission or the written permission of a responsible guardian. Even with guardian written consent one should not record a session against the expressed wishes of a client.

i. Where a child or adolescent is the primary client, the interests of the minor shall be paramount.

j. In work with families, the rights of each family member should be safeguarded. The provider of service also has the responsibility to discuss the contents of the record with the parent and/or child, as appropriate, and to keep separate those parts which should remain the property of each family member.

Principle 6. Welfare of the Consumer

Mental health counselors respect the integrity and protect the welfare of the people and groups with whom they work. When there is a conflict of interest between the client and the mental health counselors' employing institution, the mental health counselors clarify the nature and direction of their loyalties and responsibilities and keep all parties informed of their commitments. Mental health counselors fully inform consumers as to the purpose and nature of any evaluative, treatment, educational or training procedure, and they freely acknowledge that clients, students, or subjects have freedom of choice with regard to participation.

a. Mental health counselors are continually cognizant both of their own needs and of their inherently powerful position "vis-a-vis" clients, in order to avoid exploiting the client's trust and dependency. Mental health counselors make every effort to avoid dual relationships with clients and/or relationships which might impair their professional judgement or increase the risk of client exploitation. Examples of such dual relationships include treating an employee or supervisor, treating a close friend or family relative, and sexual relationships with clients.

b. Where mental health counselors work with members of an organization goes beyond reasonable conditions of employment, mental health counselors recognize possible conflicts of interest that may arise. When such conflicts occur, mental health counselors clarify the nature of the conflict and inform all parties of the nature and directions of the loyalties and responsibilities involved.

c. When acting as supervisors, trainers, or employers, mental health counselors accord recipients informed choice, confidentiality, and protection from physical and mental harm.

d. Financial arrangements in professional practice are in accord with professional standards that safeguard the best interests of the client and that are clearly understood by the client in advance of billing. This may best be done by the use of a contract. Mental health counselors are responsible for assisting clients in finding needed services in those instances where payment of the usual fee would be a hardship. No commission or rebate or other form of remuneration may be given or received for referral of clients for professional services, whether by an individual or by an agency.

e. Mental health counselors are responsible for making their services readily accessible to clients in a

manner that facilitates the client's ability to make an informed choice when selecting a service provider. This responsibility includes a clear description of what the client may expect in the way of tests, reports, billing, therapeutic regime and schedules and the use of the mental health counselor's Statement of Professional Disclosure.

f. Mental health counselors who find that their services are not beneficial to the client have the responsibility to make this known to the responsible persons.

g. Mental health counselors are accountable to the parties who refer and support counseling services and to the general public and are cognizant of the indirect or long-range effects of their intervention.

h. The mental health counselor attempts to terminate a private service or consulting relationship when it is reasonably clear to the mental health counselor that the consumer is not benefitting from it. If a consumer is receiving services from another mental health professional, mental health counselors do not offer their services directly to the consumer without informing the professional persons already involved in order to avoid confusion and conflict for the consumer.

i. The mental health counselor has the responsibility to screen prospective group participants, especially when the emphasis is on self-understanding and growth through self-disclosure. The member should maintain an awareness of the group participants' compatibility throughout the life of the group.

j. The mental health counselor may choose to consult with any other professionally competent person about a client. In choosing a consultant, the mental health counselor should avoid placing the consultant in a conflict of interest situation that would preclude the consultant's being a proper party to the mental health counselors' efforts to help the clients.

k. If the mental health counselor is unable to be of professional assistance to the client, the mental health counselor should avoid initiating the counseling relationship or the mental health counselor terminates the relationship. In either event, the member is obligated to suggest appropriate alternatives. (It is incumbent upon the mental health counselors to be knowledgeable about referral resources so that a satisfactory referral can be initiated.) In the event the client declines the suggested referral, the mental health counselor is not obligated to continue the relationship.

l. When the mental health counselor has other relationships, particularly of an administrative, supervisory, and/or evaluative nature, with an individual seeking counseling services, the mental health counselor should not serve as the counselor but should refer the individual to another professional. Only in instances where such an alternative is unavailable and where the individual's situation definitely warrants counseling intervention should the mental health counselor enter into and/or maintain a counseling relationship. Dual relationships with clients which might impair the member's objectivity and professional judgement (such as with close friends or relatives, sexual intimacies with any client, etc.) must be avoided and/or the counseling relationship terminated through referral to another competent professional.

m. All experimental methods of treatment must be clearly indicated to prospective recipients, and safety precautions are to be adhered to by the mental health counselor instituting treatment.

n. When the member is engaged in short-term group treatment/training programs, e.g., marathons and other encounter-type or growth groups, the member ensures that there is professional assistance available during and following the group experience.

Principle 7.   Professional Relationship

Mental health counselors act with due regard to the needs and feelings of their colleagues in counseling and other professions. Mental health counselors respect the prerogatives and obligations of the institutions or organizations with which they are associated.

a. Mental health counselors understand the areas of competence of related professions and make full use of other professional, technical, and administrative resources which best serve the interests of consumers. The absence of formal relationships with other professional workers does not relieve mental health counselors from the responsibility of securing for their clients the best possible professional service; indeed, this circumstance presents a challenge to the professional competence of mental health counselors, requiring special sensitivity to problems outside their areas of training, and foresight, diligence, and tact in obtaining the professional assistance needed by clients.

b. Mental health counselors know and take into account the traditions and practices of other professional groups with which they work and cooperate fully with members of such groups when research, services, and other functions are shared or in working for the benefit of public welfare.

c. Mental health counselors strive to provide positive conditions for those they employ and they spell out clearly the conditions of such employment. They encourage their employees to engage in activities that facilitate their further professional development.

d. Mental health counselors respect the viability, reputation, and the proprietary right of organizations which they serve. Mental health counselors show due regard for the interest of their present or prospective employers. In those instances where they are critical of policies, they attempt to effect change by constructive action within the organization.

e. In the pursuit of research, mental health counselors give sponsoring agencies, host institutions, and publication channels the same respect and opportunity for giving informed consent that they accord to individual research participants. They are aware of their obligation to future research workers and insure that host institutions are given feedback information and proper acknowledgment.

f. Credit is assigned to those who have contributed to a publication, in proportion to their contribution.

g. When a mental health counselor violates ethical standards, mental health counselors who know firsthand of such activities should, if possible, attempt to rectify the situation. Failing an informal solution, mental health counselors should bring such unethical activities to the attention of the appropriate state and/or national committee on ethics and professional conduct. Only after all professional alternatives have been utilized will a mental health counselor begin legal action for resolution.

Principle 8.   Utilization of Assessment Techniques

In the development, publication, and utilization of counseling assessment techniques, mental health counselors follow relevant standards. Individuals examined, or their legal guardians, have the right to know the results, the interpretations made, and where appropriate, the particulars on which final judgement was based. Test users should take precautions to protect test security but not at the expense of an individual's right to understand the basis for decisions that adversely affect that individual or that individual's dependents.

a. The client has the right to have and the provider has the responsibility to give explanations of test results in language the client can understand.

b. When a test is published or otherwise made available for operational use, it should be accompanied by a manual (or other published or readily available information) that makes every reasonable effort to describe fully the development of the test, the rationale, and specifications followed in writing items analysis or other research. The test, the manual, the record forms and other accompanying material should help users make correct interpretations of the test results and should warn against common misuses. The test manual should state explicitly the purposes and applications for which the test is recommended and identify any special qualifications required to administer the test and to interpret it properly. Evidence of validity and reliability, along with other relevant research data, should be presented in support of any claims made.

c. Norms presented in test manuals should refer to defined and clearly described populations. These populations should be the groups with whom users of the test will ordinarily wish to compare the persons tested. Test users should consider the possibility of bias in tests or in test items. When indicated, there should be an investigation of possible differences in validity for ethnic, sex, or other subsamples that can be identified when the test is given.

d. Mental health counselors who have the responsibility for decisions about individuals or policies that are based on test results should have a thorough understanding of counseling or educational measurement and of validation and other test research.

e. Mental health counselors should develop procedures for systematically eliminating from data files test score information that has, because of the lapse of time, become obsolete.

f. Any individual or organization offering test scoring and interpretation services must be able to demonstrate that their programs are based on appropriate research to establish the validity of the programs and procedures used in arriving at interpretations. The public offering of an automated test interpretation service will be considered as a professional-to-professional consultation. In this the formal responsibility of the consultant is to the consultee but his/her ultimate and overriding responsibility is to the client.

g. Counseling services for the purpose of diagnosis, treatment, or personalized advice are provided only in the context of a professional relationship, and are not given by means of public lectures or demonstrations, newspapers or magazine articles, radio or television programs, mail, or similar media. The preparation of personnel reports and recommendations based on test data secured solely by mail is unethical unless such appraisals are an integral part of a continuing client relationship with a company, as a result of which the consulting clinical mental health counselor has intimate knowledge of the client's personal situation and can be assured thereby that his written appraisals will be adequate to the purpose and will be properly interpreted by the client. These reports must not be embellished with such detailed analyses of the subject's personality traits as would be appropriate only for intensive interviews with the subjects.

Principle 9. Pursuit of Research Activities

The decision to undertake research should rest upon a considered judgment by the individual mental health counselor about how best to contribute to counseling and to human welfare. Mental health counselors carry out their investigations with respect for the people who participate and with concern for their dignity and welfare.

a. In planning a study the investigator has the personal responsibility to make a careful evaluation of its ethical acceptability, taking into account the following principles for research with human beings. To the extent that this appraisal, weighing scientific and humane values, suggests a deviation from any principle, the investigator incurs an increasingly serious obligation to seek ethical advice and to observe more stringent safeguards to protect the rights of the human research participants.

b. Mental health counselors know and take into account the traditions and practices of other professional groups with members of such groups when research, services, and other functions are shared or in working for the benefit of public welfare.

c. Ethical practice requires the investigator to inform the participant of all features of the research that reasonably might be expected to influence willingness to participate, and to explain all other aspects of the research about which the participant inquires. Failure to make full disclosure gives added emphasis to the investigator's abiding responsibility to protect the welfare and dignity of the research participant.

d. Openness and honesty are essential characteristics of the relationship between investigator and research participant. When the methodological requirements of a study necessitate concealment or deception, the investigator is required to insure as soon as possible the participant's understanding of the reasons for this action and to restore the quality of the relationship with the investigator.

e. In the pursuit of research, mental health counselors give sponsoring agencies, host institutions, and publication channels the same respect and opportunity for giving informed consent that they accord to individual research participants. They are aware of their obligation to future research workers and insure that host institutions are given feedback information and proper acknowledgment.

f. Credit is assigned to those who have contributed to a publication, in proportion to their contribution.

g. The ethical investigator protects participants from physical and mental discomfort, harm and danger. If the risk of such consequences exists, the investigator is required to inform the participant of that fact, secure consent before proceeding, and take all possible measures to minimize distress. A research procedure may not be used if it is likely to cause serious and lasting harm to participants.

h. After the data are collected, ethical practice requires the investigator to provide the participant with a full clarification of the nature of the study and to remove any misconceptions that may have arisen. Where scientific or humane values justify delaying or withholding information the investigator acquires a special responsibility to assure that there are no damaging consequences for the participants.

i. Where research procedure may result in undesirable consequences for the participant, the investigator has the responsibility to detect and remove or correct these consequences, including, where relevant, long-term aftereffects.

j. Information obtained about the research participants during the course of an investigation is confidential. When the possibility exists that others may obtain access to such information, ethical research practice requires that the possibility, together with the plans for protecting confidentiality, be explained to the participants as a part of the procedure for obtaining informed consent.

Principle 10.   Private Practice

a. A mental health counselor should assist where permitted by legislation or judicial decision the profession in fulfilling its duty to make counseling services available in private settings.

b. In advertising services as a private practitioner the mental health counselor should advertise the services in such a manner so as to accurately inform the public as to services, expertise, profession, and techniques of counseling in a professional manner. A mental health counselor who assumes an executive leadership role in the organization shall not permit his/her name to be used in professional notices during periods when not actively engaged in the private practice of counseling.

The mental health counselor may list the following: Highest relevant degree, type and level of certification or license, type and/or description of services and other relevant information. Such information should not contain false, inaccurate, misleading, partial, out-of-context or deceptive material or statements.

c. The mental health counselor may join in partnership/corporation with other mental health counselors and/or other professionals provided that each mental health counselor of the partnership or corporation makes clear the separate specialties by name in compliance with the regulations of the locality.

d. A mental health counselor has an obligation to withdraw from a counseling relationship if it is believed that employment will result in violation of the code of ethics, if their mental capacity or physical condition renders it difficult to carry out an effective professional relationship, or if the mental health counselor is discharged by the client because the counseling relationship is no longer productive for the client.

e. A mental health counselor should adhere to and support the regulations for private practice of the locality where the services are offered.

f. Mental health counselors are discouraged from deliberate attempts to utilize one's institutional affiliation to recruit clients for one's private practice. Mental health counselors are to refrain from offering their services in the private sector, when they are employed by an institution in which this is prohibited by stated policies reflecting conditions for employment.

g. In establishing fees for professional counseling services, mental health counselors should consider the financial status of clients and locality. In the event that the established fee structure is inappropriate for a client, assistance should be provided in finding services of acceptable cost.

Principle 11.   Consulting

a. The mental health counselor acting as consultant must have a high degree of self-awareness of his/her own values, knowledge, skills and needs in entering a helping relationship which involves human and/or organizational change and that the focus of the relationship be on the issues to be resolved and not on the person(s) presenting the problem.

b. There should be understanding and agreement between the mental health counselor and client for the problem definition, change goals and predicted consequences of interventions selected.

c. The mental health counselor must be reasonably certain that she/he or the organization represented have the necessary competencies and resources for giving the kind of help which is needed now or may develop later and that appropriate referral resources are available to the consultant, if needed later.

d. The mental health counselor relationship must be one in which client adaptability and growth toward self-direction are encouraged and cultivated. The mental health counselor must maintain this role consistently and not become a decision maker or substitute for the client.

e. When announcing consultant availability for services, the mental health counselor conscientiously adheres to professional standards.

f. The mental health counselor is expected to refuse a private fee or other remuneration for consultation with persons who are entitled to these services through the members' employing institution or agency. The policies of a particular agency may make explicit provisions for private practice with agency counselees by members of its staff. In such instances, the counselees must be appraised of other options open to them should they seek private counseling services.

Principle 12.   Client's Rights

The following apply to all consumers of mental health services, including both in and out-patients in all state, county, local, and private care mental health facilities, as well as patients/clients of mental health practitioners in private practice.

The client has the right:

a. to be treated with consideration and respect;

b. to expect quality service provided by concerned, competent staff;

c. to a clear statement of the purposes, goals, techniques, rules of procedure, and limitations as well as potential dangers of the services to be performed and all other information related to or likely to affect the on-going counseling relationship;

d. to obtain information about their case record and to have this information explained clearly and directly;

e. to full, knowledgeable, and responsible participation in the on-going treatment plan, to the maximum feasible extent;

f. to expect complete confidentiality and that no information will be released without written consent;

g. to see and discuss their charges and payment records; and

h. to refuse any recommended services and be advised of the consequences of this action.

Last amended April 23, 1987

AAMFT Code of Ethics

American Association for Marriage and Family Therapy

The Board of Directors of the American Association for Marriage and Family Therapy (AAMFT) hereby promulgates, pursuant to Article 2, Section 2.013 of the Association's Bylaws, the Revised AAMFT Code of Ethics, effective August 1, 1991.

The AAMFT Code of Ethics is binding on Members of AAMFT in all membership categories, AAMFT Approved Supervisors, and applicants for membership and the Approved Supervisor designation (hereafter, AAMFT Member).

If an AAMFT Member resigns in anticipation of, or during the course of an ethics investigation, the Ethics Committee will complete its investigation. Any publication of action taken by the Association will include the fact that the Member attempted to resign during the investigation.

Marriage and family therapists are strongly encouraged to report alleged unethical behavior of col-

This Code is published by:
American Association for Marriage and Family Therapy
1100 17th Street, NW, 10th Floor
Washington, DC 20036-4601
(202) 452-0109

Violations of this Code should be brought in writing to the attention of the AAMFT Ethics Committee, 1100 17th Street, NW, The Tenth Floor, Washington, DC 20036-4601 (telephone 202/452-0109).

Effective August 1, 1991.

leagues to appropriate professional associations and state regulatory bodies.

1. RESPONSIBILITY TO CLIENTS

Marriage and family therapists advance the welfare of families and individuals. They respect the rights of those persons seeking their assistance, and make reasonable efforts to ensure that their services are used appropriately.

1.1 Marriage and family therapists do not discriminate against or refuse professional service to anyone on the basis of race, gender, religion, national origin, or sexual orientation.

1.2 Marriage and family therapists are aware of their influential position with respect to clients, and they avoid exploiting the trust and dependency of such persons. Therapists, therefore, make every effort to avoid dual relationships with clients that could impair professional judgement or increase the risk of exploitation. When a dual relationship cannot be avoided, therapists take appropriate professional precautions to ensure judgement is not impaired and no exploitation occurs. Examples of such dual relationships include, but are not limited to, business or close personal relationships with clients. Sexual intimacy with clients is prohibited. Sexual intimacy with former clients for two years following the termination of therapy is prohibited.

1.3 Marriage and family therapists do not use their professional relationships with clients to further their own interests.

1.4 Marriage and family therapists respect the right of clients to make decisions and help them to understand the consequences of these decisions. Therapists clearly advise a client that a decision on marital status is the responsibility of the client.

1.5 Marriage and family therapists continue therapeutic relationships only so long as it is reasonably clear that clients are benefiting from the relationship.

1.6 Marriage and family therapists assist persons in obtaining other therapeutic services if the therapist is unable or unwilling, for appropriate reasons, to provide professional help.

1.7 Marriage and family therapists do not abandon or neglect clients in treatment without making reasonable arrangements for the continuation of such treatment.

1.8 Marriage and family therapists obtain written informed consent from clients before videotaping, audio recording, or permitting third party observation.

2. CONFIDENTIALITY

Marriage and family therapists have unique confidentiality concerns because the client in a therapeutic relationship may be more than one person. Therapists respect and guard confidences of each individual client.

2.1 Marriage and family therapists may not disclose client confidences except: (a) as mandated by law; (b) to prevent a clear and immediate danger to a person or persons; (c) where the therapist is a defendant in a civil, criminal, or disciplinary action arising from the therapy (in which case client confidences may be disclosed only in the course of that action); or (d) if there is a waiver previously obtained in writing, and then such information may be revealed only in accordance with the terms of the waiver. In circumstances where more than one person in a family receives therapy, each such family member who is legally competent to execute a waiver must agree to the waiver required by subparagraph (d). Without such a waiver from each family member legally competent to execute a waiver, a therapist cannot disclose information received from any family member.

2.2 Marriage and family therapists use client and/or clinical materials in teaching, writing, and public presentations only if a written waiver has been obtained in accordance with Subprinciple 2.1(d), or when appropriate steps have been taken to protect client identity and confidentiality.

2.3 Marriage and family therapists store or dispose of client records in ways that maintain confidentiality.

3. PROFESSIONAL COMPETENCE AND INTEGRITY

Marriage and family therapists maintain high standards of professional competence and integrity.

3.1 Marriage and family therapists are in violation of this Code and subject to termination of membership or other appropriate action if they: (a) are convicted of any felony; (b) are convicted of a misdemeanor related to their qualifications or functions; (c) engage in conduct which could lead to conviction of a felony, or a misdemeanor related to their qualifications or functions; (d) are expelled from or disciplined by other professional organizations; (e) have their licenses or certificates suspended or revoked or are otherwise disciplined by regulatory bodies; (f) are no longer competent to practice marriage and family therapy because they are impaired due to physical or mental causes or the abuse of alcohol or other substances; or (g) fail to cooperate with the Association at any point from the inception of an ethical complaint through the completion of all proceedings regarding that complaint.

3.2 Marriage and family therapists seek appropriate professional assistance for their personal problems or conflicts that may impair work performance or clinical judgement.

3.3 Marriage and family therapists, as teachers, supervisors, and researchers, are dedicated to high standards of scholarship and present accurate information.

3.4 Marriage and family therapists remain abreast of new developments in family therapy knowledge and practice through educational activities.

3.5 Marriage and family therapists do not engage in sexual or other harassment or exploitation of clients, students, trainees, supervisees, employees, colleagues, research subjects, or actual or potential witnesses or complainants in investigations and ethical proceedings.

3.6 Marriage and family therapists, because of their ability to influence and alter the lives of others, exercise special care when making public their professional recommendations and opinions through testimony or other public statements.

4. RESPONSIBILITY TO STUDENTS, EMPLOYEES, AND SUPERVISEES

Marriage and family therapists do not exploit the trust and dependency of students, employees, and supervisees.

4.1 Marriage and family therapists are aware of their influential position with respect to students, employees, and supervisees, and they avoid exploiting the trust and dependency of such persons. Therapists, therefore, make every effort to avoid dual relationships that could impair professional judgement or increase the risk of exploitation. When a dual relationship cannot be avoided, therapists take appropriate professional precautions to ensure judgement is not impaired and no exploitation occurs. Examples of such dual relationships include, but are not limited to, business or close personal relationships with students, employees, or supervisees. Provision of therapy to students, employees, or supervisees is prohibited. Sexual intimacy with students or supervisees is prohibited.

4.2 Marriage and family therapists do not permit students, employees, or supervisees to perform or to hold themselves out as competent to perform professional services beyond their training, level of experience, and competence.

4.3 Marriage and family therapists do not disclose supervisee confidences except: (a) as mandated by law; (b) to prevent a clear and immediate danger to a person or persons; (c) where the therapist is a defendant in a civil, criminal, or disciplinary action arising from the supervision (in which case supervisee confidences may be disclosed only in the course of that action); (d) in educational or training settings where there are multiple supervisors, and then only to other professional colleagues who share responsibility for the training of the supervisee; or (e) if there is a waiver previously obtained in writing, and then such information may be revealed only in accordance with the terms of the waiver.

5. RESPONSIBILITY TO RESEARCH PARTICIPANTS

Investigators respect the dignity and protect the welfare of participants in research and are aware of federal and state laws and regulations and professional standards governing the conduct of research.

5.1 Investigations are responsible for making careful examinations of ethical acceptability in planning studies. To the extent that services to research participants may be compromised by participation in research, investigators seek the ethical advice of qualified professionals not directly involved in the investigation and observe safeguards to protect the rights of research participants.

5.2 Investigators requesting participants' involvement in research inform them of all aspects of the research that might reasonably be expected to influence willingness to participate. Investigators are especially sensitive to the possibility of diminished consent when participants are also receiving clinical services, have impairments which limit understanding and/or communication, or when participants are children.

5.3 Investigators respect participants' freedom to decline participation in or to withdraw from a research study at any time. This obligation requires special thought and consideration when investigators or other members of the research team are in positions of authority or influence over participants. Marriage and family therapists, therefore, make every effort to avoid dual relationships with research participants that could impair professional judgement or increase the risk of exploitation.

5.4 Information obtained about a research participant during the course of an investigation is confidential unless there is a waiver previously obtained in writing. When the possibility exists that others, including family members, may obtain access to such information, this possibility, together with the plan for protecting confidentiality, is explained as part of the procedure for obtaining informed consent.

6. RESPONSIBILITY TO THE PROFESSION

Marriage and family therapists respect the rights and responsibilities of professional colleagues and participate in activities which advance the goals of the profession.

6.1 Marriage and family therapists remain accountable to the standards of the profession when acting as members or employees of organizations.

6.2 Marriage and family therapists assign publication credit to those who have contributed to a publication in proportion to their contributions and in accordance with customary professional publication practices.

6.3 Marriage and family therapists who are the authors of books or other materials that are published or distributed cite persons to whom credit for original ideas is due.

6.4 Marriage and family therapists who are the authors of books or other materials published or distributed by an organization take reasonable precautions to ensure that the organization promotes and advertises the materials accurately and factually.

6.5 Marriage and family therapists participate in activities that contribute to a better community and society, including devoting a portion of their professional activity to services for which there is little or no financial return.

6.6 Marriage and family therapists are concerned with developing laws and regulations pertaining to marriage and family therapy that serve the public interest, and with altering such laws and regulations that are not in the public interest.

6.7 Marriage and family therapists encourage public participation in the design and delivery of professional services and in the regulation of practitioners.

7. FINANCIAL ARRANGEMENTS

Marriage and family therapists make financial arrangements with clients, third party payors, and supervisees that are reasonably understandable and conform to accepted professional practices.

7.1 Marriage and family therapists do not offer or accept payment for referrals.

7.2 Marriage and family therapists do not charge excessive fees for services.

7.3 Marriage and family therapists disclose their fees to clients and supervisees at the beginning of services.

7.4 Marriage and family therapists represent facts truthfully to clients, third party payors, and supervisees regarding services rendered.

8. ADVERTISING

Marriage and family therapists engage in appropriate informational activities, including those that enable laypersons to choose professional services on an informed basis.

General Advertising

8.1 Marriage and family therapists accurately represent their competence, education, training, and experience relevant to their practice of marriage and family therapy.

8.2 Marriage and family therapists assure that advertisements and publications in any media (such as directories, announcements, business cards, newspapers, radio, television, and facsimiles) convey information that is necessary for the public to make an appropriate selection of professional services. Information could include: (a) office information, such as name, address, telephone number, credit card acceptability, fees, languages spoken, and office hours; (b) appropriate degrees, state licensure and/or certification, and AAMFT Clinical Member status; and (c) description of practice. (For requirements for advertising under the AAMFT name, logo, and/or the abbreviated initials AAMFT, see Subprinciple 8.15, below.)

8.3 Marriage and family therapists do not use a name which could mislead the public concerning the identity, responsibility, sources, and status of those practicing under that name and do not hold themselves out as being partners or associates of a firm if they are not.

8.4 Marriage and family therapists do not use any professional identification (such as a business card, office sign, letterhead, or telephone or association directory listing) if it includes a statement of claim that is false, fraudulent, misleading, or deceptive. A statement is false, fraudulent, misleading, or deceptive if it (a) contains a material misrepresentation of fact; (b) fails to state any material fact necessary to make the statement, in light of all circumstances, not misleading; or (c) is intended to or is likely to create an unjustified expectation.

8.5 Marriage and family therapists correct, wherever possible, false, misleading, or inaccurate information and representations made by others concerning the therapist's qualifications, services, or products.

8.6 Marriage and family therapists make certain that the qualifications of persons in their employ are represented in a manner that is not false, misleading, or deceptive.

8.7 Marriage and family therapists may represent themselves as specializing within a limited area of marriage and family therapy, but only if they have the education and supervised experience in settings which meet recognized professional standards to practice in that specialty area.

Advertising Using AAMFT Designations

8.8 The AAMFT designations of Clinical Member, Approved Supervisor, and Fellow may be used in public information or advertising materials only by persons holding such designations. Persons holding such designations may, for example, advertise in the following manner:

- *Jane Doe, Ph.D., a Clinical Member of the American Association for Marriage and Family Therapy.*

  Alternately, the advertisement could read:

  Jane Doe, Ph.D., AAMFT Clinical Member.

- *John Doe, Ph.D., an Approved Supervisor of the American Association for Marriage and Family Therapy.*

  Alternately, the advertisement could read:

  John Doe, Ph.D., AAMFT Approved Supervisor.

- *Jane Doe, Ph.D., a Fellow of the American Association for Marriage and Family Therapy.*

  Alternately, the advertisement could read:

  Jane Doe, Ph.D., AAMFT Fellow.

  More than one designation may be used if held by the AAMFT Member.

8.9 Marriage and family therapists who hold the AAMFT Approved Supervisor or the Fellow designation may not represent the designation as an advanced clinical status.

8.10 Student, Associate, and Affiliate Members may not use their AAMFT membership status in public information or advertising materials. Such listings on professional resumes are not considered advertisements.

8.11 Persons applying for AAMFT membership may not list their application status on any resume or advertisement.

8.12 In conjunction with their AAMFT membership, marriage and family therapists claim as evidence of educational qualifications only those degrees (a) from regionally accredited institutions or (b) from institutions recognized by states which license or certify marriage and family therapists, but only if such state regulation is recognized by AAMFT.

8.13 Marriage and family therapists may not use the initials AAMFT following their name in the manner of an academic degree.

8.14 Marriage and family therapists may not use the AAMFT name, logo, and/or the abbreviated initials AAMFT or make any other such representation that would imply that they speak for or represent the Association. The Association is the sole owner of its name, logo, and the abbreviated initials AAMFT. Its committees and divisions, operation as such, may use the name, logo, and/of the abbreviated initials, AAMFT, in accordance with AAMFT policies.

8.15 Authorized advertisements of Clinical Members under the AAMFT name, logo, and/or the abbreviated initials AAMFT may include the following: the Clinical Member's name, degree, license or certificate held when required by state law, name of business, address, and telephone number. If a business is listed, it must follow, not precede, the Clinical Member's name. Such listings may not include AAMFT offices held by the Clinical Member, nor any specializations, since such a listing under the AAMFT name, logo, and/or the abbreviated initials, AAMFT, would imply that this specialization has been credentialed by AAMFT.

8.16 Marriage and family therapists use their membership in AAMFT only in connection with their clinical and professional activities.

8.17 Only AAMFT divisions and programs accredited by the AAMFT Commission on Accreditation for Marriage and Family Therapy Education, not businesses nor organizations, may use any AAMFT-related designation or affiliation in public information or advertising materials, and then only in accordance with AAMFT policies.

8.18 Programs accredited by the AAMFT Commission on Accreditation for Marriage and Family Therapy Education may not use the AAMFT name, logo, and/or the abbreviated initials, AAMFT. Instead, they may have printed on their stationery and other appropriate materials a statement such as:

The (name of program) *of the* (name of institution) *is accredited by the AAMFT Commission on Accreditation for Marriage and Family Therapy Education.*

8.19 Programs not accredited by the AAMFT Commission on Accreditation for Marriage and Family Therapy Education may not use the AAMFT name, logo, and/or the abbreviated initials, AAMFT. They may not state in printed program materials, program advertisements, and student advisement that their courses and training opportunities are accepted by AAMFT to meet AAMFT membership requirements.

Appendix I

Specialty Guidelines for the Delivery of Services by Counseling Psychologists

The Specialty Guidelines that follow are based on the generic *Standards for Providers of Psychological Services* originally adopted by the American Psychological Association (APA) in September 1974 and revised in January 1977 (APA, 1974b, 1977b). Together with the generic *Standards,* these Specialty Guidelines state the official policy of the Association regarding delivery of services by counseling psychologists. Admission to the practice of psychology is regulated by state statute. It is the position of the Association that licensing be based on generic, and not on specialty, qualifications. Specialty guidelines serve the additional purpose of providing potential users and other interested groups with essential information about particular services available from the several specialties in professional psychology.

Professional psychology specialties have evolved from generic practice in psychology and are supported by university training programs. There are now at least four recognized professional specialties—clinical, counseling, school and industrial/organizational psychology.

The knowledge base in each of these specialty areas has increased, refining the state of the art to the point that a set of uniform specialty guidelines is now possible and desirable. The present Guidelines are intended to educate the public, the profession, and other interested parties regarding specialty profession practices. They are also intended to facilitate the continued systematic development of the profession.

The content of each Specialty Guideline reflects a consensus of university faculty and public and private practitioners regarding the knowledge base, services provided, problems addressed, and clients served.

Traditionally, all learned disciplines have treated the designation of specialty practice as a reflection of preparation in greater depth in a particular subject matter, together with a voluntary limiting of focus to a more restricted area of practice by the professional. Lack of specialty designation does not preclude general providers of psychological services from using the methods or dealing with the populations of any specialty, except insofar as psychologists voluntarily refrain from providing services they are not trained to render. It is the intent of these guidelines, however, that after the grandparenting period, psychologists not put themselves forward as *specialists* in a given area of practice unless they meet the qualifications noted in the Guidelines (see Definitions). Therefore, these Guidelines are meant to apply only to those psychologists who voluntarily wish to be designated as *counseling psychologists.* They do not apply to other psychologists.

These Guidelines represent the profession's best judgement of the conditions, credentials, and experience that contribute to competent professional practice. The APA strongly encourages, and plans to par-

These Specialty Guidelines were prepared by the APA Committee on Standards for Providers of Psychological Services (COSPOPS), chaired by Durand F. Jacobs, with the advice of the officers and committee chairpersons of the Division of Counseling Psychology (Division 17). Barbara A. Kirk and Milton Schwebel served successively as the counseling psychology representative of COSPOPS, and Arthur Centor and Richard Kilburg were the Central Office liaisons to the committee. Norman Kagan, Samuel H. Osipow, Carl E. Thoresen, and Allen E. Ivey served successively as Division 17 presidents. Copyright 1981 by the American Psychological Association. Reprinted by permission of the publisher.

ticipate in, efforts to identify professional practitioner behaviors and job functions and to validate the relation between these and desired client outcomes. Thus, future revisions of these Guidelines will increasingly reflect the results of such efforts.

These guidelines follow the format and, wherever applicable, the wording of the generic *Standards*.[1] (Note: Footnotes appear at the end of the Specialty Guidelines.) The intent of these Guidelines is to improve the quality, effectiveness, and accessibility of psychological services. They are meant to provide guidance to providers, users, and sanctioners regarding the best judgement of the profession on these matters. Although the Specialty Guidelines have been derived from and are consistent with the generic *Standards,* they may be used as separate documents. However, *Standards for Providers of Psychological Services* (APA, 1977b) shall remain the basic policy statement and shall take precedence where there are questions of interpretation.

Professional psychology in general and counseling psychology as a specialty have labored long and diligently to codify a uniform set of guidelines for the delivery of services by counseling psychologists that would serve the respective needs of users, providers, third-party purchasers, and sanctioners of psychological services.

The Committee on Professional Standards, established by the APA in January 1980, is charged with keeping the generic *Standards* and the Specialty Guidelines responsive to the needs of the public and the profession. It is also charged with continually reviewing, modifying, and extending them progressively as the profession and the science of psychology develop new knowledge, improving methods, and additional modes of psychological services.

The Specialty Guidelines for the Delivery of Services by Counseling Psychologists that follow have been established by the APA as a means of self-regulation to protect the public interest. They guide the specialty practice of counseling psychology by specifying important areas of quality assurance and performance that contribute to the goal of facilitating more effective human functioning.

PRINCIPLES AND IMPLICATIONS OF THE SPECIALTY GUIDELINES

These Specialty Guidelines emerged from and reaffirm the same basic principles that guided the development of the generic *Standards for Providers of Psychological Services* (APA, 1977b):

1. These Guidelines recognize that admission to the practice of psychology is regulated by state statute.

2. It is the intention of the APA that the generic *Standards* provide appropriate guidelines for statutory licensing of psychologists. In addition, although it is the position of the APA that licensing be generic and not in specialty areas, these Specialty Guidelines in counseling psychology provide an authoritative reference for use in credentialing specialty providers of counseling psychological services by such groups as divisions of the APA and state associations and by boards and agencies that find such criteria useful for quality assurance.

3. A uniform set of Specialty Guidelines governs the quality of services to all users of counseling psychological services in both the private and the public sectors. Those receiving counseling psychological services are protected by the same kinds of safeguards, irrespective of sector: these include constitutional guarantees, statutory regulation, peer review, consultation, record review, and supervision.

4. A uniform set of Specialty Guidelines governs counseling psychological service functions offered by counseling psychologists, regardless of setting or form of remuneration. All counseling psychologists in professional practice recognize and are responsive to a uniform set of Specialty Guidelines, just as they are guided by a common code of ethics.

5. Counseling psychology Guidelines establish clear, minimally acceptable levels of quality for covered counseling psychological service functions, regardless of the nature of the uses, purchasers, or sanctioners of such covered services.

6. All persons providing counseling psychological services meet specified levels of training and experience that are consistent with and appropriate to, the functions they perform. Counseling psychological services provided by persons who do not meet the APA qualifications for a professional counseling psychologist (see Definitions) are supervised by a professional counsel-

ing psychologist. Final responsibility and accountability for services provided rest with professional counseling psychologists.

7. When providing any of the covered counseling psychological service functions at any time and in any setting, whether public or private, profit or nonprofit, counseling psychologists observe these Guidelines in order to promote the best interests and welfare of the users of such services. The extent to which counseling psychologists observe these Guidelines is judged by peers.

8. These Guidelines, while assuring the user of the counseling psychologist's accountability for the nature and quality of services specified in this document, do not preclude the counseling psychologist from using new methods or developing innovative procedures in the delivery of counseling services.

These Specialty Guidelines have broad implications both for users of counseling psychological services and for providers of such services:

1. Guidelines for counseling psychological services provide a foundation for mutual understanding between provider and user and facilitate more effective evaluation of services provided and outcomes achieved.

2. Guidelines for counseling psychologists are essential for uniformity in specialty credentialing of counseling psychologists.

3. Guidelines give specific content to the profession's concept of ethical practice as it applies to the functions of counseling psychologists.

4. Guidelines for counseling psychological services may have significant impact on tomorrow's education and training models for both professional and support personnel in counseling psychology.

5. Guidelines for the provision of counseling psychological services in human service facilities influence the determination of acceptable structure, budgeting, and staff patterns in these facilities.

6. Guidelines for counseling psychological services require continual review and revision.

The Specialty Guidelines here presented are intended to improve the quality and delivery of counseling psychological services by specifying criteria for

key aspects of the practice setting. Some settings may require additional and/or more stringent criteria for specific areas of service delivery.

Systematically applied, these Guidelines serve to establish a more effective and consistent basis for evaluating the performance of individual service providers as well as to guide the organization of counseling psychological service units in human service settings.

DEFINITIONS

Providers of counseling psychological services refers to two categories of persons who provide counseling psychological services:

A. Professional counseling psychologists.[2] Professional counseling psychologists have a doctoral degree from a regionally accredited university or professional school providing an organized, sequential counseling psychology program in an appropriate academic department in a university or college, or in an appropriate department or unit of a professional school. Counseling psychology programs that are accredited by the American Psychological Association are recognized as meeting the definition of a counseling psychology program. Counseling psychology programs that are not accredited by the American Psychological Association meet the definition of a counseling psychology program if they satisfy the following criteria:

1. The program is primarily psychological in nature and stands as a recognizable, coherent organizational entity within the institution.

2. The program provides an integrated, organized sequence of study.

3. The program has an identifiable body of students who are matriculated in that program for a degree.

4. There is a clear authority with primary responsibility for the core and specialty areas, whether or not the program cuts across administrative lines.

5. There is an identifiable psychology faculty, and a psychologist is responsible for the program.

The professional counseling psychologist's doctoral education and training experience[3] is defined by the institution offering the program. Only counseling psychologists, that is, those who meet the appropriate education and training requirements, have the minimum professional qualifications to provide unsupervised counseling psychological services. A professional counseling psychologist and others providing counseling psychological services under supervision (described below) form an integral part of a multilevel counseling psychological service delivery system.

B. All other persons who provide counseling psychological services under the supervision of a professional counseling psychologist. Although there may be variations in the titles of such persons, they are not referred to as counseling psychologists. Their functions may be indicated by use of the adjective *psychological* preceding the noun, for example, *psychological associate, psychological assistant, psychological technician,* or *psychological aide.*

Counseling psychological services refers to services provided by counseling psychologists that apply principles, methods, and procedures for facilitating effective functioning during the lifespan developmental process.[4,5] In providing such services, counseling psychologists approach practice with a significant emphasis on positive aspects of growth and adjustment and with a developmental orientation. These services are intended to help persons acquire or alter personal-social skills, improve adaptability to changing life demands, enhance environmental coping skills, and develop a variety of problem-solving and decision-making capabilities. Counseling psychological services are used by individuals, couples, and families of all age groups to cope with problems connected with education, career choice, work, sex, marriage, family, other social relations, health, aging, and handicaps of a social or physical nature. The services are offered in such organizations as educational, rehabilitation, and health institutions and in a variety of other public and private agencies committed to service in one or more of the problem areas cited above. Counseling psychological services include the following:

A. Assessment, evaluation, and diagnosis. Procedures may include, but are not limited to, behavioral observation, interviewing, and administering and interpreting instruments for the assessment of educational achievement, academic skills, aptitudes, interests, cognitive abilities, attitudes, emotions, motivations, psychoneurological status, personality characteristics, or any other aspect of human experience and behavior that may contribute to understanding and helping the user.

B. Interventions with individuals and groups. Procedures include individual and group psychological counseling (e.g., education, career, couples, and family counseling) and may use a therapeutic, group process, or social-learning approach, or any other deemed to be appropriate. Interventions are used for purposes of prevention, remediation, and rehabilitation; they may incorporate a variety of psychological modalities, such as psychotherapy, behavior therapy, marital and family therapy, biofeedback techniques, and environmental design.

C. Professional consultation relating to A and B above, for example, in connection with developing in-service training for staff or assisting an educational institution or organization to design a plan to cope with persistent problems of its students.

D. Program development services in the areas of A, B, and C, above, such as assisting a rehabilitation center to design a career-counseling program.

E. Supervision of all counseling psychological services, such as the review of assessment and intervention activities of staff.

F. Evaluation of all services noted in A through E above and research for the purpose of their improvement.

A *counseling psychological service unit* is the functional unit through which counseling psychological services are provided; Such a unit may be part of a larger psychological service organization comprising psychologists of more than one specialty and headed by a professional psychologist:

A. A counseling psychological service unit provides predominantly counseling psychological services and is composed of one or more professional counseling psychologists and supporting staff.

B. A counseling psychological service unit may operate as a functional or geographics component of a larger multipsychological service unit or of a governmental, educational, correctional, health, training, industrial, or commercial organizational unit, or it may operate as an independent professional service.[6]

C. A counseling psychological service unit may take the form of one or more counseling psychologists providing professional services in a multidisciplinary setting.

D. A counseling psychological service unit may also take the form of a private practice, composed of one or more counseling psychologists serving individuals or groups, or the form of a psychological consulting firm serving organizations and institutions.

Users of counseling psychological services include:

A. Direct users or recipients of counseling psychological services.

B. Public and private institutions, facilities, or organizations receiving counseling psychological services.

C. Third-party purchasers—those who pay for the delivery of services but who are not the recipients of services.

D. Sanctioners—those who have a legitimate concern with the accessibility, timeliness, efficacy, and standards of quality attending the provision of counseling psychological services. Sanctioners may include members of the user's family, the county, the probation officer, the school administrator, the employer, the school administrator, the employer, the union representative, the facility director, and so on. Sanctioners may also include various governmental, peer review, and accreditation bodies concerned with the assurance of quality.

GUIDELINE 1: PROVIDERS

1.1 *Each counseling psychological service unit offering psychological services has available at least one professional counseling psychologist and as many more professional counseling psychologists as are necessary to assure the adequacy and quality of services offered.*

Interpretation: The intent of this Guideline is that one or more providers of psychological services in any counseling psychological service unit meet the levels of training and experience of the professional counseling psychologist as specified in the preceding definitions.[7]

When a professional counseling psychologist is not available on a full-time basis, the facility retains the services of one or more professional counseling psychologists on a regular part-time basis. The counseling psychologist so retained directs the psychological services, including supervision of the support staff, has the authority and participates sufficiently to assess the need for services, reviews the content of services provided, and assumes the professional responsibility and accountability for them.

The psychologist directing the service unit is responsible for determining and justifying appropriate ratios of psychologists to users and psychologists to support staff, in order to ensure proper scope, accessibility, and quality of services provided in that setting.

1.2 *Providers of counseling psychological services who do not meet the requirements for the professional counseling psychologists are supervised directly by a professional counseling psychologist who assumes professional responsibility and accountability for the services provided. The level and extent of supervision may vary from task to task so long as the supervising psychologist retains a sufficiently close supervisory relationship to meet this Guideline. Special proficiency training or supervision may be provided by a professional psychologist of another specialty or by a professional from another discipline whose competence in the given area has been demonstrated by previous training and experience.*

Interpretation: In each counseling psychological service unit there may be varying levels of responsibility with respect to the nature and quality of services provided. Support personnel are considered to be responsible for their functions and behavior when assisting in the provision of counseling psychological services and are accountable to the professional counseling psychologist. Ultimate professional responsibility and accountability for the services provided require that the supervisor review reports and test protocols, and review and discuss intervention plans, strategies, and outcomes. Therefore, the supervision of all counseling psychological services is provided directly by a professional counseling psychologist in a face-to-face arrangement involving individual and/or group supervision. The extent of supervision is determined by the needs of the providers, but in no event is it less than 1 hour per week for each support staff member providing counseling psychological services.

To facilitate the effectiveness of the psychological service unit, the nature of the supervisory relationship is communicated to support personnel in writing. Such communications delineate the duties of the employees, describing the range and type of services to be provided. The limits of independent action and decision making are defined. The description of responsibility specifies the means by which the employee will contact the professional counseling psychologist in the event of emergency or crisis situations.

1.3 *Whenever a counseling psychological service unit exists, a professional counseling psychologist is responsible for planning, directing, and reviewing the provision of counseling psychological services. Whenever the counseling psychological service unit is part of a larger professional psychological service encompassing various psychological specialties, a professional psychologist shall be the administrative head of the service.*

Interpretation: The counseling psychologist who directs or coordinates the unit is expected to maintain an ongoing or periodic review of the adequacy of services and to formulate plans in accordance with the results of such evaluation. He or she coordinates the activities of the counseling psychology unit with other professional, administrative and technical groups, both within and outside the institution or agency. The counseling psychologist has related responsibilities including, but not limited to, directing the training and research activities of the service, maintaining a high level of professional and ethical practice, and ensuring that staff members function only within the areas of their competency.

To facilitate the effectiveness of counseling services by raising the level of staff sensitivity and professional skills, the counseling psychologist designated as director is responsible for participating in the selection of staff and support personnel whose qualifications and skills (e.g., language, cultural and experiential background, race, sex, and age) are relevant to the needs and characteristics of the users served.

1.4 *When functioning as part of an organizational setting, professional counseling psychologists bring their backgrounds and skills to bear on the goals of the organization, whenever appropriate, by participation in the planning and development of overall services.*[8]

Interpretation: Professional counseling psychologists participate in the maintenance of high professional standards by representation on committees concerned with service delivery.

As appropriate to the setting, their activities may include active participation, as voting and as office-holding members, on the facility's professional staff and on other executive, planning, and evaluation boards and committees.

1.5 *Counseling psychologists maintain current knowledge of scientific and professional developments to preserve and enhance their professional competence.*

Interpretation: Methods through which knowledge of scientific and professional developments may be gained include, but are not limited to, reading scientific and professional publications, attendance at professional workshops and meetings, participation in staff development programs, and other forms of continuing education.[9] The counseling psychologist has ready access to reference material related to the provision of psychological services. Counseling psychologists are prepared to show evidence periodically that they are staying abreast of current knowledge and practices in the field of counseling psychology through continuing education.

1.6 *Counseling psychologists limit their practice to their demonstrated areas of professional competence.*

Interpretation: Counseling psychological services are offered in accordance with the providers' areas of competence as defined by verifiable training and experience. When extending services beyond the range of their usual practice, counseling psychologists obtain pertinent training or appropriate professional supervision. Such training or supervision is consistent with the extension of functions performed and services provided. An extension of services may involve a change in the theoretical orientation of the counseling psychologist, in the modality or techniques used, in the type of client, or in the kinds of problems or disorders for which services are to be provided.

1.7 *Professional psychologists who wish to qualify as counseling psychologists meet the same requirements with respect to subject matter and professional skills that apply to doctoral education and training in counseling psychology.*[10]

Interpretation: Education of doctoral-level psychologists to qualify them for specialty practice in counseling psychology is under the auspices of a department in a regionally accredited university or a professional school that offers the doctoral degree in counseling psychology. Such education is individualized, with due credit being given for relevant course work and other requirements that have previously been satisfied. In addition, doctoral-level training supervised by a counseling psychologist is required. Merely taking an internship in counseling psychology or acquiring experience in a practicum setting is not adequate preparation for becoming a counseling psychologist when prior education has not been in that area. Fulfillment of such an individualized educational program is attested to by the awarding of a certificate by the supervising department or professional school that indicates the successful completion of preparation in counseling psychology.

1.8 *Professional counseling psychologists are encouraged to develop innovative theories and procedures and to provide appropriate theoretical and/or empirical support for their innovations.*

Interpretation: A specialty of a profession rooted in a science intends continually to explore and experiment with a view to developing and verifying new and improved ways of serving the public and documents the innovations.

GUIDELINES 2: PROGRAMS

2.1 *Composition and organization of a counseling psychological service unit:*

2.1.1 *The composition and programs of a counseling psychological service unit are responsive to the needs of the persons or settings served.*

Interpretation: A counseling psychological service unit is structured so as to facilitate effective and economical delivery of services. For example, a counseling psychological service unit serving predominantly a low-income, ethnic, or racial minority group has a staffing pattern and service programs that are adapted to the linguistic, experiential, and attitudinal characteristics of the users.

2.1.2 *A description of the organization of the counseling psychological service unit and its lines of responsibility and accountability for the delivery of psychological services is available in written form to staff of the unit and to users and sanctioners upon request.*

Interpretation: The description includes lines of responsibility, supervisory relationships, and the level and extent of accountability for each person who provides psychological services.

2.1.3 *A counseling psychological service unit includes sufficient numbers of professional and support personnel to achieve its goals, objectives, and purposes.*

Interpretation: The work load and diversity of psychological services required and the specific goals and objectives of the setting determine the numbers of qualifications of professional and support personnel in the counseling psychological service unit. Where shortages in personnel exist, so that psychological services cannot be rendered in a professional manner, the director of the counseling psychological service unit initiates action to remedy such shortages. When this fails, the director appropriately modifies the scope or work load of the unit to maintain the quality of the services rendered and, at the same time, makes continued efforts to devise alternative systems for delivery of services.

2.2 *Policies:*

2.2.1 *When the counseling psychological service unit is composed of more than one person or is a component of a larger organization, a written statement of its objectives and scope of services is developed, maintained, and reviewed.*

Interpretation: The counseling psychological service unit reviews its objectives and scope of services annually and revises them as necessary to ensure that the psychological services offered are consistent with staff competencies and current psychological knowledge and practice. This statement is discussed with staff, reviewed with the appropriate administrator, and distributed to users and sanctioners upon request, whenever appropriate.

2.2.2 *All providers within a counseling psychological service unit support the legal and civil rights of the users.*[11]

Interpretation: Providers of counseling psychological services safeguard the interests of the users with regard to personal, legal, and civil rights. They are continually sensitive to the issue of confidentiality of information, the short-term and long-term impacts of their decisions and recommendations, and other matters pertaining to individual, legal, and civil rights. Concerns regarding the safeguarding of individual rights of users include, but are not limited to, problems of access to professional records in educational institutions, self-incrimination in judicial proceedings, involuntary commitment to hospitals, protection of minors or legal incompetents, discriminatory practices in employment selection procedures, recommendation for special education provisions, information relative to adverse personnel actions in the armed services, and adjudication of domestic relations disputes in divorce and custodial proceedings. Providers of counseling psychological services take affirmative action by making themselves available to local committees, review boards, and similar advisory groups established to safeguard the human, civil and legal rights of service users.

2.2.3 *All providers within a counseling psychological service unit are familiar with and adhere to the American Psychological Association's* Standards for Providers of Psychological Services, Ethical Principles of Psychologists, Standards for Educational and Psychological Tests, Ethical Principles in the Conduct of Research with Human Participants, *and other official policy statements relevant to standards for professional services issued by the Association.*

Interpretation: Providers of counseling psychological services maintain current knowledge of relevant standards of the American Psychological Association.

2.2.4 *All providers within a counseling psychological service unit conform to relevant statutes established by federal, state, and local governments.*

Interpretation: All providers of counseling psychological services are familiar with and conform to appropriate statutes regulating the practice of psychology. They also observe agency regulations that have the force of law and that relate to the delivery of psychological services (e.g., evaluation for disability retirement and special education placements). In addition, all providers are cognizant that federal agencies such as the Veterans Administration, the Department of Education, and the Department of Health and Human Services have policy statements regarding psychological services. Providers are familiar as well with other statutes and regulations, including those addressed to the civil and legal rights of users (e.g., those promulgated by the federal Equal Employment Opportunity Commission), that are pertinent to their scope of practice.

It is the responsibility of the American Psychological Association to maintain current files of those federal policies, statutes, and regulations relating to this section and to assist its members in obtaining them. The state psychological associations and the state licensing boards periodically publish and distrib-

ute appropriate state statutes and regulations, and these are on file in the counseling psychological service unit or the larger multipsychological service unit of which it is a part.

2.2.5 *All providers within a counseling psychological service unit inform themselves about and use the network of human services in their communities in order to link users with relevant services and resources.*

Interpretation: Counseling psychologists and support staff are sensitive to the broader context of human needs. In recognizing the matrix of personal and social problems, providers make available to clients information regarding human services such as legal aid societies, social services, employment agencies, health resources, and educational and recreational facilities. Providers of counseling psychological services refer to such community resources and, when indicated, actively intervene on behalf of the users.

Community resources include the private as well as the public sectors. Consultation is sought or referral made within the public and private network of services whenever required in the best interest of the users. Counseling psychologists, in either the private or the public setting, utilize other resources in the community whenever indicated because of limitations within the psychological service unit providing the services. Professional counseling psychologists in private practice know the types of services offered through local community mental health clinics and centers, through family-service, career, and placement agencies, and through reading and other educational improvement centers and know the costs and the eligibility requirements for those services.

2.2.6 *In the delivery of counseling psychological services, the providers maintain a cooperative relationship with colleagues and co-workers in the best interest of the users.*[12]

Interpretation: Counseling psychologists recognize the areas of special competence of other professional psychologists and of professionals in other fields for either consultation or referral purposes. Providers of counseling psychological services make appropriate use of other professional, research, technical, and administrative resources to serve the best interest of users and establish and maintain cooperative arrangements with such other resources as required to meet the needs of users.

2.3 *Procedures:*

2.3.1 *Each counseling psychological service unit is guided by a set of procedural guidelines for the delivery of psychological services.*

Interpretation: Providers are prepared to provide a statement of procedural guidelines, in either oral or written form, in terms that can be understood by users, including sanctioners and local administrators. This statement describes the current methods, forms, procedures, and techniques being used to achieve the objectives and goals for psychological services.

2.3.2 *Providers of counseling psychological services develop plans appropriate to the providers' professional practices and to the problems presented by the users.*

Interpretation: A counseling psychologist, after initial assessment, develops a plan describing the objectives of the psychological services and the manner in which they will be provided.[13] To illustrate, the agreement spells out the objective (e.g., a career decision), the method (e.g., short-term counseling), the roles (e.g., active participation by the user as well as the provider), and the cost. The plan is in written form. It serves as a basis for obtaining understanding and concurrence from the user and for establishing accountability and provides a mechanism for subsequent peer review. This plan is, of course, modified as changing needs dictate.

A counseling psychologist who provides services as one member of a collaborative effort participates in the development, modification (if needed), and implementation of the overall service plan and provides for its periodic review.

2.3.3 *Accurate, current, and pertinent documentation of essential counseling psychological services provided is maintained.*

Interpretation: Records kept of counseling psychological services include, but are not limited to, identifying data, dates of services, types of services, significant actions taken, and outcome at termination. Providers of counseling psychological services ensure that essential information concerning services rendered is recorded within a reasonable time following their completion.

2.3.4 *Each counseling psychological service unit follows an established record retention and disposition policy.*

Interpretation: The policy on record retention and disposition conforms to state statutes or federal regulations where such are applicable. In the absence of such regulations, the policy is (a) that the full record be maintained intact for at least 4 years after the completion of planned services or after the date of last contact with the user, whichever is later; (b) that if a full record is not retained, a summary of the record be maintained for an additional 3 years; and (c) that the record may be disposed of no sooner than 7 years after the completion of planned services or after the date of last contact, whichever is later.

In the event of the death or incapacity of a counseling psychologist in independent practice, special procedures are necessary to ensure the continuity of active service to users and the proper safeguarding of records in accordance with this Guideline. Following approval by the affected user, it is appropriate for another counseling psychologist, acting under the auspices of the professional standards review committee (PSRC) of the state, to review the record with the user and recommend a course of action for continuing professional service, if needed. Depending on local circumstances, appropriate arrangements for record retention and disposition may also be recommended by the reviewing psychologist.

This Guideline has been designed to meet a variety of circumstances that may arise, often years after a set of psychological services has been completed. Increasingly, psychological records are being used for forensic matters, for peer review, and in response to requests from users, other professionals, and other legitimate parties requiring accurate information about the exact dates, nature, course, and outcome of a set of psychological services. The 4-year period for retention of the full record covers the period of either undergraduate or graduate study of most students in postsecondary educational institutions, and the 7-year period for retention of at least a summary of the record covers the period during which a previous user is most likely to return for counseling psychological services in an educational institution or other organization or agency.

2.3.5 *Providers of counseling psychological services maintain a system to protect confidentiality of their records.*[14]

Interpretation: Counseling psychologists are responsible for maintaining the confidentiality of information about users of services, from whatever source derived. All persons supervised by counseling psychologists, including nonprofessional personnel and students, who have access to records of psychological services maintain this confidentiality as a condition of employment and/or supervision.

The counseling psychologist does not release confidential information, except with written consent of the user directly involved or his or her legal representative. The only deviation from this rule is in the event of clear and imminent danger to, or involving, the user. Even after consent for release has been obtained, the counseling psychologist clearly identifies such information.[15] If directed otherwise by statute or regulations with the force of law or by court order, the psychologist seeks a resolution to the conflict that is both ethnically and legally feasible and appropriate.

Users are informed in advance of any limits in the setting for maintenance of confidentiality of psychological information. For instance, counseling psychologists in agency, clinic, or hospital settings inform their clients that psychological information in a client's record may be available without the client's written consent to other members of the professional staff associated with service to the client. Similar limitations on confidentiality of psychological information may be present in certain educational, industrial, military, or other institutional settings, or in instances in which the user has waived confidentiality for purposes of third-party payment.

Users have the right to obtain information from their psychological records. However, the records are the property of the psychologist or the facility in which the psychologist works and are, therefore, the responsibility of the psychologist and subject to his or her control.

When the user's intention to waive confidentiality is judged by the professional counseling psychologist to be contrary to the user's best interests or to be in conflict to the user's civil and legal rights, it is the responsibility of the counseling psychologist to discuss the implications of releasing psychological information and to assist the user in limiting disclosure only to information required by the present circumstance.

Raw psychological data (e.g., questionnaire returns or test protocols) in which a user is identified are released only with the written consent of the user or his or her legal representative and released only to a person recognized by the counseling psychologists as qualified and competent to use the data.

Any use made of psychological reports, records, or data for research for training purposes is consistent with this Guideline. Additionally, providers of counseling psychological services comply with statutory confidentiality requirements and those embodied in the American Psychological Association's *Ethical Principles of Psychologists* (APA, 1981b).

Providers of counseling psychological services who use information about individuals that is stored in large computerized data banks are aware of the possible misuse of such data as well as the benefits and take necessary measures to ensure that such information is used in a socially responsible manner.

GUIDELINE 3: ACCOUNTABILITY

3.1 *The promotion of human welfare is the primary principle guiding the professional activity of the counseling psychologist and the counseling psychological service unit.*

Interpretation: Counseling psychologists provide services to users in a manner that is considerate, effective, economical, and humane. Counseling psychologists are responsible for making their services readily accessible to users in a manner that facilitates the users' freedom of choice.

Counseling psychologists are mindful of their accountability to the sanctioners of counseling psychological services and to the general public, provided that appropriate steps are taken to protect the confidentiality of the service relationship. In the pursuit of their professional activities, they aid in the conservation of human, material, and financial resources.

The counseling psychological service unit does not withhold services to a potential client on the basis of that user's race, color, religion, gender, sexual orientation, age or national origin; nor does it provide services in a discriminatory or exploitative fashion. Counseling psychologists who find that psychological services are being provided in a manner that is discriminatory or exploitative to users and/or contrary to these Guidelines or to state or federal statutes take appropriate corrective action, which may include the refusal to provide services. When conflicts of interest arise, the counseling psychologist is guided in the resolution of differences by the principles set forth in the American Psychological Association's *Ethical Principles of Psychologists* (APA, 1981b) and "Guidelines for Conditions of Employment os Psychologists" (APA, 1972).[16]

Recognition is given to the following considerations in regard to the withholding of service: (a) the professional right of counseling psychologists to limit their practice to a specific category of users with whom they have achieved demonstrated competence (e.g., adolescents or families); (b) the right and responsibility of counseling psychologists to withhold an assessment procedure when not validly applicable; (c) the right and responsibility of counseling psychologists to withhold services in specific instances in which their own limitations or client characteristics might impair the quality of the services; (d) the obligation of counseling psychologists to seek to ameliorate through peer review, consultation, or other personal therapeutic procedures those factors that inhibit the provision of services to particular individuals; and (e) the obligation of counseling psychologists who withhold services to assist clients in obtaining services from other sources.[17]

3.2 *Counseling psychologists pursue their activities as members of the independent, autonomous profession of psychology.*[18]

Interpretation: Counseling psychologists, as members of an independent profession, are responsible both to the public and to their peers through established review mechanisms. Counseling psychologists are aware of the implications of their activities for the profession as a whole. They seek to eliminate discriminatory practices instituted for self-serving purposes that are not in the interest of the users (e.g., arbitrary requirements for referral and supervision by another profession). They are cognizant of their responsibilities for the development of the profession, participate where possible in the training and career development of students and other providers, participate as appropriate in the training of paraprofessionals or other professionals, and integrate and supervise the implementation of their contributions within the structure established for delivering psychological services. Counseling psychologists facilitate the development of, and participate in, professional standards review mechanisms.[19]

Counseling psychologists seek to work with other professionals in a cooperative manner for the good of the users and the benefit of the general public. Counseling psychologists associated with multidisciplinary settings support the principle that members of each participating profession have equal rights and opportunities to share all privileges and responsibilities of full membership in human service facilities and to administer service programs in their respective areas of competence.

3.3 *There are periodic, systematic, and effective evaluations of counseling psychological services.*[20]

Interpretation: When the counseling psychological service unit is a component of a larger organization, regular evaluation of progress in achieving goals is provided for in the service delivery plan, including consideration of the effectiveness of counseling psychological services relative to costs in terms of use of time and money and the availability of professional and support personnel.

Evaluation of the counseling psychological service delivery system is conducted internally and, when possible, under independent auspices as well. This evaluation includes an assessment of effectiveness (to determine what the service unit accomplished), efficiently (to determine the total costs of providing the services), availability (to determine appropriate levels and distribution of services and personnel), accessibility (to ensure that the services are barrier free to users), and adequacy (to determine whether the services meet the identified needs for such services).

There is a periodic reexamination of review mechanisms to ensure that these attempts at public safeguards are effective and cost efficient and do not place unnecessary encumbrances on the providers or impose unnecessary additional expenses on users or sanctioners for services rendered.

3.4 *Counseling psychologists are accountable for all aspects of the services they provide and are responsive to those concerned with these services.*[21]

Interpretation: In recognizing their responsibilities to users, sanctioners, third-party purchasers, and other providers, and where appropriate and consistent with the users' legal rights and privileged communications, counseling psychologists make available information about, and provide opportunity to participate in, decisions concerning such issues as initiation, termination, continuation, modification, and evaluation of counseling psychological services.

Depending on the settings, accurate and full information is made available to prospective individual or organizational users regarding the qualifications of providers, the nature and extent of service offered, and where appropriate, financial and social costs.

Where appropriate, counseling psychologists inform users of their payment policies and their willingness to assist in obtaining reimbursement from a third party and are acquainted with the appropriate statutes and regulations, the procedures for submitting claims, and the limits on confidentiality of claims information, in accordance with pertinent statutes.

GUIDELINE 4:   ENVIRONMENT

4.1 *Providers of counseling psychological services promote the development in the service setting of a physical, organizational, and social environment that facilitates optimal human functioning.*

> *Interpretation:* Federal, state, and local requirements for safety, health, and sanitation are observed.

As providers of services, counseling psychologists are concerned with the environment of their service unit, especially as it affects the quality of service, but also as it impinges on human functioning in the larger context. Physical arrangements and organizational policies and procedures are conducive to the human dignity, self-respect, and optimal functioning of users and to the effective delivery of service. Attention is given to the comfort and the privacy of providers and users. The atmosphere in which counseling psychological services are rendered is appropriate to the service and to the users, whether in an office, clinic, school, college, university, hospital, industrial organization, or other institutional setting.

FOOTNOTES

[1]The footnotes appended to these Specialty Guidelines represent an attempt to provide a coherent context of other policy statements of the Association regarding professional practice. The Guidelines extend these previous policy statements where necessary to reflect current concerns of the public and the profession.

[2]The following two categories of professional psychologists who met the criteria indicated below on or before the adoption of these Specialty Guidelines on January 31, 1980, are also considered counseling psychologists: Category 1—persons who completed (a) a doctoral degree program primarily psychological in content at a regionally accredited university or professional school and (b) 3 postdoctoral years of appropriate education, training, and experience in providing counseling psychological services as defined herein, including a minimum of 1 year in a counseling setting; Category 2—

persons who on or before September 4, 1974, (a) completed a master's degree from a program primarily psychological in content at a regionally accredited university or professional school and (b) held a license or certificate in the state in which they practiced, conferred by a state board of psychological examiners, or the endorsement of the state psychological association through voluntary certification, and who, in addition, prior to January 31, 1980, (c) obtained 5 post-master's years of appropriate education, training, and experience in providing counseling psychological services as defined herein, including a minimum of 2 years in a counseling setting.

After January 31, 1980, professional psychologists who wish to be recognized as professional counseling psychologists are referred to Guideline 1.7.

[3]The areas of knowledge and training that are a part of the educational program for all professional psychologists have been presented in two APA documents, *Education and Credentialing in Psychology II* (APA, 1977a) and *Criteria for Accreditation of Doctoral Training Programs and Internships in Professional Psychology* (APA, 1979). There is consistency in the presentation of core areas in the education and training of all professional psychologists. The description of education and training in these Guidelines is based primarily on the document *Education and Credentialing in Psychology II*. It is intended to indicate broad areas of required curriculum, with the expectation that training programs will undoubtedly want to interpret the specific content of these areas in different ways depending on the nature, philosophy, and intent of the programs.

[4]Functions and activities of counseling psychologists relating to the teaching of psychology, the writing or editing of scholarly or scientific manuscripts, and the conduct of scientific research do not fall within the purview of these Guidelines.

[5]These definitions should be compared with the APA (1967) guidelines for state legislation (hereinafter referred to as state guidelines), which define *psychologist* (i.e., the generic professional psychologist, not the specialist counseling psychologist) and the *practice of psychology* as follows:

> A person represents himself [or herself] to be a psychologist when he [or she] holds himself [or herself] out to the public by any title or description of services incorporating the words "psychology," "psychological," "psychologist," and/or offers to render or renders services as defined below to individuals, groups, organizations, or the public for a fee, monetary or otherwise.

The practice of psychology within the meaning of this act is defined as rendering to individuals, groups, organizations, or the public any psychological service involving the application of principles, methods, and procedures of understanding, predicting, and influencing behavior, such as the principles pertaining to learning, perception, motivation, thinking, emotions, and interpersonal relationships; the methods and procedures of interviewing, counseling, and psychotherapy; of constructing, administering, and interpreting tests of mental abilities, aptitudes, interests, attitudes, personality characteristics, emotion, and motivation; and of assessing public opinion.

The application of said principles and methods includes, but is not restricted to: diagnosis, prevention, and amelioration of adjustment problems and emotional and mental disorders of individuals and groups, hypnosis; educational and vocational counseling; personnel selection and management; the evaluation and planning for effective work and learning situations; advertising and market research; and the resolution of interpersonal and social conflicts.

Psychotherapy within the meaning of this act means the use of learning, conditioning methods, and emotional reactions, in a professional relationship, to assist a person or person to modify feelings, attitudes, and behavior which are intellectually, socially, or emotionally maladjustive or ineffectual.

The practice of psychology shall be as defined above, any existing statute in the state of _____ to the contrary not withstanding. (APA, 1967, pp. 1098–1099)

[6]The relation of a psychological service unit to a large facility or institution is also addressed indirectly in the APA (1972) "Guidelines for Conditions of Employment of Psychologists" (hereinafter referred to as CEP Guidelines), which emphasize the roles, responsibilities, and prerogatives of the psychologist when he or she is employed by or provides services for another agency, institution, or business.

[7]This Guideline replaces earlier recommendations in the 1967 state guidelines concerning exemption of psychologists from licensure. Recommendations 8 and 9 of those guidelines read as follows:

Persons employed as psychologists by accredited academic institutions, governmental agencies, research laboratories, and business corporations consulting or offering their research finding or providing scientific information *to like organizations* for a fee should be exempted. (APA, 1967, p. 1100)

On the other hand, the 1967 state guidelines specifically denied exemptions under certain conditions, as noted in Recommendations 10 and 11:

Persons employed as psychologists who offer or provide psychological services to the public for a fee, over and above the salary that they receive for the performance of their regular duties should not be exempted.

Persons employed as psychologists by organizations that sell psychological services to the public should not be exempted. (APA, 1967, pp. 1100–1101)

The present APA policy, as reflected in this guideline, establishes a single code of practice for psychologists providing covered services to users in any setting. The present position is that a psychologist providing any covered service meets local statutory requirements for licensure or certification. See the section entitled Principles and Implications of the Specialty Guidelines for further elaboration of this point.
[8]A closely related principle is found in the APA (1972) CEP Guidelines:

It is the policy of the APA that psychology as an independent profession is entitled to parity with other health and human service professionals in institutional practices and before the law. Psychologists in interdisciplinary settings such as colleges and universities, medical schools, clinics, private practice groups, and other agencies expect parity with other professionals in such matters as academic rank, board status, salaries, fringe benefits, fees, participation in administrative decisions, and all other conditions of employment, private contractual arrangements, and status before the law and legal institutions. (APA, 1972, p. 333)

[9]See CEP Guidelines (section entitled Career Development) for a closely related statement:

Psychologists are expected to encourage institutions and agencies which employ them to sponsor or conduct career development programs. The purpose of these programs would be to enable psychologists to engage in study for professional advancement and to keep abreast of developments in their field. (APA, 1972, p. 332)

[10]This Guideline follows closely the statement regarding "Policy on Training for Psychologists Wishing to Change Their Specialty" adopted by the APA Council of Representatives in January 1976. Included therein was the implementing provision that "this policy statement shall be incorporated in the guidelines of the Committee on Accreditation so that appropriate sanctions can be brought to bear on the university and internship training programs that violate [it]" (Conger, 1976, p. 424).
[11]See also APA's (1981b) *Ethical Principles of Psychologists*, especially Principles 5 (Confidentiality), 6 (Wel-

fare of the Consumer), and 9 (Research with Human Participants); and see *Ethical Principles in the Conduct of Research with Human Participants* (APA, 1973a). Also, in 1978 Division 17 approved in principle a statement on "Principles for Counseling and Psychotherapy with Women," which was designed to protect the interests of female users of counseling psychological services.

[12]Support for this position is found in the section on relations with other professions in *Psychology as a Profession:*

> Professional persons have an obligation to know and take into account the traditions and practices of other professional groups with whom they work and to cooperate fully with members of such groups with whom research, service, and other functions are shared. (APA, 1968, p. 5)

[13]One example of a specific application of this principle is found in APA's (1981a) reviewed *APA/Champus Outpatient Psychological Provider Manual.* Another example, quoted below, is found in Guideline 2 in APA's (1973b) "Guidelines for Psychologists Conducting Growth Groups":

> The following information should be made available *in writing* [italics added] to all prospective participants:
>
> (*a*) An explicit statement of the purpose of the group;
>
> (*b*) Types of techniques that may be employed;
>
> (*c*) The education, training, and experience of the leader or leaders;
>
> (*d*) The fee and any additional expense that may be incurred:
>
> (*e*) A statement as to whether or not to follow-up service is included in the fee:
>
> (*f*) Goals of the group experience and techniques to be used:
>
> (*g*) Amounts and kinds of responsibility to be assumed by the leader and by the participants. For example, (*i*) *the degree to which a participant is free not to follow suggestions;* (*ii*) any restrictions on a participant's freedom to leave the group at any time; and
>
> (*h*) Issues of confidentiality. (p. 933)

[14]See Principle 5 (Confidentiality) in *Ethical Principles of Psychologists* (APA, 1981b).

[15]Support for the principles of privileged communication is found in at least two policy statements of the Association:

> In the interest of both the public and the client and in accordance with the requirements of good pro-

fessional practice, the profession of psychology seeks recognition of the privileged nature of confidential communications with clients, preferably through statutory enactment or by administrative policy where more appropriate. (APA, 1968, p. 8)

> Whenever possible, a clause protecting the privileged nature of the psychologist-client relationship is included.

> When appropriate, psychologists assist in obtaining general "across the board" legislation for such privileged communications. (APA, 1967, p. 1103)

[16]The CEP Guidelines include the following:

> It is recognized that under certain circumstances, the interests and goals of a particular community or segment of interest in the population may be in conflict with the general welfare. Under such circumstances, the psychologists' professional activity must be primarily guided by the principle of "promoting human welfare." (APA, 1972, p., 334)

[17]This paragraph is adapted in part from the CEP Guidelines (APA, 1972, p. 333).

[18]Support for the principle of the independence of psychology as a profession is found in the following:

> As a member of an autonomous profession, a psychologist rejects limitations upon his [or her] freedom of thought and action other than those imposed by his [or her] moral, legal, and social responsibilities. The Association is always prepared to provide appropriate assistance to any reasonable member who becomes subjected to unreasonable limitation upon his [or her] opportunity to function as a practitioner, teacher, researcher, administrator, or consultant. The Association is always prepared to cooperate with any responsible professional organization in opposing any unreasonable limitations on the professional functions of the members of that organization.

> This insistence upon professional autonomy has been upheld over the years by the affirmative actions of the courts and other public and private bodies in support of the right of the psychologist—and other professionals—to pursue those functions which he [or she] is trained and qualified to perform. (APA, 1968, p. 9)

> Organized psychology has the responsibility to define and develop its own profession, consistent with the general canons of service and with the public welfare.

> Psychologists recognize that other professions and other groups will, from time to time, seek to define the roles and responsibilities of psychologists. The APA opposes such developments on the same principle that

it is opposed to the psychological profession taking positions which would define the work and scope of responsibility of other duly recognized professions. (APA, 1972, p. 333)

[19]APA support for peer review is detailed in the following excerpt from the APA (1971) statement entitled "Psychology and National Health Care":

> All professions participating in a national health plan should be directed to establish review mechanisms (or performance evaluations) that include not only peer review but active participation by persons representing the consumer. In situations where there are fiscal agents, they should also have representation when appropriate. (p. 1026)

[20]This Guideline on program evaluation is based directly on the following excerpts from two APA position papers:

> The quality and availability of health services should be evaluated by both consumers and health professionals. Research into the efficiency and effectiveness of the system should be conducted both internally and under independent auspices. (APA, 1971, p. 1025)

> The comprehensive community mental health center should devote an explicit portion of its budget to program evaluation. All centers should inculcate in their staff attention to and respect for research findings; the larger centers have an obligation to set a high priority on basic research and to give formal recognition to research as a legitimate part of the duties of staff members.

> . . . Only through explicit appraisal of program effects can worthy approaches be retained and refined, ineffective ones dropped. Evaluative monitoring of program achievements may vary, of course, from the relatively informal to the systematic and quantitative, depending on the importance of the issue, the availability of resources, and the willingness of those responsible to take risks of substituting informed judgement for evidence. (Smith & Hobbs, 1966, pp. 21–22)

[21] See also the CEP Guidelines for the following statement: "A psychologist recognizes that . . . he [or she] alone is accountable for the consequences and effects of his [or her] services, whether as teacher, researcher, or practitioner. This responsibility cannot be shared, delegated, or reduced." (APA, 1972, p. 334).

REFERENCES

American Psychological Association. Committee on Legislation. A model for state legislation affecting the practice of psychology. *American Psychologist,* 1967, *22,* 1095–1103.

American Psychological Association. *Psychology as a profession.* Washington, D.C.: Author, 1968

American Psychological Association. Psychology and national health care. *American Psychologist,* 1971, *26,* 1025–1026.

American Psychological Association. Guidelines for conditions of employment of psychologists. *American Psychologist,* 1972, *27,* 331–334.

American Psychological Association. *Ethical principles in the conduct of research with human participants.* Washington D.C.: Author, 1973(a).

American Psychological Association. Guidelines for psychologists conducting growth groups. *American Psychologist,* 1973(b), *28,* 933.

American Psychological Association. *Standards for educational and psychological tests.* Washington D.C.: Author, 1974(a).

American Psychological Association. *Standards for providers of psychological services.* Washington D.C.: Author, 1974(b).

American Psychological Association. *Education and credentialing in psychology II.* Report of a meeting, June 4–5, 1977, Washington, D.C.:Author, 1977(a).

American Psychological Association. *Standards for providers of psychological services* (Rev. ed.). Washington, D.C.: Author, 1977(b).

American Psychological Association. *Criteria for accreditation of doctoral training programs and internships in professional psychology.* Washington, D.C.: 1979 (amended 1980).

American Psychological Association APA/CHAMPUS *outpatient psychological provider manual* (Rev. ed.). Washington, D.C.: Author, 1981(a).

American Psychological Association. *Ethical principles of psychologists* (Rev. ed.). Washington, D.C.: Author, 1981(b).

Conger, J. J. Proceedings of the American Psychological Association, Incorporated, for the year 1975; Minutes of the annual meeting of the Council of Representatives. *American Psychologist,* 1976, *31,* 406–434.

Smith, M. B., & Hobbs, N. *The community and the community mental health center.* Washington, D.C.: American Psychological Association, 1966.

References

Abbe, A. E. (1961). Consultation to a school guidance program. *Elementary School Journal, 61*, 331–337.

Adler, A. (1959). *Understanding human nature.* New York: Premier Books.

Aiello, H., & Humes, C. (1987). Counselor contact of the noncustodial parent: A point of law. *Elementary School Guidance and Counseling, 21*(3), 177–182.

Aiken, L. R. (1988). *Psychological testing and assessment* (5th ed.). Boston: Allyn & Bacon.

Ailes, R. (1988). *You are the message.* Homewood, IL: Dow, Jones-Brown.

Allen, G. J., Chinsky, J. M., Larsen, S. W., Lochman, J. E., & Selinger, H. V. (1976). *Community psychology and the schools.* Hillsdale, NJ: Erlbaum.

Allsopp, A., & Prosen, S. (1988). Teacher reactions to child sexual abuse training program. *Elementary Guidance and Counseling, 22*, 299–305.

American Association for Counseling and Development, & Association for Measurement and Evaluation in Counseling and Development. (1989). *Responsibilities of users of standardized tests.* (RUST statement revised.) Alexandria, VA: American Association for Counseling and Development.

American Association for Marriage and Family Therapy. (1983). *Membership requirements: Clinical member, associate member, student member.* Washington, DC: Author.

American Association for Marriage and Family Therapy. (1991). *AAMFT code of ethics.* Washington, DC: Author.

American Association of Retired Persons. (1988). *A profile of older Americans.* Washington, DC: Author.

American Counseling Association. (1988). *Ethical standards: American Counseling Association.* Alexandria, VA: Author.

American Mental Health Counselors Association. (1986). *Code of ethics for mental health counselors.* Alexandria, VA: American Counseling Association/Author.

American Personnel and Guidance Association. (1964). *American School Counselor Association statement of policy for secondary school counselors.* Alexandria, VA: Author.

American Psychiatric Association. (1994). *Diagnostic and statistical manual of mental disorders: DSM-IV* (4th ed.). Washington, DC: American Psychiatric Association.

American Psychological Association. (1992). *Ethical principles of psychologists and code of conduct.* Arlington, VA: Author.

American Psychological Association. (1981). *Specialty guidelines for the delivery of services by counseling psychologists.* Arlington, VA: Author.

American School Counselor Association. (1984). *The school counselor in career guidance: Expectations and responsibilities.* Alexandria, VA: Author.

American School Counselor Association. (1988). The school counselor and child abuse/neglect prevention. *Elementary School Guidance and Counseling, 22,* 261–263.

American School Counselor Association. (1990). *The American School Counselor Association role statement: The school counselor.* Alexandria, VA: Author.

Anastasi, A. (1954). The measurements of abilities. *Journal of Counseling Psychology, 1,* 164–168.

Anastasi, A. (1982). *Psychological testing* (5th ed.). New York: Macmillan.

Anastasi, A. (1988). *Psychological testing* (6th ed.). New York: Macmillan.

Anastasi, A. (1992). Tests and assessment: What counselors should know about the use and interpretations of psychological tests. *Journal of Counseling and Development, 70*(5), 610–615.

Anderson, D. J., & Cranston-Gingras, A. (1991). Sensitizing counselors and educators to multicultural issues: An interactive approach. *Journal of Counseling and Development, 70,* 91–98.

Anderson, L. S., & Lemoncelli, R. J. (1982). Meeting the needs of high-risk, difficult to reach students: Creative educational approaches. *The School Counselor, 29,* 381–387.

Applebaum, P. (1993). Legal liability and managed care. *American Psychologist, 148*(3), 251–257.

Arlow, J. A. (1979). Psychoanalysis. In R. J. Corsini (Ed.), *Current psychotherapies* (2nd ed., pp. 1–43). Itasca, IL: Peacock.

Arthur, G. L., Jr., & Swanson, C. D. (1993). *Confidentiality and privileged communication.* ACA Legal Series, 6.

Association for Specialists in Group Work. (1990). *Ethical guidelines for group counselors and professional standards for the training of group workers* (rev. ed.). Alexandria, VA: Author.

Astin, A. (1982). *Minorities in higher education.* San Francisco: Jossey-Bass.

Aubrey, R. F. (1977). Historical development of guidance and counseling and implications for the future. *Personnel and Guidance Journal, 55,* 288–295.

Axelson, J. A. (1985). *Counseling and development in a multicultural society.* Monterey, CA: Brooks/Cole.

Baker, S. B. (1977). An argument for constructive accountability. *Personnel and Guidance Journal, 456,* 53–55.

Baker, S. B. (1992). *School counseling for the 21st century.* New York: Merrill.

Baker, S., Swisher, P., Nadenichek, P., & Popowitz, C. (1984). Primary effects of primary prevention strategies. *Personnel and Guidance Journal, 62,* 459–464.

Bales, R. F., & Borgatta, E. F. (1965). *Size of group as a factor in the interaction profile.* In A. P. Hare, E. F. Borgatta, & R. F. Bales (Eds.), *Small groups: Studies in social interaction.* New York: Knopf.

Bandura, A. (1982). The psychology of chance encounters and life paths. *The American Psychologist, 37*(7), 747–755.

Barclay, J. R. (1984a). Primary prevention in schools [Special issue]. *Personnel and Guidance Journal, 62*(8).

Barclay, J. R. (1984b). Primary prevention on campuses and in communities [Special issue]. *Personnel and Guidance Journal, 62*(9).

Baruth, L., & Robinson, E. M. (1987). *An introduction to the counseling profession.* Englewood Cliffs, NJ: Prentice-Hall.

Bates, M., Johnson, C. D., & Blaker, K. E. (1982). *Group leadership: A manual for group counseling* (2nd ed.). Denver: Love.

Beers, C. (1908). *A mind that found itself.* New York: Longman Green; republished by Doubleday, 1953.

Belkin, G. S. (1975). *Practical counseling in the schools.* Dubuque, IA: Brown.

Belkin, G. S. (1981). *Practical counseling in the schools* (2nd ed.). Dubuque, IA: Brown.

Belkin, G. S. (1988). *Introduction to counseling* (3rd ed.). Madison, WI: Brown & Benchmark.

Belkin, G. S. (1984). *Practical counseling in the schools* (3rd ed.). Dubuque, IA: Brown.

Bell, A., & Weinberg, M. (1978). *Homosexualities.* New York: Simon & Schuster.

Bell, T. (1983). *A nation at risk: The imperative for educational reform.* Washington, DC: The National Commission of Excellence in Education.

Belloc, N. B. (1973). Relationship of health practices and mortality. *Preventative Medicine, 2,* 67–81.

Belloc, N. B., & Breslow, L. (1972). Relationship of physical health status and health practices. *Preventative Medicine, 1,* 409–421.

Berk, J., & Berk, S. (1991). *Managing effectively: A handbook for first-time managers.* New York: Sterling.

Berven, N. L. (1979). The roles and functions of the rehabilitation counselor revisited. *Rehabilitation Counseling Bulletin, 23,* 84–88.

Biegel, D. E., & Naparstek, A. J. (Eds.). (1982). *Community support systems and mental health.* New York: Springer.

Biggs, D., & Blocher, D. (1987). *Foundations of ethical counseling.* New York: Springer.

Bissell, L., & Royce, J. E. (1992). Ethics for addiction professionals. *Professional Counselor, 6*(4).

Blackham, G. J. (1977). *Counseling: Theory, process, and practice.* Belmont, CA: Wadsworth.

Blackham, G. J., & Silberman, A. (1980). *Modification of child and adolescent behavior* (3rd ed.). Belmont, CA: Wadsworth.

Blake, R., & Peterson, D. (1979). Module I: Demographic aspects of aging: Implications for counseling. In M. L. Ganikos (Ed.), *Counseling the aged: A training syllabus for educators* (pp. 1–27). Washington, DC: American Personnel and Guidance Association.

Blanchard, K. H. (1982). *The one minute manager.* New York: Morrow.

Blatt, I. (1976). Counseling the Puerto Rican client. In G. S. Belkin (Ed.), *Counseling: Directions in theory and practice.* Dubuque, IA: Kendall/Hunt.

Blau, P. M., Gustad, J. W., Jessor, R., Parnes, H. S., & Wilcock, R. G. (1956). Occupational choice: A conception framework. *Industrial and Labor Relations Review, 9,* 531–543.

Bleck, R. T., & Bleck, B. L. (1982). The disruptive child play group. *Elementary School Guidance & Counseling, 17,* 137–141.

Blocher, D. H. (1987). *The professional counselor.* New York: Macmillan.

Blocher, D. H., & Biggs, D. A. (1983). *Counseling psychology in community settings.* New York: Springer.

Bloland, P. A., & Edwards, P. B. (1981). Work and leisure: A counseling synthesis. *Vocational Guidance Quarterly, 30,* 101–108.

Bloom, B. L. (1984). *Community mental health: A general introduction* (2nd ed.). Belmont, CA: Brooks/Cole.

Bloom, B. S. (1976). *Human characteristics and school learning.* New York: McGraw-Hill.

Bloom, J., Gerstein, L., Tarvydas, V., Conaster, J., Davis, E., Kater, D., Sherrard, P., & Esposito, R. (1990). Model legislation for licensed professional counselors. *Journal of Counseling and Development, 68,* 511–523.

Bloom, M. (1981). *Primal prevention: The possible science.* Englewood Cliffs, NJ: Prentice-Hall.

Blum, L. (1986). Building constructive counselor-teacher relationships. *Elementary School Guidance & Counseling, 20,* 236–239.

Bogardus, E. S. (1925). Measuring social distance. *Journal of Applied Sociology, 9,* 299–308.

Borow, H. (1964). *Man in a world at work.* Ellicott City, MD: National Career Development Association.

Bowman, S. L. (1993). Career intervention strategies for ethnic minorities. *Career Development Quarterly, 42,* 14–25.

Boy, A. V., & Pine, G. J. (1982). *Client-centered counseling: A renewal.* Boston: Allyn & Bacon.

Brabeck, M. M., & Welfel, E. R. (1985). Counseling theory: Understanding the trend toward eclecticism from a developmental perspective. *Journal of Counseling and Development, 63*(6), 343–347.

Brammer, L. M. (1988). *The helping relationship: Process and skills* (4th ed.). Englewood Cliffs, NJ: Prentice-Hall.

Brammer, L. M., & Shostrom, E. L. (1982). *Therapeutic psychology: Fundamentals of counseling and psychotherapy* (4th ed.). Englewood Cliffs, NJ: Prentice-Hall.

Brammer, L. M., Shostrom, E. L., & Abrego, P. J. (1989). *Therapeutic psychology: Fundamentals of counseling and psychotherapy* (5th ed.). Englewood Cliffs, NJ: Prentice-Hall.

Brandt, J. E., & Hood, A. B. (1968). Effect of personality adjustment on the predictive validity of the Strong Vocational Interest Blank. *Journal of Counseling Psychology, 15,* 547–551.

Braucht, S., & Weime, B. (1990). Establishing a rural school counseling agenda: A multiagency needs-assessment model. *The School Counselor, 37,* 179–183.

Brewer, J. M. (1932). *Education as guidance.* New York: Macmillan.

Brockopp, G. W. (1973). Crisis intervention: Theory, process and practice. In D. Lester & G. W. Brockopp (Eds.), *Crisis intervention and counseling by telephone.* Springfield, IL: Thomas.

Bronfenbrenner, U. (1979). *The ecology of human development: Experiments by nature and design.* Cambridge, MA: Harvard University Press.

Brown, D., & Feit, S. S. (1978). Making job placement work. *Vocational Guidance Quarterly, 27,* 176–183.

Brown, D., & Kurpius, D. J. (Eds.). (1985). Consultation. *The Counseling Psychologist, 13*(3).

Brown, D., Kurpius, D. J., & Morris, J. R. (1988). *Handbook of consultation with individuals and small groups.* Alexandria, VA: Association for Counselor Education and Supervision.

Brown, D., & Srebalus, D. J. (1988). *An introduction to the counseling profession.* Englewood Cliffs, NJ: Prentice-Hall.

Brown, J. A., & Pate, R. H., Jr. (1983). *Being a counselor.* Belmont, CA: Brooks/Cole.

Brown, J. H., & Christensen, D. N. (1986). *Family therapy: Theory and practice.* Monterey, CA: Brooks/Cole.

Bruce, P. (1984). Continuum of counseling goals: A framework for differentiating counseling strategies. *Personnel and Guidance Journal, 62,* 259–263.

Burn, D. (1992). Ethical implications in cross-cultural counseling and training. *Journal of Counseling and Development, 70,* 578–583.

Burnette, C., Williams, R. L., & Law, J. G. (1987). Therapeutic and lifestyle reduction of aggressiveness in Vietnam veterans, *Group, 11*(1), 3–14.

Burnham, S., & Satcher, J. (1990). *Guide to community colleges serving students with learning disabilities (Mississippi, Alabama, Georgia, Tennessee, and Florida.* (ERIC Document Reproduction Service No. ED 320098)

Burns, J. M. (1978). *Leadership.* New York: Harper & Row.

Busch, E. J., Jr. (1981). Developing an employee assistance program. *Personnel Journal, 60,* 708–711.

Campbell, N. J., & Dobson, J. E. (1987). An inventory of student computer anxiety. *Elementary School Guidance and Counseling, 22,* 149–156.

Caplan, G. (1963). Types of mental health consultation. *American Journal of Orthopsychiatry, 33,* 470–481.

Caplan, G. (1970). *The theory and practice of mental health consultation.* New York: Basic Books.

Caplow, T. (1954). *The sociology work.* Minneapolis: University of Minnesota Press.

Caplow, T. (1968). *Two against one coalitions in triad.* Englewood Cliffs, NJ: Prentice-Hall.

Capuzzi, D., & Gross, D. R. (1991). *Introduction to counseling: Perspectives for the 1990s.* Needham Heights, MA: Allyn and Bacon.

Carlson, J. (1993). Marriage and family counseling. In G. R. Walz & J. C. Bleuer (Eds.), *Counselor efficacy: Assessing and using counseling outcome research.* Ann Arbor, MI: ERIC Counseling and Personnel Services Clearinghouse.

Carnegie Forum on Education and the Economy. (1986). *A nation prepared: Teachers for the 21st century.* Washington, DC: Author.

Casey, J. A. (1992, February). *Macmentoring: Using technology and counseling with at-risk youth.* Paper presented at the meeting of the California Association for Counseling and Development, San Francisco.

Casey, J., & Ramsammy, R. (1992, February). *Macmentoring: Using technology and counseling with at-risk youth.* Paper presented at the Annual Conference of the California Association for Counseling and Development, San Francisco.

Casteneda, C. (1974). *Tales of power.* New York: Simon & Schuster.

Caublin, L., & Prout, H. (1983). School counselors and the reporting of child abuse: A survey of state laws and practices. *The School Counselor, 30*(5), 358–367.

Cavanaugh, M. E. (1982). *The counseling experience: A theoretical and practical approach.* Belmont, CA: Brooks/Cole.

Cetron, M. J. (1985). *Schools of the future: How American business and education can cooperate to save our schools.* (Sponsored by the American Association of School Administrators.) New York: McGraw-Hill.

Chandler, C. L., Weissberg, R. P., Cowen, E. L., & Guarez, J. (1984). Long term effects of school-based secondary prevention program for young maladapting children. *Journal of Consulting and Clinical Psychology, 52*(2).

Chase, C. I. (1984). *Elementary statistical procedures* (3rd ed.). New York: McGraw- Hill.

Chomsky, N. (1971). *Problems of knowledge and freedom.* New York: Vintage.

Christensen, C. P. (1989). Cross-cultural awareness development: A conceptual model. *Counselor Education and Supervision, 28,* 270–287.

Clifton, J. A. (Ed.). (1970). *Applied anthropology: Readings into the uses of the science of man.* Boston: Houghton-Mifflin.

Cobb, H. C., & Richards, H. C. (1983). Efficacy of counseling services in decreasing behavior problems of elementary school children. *Elementary School Guidance & Counseling,* 17(3), 180–187.

Cohen, R. I, Montague, P., Nathanson, L. S., & Swerdlik, M. E. (1988). *Psychological testing: An introduction to tests and measurement.* Mountain View, CA: Mayfield.

Coie, J. D., Watt, N. F., West, S. G., Hawkins, J. D., Asarnow, J. R., Markham, H. J., Ramey, S. L., Shure, M. B., & Long, B. (1993). The science of prevention: A conceptual framework and some directions for a national research program. *American Psychologist, 48,* 1013–1022.

Coleman, J. S., & James, J. (1961). The equilibrium size distribution of freely forming groups. *Sociometry, 24,* 36–45.

College Entrance Examination Board. (1986, October). *Keeping the options open: Recommendations. Final report of the Commission on Precollege Guidance and Counseling.* New York: Author.

Commission on Precollege Guidance & Counseling. (1986). *Keeping the options open: Final report recommendations* (pp. 5-6). New York: College Entrance Examination Board.

Conant, J. (1959). *The American high school today.* New York: McGraw-Hill.

Conyne, R. K. (1983). Two critical issues in primary prevention: What it is and how to do it. *Personnel and Guidance Journal, 61,* 331–340.

Conyne, R. K. (1984). Primary prevention through a campus alcohol education project. *Personnel and Guidance Journal, 62,* 524–528.

Conyne, R. K. (1985). The counseling ecologist: Helping people and environments. *Counseling and Human Development, 18*(2), 1–12.

Conyne, R. K. (1987). *Primary preventative counseling.* Muncie, IN: Accelerated Development.

Cooney, J. (1991). *Coping with sexual abuse.* New York: Rosen Publishing Group.

Corey, G. (1977). Theory and practice of counseling and psychotherapy (1st ed.). Monterey, CA: Brooks/Cole.

Corey, G. (1981). *Theory and practice of group counseling.* Monterey, CA: Brooks/Cole.

Corey, G. (1986). *Theory and practice of counseling and psychotherapy* (3rd ed.). Monterey, CA: Brooks/Cole.

Corey, G. (1990). *Theory and practice of group counseling (3rd ed.).* Pacific Grove, CA: Brooks/Cole.

Cormier, L. S., & Hackney, H. (1993). *The professional counselor: A process guide to helping.* Needham Heights, MA: Allyn & Bacon.

Cottle, W. C., & Downie, E. M. (1970). *Preparation for counseling* (2nd ed.). Englewood Cliffs, NJ: Prentice-Hall.

Council for the Accreditation of Counseling and Related Educational Programs (1994). *CACREP accreditation standards and procedures manual.* Alexandria, VA: Author.

Cowen, E. L. (1982). Primary prevention research: Barriers, needs, and opportunities. *Journal of Primary Prevention, 2,* 131–137.

Cramer, S. H., Herr, E. L., Morris, C. N., & Frantz, T. T. (1970). *Research and the school counselor.* Boston: Houghton Mifflin.

Cristiani, T. S., & Cristiani, M. F. (1979). The application of counseling skills in the business and industrial setting. *Personnel and Guidance Journal, 58,* 166–169.

Crocker, E. C. (1964). Depth consultation with parents. *Young Children, 20,* 91–99.

Crosbie-Burnett, M. C., & Pulvino, C. J. (1990). Pro-tech: A multimodal group intervention for children with reluctance to use computers. *Elementary School Guidance and Counseling, 24,* 272–280.

Cross, H. I. (1964). The outcome of psychotherapy: A selected analysis of research findings. *Journal of Consulting Psychology, 28,* 413–417.

Crouch, R. C. (1979). Social work defined. *Social Work, 24*, 46–48.

Crow, L. D., & Crow, A. (1960). *An introduction to guidance* (2nd ed.). New York: American.

Crowe, W. L. (1994). A day in the life of a middle school counselor. Unpublished account. Bloomington, IN.

Cubberly, E. P. (1934). *Public education in the United States.* Boston: Houghton Mifflin.

Curran, D. J., & Renzetti, C. M. (1990). *Social problems* (2nd ed.). Boston: Allyn & Bacon.

Daly, M. (1979). How good is your child's school counselor? *Better Homes and Gardens, 57*, 15–22.

Daniels, J. L. (1981). World of work in disabling conditions. In R. M. Parker & C. E. Hansen (Eds.), *Rehabilitation counseling* (pp. 169–199). Boston: Allyn & Bacon.

Delco, W. (1988). *Access plus quality: The formula for student success.* Paper presented at the Third Annual Harry S. Truman Lecture, Washington, DC.

Dickman, F., & Emener, W. G. (1982). Employee assistance programs: Basic concepts, attributes and an evaluation. *Personnel Administration, 27*(8), 55–62.

Dodge, K. (1983). Promoting social competence in school children. *Schools and Teaching, 1*(2).

Dolliver, R. H. (1982). Review of card sorts. In J. T. Kapes & M. M. Mastie (Eds.), *A counselor's guide to vocational guidance instruments* (pp. 147–160). Falls Church, VA: National Vocational Guidance Association.

Donovan, C. E. (1959). A new era of guidance. *School and Society, 87*, 241.

Drasgow, J., & Carkhuff, R. R. (1964). Juder neuropsychiatric keys before and after psychotherapy. *Journal of Counseling Psychology, 11*, 67–69.

Driver, H. I. (1958). *Counseling and learning through small group discussions.* Madison, WI: Monona.

Drucker, P. (1954). *The practice of management.* New York: Harper.

Drum, D. J. (1984). Implementing theme-focused prevention: Challenge for the 1980's. *Personnel and Guidance Journal, 62*, 509–514.

Drummond, R. J. (1988). *Appraisal procedures for counselors and helping professionals.* Columbus, OH: Merrill.

Dugan, W. (1962). An inward look: Assumptions and expectations. *Counselor Education and Supervision, 1*(4), 174–180.

Dunn, L. (1994). Typical day of a counselor at a community mental health center. Unpublished account. Bloomington, IN.

Dusay, J. M., & Steiner, C. (1971). Transactional analysis in groups. In H. I. Kaplan & B. J. Sadock (Eds.), *Comprehensive groups psychotherapy.* Baltimore: Williams & Wilkins.

Dyer, W. W., & Vriend, J. (1977). A goal-setting checklist for counselors. *Personnel and Guidance Journal, 55*, 469–471.

Dymond, R. F. (1953). Can clinicians predict individual behavior? *Journal of Personality, 22*, 151–161.

Dziekan, K. I., & Okocha, A. A. G. (1993, June). Accessibility of rehabilitation services: Comparison by racial-ethnic status. *Rehabilitation Counseling Bulletin, 36*, 183–189.

Eckerson, L., & Smith, H. (1962). *Elementary school guidance: The consultant.* (Reprint of three articles in *School Life*). Washington, DC: U.S. Department of Health, Education and Welfare, Office of Education.

Edgerton, R. B., & Karno, M. (1971). Mexican-American bilingualism and the perception of mental illness. *Archives of General Psychiatry, 24*, 286–290.

Education for All Handicapped Children Act of 1975: Implementation of Part B. (1977). *Federal Register, 42*, 42474–42518.

Education for All Handicapped Children Act of 1975, *20* (1977). U.S.C. 1401–1415.

Edwards, A. (1987, July). Black working women: A report from the front. *Glamour*, pp. 162–163, 218.

Egan, G. (1977). *You and me: The skills of communicating and relating to others.* Monterey, CA: Brooks/Cole.

Egan, G. (1982). *The skilled helper: Model, skills, and methods for effective helping* (2nd ed.). Monterey, CA: Brooks/Cole.

Ehrhart, J., & Sandler, B. (1987). *Looking for more than a few good women in traditionally male fields. Project on the status and education of women.* Washington, DC: Association of American Colleges.

Eisenberg, S., & Delaney, D. J. (1983). *The counseling process* (3rd ed.). Boston: Houghton Mifflin.

Ellis, A. (1957). Outcome of employing three techniques of psychotherapy. *Journal of Clinical Psychology, 13*, 334–350.

Engen, H. B., Lamb, R. R., & Prediger, D. (1982). Are secondary schools still using standardized tests? *Personnel and Guidance Journal, 60*, 287–290.

Entine, A. D. (1977). Counseling for mid-life and beyond. *Vocational Guidance Quarterly, 25*, 332–336.

Entine, A. D. (1984). Voluntary mid-life career change: Family effects. In S. H. Cramer (Ed.), *Perspectives on work and the family.* Rockville, MD: Aspen Systems.

Erickson, S. H. (1993). Ethics and confidentiality in AIDS counseling: A professional dilemma. *Journal of Mental Health Counseling, 15*, 118–131.

Esters, P., & Levant, R. F. (1983). The effects of two parent counseling programs on rural low-achieving children. *The School Counselor, 31*, 159–166.

Ethics Committee of APA. (1988). Trends in ethics cases: Common pitfalls and published resources. *American Psychologist, 43*(7), 564–572.

Ewing, D. B. (1975). Direct from Minnesota—E. G. Williamson. *Personnel and Guidance Journal, 54*, 77–87.

Fagan, T. K., & Jenkins, W. M. (1989). People with disabilities: An update. *Journal of Counseling and Development, 68*, 140–144.

Fagan, T. K., & Wise, P. S. (1994). *School psychology: Past, present and future.* New York: Longman.

Family Rights and Privacy Act. (1974). *United States Code of Congressional and Administrative News: Vol. I.* St. Paul, MN: West.

Fassiner, R. E. (1991). The hidden minority: Issues and challenges in working with lesbian women and gay men. *Counseling Psychologist, 19*, 157–176.

Faust, V. (1967). The counselor as a consultant to teachers. *Elementary School Guidance and Counseling, 1*, 112–117.

Faust, V. (1968a). *The counselor-consultant in the elementary school.* Boston: Houghton Mifflin.

Faust, V. (1968b). *The history of elementary school counseling: Overview and critique.* Boston: Houghton Mifflin.

Feingold, G. A. (1947). A new approach to guidance. *School Review, 4*, 542–550.

Feller, J. L. (1978). *Impact of sex-role stereotypes and biases on the vocational development and counseling of women.* Unpublished manuscript. Indiana University, Bloomington.

Felner, R. D., Jason, L. A., Moritsugu, J. N., & Farber, S. S. (Eds.). (1983). *Preventive psychology: Theory, research, and practice.* New York: Pergamon.

Fine, R. (1973). Psychoanalysis. In R. J. Corsini (Ed.), *Current psychotherapies* (pp. 1–33). Itasca, IL: Peacock.

Finkel, N. J. (1976). *Mental illness and health: Its legacy, tensions, and changes.* New York: Macmillan.

Finkelhor, D. (1984). *Child sexual abuse.* New York: Free Press.

Fischer, L., & Sorenson, G. P. (1985). *School law for counselors, psychologists and social workers.* New York: Longman.

Fischer, L., & Sorenson, G. P. (1991). *School law for counselors, psychologists and social workers* (2nd ed.). New York: Longman.

Fischer, P. H. (1953). An analysis of the primary group. *Sociometry, 16,* 272–276.

Fiske, E. B. (1988). America's test mania. *New York Times,* Education Life, Section 12, 16–20.

Flaherty, J. A., & Meagher, R. (1980). Measuring racial bias on inpatient treatment. *American Journal of Psychiatry, 137,* 679–682.

Flygare, T. (1975). *The legal rights of students.* Bloomington, IN: Phi Delta Kappa Educational Foundation.

Fong, M. L., & Amatea, E. S. (1992). Stress and single professional women: An exploration of causal factors. *Journal of Mental Health Counseling, 14,* 20–29.

Forrest, D. V. (1983). Employee assistance programs in the 1980's: Expanding career options for counselors. *Personnel and Guidance Journal, 62,* 105–107.

Forster, J. R. (1977). What shall we do about credentialing? *Personnel and Guidance Journal, 55,* 573–576.

Fretz, B. R. (1988). Third National Conference for Counseling Psychology: Planning the future. *Counseling Psychologist, 16*(3).

Frey, D. H., & Raming, H. E. (1979). A taxonomy of consulting goals and methods. *Personnel and Guidance Journal, 58,* 26–33.

Frieden, B. (1993). *The fountain of age.* New York: Simon & Schuster.

Froehlich, C. P. (1958). *Guidance services in schools* (2nd ed.). New York: McGraw-Hill.

Fullerton, H., Jr. (1987, September). *Projections 2000: Labor force projections—1986 to 2000. Monthly Labor Review.* Washington, DC: U.S. Department of Labor.

Fuqua, D. R., & Kurpius, D. J. (1993). Conceptual models in organization consultation. *Journal of Counseling and Development, 71*(6), 607–618.

Galfo, A. J. (1975). *Interpreting educational research* (3rd ed.). Dubuque, IA: Brown.

Gallessich, J. (1982). *The profession and practice of consultation.* San Francisco: Jossey-Bass.

Gandara, P. (1989, January). Those children are ours: Moving towards community. *National Education Journal,* pp. 38–43.

Garmezy, N. (1978). DSM III: Never mind the psychologists—Is it good for the children? *Clinical Psychologist* (Spring–Summer), *31*(3-4), 1, 4–6.

Garrett Park Press. (1987). *Minority student enrollments in higher education.* Garrett Park, MD: Author.

Gay, L. R. (1976). *Educational research: Competencies for analysis and application* (2nd ed.). Columbus, OH: Merrill.

Gazda, G. M. (1984). *Group Counseling: A developmental approach.* (3rd ed.). Boston: Allyn & Bacon.

Gazda, G. M. (1989). *Group counseling: A developmental approach* (4th ed.). Boston: Allyn & Bacon.

Gazda, G. M., Asbury, F. R., Balzer, F. J., Childers, W. C., & Walters, R. P. (1977). *Human relations development: A manual for educators.* Boston: Allyn & Bacon.

Gelso, C. J., & Fretz, B. R. (1992). *Counseling psychology.* New York: Harcourt Brace Jovanovich.

George, R. L., & Cristiani, T. S. (1995). *Counseling: Theory and practice* (4th ed.). Englewood Cliffs, NJ: Prentice-Hall.

George, R. L., & Dustin, D. (1988). *Group counseling: Theory and practice.* Englewood Cliffs: Prentice-Hall.

Getson, R., & Schweid, R. (1976). School counselors and the Buckley Amendment—Ethical Standards squeeze. *The School Counselor, 24*, 56–58.

Gibbs, J. T., Huang, L., & Associates. (1989). *Children of color: Psychological intervention with minority youth.* San Francisco: Jossey-Bass.

Gibson, R. L. (1973). The counselor as curriculum consultant. *American Vocational Journal, 48*, 50–51, 54.

Gibson, R. L. (1989). Prevention and the elementary school counselor. *Elementary School Guidance and Counseling Journal, 24*, 30–36.

Gibson, R. L. (1990). Teachers' opinions of high school counseling and guidance programs: Then and now. *The School Counselor, 37*, 248–255.

Gibson, R. L., & Higgins, R. E. (1966). *Techniques of guidance: An approach to pupil analysis.* Chicago: Science Research Associates.

Gibson, R. L., & Mitchell, M. H. (1976). *Identification of effective concepts in placement and follow-up: A technical report.* Indianapolis: State of Indiana and Indiana University.

Gibson, R. L., Mitchell, M. H., & Basile, S. K. (1993). *Counseling in the elementary school: A comprehensive approach.* Boston: Allyn & Bacon.

Gibson, R. L., Mitchell, M. H., & Higgins, R. E. (1983). *Development and management of counseling programs and guidance services.* New York: Macmillan.

Gibson, R. L., Mitchell, M. H., Stockton, R., Gerster, D., & Shafe, M. (1977). *The dissemination and implementation of effective concepts and practices in placement and follow-up services for school guidance programs.* Unpublished manuscript.

Gifford, B. R. (1991, August). The learning society: Serious play. *Chronicle of Higher Education,* p. 7.

Gilbert, S. P. (1992). Ethical issues in the treatment of severe psychopathology in university and college counseling centers. *Journal of Counseling and Development, 70*, 695–699.

Gilbride, D. D. (1993). Parental attitudes toward their child with a disability: Implications for rehabilitation counselors. *Rehabilitation Counseling Bulletin, 36*, 139–150.

Gill, S. J., & Barry, R. A. (1982). Group-focused counseling: Classifying the essential skills. *Personnel and Guidance Journal, 60*, 302–305.

Gilliland, B. E., James, R. K., & Bowman, J. T. (1989). *Theories and strategies in counseling and psychotherapy* (2nd ed.). Englewood Cliffs, NJ: Prentice-Hall.

Ginzberg, E., Ginsburg, S. W., Axelrod, S., & Herma, J. L. (1951). *Occupational choice: An approach to a general theory.* New York: Columbia University Press.

Gladding, S. T. (1991). *Group work: A counseling specialty.* New York: Macmillan.

Gladding, S. T., Burgraf, M., & Fennell, D. R. (1987). Marriage and family counseling in counselor education: National trends and implications. *Journal of Counseling and Development, 66*(2), 90–92.

Glasser, W. (1965). *Reality therapy: A new approach to psychiatry.* New York: Harper & Row.

Glasser, W. (1969). *Schools without failure.* New York: Harper & Row.

Glasser, W. (1981). *Stations of the mind.* New York: Harper & Row.

Glasser, W. (1984). Reality therapy. In R. J. Corsini (Ed.), *Current psychotherapies* (3rd ed., pp. 320–353). Itasca, IL: Peacock.

Goeke, J. D., & Salomone, P. R. (1979). Job placement and the school counselor. *Vocational Guidance Quarterly, 27*, 209–215.

Goldman, L. (Ed.). (1978). *Research methods for counselors.* New York: Wiley.

Goldenberg, I., & Goldenberg, H. (1991). *Family therapy: An overview.* Pacific Grove, CA: Brooks/Cole.

Good, L. (1982). *The employee assistance program from school district I.* Wheatland, WY: Southeast Wyoming Mental Health Center.

Goodwin, D. K. (1978, October). True leadership. *Psychology Today,* 46–48, 50, 53–54, 57–58, 110.

Goodyear, R. K. (1976). Counselors as community psychologist. *Personnel and Guidance Journal, 54,* 512–516.

Gordon, T. (1970). *Parent effectiveness training: The no-lose program for raising responsible children.* New York: Wyden.

Goshen, C. E. (1967). *Documentary history of psychiatry: A sourcebook on history principles* (pp. 501–504). New York: Philosophical Library.

Gross, M. L. (1963). The brain watchers. New York: Signet Books.

Gross, B., & Gross, R. (1974). *Will it grow in a classroom?* New York: Dell.

Gummere, R. (1988). The counselor as prophet: Frank Parsons. *Journal of Counseling and Development, 66*(9), 402–405.

Gysbers, N. C., & Henderson, P. (1994). *Developing and managing your school guidance program* (2nd ed.). Alexandria, VA: American Counseling Association.

Gysbers, N. C., Hughey, K. F., Starr, M., & Lapan, R. T. (1992). Improving school guidance programs: A framework for program, personnel, and results evaluation. *Journal of Counseling & Development, 70,*(5), 565–570.

Hackney, H., & Cormier, L. S. (1988). *Counseling strategies and objectives* (3rd ed.). Englewood Cliffs, NJ: Prentice-Hall.

Hagedorn, H. J., Beck, K. J., Neubert, S. F., & Werlin, S. H. (1976). *Working manual of simple program evaluation techniques for community mental health centers.* Rockville, MD: Arthur D. Little (for National Institute of Mental Health).

Hall, E. T. (1976). *Beyond culture.* New York: Anchor Press.

Hall, O. C. N., & Maloney, H. N. (1983). Cultural control in psychotherapy with minority clients. *Psychotherapy: Theory, Research and Practice, 20*(2), 131–142.

Hamilton, M. H. (1988, July 10). Employing new tools to recruit workers. *Washington Post,* pp. H1, H3.

Hansen, J. C., Stevic, R. R., & Warner, R. W., Jr. (1986). *Counseling: Theory and process* (4th ed.). Boston: Allyn & Bacon.

Hansen, J. C., Warner, R. W., & Smith, E. M. (1980). *Group counseling: Theory and process* (2nd ed.). Englewood Cliffs, NJ: Prentice-Hall.

Hardy, R. E., & Cull, J. G. (1974). *Group counseling and therapy techniques in special settings.* Springfield, IL: Thomas.

Hare, A. P. (1976). *Handbook of small group research* (2nd ed.). New York: Free Press.

Hartman, K. D. (1988). Role of the school counselor. *Education Week, 7*(36), 32.

Hatch, R. N., & Costar, J. W. (1961). *Guidance services in the elementary school.* Dubuque, IA: Brown.

Havighurst, R. J. (1953). *Human development and education.* New York: Longmans, Green.

Havighurst, R. J. (1964). Youth in exploration and man emergent. In H. Borow (Ed.), *Man in a world at work* (pp. 215–236). Boston: Houghton Mifflin.

Hawes, G. R. (1973). Criterion referenced testing—No more losers, no more norms, no more parents raising storms. *Nation's Schools, 91*(2), 35–41.

Hawks, B. K., & Muha, D. (1991). Facilitating the career development of minorities: Doing it differently this time. *Career Development Quarterly, 39,* 251–260.

Henderson, A. (1988, October). Best friends. *Phi Delta Kappan,* 149–153.

Henderson, H. J. (1989). *Counseling with computers: Technology and techniques.* Lancaster, TX: 3S.

Heppner, P. P., Gelso, C. J., & Dolliver, R. H. (1987). Three approaches to research training in counseling. *Journal of Counseling & Development, 66,* 45–49.

Heppner, P. P., Kivlighan, D. M., Jr., & Wampold, B. E. (1992). *Research design in counseling.* Pacific Grove, CA: Brooks/Cole.

Herlihy, B. (1994). Licensure, registration, or certification for counselors. Personal communication to authors.

Herlihy, B., Healy, M., Cook, E. P., & Hudson, P. (1987). Ethical practices of licensed professional counselors: A survey of state licensing boards. *Counselor Education and Supervision, 27*(1), 69–76.

Herlihy, B., & Sheeley, V. L. (1987). Privileged communication in selected helping professions: A comparison among statutes. *Journal of Counseling and Development, 65*(19), 479–483.

Herlihy, B., & Sheeley, V. L. (1988). Counselor liability and the duty to warn: Selected cases, standards, trends, and implications for practice. Counselor Education and Supervision, 27(2), 203-215.

Herndon, T. (1976). Standardized tests: Are they worth the cost? *Educational Digest, 42,* 13–16.

Herr, E. L. (1979). *Guidance and counseling in the schools: The past, present, and future.* Falls Church, VA: American Personnel and Guidance Association.

Herr, E. L., & Cramer, S. H. (1988). *Career guidance and counseling through the life span: Sys-*tematic approaches (3rd ed.). Boston: Scott, Foresman.

Hershenson, D. B., & Power, P. W. (1987). *Mental health counseling: Theory and practice.* New York: Pergamon.

Higbee, J. L., Dwinell, P. L., McAdams, C. R., GoldbergBelle, E., & Tardola, M. E. (1991). Serving underprepared students in institutions of higher education. *Journal of Humanistic Education and Development, 30,* 73–80.

Hinkeldey, N., & Spokane, A. (1985). Effects of pressure and legal guideline clarity on counselor decision making in legal and ethical conflict situations. *Journal of Counseling and Development, 64*(4), 240–245.

Hinshaw, R. P. (1942). The concept of adjustment and problems of norms. *Psychological Review, 49,* 284–292.

Hirshberg, D. (1991). *The role of the community college in economic and workforce development.* Los Angeles, CA: ERIC Clearinghouse for Junior Colleges. (ERIC Document Reproduction Service No. ED 339443)

Hodgkinson, H. (1985). *All one system: Demographics of education, kindergarten through graduate school.* Washington, DC: Institute for Educational Leadership.

Hoffman, M.A. (1991). Counseling the HIV-infected client: A psycho-social model for assessment and intervention. *The Counseling Psychologist, 19,* 467–542.

Holland, J. L. (1966). *The psychology of vocational choice.* Lexington, MA: Blaisdell/Ginn.

Holland, J. L. (1973). *Making vocational choices: A theory of careers.* Englewood Cliffs, NJ: Prentice-Hall.

Holland, J. L. (1975). The use and evaluation of interest inventories and simulations. In E. E. Diamond (Ed.), *Issues of sex bias and sex fairness in career interest measurement and evaluation* (6th ed.). Englewood Cliffs, NJ: Prentice-Hall.

Holland, J. L. (1985a). *Making vocational choices: A theory of careers* (2nd ed.). Englewood Cliffs, NJ: Prentice-Hall.

Holland, J. L. (1985b). *The self-directed search: Professional manual—1985 edition.* Odessa, FL: Psychological Assessment Resources.

Hollis, J. W., & Wantz, R. A. (1994). *Counselor preparation 1993-95: Vol. II. Status, trends, and implications* (8th ed.). Muncie, IN: Accelerated Development.

Hood, A. B., & Johnson, R. W. (1991). *Assessment in counseling: A guide to the use of psychological assessment procedures.* Alexandria, VA: American Association for Counseling and Development.

Hopkins, B. R., & Anderson, B. S. (1990). *The counselor and the law* (3rd ed.). Alexandria, VA: American Association for Counseling and Development.

Hopkins, K. D., & Stanley, J. C. (1981). *Educational and psychological measurement and evaluation* (6th ed.). Englewood Cliffs, NJ: Prentice-Hall.

Horan, J. J. (1979). *Counseling for effective decision making.* North Scituate, MA: Duxbury.

Horowitz, F. D., & O'Brien, M. (1989). In the interest of the nation: A reflective essay on the state of our knowledge and challenges before us. *American Psychologist, 44,* 441–445.

Hosie, T. W., Patterson, J. B., & Hollingsworth, D. K. (1989). School and rehabilitation counselor preparation: Meeting the needs of individuals with disabilities. *Journal of Counseling and Development, 68,* 171–176.

Hotchkiss, L., & Borow, H. (1984). Sociological perspectives on career choice and attainment. In D. Brown, L. Brooks, & Associates (Eds.), *Career choice and development.* San Francisco: Jossey-Bass.

Hotchkiss, L., & Borow, H. (1990). Sociological perspectives on work and career development. In D. Brown, L. Brooks, & Associates

(Eds.), *Career choice and development* (2nd ed.). San Francisco: Jossey-Bass.

Howard G. S. (1992). Behold our creation! What counseling psychology has become and might yet become. *Journal of Counseling Psychology, 39*(4), 419–442.

Howe, L. W., & Howe, M. M. (1975). *Personalizing education: Values clarification and beyond.* New York: Hart.

Hoyt, K. B. (1974). *An introduction to career education.* Washington, DC: U.S. Office of Education, Department of Health, Education and Welfare.

Hoyt, K. B. (1988). The changing workforce: A review of projections—1986 to 2000. *Career Development Quarterly, 37*(1), 31–38.

Hoyt, K. (1993). Guidance is not a dirty word. *The School Counselor, 40*(4), 267–274.

Huey, W. (1987). Ethical standards for school counselors: Test your knowledge. *The School Counselor, 34*(5), 331–335.

Humes, C. W. (1987). *Contemporary counseling: Services, applications, issues.* Muncie, IN: Accelerated Development.

Humes, C. W., II. (1978). School counselors and PL 94-142. *The School Counselor, 25,* 193–195.

Humes, C. W., & Hohenshil, T. H. (1987). Elementary counselors, school psychologists, school social workers: Who does what? *Elementary School Guidance and Counseling, 22,* 37–45.

Hummel, D. L. (1985). Law and ethics for practitioners in counseling and guidance. *Educational Perspectives, 23*(3), 3–12.

Hummel, D. L., & Humes, C. W. (1984). *Pupil services: Development, coordination, administration.* New York: Macmillan.

Hutson, P. W. (1958). *The guidance function in education.* New York: Appleton-Century-Crofts.

Iacocca, L., & Novack, W. (1984). *Iacocca: An autobiography.* New York: Bantam Books.

Isaacson, L. E. (1985). *Basics of career counseling.* Boston: Allyn & Bacon.

Isaacson, L. E., & Brown, D. (1993). *Career information, career counseling, and career development.* Boston: Allyn & Bacon.

Ivey, A. E. (1980). Counseling 2000: Time to take charge! *The Counseling Psychologist,* 8(4), 12–16.

Ivey, A. E., Ivey, M. B., & Simek-Downing, L. (1987). *Counseling and psychotherapy: Integrating skills, theory, and practice* (2nd ed.). Englewood Cliffs, NJ: Prentice-Hall.

Ivey, A. E., Ivey, M. B., & Simek-Morgan, L. (1993). *Counseling and psychotherapy: A multicultural perspective* (3rd ed.). Boston: Allyn & Bacon.

Jackson, R. M., Cleveland, J. C., & Meranda, P. F. (1975). The longitudinal effects of early identification and counseling of underachievers. *Journal of School Psychology, 13,* 119–128.

Jacques, M. E. (1969). *Rehabilitation counseling: Scope and services.* Boston: Houghton Mifflin.

James, W. (1890). *The principles of psychology: Vol. I.* New York: Holt.

Jeger, A. M., & Slotnick, R. S. (1982). *Community mental health and behavioral ecology: A handbook of theory, research and practice.* New York: Plenum.

Jemerin, M. D., & Philips, I. (1988). Changes in inpatient child psychiatry: Consequences and recommendations. *Journal of the American Academy of Child and Adolescent Psychiatry, 27,* 397–493.

Jenkins, D. E. (1985). Ethical and legal dilemmas of working with students with special needs. *Elementary School Guidance and Counseling, 19,* 202–209.

Johansen, J. H., Collins, H. W., & Johnson, J. A. (1975). *American education* (2nd ed.). Dubuque, IA: Brown.

Johansson, C. B., & Campbell, D. P. (1971). Stability of the Strong Vocational Interest Blank for Men. *Journal of Applied Psychology, 55,* 34–36.

Johnson, A. A. (1990). Relocating two-earner couples: What companies are doing. *The Conference Board,* Research Bulletin Number 247.

Johnson, D. W., & Johnson, F. P. (1982). *Joining together: Group theory and skills* (2nd ed.). Englewood Cliffs, NJ: Prentice-Hall.

Johnston, W., & Packer, A. (1987). *Workforce 2000: Work and workers for the twenty-first century.* Indianapolis: The Hudson Institute.

Jones, A. J. (1963). *Principles of guidance* (5th ed.). New York: McGraw-Hill.

Jones, B. A. P. (1986). Black women and labor force participation: An analysis of sluggish growth rates. In M. C. Simms & J. M. Malveaux (Eds.), *Slipping through the cracks: The status of black women* (pp. 11–32). New Brunswick, NJ: Transaction Books.

Kalish, R. A., & Collier, K. W. (1981). *Exploring human values: Psychological and philosophical considerations.* Monterey, CA: Brooks/Cole.

Kameen, M. C., Robinson, E. H., & Rotter, J. C. (1985). Coordination activities: A study of perceptions of elementary and middle school counselors. *Elementary School Guidance & Counseling, 20,* 97–104.

Kazdin, A. E. (1981). Behavioral observation. In M. Hersen & A. S. Bellack (Eds.), *Behavioral assessment: A practical handbook* (2nd ed., pp. 101–124). New York: Pergamon.

Kelly, G. (1955). *The psychology of personal constructs.* New York: Norton.

Kennedy, E. (1977). *On becoming a counselor: A basic guide for non-professional counselors.* Dublin: Gill & Macmillan.

Kennedy, E. M. (1990, November). Community-based care for the mentally ill: Simple justice. *American Psychologist, 45*(11), 1238–1240.

Kielder, T. (1993). *Old friends.* Boston: Houghton Mifflin.

Kiley, M. A. (1975). *Personal and interpersonal appraisal techniques.* Springfield, IL: Thomas.

Kinney, J., & Leaton, G. (1978). *Loosening the grip: A handbook of alcohol information.* St. Louis: Mosby.

Kinzer, L. (1961). The educated counselor. *Journal of Counseling Psychology, 8*(1), 1416.

Kitchener, K. S. (Ed.). (1984). Ethical decision making in counseling psychology [Special issue]. *Counseling Psychologist, 12*(3)19–98.

Klocke, D. (1994). Typical day's activities of a high school counselor. Unpublished personal account. Fort Wayne, IN.

Klopf, G. (1960). The expanding role of the high-school counselor. *School and Society, 88,* 417–419.

Knox, H. (1977). *Cracking the glass slipper: PEER's guide to ending sex bias in your schools.* Washington, DC: The National Organization for Women Legal Defense and Education Fund.

Kotter, J. (1988). *The leadership factor.* New York: Free Press.

Kottler, J. A., & Brown, R. W. (1985). *Introduction to therapeutic counseling.* Monterey, CA: Brooks/Cole.

Krieshok, T. (1987). Psychologists and counselors in the legal system: A dialogue with Theodore Blau. *Journal of Counseling and Development, 66*(2), 69–72.

Krumboltz, J. D. (Ed.). (1966). *Revolution in counseling: Implications of behavioral science.* Boston: Houghton Mifflin.

Krumboltz, J. D. (1974). An accountability model for counselors. *Personnel and Guidance Journal, 52,* 639–646.

Krumboltz, J. D. (1976). Behavior goals for counseling. In G. S. Belkin (Ed.), *Counseling direc-*

tions in theory and practice (pp. 171–178). Dubuque, IA: Kendall/Hunt.

Krumboltz, J. D., Mitchell, A., & Gelatt, H. G. (1975). Applications of social learning theory of career selection. *Focus on Guidance, 8,* 1–16.

Kubiszyn, T., & Borich, G. (1987). *Educational testing and measurement: Classroom application and practice* (2nd ed.). Glenview, IL: Scott, Foresman.

Kurpius, D. (1978). Consultation theory and process: An integrated model. *Personnel and Guidance Journal, 56,* 335–338.

Kurpius, D. (1985). Consultation interventions: Success, failures and proposals. *The Counseling Psychologist, 13*(3), 368–389.

Kurpius, D. J. (Ed.) (1978). Consultation II: Dimensions-training-bibliography [Special issue]. *Personnel and Guidance Journal, 56*(7).

Kurpius, D. J., & Brown, D. (1988). *Handbook of consultation: An intervention for advocacy and outreach.* Alexandria, VA: Association for Counselor Education and Supervision.

Kurpius, D. J., & Fuqua, D. R. (Eds.). (1993a). Consultation: A paradigm for helping: Consultation I: Conceptual, structural, and operational dimensions [Special issue]. *Journal of Counseling and Development, 71*(6).

Kurpius, D. J., & Fuqua, D. R. (1993b). Fundamental issues in defining consultation. *Journal of Counseling and Development, 71,* 598–600.

Kurpius, D. J., & Fuqua, D. R. (Eds.). (1993c). Consultation: A paradigm for helping: Consultation II: Prevention, preparation and key issues [Special issue]. *Journal of Counseling and Development, 72*(2).

Kurpius, D., & Lewis, J. (1988). Introduction to consultation: An intervention for advocacy and outreach. In D. Kurpius & D. Brown (Eds.), *Handbook of consultation: An interven-*

tion for advocacy and outreach (pp. 1–4). Alexandria, VA: Association for Counselor Education and Supervision.

Kurpius, D. J., & Robinson, S. E. (Eds.). (1978). Consultation I: Definition-models-programs [Special issue]. *Personnel and Guidance Journal, 56*(6).

Kutscher, R. (1987a, September). Projections 2000: Overview and implications of the projections to 2000. *Monthly Labor Review, 110*(9), 3–9. Washington, DC: U.S. Department of Labor.

Kutscher, R. (1987b). The impact of technology on employment in the United States: Past and future. In G. Burke & R. Rumberger (Eds.), *The future impact of technology on work and education.* Philadelphia: Fullmer.

L'Abate, L. (1981). Classification of counseling and therapy theorists, methods, processes and goals: The E-R-A model. *Personnel and Guidance Journal, 59*(5), 263–265.

La Forge, J., & Henderson, P. (1990). Counselor competency in the courtroom. *Journal of Counseling and Development, 68*, 456–459.

Lee, C. C. (1991). Multicultural counseling: New perspectives for the 1990's and beyond. *Counseling and Human Development, 23*(5), 1–8.

Leedy, P. D. (1974). *Practical research: Planning and design* (2nd ed.). New York: Macmillan.

Leitenberg, H., Agras, W. S., Thompson, L. D., & Wright, D. E. (1968). Feedback in behavior modification: An experimental analysis in two phobic cases. *Journal of Applied Behavior Analysis, 1*, 131–137.

Lessinger, L., Cunningham, E., & Sabine, D. D. (1973). *Accountability: Systems planning in education.* Homewood, IL: ETC.

Leung, P., & Eargle, D. (1980). Counseling with the elderly living in public housing. *Personnel and Guidance Journal, 58*, 442–445.

Lewin, K. (1936). *Principles of topological psychology.* New York: McGraw-Hill.

Lewis, M. D., Hayes, R. L., & Lewis, J. A. (1986). *An introduction to the counseling profession.* Itasca, IL: Peacock.

Lewis, J. A., & Lewis, M. D. (1983). *Community counseling: A human services approach* (2nd ed.). New York: Wiley.

Lewis, J. A., Lewis. M. D., & Souflee, F., Jr. (1993). *Management of human service programs.* Pacific Grove, CA: Brooks/Cole.

Lewis, M. D., Hayes, R. L., & Lewis, J. A. (1986). *An introduction to the counseling profession.* Itasca, IL: Peacock.

Lewis, M. D., & Lewis, J. A. (1991). *Management of human service programs* (2nd ed.). Pacific Grove, CA: Brooks/Cole.

Lodish, D. (1985). Preventing smoking. In L. D. Gilchrist & S. P. Schinke (Eds.), *Preventing social and health problems through life skills training.* Seattle: University of Washington School of Social Work.

London, P. (1987, May). Character education and clinical intervention: A paradigm shift for U.S. schools. *Phi Delta Kappan,* pp. 211–215.

Lieberman, M. A., Yalom, I., & Miles, M. (1973). *Encounter groups: First facts.* New York: Basic Books.

Lucking, R., & Mitchum, N. (1990). Desktop publishing for counselors. *The School Counselor, 37*, 270–272.

Luft, J. (1984). *Group process: An introduction to group dynamics* (3rd ed.). Palo Alto, CA: Mayfield.

Mabe, A. R., & Rollin, S. A. (1986). The role of a code of ethical standards in counseling. *Journal of Counseling and Development, 64*(5), 294–297.

Maccoby, E. E., & Jacklin, C. N. (1974). *The psychology of sex differences: Vol. 1.* Stanford, CA: Stanford University Press.

Mallart, M. (1955). *The history of the guidance movement: Western civilization—1955.* Cleveland: Collins & World.

Manaster, O. S., & Corsini, R. J. (1982). *Individual psychology: Theory and practice.* Itasca, IL: Peacock.

Mannino, F. V., & MacLennan, B. W. (1978). *Monitoring and evaluating mental health consultation and education services.* DHEW Pub. No. (ADM) 77-550. Washington, DC: U.S. Government Printing Office.

Mappes, D., Robb, G., & Engels, D. (1985). Conflicts between ethics and law in counseling and psychotherapy. *Journal of Counseling and Development, 64*(4), 246–252.

Mark, J. (1987, April). Technological change and employment: Some results from BLS research. *Monthly Labor Review,* pp. 26–29.

Marshall, J. (1983). Reducing the effects of work oriented values on the lives of male American workers. *Vocational Guidance Quarterly, 32,* 109–115.

Martin, A., & Martin, M. (1982). Nutritional counseling: A humanistic approach to psychological and physical health. *Personnel and Guidance Journal, 61,* 21–24.

Maslow, A. H. (1970). *Motivation and personality* (2nd ed.). New York: Harper & Row.

Mason, J. (1985). Public health service plan for the prevention & control of acquired immunodeficiency syndrome. *Public Health Reports, 100,* 453–455.

Matarazzo, J. D. (1986). Computerized clinical and psychological test interpretations: Unvalidated plus all mean and no sigma. *American Psychologist, 41,* 14–24.

Matheny, K. B., Aycock, D. W., Pugh, J. L., Curlette, W. L., & Cannella, K. A. S. (1986). Stress coping: A qualitative and quantitative synthesis with implications for treatment. *The Counseling Psychologist, 14*(4), 499–549.

Mayo, A. D. (1872). Moral instruction in common schools. *National Education Association Journal of Addresses and Proceedings,* 11–24.

McCandless, B. R., & Coop, R. H. (1979). *Adolescents: Behavior and development* (2nd ed.). New York: Holt, Rinehart & Winston.

McCully, C. H. (1962). The school counselor: Strategy for professionalization. *Personnel and Guidance Journal, 61,* 597–601.

McCully, C. H. (1965). The counselor: Instrument of change. *Teachers College Record, 66,* 405–412.

McCully, C. H. (1969). *Challenges for change in counselor education.* (Compiled by L. L. Miller.) Minneapolis, MN: Burgess.

McKown, H. C. (1934). *Home room guidance.* New York: McGraw-Hill.

McWhirter, J. J., & McWhirter, B. T. (1991). A framework for theories in counseling. In D. Capuzzi & D. R. Gross (Eds.), *Introduction to counseling: Perspectives for the 1990s* (pp. 69–88). Boston: Allyn & Bacon.

Meares, P. A. (1977). Analysis of tasks in school social work. *Social Work, 22,* 196–201.

Mehrens, W. A., & Lehmann, I. J. (1984). *Measurement and evaluation in education and psychology* (3rd ed.). New York: Holt, Rinehart & Winston.

Mejta, C. L. (1987). Acquired Immunodeficiency Syndrome (AIDS): Implications for counseling and education. *Counseling and Human Development, 20*(2), 1–12.

Mercurio, J. M., & Weiner, M. (1975). The minigroup in counseling. *Personnel and Guidance Journal, 54,* 227–228.

Meyerson, L., & Jack, M. (1962). A behavioral approach to counseling and guidance. *Harvard Educational Review, 32*(4), 382–402.

Miringoff, M. L. (1980). *Management in human services.* New York: Macmillan.

Moles, O. C. (1991). Guidance programs in American high schools: A descriptive portrait. *The School Counselor, 38,* 163–177.

Monahan, J., & Walker, L. (1988). Social science research in law: A new paradigm. *American Psychologist, 43*(6), 465–472.

Moreno, J. L. (Ed.). (1960). *The sociometry reader.* New York: Free Press.

Mosak, H. H. (1979). Adlerian psychotherapy. In R. J. Corsini (Ed.), *Current psychotherapies* (2nd ed., pp. 44–94). Itasca, IL: Peacock.

Moses, A., & Hawkins, R. (1982). *Counseling lesbian women and gay men: A life issues approach.* St. Louis, MO: Mosby.

Mudore, C. (1988). Computers, ethics, and the school counselor. *Clearing House, 61,* 283–284.

Mueller, C. G. (1979). Some origins of psychology as science. In M. R. Rosenzweig & L. W. Porter (Eds.), *Annual review of psychology* (Vol. 30, pp. 9–29). Palo Alto, CA: Annual Reviews.

Munson, H. L. (1971). *Foundation of developmental guidance.* Boston: Allyn & Bacon.

Murphy, G. (1955). The cultural context of guidance. *Personnel and Guidance Journal, 34,* 4–9.

Murray, H., Barrett, W. G., & Honburger, E. (1938). *Explorations in personality: A clinical and experimental study of fifty men of college age.* New York: Oxford University Press.

Muthard, J. E., & Salomone, P. R. (1969). The roles and functions of the rehabilitation counselor. *Rehabilitation Counseling Bulletin, 13,* 81–168.

Myers, J. E. (July, 1990). Aging: An overview for mental health counselors. *Journal of Mental Health Counseling, 12*(3), 245–259.

Myers, J. E. (1992a). Competencies, credentialing, and standards for gerontological counselors: Implications for counselor education. *Counselor Education and Supervision, 32,* 34–41.

Myers, J. E. (1992b). Wellness, prevention, development: The cornerstone of the profession. *Journal of Counseling and Development, 71,* 136–139.

Myers, J. E., Emmerling, D., & Leafgren, F. (1992). Wellness throughout the lifespan [Special issue]. *Journal of Counseling and Development, 71*(2).

Myers, G. E., & Myers, M. T. (1973). *The dynamics of human communication.* New York: McGraw-Hill.

Myrick, R. D., & Dixon, R. W. (1985). Changing student attitudes and behavior through group counseling. *The School Counselor, 32,* 325–330.

Myrick, R. D., Merbell, H., & Swanson, L. (1986). Changing student attitudes through classroom guidance. *The School Counselor, 33,* 244–252.

Naisbitt, J., & Aburdene, P. (1990). *Megatrends 2000.* New York: Morrow.

Namir, S. (1986). Treatment issues concerning persons with AIDS. In L. McKusick (Ed.), *What to do about AIDS* (pp. 87–94). Berkeley: University of California Press.

National Alliance of Business. (1986, September 20). A critical message for every American who plans to work or do business in the 21st century. *New York Times Magazine.*

National Board of Certified Counselors. (1990). *NBCC Counselor Certification 1991–1992.* Alexandria, VA: Author.

National Commission on the Reform of Secondary Education. (1973). *The reform of secondary education.* New York: McGraw-Hill.

National Education Association. (1987). *Report of the Hispanic concerns study committee.* Washington, DC: Author.

National Employment Counselors Association. (1975). Role of the employment counselor. *Journal of Employment Counseling, 12,* 148–153.

National Governors' Association. (1986). *Time for results: The governors' report on education.* Washington, DC: Author.

National Vocational Guidance Association. (1973). *Career development: NVGA-AVA position paper.* Washington, DC: American Personnel and Guidance Association.

Nelson, R. C. (1992). Spa in counseling. *Journal of Counseling & Development, 71*(2), 214–220.

New York State Teachers Association. (1935). *Guidance in the secondary school.* New York State Teachers Association Educational Monograph #3. New York: Author.

Nixon, H. L., II. (1979). *The small group.* Englewood Cliffs, NJ: Prentice-Hall.

Nolte, M. C. (1975). Use and misuse of tests in education: Legal implications. *Evaluation Horizons, 54,* 10–16.

Obermann, C. E. (1965). *A history of vocational rehabilitation in America.* Minneapolis: Denison.

Odegaard, C. (1987). A historical perspective on the dilemmas confronting psychologists. *American Psychologist, 42*(12), 1048–1051.

Offerman, L. R., & Gowing, M. K. (1990). Organizations of the future: Changes and challenges. *American Psychologist, 45,* 95–108.

Ohlsen, M. M. (1955). *Guidance: An introduction.* New York: Harcourt Brace Jovanovich.

Ohlsen, M. M. (1977). *Group counseling.* (2nd ed.). New York: Holt, Rinehart, & Winston.

Ohlsen, M. M. (1983). *Introduction to counseling.* Itasca, IL: Peacock.

Okun, B. E (1987). *Effective helping: Interviewing and counseling techniques* (3rd ed.). Monterey, CA: Brooks/Cole.

Okun, B. E., & Rappaport, L. (1980). *Working with families: An introduction to family therapy.* Belmont, CA: Duxbury.

Omizo, M. M., Omizo, S. A., & D'Andrea, M. J. (1992). Promoting wellness among elementary school children. *Journal of Counseling & Devlopment, 71*(2), 194–198.

Ornstein, A. C. (1976). 10 tests and the culture issue. *Phi Delta Kappan, 57,* 403–404.

Osipow, S. H. (1983). *Theories of career development.* Englewood Cliffs, NJ: Prentice-Hall.

Page, R. C., Smith, M., & Beamish, P. (1977). Establishing a drug rehabilitation center. *Personnel and Guidance Journal, 56,* 180–183.

Paradise, L. V., & Long, T. J. (1981). *Counseling in the community college.* New York: Praeger.

Parker, C. A. (Ed.). (1975). *Psychological consultation: Helping teachers meet special needs.* Minneapolis: University of Minnesota, Leadership Training Institute.

Parsons, E. (1909). *Choosing a vocation.* Boston: Houghton-Mifflin.

Partin, R. L. (1993). School counselors' time: Where does it go? *The School Counselor, 40,* 274–281.

Pascal, A. H., Bell, D., Dougherty, L. A., Dunn, W. L., & Thompson, V. M. (1975). *An evaluation of policy-related research on programs for mid-life career redirection: Vols. I & II. Major findings* (R-1582/2-NSF). Washington, DC: National Science Foundation.

Passons, W. R. (1975). *Gestalt approaches in counseling.* New York: Holt, Rinehart & Winston.

Patterson, C. H. (1980). *Theories of counseling and psychotherapy* (3rd ed.). New York: Holt, Rinehart & Winston.

Patton, M. J. (1984). Managing social interaction in counseling: A contribution from the philosophy of science. *Journal of Counseling Psychologist, 17,* 442–456.

Pedersen, P. (1988). *A handbook for developing multicultural awareness.* Alexandria, VA:

American Association for Counseling & Development.

Pedersen, P. B. (1991). Multiculturalism as a generic approach to counseling. *Journal of Counseling and Development, 70,* 6–12.

Peeks, B. (1993). Revolutions in counseling and education: A systems perspective in the schools. *Elementary School Guidance and Counseling, 27,* 245–251.

Peltier, S. W., & Vale, S. O. (1986). A national survey of counselor education department: Course offerings on marriage and family. *Counselor Education and Supervision, 25,* 313–318.

Perls, F. (1948). Theory and technique of personality integration. *American Journal of Psychotherapy, 2,* 565–586.

Permian Basin Regional Planning Commission. (1980). *1980–1981 regional plan for prevention, treatment and control of alcohol abuse and alcoholism in the Permian Basin.* Midland, TX: Author.

Peter, L. I., & Hull, R. (1959). *The Peter principle.* New York: Harper & Row.

Peters, T. J., & Waterman, R. H., Jr. (1982). *In search of excellence.* New York: Harper & Row.

Phelps, R. J., Peer, G. G., & Canada, R. M. (1973). Training employment personnel in basis counseling skills. *Journal of Employment Counseling, 10,* 173–179.

Phillips, E. L. (1968). Achievement place: Token reinforcement procedures in a home-style rehabilitation setting for "pre-delinquent" boys. *Journal of Applied Behavior Analysis, 1,* 213–223.

Pietrofesa, J. J., Hoffman, A., Splete, H. H., & Pinto, D. V. (1984). *Counseling: An introduction.* (2nd ed.). Boston: Houghton-Mifflin.

Ponzo, Z. (1992). Promoting successful aging: Problems, opportunities, and counseling guidelines. *Journal of Counseling & Development, 71*(2), 210–213.

Price, R., Omizo, M., & Hammett, V. (1986). Counseling clients with AIDS. *Journal of Counseling and Development, 65*(2), 96–97.

Proctor, W. M., Benefield, W., & Wrenn, C. G. (1931). *Workbook in vocations.* Boston: Houghton Mifflin.

Pyle, K. R. (1985). High tech/high touch: A synergy applicable to career development. *Journal of Career Development, 12,* 145–156.

Pyszowski, I. S. (1986). Moral values and the schools: Is there a way out of the maze? *Chronicle Guidance, 107*(1), 87–92.

Quimbita, G. (1991). *Preparing women and minorities for careers in math and science: The role of community colleges.* Los Angeles: ERIC Clearinghouse for Junior Colleges. (ERIC Document Reproduction Service No. ED 333943.)

Rapoport, R., & Rapoport, R. N. (1976). *Dual-career families re-examined: New interpretations of work and family.* London: Martin Robertson.

Raths, L. E., Harmin, M., & Simon, S. B. (1978). *Values and teaching: Working with values in the classroom.* Columbus, OH: Merrill.

Rauch, J. (1989, August). Kids as capital. *The Atlantic,* pp. 56–61.

Rawlings, E. I., & Carter, D. K. (Eds.). (1977). *Psychotherapy for women: Treatment toward equality.* Springfield, IL: Thomas.

Remley, T. (1988). More explanation needed in ethical and legal topics. *Mental Health Counseling, 10*(3), 167–170.

Remley, T. P., Jr. (1991, August). On being different. *Guidepost,* p. 2.

Remley, T. P., Jr. (1993). Consultation contracts. *Journal of Counseling & Devlopment, 72,* 157–159.

Rencken, R. H. (1989). *Intervention strategies for sexual abuse.* Alexandria, VA: American Association for Counseling and Development.

Reschly, D. J., & Wilson, M. S. (1993). *Demographics, job satisfaction, system reform, and current/ideal roles: 1986–1995 comparisons.* Unpublished manuscript.

Ridley, C. R. (1978). Cross-cultural counseling; A multivariate analysis. *Viewpoints in Teaching and Learning* (Journal of the School of Education, Indiana University), *54*(1), 43–50.

Ritchie, M. H. (1982). Parental consultation: Practical considerations. *The School Counselor, 29*(5), 402–410.

Roberts, A. R. (1984). *Battered women and their families: Vol. 1.* New York: Springer.

Robinson, S. (1988). Counselor competence and malpractice suits: Opposite sides of the same coin. *Counseling and Human Development, 20*(9), 1-7.

Robinson, S. E. (1983). Nader versus ETS: Who should we believe? *Personnel and Guidance Journal, 61,* 260–262.

Robinson, S. E., & Roth, S. L. (1992). Women and health [Special issue]. *Journal of Mental Health Counseling, 14*(1).

Rockwell, P. J., & Rothney, J. W. M. (1961). Some social ideas of pioneers in the guidance movement. *Personnel and Guidance Journal, 40,* 349–354.

Roe, A. (1956). *The psychology of occupation.* New York: Wiley.

Roe, A., & Lunneborg, P. W. (1984). Personality development and career choice. In D. Brown & L. Brooks (Eds.), *Career choice and development: Applying contemporary theories to practice.* San Francisco: Jossey-Bass.

Rogers, C. R. (1967a). The conditions of change from a client-centered viewpoint. In B. G. Berenson & R. R. Carkhuff (Eds.), *Sources of gain in counseling and psychotherapy.* New York: Holt, Rinehart & Winston.

Rogers, C. R. (1967b). The process of the basic encounter group. In J. F. T. Bugental (Ed.), *Challenges of humanistic psychology* (pp. 261–276). New York: McGraw-Hill.

Rogers, C. R. (1942). *Counseling and psychotherapy.* Cambridge, MA: Riverside.

Rogers, C. R. (1951). *Client-centered therapy.* Boston: Houghton Mifflin.

Rogers, C. R. (1959a). A theory of therapy, personality and interpersonal relationships as developed in the client-centered framework. In S. Koch (Ed.), *Psychology: A study of science: Vol. 3* (pp. 184-256). New York: McGraw-Hill.

Rogers, C. R. (1959b). Significant learning: In theory and in education. *Educational Leadership, 16,* 232–242.

Rowntree, D. (1987). *Assessing students: How shall we know them?* London: Nichols.

Rude, S. S., Weissberg, M., & Gazda, G. M. (1988). Looking to the future: Themes from the third national conference for counseling psychology. *The Counseling Psychologist, 16,* 423–430.

Rutter, M. (1980). School influences on children's behavior and development: The 1979 Kenneth Blackfan Lecture, Children's Hospital Medical Center, Boston. *Pediatrics, 65*(2), 208–220.

Sampson, J. P., Jr., & Pyle, K. R. (1983). Ethical issues involved with the use of computer-assisted counseling, testing and guidance systems. *Personnel and Guidance Journal, 61,* 283–287.

Satir, V. (1964). *Conjoint family therapy: A guide to theory and technique.* Palo Alto, CA: Science and Behavior Books.

Sattler, J. M. (1992). *Assessment of children* (3rd ed.). San Diego, CA: Sattler.

Schein, E. H. (1978). The role of the consultant: Content expert or process facilitator? *Personnel and Guidance Journal, 56,* 339–345.

Schein, E. H. (1991). Process consultation. *Consulting Psychology Bulletin, 43,* 16–18.

Schinke, S. P., Gilchrist, L. D., & Small, R. W. (1979). Preventing unwanted adolescent pregnancy: A cognitive behavioral approach. *American Journal of Orthopsychiatry, 49,* 81–88.

Schlossberg, N. K. (1984). *Counseling adults in transition.* New York: Springer.

Schmidt, J. J. (1993). *Counseling in schools: Essential services and comprehensive programs.* Boston: Allyn & Bacon.

Schmolling, P., Jr., Youkeles, M., & Burger, W. R. (1989). *Human services in contemporary America* (2nd ed.). Pacific Grove, CA: Brooks/Cole.

Sekaran, U. (1986). *Dual-career families.* San Francisco: Jossey-Bass.

Seligman, L. (1983). An introduction to the new DSM-II. *Personnel and Guidance Journal, 61*(10), 601–605.

Sexton, T. L., Montgomery, D., Goff, K., & Nugent, W. (1992). Ethical, therapeutic, and legal considerations in the use of paradoxical techniques: The emerging debate. *Journal of Mental Health Counseling, 15,* 260–277.

Shafe, M., Gerster, D., & Moore, B. (1976). *School based placement programs.* Unpublished manuscript, State of Indiana and Indiana University, Bloomington.

Shane, J. G., Shane, H. G., Gibson, R. L., & Munger, P. F. (1971). *Guiding human development: The counselor and the teacher in the elementary school.* Worthington, OH: Jones.

Shanker, A. (1988, April 24). Where we stand. Time for truth in testing: Exams fail the test. *New York Times,* p. E7.

Shaw, M. C. (1986). The prevention of learning and interpersonal problems. *Journal of Counseling and Development, 64*(10), 624–627.

Sheeley, V. L., & Jenkins, D. (1985). *Tomorrow's school counselors. Directions revealed for their education.* Bowling Green: Western Kentucky University.

Shein, E. H. (1992). Process consultation. *Consulting Psychology Bulletin, 43,* 16–18.

Sheldon, C., & Morgan, C. D. (1984). The child development specialist: A prevention program. *Personnel and Guidance Journal, 62,* 470–474.

Shertzer, B., & Stone, S. C. (1980). *Fundamentals of counseling* (3rd ed.). Boston: Houghton Mifflin.

Shertzer, B., & Stone, S. C. (1981). *Fundamentals of guidance* (4th ed.). Boston: Houghton Mifflin.

Shifron, R., Dye, A., & Shifron, G. (1983). Implications for counseling the unemployed in a recessionary economy. *Personnel and Guidance Journal, 61,* 527–529.

Silvestri, G., & Lukasiewicz, J. (1987, September). A look at occupational employment trends to the year 2000. *Monthly Labor Review,* Washington, DC: U.S. Department of Labor.

Simmel, G. (1955). *The web of group affiliations.* Glencoe, IL: Free Press.

Simon, S. B., & deSherbinin, P. (1975). Values clarification: It can start gently and grow deep. *Phi Delta Kappan, 56,* 679–683.

Smith, D. K. (1984). Practicing school psychologists: Their characteristics, activities, and populations served. *Professional Psychology: Research and Practice, 15,* 798–810.

Smith, D., & Peterson, J. (1977). Values: A challenge to the profession. *Personnel and Guidance Journal, 55,* 227–231.

Solomon, C., & Jackson-Jobe, P. (Eds.). (1992). *Helping homeless people: Unique challenges and solutions.* Alexandria, VA: American Association for Counseling and Development.

Southern, S., & Hannaford, C. (1981). Health counseling: An emergent specialization. *Counselor Education and Supervision, 20*(4), 253–261.

Spivack, G., & Shure, M. B. (1974). *Social adjustment of young children.* San Francisco: Jossey-Bass.

Sprinthall, N. A. (1990). Counseling psychology from Greyston to Atlanta: On the road to Armageddon? *The Counseling Psychologist, 18,* 454–462.

St. John, W. D., & Walden, J. (1976). Keeping student confidence. *Phi Delta Kappan, 57,* 682–684.

Stefflre, B., & Grant, W. H. (1972). *Theories of counseling* (2nd ed.). New York: McGraw-Hill.

Stevens, R., & Phil, R. O. (1982). The identification of the student-at-risk for failure. *Journal of Clinical Psychology, 38,* 298–301.

Stockton, R. A., Barr, J. E., & Klein, R. (1981). Identifying the group dropout: A review of the literature. *Journal for Specialists in Group Work, 6,* 75–82.

Stockton, R., & Hulse, D. (1983). The use of research teams to enhance competence in counseling research. *Counselor Education and Supervision, 22*(4), 303–310.

Stockton, R. & Morran, D. K. (1982). Review and perspective of critical dimensions in therapeutic small group research. In G. M. Gazda (Ed.) *Basic approaches to group psychotherapy and group counseling.* (3rd ed.). Springfield, IL: Charles C. Thomas.

Stockton, R., & Morran, K. (1985). Perceptions on group research programs. *Journal for Specialists in Group Work, 10*(4), 186–191.

Stockton, R., & Toth, P. (1993). Small group counseling in school settings. In J. Wittmer (Ed.), *Managing your school counseling program: K–12 developmental strategies.* Minneapolis: Educational Media Corporation.

Stockton, R. A. (1980). The education of group leaders: A review of the literature with suggestions for the future. *Journal for Specialists in Group Work, 5,* 55–62.

Stoltz-Loike, M. (1992). *Dual career couples: New perspectives in counseling.* Alexandria, VA:

American Association for Counseling and Development.

Strosnider, J. S., & Grad, J. D. (1993). *Third-party payments.* American Counseling Association Legal Series 9.

Sturtevant, S. M. (1937). Some questions regarding the developing guidance movement. *School Review, 58,* 14–23.

Sue, D. W. (1977). Community health services to minority groups: Some optimism, some pessimism. *American Psychologist, 32,* 616–624.

Sue, D. W. (1978). Editorial. *Personnel and Guidance Journal, 56*(8), 451.

Sue, D. W. (1981). *Counseling the culturally different: Theory and practice.* New York: Wiley.

Sue, D., & Sue, D. M. (1989). Multicultural counseling. *Counseling and Human Development, 22*(3), 1–12.

Sue, D. W. & Sue, S. (1972). Counseling Chinese-Americans. *Personnel and Guidance Journal, 50*(8), 637–644.

Super, D. E. (1975). *The psychology of careers.* New York: Harper & Row.

Super, D. E. (1990). A life-span, life-space approach to career development. In D. Brown, L. Brooks, & Associates (Eds.), *Career choice and development* (2nd ed.). San Francisco: Jossey-Bass.

Super, D. E., Starishevsky, R., Matlin, N., & Jordaan, J. P. (1963). *Career development: Self-concept theory.* New York: College Entrance Examination Board.

Super, D. E., & Thompson, A. S. (1979). A six-scale, two factor measure of adolescent career or vocational maturity. *Vocational Guidance Quarterly, 27,* 6–15.

Sweeney, T. J. (1989). *Adlerian counseling: A practical approach for a new decade* (3rd ed.). Muncie, IN: Accelerated Development, Inc.

Tableman, B., Marceniak, D., Johnson, D., & Rodgers, R. (1982). Stress management training for women on public assistance. *American Journal of Community Psychology, 10,* 357–367.

Taeuber, C. M., & V. Valdisera. (1986) *Women in the American economy.* Current Population Reports, Series P-23, 146. Washington, DC: U.S. Government Printing Office.

Tannenbaum, A. S. (1962). Reactions of member of voluntary groups: A logarithmic function of size and group. *Psychological Reports, 10,* 113–114.

Taylor, S. E., Falke, R. L., Shapton, S. J., & Lichtman, R. R. (1986). Social support, support groups, and the cancer patient,. *Journal of Consulting and Clinical Psychology, 54,* 608–615.

Teague, J. B. (1992). Issues related to the treatment of adolescent lesbians and homosexuals. *Journal of Mental Health Counseling, 14,* 422–439.

Texas Rehabilitation Commission. (1984). *Eligibility requirements of rehabilitation.* Austin: Author.

Tharp, R. G., & Wetzel, R. (1969). *Behavior modification in the natural environment.* New York: Academic Press.

Thelen, H. A. (1954). *Dynamics of groups at work.* Chicago: University of Chicago Press.

Thomas, E. J., & Fink, C. E. (1961). Models of group problem solving. *Journal of Abnormal and Social Psychology, 63,* 1.

Thomas, D. R. (1973). *The schools next time.* New York: McGraw-Hill.

Thomson-Rountree, P., & Woodruff, A. E. (1982). An examination of Project Aware: The effects on children's attitudes toward themselves, others and school. *Journal of School Psychology, 20,* 20–31.

Thornburgh, H. D. (1986). The counselor's impact on middle grade students. *The School Counselor, 33,* 175–176.

Thorndike, R. L., & Hagen, E. (1977). *Measurement and evaluation in psychology and education* (4th ed.). New York: Wadsworth.

Tiedeman, D. V., & Field, F. L. (1962). Guidance: The science of purposeful action applied through education. *Harvard Educational Review, 32*(4), 483–501.

Tiger, L. (1979). *Optimism: The biology of hope.* New York: Simon & Schuster.

Tinsley, H. E. A., Hinson, J. A., Tinsley, D. J., & Holt, M. S. (1993). Attributes of leisure and work experiences. *Journal of Counseling Psychology, 40,* 447–455.

Tinsley, H. E. A., & Tinsley, D. J. (1986). A theory of the attributes, benefits and causes of leisure experience. *Leisure Sciences, 8,* 1–45.

Tinsley, H. E. A., & Tinsley, D. J. (1988). An expanded context for the study of career decision-making, development, and maturity. In W. B. Walsh & S. H. Osipow (Eds.), *Career decision making* (pp. 213–264). Hillsdale, NJ: Erlbaum.

Tolbert, E. L. (1972). *Introduction to counseling* (2nd ed.). New York: McGraw-Hill.

Toomer, J. E. (1982). Counseling psychologists in business and industry. *The Counseling Psychologist, 10*(3), 9–18.

Traxler, A. E. (1950). Emerging trends in guidance. *School Review, 58,* 14–23.

Turnbull, A. P., & Turnbull, H. R. (1990). *Families, professionals and exceptionality: A special partnership.* Columbus, OH: Merrill.

Turner, A. N. (1982). Consulting is more than giving advice. *Harvard Business Review, 60*(5), 120–129.

Tyler, L. E. (1980). The next twenty years. *The Counseling Psychologist, 8*(4), 19–21.

Ulrici, D., L'Abate, L., & Wagner, V. (1981). The E-R-A model: A heuristic framework for classification of social skills training programs for couples and families. *Family Relations, 30*(2), 307–315.

U.S. Bureau of Census. (1980). *Census of population supplementary report* (PC 80–S13). Washington, DC: U.S. Government Printing Office.

U.S. Bureau of Census. (1980–1989). *Statistical abstract of the United States.* Washington, DC: U.S. Government Printing Office.

U.S. Centers for Disease Control. (1991). *HIV/AIDS surveillance report* (1–22). Atlanta, GA: Author.

U.S. Department of Education. (1986). *Schools without drugs.* Washington, DC: Author.

U.S. Government Printing Office. 1970. *General Aptitude Test Battery.* Washington, DC: U.S. Government Printing Office.

Vaac, N. A., & Wittmer, J. P. (1980). *Let me be me: Special populations and the helping professions.* Muncie, IN: Accelerated Development.

Vander Kolk, C. J. (1985). *Introduction to group counseling and psychotherapy.* Columbus, OH: Merrill.

VanderCreek, L., & Knapp, S. (1984). Counselors, confidentiality and life-endangering clients. *Counselor Education and Supervision, 24*(1), 51–57.

Veninga, R. L., & Spradley, J. P. (1981). *The work stress connection: How to cope with job burnout.* Boston: Little, Brown.

Waldron, N. (1994). School counselors work with school psychologists. Unpublished information provided by personal interview. Bloomington: Indiana University.

Wallace, W. A. (1986). *Theories of counseling and psychotherapy: A basic issues approach.* Newton, MA: Allyn & Bacon.

Walz, G. R. (1987). *Current issues and trends in guidance and counseling* (Report No. UD 025 435). Ann Arbor, MI: ERIC Clearinghouse on Counseling and Personnel Services. (ERIC Document Reproduction Service No. ED 281 900.)

Walz, G. R., & Bleur, J. (1985). Putting the byte into career development. *Journal of Career Development, 12,* 187–198.

Watson, J. B. (1913). Psychology as the behaviorist views it. *Psychological Review, 20,* 159–170.

Weikel, W. J., & Hughes, P. R. (1993). *The counselor as expert witness.* American Counseling Association Legal Series, 5. Alexandria, VA: American Counseling Association.

Weiner, H. J., Akabas, S. H., & Sommer, J. J. (1973). *Mental health care in the world of work.* New York: Association Press.

Weiner, M. F. (1984). *Techniques of group psychotherapy.* Washington, DC: American Psychiatric Press.

Weissberg, R. P., & Gesten, E. L. (1982). Considerations for developing effective school-based social problem solving (SPS) training programs. *School Psychology Review, 11*(1), 56–63.

Werner, J. L. (1978). Community mental health consultation with agencies. *Personnel and Guidance Journal, 56,* 364–368.

Werner, J. L., & Tyler, M. M. (1993). Community-based interventions: A return to community mental health centers' origins. *Journal of Counseling & Development, 71*(6), 689–692.

Wetzel, J. (1987). *American youth: A statistical snapshot.* Washington, DC: William T. Grant Foundation Commission on Work, Family and Citizenship.

White, B. L. (1985). *The first three years of life.* Englewood Cliffs, NJ: Prentice-Hall.

Whiteley, J. M. (1980). Counseling psychology in the year 2000 A.D. *The Counseling Psychologist, 8*(4), 2–8.

Whiteley, J (Ed.). (1984). Counseling psychology: A historical perspective. *The Counseling Psychologist, 12*(1), 1–126.

Wilcoxon, S. A. (1987). Client consent in departures from customary and suggested treatment formats. *American Mental Health Counselors Association Journal, 9*(2), 77–83.

Wilcoxon, S. A. (1992). The revised AACD Ethical Standards: New clarity and new uncertainty. *The School Counselor, 40,* 4–9.

Wilcoxon, S. A., & Puleo, S. G. (1992). Professional development needs of mental health counselors: Results of a national survey. *Journal of Mental Health Counseling, 14,* 187–195.

Wilhelm, C. D., & Case, M. (1975). Telling it like it is—Improving school records. *The School Counselor, 23,* 84–90.

Williamson, E. G. (1939). *How to counsel students: A manual of techniques for clinical counselors.* New York: McGraw-Hill.

Williamson, E. G. (1964). An historical perspective of the vocational guidance movement. *Personnel and Guidance Journal, 42,* 854–859.

Windle, C., & Neigher, W. (1978). Ethical problems in program evaluation: Advice for trapped evaluators. *Evaluation and Program Planning, 1*(2), 97–107.

Wirth-Bond, S., Coyne, A., & Adams, M. (1991). A school counseling program that reduces dropout rate. *The School Counselor, 39,* 131–137.

Witmer, J. M., & Sweeney, T. J. (1992). A holistic model for wellness and prevention over the life span. *Journal of Counseling & Development, 71,* 140–148.

Wittmer, J., Lanier, I. E., & Parker, M. (1976). Race relations training with correctional officers. *Personnel and Guidance Journal, 54,* 302–306.

Woody, R. H., Hansen, J. C., & Rossberg, R. H. (1989). *Counseling psychology: Strategies & services.* Pacific Grove, CA:Brooks/Cole.

Worthen, B. R., White, K. R., & Borg, W. R. (1993). *Measurement and evaluation in the schools.* New York: Longman.

Worthen, B. R., & Sanders, J. R. (1973). *Educational evaluation: Theory and practice.* Worthington, OH: Jones.

Wrenn, C. G. (1962). *The counselor in a changing world.* Washington, DC: American Personnel and Guidance Association.

Wrenn, C. G. (1973). *The world of the contemporary counselor.* Boston: Houghton Mifflin.

Yalom, I. D. (1985). *The theory and practice of group psychotherapy* (3rd ed.). New York: Basic Books.

Zavella, P. (1987). *Women's work and Chicano families.* Ithaca, NY: Cornell University Press.

Zeran, F. R., & Riccio, A. C. (1962). *Organization and administration of guidance services.* Skokie, IL: Rand McNally.

Ziegler, W. L. (1972). If we do not speak out on behalf of mankind, who will? Penney's Forum.

Zins, J. E., & Curtis, M. J. (1984). Building consultation into the educational service delivery system. In C. A. Maher, R. J. Illback, & J. E. Zins (Eds.), *Organizational psychology in the schools: A handbook for professionals* (Chap. 10). Springfield, IL: Thomas.

Zunker, V. G. (1990). *Career counseling: Applied concepts of life planning* (3rd ed.) Pacific Grove, CA: Brooks/Cole.

Zytowski, D. G. (1972). Four hundred years before Parsons. *Personnel and Guidance Journal, 50,* 443–450.

Name Index

Subject Index